THE GOLDEN LEGEND

Jacobus de Voragine

The Golden Legend

Readings on the Saints

TRANSLATED BY

William Granger Ryan

VOLUME II

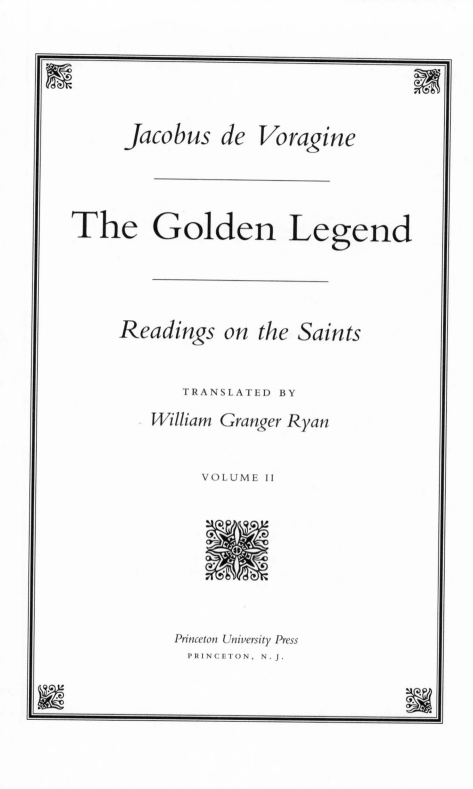

Princeton University Press
PRINCETON, N.J.

Copyright © 1993 by Princeton University Press
Published by Princeton University Press, 41 William Street,
Princeton, New Jersey 08540
In the United Kingdom: Princeton University Press,
Chichester, West Sussex

Library of Congress Cataloging-in-Publication Data

Jacobus de Voragine, ca. 1229-1298.
[Legenda aurea. English]
The golden legend: readings on the saints / Jacobus de Voragine;
translated by William Granger Ryan.
p.   cm.
Includes bibliographical references and index.
ISBN 0-691-00865-5 (v.1, hardback)
ISBN 0-691-00153-7 (v.1, paperback)
ISBN 0-691-03178-9 (v.2, hardback)
ISBN 0-691-00154-5 (v.2, paperback)
1. Christian saints—Biography.   I. Ryan, William Granger,
1905–.   II. Title.
BX4654.J334   1993
282'.092'2—dc20
[B]   92-300068

This book has been composed in Adobe Bembo
Designed by Jan Lilly

Princeton University Press books are printed on acid-free paper
and meet the guidelines for permanence and durability of the Committee
on Production Guidelines for Book Longevity of the
Council on Library Resources

Printed in the United States of America

Fifth printing, and first paperback printing, 1995

8   10   9   7

TO

Dominique de Menil

CONTENTS

CONTENTS

CONTENTS

INDEX
389

VOLUME II

CONTENTS

THE GOLDEN LEGEND

99. Saint James the Greater

The apostle James was called James of Zebedee, James brother of John, *Boan-erges*, i.e., son of thunder, and James the Greater. He is called James of Zebedee, namely, the son of Zebedee, not only because he was his son in the flesh but also by the interpretation of the name. *Zebedaeus* is interpreted as giving or given, and blessed James gave himself to Christ through the martyrdom of death and was given to us by God as a spiritual patron. He is called James the brother of John because he was his brother not only in the flesh but in the similarity of their character and virtues, for both had the same zeal, the same desire to learn, and the same ambition. They had the same zeal, namely, the same eagerness to avenge the Lord. When the Samaritans refused to welcome Christ, James and John said: "Lord, do you want us to bid fire to come down from heaven and consume them?" They had the same desire to learn: hence they were ahead of the others in questioning Christ about the Day of Judgment and other things to come. They had the same ambition, because they both wanted to be seated one on the right and the other on the left of Christ. James is called son of thunder by reason of the thunderous sound of his preaching, which terrified the wicked, roused up the sluggish, and by its depth attracted the admiration of all. So Bede says of John:[1] "He spoke so loudly that if he thundered but a little more loudly, the whole world would not have been able to contain him." James is called the Greater, as the other James is called the Less, first, because he was the first of the two to be called by Christ, secondly, because of his intimacy with Christ, who seems to have had a closer relationship with this James than with the other, admitting him to his secrets, as at the raising of the daughter of Jairus and at the Lord's glorious transfiguration. He is called the Greater, thirdly, by reason of his martyrdom, because he suffered first among the apostles. Therefore as he is designated greater than the other James because he was called earlier to the grace of apostleship, so he can be called greater because summoned earlier to the glory of eternity.

James the apostle, son of Zebedee, preached throughout Judea and Samaria after the Lord's ascension, then went to Spain to sow the word of God there. But he felt that he was making no headway there and had gained only nine disciples, so he left two of them to preach in Spain and returned to Judea, taking the other seven with him. Master John Beleth says, however, that James converted only

---

[1] Also called *Boanerges* (Mark 3:17).

one disciple in Spain. While he was preaching the word of God in Judea, a certain magician named Hermogenes, who was allied with the Pharisees, sent one of his followers, whose name was Philetus, to James. Philetus was to confront the apostle and convince him, in the presence of the Jews, that his preaching was false. But James, by well-reasoned argument, showed Philetus that he preached the truth, and wrought many miracles for everyone to see. Philetus returned to Hermogenes, saying that he agreed with James's doctrine and relating his miracles. He further declared that he intended to become a disciple of James, and urged his master to do likewise.

Hermogenes was furious. By his magical skills he made Philetus so immobile that he could not make the slightest movement, and said: "Now we shall see whether your James can release you!" Philetus sent word of this to James by his servant, and James sent him his kerchief, saying: "Have him hold this cloth and say, 'The Lord upholds all who are falling; he sets the prisoners free.'" As soon as Philetus touched the kerchief, he was freed of his invisible bonds, mocked Hermogenes' magic arts, and hastened to join James.

Hermogenes' anger knew no bounds. He summoned the demons and commanded them to bring James himself in chains, together with Philetus, to him, in order that he might avenge himself upon them and also to be sure that his other disciples would not dare to visit such insults on him. The demons swarmed in the air around James and began to howl, saying: "Apostle James, have mercy on us, because we are already on fire before our time has come!" James asked them: "For what purpose have you come to me?" They answered: "Hermogenes sent us to bring you and Philetus to him, but as soon as we reached you, an angel of God bound us with fiery chains and tormented us sorely!" James: "Let the angel of God release you, and go back to him and bring him to me, bound but unharmed!" Off they went and seized Hermogenes, tied his hands behind his back, and brought him thus shackled to James, saying to their captive: "You sent us, and where we went we were burned and sorely tormented!" To James the demons said: "Give us power over him, so that we can get revenge for the wrongs he has done you and for our own fiery torments!" James said to them: "Here is Philetus standing before you! Why don't you lay hold of him?" They answered: "We cannot lay a finger on as much as an ant, as long as it is in your house!"

James said to Philetus: "Let us return good for evil, as Christ taught us to do. Hermogenes put you in bonds, now you unbind him!" Hermogenes, released, stood there not knowing what to do, and James said to him: "You are free, go wherever you want to! It is not in our religion to convert anyone against his will!" The magician replied: "I know the anger of the demons! They will kill me unless you give me something I can have with me to keep me safe!" James gave him his staff, and he went and brought all his books on magic to the apostle to be burned. But James, fearful that the smoke from the fire might do some harm to those unaware of the danger, ordered him to throw them into the sea. He did so and, coming back to the apostle, prostrated himself and clung to James's feet, saying: "Liberator of men's souls! You have borne with me while I envied you and sought to do you harm! Receive me now as a penitent!" Thereafter he began to live perfectly in the fear of God, so much so that many miracles took place through him.

Now the Jews, indignant at seeing Hermogenes a convert to the faith, went to James and inveighed against him for preaching Christ crucified. James, however, quoted the Scriptures to prove conclusively to them the coming of Christ and his passion, and many of them believed. Abiathar, who was the high priest of that year, incited an uprising among the people, then put a rope around the apostle's neck and had him brought before Herod Agrippa. At Herod's command he was led away to be beheaded. Along the road there lay a paralyzed man who called out to James, begging him to cure him. James said to him: "In the name of Jesus Christ, for whose faith I am led to execution, stand up cured and bless your Creator!" The man stood up and blessed the Lord.

The scribe who had put the rope around James's neck, and whose name was Josiah, saw this, knelt at the apostle's feet, asked for his pardon, and requested that he be made a Christian. Observing this, Abiathar had him held and said to him: "Unless you curse the name of Christ, you will be beheaded with James!" Josiah answered: "Cursed be you and all your days, and blessed be the name of the Lord Jesus Christ forever!" Abiathar had him punched in the mouth, and sent a messenger to Herod to obtain an order for his beheading. While the two were waiting to be executed, James asked the headsman for a jug of water. He then baptized Josiah, and both of them had their heads struck off and thus achieved martyrdom.

James was beheaded on 25 March, the feast of the Lord's annunciation, and was transferred to Compostella on 25 July. He was buried on 30 December, because the construction of his tomb took from August to the end of December.

According to John Beleth, who wrote a thorough account of this transferral, after John was beheaded, his disciples went at night, for fear of the Jews, got his body, and put it aboard a rudderless boat. Commending the burial to divine providence they set sail, an angel of the Lord being their pilot, and made port in Galicia, Spain. They landed in the realm of Queen Lupa, whose name, which means she-wolf, fitted her well. They carried the saint's body off the boat and laid it on a large rock, and the rock promptly softened, miraculously shaping itself into a sarcophagus for the body.

The disciples then presented themselves to Queen Lupa and said to her: "The Lord Jesus Christ sends you the body of his apostle, in order that you may welcome dead him whom you would not welcome alive!" They told her about the miracle, namely, how they had reached her territory in a rudderless ship, and asked her to grant them a suitable place for his burial. John Beleth continues that the queen, having heard all this, treacherously sent them to a man known for his cruelty—who, according to other sources, was the king of Spain—in order to gain his consent to the burial; but he took them prisoners and put them in jail. While he slept, however, an angel of the Lord opened the prison and allowed them to go free. When the cruel despot learned of this, he sent soldiers after them to bring them back, but as the soldiers were crossing a bridge, the bridge collapsed and all were drowned in the river. Word of this reached the tyrant, and he, repentant and fearful for himself and his people, sent messengers to ask James's people to come back to him, with the promise that he would grant them whatever request they made. They went back and converted all the people of that city to the Lord.

Lupa heard of this and took the news badly, and when the disciples came to tell her that the king had given his consent, she answered: "Go and take the oxen that I have in a place in the mountains, put together a wagon to carry your master's body, and build a tomb for him wherever you choose!" This was wolfish thinking, because she knew the oxen were really wild, untamed bulls, and thought they could be neither yoked nor harnessed, and if they were harnessed, would run off in different directions, demolishing the wagon, losing the body, and killing the disciples themselves.

But no wisdom can prevail against God. The disciples, not suspecting the queen's ruse, went up into the mountain. A fire-breathing dragon came charging upon them, but they met him with the sign of the cross and split him up the middle. They then made the sign of the cross over the bulls, which suddenly became gentle and submitted to the yoke. Next they put Saint James's body, with the rock upon which they had laid it, on the wagon. The oxen, with no one guiding them, hauled the body into the middle of Lupa's palace. This was enough for the queen. Recovering from her astonishment, she believed and became a Christian, granted everything the disciples asked for, gave her palace to be a church dedicated to Saint James, endowed it magnificently, and spent the rest of her life doing good works.

Pope Callistus tells us that a man named Bernard, of the diocese of Modena, was captured and chained in the bottom of a tower. There he prayed continually to Saint James, who appeared to him and said: "Come, follow me to Galicia!" The apostle broke the man's chains and then disappeared. Bernard, with the chains still hanging around his neck, climbed to the top of the tower and jumped to the ground, sustaining no injury though the tower was sixty cubits high.

Bede writes that a certain man had committed a truly enormous sin, a sin so grave that his bishop feared to absolve him and sent him to Saint James with a paper on which that sin was written. On the saint's feast day the man laid the paper on the altar and prayed to Saint James to erase the sin by his merits. He unfolded the paper afterwards and found that the sin was completely erased, so he thanked God and Saint James, and spread the word about what had happened.

We learn from Hubert of Besançon that about the year 1070 thirty men from Lorraine went on pilgrimage to Compostella, to the tomb of Saint James. All of them except one had sworn to help each other. One of the thirty fell ill, and the rest waited for him for a fortnight, after which they all left him except the one who had not made the promise. This man stayed with him at the foot of the mountain of Saint Michael, where, as evening drew on, the sick man died. The other was frightened by the loneliness of the place, the presence of the dead man, the darkness of the night, and the fierceness of the local population; but of a sudden Saint James appeared to him in knightly array, comforted him, and said: "Lift the corpse up to me, and you come up behind me on my horse!" They rode on and before dawn had traveled a fifteen days' journey, arriving at Mount Joy, a short distance from Compostella and the apostle's tomb. The saint set both the living and the dead down there, ordering the survivor to call upon the canons of Saint James to bury the dead pilgrim, and to tell those who had traveled with him that their pilgrimage was worthless because they had broken their oath. The man carried out his orders and told his astonished companions what Saint James had said.

Pope Callistus says that a certain German and his son set out, around the year 1020, on a pilgrimage to the tomb of Saint James, and stopped overnight in the city of Toulouse, where the innkeeper got the older man drunk and hid a silver drinking cup in their baggage. The two left in the morning, but the host pursued them as if they were thieves, accusing them of stealing his silver cup. They said he could have them punished if he found the cup on them, and when the article was found in their baggage, they were haled before the magistrate. They were sentenced to surrender everything they had to the innkeeper, and one of them to be hanged. The father wanted to die in place of his son and the son in the father's place, but in the end the son was hanged and the father, grief-stricken, went on to Saint James. Thirty-six days later, going back through Toulouse, he turned aside to where his son's body hung and broke out in loud lamentations. And behold, the son, still hanging, began to console his father, saying: "Dearest father, don't cry! I have never been so well off, because Saint James has borne me up and has refreshed me with heavenly sweets!" Hearing this, the father ran into the city, and the people came, took his son down from the gallows unhurt, and hanged the innkeeper.

Hugh of Saint Victor tells the story of a pilgrim on the way to Saint James, to whom the devil appeared in the guise of the saint, and, bemoaning the misery of this present life, said he would be happy if the pilgrim was willing to kill himself in his honor. The pilgrim grasped a sword and killed himself forthwith. But now the man in whose house he had been a guest was suspected of murdering him and feared for his own life. However, the man who had died came back to life and declared that while the devil who had persuaded him to kill himself was leading him to the torments of hell, Saint James met them, snatched the man away, brought him before the heavenly judge, and, despite the demon's accusations, obtained his restoration to life.

Abbot Hugh of Cluny tells us that a young man from the Lyons district, who used to go to the tomb of Saint James regularly and with great devotion, was on his way there when one night he lapsed into the sin of fornication. As he continued his journey, the devil, having assumed the appearance of Saint James, appeared to him and said to the young man: "Do you know who I am?" The youth asked who he was, and the devil said: "I am James the apostle, whom you have been visiting yearly, and I want you to know that your devotion gave me much joy; but recently you left your house and fell into fornication, yet, not having confessed your sin, you presume to come to me, as if your pilgrimage could possibly please God and me. That will do you no good. Anyone who desires to come to me as a pilgrim must first reveal his sins in confession and then do penance for them by making the pilgrimage!" After having said this, the devil vanished.

The young man was troubled in spirit and decided that he would go home, confess his sin, and then start out again on his pilgrimage. But again the devil appeared to him in the guise of Saint James and advised against this plan, asserting that his sin would not be remitted unless he cut off his male member, or made up his mind, in order to be still more blessed, to kill himself and become a martyr in his, James's, honor. Therefore one night, while his companions slept, the young man took a knife and castrated himself, then drove the knife through his belly. When his companions woke up and saw what had happened, they made ready to decamp, fearing that they might be suspected of murder. Meanwhile, a grave was being dug for the dead man, but he came to life and spoke to those who were about to get away, and who were astounded at seeing him alive. He told them what had happened to him, and said: "When I took the devil's advice and killed myself, demons laid hold of me and carried me off toward Rome; but lo and behold, Saint James came riding after us and roundly upbraided the evil spirits for lying to me. When the demons kept arguing, Saint James herded all of us to a nearby meadow where the Blessed Virgin sat in conversation with a large number of saints. Saint James appealed to her on my behalf, and she rebuked the demons severely and commanded that I be restored to life." Three days later, with nothing left of his wounds except the scars, the youth took to the road with his companions and told them the whole story in full detail.

Pope Callistus tells us that about the year 1100, a certain Frenchman set out with his wife and children to go to the tomb of Saint James, partly to escape the plague that was raging in France, but also out of a pious wish to visit the saint. When they reached the city of Pamplona, his wife died, and the innkeeper stole all his money and even the ass his children rode on. Grieving for his lost wife he continued his journey, carrying some of his children on his shoulders and leading the others by the hand. A man came along leading an ass, was moved to compassion by the pilgrim's plight, and lent him the beast to carry the children. When he came to the shrine of Saint James and was watching and praying beside the apostle's tomb, the saint appeared to him and asked whether he recognized him. The man said no, and the saint said: "I am the apostle James, who lent you my beast on your way here, and now I lend it to you for the return journey; but you should know in advance that that innkeeper will fall off the roof and die, and all he stole from you will be returned to you!" Everything happened as the saint had foretold. The man got home safe and happy, and when he lifted his children from the ass's back, the animal vanished.

A certain tyrant had unjustly despoiled a tradesman of his goods and kept him in confinement, and this man devoutly besought Saint James's aid. The saint appeared while the guards looked on, and led the man to the top of the tower. The tower then bent over until the top was level with the ground, and the prisoner stepped off without jumping and went his way. The guards went after him, but, though they passed close to him, they could not see him.

Hubert of Besançon tells us that three soldiers from the diocese of Lyons were on the pilgrimage road to Saint James, and an old woman asked one of them, for the love of Saint James, to load the sack she was carrying onto his horse, which he did. Then he came upon a sick man lying beside the road. The soldier put him on his horse and followed the horse on foot, carrying the old woman's sack and the sick man's staff. But the sun's heat and the toil of the journey were too much for him, and when he reached Galicia he fell gravely ill. His companions asked him about the state of his soul with regard to eternal salvation, but he did not utter a single word for three days. On the fourth day, when his friends were expecting him to die at any moment, he sighed heavily and said: "Thanks be to God and Saint James, because of whose merits I am set free. When you warned me about my salvation, I wanted to do what you suggested, but demons came and held me by the throat so tightly that I could not say a word for the good of my soul. I heard you but I simply could not answer. Then Saint James came in, carrying the old woman's sack in his left hand and the poor man's staff in his right—the two I helped on the road. He wielded the staff like a spear and held the sack as a shield, and set upon the demons as if in anger, threatening them with his raised staff and putting them to rout. Now you see that I am freed and can speak again. Call a priest for me, because I have not long to live." Then he turned to one of the two soldiers and said: "Don't stay in your master's service any longer, because truly he is damned and will shortly come to a bad end." After his companion was buried, this soldier told his master what the dying man had said. The master scoffed and made no effort to amend his ways, and not long afterwards was pierced with a lance in battle and perished.

According to Pope Callistus, a man from Vézelay was on a pilgrimage to Saint James when his money ran out, and he was ashamed to beg. He lay down under a tree to rest, and fell asleep and dreamed that Saint James was providing him with food. Upon awaking he discovered a cinder-baked loaf beside his head. The loaf sustained him for two weeks, until he reached home. Twice each day he ate as much of the bread as he needed, but the following day he found the loaf whole and intact in his sack.

Pope Callistus reports that about the year 1100 a citizen of Barcelona went on pilgrimage to Saint James and prayed for just one favor, namely, that thenceforth he might never be taken captive by an enemy. He was returning home via Sicily when he was captured by Saracens at sea and was sold several times as a slave, but the chains with which he was fettered always fell apart. When he had already been sold thirteen times and was bound with double chains, he called upon Saint James for help, and the saint appeared to him and said: "When you were in my church, with no thought for your soul's salvation you asked only for your body's liberation, and that is why all these misfortunes have beset you. But because the Lord is merciful, he has sent me to redeem you." At once his chains were broken, and he passed through the lands and strongholds of the Saracens carrying a part of the chain as proof of this miracle. So he returned home, where his own saw him and marveled. When anyone tried to take him captive, the sight of the chain sent him flying; and when lions and other wild beasts were about to attack him as he went about in desert places, they saw the chain, were stricken with stark terror, and turned and ran at once.

In the year 1238, in the town of Prato, which is situated between Florence and Pistoia, on the vigil of the feast of Saint James, a feebleminded youth, misled by his own simplicity, set fire to the crops of his guardian, who intended to deprive him of his inheritance. The youth was apprehended and admitted his crime, and was sentenced to be tied to a horse's tail and dragged through the streets, then burned at the stake. He confessed his sin and prayed devoutly to Saint James. Then, clad only in a shirt, he was dragged over stony ground, but neither his body nor his shirt sustained any damage. Then he was bound to the stake and wood was piled all around him. The fire was lit, the bonds were burned away, but he continued to invoke Saint James and both his body and his shirt remained unscathed. They wanted to light a new fire around him, but the people got him away and God was magnificently praised in his apostle.

100. Saint Christopher

Before Christopher was baptized, he was called Reprobus, meaning outcast, but afterwards he was called Christophoros, the Christ-bearer. He bore Christ in four ways, namely, on his shoulders when he carried him across the river, in his body by mortification, in his mind by devotion, and in his mouth by confessing Christ and preaching him.

Christopher was a Canaanite by birth, a man of prodigious size—he was twelve feet tall—and fearsome of visage. According to some accounts of his life it happened one day, when he was in the presence of a certain Canaanite king, that the idea came to him of going in quest of the greatest prince in the world and staying with him. He came to a mighty king who was regarded generally as the world's greatest ruler. When this king saw Christopher, he received him gladly and made him a member of his court.

Then one day the court jester sang some ditty before the king, in which frequent mention was made of the devil. The king was a Christian and made the sign of the cross on his forehead when he heard the devil spoken of. Christopher noticed this, and wondered why the king did it and what the sign meant. He asked the king about it and, when the ruler did not answer, said to him: "Unless you answer my question I will not stay with you any longer!" The king, thus pressed, told him: "Whenever I hear the devil mentioned, I defend myself with this sign, for fear the devil might get some power over me and do me harm!" Christopher: "If you're afraid of being harmed by the devil, this proves that he is greater and more powerful than you are, or you wouldn't be afraid of him. Therefore I am frustrated in my hope that I had found the greatest and most powerful lord in the world. So now farewell! I'll go and look for the devil, accept him as my master, and become his servant!"

Christopher left that king and went in search of the devil. He was going through a desert when he saw a great host of soldiers, and one of them, fiercer and more terrible than the rest, came to him and asked where he was going. Christopher answered: "I'm looking for the lord devil! I want to take him as my master." The other said to him: "I'm the one you're looking for!" Christopher was happy to hear this and pledged himself to serve him forever, acknowledging him as his lord and master.

They marched along the highway until they came to a cross erected at roadside. When the devil saw it, he was terror-stricken, left the road, and led Christopher over a wild and desolate tract before returning to the road. Christopher was surprised at this, and asked the devil what made him so afraid that he left the highroad and took another way through a rough wilderness. The devil refused to state his reason, and Christopher said: "Unless you tell me what this is about, I shall leave you immediately!" The demon, no longer able to evade the question, said: "There was a man named Christ who was nailed to a cross, and when I see the sign of his cross, I am filled with terror and run away!" Christopher: "Well, then, this Christ, whose sign you dread so much, is greater and more powerful than you are! Therefore I have labored in vain and have not yet found the greatest prince in the world! So good-bye to you! I'm leaving you and going in search of Christ!"

He looked long and far for someone who could give him word of Christ. Finally he came upon a hermit who preached Christ to him and instructed him

11

diligently in the Christian faith. He said to Christopher: "This king whom you wish to serve requires that you do his will in many ways. For instance, you will have to fast frequently." Christopher: "Let him require some other form of obedience! That one I just can't do!" Again the hermit: "You will also have to offer him many prayers." Christopher: "I don't even know what that means, so I can't perform that kind of service!" The hermit than asked him: "Do you know the famous river, where many people, trying to get across, go under and perish?" "Yes I do!" said Christopher. The hermit: "You're big enough and strong enough! Go dwell by the river, and if you help those who wish to cross it, that will greatly please Christ the king whom you wish to serve, and I hope he might show himself to you there!" Christopher: "Good! That kind of service I can give, and I promise to serve him that way!"

He went to the river and built himself a shelter to live in. Instead of a staff he used a long pole to steady himself in the water, and carried across all those who wished to go. Many days later he was resting in his shelter when he heard a child's voice calling him: "Christopher, come out and carry me across!" He jumped to his feet and went out, but found no one. He went indoors and again heard the same voice calling him, but ran out and again saw no one. The third time he responded to the same call and found a child standing on the riverbank. The child begged him to carry him across the river, and Christopher lifted him to his shoulders, grasped his great staff, and strode into the water. But little by little the water grew rougher and the child became as heavy as lead: the farther he went, the higher rose the waves, and the weight of the child pressed down upon his shoulders so crushingly that he was in dire distress. He feared that he was about to founder, but at last he reached the other bank.

Setting the child down he said to him: "My boy, you put me in great danger, and you weighed so much that if I had had the whole world on my back I could not have felt it a heavier burden!" The child answered him: "Don't be surprised, Christopher! You were not only carrying the whole world, you had him who created the world upon your shoulders! I am Christ your king, to whom you render service by doing the work you do here. And if you want proof that what I am saying is true, when you get back to your little house, plant your staff in the earth, and tomorrow you will find it in leaf and bearing fruit!" With that the child vanished. Christopher crossed over and thrust his staff into the earth near his shelter. The next morning he rose and found the staff bearing leaves and fruit like a palm tree.

After that, Christopher went to Samos, a city in Lycia. He did not understand the language spoken there, and prayed the Lord to make him able to understand it. As he prayed, the judges thought he was insane and left him alone; but when the favor he had prayed for was granted, he covered his face and went to the place where Christians were being tortured and executed, to speak to them and give them courage in the Lord. One of the judges struck him in the face, and Christopher, uncovering his face, said: "If I were not a Christian, I would quickly have revenge for this insult!" Then he planted his staff in the earth and prayed the Lord that it might burst into leaf and thus help to convert the people. Leaves sprouted instantly, and eight thousand men believed and became Christians.

The king now sent two hundred soldiers to bring Christopher to him, but they found him at prayer and were afraid to tell him why they had come. The king sent as many more, but they, when they found him praying, prayed with him. Christopher rose and said to them: "For whom are you looking?" Seeing his face, they said: "The king sent us to bring you to him in bonds!" Christopher: "If I did not wish to go, you could not take me, bound or not!" They said: "Well, then, if you don't want to come, take your leave and go wherever you wish, and we'll tell the king that we could not find you anywhere." "Not so!" he replied, "I will go with you!"

So Christopher converted the soldiers to the faith, and had them tie his hands behind his back and present him, thus bound, to the king. The sight of him terrified the king, who fell from his seat. His servitors raised him, and he asked Christopher his name and country of origin. Christopher replied: "Before baptism I was called Reprobus but now am called Christopher." The king: "You have taken a foolish name, calling yourself after Christ, who was crucified and could do nothing to save himself, and now can do nothing for you! Now, then, you trouble-making Canaanite, why do you not sacrifice to our gods?" Christopher: "You are rightly called Dagnus, because you are the death of the world and the devil's partner, and your gods are the work of men's hands!" The king: "You were brought up among wild beasts, and you can do only the works of savages and talk only of things unknown to men! Now, however, if you are ready to sacrifice, I will bestow great honors upon you. If not, you will be tortured to death!" Christopher refused to sacrifice, and the king put him in jail. As for the soldiers whom he had sent after Christopher, he had them beheaded for the name of Christ.

Now the king had two shapely young women, one named Nicaea and the other Aquilina, put into the cell with Christopher, promising them large rewards if they succeeded in seducing him. Christopher quickly saw through the stratagem and knelt to pray. When the women tried to arouse him by stroking him and putting their arms around him, he stood up and said to them: "What are you trying to do and for what reason were you sent in here?" The two were frightened by the radiance of his face and said: "Saint of God, pity us! Make us able to believe in the God whom you preach!"

Word of this reached the king, who had the women brought to him, and said: "So you too have been seduced! I swear by the gods that unless you sacrifice to the gods, you will die an awful death!" They answered: "If your will is that we offer sacrifice, have the streets cleared and order all the people into the temple!" This done, they went into the temple, loosened their girdles, and threw them around the necks of the idols, pulling them to the ground and reducing them to dust. Then they said to the assistants: "Call your doctors and let them heal your gods!"

By order of the king, Aquilina was then hung up by the wrists and a huge stone was tied to her feet, thus breaking all her limbs. When she had breathed her last in the Lord, her sister Nicaea was thrown into the fire, but when she emerged unscathed, she was beheaded at once.

Christopher was then brought before the king, who ordered him to be beaten with iron rods, and to have an iron helmet, heated in the fire, placed on his head. Then he had an iron chair made. The saint was bound into it, then a fire was lighted underneath and pitch thrown on the flames. But the chair crumbled like wax, and Christopher came away from it unharmed. Then the king had him lashed to a pillar and ordered four hundred bowmen to shoot arrows at him, but the arrows hung in midair and not a single one of them could touch him. But when the king, thinking that he had been mortally wounded, came to mock him, suddenly one of the arrows came through the air, turned back, and struck the tyrant in the eye, blinding him. Christopher said to him: "Tyrant, I will be dead by tomorrow. Then make a paste with my blood and rub it on your eyes, and you will recover your sight!"

By the king's order the saint was led away to the place of execution, where after praying he was beheaded. The king took a little of his blood and rubbed it on his eyes, saying: "In the name of God and Saint Christopher," and his sight was restored immediately. Then he was baptized and issued a decree that whoever blasphemed against God or Saint Christopher was to be beheaded at once.

Ambrose in his Preface says of this martyr: "O Lord, you granted such a wealth of virtue and such grace of teaching to Christopher that by his gleaming miracles he recalled forty-eight thousand men from the error of paganism to the cult of Christian dogma. Nicaea and Aquilina had been engaged in prostitution in a public brothel, but he won them over to the practice of chastity and schooled them to receive the crown of martyrdom. For this he was strapped into an iron chair in the middle of a blazing fire but feared no harm from the heat. For a whole day the storm of arrows shot by the soldiers could not pierce him; yet one arrow struck the executioner in the eye, and the blessed martyr's blood mixed with earth restored his sight and by removing the body's blindness also illumined his mind; for the saint besought your forgiveness and by his supplications obtained the cure of diseases and infirmities."

101. The Seven Sleepers

The Seven Sleepers were natives of the city of Ephesus. The emperor Decius, who decreed the persecution of Christians, came to Ephesus and gave orders to build temples in the center of the city, so that all the people might join him in worshiping the false gods. He further ordered that all Christians were to be rounded up and put in chains, either to sacrifice to the gods or to die; and the Christians in Ephesus were so afraid of the threatened punishments that friends betrayed friends, fathers their sons, and sons their fathers.

In the city there were seven young Christian men named Maximianus, Malchus, Marcianus, Dionysius, Johannes, Serapion, and Constantinus, who were sorely distressed about what was happening among the Christian faithful. The seven held high rank in the palace but refused to sacrifice to the idols. Instead they hid in their houses and devoted themselves to fasting and prayer. For this they were denounced and brought before Decius. They affirmed their Christian faith, but the emperor gave them time to come to their senses before he came back to the city. On the contrary, they distributed their wealth to the poor, and by common consent withdrew to Mount Celion and kept out of sight there. They lived that way for a long time, while Malchus, one of their number, took it upon himself to provide for their needs. Whenever he had to go into the city for supplies, he put on the dress and appearance of a beggar.

Decius in time returned to Ephesus and commanded that the seven be sought out and forced to sacrifice. Malchus was alarmed when he heard this in the city and reported the emperor's will to his friends. This aroused their fears, but Malchus set before them the food he had brought, to give them strength to face the coming trials. After they had eaten and were talking together with sighs and tears, they suddenly, by the will of God, fell asleep. The next morning the search was on but they could not be found, and Decius was disturbed at the loss of such fine young men. Then they were denounced for concealing themselves on Mount Celion, and, moreover, for giving their property to the Christian poor and persisting in the adherence to the faith. Decius therefore ordered their parents to appear before him and threatened them with death unless they told all they knew regarding their sons' whereabouts. The parents, instead, repeated the same charges against the youths and complained that their wealth had been given away to the poor. The emperor thought about what he ought to do to the seven, and decided, by the will of God, to have the cave in which they were hiding walled up with stones, so that, thus immured, they would die of hunger and need. This was done, but two Christians, Theodorus and Rufinus, wrote an account of the martyrdom and left it concealed among the stones that closed the cave.

Three hundred and seventy-two years later, long after Decius and his whole generation had passed away, in the thirtieth year of the reign of the emperor Theodosius, there was an outbreak of heresy and widespread denial of the resurrection of the dead. This deeply aggrieved the most Christian emperor, who, seeing how the true faith was so impiously distorted, sat day after day in an inside room of his palace, wearing a hair shirt and weeping inconsolably. God in his mercy saw this and, wishing to assuage the grief of those who mourned and to confirm their faith in the resurrection of the dead, opened the treasury of his loving-kindness and awakened the aforesaid martyrs. He inspired a certain citizen of Ephesus to build a shelter for his sheepherders on Mount Celion, and to do this the masons took away the stones from the mouth of the cave and thus awakened the saints. They greeted each other, thinking that they had simply slept through the night. Then they remembered their sadness of the day before and questioned Malchus about Decius's decision concerning them. He answered as he had on the previous evening: "They're looking for us to make us sacrifice to the idols. That's what the emperor has in mind for us!" "And God knows," Maximianus responded, "we will not offer sacrifice!" Having encouraged his companions, he asked Malchus to go down to the city and buy more loaves than he had the day before, and to find out what the emperor had ordered and report what he learned.

Taking five coins with him, Malchus left the cave. He wondered for a moment about the stones lying around but, having other things on his mind, thought no more about it. He approached the city cautiously and marveled at seeing a cross over the gate. Going to another gate and another, he was dumbfounded at the sight of a cross over each of them and at the different appearance of the city itself. He crossed himself and returned to the first gate, thinking that he must be dreaming; but gathering his wits and covering his face he went in. When he came to the bread sellers, he heard people talking about Christ, and was more and more bewildered. "What's going on?" he thought. "Yesterday no one dared to utter the name of Christ, and today everybody confesses him! I don't think I'm in Ephesus at all, because the city looks different, but I don't know any other city like this!" He asked someone and was assured that he was in Ephesus, but kept thinking that there was some mistake and that he had better go back to his companions.

First, however, he went to buy bread, but when he offered his money, the sellers, surprised, told each other that this youth had found some ancient treasure. Seeing them talking about him, Malchus thought they were getting ready to turn him over to the emperor, and, more frightened than ever, asked them to let him go and told them to keep the bread and the money. But they laid hold of him and said: "Where are you from? Tell us where you found these coins of the old emperors, and we'll share with you and hide you. There's no other way you can be hidden." Malchus was so frightened that he could find nothing to say to them, and the men, seeing that he would not answer, put a rope around his neck and led him through the streets to the middle of town. Meanwhile the rumor spread that this young man had discovered a treasure. Crowds gathered round and gaped at him. He wanted to convince them that he had not found anything, and looked all around him, hoping that someone would recognize him or he would see some of his relatives, who, he thought, must be alive. But no such thing happened, and he stood there like one demented, in the middle of the crowd.

Word of this reached Saint Martin, the bishop, and Antipater, the proconsul, a recent arrival in the city. They ordered the citizens to be careful and to bring the youth and his money to them. When he was hauled along to the church, he thought that he was being brought to the emperor. The bishop and the proconsul, amazed when they saw the coins, asked him where he had found this unknown treasure. He answered that he had not found anything at all but had taken the money out of his parents' purse. They asked him what city he came from, and he replied: "I am sure I belong to this city, if indeed this is the city of the Ephesians." "Get your parents here to vouch for you!" the consul said; but when Malchus gave their names, they said he was pretending to be someone else in order to escape. "How can we believe you," the proconsul asked, "when you say the money belonged to your parents? The inscription on the coins is more than 370 years old. They go back to the first days of the emperor Decius and are not at all like our coinage. And how can your parents be that old and you so young? You are just trying to fool the wise men and elders of Ephesus. Therefore I order you to be held until you confess what you found."

Malchus then threw himself at their feet and said: "In God's name, my lords, tell me what I ask you, and I will tell you all I have in my heart. The emperor Decius who was here in this city . . . where is he now?" The bishop answered: "My son, today there is nobody on earth who is called Decius, but there was an emperor Decius long, long ago!" "My lord," Malchus replied, "what you say leaves me confused, and no one believes what I say. But come with me and I will show you my friends who are with me on Mount Celion, and believe them! For I know this, that we fled from the face of the emperor Decius, and yesterday evening I saw the emperor come into this city, if this is the city of Ephesus!"

The bishop thought this over, then told the proconsul that God was trying to make them see something through this youth. So they set out with him and a great crowd followed them. Malchus went ahead to alert his friends, and the bishop came after him and found among the stones the letter sealed with two silver seals. He called the people together and read the letter to them. They marveled at what they heard, and, seeing the seven saints of God, their faces like roses in bloom, sitting in the cave, all fell to their knees and gave glory to God.

Now the bishop and the proconsul sent word to the emperor Theodosius, bidding him come quickly to see this new miracle. He rose at once, laid aside

17

the sackcloth in which he had been grieving, and, glorifying God, hurried from Constantinople to Ephesus. All the people went out to meet him, and together they went up to the cave. The minute the saints saw the emperor, their faces shone like the sun. The emperor prostrated himself before them and gave praise to God, then rose and embraced each one and wept over them, saying: "Seeing you thus, it is as if I saw the Lord raising Lazarus from the dead!" Saint Maximianus said to him: "Believe us, it is for your sake that God has raised us before the day of the great resurrection, so that you may believe without the shadow of a doubt in the resurrection of the dead. We have truly risen and are alive, and as an infant is in his mother's womb and lives feeling no pain, so were we, living, lying here asleep, feeling nothing!"

Then, while all looked on, the seven saints bowed their heads to the ground, fell asleep, and yielded up their spirits as God willed that they should do. The emperor rose and bent over them, weeping and kissing them, and ordered golden coffins to be made for them. That very night, however, they appeared to Theodosius and said that as hitherto they had lain in the earth and had risen from the earth, so he should return them to the earth until the Lord raised them up again. Therefore the emperor ordered the cave to be embellished with gilded stones, and also decreed that all the bishops who now professed faith in the resurrection should be absolved.

There is reason to doubt that these saints slept for 372 years, because they arose in the year of the Lord 448. Decius reigned in 252 and his reign lasted only fifteen months, so the saints must have slept only 195 years.

102. Saints Nazarius and Celsus

Nazarius is interpreted to mean consecrated, or clean, or separated, or flowering, or guarding. In man five things are required, namely, thought, affection, intention, action, and speech. A man should be holy in his thought, clean in affection, straight in intention, just in action, and moderate in speech. All these virtues were in Saint Nazarius. He was holy in his thought and therefore is called consecrated, clean in his affections and is called clean. He was straight in intention and is called separated, for it is the intention that separates works: if the eye is sound, the whole body will be full of light, but if the eye is not sound, the whole body will be full of darkness. He was just in action and therefore is called flowering, because the just shall blossom as the lily. He was moderate in speech and therefore is called guarding, because he guarded his ways and sinned not with his tongue.

Celsus, like *excelsus*, means exalted, and Saint Celsus lifted himself above himself, rising above his childhood age by the strength of his spirit.

It is said that Ambrose found an account of the life and passion of these saints in the book of Gervasius and Protasius; but in other books we read that a certain philosopher who was devoted to Nazarius wrote his passion, and that Ceratius, who buried the saints' bodies, placed the writing at their head.

Nazarius was the son of a man of high distinction, but a Jew, whose name was Africanus, and of blessed Perpetua, a most Christian woman of the highest Roman nobility, who had been baptized by Saint Peter the apostle. When Nazarius was nine years old, he began to wonder about how differently his father and mother practiced their religion, since his mother followed the law of baptism and his father the law of the Sabbath. He hesitated for a long time over which of the two he should follow, his father trying to draw him to his faith and his mother to hers. Finally, by God's will, he went his mother's way and received holy baptism from Pope Linus. His father, understanding what he had done, nevertheless tried to turn him away from his holy resolution, describing to him in detail the kinds of tortures that Christians were forced to undergo. We should note that while it is said that he was baptized by Pope Linus, this should perhaps be understood to mean not that Linus was pope when he baptized Nazarius, but that he was destined to be pope later on. As we shall see below, Nazarius lived many years following his baptism and was martyred by Nero, who in the last year of his reign had Saint Peter crucified. Linus succeeded Peter as pope.

Nazarius did not accede to his father's wish. On the contrary, he was committed to preaching Christ, and his parents feared that he would be put to death. Therefore at their urging he left the city of Rome with seven mules laden with his possessions, and, as he passed through the cities of Italy, he gave away all his wealth to the poor. In the tenth year of his wandering he arrived in Piacenza and later in Milan, where he learned that Saints Gervasius and Protasius were detained in prison. It became known that he was visiting these martyrs and exhorting them to perseverance, and he was denounced to the prefect. Persisting as he did in confessing Christ, he was beaten with cudgels and driven out of the city. As he moved about from place to place, his mother, who had died, appeared to him and comforted her son, advising him to go as quickly as possible into Gaul. He came to a city of Gaul called Gemellus,[1] where he made a great many converts. There a lady brought her son, a charming adolescent named Celsus, and

---

[1] Possibly Geneva.

asked Nazarius to baptize the boy and to take him along with him. When this came to the ears of the prefect of Gaul, he had both Nazarius and Celsus arrested and jailed with their hands tied behind their backs, intending to subject them to torture the next day. His wife, however, sent word to him that it was unjust to sentence innocent men to death and to presume to avenge the almighty gods in this way. Her words made the prefect change his mind and he released the two saints, but warned them and strictly forbade them to preach there any longer.

Nazarius then went to the city of Trier. He was the first to preach the faith there and converted many to Christ. He also built a church dedicated to Christ. When Cornelius the governor heard of this he reported it to Emperor Nero, who sent a hundred soldiers to take Nazarius prisoner. When they found him at the oratory he had built for himself, they bound his hands and told him: "The great Nero calls for you!" Nazarius answered them: "Why didn't you come to me like honest men and say, 'Nero is calling for you,' and I would have come!"

The soldiers took him to Nero in bonds. The boy Celsus cried, and they slapped him and made him follow them. When Nero saw them, he ordered them to be shut up in prison until he devised ways of torturing them to death. Meanwhile, the emperor had sent hunters to capture wild animals, and suddenly a great pack of beasts burst into his gardens and injured and killed many people. The emperor himself was wounded in the foot and had difficulty getting away to his palace. The pain of the wound kept him immobile for many days, until he remembered Nazarius and Celsus and thought the gods were angry with him for allowing them to live so long. So, by the emperor's orders, the soldiers took the two out of prison, kicking and whipping them along, and set them down in Nero's presence. Nero saw the face of Nazarius shining like the sun and thought that this was some magic trick, so he told Nazarius to have done with his wizard-ries and to sacrifice to the gods. Nazarius was brought to the temple and asked all present to go outside while he stayed behind and prayed; and the idols crum-bled to dust. Nero, learning of this, ordered him to be thrown into the sea, and, if by chance he escaped, to be burned alive and his ashes to be scattered over the waters.

Nazarius and Celsus were therefore put into a ship, carried out to sea, and thrown overboard. At once a violent storm broke out around the ship, while a perfect calm surrounded the two saints. The ship's crew feared for their lives and repented the wrongs they had done the saints; and behold, Nazarius and Celsus came walking over the water and boarded the ship. The crew professed the Christian faith, Nazarius prayed, the sea fell calm, and the whole company landed at a place not far from the city of Genoa.

Nazarius preached for a considerable time in Genoa, then proceeded to Milan, where he had left Gervasius and Protasius. When Anolinus, the prefect, heard of this, he ordered Nazarius into exile, while Celsus stayed in the custody of a Milanese matron. Nazarius got to Rome and found his father, now far advanced in age and a Christian. He asked his father how he had come to accept the Christian faith, and the old man replied that Saint Peter had appeared to him and counseled him to follow his wife and son.

The temple priests forced Nazarius to go back to Milan, whence he had been sent to Rome. In Milan he and Celsus were brought before the judge. Then they were led outside the Porta Romana to a place called Tres Muri, and there beheaded. Christians carried the bodies away and buried them in their gardens, but that night the saints appeared to a man named Ceratius and told him to bury their bodies deep down under his house, for fear of Nero. Ceratius said to them: "My lords, please cure my daughter first; she is paralyzed!" The girl was cured immediately, and he took the bodies and buried them as the martyrs had commanded. Long afterwards, the Lord revealed the whereabouts of the bodies to Saint Ambrose, who left Celsus's remains where they were, but found the body of Nazarius looking as if it had been buried that same day, incorrupt, giving forth a wonderful perfume, the blood fresh, the hair and beard growing. Ambrose transferred the sacred relic to the church of the Apostles and there buried it with honors. The martyrs, however, suffered under Nero, whose reign began about A.D. 57.

About this martyr Ambrose says in his Preface: "The holy martyr Nazarius by his merits ascended to the celestial realm, cleansed by his rosy blood. While he was being cruelly subjected to countless forms of torture, he withstood the tyrant's fury with unshaken constancy and could not flinch before the persecutor's threats since the real agent of victory, Christ himself, fought for him. He is led to the temple to offer a libation to the profane idols, but, strengthened by divine help, he reduced their images to dust as soon as he entered. For doing this he was projected into the flowing waters of the sea far from land, but by the help of angelic support he fashioned solid footing amidst the billows. O happy, renowned battler for the Lord, who, attacking the prince of this world, made an innumerable multitude of people participants of eternal life! O great and glorious mystery, that it is rather the Church rejoicing over their salvation than the world exalting over their damnation! O beloved mother, glorified by her children's torments—the children whom she does not consign to hell with loud grieving and groaning, but follows with perpetual laud as they pass over into the eternities of heaven! O most fragrant witness, glowing with heavenly brilliance, whose precious aroma overpowers the perfumes of Saba! Ambrose found thee and made thee his perpetual patron and physician, defender of the faith, warrior in the sacred strife":

> Tu dudum multo latitantem pulvere dragma
> Invenis accensa verbi virtute superna,
> Ut pateant cunctis tua, Christe, munera sedis,
> Angelicos cernant humanaque lumina vultus.[2]

---

[2] This coin, long hid in depth of dust / Lit by the heavenly power of the word, you lately found / That all may know, O Christ, the rewards of your abode / And human eyes may look upon angel faces.

103. Saint Felix, Pope

Felix was elected and ordained pope to fill the place of Pope Liberius, who had refused to approve the Arian heresy and had been exiled by Constantius, son of Constantine, and remained in exile for three years. For this reason the clergy of Rome, with the approval and consent of Liberius, ordained Felix to fill the latter's place. Felix then convoked a council of forty-eight bishops, before whom he condemned Emperor Constantius, and two priests who sided with him, as Arian heretics. This angered Constantius, who deposed Felix from his episcopacy, and reinstated Liberius on condition that the latter be in communion only with the emperor and those whom Felix had condemned. Liberius, weary of exile, subscribed to the perverse errors of the heretics. There ensued a persecution so savage that a great many priests and clerics within the Church were killed. Liberius did nothing to prevent this. Felix was deposed from his office and retired to his private estate, and was seized there and merited martyrdom by decapitation, about A.D. 340.[1]

104. Saints Simplicius and Faustinus

Simplicius and Faustinus were brothers. In Rome, under Emperor Diocletian, they refused to offer sacrifice and endured many kinds of torture. Finally they were sentenced and beheaded, and their bodies were thrown into the Tiber. Their sister, whose name was Beatrice, recovered their bodies from the river and gave them honorable burial. The prefect Lucretius and his vicar, who coveted

[1] This brief chapter is almost totally at variance with now known historical facts that were not known to Jacobus. For instance, Felix is now listed in the *Annuario pontificio* as an antipope, and he did not die a martyr in 340, but died, of unknown but presumably natural causes, in 365. For a useful brief summary of the known facts concerning Popes Liberius and Felix, see *The Oxford Dictionary of the Popes* (New York: Oxford University Press, 1989), 30–32. L. Duchesne, in his edition of the *Liber pontificalis*, pars. 59–66, discusses the situation in more detail.

their estate, had Beatrice arrested and ordered her to sacrifice to the idols. This she refused to do, and Lucretius commanded her slaves to suffocate her by night. The virgin Lucia got possession of her body and buried her beside her brothers.

Lucretius the prefect moved into the coveted property and gave a great banquet for his friends, at which he spoke disdainfully of the martyrs. Then a newborn infant, wrapped in swaddling clothes and resting in his mother's lap, exclaimed for all to hear: "Lucretius, you have killed and you have usurped, and now you are given into the possession of the enemy!" Straightaway Lucretius, fearful and trembling, was seized by the demon and for three hours was so grievously tortured that there, in the midst of the feast, he died. Seeing this, those present were converted to the faith and told everyone how the martyrdom of the virgin Beatrice had been avenged at the banquet. These martyrs suffered about the year of the Lord 287.

✳

105. Saint Martha

Martha, who was Christ's hostess, was of royal lineage. Her father was named Syrus, and her mother, Eucharia. Her father was governor of Syria and many maritime lands. By inheritance through her mother she possessed three towns, namely Magdalum, and the two Bethanys, as well as parts of Jerusalem. Nowhere do we read that she had a husband or ever lived intimately with men. This noble hostess waited on the Lord and wanted her sister to do likewise, because, as she saw it, the whole world would not be enough to serve so great a guest.

After the Lord's ascension, when the dispersion of the disciples occurred, Martha, with her brother Lazarus, her sister Mary Magdalene, blessed Maximinus, who had baptized the sisters and to whom the Holy Spirit had entrusted them, and many others, were put on rafts by the infidels without oars, sails, rudders, or food; but with the Lord as pilot they made port at Marseilles. Then they went to the region around Aix and converted the local populace to the faith. Martha spoke eloquently and was gracious to all.

At that time, in the forest along the Rhone between Arles and Avignon, there was a dragon that was half animal and half fish, larger than an ox, longer than a horse, with teeth as sharp as horns and a pair of bucklers on either side of his body. This beast lurked in the river, killing all those who tried to sail by and

23

sinking their vessels. The dragon had come from Galatia in Asia, begotten of Leviathan, an extremely ferocious water-serpent, and Onachus, an animal bred in the region of Galatia, which shoots its dung like darts at pursuers within the space of an acre: whatever this touches is burned up as by fire. The people asked Martha for help, and she went after the dragon. She found him in the forest in the act of devouring a man, sprinkled him with blessed water, and had a cross held up in front of him. The brute was subdued at once and stood still like a sheep while Martha tied him up with her girdle, and the people killed him then and there with stones and lances. The inhabitants called the dragon *Tarasconus*, and in memory of this event the place is still called Tarascon, though previously it had been called Nerluc, i.e., black place, because the forest thereabouts was dark and shadowy.

With the permission of Saint Maximinus and her sister, Martha stayed there and devoted herself continually to prayer and fasting. Eventually a large congregation of sisters formed around her, and a great basilica dedicated to Blessed Mary ever Virgin was built. The sisters avoided meat, fats, eggs, cheese, and wine, took food only once a day, and genuflected a hundred times a day and the same number of times at night.

It happened one day when Martha was preaching between Avignon town and the Rhone river that a youth who was standing on the other side of the river wanted to hear what she was saying; but he had no boat, so he jumped in nude and started to swim across. But the swift current caught him and he drowned. It took two days to find his body, which was brought to Martha and laid at her feet. She then lay prone on the ground, her arms extended in the form of a cross, and prayed: "Adonai, Lord Jesus Christ, you once raised my brother Lazarus, your friend, to life! My dear guest, look upon the faith of these people gathered here, and give life to this boy!" She took the lad's hand, and he stood up and received holy baptism shortly thereafter.

Eusebius reports in the fifth book of his *Ecclesiastical History* that a woman who had been miraculously cured of an issue of blood erected in her garden a statue of Christ dressed in the same garment as she had seen him in, and prayed before it devoutly. The grass that grew around the statue had never had any curative power, but now any grass that touched the hem of the garment was so filled with power that it cured many of their illnesses. Ambrose says that the woman whom the Lord cured of the issue of blood was Martha herself.

Jerome has a story, also reported in the *Tripartite History*, about the emperor Julian the Apostate. The emperor, so this story goes, took away the statue of Christ above referred to and substituted one of himself, which was struck by lightning and destroyed.

During the year before her death, the Lord revealed to Martha the time of her passing. Throughout that year she suffered continually from fevers. Then, a week before she died, she heard the angelic choirs bearing her sister's soul to heaven. She called all her brothers and sisters in religion together and said: "My companions and dear friends, rejoice with me, I beg of you, because I rejoice at the sight of the choirs of angels bearing my sister's soul to the promised mansions! O my beautiful and beloved sister, may you live in the blessed abode with him who was your master and my guest!"

At that very moment Saint Martha sensed the nearness of her own death, and cautioned her companions to keep the lamps lighted and to watch with her until she died. At midnight before the day of her passing, however, when those watching with her had fallen asleep, a strong wind swept through and blew out all the lamps. She perceived a swarm of evil spirits surrounding her and began to pray: "My father Eloi, my dear Guest! My seducers, holding lists of all the wrongs I have done, are gathered to devour me! Eloi, do not abandon me, hasten to help me!" Then she saw her sister coming to her, carrying a torch with which she lighted all the candles and lamps, and while they called to each other by name, behold, Christ came, saying: "Come, beloved hostess, and where I am, there you will be with me! You welcomed me into your house, I shall welcome you into my heaven, and for love of you I shall listen favorably to those who invoke you!"

As the hour of her death drew near, she had herself carried out of doors so that she might see the heavens, and asked that she be laid down upon ashes and a cross be held before her eyes. Then she prayed in the following words: "My dear Guest, take care of your poor little servant, and, as you deigned to accept my hospitality, receive me now into your heavenly dwelling!" Then she asked to have the passion according to Luke read to her, and at the words: "Father, into thy hands I commend my spirit," she breathed her last in the Lord.

The following day, which was a Sunday, the office of lauds was being chanted around the body of the saint, while in Perigueux, at the third hour, blessed Fronto was celebrating a solemn mass. At the reading of the epistle he fell asleep, and the Lord appeared to him and said: "My beloved Fronto, if you want to fulfill the promise you once made to our hostess, rise quickly and follow me!" In an instant they were in Tarascon and led the singing of the whole office around Martha's body while those assisting sang the responses; then, with their own hands, they laid her body in the tomb. Meanwhile, in Perigueux, the deacon, who was about to chant the gospel, woke Bishop Fronto to ask his blessing, and Fronto, barely awake, answered: "My brothers, why did you awaken me? The Lord Jesus Christ brought me to the body of Martha his hostess and we carried her to her burial! Quick, send messengers there to bring back our gold ring and silver gloves. I entrusted them to the sacristan as I prepared to bury her, and forgot to retrieve them, you woke me up so suddenly!" The messengers went and found things as the bishop had said, and brought back the ring but only one glove: the sacristan kept the other in memory of the event. Saint Fronto added a detail, saying: "As we were leaving the church after the burial, a brother from that place, who was learned in letters, followed us and asked the Lord what his name was. The Lord said nothing but showed the man an open book he was carrying in his hand, on which nothing was written except this verse: 'In perpetual memory: my hostess will be just, she will not be afraid of hearing evil on the last day'; and when the book was closed, he found that the same verse was written on each page."

Many miracles took place at the saint's tomb. Clovis, king of the Franks, had become a Christian and been baptized by Saint Remy. Suffering from a grave malady of the kidneys, he went to Martha's burial place and there recovered his health. In return for that favor he endowed the place and all the land, including villas and strongholds, for three miles around on both banks of the Rhone, declaring the area free of taxes and services.

Martilla, a servingmaid to Martha, wrote her life. Later she went to Slavonia and preached the Gospel of God there, and, ten years after Martha's death, fell asleep in the Lord.

106. Saints Abdon and Sennen

Abdon and Sennen suffered martyrdom under the emperor Decius. When Decius had conquered Babylonia and other provinces, he found some Christians in these regions, brought them to the town of Cordoba, and put them to death with various tortures. Two officials of that area, whose names were Abdon and Sennen, took the martyrs' bodies and buried them. When the two were denounced and brought before Decius, he had them bound with chains and brought to Rome with him. There, in the presence of the emperor and the Senate, they were ordered either to sacrifice and receive their freedom and goods, or to be devoured by wild beasts. They scoffed at the idea of sacrificing and spat upon the idols, so they were dragged to the circus, and two lions and four bears were loosed upon them. The beasts, however, would not touch the saints but rather stood guard around them, so they were put to death by the sword. Then their feet were tied together and their bodies dragged into a temple and thrown in front of an idol representing the sun god. When the bodies had lain there for three days, a subdeacon named Quirinus took them away and buried them in his house. They suffered about A.D. 253.

Later, in the reign of Constantine, the martyrs themselves revealed the whereabouts of their bodies, and Christians transferred them to the cemetery of Pontianus, where the Lord granted many benefits to the people through them.

107. Saint Germain, Bishop

The name Germanus, or Germain, is formed of *germen*, seed, and *ana*, above, hence a seed from above. Three things are found in the sprouting seed, namely, a natural warmth, a nourishing fluid, and a generative power. Saint Germain is called, as it were, a germinating seed, because in him there was warmth in the fervor of his love, fluid in the richness of his devotion, and generative power in the power of his preaching, by which he begot many in faith and morals.

His life was written by the priest Constantine and addressed to Saint Censurius, bishop of Auxerre.

Germain, noble by descent, was born in the city of Auxerre and was well instructed in the liberal studies. Then he went to Rome to study law and achieved such success that the Senate sent him to Gaul, where he attained high office in the duchy of Burgundy and took special interest in governing the city of Auxerre. In the center of that city he had a pine tree, from the branches of which he used to hang the heads of the wild beasts he had killed, as trophies of his skill as a huntsman. Saint Amator, bishop of the city, often protested against this display of vanity, warning that he would have the tree itself cut down lest some bad outcome overtake the Christians on that account, but Germain turned a deaf ear. The time came, however, when in Germain's absence the bishop ordered the tree cut down and burned, and Germain, forgetting his Christian principles, deployed soldiers to besiege the city and threatened the bishop with death. Amator, however, knew by a revelation from God that Germain was to be his successor, so he yielded to the angry governor and retired to Autun. Later he returned to Auxerre, managed to close Germain up in his church, tonsured him,[1] and predicted that he would be the next bishop. That is what happened. A short time later the bishop died a happy death, and the whole populace chose Germain to succeed him.

Germain thereupon distributed his wealth to the poor, lived with his wife as brother and sister, and for thirty years subjected his body to the strictest austerity. He never ate wheaten bread or vegetables, drank no wine, did not flavor his food with salt. He took wine only twice a year, at Easter and Christmas, but even then did away with the taste by adding too much water. He began a meal by swallowing some ashes, following this with a barley loaf; and he fasted always, never eating before evening. Winter and summer he wore only a hair shirt, a

---

[1] The tonsure, a shaved area of the scalp, was the mark of clerical status.

tunic, and a hood, and unless he gave a garment away, he kept it until it was worn to shreds. He spread ashes on his bed: its only covering was a hair shirt and a sack, and there was no pillow to rest his head on. He wept a great deal, carried relics of the saints in a pouch around his neck, never took his clothes off, and seldom loosed his belt or the fastening of his shoes. Everything he did was superhuman. Indeed, such was his life that if there had not been miracles, it would have been unbelievable; and there were in fact so many miracles that, had they not been preceded by his merits, they would have seemed figments of the imagination.

Once when he was a guest in a certain house, after the evening meal he noticed that preparations were made for another meal. Germain wondered about this and asked for whom the preparations were made. He was told that some nice women came at night, and Saint Germain decided to stay awake that night. He did and saw a troop of demons coming to the table in the guise of men and women. Germain ordered them to stay where they were, then awakened the family and asked them whether they recognized the visitors. They answered yes, that they were all neighbors. Then, after again telling the demons not to go away, he sent to the neighbors' houses and they were all found at home and in their beds. Finally, at his command, the visitors admitted that they were demons, and that this was the way they fooled humans.

At that time blessed Lupus flourished as the bishop of Troyes. When King Attila laid siege to his city, Lupus mounted above the city gate and called out to the aggressor, asking who he was who presumed to besiege them. "I am Attila, the scourge of God!" was the answer. Weeping, God's humble prelate said: "And I am Lupus, the ravager of God's flock, alas, and I deserve the scourge of God!" Then he ordered the city gates flung open. The attackers were blinded by divine power, and rushed in by one gate and out by another, seeing no one and harming no one.

Blessed Germain took Bishop Lupus with him to Britain, where heretics swarmed. While they were at sea, a wild storm came up, but Germain prayed and a serene calm settled on the waters. The people gave honorable welcome to the two bishops, whose arrival had been foretold by the demons whom Saint Germain had driven out of the possessed. The bishops convinced the heretics of their errors, brought them back to the true faith, and returned to their own sees.

Germain lay ill in a certain place when it happened that a sudden fire swept through the whole area. The people asked him to let them carry him away so as to escape the flames, but the saint stood up and faced the fire, which consumed everything around but spared the house where he lay.

He was journeying back to Britain to refute the heretics, and one of his disciples, who had hastily followed him, fell ill in the town of Tonnerre. On his way home Blessed Germain had the disciple's tomb opened, called the dead man by name, and asked him whether he wanted to come back and continue to do battle at his side. The dead man sat up and answered that he was happy as he was and had no wish to be recalled to life. The saint agreed that he should resume his rest, and he again laid his head down and fell asleep in the Lord.

On one occasion while he was preaching in Britain, the king of Britain refused to give shelter to him and his companions. One of the king's swineherds, after feeding his charges and receiving his wage at the palace, was on the way home and saw Germain and his fellows in sorry straits due to hunger and the cold. He kindly took them to his cottage and had his one and only calf killed for their supper. When the meal was finished, the bishop had all the calf's bones laid upon the hide, and as he prayed over them, the calf stood up whole and entire. The next day Germain accosted the king and asked him bluntly why he had refused him hospitality. The king, overcome with astonishment, could think of nothing to say in response. Germain said: "Begone then, and leave the kingdom to a better man!" Then, by God's command, he had the swineherd and his wife summoned, and, to the amazement of all, proclaimed him king. Hence the monarchs who have ruled the British people since then are descendants of that swineherd.

Once when the Saxons were making war on the Britons and found that they were undermanned, they called to the two saints, who were passing that way. The saints preached the faith of Christ to them, and all hastened eagerly to receive the grace of baptism. On Easter Sunday their fervor was so great that they threw away their weapons and proposed to fight without them. The Britons heard this and moved swiftly against the disarmed foe, but Germain, who was in among the Saxons, told them that when he shouted *Alleluia!* they should shout *Alleluia!* all together. They did this, and their enemies were so terrified by what they took to be not only the mountains but heaven itself falling upon them that they threw down their arms and retreated on the run.

One time when Germain was passing through Autun, he visited the tomb of Bishop Saint Cassian and asked the deceased bishop how it was with him. At once Cassian responded from the tomb for all to hear, saying: "I taste my sweet repose to the full and await the coming of my redeemer!" Germain: "Rest for a long time in Christ, and intercede earnestly for us, that we may merit the joy of the sacred resurrection!"

He had occasion to go to Ravenna, and Queen Placidia and her son Valentinian welcomed him with honor. At the dinner hour the queen sent him a large silver platter packed with the most exquisite viands. He accepted this gladly, gave the food to his servants, and kept the silver platter to give to the poor. By way of a return gift he sent the queen a small wooden dish containing a barley loaf. The queen was delighted with the present and later had the dish covered with silver.

Another time the aforesaid queen had invited him to dine and he graciously accepted, but he was so weakened with praying and fasting that he had to ride an ass to the palace. Then, while the banquet was in progress, the beast of burden died. The queen learned of this and had a marvelously gentle horse caparisoned and presented to the bishop, who looked at the horse and said: "Let me have my little ass back! He brought me here, he will carry me home!" He went to the cadaver and said: "Up with you, ass, and let us get back to our inn!" The animal got to its feet, shook itself as if nothing had gone amiss, and carried Germain to his lodgings.

Before he left Ravenna, the bishop predicted that he did not have long to linger in this world. Shortly thereafter, he was stricken with fever and died in the Lord seven days later. His body was transported into Gaul, as he had requested of the queen. He died about A.D. 430.

Saint Germain had promised blessed Eusebius, bishop of Vercelli, that he would assist him in dedicating a church which Eusebius had just built. When this bishop understood that blessed Germain had died, he ordered the candles to be lighted for the dedication of the church; but as often as they were lighted, they were immediately blown out. Eusebius saw this as a sign indicating either that the dedication should take place at another time or that it should be reserved for another bishop. Then Saint Germain's body was carried into Vercelli and brought into the aforesaid church, and instantly all the candles were lighted by divine power. Then Saint Eusebius remembered Saint Germain's promise and realized that what he had promised to do while living he was doing after death. This, however, should not be understood as relating to the great Eusebius of Vercelli, or that this had happened in his time, because that Eusebius died under the emperor Valens, and more than fifty years elapsed between his death and that of Saint Germain. What we have narrated took place, therefore, under another Eusebius.

---

108. Saint Eusebius

The name Eusebius is composed of *eu*, which means good, and *sebe*, which means eloquent or standing. Or *eusebius* can mean good worship. The saint had goodness in his constant effort to sanctify himself, and eloquence in his defense of the faith; he stood firm when he faced martyrdom, and offered good worship in his reverence for God.

Eusebius lived a virginal life even when he was still a catechumen, and received both baptism and his name from Pope Eusebius. At his baptism the hands of angels were seen lifting him from the sacred font. A certain lady, captivated by his good looks, wanted to make her way into his bedroom, but his guardian angels forestalled her entering, and when morning came, she prostrated herself at his feet and begged his forgiveness. He was ordained to the priesthood and shone with such holiness that when he celebrated mass the hands of angels were seen serving him.

Later, when the Arian pestilence was infesting all Italy and Emperor Constantius himself abetted the heresy, Pope Julian consecrated Eusebius to be bishop of Vercelli, which at that time stood first among the cities of Italy. When the heretics heard of this, they had the doors of the principal church, which was dedicated to Blessed Mary, closed and locked; but when Eusebius entered the city, he knelt before the main portal of this church, and in answer to his prayer all the doors flew open.

Eusebius deposd Auxentius, the bishop of Milan, who was corrupted by the Arian heresy, from his see, and ordained Dionysius, a true Catholic, in his place. Thus Eusebius purged the whole Western Church of the Arian plague, as Athanasius did for the Eastern Church. Arius was a priest of Alexandria, who said that Christ was purely a creature, and declared that there had been a time when Christ did not exist and that he was made for our sake: thus God created us through Christ, using him as his instrument. Therefore Constantine the Great caused the Council of Nicaea to be convened, and there the Arian heresy was condemned. Arius himself died a miserable death in a privy.

Emperor Constantius, son of Constantine, was infected by this heresy. He was extremely angry at Eusebius, and called a large number of bishops to a council to which he summoned Dionysius. He also wrote several times to Eusebius, urging him to attend the council; but Eusebius knew that malice throve in multitude, and refused to attend, pleading his advanced age as an excuse. In response to this excuse the emperor decreed that the council would be held in the city of Milan, which was not far from Vercelli. When he saw that Eusebius was still absent, he commanded the Arians to write out a statement of their faith, and ordered Dionysius, bishop of Milan, and thirty-three other bishops, to subscribe to that statement. When word of this reached Eusebius, he left his own city and set out for Milan, predicting that he would soon suffer many hardships. He came to a river that he had to cross in order to reach Milan. There was a boat far off on the other side of the river, and at his command the boat came to him with neither rudder nor pilot, and carried him and his companions across. Then the aforesaid Dionysius came to meet him, fell to his knees, and asked for his pardon.

Eusebius continued to be unmoved by either the threats or the blandishments of the emperor, and said for all to hear: "You say that the Son is inferior to the Father. Why then do you put Dionysius, my son and disciple, ahead of me? The disciple is not above the teacher nor the slave above the master nor the son above the father." Taken aback by this reasoning, the Arians brought out the profession of faith that they had written and Dionysius had signed, and put it before Eusebius. But he said: "Never will I put my signature below that of my son, to whom I am superior in authority! So burn this document and write a new one, to which I may subscribe if you wish!" So the written statement that Dionysius and the other thirty-three bishops had signed was by God's will destroyed. The Arians immediately wrote a new copy of their profession and submitted it to Eusebius and the other bishops for their signature, but these, encouraged by Eusebius, refused to sign and rejoiced together when they saw the earlier statement, to which they had subscribed, consumed by fire.

This turn of events angered Emperor Constantius, and he handed Eusebius over to the Arians to do with as they pleased. Immediately they snatched him away from the other bishops, beat him savagely, and dragged him from the top to the bottom of the palace steps and back to the top. He lost much blood from wounds in his head but still refused to give in to them, so they bound his hands behind his back and dragged him by a rope tied around his neck. The bishop, however, gave thanks and said that he was ready to die for professing the Catholic faith.

Constantius now sent into exile Pope Liberius, Dionysius, Paulinus, and all the other bishops who had acted following Eusebius's example. The Arians brought Eusebius to Scythopolis, a town in Palestine, and confined him in a cell so low-ceilinged that he could not stand erect and so narrow that he could neither stretch out his legs nor turn from one side to the other, but crouched with bent head, able to move only his shoulders and his elbows.

Constantius died and was succeeded by Julian, who wanted to please all parties and ordered the exiled bishops to be recalled, the temples to be reopened, and everyone to live in peace under whichever law he preferred. Eusebius, now free, went to Athanasius in Alexandria and told him all that he had suffered. When Julian died and Jovinian reigned, the Arians were quiet and Eusebius returned to Vercelli, where the people welcomed him with great rejoicing. But then, in the reign of Valens, the Arians, who had increased in numbers, surrounded the bishop's house, dragged him outside on his back, and stoned him. Thus he died in the Lord and was buried in the church that he himself had built. It is said that Eusebius prayed God that a grace be granted to his city, namely, that no Arian could ever live in it. According to the chronicle he lived at least eighty-eight years. He flourished about the year A.D. 350.

109. The Holy Maccabees

The Maccabees were seven brothers who, with their venerable mother and the priest Eleazar, refused to eat pork flesh and were subjected to unheard-of tortures, as is told in full detail in the second Book of Maccabees.

It is worthy of note that the Eastern Church celebrates the feasts of saints of both the Old and the New Testaments. The Western Church, on the other hand, does not celebrate feasts of saints of the Old Testament, on the ground that they descended into hell—exceptions being made for the Holy Innocents, in each of whom Christ was put to death, and for the Maccabees.

There are four reasons for the Church's solemnizing the feast of these Maccabees despite the fact that they descended into hell. The first is that they had the privilege of martyrdom. Because among all the Old Testament saints these suffered unheard-of tortures, they are accorded the privilege of having their passion celebrated. This reason is proposed in the *Scholastic History*.

The second reason is the mystical significance of their number. The number 7 is the number of universality. In these seven saints are represented all the Old Testament fathers who deserve to be celebrated. While the Church observes no feasts for them—both because they descended into limbo and because the great multitude of new saints has slipped into their places—nevertheless in these seven she pays reverence to all, because, as has been said, seven is the number by which a universality is designated.

The third reason is the example of patience under suffering. These martyrs are set before the faithful as examples, in order that their constancy may encourage the faithful to be zealous for the faith, and to be ready to suffer for the law of the Gospel as the Maccabees girded themselves steadfastly to live by the law of Moses.

The fourth reason is the cause for which they suffered. They bore tortures for the defense of their Law, just as Christians suffer in defense of the law of the Gospel.

These last three reasons are offered by Master John Beleth in his *Summa of the Divine Offices*, chapter 5.

110. Saint Peter in Chains

The feast called (in English)[1] "Saint Peter in Chains" is thought to have been established for four reasons: to commemorate Peter's liberation, in memory of Alexander's liberation, to commemorate the destruction of a pagan rite, and to obtain release from spiritual bondage.

Firstly, the feast commemorates Saint Peter's liberation. We read in the *Scholastic History* that Herod Agrippa went to Rome and became the close friend of Caius, grandson of the emperor Tiberius.[2] One day when Herod was riding in a chariot with Caius, he raised his hands to heaven and said to his friend: "Would that I might see the death of the old man, and you the master of the whole world!" The charioteer heard this and hastened to report it to Tiberius, who resented what he heard and shut Herod up in prison. Then one day when Herod was resting against a tree in whose branches an owl was perched, a fellow prisoner who was skilled in divination told him: "Have no fear, you will be set free, and you will rise to such heights that your friends will envy you; and in the midst of this prosperity you will die. As soon as you see a bird like this one hovering over you, you will know that you have not more than five days to live!"

Not long thereafter, Tiberius died and Caius succeeded him. He freed Herod, showered him with favors, and sent him to Judea to rule as king. When Herod arrived in Judea, he set his hand to afflict members of the Church. Before the days of unleavened bread he had James, the brother of John, put to death by the sword, and then, seeing how this pleased the Jews, he arrested Peter also. That was during the days of unleavened bread, and his intention was to bring him out to the people after the Passover. An angel, however, came to Peter's assistance in the night, miraculously freed him of his chains, and ordered him to go and resume his ministry of preaching. But there could be no delay in avenging a

---

[1] In Latin it is called *festum sancti Petri ad vincula*, feast of Saint Peter *at the chains*, or *where the chains are*. Despite the somewhat confused account set forth in this chapter, the only fairly probable historical reason for the title of the feast is that it commemorated the rededication of an ancient church in Rome, which originally was dedicated to Saints Peter and Paul. This church is said to have become the repository of the miraculous chains of the apostle in the fifth century, and began to be referred to in the sixth century as the church of Saint Peter *ad vincula*; cf. the paragraph that begins "Saint Alexander subsequently . . ." below, and the paragraph that begins "Eudoxia, daughter of Theodosius . . ." and the following paragraph. The feast was eliminated from the Roman calendar by decision of Pope John XXIII in 1960. I borrow these details from the informative account in *Butler's Lives of the Saints* (New York: P. J. Kenedy & Sons, 1963), 3:236–237.

[2] More exactly, Gaius Caesar, third son of Tiberius, also known as Caligula.

crime against the king, and the next day Herod had the prison guards brought before him so that he could punish them as painfully as possible for letting Peter get away; but he was prevented from doing so, lest Peter's escape bring harm to anyone. Instead Herod hurried down to Caesarea, and there was struck by an angel and died.

Of this last event Josephus, in Book 19 of the *Antiquities*, gives the following account. When Herod came to Caesarea and the populace of the entire province gathered to greet him, he put on a resplendent costume wondrously woven of gold and silver, and came into the theater early in the day. When the rays of the sun struck the silvery garment, the gleam of the shimmering metal and the reflected brilliance cast a redoubled light upon the spectators. The king's formidable appearance blinded the eyes of those who gazed upon him, and his artful arrogance deceived them into thinking that there was something more than human about him. Then the voices of the flattering crowd rolled and rattled around him: "Until now we thought of you," they intoned, "as being just a man, but now we avow that you are above the nature of man!" The king took pleasure in the thought that these eulogies were no more than his due, and made no effort to disown the divine honors offered to him. Then, looking up, he spied, perched on a rope over his head, an angel—that is, an owl. He realized that this was a harbinger of approaching death, and, looking out over the assembled throng, he said: "Behold, I your god am about to die!" He knew by the soothsayer's prediction that death would claim him shortly: he was stricken immediately, for five days worms fed upon him, and he died. Thus Josephus.

To commemorate the miraculous liberation of the prince of the apostles from his chains, and the dreadful vengeance that so soon fell upon the tyrant, the Church solemnly celebrates the feast of Saint Peter *ad vincula*. The epistle sung in the mass of the feast tells how this liberation came about, and it would seem from this that the feast should be called Saint Peter *out of* chains.

Secondly, the feast commemorates the liberation of Pope Alexander, who, sixth after Saint Peter, ruled the Church. Alexander and Hermes, the prefect of the city of Rome whom the pope had converted to the faith, were held in custody in different places by Quirinus the tribune. The tribune said to Hermes: "I marvel that you, a sensible, prudent man, would put aside the honor of being prefect and dream of another life!" Hermes answered him: "Years ago I too scoffed at all those dreams and thought that this present life was the only life!" Quirinus: "Show me how you know there is another life than this one, and you will have me for a disciple of your faith!" Hermes: "Holy Alexander, whom you hold in chains, can teach you better than I can!" At this Quirinus cursed Hermes and said: "I told you to give me proof of this, and now you're sending me to Alexander, whom I hold enchained for his crimes! Anyhow I'm going to double the guards on both you and Alexander, and if by any chance I see you with him and him with you, I'll pay attention to what each of you has to say and teach!"

Quirinus doubled the guards, and Hermes got word to Alexander. Then, while the pope was at prayer, an angel came to him and brought him to Hermes' cell. Quirinus was startled to find them together. Hermes proceeded to tell Quirinus how Alexander had raised his dead son to life, and Quirinus said to Alexander: "I have a daughter—her name is Balbina—and she has a goiter. I promise you that if you can obtain a cure for her, I will accept your faith!" Alexander: "Hurry and bring her to my cell!" Quirinus: "You're here, so how will I find you in your cell?" Alexander: "Go quickly! The one who brought me here will take me back there this minute!"

Quirinus fetched his daughter and went with her to Alexander's prison, where he found the pope and knelt at his feet. Meanwhile the girl began to kiss Saint Alexander's chains devoutly, in the hope of regaining her health. Alexander said to her: "My child, do not kiss my chains, but try to find Saint Peter's bonds, kiss them reverently, and you will be cured." Quirinus therefore had the prison where Peter had been held searched for the chain with which the apostle had been bound, and when it was found, he gave it to his daughter to kiss. No sooner had she done so than she was blessed with perfect health. Quirinus thereupon besought Alexander's pardon and released him from jail, and then was baptized with his household and many other persons.

Saint Alexander subsequently instituted this feast, to be celebrated on the first day of August. He also built a church in honor of Saint Peter the apostle, enshrined the saint's chains there, and called it the church of Saint Peter *ad vincula*. This feast day brings a great concourse of people to the church, where they venerate the chains.

According to Bede, the third reason for the establishment of the feast was this. Emperor Octavian and Antony, who was his relative by marriage, divided the whole empire between them in such a way that Octavian kept Italy, Gaul, and Spain in the West, and, in the East, Asia, Pontus, and Africa belonged to Antony. Antony, however, was a debauched, lascivious man. He was married to Octavian's sister, but repudiated her and took Cleopatra, queen of Egypt, as his wife. Octavian, indignant at this outrage, marched with an army into Asia and routed Antony completely. Antony and Cleopatra fled in defeat and, overwhelmed by misfortune, took their own lives.

Octavian then destroyed the Egyptian kingdom and made Egypt a Roman province. He went to Alexandria and stripped the city of its wealth, transferring the booty to Rome, and enriched the republic so much that now one denarius bought what previously had cost four. Furthermore, since the city of Rome had been devastated by the civil wars, he rebuilt it and was able to say: "I found a city of brick, I left it a city of marble." Because he had done so much to enhance the republic, he was the first to be called Augustus, and his successors were also given that title, just as they were called Caesar after Julius Caesar, Octavian's uncle. And the month that previously had been named Sextilis (because it was the sixth counting from March) was renamed August. So it was to commemorate and honor the victory which Octavian had won on the first day of August that the Romans adopted the custom of celebrating this day until the time of Emperor Theodosius, whose reign began in the year of the Lord 426.

Eudoxia, daughter of Theodosius and wife of Emperor Valentinian, made a pilgrimage to Jerusalem in fulfillment of a vow, and there a Jew offered her, for a very high price, the two chains with which Peter the apostle had been bound in the reign of Herod. She returned to Rome on the first day of August and saw the pagan Romans celebrating the day in honor of a pagan emperor. She grieved to see so much honor paid to a man who was damned, but realized that it would not be easy to turn people away from established culture and custom. Eudoxia therefore managed the affair in such a way that the observance went on, but thenceforth in honor of Saint Peter, and that all the people would name the day *ad vincula*. She consulted with blessed Pelagius, the pope, and together they persuasively exhorted the people to allow the memory of a prince of the pagans to lapse into oblivion, and to celebrate instead the memory of the prince of the apostles.

This train of thought pleased all parties, and Eudoxia produced the chains that she had brought from Jerusalem and showed them to the people. The pope, for his part, brought out the chain with which the same apostle had been bound under Nero. When the two chains were put down side by side, they miraculously joined together, as if there had always been the one chain. The pope and the queen thereupon decided that the worship which men had wrongly given to a pagan who was damned would better be altered and given to Peter the prince of the apostles. They therefore placed the newly joined chains in the church of Saint Peter *ad vincula*, and endowed the church with many gifts and privileges, and decreed that this particular day should be celebrated everywhere. So runs Bede's account, and Sigebert's agrees with it.

The power that was in this chain became apparent in the year 964. The devil had seized upon one of the emperor Otto's counts so cruelly that in sight of everyone the man tore his own flesh with his teeth. By the emperor's order the count was brought to Pope John in order to have Saint Peter's chain placed around his neck; but when another chain was laid on the raving man, nothing good happened—and no wonder, since this chain had no power. Then, however, the true chain of Saint Peter was produced and put about the afflicted man's neck. The devil could not bear the weight of so much power, cried out, and departed while all looked on. Then Theodoric, bishop of Metz, laid hold of the chain and declared that he would not give it up unless they cut off his hand. This started a serious controversy between the bishop on one side and the pope and other clerics on the other, until the emperor put an end to the quarrel by obtaining from the pope one link of the chain for the bishop.

Miletus tells us in his *Chronicle*—and we find the same story in the *Tripartite History*—that in those days a huge dragon appeared in Epirus. Bishop Donatus, who was renowned for his virtue, first made the sign of the cross with his fingers so that the dragon could see it, then spat in the beast's maw and killed it. Eight yoke of oxen were needed to haul the carcass to the place where it was to be burned: this was necessary to avoid polluting the air with the stench of its rotting.

We read in the same two sources that the devil appeared in Crete in the guise of Moses, called together Jews from all over, and led them to the top of a precipitous mountain by the sea. He promised to go ahead of them and lead them dry-shod over the water to the Promised Land. Many followed him and were killed. It is believed that he was angry because, due to the action of the Jew who had given the chain to the queen, the honor paid to Octavian had ceased, and the devil took this means of getting his revenge. Not all those Jews, however, perished on this occasion, and many who escaped hastened to receive the grace of baptism. The mountain sloped steeply toward the sea, and when people began to roll down its face, some were torn apart by sharp rocks, others fell into the water. All died. Those who were still on the summit of the mountain, and did not know what had befallen the others, wanted to go in their turn, but some fishermen, who had seen what had happened, warned them, and so they were converted. That is what we read in the *Tripartite History*.

The fourth reason for the institution of this feast may be set forth here. The Lord miraculously loosed Peter's bonds and gave him the power to bind and to loose. We, on the other hand, are held and bound by the bonds of sin, and need to have those bonds loosed. Therefore we honor Peter on the feast called *ad vincula*, in order that as he merited to be freed of his bonds and received from the Lord the power of loosing, he may absolve us of the bonds of sin. That this really constituted a reason for the establishment of the feast is clear from the liturgical readings in the day's mass. The epistle commemorates the apostle's liberation from his chains, and the gospel narrates the conferring upon him of the power of absolution, while the prayer of the mass asks that absolution be given to us through him.

Moreover, that at times he may, by the keys he received, absolve those who are liable to damnation, is clearly demonstrated by a miracle about which we read in the *Book of the Miracles of the Blessed Virgin*. In the monastery of Saint Peter in the city of Cologne there was a monk who was light-headed, lustful, and lascivious. When he was suddenly overtaken by death, the demons accused him and loudly brought charges of all sorts of sins against him. One said: "I am your greed, which often made you covetous, contrary to God's commandments." Another called out: "I am your vain pride, which made you exalt yourself boastfully before others!" Another: "I am mendacity, in which you sinned by lying." And from others, more in the same vein. To the contrary, some good works that he had done spoke up for him in defense, saying: "I am obedience, which you paid to your spiritual elders!" . . . "I am the sacred chant, and you often chanted the Psalms to God!"

Now Saint Peter, to whose monastery the monk belonged, came before God to intercede for him. To Peter the Lord replied: "Did not the prophet, inspired by me, say, 'Lord, who shall abide in thy tabernacle? Who shall dwell on thy holy hill? He who walks blamelessly, and does what is right.'[3] How can this monk be saved, since he neither walked blamelessly nor did what is right?" But the Virgin Mother joined Peter in his pleading, and the Lord gave his judgment, namely, that the monk should return to his body and do penance. Then suddenly Peter threatened the devil with the key he held in his hand, and the demon turned and fled. Peter entrusted the monk's soul to the hands of one who had been a monk in the aforesaid monastery, ordering him to replace it in the body. The second monk demanded, as a reward for transporting the soul, that his brother monk daily recite the Psalm *Miserere mei Deus*,[4] and that he sweep out his tomb from time to time. So the monk came back from death and related all the things that had happened to him.

✳

111. Saint Stephen, Pope

Pope Stephen converted a great many pagans by his work and example, and buried the bodies of many holy martyrs. For this double reason Emperors Valerianus and Gallienus, in A.D. 260, launched a relentless search for him and his clerics, either to compel them to sacrifice to the idols or to punish them with torture and death. The emperors also issued an edict to the effect that anyone who exposed their whereabouts could take over all their property. Ten of Stephen's clerics were apprehended and beheaded without a hearing. The following day Pope Stephen was captured and led to the temple of Mars, there to worship the god or to be sentenced to death. But as he entered the temple, he prayed God to destroy it, and at once a large section of the building collapsed and all those present fled in terror. Stephen, however, went to the cemetery of Saint Lucy.

Valerianus heard of the pope's escape and sent more soldiers than before to arrest him. They found him celebrating mass in his house. When he had finished the mass, he faced the soldiers fearlessly, and they beheaded him at his throne.

[3] Ps. 14(15):1.
[4] Have mercy on me, O God; Ps. 50(51).

112. The Finding of Saint Stephen, the First Martyr

We are told that the body of Stephen the Protomartyr was found in the year A.D. 417, in the reign of the emperor Honorius. The whole story of the finding of his body includes its transfer and its being united with the body of Saint Laurence.

The finding came about as follows. In the territory of Jerusalem there was a priest named Lucian, whom Gennadius numbered among illustrious men and who wrote the present account. One Friday evening he went to bed and was half-asleep when there appeared to him an aged man, tall, comely of feature, richly bearded, wearing a white mantle adorned with crosses and small gems, shod in gilded boots. He held in his hand a gold rod with which he touched Lucian and said: "Open our tomb with great care, because we were laid away in a very unsuitable place. Go therefore and tell Bishop John of Jerusalem that we are to be reburied in an honorable setting, because, now that the world is stricken with drought and tribulation, God has decreed that he will have mercy if our help is prayed for." The priest Lucian asked: "Sir, who are you?" "I am Gamaliel," came the answer. "I nurtured Paul and taught him the Law. And the one who lies buried beside me is Stephen, who was stoned by the Jews and cast outside the city to be eaten by birds and wild beasts; but this was prevented by him for whom the martyr kept his faith intact. I therefore took up his body with all reverence and buried it in my own new tomb.

"Also buried with me is my nephew Nicodemus, who came to Jesus by night and who received sacred baptism from Peter and John. The chief priests were angry about that and would have killed him, but were deterred by their respect for our relationship. They did, however, take away all his possessions, deposed him from his high office, beat him long and hard, and left him half dead. I carried him into my house, he lived for some days, and when he died, I had him buried at Saint Stephen's feet.

"The third body in my tomb is that of my son Abibas, who at the age of twenty was baptized with me, remained a virgin, and studied the Law with my disciple Paul. My wife Aethea and my son Selemias, who refused to accept the faith of Christ, were not worthy to be buried with us. You will find them buried elsewhere, and their places in my tomb will be found empty and bare." Having said as much, Gamaliel disappeared.

Lucian woke and prayed the Lord that if this had been a true vision, it might occur a second and third time. On the following Friday Gamaliel appeared to him as before and asked him why he had neglected to do as he had directed. "It was not that I was negligent, Sir," he answered. "I had asked the Lord to let the vision be repeated a second and third time if it was truly from God." Gamaliel said: "You have thought about how, if you found us, you would be able to distinguish the relics of each of us. I now give you clues by which you will recognize the coffin and relics of each one!" He showed Lucian three gold baskets and a fourth one of silver. One of the first three was filled with red roses, the other two with white roses; the fourth was filled with saffron. "These baskets are our coffins," Gamaliel said, "and the roses are our relics. The one with the red roses is Saint Stephen's, since he was the only one of us who merited the crown of martyrdom. The baskets filled with white roses are my coffin and Nicodemus's, because we persevered with sincere hearts in confessing Christ. The silver basket filled with saffron belongs to my son Abibas, who shone by his virginity and departed this life pure." With these words Gamaliel again disappeared.

On Friday of the following week he appeared again, angry, and sternly rebuked Lucian for his hesitancy and negligence. Lucian therefore set out immediately for Jerusalem and told Bishop John all that had happened. They called some other bishops and all went together to the place that had been made known to Lucian. As soon as they began to dig, the earth shook and a sweet odor spread, and its fragrance, by the merits of the saints, freed seventy sick people of their infirmities. The relics of the saints were transferred with great rejoicing to the church of Sion in Jerusalem, where Saint Stephen had functioned as archdeacon, and were given honorable burial there. At that very hour a great rainstorm relieved the drought.

Bede, in his chronicle, mentions this vision and the finding of the relics. Stephen's body was found on the same day of the year on which his martyrdom is commemorated and is said to have occurred.[1] The Church, however, changed the dates of the feast days for two reasons. The first was that Christ was born on earth in order that man could be born in heaven. It was appropriate, therefore, that the feast of Stephen's birth in heaven should fall close after Christ's birthday, since he was the first to suffer martyrdom for Christ, and martyrdom is the martyr's heavenly birth and follows as a consequence upon Christ's birth. Therefore the Church sings: "Yesterday Christ was born on earth, in order that today Stephen might be born in heaven."

The second reason was that earlier the finding of Stephen's body was more solemnly celebrated than was his martyrdom, so as not to diminish the reverence due to the Lord's nativity and also on account of the many miracles by which God marked the finding of the relics. But since Stephen's martyrdom was more worthy of veneration than the finding, and therefore ought to be more solemnly

---

[1] 26 December. In the old Roman calendar the Finding was celebrated on 3 August.

observed, the Church transferred the feast of his passion to Christmas week, a time when it would be held in fuller reverence.

Augustine tells us about the translation of the saint's body. He says that Alexander, a senator of Constantinople, went to Jerusalem with his wife and built a beautiful oratory in honor of Stephen the Protomartyr, stipulating that when he died, he was to be buried beside the saint. Seven years after his death Juliana, his wife, decided to return to her own homeland because some prominent men had treated her badly. She wanted to take her husband's remains with her and sought the bishop's permission. The bishop placed two silver coffins in front of her and said: "I do not know which of these is your husband's!" "I know!" she exclaimed, and, hurrying forward, took the body of Saint Stephen in her arms. So it happened that she received the first martyr's body, thinking that it was her spouse's.

When she boarded the ship for her homeward journey, having the sacred relic with her, angels' hymns were heard and a fragrant odor spread abroad. Then demons stirred up a wild storm and cried out: "Woe to us, Stephen the Protomartyr is passing by and is tormenting us with dreadful fire!" The crews were afraid the ship would be sunk, and they invoked the saint, who instantly appeared and said: "Do not be afraid, I am here!" At once a great calm stilled the tempest. Then the demons' voices were heard as they shouted: "Wicked prince, burn the ship, because Stephen our adversary is aboard!" Their prince sent five demons to set fire to the ship, but an angel of the Lord thrust them into the deep. When the vessel put in at Chalcedon, the evil spirits called out: "The servant of God whom the Jews stoned is coming!" Finally the company reached Constantinople safely and installed the body of Saint Stephen in a selected church with all due reverence. This from Augustine.[2]

The bringing together of the bodies of Saint Stephen and Saint Laurence came about in the following manner. It happened that Eudoxia, daughter of the emperor Theodosius, was sorely tormented by a demon. When news of this came to her father, who was in Constantinople, he gave orders to bring the young woman to the city and have her touch the relics of Saint Stephen; but the demon who was in her cried: "I will not go out of her unless Stephen comes to Rome, because this is the will of the apostle!" When the emperor heard this, he persuaded the clergy and people of Constantinople to agree to give Saint Stephen's body to the Romans and to accept Saint Laurence's body in exchange. The emperor wrote a letter to Pope Pelagius about this, and the pope, after consulting the cardinals, acceded to the emperor's petition. Cardinals were

---

[2] The above descriptions, here attributed to Augustine, are composed for the most part of excerpts—words, phrases, sentences, passages—taken piecemeal from several documents, none of them by Augustine, including an *Epistola Luciani ad omnem ecclesiam*, an *Epistola Anastasii ad Landuleum de scriptura translationis protomartyris*, and a *Scriptura de translatione sancti Stephani*, which are published as appendixes in vol. 7 of Augustine's *Opera omnia*, St. Maur edition (Paris, 1838).

sent to Constantinople and took Saint Stephen's body to Rome, and Greeks went there to receive Saint Laurence's remains.

The protomartyr's body was welcomed at Capua, and in response to the Capuans' pious request his right arm was left to them, and the metropolitan church was built in his honor. Then the cortege arrived in Rome. The intention was to enshrine the holy relic in the church of Saint Peter in Chains, but the bearers stopped at the door and could not move a step farther. The emperor's daughter was there, and the demon in her called out: "You labor in vain, because Stephen has chosen his resting place not here but with his brother Laurence!" They carried the body to its new destination, and when Eudoxia touched it, she was freed of the demon. Saint Laurence, as if he were congratulating himself and smiling at the arrival of his brother Stephen, moved to one side of his tomb and left the middle vacant for his brother.

When the Greeks raised their hands to carry Laurence's body away, they sank to the ground as if in a faint, but the pope, with the clergy and the people, prayed for them, and toward evening they revived; yet within ten days they were all dead. As for the Latins who had sided with the Greeks in this matter, they were seized with a frenzy and could not be cured until the bodies of the two saints were entombed together. Then a voice was heard in the heavens: "O happy Rome! You now hold within yourself the bodies of Laurence of Spain and Stephen of Jerusalem, those glorious pledges!" This joining was carried out on 20 April about the year A.D. 425.

In Book XXII of *The City of God*, Augustine tells about six dead persons who were brought to life by invoking Saint Stephen. Item: one man had been dead long enough that his thumbs were tied together, but Saint Stephen's name was invoked over him and he immediately came to life. Item: a boy had been crushed to death by a wagon, but his mother carried him to Saint Stephen's church and he was restored to her alive and well. Item: a nun who was in her last agony had been carried to Saint Stephen's church and had expired there, and then, in the sight and to the astonishment of all, rose up in good health. Item: a girl in Hippo had died. Her father took her tunic to Saint Stephen's church and later threw it over the dead girl: she rose immediately. Item: a youth whose dead body was anointed with Saint Stephen's oil came to life forthwith. Item: a boy was carried dead into Saint Stephen's church and was restored to life at once.

About this martyr Augustine says: "Gamaliel, clothed in a richly adorned garment, revealed the location of the martyr's body; Saul, stripped, stoned him; Christ, wrapped in swaddling clothes, enriched him and crowned him with precious stones." Augustine again: "In Stephen shone beauty of body, the flower of age, the eloquence of the preacher, the wisdom of a most holy mind, and the operation of divinity." Again: "This strong column of God, when he was held between the hands of stoners as by a giant vise, was enkindled by his white-hot faith, was struck down yet stood up, was strangled, throttled, beaten, yet could not be conquered." Augustine on the text *You stiff-necked people. . . :*[3] "He does not flatter, he attacks with words; does not pamper, he provokes; does not tremble, he incites." And still Augustine: "Consider Stephen, your fellow servant! He was a man, as you are, came from the mass of sin, as you did, was redeemed at the same price as you were; when he was a deacon, he read the Gospel that you read or hear, and there he found written, 'Love your enemies.' He learned this by reading, he accomplished it by obeying."

113. Saint Dominic

Dominic, or Dominicus, is like *Domini custos*, the guardian of the Lord, or *a Domino custoditus*, guarded by the Lord; or the name may be interpreted according to the etymology of the word *dominus*. Dominic is therefore called the guardian of the Lord in three ways. With regard to God, he guarded the Lord's honor. With regard to his neighbor, he guarded the Lord's vineyard or his flock. With regard to himself, he minded the Lord's will and kept his commandments. He is called Dominic as being guarded by the Lord because God guarded him in each of his states of life, as a layman, a canon regular, and an apostle. The Lord guarded him in his first state by having him start out in a praiseworthy manner, in his second by making him go forward with fervor, and in the third by enabling him to achieve perfection. And lastly, he is called Dominic according to the etymology of the word *dominus*, which is equivalent to *donans minas*, condoning threats, of *donans minus*, giving less, or *donans munus*, giving a gift. For Saint Dominic was *donans minas* because he forgave injuries, *donans minus* by mortifying his body, to which he always gave less than it desired, and *donans munus* because he not only gave what was his to the poor but also sought several times to sell himself for them.

Dominic, the illustrious leader and father of the Order of Preachers, was born in Spain, in the village of Calaroga, diocese of Osma. His father's name was Felix and his mother's Joanna; from them he took his bodily origin. Before he was born, his mother dreamed that she carried in her womb a little dog which held a lighted torch in his mouth, and when the dog came forth from her womb, he

[3] Acts 7:51.

set fire to the whole fabric of the world. And when Dominic's godmother lifted him from the sacred font, it seemed to her that he had on his forehead a brilliant star which shed its light over the whole world. While he was still a child in the care of his nurse, he often got out of bed at night and lay on the bare ground.

For his studies he was sent to Palentia. He was so eager for knowledge that for ten years he never drank wine. When a great famine befell the city, he sold his books and furniture and gave the proceeds to the poor. His fame spread, and the bishop of Osma made him a canon regular;[1] and later on, because his life was a mirror of virtue for all, the canons appointed him to be their subprior. He devoted himself day and night to reading and prayer, ceaselessly beseeching God to deign to give him the grace to spend himself totally for the salvation of his neighbor. He also studiously read the book of the *Conferences of the Fathers* and advanced to a high degree of perfection.

With his bishop he went to Toulouse and perceived that his host there had become tainted with heretical perversity. Dominic converted him to the faith of Christ and presented him to the Lord as a sheaf of the first fruits of the harvest to come.

We read in the *Acts of Count de Montfort* that on one occasion when Dominic had preached against the heretics, he wrote out the arguments and proofs he had used in his discourse, and gave the paper to one of the heretics so that he could give thought to his objections. That night the man showed the paper he had received to his fellow heretics as they sat around a fire. They told him to throw the document into the fire: if it burned, they said, their faith (or rather their false faith) would be proven true, but if it could not be burned up, they would preach the true faith of the Roman church. The paper was tossed into the flames, but after some minutes it sprang out of the fire intact. They were all astonished, but one, more hardheaded than the rest, said: "Throw it in again, repeat the test, and we will be surer of the truth." The writing was thrown in again and again came out unscathed. But the stubborn one said: "Try it a third time and then we will have no doubt about the outcome." Back went the paper, and again it bounced out unscorched and unharmed. The heretics, however, persisting in their willfulness, bound themselves with the strictest of oaths not to make this known. But there was a soldier present who felt drawn to our faith, and he later made the miracle public. This took place near Montréal, and it is said that a similar thing happened about that time at Fanjeaux, where a formal debate with the heretics was held.

The bishop of Osma died and most of his entourage went back home, but Saint Dominic, with a few companions, stayed on and continued to preach the word of God against the heretics. The enemies of the truth made fun of him, spat at him, threw mud and ordure at him, and in derision tied a tail of straw

---

[1] Member of a body of priests not belonging to a religious order but attached to a cathedral or other church and living in community under a rule, usually the Rule of Saint Augustine.

behind him. When they threatened to kill him, he fearlessly responded: "I am not worthy of the glory of martyrdom, I have not yet merited the death you threaten me with." So, passing through a place where they were waiting to waylay him, he went ahead not only without fear, but jauntily, singing a song. They marveled at him and said: "Are you not stricken with horror at the thought of death? What would you have done if we had laid hold of you?" He answered: "I would have asked you to put me to death not with swift, sudden blows, but slowly, cutting me to pieces, bit by bit, holding up before my eyes the pieces you had cut off, then putting my eyes out and leaving my half-dead body to welter in its own blood—or else to kill me any way you please."

Once, when he found a man who, suffering from dire poverty, had yielded to the heretics' persuasion, Dominic decided to sell himself, so that with the price he got for his own person he might put an end to the man's indigence and free him from the error into which his need had driven him. And the saint would have done it, had not God's mercy provided otherwise for the poor man.

Another time a woman, loud in her lamentations, told him that her brother was held in captivity by the Saracens, and declared that she could no longer find any means of obtaining his freedom. Dominic, moved to compassion, offered to sell himself and thus redeem the captive, but God did not allow this, foreseeing that the saint would be needed for the spiritual redemption of many captives.

In the Toulouse area Dominic was the guest of some ladies who had been led into error by the heretics' ostentatious show of religiousness. Fighting fire with fire, the saint and his companion fasted all during Lent on bread and cold water and watched throughout the night, resting their weary limbs only when necessity compelled them. Thus the ladies were led to recognize the true religion.

Now Dominic began to think about establishing a religious order whose mission it would be to go from place to place, preaching and strengthening the faith against the heretics. After he had spent ten years in and around Toulouse, from the death of the bishop of Osma to the calling of the council of the Lateran, he went to Rome with Fulk, the bishop of Toulouse, to assist at the general council. In Rome he sought permission of Pope Innocent, for himself and his successors, to found an order that would be called, and would be in fact, the Order of Preachers. The pope withheld his assent for some time. Then one night in a dream he saw the Lateran basilica about to fall in ruins; but, while he watched fearfully, Dominic, the man of God, came running from the opposite side, placed his shoulders against the tottering building, and held up the whole structure. When the pope awoke, he understood the meaning of the vision and happily entertained the petition of the man of God, advising him to return to his brethren and to choose some one of the approved rules, and then to come back to him and receive his approval. Dominic therefore returned to his brothers and informed them of the pontiff's word; whereupon they, sixteen in number, invoked the Holy Spirit, and with one mind chose the rule of Saint Augustine, the renowned doctor and preacher, and decided that they would be preachers in

name and in action. To the rule of Augustine they added certain stricter practices that would be observed as constitutions. As Innocent had died in the meantime and Honorius had been elevated to the supreme pontificate, Dominic obtained confirmation of the Order from Honorius in the year of the Lord 1216.

One day while he was praying in the church of Saint Peter for the expansion
of his Order, Peter and Paul, the glorious princes of the apostles, appeared to
him. Peter gave him a staff, and Paul a book, and they said: "Go forth and
preach, for God has chosen you for this ministry." In a moment it seemed to him
that he saw his sons setting out two by two and dispersed throughout the world.
He therefore returned to Toulouse and sent his brethren forth, some to Spain,
others to Paris, still others to Bologna; and he himself went back to Rome.

One day, before the institution of the Order of Preachers, a certain monk was
rapt in ecstasy and saw the Blessed Virgin kneeling with clasped hands, praying
to her Son for the human race. Several times he seemed to resist his loving
mother, but she insisted, and he said: "Dear mother, what more can I do or
ought I do for them? I have sent them patriarchs and prophets, and little have
they amended their ways. I came to them myself and then sent my apostles, and
they put me and them to death. I sent them martyrs, doctors, and confessors, and
they paid no attention to them. But it would not be right for me to refuse you
anything. Therefore I shall send them my preachers, through whom they can be
enlightened and cleansed. If they are not, I shall come against them."

Another monk had a similar vision about that time, when twelve abbots of
the Cistercian Order had been sent to Toulouse to combat the heretics. In this
vision, when the Son had given the above-mentioned answer to his mother, the
Virgin said to him: "Dear Son, you must not deal with them in accordance with
their evil deeds, but as your mercy dictates!" Conquered by her prayers, he
replied: "At your appeal I shall grant them this mercy, that I send them my
preachers to instruct and admonish them. If then they do not change their ways,
I shall spare them no longer."

A Friar Minor, who had long been a companion to Saint Francis, told the
following story to several friars of the Order of Preachers. While Dominic was
in Rome, waiting upon the pope for approval of his Order, one night in a vision
he saw Christ, aloft in the air, holding three spears that he brandished over the
world. His mother ran to him and asked what he was about to do. He said: "The
whole world is full of three vices, pride, concupiscence, and avarice: therefore
I will destroy it with these three lances." The Virgin fell to her knees and said:
"Dearest Son, have pity, and temper your justice with mercy!" Christ replied:
"But do you not see the wrongs they wreak upon me?" Mary answered: "My
Son, curb your wrath and wait a little, for I have a faithful servant and valiant
warrior, who will go all over the world and conquer it and subjugate it to your
rule! And I will give him another servant to help him, who will fight loyally at
his side." Jesus said: "My anger is appeased and I yield to your plea, but I would
be pleased to see these men whom you wish to commit to so high a destiny." At

this she presented Saint Dominic to Christ, who said: "This is a good, strong battler, and he will be zealous in doing all that you have said." Then she brought Saint Francis to him, and Christ commended him as he had the first. Saint Dominic studied this ally whom he had not known before, and the next day, finding him in the church and recognizing him without any clue other than what he had seen the night before, hurried to him and embraced and kissed him affectionately, saying: "You are my partner, you will run with me stride for stride. Let us stand together and no adversary will prevail against us." He then told Francis about the aforesaid vision in detail. Thenceforward they were of one heart and soul in the Lord, and they made it a rule that those who would follow them should live in the same harmony for all time.

Dominic had received as a novice in his Order a certain youth from Apulia, but some of the young man's former cronies demoralized him to such an extent that he decided to return to the world and insisted on resuming his ordinary clothes. When Saint Dominic heard of this, he resorted at once to prayer; and when they had stripped the youth of his religious habit and had put on his shirt, he began to cry out with loud shouts: "Help! I am burning, I am on fire, I am totally consumed! Quick, take off this accursed shirt! It's burning me alive!" He could not be quieted until the shirt was taken off, and he was clothed again in his religious garb and led back to the cloister.

One night when Saint Dominic was in Bologna and the brothers had already gone to bed, one lay brother began to be tormented by the devil. His master, Friar Rainier of Lausanne, heard this and was careful to report it to Dominic, who ordered the brother to be carried into the church and set down before the altar. When ten of the brothers had brought him in and barely managed to hold him down, Dominic addressed the devil: "I adjure you, you wretch, to tell me why you are tormenting this creature of God, and why and how you got into him!" The evil spirit answered: "I torture him because he deserves it. Yesterday in town he drank without the prior's permission and without making the sign of the cross over the wine. So I entered him in the shape of a gnat, or rather he drank me in with the wine"; and it was ascertained that the brother had been guilty of this fault. While all this was going on, however, the first bell for matins rang, and at the sound the devil, who was speaking from inside the brother, said: "Now I cannot stay here any longer, because those cowl-heads are getting up!" Thus, at Saint Dominic's prayer, the demon was forced to come out of the man.

The saint was crossing a river in the vicinity of Toulouse, and his books, which had no wrapping around them, fell into the water. Three days later a fisherman cast his line into the river and, thinking he had hooked a big fish, hauled in the books as unharmed as if they had been carefully stowed in a cupboard.

One night Dominic arrived at the door of a monastery after the brothers had gone to bed. The saint did not want to disturb their rest, so he prayed, and he and his companion went in through the locked doors. It is also related that once when, with a Cistercian lay brother, he was engaged in combating the heretics, they reached a certain church in the evening and found it closed; but the saint prayed, and they suddenly found themselves inside the church, where they spent the whole night in prayer.

After the fatigues of a journey and before he accepted hospitality, it was his custom to quench his thirst at a spring, so that once he was in the house, his host would not think that he drank more than was usual.

A scholar who suffered temptations of the flesh came, on a certain feast day, to a house of the Order to hear mass. It happened that on that day Dominic was the celebrant of the holy sacrifice. When the time came for the offering, the scholar went forward and kissed the saint's hand with deep devotion. When he had kissed it, he sensed a perfume coming from the hand, an odor sweeter than any he had ever experienced in his life; and thereafter the heat of carnal passion was marvelously cooled in him, to the point that the young man, who had been vain and lubricious, became continent and chaste. Oh, how great was the purity and cleanness that strengthened the body of him whose odor so wondrously purged away all dirt from a soul!

A certain priest, seeing the zeal with which Dominic and his friars preached, considered joining them, if only he could obtain a New Testament that he needed for his preaching. As he thought about this, a young man came along with a Testament under his coat and offered to sell it to the priest, who bought it immediately and joyfully. But as he still hesitated a little, he offered a prayer to God, made the sign of the cross on the cover of the book, and opened it. What first met his eye was the tenth chapter of the Acts of the Apostles, and he read the words that the Holy Spirit spoke to Peter: "Rise and go down, and accompany them without hesitation; for I have sent them." He rose at once and joined the friars.

At that time there was in Toulouse a master of theology, renowned for his knowledge and good name. One morning before dawn he was preparing his lectures for the day, but felt sleepy and drowsed a little in his chair; and in a vision he saw seven stars being offered to him. Marveling at the novelty of such a present, he then saw the stars grow in size and number until they lighted up the whole world. He woke up still wondering what this meant. Behold! when he had entered the school and began his lesson, Saint Dominic and six of his friars, all wearing the same habit, humbly approached the master and, submitting their proposal to him, said that they wanted to attend his lectures. He recalled his vision and had no doubt that these were the seven stars he had seen.

While Dominic, the man of God, was in Rome, a certain Master Reginald, who was dean of Saint Amianus in Orleans and had taught canon law in Paris for five years, came to Rome with the bishop of Orleans on his way to cross the sea. The master had it in mind to leave everything else and devote himself to preaching, but did not yet see how he might go about realizing this wish. He made his desire known to a certain cardinal, who told him about the establishment of the

Order of Preachers. Summoning Dominic, Reginald informed him of his intention, and decided then and there to enter the Order. But then he was stricken with a fever so grave that his life was despaired of. Saint Dominic, however, persevered in prayer and implored the Blessed Virgin, to whom he had entrusted the care of the Order as its special patroness, to deign to grant the master to him at least for a short time.

Then Reginald, awake and awaiting death, saw the Queen of mercy coming to him accompanied by two beautiful maidens. The Queen turned her smiling face to him and said: "Ask whatever you will and I will give it to you." As he pondered what to ask for, one of the maidens counseled him to make no request, but to commend himself wholly to the Queen of mercy. He did this. The Queen extended her virginal hand and anointed his ears and nostrils, his hands and feet, with a health-giving ointment she had brought, pronouncing the proper formula at each anointing. Thus at the loins she said: "May your loins be girt with the cincture of chastity"; at the feet: "Anoint the feet in preparation of the gospel of peace." She added: "Three days from now I shall send you a phial of ointment that will restore you to full health." Then she showed him a religious habit. "Look," she said, "this is the habit of your Order." This same vision came to blessed Dominic while he was at prayer.

The next day Dominic visited Reginald and found him in health. He heard all about the master's vision and adopted the habit the Virgin had shown: the friars had been using surplices. On the third day the mother of God came and anointed Reginald's body, with the result that not only the heat of the fevers but also the fires of concupiscence were extinguished in him, so that, as he later confessed, he no longer felt the slightest movement of lust. A religious of the order of the Hospitalers also saw this second vision with his own eyes, in Dominic's presence, and was astonished. After Reginald's death the saint told many of the brothers about the vision. Meanwhile Reginald was sent to Bologna, where he devoted himself to ardent preaching, and the number of friars increased markedly. Afterwards he was sent to Paris and fell asleep in the Lord some days later.

A young man, the nephew of Cardinal Stephen of Fossa Nova, fell headlong with his horse into a ditch and was lifted out dead, but was taken to Dominic, and at the saint's prayer was brought back to life. And a master builder was conducted by the brothers into the crypt of the church of Saint Sixtus, and was crushed by the fall of a ruined ceiling and died under the debris; but Dominic, the man of God, had the body brought up from the vault and by his prayers restored the man to life and health.

One day the friars who lived at this same church, about forty in number, found that they had very little bread. Saint Dominic ordered them to put the little they had on the table and divide it into small pieces. While each friar was breaking his morsel with joy, two young men, alike in form and vesture, entered the refectory with the pockets of the cloaks that hung from their necks filled with loaves. They silently laid the loaves at the head of the table where sat Dominic, the man of God, and suddenly disappeared: no one ever found out where they came from or where they went. Dominic waved his hand all around to the friars and said: "Now, my brothers, eat!"

One day when the saint was on a journey and the rain was falling in torrents, he made the sign of the cross, and it held the rain off from him and his companion as if the cross were a sort of canopy. Though the ground was flooded by the heavy downpour, not a drop fell within three or four feet around them.

Another time he was crossing a river near Toulouse in a boat, and the boatman demanded payment of his fare. The saint promised him the kingdom of heaven for the service he was providing, and added that he himself was a disciple of Christ and carried neither gold nor money. The man, however, tugged at Dominic's cape and said: "Pay the fare or hand over your cape!" The man of God raised his eyes to heaven and prayed inwardly for a few moments, then looked down and saw a coin at his feet, put there, no doubt, by the will of God. "There is what you are demanding, brother," he said. "Take it and let me go freely and in peace."

Again in his travels it happened that he was joined by another religious who was congenial in the holiness of his life but completely foreign in speech and language. Dominic was aggrieved that he could not be warmed by a mutual exchange of holy thoughts, and prayed the Lord to grant that when they conversed, each of them might speak the language of the other; and so they understood each other during the three days they traveled together.

Once a man who was possessed by many demons was brought to Dominic. He took a blessed stole and wrapped one end around his own neck and the other around the neck of the possessed man, and commanded the demons to stop molesting the man and not to bother him any longer. But the spirits began to be tortured in the man's body and cried out: "Let us go free! Why do you force us to stay here and be tortured?" The saint answered: "I will not let you go until you give me a surety that you will not enter him again." "Who would stand surety for us?" they asked. He answered: "The holy martyrs, whose bodies rest in this church!" The demons said: "We cannot give them as surety because our deserts are against it." "You had better give them," he said, "because otherwise I will by no means release you from torment." To this they responded that they would try, and after a while they said: "Despite our unworthiness we have obtained the help of the holy martyrs, and they will be our surety." He required a sign to confirm this, and they said: "Go to the casket in which the martyrs' heads are preserved, and you will find it turned around." And it was found that what they said was true.

Once when he was preaching, some women who had been led into error by the heretics threw themselves at his feet and said: "Servant of God, help us! If what you preached today is true, our minds have long been blinded by the spirit of error." He replied: "Be of good heart and wait a moment, and you will see what sort of god you have followed." At once they saw a hideous cat leap out from their midst: he was as big as a large dog, had huge, flaming eyes, a long, wide, bloody tongue that reached to his navel, and a short tail that stood up and exposed the filth of his hind parts whichever way he turned, and emitted an intolerable stench. After the beast had stalked to and fro around the women for some time, he climbed up the bell rope and disappeared into the belfry, leaving foul traces behind him. The women therefore gave thanks and were converted to the Catholic faith.

At Toulouse, Saint Dominic once convicted a number of heretics, and they were condemned to be burned alive. Looking over them, he saw a certain man, whose name was Raymond, and said to the executioners: "Save that man, do not let him be burned with the rest." Then he turned to Raymond and said to him kindly: "I know, my son, I know that one day, even though it may be years away, you will be a good man and a saint!" Raymond was freed, therefore, and persisted in heresy for twenty years. Then he was converted and entered the Order of Preachers, led an admirable life, and died a happy death.

When Dominic was in Spain with some of the friars as companions, he saw in a vision a monstrous dragon trying to draw the brothers into its open jaws. He understood the meaning of the vision and exhorted the friars to be firm in the faith, but later all of them, except Friar Adam and two lay brothers, left him. When he asked one of those who remained if he too wished to depart as the others had done, he answered: "God forbid, father, that I should leave the head to follow the feet!" The saint prayed and prayed, and within a short time, through his prayer, he converted almost all of those who had defected.

He was with the friars at Saint Sixtus in Rome when suddenly the Holy Spirit came over him. He brought the brothers together in chapter and publicly announced to all of them that four of their number would soon die, two the death of the body and two the death of the soul. Shortly thereafter, two friars migrated to the Lord and two others left the Order.

Dominic was in Bologna, where there was a certain Master Conrad the Teuton, whose entrance into the Order the friars very much desired. On the vigil of the feast of the assumption of the Blessed Mary the saint was exchanging confidences with the prior of the Cistercian monastery of Casa Mariae, and among other things he said to him: "Prior, I am going to tell you something I have never revealed to anyone, and that you must not tell anyone else as long as I live; and that is that I have never in this life asked God for anything which I did not obtain according to my wish." The prior remarked that he himself might come to the end of his life before the saint, but Dominic, moved by the spirit of prophecy, told him that, on the contrary, he would long survive him; and that is the way it turned out. Then the prior said: "Father, ask God to give Master Conrad to the Order, since the brothers so earnestly want him to enter." Dominic answered: "Good brother, you are asking for a very hard thing!" But after the hour of compline, when all had gone to rest, Dominic remained in the church and, as he usually did, prayed throughout the night.

In the morning, when the community came together for prime and the cantor intoned the hymn *Jam lucis orto sidere* (The star of light being already risen), Master Conrad, who was to be the new star of a new light, suddenly came up, prostrated himself at Saint Dominic's feet, and begged to receive the habit of the Order, which he received forthwith. Thereafter there was no more devout religious than he in the Order, nor any master whose lessons were received with more favor. And when at last he lay dying and had closed his eyes, so that the friars thought he had expired, he opened his eyes and looked around at the brothers, and said: "*Dominus vobiscum!*" They responded: "*Et cum spiritu tuo!*" Conrad added: "*Fidelium animae per misericordiam Dei requiescant in pace*" and fell asleep in the Lord.

In Dominic, the servant of God, there was a firm evenness of spirit, except when he was moved by compassion or pity; and since a joyous heart makes for a glad countenance, he manifested his inward composure by his outward gentleness. By day, when he was with his brothers and associates, there was none more affable, though with due modesty and discretion; in the night hours none was more constant in watchings and prayers. Thus he gave the day to his neighbor and the night to God. From his eyes there flowed what seemed to be a fountain of tears. Oftentimes, when the Body of the Lord was lifted up in the mass, he was rapt in such an ecstasy of spirit that he might have been looking upon Christ present in the flesh. For this reason he did not usually hear mass with the others. It was his frequent custom to pass the night in the church, so that he scarcely ever seemed to have a fixed place to rest; and when weariness overcame him and he yielded to the need for sleep, he lay down for a little while either before the altar or resting his head on a stone. Three times in the night he took the discipline with his own hand, using an iron chain—once for himself, once for sinners still in this life, and once for those who were suffering in purgatory.

He was once elected bishop of Conserano but refused absolutely to accept, declaring that he would rather quit the earth than consent to any such preferment. And sometimes, when he was in the diocese of Carcassonne, he was asked why he would not more willingly stay in his own diocese of Toulouse, and his answer was: "Because in Toulouse I find many who honor me, whereas in Carcassonne, on the contrary, everyone attacks me!" And when someone asked him in what book he had studied the most, he replied: "In the book of love."

One night while Dominic, the man of God, was praying in his church in Bologna, the devil appeared to him in the guise of a friar. The saint, thinking that he was one of his brethren, nodded to him to go to his rest with the others; but the devil mocked him by making the same sign. Then the saint, wishing to learn who it was that treated his orders so lightly, lit a candle at one of the lamps and, looking into the other's face, recognized him as the evil spirit. He reproached him vehemently, and the devil in turn upbraided him for breaking the rule of silence by speaking to him. But the saint declared that as master of the brethren he was permitted to speak, and then commanded him to say how he tempted the friars in choir. The demon answered: "I make them come too late and leave too soon!" Dominic led him to the dormitory, asking how he tempted the brothers there. The reply: "I make them sleep too long and rise late so that they miss the office, and I give them impure thoughts." Next to the refectory, Dominic asking the same question: the devil hopped about among the tables, saying over and over: "More and less, more and less!" Dominic inquired what that meant, and the devil replied: "I tempt some of the brothers to eat too much, and so they sin by gluttony, and others I tempt to eat too little and so they become weak in the service of God and the observance of the rule." Dominic led him to the parlor and again asked how he tempted the brothers there. In reply he rolled his tongue rapidly, producing a weird confusion of sounds; and being asked what this meant, he said: "This place belongs entirely to me! When the friars come here to talk, I studiously tempt them to prattle all at the same time, to confuse each other with idle words, and never to wait to hear what the other is saying." Finally, the saint led his adversary to the chapter room, but when he stood before the door, the devil would not enter and said: "Never will I go in there! For me it is a place of malediction, a hell! All that I gain elsewhere I lose there! For when I have caused a brother to sin by some negligence, quickly he comes to this accursed place and purges himself of his fault, admitting it before all. Here they are admonished, here they confess, here they are accused, here they are whipped, here they are absolved! And so, to my chagrin, I lose all I had been so happy to win elsewhere!" and with that he vanished.

When at last the term of his earthly pilgrimage drew near, Saint Dominic, being at the time in Bologna fell seriously ill. The imminent dissolution of his body was shown to him in a vision in which he saw a youth of surpassing beauty, who said to him: "Come, my beloved, come to joy, come!" He therefore called together the twelve friars of the priory at Bologna, and, so as not to leave them orphaned and without a heritage, gave them his testament. He said: "These are the things I bequeath to you in rightful possession, as my sons and heirs: have charity, keep humility, possess poverty!" He sternly forbade that anyone should bring temporal possessions into his Order, laying almighty God's terrible curse and his own on whoever might dare to besmirch the Order of Preachers with the dust of earthly riches. And as the friars were mourning inconsolably at being abandoned by him, he comforted them gently, saying: "Do not let my departure in the flesh trouble you, my sons, and be sure that I shall serve you better dead than alive!" Thereupon, being brought to his last hour, he fell asleep in the Lord in the year 1221.

His death was revealed to Gualis, the prior of the Friars Preachers at Brescia and later bishop of that city. Gualis had fallen into a light slumber, leaning against a wall in the belfry of the convent, when he saw the heavens opened and two white ladders let down to the earth, the one being held by Christ and the other by the Blessed Virgin; and angels joyously mounted and descended. Between the ladders, at the bottom, was a seat upon which a friar, his head covered, was seated. Jesus and his mother drew up the ladders until the friar was lifted into heaven, and the opening closed behind him. Gualis set out at once for Bologna and there learned that Dominic had died the very day and hour of his vision.

A friar named Rao went to the altar, in Tibur, to celebrate mass, at the very hour of the father's death. He had heard that the saint was ill in Bologna, and, when he came to the commemoration of the living in the canon of the mass, wished to pray for his recovery; but at that moment he was rapt in ecstasy, and saw Dominic, the man of God, crowned with a gold crown and shining with wondrous brightness, setting out from Bologna on the royal road, accompanied by two venerable men. Rao noted the day and the hour, and found that Dominic had departed this life at the time of the vision.

When his body had already lain underground for a long time, and his sanctity could no longer be hidden because of his miracles, which increased daily in number, the devotion of the faithful led them to transfer the saint's relics to a more honorable place. When with great effort and the use of iron tools the mortar had been broken, the stone removed, and the sarcophagus opened, an odor of such sweetness came forth that it might have come from a storeroom of perfumes rather than from a tomb. This odor was more powerful than any aromatic, and unlike the odor of any natural thing; and it penetrated not only the bones and dust of the sacred body and the coffin in which it was buried, but also the earth that was heaped around it, so that when later the earth was carried to distant places, it still retained the aroma for a long time. The fragrance also clung to the hands of the brothers who had touched the relics, so that no matter how often they were washed or rubbed together, the evidence of the perfume lingered.

In the province of Hungary a certain nobleman came with his wife and little son to visit the relics of Saint Dominic, which were preserved in Silon. But the child fell ill and died, and his father carried his body before the saint's altar and began to lament, saying: "Saint Dominic, merry I came to you and mournful I go away, for I came with my son and I go home having lost him. I beg of you, give back the joy of my heart!" And at midnight the boy returned to life and walked around in the church.

Another time a young man, the slave of a noble lady in Hungary, was fishing when he fell into the river and drowned, and his body was recovered only after a long time. The lady prayed Saint Dominic to restore him to life, and promised in return to go barefoot to venerate his relics and to give the slave his freedom. The youth was promptly brought back to life and leapt up in the sight of all, and the lady fulfilled her vow.

In the same province of Hungary a man was weeping bitterly over the death of his son and called upon Saint Dominic to bring him to life. At cockcrow the boy who had died opened his eyes and said to his father: "How is it, father, that my face is wet?" The man replied: " Your father's tears have fallen upon it, my son, because you were dead and I was left alone, bereft of all joy." The boy said: "You have shed many tears, father, but Saint Dominic took pity on your grief and by his merits obtained my return to life."

A man who had lain sick and blind for eighteen years wanted to visit the relics of Saint Dominic, and rose from his bed as if to go and do so. Suddenly he felt a surge of strength and set out at a rapid pace, and the farther he went day after day, the more both his bodily condition and his eyesight improved, until at last, when he reached his destination, he was fully cured of both infirmities.

Again in Hungary, a matron wished to have a mass celebrated in honor of Saint Dominic, but when the time for mass came there was no priest available; so she took the three candles she had prepared, wrapped them in a clean towel, and put them in a vase. She left for a short time and, coming back, saw the candles burning brightly. Many ran to see this great sight, and stood trembling and praying until the candles had burned out without damaging the towel in the least.

In Bologna a scholar whose name was Nicholas suffered such pain in the loins and the knees that he could not get out of bed, and his left thigh was so withered that he had lost all hope of cure. He therefore dedicated himself to God and Saint Dominic. Then, measuring his own full length with thread used for candles, he wound the thread around his body, neck, and chest. When he bound his knee with it, calling at each turn upon the names of Jesus and Dominic, he suddenly felt relief from his pain and cried out: "I am freed!" Then, weeping for joy and needing no crutch, he went to the church where Saint Dominic's body reposed.—In that city God, through his servant Dominic, worked miracles almost beyond counting.

At Augusta in Sicily there was a girl who suffered from the stone and was about to have it cut out; and her mother, in this dangerous situation, commended her to God and Saint Dominic. The following night the saint appeared to the girl, placed in her hand the stone that had causd her so much pain, and departed. When she awoke and found herself cured, she gave the stone to her mother and told her all about the vision. The mother took the stone to the friars' house and, to commemorate this great miracle, hung it in front of an image of Saint Dominic.

In the city of Augusta some women, after attending the solemn mass for the feast of the Translation of Saint Dominic in the friars' church, were on the way home when they saw a woman spinning wool on her doorstep. They chided her charitably for not abstaining from servile work on the great saint's feast, but she was indignant and retorted: "Observe your saint's feast yourselves, you friars' pets!" Instantly her eyes were infected with an itching tumor and worms began to wriggle out, until a neighbor woman pulled off eighteen of them. Stricken with remorse, the afflicted woman went to the friars' church, confessed her sins, and made a vow never again to speak ill of Dominic the servant of God and to observe his feast devoutly. At once she was restored to the health that had been hers.

In Tripoli, in a monastery named for the Magdalene, there was a nun called Maria, who was gravely ill and for five months had suffered from an infected leg so painful that her death was expected hour by hour. She gathered her thoughts and prayed as follows: "Dear Lord, I am not worthy to pray to you or to be heard by you, but I ask my lord the blessed Dominic to be my mediator with you and to obtain for me the blessing of recovery." When she had prayed, weeping, for a long time, she was rapt in ecstasy and saw Saint Dominic with two friars. He drew back the curtain that hung around her bed and said to her: "Why are you so eager to be healed?" She answered: "My lord, so that I may be able to serve God more devoutly." The saint then took out a marvelously fragrant ointment from under his cape and anointed her leg, and it was cured instantly. Then Dominic said: "This ointment is very precious, very sweet, and very hard to preserve." The nun asked him his reason for saying this, and he replied: "This ointment is a sign of love, and love is precious because it cannot be bought at any price, and because of all God's gifts none is better than love. It is sweet because nothing is sweeter than love, and hard to preserve because it is quickly lost if not kept with great care."

That night the saint also appeared to the nun's sister, who was asleep in the dormitory, and said: "I have cured your sister." She ran to her sister and found her in good health. Meanwhile Maria, knowing that her leg had been anointed, dried it reverently with a silk cloth. When she had told her abbess, her confessor, and her sister all that had happened, she produced the silk cloth with the ointment still on it; they were so struck with the strength and strangeness of its fragrance that they could think of no perfume with which to compare it, and put away the cloth to be preserved with reverence.

How pleasing to God the place is where the sacred body of Saint Dominic rests one miracle will suffice to show, though many miracles have made it famous. Master Alexander, bishop of Vendôme, in his notes on the text (Ps. 85:11) *Mercy and truth have met each other: justice and peace have kissed*, tells us that a certain student, who lived in Bologna and was given to worldly pleasures, saw a vision. It seemed to him that he was standing in a wide field, and a huge storm cloud hung over him. He ran to escape the tempest and came to a house, which he found closed. He knocked at the door and asked for shelter, but a woman's voice answered from within: "I am Justice, I live here and this is my house, and you cannot come in because you are not a just man!" Grieved by these words he went along and spied another house farther on. He knocked and asked admittance, but a lady inside answered: "I am Truth, I live here and this is my house, and I will not admit you because truth sets no one free who does not love truth."

Going farther he came to a third house and again begged for shelter from the storm. The lady of the house replied: "I am Peace, I live here, and there is no peace for the impious but only for men of good will. But because I think thoughts of peace and not affliction, I shall give you a word of good advice. My sister lives close by and she always offers help to those in need. Go to her and do as she tells you." When he got to the house, a voice answered: "I am Mercy, and I live here. If you want to be saved from the coming storm, go to the house where the Friars Preachers live. There you will find the stable of penance and the manger of continence and the pap of doctrine, the ass of simplicity with the ox of discretion; and Mary will enlighten you, Joseph will perfect you, and the Child Jesus will save you." When the scholar awoke, he therefore went to the friars' house, recited his vision, asked for admission to the Order, and received the habit.

---

114. Saint Sixtus

Sixtus comes from *Sios*, meaning God, and *status*, state or condition; hence, divine state. Or it comes from *sisto, sistis*, the verb that means to stand; hence Sixtus was one who stood fixed and firm in faith, or suffering, or doing good.

Pope Sixtus, an Athenian by birth, began as a philosopher, but later became a disciple of Christ and was elected supreme pontiff. With two of his deacons, Felicissimus and Agapitus, he was brought before the emperor Decius. The emperor, failing to persuade him to change his mind, had him led to the temple of Mars to offer sacrifice there, or, if he refused, to be imprisoned. Blessed Laurence followed him, calling out: "Where are you going, father, without your son? Whither are you hurrying, holy priest, without a minister?" Sixtus answered: "I am not deserting you, my son, nor abandoning you, but greater trials for the faith of Christ await you! Three days from now you, the levite,[1] will follow me, the priest! Meanwhile take the church's treasure and distribute it as you see fit." When Laurence had distributed the treasure among the Christian poor, the prefect Valerianus decreed that Sixtus was to be brought to the temple

---

[1] Under Jewish law the term *levite* was eventually reserved for sanctuary ministers who were not priests (descendants of Aaron) but were considered to be of the family of the patriarch Levi. In the Middle Ages deacons were called levites.

of Mars to offer sacrifice, or, if he refused, to be beheaded there. As he was led to the temple, blessed Laurence began to call after him: "Do not forsake me, holy father, because I have already given away your treasures, which you handed over to me!" The soldiers, hearing money mentioned, took Laurence prisoner, but beheaded Sixtus, Felicissimus, and Agapitus then and there.

This day is also the feast of the Lord's transfiguration. In some churches, on this day, the Blood of Christ is consecrated from new wine—when new wine can be made and is available—or at least a ripe grape is squeezed into the chalice. Also on this day clusters of grapes are blessed, and the people consume them as a form of communion. The reason for this is that the Lord, at the Last Supper, said to his disciples: "I shall not drink again of this fruit of the vine until that day when I drink it new with you in my Father's kingdom."[2] His transfiguration, and the new wine of which he spoke, represent Christ's glorious renewal after his resurrection; and therefore it is on this feast of the transfiguration, which represents the resurrection, that new wine is called for—not because the transfiguration happened on this day, as some say, but because the apostles made it known on this day. It is said, indeed, that the Lord's transfiguration took place early in the spring of the year, but that the disciples, having been forbidden to tell anyone of the vision until Christ was raised from the dead,[3] kept it a secret until they made it known on this day. This is what we read in the book called *On the Mitral Office*.

115. *Saint Donatus*

Donatus comes from *a Deo natus*, born of God, and this birth is threefold—by rebirth, by infusion of grace, and by glorification, hence a threefold generation by the Spirit or by God. For when saints die, it is then that they are said to be born, so the demise of a saint is not called death but birthday. A child strives to be born, so as to have more room to live in, more food to feed on, a freer air to breathe, and light to see by. And because saints issue from the womb of Mother Church through death, they gain these four things according to the mode of each and therefore are said to be born. . . . Or the name Donatus is equivalent to *dono Dei datus*, given by the gift of God.

[2] Matt. 26:29.   [3] Matt. 17:9.

Donatus was reared and nurtured with the emperor Julian up to the time when the said Julian was ordained subdeacon; but when he was elevated to the empire, he put the saint's father and mother to death, and Donatus took flight to Arezzo, lived with the monk Hilary, and wrought many miracles. When, for instance, the prefect brought his son, who was possessed of a demon, to Donatus, the unclean spirit began to cry out, saying: "In the name of the Lord Jesus Christ, do not make trouble for me or drive me out of my house, O Donatus! Why do you torment me and expel me?" And when Donatus prayed for the boy, he was soon liberated.

Then there was a man named Eustochius, a tax-collector in Tuscany, who left the public monies in the care of his wife, Euphrosina. But when the province was overrun by enemies, the woman hid the funds, and shortly afterwards illness carried her off. When the husband returned, he could not find the money and was due to be put to the torture with his sons, but he resorted to Donatus for help. Donatus went with him to his wife's tomb, prayed there, and then said in a loud voice: "Euphrosina, I adjure you by the Holy Spirit, tell us where you put that money!" And a voice came from the tomb, saying: "I buried it near the door of my house!" They went there and found the money as she had said.

Some days later Bishop Satyrus fell asleep in the Lord, and the clergy unanimously elected Donatus to succeed him. Gregory tells us in his *Dialogues* that once, when the mass was being celebrated and at communion time the deacon was ministering the Blood of Christ to the people, some pagans pushed the deacon and he fell, and the holy chalice was broken. The deacon and all the people were saddened by this accident, but Donatus gathered up the fragments, prayed over them, and restored the chalice to its former condition. The devil, however, hid one fragment and it was lacking in the repaired chalice, but its absence proves the reality of the miracle. The pagans saw the miracle, and eighty of them were converted and received baptism.

A certain spring was so polluted that anyone who drank from it died immediately. Saint Donatus, mounted on his ass, was passing that way and purified the water by his prayer, whereupon a frightful dragon burst out of the spring, coiled its tail around the ass's legs, and reared itself up against Donatus. The saint struck the beast with his whip, or, as we read elsewhere, spat in its mouth, and killed it. He also prayed to the Lord, and all the poison was gone from the spring. Another time, when he and his companions were suffering from thirst, he prayed and a spring gushed from the earth at their feet.

A daughter of the emperor Theodosius was possessed of the devil and was brought to Saint Donatus, who said: "Foul spirit, go out of her, and dwell no longer in this handiwork of God!" The demon: "Give me a way out and some place to go!" Donatus: "Where did you come from?" The demon: "From the desert!" Donatus: "Go back there!" The demon: "I see the sign of the cross on you, and fire comes out of it and burns me! I'm so afraid that I don't know where to go, but give me a clear way out and I'll go!" Donatus: "There's your clear way! Go back where you belong!" The demon left, shaking the whole house as he left.

A dead man was being carried to his grave, when another man appeared with a written bill in his hand and declared that the deceased owed him two hundred sols, and that he could not be buried until the money was paid. The widow, in tears, told blessed Donatus about this, adding that the man had already been paid in full. Donatus came to the bier, touched the dead man with his hand, and said: "Listen to me!" The deceased responded: "I'm listening!" Saint Donatus said to him: "Get up and settle your accounts with this man who won't let you be buried!" The dead man sat up, proved to everybody that he had paid his debt, took the bill, and tore it to pieces. Then he said to Saint Donatus: "Father, command me to go back to sleep!" Donatus: "Go now, my son, and take your rest!"

At that time no rain had fallen for almost three years, and the land was utterly barren. The infidels flocked to Emperor Theodosius, asking him to turn Donatus over to them, on the ground that he had brought on the drought by his magical art. At the emperor's request, therefore, Donatus came out and prayed the Lord, bringing down great floods of rain. Then, while all the others were drenched by the downpour, he went back to his house as dry as before.

The Goths were ravaging Italy at the time, and many Christians had abandoned the faith of Christ. Saint Donatus and Saint Hilarian went to the prefect Evadracianus and took him to task for his apostasy, but he arrested the two saints and tried to make them sacrifice to Jupiter. When they refused, he had Hilarian stripped and beaten until he breathed his last. Donatus he shut up in prison, and later had him beheaded, about the year A.D. 380.

---

116. Saint Cyriacus and His Companions

Cyriacus, who was ordained a deacon by Pope Marcellus, was apprehended with his companions and brought before Maximian, who ordered them to dig and carry the earth on their shoulders at a place where a public bath was under construction. There they found the aged Saint Saturninus, and Cyriacus and Sisinnius helped him with the carrying. Finally Cyriacus was put in prison, and the prefect called for his presence. Apronianus was leading him in when suddenly a voice coming with light from heaven said: "Come, O blessed of my

Father, inherit the kingdom prepared for you!" Apronianus believed, had himself baptized, and came before the prefect confessing Christ. The prefect: "What! Have you too become a Christian?" Apronianus: "Woe is me, that I lost so many days before I believed!" "Right you are!" the prefect retorted. "You'll lose all your days now!" And he dispatched him to be beheaded. When Saturninus and Sisinnius refused to offer sacrifice, they suffered various tortures and were beheaded.

Diocletian's daughter Arthemia was tormented by a demon, and the demon in her cried out: "I will not go out of her unless Cyriacus the deacon comes here!" So Cyriacus was brought, and when he commanded the demon to go away, the spirit answered: "If you want me to come out, give me some container to go into!" "Here's my body," Cyriacus replied. "If you can, come in!" The demon: "I can't come into your body, because it is sealed and closed on all sides. But if you force me out, know that I will make you go to Babylonia!" The demon was compelled to leave her, and Arthemia declared that she saw the God whom Cyriacus preached. The saint baptized her and went to live in security in a house graciously granted him by Diocletian and his wife Serena.

Shortly thereafter a messenger came from the king of the Persians, with the request that Diocletian send Cyriacus to him, because his daughter was possessed of a devil. The emperor asked Cyriacus to go, and the saint, taking Largus and Smaragdus with him, embarked in a well-provisioned ship and happily went off to Babylonia. When he came to the young woman, the demon called out through her mouth, saying: "Are you tired, Cyriacus?" "No, I'm not tired," said Cyriacus, "but wherever I go, I am governed by God's help!" "Yet I made you come where I wanted you to come!" said the demon.

Now Cyriacus said to the evil spirit: "Jesus commands you to come out!" And the demon, coming out at once, said: "Oh, that dread name! It forces me to go!" So the girl was cured, and the saint baptized her with her father and mother and a number of others. Many gifts were offered him, but he refused to accept them. Then he fasted on bread and water for forty-five days, after which he returned to Rome.

Two months later Diocletian died and Maximian succeeded him. Maximian was angry about his sister Arthemia and had Cyriacus arrested, then ordered him to be dragged, naked and loaded with chains, in front of the emperor's chariot. This Maximian could be called Diocletian's son in that he was his successor and was married to his daughter Valeriana. He next commanded his deputy, Carpasius, to compel Cyriacus and his companions to offer sacrifice, or else to put him to death with torture. So Carpasius had boiling pitch poured over the saint's head, hung him on the rack, and had him beheaded with all his companions.

Carpasius then got possession of Saint Cyriacus's house. In mockery of the Christians he bathed in the place where Cyriacus had usually baptized, and gave a banquet for nineteen of his cronies, at which, at the same moment, all of them died. After that the bath was closed and the pagans began to fear and respect the Christians.

117. Saint Laurence, Martyr

Laurence, or Laurentius, comes from *lauream tenens*, holder of a laurel wreath, because in the past victors or winners were crowned with laurel wreaths. The laurel tree is symbolic of victory, being delightful for its continuous greenness, and having a pleasant odor and powerful efficacy. So blessed Laurence is named for the laurel because he won victory in his martyrdom, which moved the emperor Decius, astonished, to say: "I really think we are already defeated." He had greenness in the cleanness and purity of his heart, whence he said: "My night has no darkness." He had a lasting odor of sweetness because the memory of him is perpetual, as the Psalm says: "He has distributed freely, he has given to the poor; his righteousness endures for ever."[1] Blessed Maximus says: "How would the righteousness of such a man not live on eternally—righteousness brought to perfection in his work and consecrated in his glorious martyrdom?" His efficacy showed in his powerful preaching, by which he convinced Lucillus, Hippolytus, and Romanus. The effiacy of the laurel tree consists in that it breaks up the stone, remedies deafness, and wards off lightning. Thus Laurence broke down hardness of heart, restored spiritual hearing, and provided protection against the lightning of a sentence of damnation.

Laurence, martyr and levite,[2] a native of Spain, was brought to Rome by Pope Saint Sixtus. Master John Beleth has it that this Saint Sixtus went to Spain and there came across two young men, Laurence and Vincent his cousin, both distinguished for their honorable lives and actions. He took both of them to Rome, and one of them, Laurence, stayed with him in Rome, while Vincent went back to Spain and finished his life by a glorious martyrdom. However, the dates of the martyrdoms of both Vincent and Laurence make Master Beleth's opinion questionable. Laurence suffered under Decius, and Vincent, still young in age, under Diocletian and Dacian. But between Decius and Diocletian there was an interval of forty years, during which seven emperors reigned, so that Vincent could not still have been a young man.

Blessed Sixtus ordained Laurence his archdeacon. At that time the emperor Philip and his son Philip accepted the faith of Christ and, having become Christians, did their best to exalt the Church. This Philip was the first emperor to accept the Christian faith. It is said that it was Origen who converted him,

---

[1] Ps. 111(112):9.

[2] Deacons were called levites, and Laurence was one of the seven deacons of Rome in the pontificate of Sixtus II (257–258).

although elsewhere we read that it was Saint Pontius. Philip reigned in the
thousandth year from the foundation of the city of Rome, so that Rome's thousandth year might be dedicated to Christ rather than to the false gods. The
millennium was celebrated by the Romans with a huge display of games and
spectacles.

Emperor Philip had a certain general named Decius, skilled in the arts of war
and famous. Gaul was rebelling at the time, and the emperor sent Decius to
bring the rebellious province securely under the yoke of the Roman Empire.
Decius carried out his mission successfully and, having achieved the victory he
desired, started back to Rome. The emperor learned that he was on his way and,
wishing to pay him honor, went from Rome to Verona to meet him. But when
bad men feel themselves honored, they become elated with pride, and Decius
began to covet the empire and to ponder how he might get rid of his master. So,
one day when the emperor was resting on his bed, Decius stole into the tent and
strangled his sleeping lord. Now he had to win over the army that had come
north with the emperor. He did this with pleas and bribes, gifts and promises,
and then led them by forced marches to the royal city.

When the younger Philip heard this, he was afraid and, as Sicardus says in his
Chronicle, placed all his father's wealth and his own in the care of Saint Sixtus and
Saint Laurence, so that, in case Decius killed him also, they could distribute the
treasure to the churches and the poor. Do not let it bother you that the treasure
which blessed Laurence dispensed is not called the emperor's but the Church's,
because it might well be that he did dispense some of the Church's wealth along
with that of Emperor Philip; or perhaps the distributed wealth is called the
Church's in view of the fact that Philip had left it to the Church to be given to
the poor. Moreover, there is serious doubt, as will be noted further on, that
Sixtus was alive at that time.

However that may be, Philip got away and hid from Decius, and the Senate
proceeded to confirm the latter as emperor. Decius wanted the killing of his lord
to appear not as treason but as zeal for the gods of Rome. He therefore began a
savage persecution of the Christians, ordering that they were to be slaughtered
without mercy. Many thousands of martyrs fell in this persecution, and the
younger Philip himself won the crown of martyrdom.

Decius now inaugurated a search for the emperor Philip's wealth, and blessed
Sixtus was pointed out to him as one who worshiped Christ and had possession
of the emperor's treasure. Decius ordered him to be jailed and tortured until he
denied Christ and gave up the treasure. As he was led away, blessed Laurence
followed him and called out: "Where are you going, father, without your son?
Whither are you hurrying, holy priest, without a deacon? You never used to
offer the holy sacrifice without a minister! What is it about me that has displeased your paternity? Have you tested me and found me unworthy to be your
son? Try me, surely, to see whether you have chosen a minister suitable to have
the dispensing of the Lord's Blood entrusted to him!" Saint Sixtus answered: "I

am not deserting you, my son, nor abandoning you, but greater trials await you for the faith of Christ! We old men reach the goal by an easier race. The more glorious triumph over the tyrant is left to you as a young man. Three days from now you, the levite, will follow me, the priest!" And he gave all the treasures into Laurence's care to be dispensed to the poor.

Blessed Laurence then sought out Christians by day and by night, and ministered to all according to their needs. He came to the house of a certain widow who had hidden many Christians in her house. She had long suffered from pains in her head, and Saint Laurence, by laying on his hands, freed her of that pain. He also washed the feet of the poor and gave alms to all. The same night he came to the house of another Christian and found a blind man there, over whom he made the sign of the cross, restoring his sight.

Meanwhile blessed Sixtus refused to yield to Decius or to sacrifice to the idols, and the emperor commanded that he be led to execution. Blessed Laurence ran after him and called out: "Do not abandon me, holy father, because I have already given away the treasures that you entrusted to me!" The soldiers, hearing of money, took Laurence and passed him on to the tribune Parthenius. He in turn presented him to Decius, and Decius Caesar said to him: "Where is the Church's money, which we know is hidden with you?" When Laurence did not answer, Decius handed him over to the prefect Valerian, with orders to make him give up the treasure and sacrifice to the idols, or to die under torture. Valerian put another prefect, named Hippolytus, in charge of him, and he shut Laurence up in jail with a number of other prisoners. Among them was a pagan named Lucillus, who had wept so much that he had lost his sight. Laurence promised that he would make him see again if he believed in Christ and received baptism, and Lucillus begged to be baptized as soon as possible. Laurence got some water and said to him: "Confession of faith washes all clean!" He then questioned Lucillus closely about the articles of faith, and Lucillus confessed that he believed all of them, whereupon Laurence poured the water over his head and baptized him in the name of Christ. For this reason many who were blind came to him and went away with their sight restored.

Now Hippolytus, having observed all this, said to Laurence: "Show me the treasure!" Laurence: "O Hippolytus, if you believed in the Lord Jesus Christ I would show you the treasure and also promise you eternal life!" Hippolytus: "If you do what you say, I will do what you are urging me to do!" That same hour Hippolytus believed and received baptism with his family; and after being baptized he said: "I have seen the souls of the innocents rejoicing!"

After that, Valerian ordered Hippolytus to bring Laurence before him. Laurence said to Hippolytus: "Let us walk side by side, because glory is prepared for me and for you!" They came to the tribunal and again were asked about the treasure, and Laurence requested a delay of three days, which Valerian granted, leaving the saint with Hippolytus. During the three days Laurence brought together the poor, the lame, and the blind, and then presented them before Decius in the Sallustian palace, saying: "See here the eternal treasure, which never diminishes but increases. It is divided among these people and is found in all of them, for their hands have carried the treasure off to heaven!" Valerian: "You talk too much! Stop talking, sacrifice now, and leave your magic aside!" Laurence: "Who ought to be adored, the one who is made or the Maker?" This aroused Decius's anger, and he ordered Laurence to be whipped with scorpions and punished before him with all sorts of tortures. The saint was told to sacrifice in order to escape this treatment but answered: "Unhappy man, this is the banquet I have always desired!" Decius: "If this is a banquet, name some others as impious as yourself, and they can come and feast with you!" Laurence: "They have already given their names in heaven, and therefore you are not worthy to look upon them!"

Decius ordered the headsmen to strip Laurence and beat him with clubs, and to press hot blades to his sides. Laurence said: "Lord Jesus Christ, God from God, have mercy on me your servant, because, being accused, I have not denied your holy name, and being put to the question I have confessed you as my Lord!" Decius said to him: "I know you have eluded these torments by means of your magic, but you're not going to elude me any longer! I swear by the gods and goddesses that unless you offer sacrifice, you will die a slow and painful death!" He then commanded that Laurence be beaten long and hard with lead-laden whips. Laurence prayed: "Lord, receive my spirit!" But a voice, which Decius heard, sounded from heaven, saying: "You have still to endure many trials!" Decius, filled with rage, said: "Men of Rome, you have heard the demons consoling this blasphemer, who does not worship our gods, does not fear torments, does not quail before angry princes!" He ordered him beaten again with scorpions. Laurence smiled, gave thanks, and prayed for those who stood by.

At this time a soldier named Romanus received the faith and said to blessed Laurence: "I see a beautiful young man standing in front of you and wiping your limbs with a towel! I adjure you by God, do not abandon me, baptize me quickly!" And Decius said to Valerian: "I really think we are defeated by this man's magic art!" At his command, Laurence was taken from the stake and again confined in care of Hippolytus. Romanus brought a jar of water, knelt at Laurence's feet, and was baptized by him. Decius learned of this and had Romanus beaten with cudgels; and when Romanus freely professed that he was a Christian, Decius had him beheaded.

That same night the saint was haled before Decius. When Hippolytus wept and cried out that he was a Christian, Laurence said to him: "Hide Christ in the inner man, listen, and when I call, come!" Decius said to Laurence: "Either you will sacrifice to the gods, or you will spend the night being tortured!" Laurence: "My night has no darkness, and all things gleam in the light!" Decius gave his orders: "Let an iron bed be brought, and let this stubborn Laurence rest on it!" The executioners therefore stripped him, laid him out on the iron grill, piled burning coals under it, and pressed heated iron pitchforks upon his body. Laurence said to Valerian: "Learn, wretched man, that your coals are refreshing to me but will be an eternal punishment to you, because the Lord himself knows that being accused I have not denied him, being put to the question I have confessed Christ, and being roasted I give thanks!" And with a cheerful countenance he said to Decius: "Look, wretch, you have me well done on one side, turn me over and eat!" And giving thanks, he said: "I thank you, O Lord, because I have been worthy to pass through your portals!" And so he breathed his last. Confounded, Decius went off with Valerian to the palace of Tiberius, leaving the body on the fire, and Hippolytus took it away in the morning, anointed it with spices, and, with the priest Justin, buried it in the Veranus field. Christians kept vigil, fasting, for three days, lamenting and weeping.

There are many who question whether it is true that Laurence suffered martyrdom under this Emperor Decius, since we read in the chronicles that Sixtus came long after[3] Decius. Eutropius, however, makes this assertion: "When Decius moved to persecute the Christians, among others he slew the blessed levite and martyr Laurence." In another fairly authentic chronicle it is said that it was not under Emperor Decius, who succeeded Philip, that Laurence suffered martyrdom, but under a younger Decius, who was caesar but not emperor; for between the emperor Decius and this younger Decius, under whom Laurence is said to have suffered, a number of emperors and popes intervened. This chronicle also says that Emperor Decius was succeeded by Gallus and his son Volusianus, and they in turn by Valerian and Gallienus. The said Valerian and Gallienus set up the younger Decius as caesar but did not make him emperor. Sometimes, in antiquity, some emperors were made *Caesares* but not *Augusti*, or emperors in the full sense. Thus we read in the chronicles that Diocletian made Maximian a caesar, and later raised him to Augustus. At the time of the emperors Valerian and Gallienus, Sixtus occupied the see of Rome. Therefore this Decius Caesar, so called, who subjected blessed Laurence to martyrdom, was not made an emperor and is never called *Decius imperator*, but only *Decius Caesar*, in the legend of Saint Laurence.

The emperor Decius reigned only two years,[4] and he put Pope Fabian to death. Cornelius succeeded Fabian and suffered martyrdom under Volusian and Gallus. Cornelius was succeeded by Lucius and Lucius by Stephen. Pope Stephen suffered under Valerian and Gallienus, who ruled fifteen years, and Sixtus succeeded Stephen. This is what we read in the chronicle mentioned above. All the chronicles, including those by Eusebius, Bede, and Isidore, agree that Pope Sixtus did not reign in the time of Emperor Decius but in that of Gallienus. In another chronicle, however, we read that the said Gallienus went

---

[3] Graesse notes (493) that the Ed. Pr. has *ante* (before), while "others" have *post* (after). What follows in the text shows that *post* is correct.

[4] 249–251.

by two names, for he was called Gallienus and Decius, and under him Sixtus and Laurence suffered about A.D. 257.[5] Godfrey, in his book called *Pantheon*, says the same thing, namely, that Gallienus was called by another name, Decius, and that Sixtus and Laurence suffered under him. And if this is true, then Master John Beleth's position can also be true.

In his *Dialogues* Gregory says that there was a nun in Sabina who practiced continence in the flesh but made no effort to control her tongue. She had been buried in the church of Saint Laurence before the martyr's altar, but demons cut her body in half, and one half remained unscathed but the other was burned, so that in the morning the scorching was apparent to the eye.

Gregory of Tours says that a certain priest was repairing the church of Saint Laurence and found that one of his timbers was too short. He prayed to the saint, reminding him that he always helped the poor and asking him to supply this particular need. Suddenly the timber grew not only to the desired length but beyond it, so the priest sawed off the extra piece and cut it into small bits, with which many infirmities were cured subsequently. Blessed Fortunatus also testifies to this miracle, which occurred in the place in Italy called Brione.

Pope Gregory, in his *Dialogues*, has the story of another priest, Sanctulus by name, who was rebuilding a church of Saint Laurence that had been burned down by the Lombards, and hired a number of craftsmen to do the work. Then one day he had no food to give them. He prayed, then looked into his oven and found a fine loaf of white bread. It did not look big enough to make one meal for three people, but Laurence, unwilling to let the workmen go hungry, multiplied the loaf in such a way that it fed them all for ten days.

Vincent, in his chronicle, reports that the church of Saint Laurence in Milan possessed a crystal chalice of extraordinary beauty. The deacon was carrying this chalice to the altar in the course of some solemn ceremony, when the chalice slipped out of his hands, fell to the floor, and was shattered. The deacon, grief-stricken, collected the fragments, put them on the altar, and prayed to Saint Laurence; and the chalice came together whole and undamaged.

We also read in the *Book of the Miracles of the Blessed Virgin* that in Rome there was a judge named Stephen, who gladly accepted bribes and in return rendered crooked decisions in many cases. Thus, for instance, he alienated three houses belonging to the church of Saint Laurence and a garden belonging to the church of Saint Agnes, and held them unjustly in his possession. Then he died and went before the judgment seat of God. Laurence came up wrathful and twisted the man's arm three times, so hard that the pain was excruciating. Saint Agnes and other virgins could not bear to look at the miscreant and turned their faces away. Then the Judge pronounced sentence upon him, saying: "Since this Stephen

---

[5] The year usually given is 258, but history knows the emperor as Publius Licinius Egnatius Gallienus (not Decius), who reigned with his father Valerian from 253 to 260, and alone, after Valerian's death, from 260 to 268.

appropriated what did not belong to him, and by taking bribes sold the truth, let him be held in the same place with Judas the traitor." But now Saint Projectus, to whom the said Stephen had been very devoted in his lifetime, went to Saint Laurence and Saint Agnes and pleaded for their pardon. The two saints and the Blessed Virgin prayed for the culprit, and it was granted that his soul should return to his body and he should do penance for thirty days. From the Blessed Virgin he received the added command to recite the Psalm *Beati immaculati in via*[6] every day. When he came back to life in his body, his arm was black and burned, as if he had suffered this in the flesh, and that mark was on him as long as he lived. He made restitution of all his ill-gotten goods, did penance, and on the thirtieth day migrated to the Lord.

We read in the life of the emperor Saint Henry[7] that, though he and his wife Saint Cunegund lived as virgins, the emperor, at the devil's instigation, once suspected her of infidelity with a certain knight. He therefore made her walk barefoot a distance of fifteen feet over plowshares reddened in the fire, and as she stepped forward to do so, she said: "O Christ, as you know that I have never been touched by Henry or any other man, help me now!" But Henry was ashamed of her and struck her in the face, whereupon a voice said to her: "The virgin Mary has delivered you, a virgin!" So she strode over the glowing mass unharmed. When the emperor died, a huge crowd of demons passed by the cell of a hermit, who opened his window and asked the last demon in line who they were. "We are a legion of demons," he answered, "hurrying to be in at the death of the caesar, if by chance we can discover anything in him that belongs to us!" The hermit adjured him to stop on the way back; and on his return the demon told him: "We gained nothing, because when his false suspicion and other misdeeds were put on our side of the scale, that roasted Laurence came up with a very heavy gold bowl, and, just as we seemed to have won, he tossed the bowl on the other side and it far outweighed ours. I was so angry that I broke off a piece of the gold bowl!" What the demon called a bowl was a chalice, which the said emperor had ordered for the church at Eichstätt in honor of Saint Laurence, whom he held in special veneration. The chalice was so large that it had two handles, and it was discovered that at the moment of the emperor's death one of the handles had broken off.

Pope Gregory reports in his *Register* that when his predecessor wanted to obtain a cure for someone at Saint Laurence's body but did not know where the body was, suddenly the saint's body came to light where they had not known it to be, and all, monks and those who were attached to the church, who were present and saw the body, died within ten days.[8]

---

[6] Ps. 118(119):1, "Blessed are those whose way is blameless."

[7] Henry II, emperor of the Holy Roman Empire 1002–1024.

[8] Graesse notes (495) that the Ed. Pr. "omits" this episode. He does not say where he found it, nor why he saw fit to include this incongruous tale.

It may be noted that the passion of Saint Laurence is seen to stand out above the passions of the other martyrs, and this for four aspects of it, as we gather from the writings of Saint Maximus and Saint Augustine. The first aspect is the bitterness of his sufferings, the second, their effectiveness or usefulness, the third, his constancy or fortitude, the fourth, his wonderful fight and the mode of his victory.

First, then, his martyrdom stands out by the bitterness of his sufferings, as the holy bishop Maximus—or, according to some books, Ambrose—says: "Blessed Laurence did not undergo some brief or simple suffering. Anyone who dies by the sword dies once: one who is thrust into a furnace is liberated by one push: but Laurence was smitten with long and multiple tortures, so that he was dying all through his suffering yet did not die to end it. We read that the holy youths walked in the flames to which they were sentenced and trod upon glowing balls of fire, but Saint Laurence earned more glory than they. If they walked amid the flames, he lay stretched over the fire of his torture; and if they could trample down the fires with the soles of their feet, he contained the fire by the way his body was spread over it." They stood in pain with their hands uplifted, praying to the Lord; he, prostrate in his pain, prayed the Lord with his whole body.

Remark also that blessed Laurence is said to stand with Saint Stephen in first place among the martyrs, not because he bore greater pain than they, since we read that many of them bore as much pain and some even more. What is said above is said for six concurrent reasons. Firstly, due to the place where the saint suffered, which was Rome, the capital of the world and the apostolic see. Secondly, because of his ministry of preaching, since he fulfilled that ministry diligently. Thirdly, there is his praiseworthy distribution of the treasures, all of which he judiciously handed out to the poor. Those three reasons are put forth by Master William of Auxerre. Fourthly, his martyrdom is authenticated and approved, because, while greater torments are attributed to some others, their authenticity is uncertain and is sometimes held to be doubtful. In the Church, on the other hand, Laurence's passion is very solemnly celebrated and approved, and many saints certify and confirm it in their sermons. Fifthly, his high rank, because he was the archdeacon of the apostolic see, and after him, it is said, there was no longer an archdeacon in the see of Rome. Sixthly, there was the severity of his torments, because he endured the most painful tortures, being roasted on an iron grid. About this martyr Saint Augustine says: "[The prefect] ordered that his limbs, cut and torn by the blows of the scourges, be placed over a fire and alternately turned from one side to the other, so that, by means of the iron grill, which, because of its continual firing, had power in itself to burn, the pain would be made more violent and would last longer."

The second aspect that confirms the high eminence of his passion among martyrs is its effectiveness or usefulness. The bitterness of his suffering, according to Augustine and Maximus, made him sublime in glorification, celebrated in esteem and fame, praiseworthy by the devotion in which he was held, and distinguished for the imitation he attracted.

Firstly, he was sublime in glorification, whence Augustine says: "You raged, O persecutor, against the martyr, you planted his palm and made it grow as you heaped up his pains." Again Maximus, or, according to some, Ambrose: "Although you reduced his members to ashes, the fortitude of his faith was not reduced: he endured the loss of his body but won the prize of salvation." And again Augustine: "O truly blessed body, which torment could not turn from the faith of Christ, but holy religion crowned unto eternal rest in heaven!"

Secondly, he was celebrated in esteem and fame. Maximus, or, according to some books, Ambrose: "We may compare the blessed martyr Laurence to the mustard seed, because, rubbed and crushed by many sufferings, he merited to spread throughout the whole earth the fragrance of his mystery. Previously he was unimpressive in body, unknown and unrecognized, a nobody: after he was tortured, torn apart, roasted, he infused all the churches throughout the world with the aroma of his nobility." Again Augustine: "It is a holy thing and pleasing to God that we venerate the birthday of Saint Laurence with special devotion, because the Church of Christ, victorious by his radiant flames, on this day beams her light over the world." And again: "This noble martyr has gained so much glory in his passion that he has illuminated the entire world."

Thirdly, he was praiseworthy for the devotion in which he was held. Augustine explains why he should be praised and held in such devotion, giving three reasons. He says: "We should look to the blessed man with wholehearted devotion, first because he shed his precious blood for God, next because it won for him the high privilege before our God of showing what the Christian faith should be since the martyrs were worthy to come from its society, and thirdly, that his way of living was so holy that he found the crown of martyrdom in the time of peace."

Fourthly, his passion made him a model inviting imitation. Augustine: "The motive behind his whole passion, the motive by which the holy man was bound and committed to die, was to exhort others to be like him." He showed us three ways in which we could imitate him. The first is the strength with which he endured adversity. Augustine: "Eloquence is an easy means of exhortation and an effective means of persuasion; but examples are stronger than words, and deeds teach more powerfully than speech." His persecutors themselves could sense how glorious and worthy the blessed martyr Laurence was in this most excellent kind of teaching: his marvelous fortitude of spirit not only did not weaken, but by the example of his tolerance gave strength to others. The second way is the greatness and fervor of his faith. Maximus or Ambrose: "In his faith he conquered the persecutor's flames, and showed us that the fire of faith can overcome the fires of hell and the love of Christ can banish fear of the Day of Judgment." The third way is the ardor of his devotion. Maximus or Ambrose:

"Laurence shed light on the whole world in the light by which he was burned, and warmed the hearts of all Christians by the flames he endured." Regarding these three ways of imitating him, Maximus—or, as some books have it, Ambrose—says: "By blessed Laurence's example we are called to martyrdom, enkindled to faith, and warmed to devotion."

The third aspect by which Saint Laurence's passion stands out above the passions of other martyrs is his excellent constancy or fortitude in suffering. Saint Augustine says about his constancy and fortitude: "Blessed Laurence stayed firm in Christ throughout the tyrant's interrogation and fierce threatening, all the way to death itself. And because he had well eaten and drunk of that long-drawn-out death, being fattened by that food and drunk with that chalice he felt no torment, yielded no whit, but rose to the kingdom." So constant was he that he not only did not succumb to torture, but through the torture, as Saint Maximus says, he became more powerful in fear of the Lord, more fervent in love, more joyous in ardor. About the first of these he says: "He was stretched out over the flaming coals and often turned from side to side, but the more pain he suffered, the more patient he became in the fear of Christ the Lord." As to the second, Maximus, or, according to some books, Ambrose, says: "The mustard seed grows hot when rubbed: Laurence, when he suffers, is inflamed." Again: "A new kind of wonder! One persecutor tortured him and others, enraged, tried to improve their ways of tormenting him, but all that these keener sufferings did was to make Laurence more devoted to his Savior." Regarding the third way the same author says: "His heart was so strengthened by his faith in the greatheartedness of Christ that, paying no attention to the pain his body was suffering, he joyfully and triumphantly taunted his insane tormentor and his fires."

The fourth aspect under which Laurence's passion stands out in excellence is his wonderful fight and the mode of his victory. Blessed Laurence, as we gather from Maximus and Augustine, fought in some way against five external fires, which he bravely overcame and extinguished. The first was Gehenna, the fire of hell; the second, the fire of material flame; the third, the fire of carnal concupiscence; the fourth, that of grasping greed; the fifth, that of raging madness.

As to the extinguishing of the first of these fires, namely, the fire of hell, Maximus says: "Could one whose faith extinguished the eternal fire of Gehenna flinch from a momentary burning of the body?" The same: "He passed through a brief earthly fire but avoided the flame of the eternal fire of hell." Regarding the extinction of the second fire, namely, that of material flame, Maximus, or Ambrose according to some books: "He suffers a bodily fire, but divine love cools the material heat." Again: "A wicked king may throw wood on and build up a fiercer fire, but blessed Laurence does not feel those flames, due to the heat of his faith." Augustine: "The love of Christ could not be conquered by any flame, and the fire that burned on the outside was less ardent than the fire within."

About the extinguishing of the third fire, namely, carnal concupiscence, Maximus says: "Behold, Laurence passed through that fire, which, though it did not burn him, made him cringe but also gave him light by its light; it burned lest it burn, and he burned lest he be burned." As for the fire of avarice, and how the greed of those who coveted the Church's wealth failed and was frustrated, Augustine says: "The man who is greedy for money and an enemy of truth is armed with two torches—avarice, which seizes gold, and impiety, which takes away Christ. Cruel man, you gain nothing, you make no profit! The mortal material you looked for is taken from you, Laurence is gone away to heaven, and you perish in your flames."

As for the fifth fire, namely, the madness of the furious persecutor, Maximus tells how it was frustrated and brought to nothing: "Having conquered those who kept the fires burning, he extinguished the fire of madness that was spreading on all sides. Thus far the devil's effort had produced just one result, namely, that the faithful man ascended in glory to his Lord; and the cruelty of his persecutors sputtered and went out with their fires." He shows that the rage of the persecutors was a fire when he says: "The fury of the pagans, being enkindled, prepares a fired grill, in order to avenge by fire the flames of their indignation."

It should cause no surprise that Saint Laurence mastered these five external fires, since, as the aforementioned Maximus says, he carried three refrigerants within himself as well as three fires in his heart, by which he moderated all external fire by cooling it, and surpassed it with the greater heat of his ardor. The first refrigerant was the longing for the kingdom of heaven; the second, meditation on the divine law; and the third, purity of conscience. Through this triple refrigeration he cooled and put out all external fires. Of the first refrigerant, the desire of heaven, Maximus, or, according to some books, Ambrose, says: "Blessed Laurence, who in his senses possessed the coolness of paradise, could not feel the torment of fire." The same: "At the tyrant's feet lies Laurence's burned flesh, his lifeless body; but he whose soul already dwells in heaven suffers no harm on earth." Of the second refrigerant, meditation on the divine law, Maximus, or Ambrose, says: "While his thoughts are of Christ's precepts, anything he suffers is cool." Of the third, purity of conscience, the same author says: "This bravest of martyrs is hot and burned in every fiber of his body, but his mind is fixed on the kingdom of heaven, and by the coolness of his conscience he emerges an exultant victor."

As the same Maximus shows, Laurence also had three internal fires, by the greater heat of which he conquered all external fires. The first of the three was the greatness of his faith; the second, his ardent love; the third, his true knowledge of God, which irradiated him like fire. Of the first, the same author or Ambrose says: "As much as the ardor of his faith burned, by so much the flame of torture was cooled." That the ardor of faith is the Savior's fire we read in the Gospel: "I came to cast fire on the earth."[9] With that fire in him, Laurence did not feel the heat of flames. Of the second inner fire, the same or Ambrose says: "Laurence the martyr was burned externally by the raging tyrant's fires, but the greater flame of the love of Christ heated him inwardly." Of the third fire he says: "The persecutor's fiercest fire could not defeat this mighty martyr, because his mind was heated far more warmly by the rays of truth. Being afire with hatred of perfidy and with love of truth, he either did not feel or overcame the flames that burned him outwardly."

The office of Saint Laurence has three privileges that do not apply to the offices of other martyrs. The first is that alone among the feasts of martyrs, his feast has a vigil. The vigils of feasts of the saints have now been replaced by fasts because of many disorders. In the past, as Master John Beleth reports, the custom was that on the feasts of the saints the men, with their wives and daughters, went to the church and there spent the night by torchlight; but because many adulteries occurred during these vigils, it was decreed that the vigils be converted into fasts. The old name persisted, however, and the fasts are still called vigils. The second privilege is that Laurence's feast has an octave, as no other martyr's does except Saint Stephen, and no confessor's except Saint Martin. The third consists of the repetition of antiphons, which only Saint Laurence and Saint Paul have— Paul on account of the excellence of his preaching, Laurence for the excellence of his passion.

——————————— ✳ ———————————

118. Saint Hippolytus and His Companions

——————————

The name Hippolytus comes from *hyper*, above, and *litos*, stone or rock; hence one who is founded on rock, the rock being Christ. Or the name comes from *in* and *polis*, city, and the word is equivalent to *politus*, polished, refined. Saint Hippolytus was indeed well founded on Christ the rock by his constancy and firmness, was in the city on high by desire and eagerness, and was polished and made smooth by the bitterness of the torments he endured.

[9] Luke 12:49.

After he buried Saint Laurence's body, Hippolytus went back to his house, gave the peace to his servants, men and women, and gave them all communion with the Sacrament of the Altar that the priest Justin had consecrated. The table was then set, but before he took food, soldiers came, arrested him, and led him to the emperor. When Decius Caesar saw him, he sneered and said: "So you too have become a sorcerer, and you took away Laurence's body!" Hippolytus: "I did not do that as a sorcerer but as a Christian!" Decius, beside himself with fury, ordered him to be stripped of the garment he wore as a Christian, and to be beaten about the face with stones. Hippolytus said to him: "You haven't stripped me, rather you've clothed me!" Decius: "How can you be so stupid, not even blushing at your nakedness? Now offer sacrifice and you will live, or else perish with your Laurence!" Hippolytus: "May I be made worthy to follow the example of Laurence, whose name you dare to pronounce with your filthy mouth!"

Decius had him beaten with rods and torn with iron rakes, but Hippolytus continued to proclaim loudly that he was a Christian. When he scorned the torments, the emperor made him put on the military apparel he had previously worn, reminding him of his military status and friendships. Hippolytus retorted that he soldiered for Christ, and Decius, his anger rising, turned him over to the prefect Valerian with orders to take possession of everything he owned and to put him to death. When it was learned that his whole household was Christian, they were all brought before the prefect and ordered to sacrifice to the idols. Concordia, his nurse, answered for all: "We wish to die chastely with our master, rather than to live dishonorably." Valerian: "Slaves can be corrected only by severe punishment!" While Hippolytus watched and rejoiced at the sight, the prefect had Concordia beaten with leaded whips until she breathed her last. Hippolytus exclaimed: "I give you thanks, O Lord, because you have sent my nurse ahead to enjoy the vision of your saints!"

Valerian now had Hippolytus and all his people led out beyond the Porta Tiburtina, and Hippolytus, to strengthen their resolve, said: "My brothers and sisters, don't be afraid! You and I have one and the same God!" Valerian commanded that all of them be beheaded while Hippolytus looked on, and that Hippolytus be tied by the feet to the necks of untamed horses and dragged over thistles and thorns until he expired. This happened about A.D. 256.

The priest Justin retrieved their bodies and buried them beside the body of Saint Laurence, but he could not find Saint Concordia's body because it had been thrown into the sewer. One of the soldiers, whose name was Porphyrius, thought Concordia might have been carrying gold or gems in her clothing, and he sought out one Ireneus, who secretly was a Christian, and said to him: "Keep this secret and get Concordia out of the sewer! I hope she had money and jewels in her clothes!" Ireneus said: "Show me the place! I'll keep the secret, and I'll let you know what I find!" But when he had pulled the body out of the sewer and found nothing, the soldier made his escape at once, and Ireneus, after calling in a Christian named Abundus, took the body to Saint Justin, who accepted it piously and buried it beside those of Saint Hippolytus and the others. When Valerian found out about this, he arrested Ireneus and Abundus and threw them alive into the sewer, and Justin rescued their bodies and buried them with the rest.

After that, Decius and Valerian mounted a golden chariot and rode into the circus to watch the Christians being tortured. But Decius was seized by a demon, and he cried out: "O Hippolytus, you are holding me bound in rough chains!" Valerian likewise cried: "O Laurence, you are dragging me with fiery chains!" Valerian died then and there, but Decius got back to his house. He was tormented for three days by the demon and pleaded: "I adjure you, Laurence, don't torture me this way!" But he died a miserable death nonetheless.

Now Triphonia, the wife of Decius, seeing what had happened, received the faith. She dismissed her people and went to Saint Justin with her daughter Cyrilla, and had the priest baptize them and many others with them. A few days later Triphonia expired while at prayer, and Justin buried her body beside that of Hippolytus. Forty-seven soldiers heard that the queen and her daughter had become Christians, so they went with their wives to Justin the priest, asking to be baptized; and Dionysius, who had succeeded Sixtus as pope, baptized them all. Claudius, now the emperor, had Cyrilla strangled when she refused to sacrifice, and ordered the soldiers beheaded. The bodies of all of them were buried with the rest in the Veranus field.

Note that here it is explicitly stated that Claudius succeeded the Decius who martyred Laurence and Hippolytus. This Decius was succeeded, according to the chronicles, by Volusianus, Volusianus by Gallienus, and Gallienus by Claudius. Therefore we should say (or so it seems) that previously Gallienus had two names and was called both Gallienus and Decius, as Vincent says in his chronicle and Godfrey in his book. Or it may be that Gallienus, to provide himself with an assistant, made someone named Decius a caesar but not the emperor: this is what Richard says in his chronicle.

Ambrose, in his Preface, says of this martyr: "The blessed martyr Hippolytus considered Christ to be his commander and preferred to be a soldier of Christ rather than to be commissioned a commander of troops. When Saint Laurence was entrusted to him to be held under guard, he did not persecute the saint but became his follower. When the treasures of the Church were distributed, he found one treasure that no tyrant could snatch from him, a treasure from which true riches could be hoped for. He spurned the tyrant's favor in order to be confirmed by the grace of the eternal King. He did not resist having his limbs torn asunder, lest he be mangled with eternal hooks."

There was an ox-driver named Peter, who, on the feast of Saint Mary Magdalene, had hitched up his team to the plow and was driving the oxen with goads and curses, when suddenly a bolt of lightning consumed both oxen and plow. Peter himself, who had been doing the cursing, was now afflicted with atrocious pain: the flesh and sinews of his leg were burned away, the bones were left bare, and the shinbone came clear out of its joint. The man went to a church of the Blessed Virgin, hid the bone in a hole in the wall, and tearfully prayed the Blessed Virgin for his healing. Then in the night the Virgin appeared to him with blessed Hippolytus, and the Virgin asked the saint to restore Peter to his former health. At once Hippolytus took the shinbone from its hiding place and inserted it in its place in the leg as a shoot is grafted into a tree. Peter suffered such pain as the insertion was done that his screams awoke the whole household, and all came with a lamp and found Peter asleep with two whole legs and two shins. The family could not believe their eyes and felt his legs again and again until they were sure the limbs were real and sound. They woke him and asked how this had happened to him. He thought they were making fun of him until, seeing that what they said was true, he was convinced and astonished. The new leg, however, was weaker than the old one and could not support his weight with good balance. Hence he walked with a limp for a whole year as testimony to the miracle, after which he again sought the Blessed Virgin's help. She appeared to him with Saint Hippolytus and told the saint that he ought to supply what was lacking in the cure. Peter awoke and saw that he was completely mended.

Peter now withdrew to a hermitage. There the devil frequently appeared to him in the form of a nude woman and forced herself upon him. The more stoutly he resisted her, the more shamelessly she threw herself upon him, tormenting him so much that finally he got hold of a priest's stole and wound it around her neck. This drove the devil away. What was left was a rotting body, and the stench was so foul that no one who saw the corpse could doubt that this was the body of a dead woman, which the devil had assumed as a disguise.

✳

119. The Assumption of the Blessed Virgin Mary

The manner of the assumption of the Blessed Virgin Mary is related in a small apocryphal book attributed to John the Evangelist. In this book we read that after the apostles had gone off to various regions of the world to preach the Gospel, the Blessed Virgin dwelt in a house close by Mount Sion. As long as she lived, she diligently and devoutly visited all the places sacred to the memory of her Son—where he had been baptized, had fasted, had prayed, had suffered, died, and been buried, had risen and ascended into heaven. According to what Epiphanius says, she lived for twenty-four years after her Son's ascension. Epiphanius calculated that she was fourteen years old when she conceived Christ and fifteen when she gave birth; she lived with him for thirty-three years and survived him by twenty-four, so she died at the age of seventy-two. It seems probable, however, as we read elsewhere, that she lived only twelve years after her Son's death and resurrection, and so was assumed into heaven at the age of sixty, since, as the *Ecclesiastical History* has it, the apostles preached for twelve years in Judea and the surrounding country.

One day the Virgin's heart was aflame with desire to be with her Son; she was so deeply stirred in spirit that her tears flowed abundantly. She could not with serenity of soul bear his being taken away for a time and the loss of his consoling presence. Then behold, an angel stood before her amid a great light and greeted her reverently as the mother of his Lord. "Hail, blessed Mary!" he said, "receive the blessing of him who bestowed salvation on Jacob. See, Lady, I have brought you a palm branch from paradise, and you are to have it carried before your bier. Three days from now you will be assumed from the body, because your Son is waiting for you, his venerable mother."

Mary replied: "If I have found favor in your eyes, I beg you to deign to tell me your name. Even more urgently I ask that my sons and brothers the apostles be brought together here with me, so that before I die, I may see them again with my bodily eyes, and may be buried by them and render my spirit to God in their presence. And I also plead and pray that when my soul leaves this body, it may see no foul spirit, and that no power of Satan may confront me."

The angel said: "Why, Lady, do you want to know my name, which is great and admirable? Know, however, that all the apostles will gather and come to you today. They will give you noble burial, and you will breathe forth your spirit in the sight of all of them. Indeed, there is no doubt that he who long ago picked up the prophet by the hairs of his head and carried him from Judea to Babylon will be able to bring the apostles to you in an instant. And why are you afraid of seeing the wicked spirit, since you crushed his head and stripped him of his imperial power? But as you wish: you will see no demons." Having said all this, the angel ascended to heaven surrounded by much light. Moreover, the palm branch shone very brightly: the stem was green like any other branch, but the leaves gleamed like the morning star.

Now it happened that John was preaching in Ephesus when suddenly there was a clap of thunder, and a shining cloud picked him up and whisked him to Mary's door. He knocked and went in, and the virgin reverently greeted the Virgin. Seeing him, Mary was so astonished and happy that she could not contain her tears for joy, and said: "My son John, remember your master's words, by which he commended me to you as your mother and you to me to be my son. I must tell you that I have been summoned by the Lord. I am about to pay the debt of the human condition, and I commend my body to your heedful care, for I have heard that some Jews have conspired together, saying, 'Men and brothers, let us wait until the woman who bore Jesus dies. Then we will seize her body, throw it into the fire, and burn it up!' Therefore you, John, must have someone carry this palm branch in front of the litter when you convey my body to the sepulcher."

"Oh!" said John, "if only all my brother apostles were here to prepare proper obsequies for you and pay you the honors you deserve!" Even as he was speaking, all the apostles were snatched up into the clouds from wherever they were preaching, and deposited at Mary's door. They marveled to find themselves brought together, and said: "What can be the Lord's reason for assembling us in this place?" John then came out to them, told them that Mary was soon to leave the body, and added: "Take care, brothers, no one is to weep for her when she dies. Otherwise people might be troubled and say: 'See how these men fear death, for all their preaching to others about the resurrection!'"

Dionysius, the apostle Paul's disciple, gives a like account in his book *On the Divine Names*. He says that the apostles came together at the dormition of the Virgin, that he himself was there, and that each one spoke in praise of Christ and the Virgin. He writes to Timothy[1] as follows: "As you know, we and he [Hierotheus] himself and many of our holy brothers came together to view that life-giving body which had received God. James the brother of God was there also, and Peter, the highest and most perfect summit among those who speak about God [*theologoi*, theologians].[2] Afterwards it seemed good that all the hierarchs present, each according to his capacity, should praise the infinitely powerful goodness of that God-bearing frailty." So far Dionysius.

When blessed Mary saw all the apostles assembled, she thanked the Lord and sat in their midst, surrounded by lighted torches and lanterns. About the third hour of the night Jesus came with companies of angels, troops of prophets, hosts of martyrs, a legion of confessors and choirs of virgins, and all took their places before the Virgin's throne and sang dulcet canticles.

The book ascribed to John, already mentioned, tells us how the obsequies were celebrated. First, Jesus himself began and said: "Come, my chosen one, and I will set you upon my throne, because I have desired your beauty." The Virgin responded: "My heart is ready, O Lord, my heart is ready."[3] Then all those who had come with Jesus softly sang: "This is she who knew no bed in sin;

---

[1] Graesse notes that the Ed. Pr. has "Timothy" here, whereas Jacobus has "Hierotheus." In fact the whole book *De divinis nominibus* is addressed to Timothy the fellow Elder. "Hierotheus" is someone whom Pseudo-Dionysius praises as his famous, even divine, teacher, and who may be fictitious.

[2] The text adds "Paul" here; Graesse notes that the Ed. Pr. omits him. A helpful English translation of the present passage by Colm Luibheid is in Pseudo-Dionysius, *The Complete Works* (New York: Paulist Press, 1987), 70.

[3] Ps. 108:1.

she shall have fruit in the visitation of holy souls."[4] Mary then sang about herself, saying: "All generations shall call me blessed, because he that is mighty has done great things for me, and holy is his name."[5] The cantor, taking a higher pitch, intoned: "Come from Lebanon, my spouse, come from Lebanon; thou shalt be crowned."[6] And Mary: "Behold I come! In the head of the book it is written of me that I should do thy will, O God, because my spirit has rejoiced in thee, God my Savior."[7]

Then Mary's soul went forth from her body and flew to the arms of her Son, and was spared all bodily pain, just as it had been innocent of all corruption. Christ said to the apostles: "Carry the body of the Virgin my mother to the valley of Josaphat and place it in a new monument that you will find there. Then wait for me there until I come back to you three days from now." At once the Virgin was surrounded with red roses, signifying the army of the martyrs, and with lilies of the valley, signifying the hosts of angels, confessors, and virgins. The apostles called after her, saying: "Where are you going, most prudent of virgins? Be mindful of us, O Lady!"

The spirits who had stayed in heaven, wondering at the singing of the ascending throngs, set forth in haste to meet them. They saw their King carrying the soul of a woman in his arms and observed her leaning upon him. This surprised them and they began to cry out, saying: "Who is this who comes up from the wilderness, flowing with delights, leaning upon her beloved?"[8] To them her attendants replied: "She is beautiful among the daughters of Jerusalem, as you have seen her full of charity and love." And so, rejoicing, she was taken into heaven and seated upon a throne of glory to the right of her Son; and the apostles saw that her soul was of a whiteness so bright that no mortal tongue could describe it.

There were three virgins at hand, and they removed Mary's robe in order to wash the body, which immediately shone with such effulgence that, while it could be touched and bathed, it could not be seen; and the light shone for as long as it took the virgins to perform their task. Then the apostles reverently lifted the body and placed it on a bier. John said to Peter: "Peter, you will carry this palm branch before the litter, because the Lord set you over us and ordained you as the shepherd and leader of his flock." Peter answered: "You should be the one to carry it, since you, a virgin, were chosen by the Lord, and it is fitting that a virgin should carry the Virgin's palm. You were worthy to lean on the Lord's bosom, and from there received a greater stream of wisdom and grace than the others; so it seems right that the one who received the greater gift from the Son should pay the greater honor to the Virgin. Therefore you must carry this palm of light at the funeral of her sanctity, as you have drunk from the cup of light and the source of perpetual clarity. I will carry the holy body on the bier,

---

[4] Wisd. 3:13. [5] Luke 1:48–49. [6] Song of Sol. 4:8.
[7] Ps. 40:8; Luke 1:47. [8] Song of Sol. 8:5.

and the rest of our brothers will surround it and raise songs of praise to God." Paul then said to him: "And I, who am the least of all of you, will carry it with you."

Peter and Paul then lifted the bier, and Peter began to sing with the words: *Exiit Israel de Aegypto, alleluia.*[9] The other apostles sweetly took up the chant. The Lord covered the litter and the apostles with a cloud in such a way that they could not be seen and only their voices were heard. Angels were present, too, singing with the apostles and filling the whole earth with the sound of their sweet song.

The populace was excited by such dulcet sound and melody, and came rushing out of the city to see what was going on. Then someone said: "The disciples of Jesus are carrying Mary away dead, and singing around her the melody you hear." At once they hurried to take arms and exhorted each other, saying: "Come on, let us kill all those disciples and burn the body that bore the seducer." The chief priest, seeing what was happening, was astounded and filled with rage, and said: "Look at the tabernacle of that man who disturbed us and our people so much! Look at the glory that is now paid to that woman!" After saying this he put his hands on the litter, intending to overturn it and throw the corpse to the ground. But suddenly his hands withered and stuck to the bier, so that he was hanging by his hands; and he moaned and cried in great pain, while the rest of the people were stricken with blindness by angels who were in the cloud.

The chief priest cried out: "Holy Peter, do not scorn me in this extremity! Pray the Lord for me, I beg of you! You must remember how I stood by you and defended you when the portress accused you." Peter answered: "We're busy seeing to our Lady's burial and can't do anything about curing you. However, if you believe in our Lord Jesus Christ and in this woman who conceived and bore him, I hope you will quickly receive the benefit of health." The chief priest: "I believe that the Lord Jesus is the true Son of God, and that this woman was his most holy mother." At once his hands were loosed from the bier, but his arms were still withered and the pain was as severe as before. Peter told him: "Kiss the bier and say, 'I believe in Jesus Christ God, whom this woman carried in her womb and remained a virgin after she delivered her child.'" He did as he was told and was cured instantly. Peter then told him: "Take the palm from the hand of our brother John and hold it up over the people who have been blinded. Those who are willing to believe will receive their sight, those who refuse will never see again."

The apostles now took Mary's body and laid it in the tomb. Then, as the Lord had commanded, they sat around the sepulcher. On the third day Jesus came with a multitude of angels and greeted them, saying: "Peace be with you!" They answered: "Glory to you, O God, who alone do great wonders!" The Lord then

[9] Cf. Ps. 114:1; Israel went forth from Egypt. . . .

asked the apostles: "What grace and honor do you think I should now confer on my mother?" They answered: "To your servants it seems just that as you have conquered death and now reign forever, you, Jesus, should bring your mother's body to life and enthrone her at your right hand for eternity."

Christ nodded his consent and immediately Michael the archangel came forward and presented Mary's soul before the Lord. Then the Savior spoke and said: "Arise, my dear one, my dove, tabernacle of glory, vessel of life, heavenly temple! As you never knew the stain of sin through carnal intercourse, so you shall never suffer dissolution of the flesh in the tomb." Thereupon Mary's soul entered her body, and she came forth glorious from the monument and was assumed into the heavenly bridal chamber, a great multitude of angels keeping her company. Thomas, however, was absent, and when he came back refused to believe. Then suddenly the girdle that had encircled her body fell intact into his hands, and he realized that the Blessed Virgin had really been assumed body and soul.

All that has been said so far, however, is apocryphal. Jerome, in his letter to Paula and Eustochium, says: "That little book must be judged to be apocryphal, except regarding some things in it that are credible because they seem to be approved by the saints. There are nine of these: every sort of consolation being promised and granted to the Virgin; the gathering of all the apostles; Mary's painless death; the preparation of a burial place in the valley of Josaphat; Christ's devout attendance; the assistance of the whole heavenly court; persecution by the Jews; the flash of miracles in every deserving case; the assumption in soul and body. But there are a lot of things narrated in the book that are pure invention rather than fact, for instance, that Thomas was not present and doubted when he came, and other like things that obviously are to be repudiated rather than maintained."

It is said that the Virgin's garments were left behind in the tomb for the consolation of the faithful, and that the following miracle was brought about by an article of her clothing. The duke of Normandy was besieging the city of Chartres. The Virgin's tunic was preserved there, and the bishop of the city attached it to a spear, thus making a sort of banner. With this for protection he went out to confront the hostile troops, with the townspeople following him. At the sight of this display the attackers were bereft of their senses, blinded, shaken to the core, thrown into disarray. The townsfolk thereupon went far beyond the divine judgment, fell upon the opposing troops, and slaughtered them unmercifully. This greatly displeased Mary, as was proved by the sudden disappearance of her tunic and the fact that the enemy militia promptly recovered their sight.

In Saint Elizabeth's *Revelations* we read that once when the saint was rapt in ecstasy, she had a vision. She saw, at a great distance, a sepulcher upon which a brilliant light fell. In the sepulcher lay a form that looked like a woman, surrounded by a multitude of angels. Shortly the woman was taken out of the tomb and lifted on high together with her many attendants; and a splendid, glorious man, carrying the banner of the cross in his right hand and accompanied by countless thousands of angels, came from heaven to meet her. Quickly taking her they led her off to heaven amidst a great chorus of song. Not long afterwards Elizabeth asked the angel with whom she frequently talked what the vision had meant. The angel answered: "You were shown how our Lady was assumed into heaven in the flesh as well as in the spirit."

In the same *Revelations* Elizabeth says it was revealed to her that Mary's assumption in the body took place forty days after her death. Blessed Mary herself, talking with Elizabeth, said: "I lived on after the Lord's ascension for a year and as many days as there are between the feast of the Ascension and the feast of my Assumption. All the apostles were with me when I fell asleep, and they reverently gave burial to my body, but I rose again after forty days." Elizabeth asked the Blessed Virgin whether she should make this known or keep it secret, and Mary replied: "It is neither to be revealed to carnal, unbelieving people, nor hidden from the devout and the faithful."

It is noteworthy that the glorious Virgin Mary was assumed and exalted integrally, honorably, joyfully, and splendidly.

She was assumed integrally in soul and body, as the Church piously believes, and as many saints not only assert but make it their business to prove, offering a number of reasons. Bernard's reasoning is as follows: the bodies of the saints are precious in the sight of God, and he makes the places where their bodies are preserved—for instance, the shrines of Saint Peter and Saint James—worthy of such reverence that the whole world comes hurrying to venerate them. Therefore if Mary's body is supposed to be on earth and yet is not visited and venerated by the faithful, it would seem (and this surely is not true) that Christ cares little about the honor due his mother's body, whereas he gives so much honor to the bodies of other saints on earth.

Jerome also says that on the fifteenth day of August Mary ascended to heaven: he says this, meaning that the Virgin was assumed bodily. On this point the Church prefers to hesitate reverently rather than define something hastily. Jerome goes on to prove that what he says should be believed. There are some, he declares, who say that for those who have risen with Christ, the final, perpetual resurrection is complete, and there are those who hold that Saint John, the guardian of Mary, also rejoices in his glorified body with Christ. Why, therefore, is this not all the more credible regarding the mother of the Savior? He who said: "Honor your father and your mother," and "I have not come to destroy the Law but to fulfill the Law," surely has honored his mother above all others: nor do we ourselves doubt that he has so honored his mother.

Augustine also affirms this belief, giving three reasons for holding it. The first is the oneness of Christ's flesh and the Virgin's. He says: "Putrescence and the worm are the shame of the human condition. Since Jesus has no part in that shame, Mary's nature, which Jesus, as we know, took from her, is exempt from it." His second reason is the dignity of her body, so he says: "The throne of God, the bridal chamber of the Lord, the tabernacle of Christ is worthy to be kept in heaven rather than on earth." Thirdly, he proposes the perfect integrity of her virginal flesh, saying: "Rejoice, Mary, with unutterable joy, body and soul, in Christ your own Son, with your own Son and through your own Son. The bane of corruption ought not to overtake her who suffered no corruption of her integrity when she gave birth to so great a Son. So she, upon whom so much grace was poured, should always be incorrupt; she who begot the integral and perfect life of all should be fully and wholly living; she should be with him whom she had borne in her womb, be beside him whom she had engendered and fed and kept warm—Mary, the mother of God, God's minister and handmaid. Since I dare not think otherwise about her, I do not presume to speak otherwise."

Here we may quote the eminent poet:

> Scandit ad aethera
> Virgo puerpera,
> virgula Jesse.
> Non sine corpore
> sed sine tempore
> tendit adesse.[10]

Mary was assumed amidst rejoicing. Saint Gerard, bishop and martyr, says about this in his homilies: "Today the heavens welcomed the Blessed Virgin joyfully, Angels rejoicing, Archangels jubilating, Thrones exalting, Dominations psalming, Principalities harmonizing, Powers lyring, Cherubim and Seraphim hymning and leading her to the supernal tribunal of the divine majesty."

High honors attended her assumption. Jesus and the whole host of the celestial army went forth to meet her. Hence Jerome says: "Who might be able even to think how gloriously the queen of the world advanced, with what stirring of devotion the multitude of the heavenly legions came forth to meet her, with what chants she was conducted to her throne, with what placid mien and serene visage and what divine embraces her Son received her and exalted her above every creature!"

Jerome also says: "We must believe that on this day the celestial militia came to meet the mother of God with festive celebration and shone round about her with dazzling light, leading her up to the throne of God with lauds and spiritual canticles, and that the army of the heavenly Jerusalem exulted with indescribable joy, and welcomed her with ineffable devotion and boundless rejoicing. We celebrate this feast as it comes round once a year, but it is celebrated unceasingly in heaven. We also believe that the Savior himself went to meet his mother joyfully and gladly placed her on a throne at his side. Otherwise he would not

---

[10] She mounts to the skies / the virgin mother / the shoot of Jesse. / Not without her body / but outside of time / she goes to be present.

have fulfilled what he himself had commanded in the Law: 'Honor your father and your mother.'" So far Jerome.

Finally, it was a splendid reception. Jerome: "This is the day the inviolate mother and virgin ascended the heights to her throne, and, being raised in rank next to Christ's in the kingdom, took her place in glory." Indeed, Gerard in his homilies tells to what height of heavenly glory and honor she was elevated: "The Lord Jesus Christ alone can give such greatness as he gave to his mother—greatness such that she continuously receives praise and honor from the divine majesty itself, is attended by choirs of Angels, compassed about by troops of Archangels, accompanied on all sides by the jubilation of Thrones, encircled by the dances of Dominations, by the plaudits of Powers, by the honors of Virtues, the hymns of the Cherubim and the chants of the Seraphim. The ineffable Trinity also applauds her with unceasing dance, and the grace with which the three Persons totally infuse her draws the attention of all to her. The illustrious order of the apostles extols her with praise beyond expression, the throng of the martyrs offers every kind of worship to so great a queen, the innumerable army of confessors sounds a continuous chant to her, the shining assembly of virgins sings a ceaseless chorus in honor of her glory, unwilling Hell howls to her and the impudent demons add their shrieking."

A certain clerk who had great devotion to the Virgin Mary tried every day to console her, so to speak, for the pain of the five wounds of Christ by repeating these words: "Rejoice, mother of God, Virgin immaculate, rejoice! You received joy from the angel, rejoice! You begot the brightness of eternal light, rejoice, O mother, rejoice, holy virgin mother of God! You alone are mother without spouse, all that is created and made praises you! Mother of light, be for us, we pray you, our perpetual mediatrix!" In time this clerk was stricken with an illness so grave that his end was near, and he began to be very much afraid. The Virgin appeared to him and said: "My son, you often bade me rejoice. Why do you now tremble with fear? You too rejoice, and rejoice eternally! Come with me!"

A very rich and valiant knight had squandered all his wealth with careless liberality and was reduced to such poverty that he, accustomed as he was to giving his money away, began to want for the barest necessities. His wife was a most virtuous woman and very devoted to blessed Mary. Now a solemn feast day was approaching, a day on which the knight had always made many large donations, but now he had nothing to give. Driven by embarrassment and shame, he went out to a desert place to let the feast day go by, hoping also to find some companion in misery with whom he could bemoan his bad luck and escape his feeling of humiliation.

Suddenly a fearful horse, with a still more fearful rider in the saddle, galloped up to the knight. The rider addressed him and asked the reason for his woebegone look. The knight told him everything that had happened to him, and the rider said: "If you are willing to do me a small favor, you will enjoy greater fame and more riches than ever." The knight answered the prince of darkness that he would gladly do whatever he was asked to, provided the other would fulfill his promises. The demon said: "Go home and look in a certain cupboard in your house, and you will find large amounts of gold, silver, and precious stones. And here is what you will do for me: bring your wife to me on the day I tell you."

After that exchange of promises the knight went home, found the treasures as directed, and proceeded to buy palaces, make lavish gifts, redeem his lands, and purchase slaves. Then, as the appointed day drew near, he called to his wife and said: "Get up behind me, we have a long ride ahead of us." She shook with fear but dared not refuse, so she devoutly commended herself to the Blessed Virgin and set out with her husband. They had ridden a long distance when they came to a church beside the road, and the lady dismounted and went in while her spouse waited outside. Then, as she prayed earnestly to blessed Mary, she fell asleep. Next, the glorious Virgin, dressed as the matron was and looking exactly like her, came down from the altar, went out of the church while the woman slept on inside, and mounted behind the knight. He, thinking it was his wife, continued the journey.

When they reached the place agreed upon, the prince of darkness hurried up to meet them, but when he saw who was there, he dared come no closer and said to the knight: "You treacherous fellow, why have you tricked me this way after all I did for you? I told you to bring your wife to me, and instead you have brought me the mother of the Lord. I wanted your spouse and you come here with Mary! Your wife has done me great harm and I wanted to take my revenge, and now you bring this woman to torment me and send me to hell!" The knight was stupefied at what he heard and could not say a word for fear and wonderment. Mary, however, spoke: "Wicked spirit, what rashness led you to presume to harm my devoted follower? You will not go unpunished for this, and I now impose this sentence upon you. Go down to hell, and never again dare to do injury to anyone who invokes me with devotion!"

The devil vanished, loudly lamenting his frustration. The knight got down from his horse and prostrated himself at the Virgin's feet. She rebuked him and ordered him to go to his wife, who was still asleep in the church, and to throw away all the demon's riches. He went into the church, awakened his sleeping spouse, and told her all that had occurred. They then returned home, threw out all the ill-gotten treasures, and lived thereafter praising the Virgin most devoutly. In time they acquired much wealth, blessed Mary herself bestowing it.

A certain man, whose sins weighed heavily upon him, had a vision in which he came before God's judgment seat. Satan was present and said: "You have no rights in this man's soul. He belongs entirely to me, and I have a warrant to prove it." "Where is your warrant?" the Lord asked. Satan: "I have it because you yourself dictated it and confirmed it in perpetuity, for you said: 'At whatever hour you eat of this, you shall die the death.'[11] Since this man is of the

[11] Cf. Gen. 2:17.

progeny of those who ate the forbidden food, by this public warrant I have title to him and he should be sentenced to die with me." The Lord said: "O man, you have permission to speak for yourself," but the man said nothing. The demon spoke again: "He is mine also by right of prescription, because I owned him for thirty years and he obeyed me as a slave should." But the man still remained silent. Again the demon spoke: "His soul is mine also because though he did some good, the evil he did far outweighs the good."

God, however, did not wish to pronounce sentence against him so quickly and granted him a week's reprieve, at the end of which he would again appear to refute all the devil's allegations. As he left the Lord's presence frightened and grief-stricken, he met someone who asked the reason for his sadness. The man told him the situation he was in, and the other answered: "Don't be afraid, you have nothing to fear. I will help you manfully in answering the first charge." The man asked the other's name, and the reply was: "My name is Truth." Then he came upon a second person, who promised to defend him staunchly against the second charge, and, being asked his name, said: "I am called Justice."

On the eighth day, therefore, the man again came before the judgment seat and the demon repeated his first claim, to which Truth responded: "We know that there are two deaths, the death of the body and the death of the soul in hell. The warrant you quote in your favor, O demon, does not speak of the death of hell, but only of that of the body. It is obvious that all fall under the first sentence, namely, that all must die the death of the body, but all do not die the death of hell. Your instrument, therefore, applies in perpetuity regarding bodily death, but with regard to the death of the soul it has been revoked by the blood of Christ!" So, seeing that he had lost his first point, the devil started to restate the second one, but Justice was there and answered him as follows: "Granted that you owned him as a slave for many years, his reason always opposed you, because reason always murmured against serving so cruel a master."

The man had no one to take his part against the third charge, and God said: "Let the scales be brought and all his good and bad deeds be weighed." Truth and Justice said to the sinner: "You see there the mother of mercy, seated beside the Lord. Call upon her with your whole heart and try to win her help." He did this, and blessed Mary came to his aid. She put her hand on the side of the scale where the few good deeds were, while the devil tried to pull the other side down; but the mother of mercy prevailed and the sinner was freed. He thereupon came to himself and led a better life from then on.

In the city of Bourges, about the year of the Lord 527, the Christians were receiving holy communion on Easter Sunday, and a Jewish boy went to the altar and received the Lord's Body with the others. When he went home, his father asked him where he had been, and he answered that he had gone to church with his schoolmates and had taken communion with them. The father, furious, picked the lad up and threw him into a white-hot furnace. At once, however, the mother of God, looking like a painting that the boy had seen on the altar, came to his side and kept him unharmed by the fire. The boy's mother's outcries brought together a number of Christians and Jews, and seeing the lad unscathed in the furnace they pulled him out and asked him how he had been able to escape the flames. "That venerable lady who stood above the altar," he answered, "helped me and held the fire away from me." The Christians present, understanding that he referred to the image of the Blessed Virgin, seized the boy's father and cast him into the furnace, where he was immediately burned up and reduced to ashes.

Several monks were standing on a riverbank before dawn, gossiping and exchanging idle banter, when they heard oarsmen rowing down the river at top speed. The monks asked them who they were. "We are devils," they replied, "and we are taking to hell the soul of Ebroïn, mayor of the palace to the king of the Franks and a renegade from the monastery of Saint Gall." Hearing this the monks were terror-stricken and cried out at the top of their voices: "Holy Mary, pray for us!" "You do well to call on Mary!" said the demons. "We intended to tear you to pieces and drown you, because we found you chattering away at a time forbidden by the rule." The monks went back to the cloister and the demons sped off to hell.

There was a monk much given to lechery but very devoted to blessed Mary. One night, on his way to commit the usual mischief, he passed before the altar and greeted the Blessed Virgin, then left the church. He had to cross a river, but fell in and drowned. When devils came to take away his soul, angels were there to keep it free. The devils said to them: "What are you doing here? you have no claim to this soul!" Instantly blessed Mary was present and reproached the evil spirits for presuming to lay hands on the monk's soul; but they said that they had found him about to die and bent on wrongdoing. Mary retorted: "Your accusations are false! I know that whenever he was going somewhere he first greeted me, and did the same on his way back. But if you say that you are being treated unjustly, we will submit the case to the judgment of the King of kings." When the question was argued before God, it pleased him to have the soul return to the sinner's body and there do penance for his actions. Meanwhile his brother monks noticed that matins had not been rung, so they looked for the sacristan and found him drowned in the river. They pulled the body out and wondered what had happened, when he suddenly came to life and told the whole story. Thereafter he lived out his life in good works.

There was a certain woman to whom the devil appeared in the form of a man, harassing her continually. She resorted to many remedies, sometimes sprinkling blessed water, at other times trying this and that, but nothing made the demon desist. Finally a holy man advised her to raise her hands when the evil spirit appeared and to say aloud: "Holy Mary, help me!" She did this, and the demon, as if hit by a stone, stood terrified and said: "May a bad devil enter the mouth of the one who taught you that!" And straightway he vanished and came back no more.

HOW MARY WAS ASSUMED INTO HEAVEN

The manner and circumstances of the blessed Virgin Mary's assumption are related in a sermon that was compiled from various sayings of saints and is solemnly read in many churches. In it we read: "I have kept a careful record of all that I could find in the writings of the holy fathers throughout the world concerning the venerable migration of the mother of God." Saint Cosmas Vestitor says that he had accurately preserved what he learned from persons who came after those who had been present at the sacred event, and that this must not be omitted. He says that when Christ decided to bring to himself the mother who had given him life, he sent the usual angel to announce to her the manner of her falling asleep, for fear that death, coming unexpectedly, should cause her any disturbance. His mother had implored him face to face, when her Son was still living on earth, not to let her see any malignant spirit. He therefore sent the angel ahead to deliver this message to her: "The time has come for me to take you, my mother, to myself. As you have filled the earth with joy, now make my Father's mansions joyful; console the spirits of my saints. And now that you are about to dwell in the palace of heaven, do not be disturbed at leaving the corruptible world with its vain desires. Do not, O my mother, let separation from the body frighten you, because you are called to perpetual life, to a joy that never fails, to peaceful rest, to untroubled ease, to unending refreshment, to inaccessible light, to the day that has no evening, to indescribable glory, to myself, your Son, the maker of all that is. For I am life eternal, love without compare, the ineffable dwelling, light that knows no darkness, bounty immeasurable. Give to the earth what is the earth's, without anxiety. No one will snatch you from my hand, because in my hand are all the bounds of the earth. Commit your body to me, because I deposited my divinity in your womb. Death will have no boast over you, because you begot life. No shadow of darkness will come upon you, because you gave birth to light. No damage or breakage will touch you, because you were worthy to become the vessel that held me. Come now to him who was born of you: you are about to receive the reward of motherhood, the guerdon for raising your child, the return for nursing him and keeping him warm. Dwell with your only-begotten, hasten to cling to your Son; for I know that you will not be torn by love for another son. I have shown you to be a virgin mother: now I show that you are the sustaining wall of the whole world, the ark of those who are to be saved, the raft of those tossed about by the sea, the staff of the feeble, the ladder of those mounting to heaven, the mediatrix of sinners. I will bring the apostles to you, and they will bury you as if their hands were my own. For it is fitting that these sons of my spiritual light, to whom I have given the Holy Spirit, should bury your body and take my part in your honorable obsequies."

Having said all this, the angel gave the Virgin a palm branch sent from heaven as assurance of victory over the corruption of death, and the clothing for her burial, and then repaired to heaven whence he had come. Blessed Mary called her friends and relatives together and said: "I must tell you that today I am to pass out of this life of time. Therefore we must be watchful, because when someone is dying, both the godly power of angels, and wicked spirits, come to the death-bed." At these words all began to weep and said: "You were worthy to become the mother of the author of all things, you bore him who harrowed hell, you have merited a throne above the Cherubim and Seraphim, and are you now afraid of the presence of spirits? Then what shall we do? How can we escape?" And the crowd of women wept and begged Mary not to leave them orphans. The Blessed Virgin comforted them, saying: "If you, mothers of corruptible sons, cannot bear to be separated from them even for a short while, how should I, virgin mother as I am, not wish to go to my Son, the only-begotten of God the Father? If any one of you is bereaved of a son, she will be consoled by a surviving son or one still to be born, but I have only one Son and remain a virgin; how could I not be eager to hurry to him who is the life of all?"

While these things were going on, Saint John arrived and asked how matters stood. When the Virgin told him that she was about to migrate to heaven, he prostrated himself and cried out: "What are we, O Lord, that you afflict us with such tribulations? Why did you not take me out of the body and have me buried by the mother of my Lord, rather than have me present at her funeral?" The Blessed Virgin led him still weeping into her chamber and showed him the palm branch and the clothes, and then lay down on the bed that had been prepared for the burial.

Now a tremendous clap of thunder was heard, a whirlwind descended like a white cloud, and the apostles came down like a rain shower before the door of the Virgin's house. They did not know what to make of this until John came out and revealed to them what the angel had announced to Mary. They all wept, but John consoled them. Then, wiping away their tears, they went in, reverently greeted the Virgin, and knelt to her. She welcomed them, saying: "Hail to you, sons of my only-begotten Son!" And while she heard from them the manner of their getting there, she told them all that had happened. To her the apostles said: "Looking at you in the past, O most renowned Virgin, it was as though we were seeing our Lord and master, and we were consoled. Now our only comfort is that we hope to have you as our mediatrix with God." Mary called upon Paul by name, and he said: "Hail, queen of my solace! True, I never saw Christ in the flesh, yet, seeing you in the flesh, I am consoled as if I saw him. To this day I have preached to the Gentiles that you begot God; now I shall teach them that you have been taken up to him."

After that the Virgin showed them the things the angel had brought. She also gave orders that the lamps should not be extinguished until after her death. A hundred and twenty virgins were present to attend to her burial. She put on the funeral clothes, and, bidding all farewell, composed herself on the bed, ready to die. Peter stood at the head of the bed, John at the foot, the other apostles ranged themselves at the sides, all praising the mother of God as Peter began: "Rejoice, spouse of the heavenly bridal chamber, three-branched candelabrum of the light from on high, through whom the eternal clarity is made manifest!"

This gathering of the apostles at the dormition of the most holy Virgin is attested by Saint Germanus, archbishop of Constantinople, who says: "O mother of God, you accepted the death that is inevitable to human nature, yet your eye, which watches over us, will neither slumber nor sleep. For your transmigration was not without witnesses nor was your falling asleep a lie: heaven narrates the glory of those who sang over you, the earth exhibits the truth of them, the clouds proclaim the honor that by them was paid you, the angels tell the obsequies performed for you when the apostles together came to you in Jerusalem." The great Dionysius the Areopagite gives the same testimony, saying: "As you know, we and he and many from among our brothers came together to see the body that received the Lord. James the brother of God was there, and Peter the renowned, highest summit of theologians. It was agreed that after the viewing, all these high priests, so far as each one was of immense virtue, should sing the praises of this life-giving goodness and weakness."

Cosmas again takes up the story, saying: "After this great thunderclap the whole house shook and a fragrant breeze filled the house with so much sweetness that a deep sleep overcame all present except the apostles and three virgins who carried lamps. Then the Lord descended with a multitude of angels and took up the soul of his mother. Her soul shone with such effulgence that none of the apostles could look at it. Christ said to Peter: 'Bury my mother's body with all reverence and guard it diligently for three days. Then I will come and transfer it out of reach of corruption. I will wrap it in brightness like my own in order to put union and harmony between that which was received and that which received.'" The same Saint Cosmas goes on to record a fearful, marvelous mystery, which does not lend itself to natural discussion or curious investigation, since everything that is said about the mother of God is supernatural and wondrous and awesome rather than subject to curious scrutiny. "When the soul had gone out of her body," he says, "the body pronounced these words: 'O Lord, I, who am worthy of your glory, thank you. Remember me, because I am the work of your hands and have cared for that which you entrusted to me.'

"When the others woke and saw the lifeless body of the Virgin," Cosmas continues, "they began to grieve and mourn. Then the apostles took up the body and carried it to the tomb, Peter leading off with the Psalm *In exitu Israel de Aegypto*. Choirs of angels, too, sang the Virgin's praises, so that all Jerusalem was amazed at such glorification. Then the chief priests sent a crowd armed with swords and clubs. One of them rushed at the bier, hoping to drag the body of God's mother to the earth; but because he had impiously tried to touch the corpse, his hands lost the power of touch. Both hands tore away at the elbows and clung to the litter, and the attacker was stricken with horrible pain. He begged for pardon and promised amendment. Peter said to him: 'You will never obtain pardon unless you kiss the body of the ever Virgin and confess that Christ, born of her, is the Son of God.' The culprit obeyed, and his hands were rejoined to the elbows. Peter then plucked a date from the palm branch and gave it to him, saying: 'Go into the city and touch the sick with this date. Those who believe will be cured.'"

When the apostles reached the field of Gethsemane, they found there a tomb like Christ's life-restoring sepulcher. In it they deposited the body with much reverence. They did not dare to touch this sublime vessel of God but set it down by holding the corners of the shroud. Then they closed the tomb securely and the apostles and disciples of the Lord, following his orders, stood guard around it. On the third day a shining cloud enveloped them, angelic voices sounded, an ineffable perfume spread abroad, and all were wonderstruck when they saw that the Lord had come down and was carrying away the Virgin's body in glory.

The apostles therefore kissed the sepulcher and went back to the house of John the evangelist and theologian, praising him for having been the guardian of so great a virgin. But one of the apostles had missed the ceremonies and, marveling at what he heard about them, insisted that the tomb be opened so that he could ascertain the truth of what he had been told. The apostles refused, declaring, first, that the testimony of so many witnesses ought to be enough, and second, that if the infidels got wind of this, they might spread a rumor that the body had been stolen. But the doubter sadly asked: "Why do you defraud me, your equal, of the treasure that is ours in common?" In the end they opened the tomb and found not the body but the garments and the shroud.

In the *Historia Euthimiata*, Book III, chapter XL, Saint Germanus, archbishop of Constantinople, says he had discovered—and the great John of Damascus also attests to this—that the empress Pulcheria of blessed memory built many churches in and around Constantinople during the reign of Emperor Marcianus, among them a very beautiful one at Balcherna dedicated to the Virgin Mary. She then summoned Juvenal, archbishop of Jerusalem, and other bishops from Palestine who were in the royal capital because of the council in progress at Chalcedon, and said to them: "We have heard that the body of the all-holy Virgin was buried in the Garden of Gethsemane, and it is our wish that for the protection of this city the body be transferred here with all due reverence." Juvenal stated that Mary's body, as he had learned from ancient records, had been taken up to glory, only the clothing and the burial shroud being left in the tomb. Juvenal later sent the garments to Constantinople, and they are preserved with honor in the aforementioned church. Let no one judge that I have made up this story out of my own imagination. I have put down the things I learned by studious reading of the writings of those who in turn had received their knowledge from their predecessors through a true and certain tradition. So far I have reported the words found in the sermon to which I referred.

John of Damascus, who also was a Greek, adds still other wondrous details concerning the sacred assumption of the Virgin. In his sermons he says: "Today the most holy Virgin is borne aloft to the celestial bridal chamber. Today the sacred, living ark, which carried within itself the One who fashioned it, is given its place in a temple not made with hands. Today that most sacred dove, innocent and simple, flying out of the ark—that is, out of the body that received God—has found rest for its feet. Today the immaculate Virgin, who knew no earthly passion—nay, more was instructed by heavenly intelligences—has not gone down into the earth, but, being rightly called a living heaven, dwells in celestial mansions.

"Yes, your holy, blessed soul was naturally separated from your glorious body and your body was buried in the tomb; but it does not remain in death nor is it dissolved in corruption. Your virginity remained inviolate through childbirth; now, at your migration, your body rises above all and is transferred to a better and holier life, not corrupted by death but to be the same for eternal ages. For as the radiant, luciferous sun, hidden behind a sublunar body, seems for a brief hour somehow to fail, though it is not deprived of its light since in itself it has a perennial fount of light, so you, font of the true light, inexhaustible treasure of life, though for a brief moment of time you were allowed to die bodily, you still abundantly pour into us the brightness of inextinguishable light. This your sacred dormition ought not to be called death but transmigration, or a withdrawal, or, still better, an arrival. For leaving the body you come to heaven, angels and archangels meet you, the unclean spirits quake at your ascension. You, blessed Virgin, have not simply gone to heaven like Elijah, nor mounted like Paul to the third heaven: you have risen all the way to the royal throne of your Son.

"The death of other saints is blessed because it shows that they are blessed, but this is not so for you. It is not your death nor your blessedness, nor your transmigration nor your setting out, nor yet your withdrawal, that has bestowed upon you the surety of your blessedness, because you are the beginning, the middle, and the end of all the goods that transcend the thought of man. Your protection, your perfection, your conceiving without seed, all this is God dwelling in you! So you said truly that you will be and will be called blessed, not beginning with your death but from the moment you were conceived. It is not that death beatified you but that you glorified death, banishing its sadness and converting death to joy. For if God said: 'Lest the first man put out his hand and pluck the fruit and live forever,' how could the one who carried life itself, the life with no beginning, the life that has no ending—how could such a one not live forever and ever?

"Of old, God expelled and exiled from paradise the first parents of the human race, asleep in the death of sin, already buried under a mountain of disobedience, already rotting in the drunkenness of sin: now, conversely, this woman, who brought life to the whole human race, who manifested obedience to God the Father, who rooted out all passion . . . how could paradise not welcome her? Eve lent her ear to the serpent, drank the poisonous draft, was entrapped by pleasures, subjected to the pangs of childbirth, and condemned with Adam. But this truly blessed woman, who bent her ear to God, whom the Holy Spirit filled, who bore the Father's mercy in her womb, who conceived without contact with a husband and gave birth without pain, how shall death swallow her, how shall corruption dare to do anything to the body that bore life itself?"

The same Damascenus adds in his sermons: "Of a truth, the apostles were scattered worldwide to labor at fishing for men, drawing them by the net of the word out of the depths of darkness to the table of the heavenly court or to the Father's marriage feast, when God's command, like a fishing net or a cloud, brought them to Jerusalem, gathering and collecting them from beyond the seas. Then Adam and Eve, our first parents, called out: 'Come to us, O sacred, salutary vessel, you have made our joy complete!' On the other hand a throng of saints who were corporeally present said: 'Stay here with us, you our consolation! Do not leave us orphans, you whom we have as our solace in struggle, our refreshment in toil! For how can our life be life if we are deprived of your presence?' I think that the apostles and the rest who filled the church uttered these and similar pleas while sobs often interrupted their protestations.

"Mary then turned to her Son and said: 'Be the consoler of these beloved sons whom it has pleased you to call brothers. Comfort their grief at my departure, and as I lay my hands on them, heap blessing upon blessing on them.' Then she stretched out her hands, blessed the gathering of believers, and said: 'Into your hands, O Lord, I commend my spirit. Receive my soul, which you love, which you have kept free of any guilt. Not to the earth but to you I commit my body. Keep whole this body in which it pleased you to dwell. Take me to yourself, so that where you are, you the fruit of my loins, there I may live with you!' Thereupon words like these were heard: 'Arise, come then, my beloved, O beautiful among women! You are beautiful, my dear, and in you there is no stain.'

"Hearing this summons, the most holy Virgin commended her spirit into the hands of her Son, as the apostles, weeping, kissed the tabernacle of the Lord and were filled with blessing and holiness by their contact with the sacred body. Then diseases and demons fled, air and sky were purified by the soul's ascension and the body's commitment to the earth, and water by the washing of the body; for the body was washed with exceedingly clean water—not that the body was cleansed by the water but that the body sanctified the water. Then the sacred body was wrapped in a clean shroud and placed upon a bed, lamps gleamed, ointments sweetened the air, angel hymns resounded. As the disciples and other saints who were present intoned heavenly hymns, the ark of the Lord was set upon the sacred shoulders of the apostles and carried from Mount Sion to the holy ground of Gethsemane. Angels led the way and followed after, others kept the holy body covered, and the whole community of the church accompanied the cortege.

"Some Jews, hardened in their old malevolence, also showed themselves. It is said that as the sacred body of the mother of God was carried down from Mount Sion, a Hebrew, a true limb of Satan, ran up to the body which angels feared to approach, and in a spasm of fury laid both hands on the litter and dragged it to the ground. It is further said that one hand fell off as dry as a stick, and it was a sight to see the man standing there with his useless stump, until faith changed his mind and he repented, bemoaning his crime. The bearers of the litter stood still, however, until the poor man put his hand on the most holy body, and at the touch it was restored to its pristine condition.

"So the procession reached Gethsemane, and there were kisses and embraces, sacred hymns, tears, drops of sweat, as the holy body was placed in the venerable tomb: but your soul was not abandoned in hell, nor did your body see corruption. It was fitting that the shrine of God, the spring undug, the field unplowed, the vineyard unwatered, the fruit-bearing olive, should not be detained in the bosom of the earth. It was proper that the mother be raised up by the Son, so that she might ascend to him as he had descended to her; that the body of the woman who had kept her virginity in childbirth should never see corruption; that she who had borne her Creator in her womb should abide in heavenly dwellings; that she whom the Father had made his bride should reside in celestial bridal chambers; and that what belonged to the Son should be possessed also by his mother." Thus far John of Damascus.

Saint Augustine, in one of his sermons, discusses this sacred assumption from several points of view, saying: "As we undertake to speak of the most holy body of Mary ever virgin and of the assumption of her sacred soul, we say first that in the Scriptures, after the Lord on the cross commended her to the disciple, nothing is found about her except what Luke commemorates in the Acts: 'All these were persevering with one mind in prayer with Mary the mother of Jesus.' What, therefore, should we say about her death or about her assumption? Since Scripture tells us nothing, we must seek by reason what accords with truth. Thus truth itself becomes our authority, and without truth there is no valid authority.

"So then, having in mind the human condition, we have not been afraid to say that Mary underwent temporal death; but if we say that she was subjected to the common putrefaction, to the worm and the dust, we must stop to ponder whether all this is compatible with such great sanctity, with the prerogatives of this woman in whom God dwelt. We know what was said to our first parents: 'You are dust and to dust you shall return.'[12] The body of Christ was spared this condition, since it was not subjected to corruption. Thus the nature taken from the Virgin was exempt from the general sentence. To the woman God said: 'I will greatly multiply your pain in childbirth.'[13] Mary bore pain; her soul was pierced with a sword; but she gave birth without pain. Therefore, although she shared pain with Eve, she did not share the pain of childbirth; so great a prerogative of dignity raised her up that she was exempted from some general laws. Therefore, if she is said to have undergone death but was not held fast in its bonds, is there anything impious about that? If God has willed to preserve incor-

[12] Gen. 3:19.   [13] Gen. 3:16.

95

rupt the modesty of his mother's virginity, why would he not wish to save his mother from the foulness of putrefaction? Does it not befit the Lord's loving-kindness to preserve his mother's honor, since he came not to abolish the Law but to fulfill it?

"It is true piety, therefore, to believe that he who honored her in her lifetime before all women with the grace of his conception, honored her in death with a salvation all her own and with special grace. To rot away and feed the worm is the shame of the human condition. Since Jesus is immune to this shame, Mary's nature is exempt from it—the nature that Jesus is proved to have assumed from her. For the flesh of Jesus is Mary's flesh, which he raised above the stars, honoring all human nature but above all his mother's. If a mother's nature be the son, it is fitting that the son's be the mother, not in the sense of a unity of person but of a unity of bodily nature. For if grace can effect a unity without the property of a special nature, how much the more so when there is unity of grace and a special bodily birth. The unity of the disciples in Christ is an example of union in grace; of them he says: 'That they may be one as we also are';[14] and again, 'Father, I will that where I am, they also may be with me.'[15] If, therefore, he wills to have with him those who are judged to be joined in union with him here by their faith, what is to be thought of his mother? Where is she worthy to be if not in the presence of her Son?

"As far as I am able to understand, therefore, this is what I believe: Mary's soul is honored by her Son with a more excellent privilege, possessing in Christ his body, which she engendered, glorified. And why not therefore her own body, through which she engendered? If no recognized authority stands in the way, I truly believe that the body through which she engendered Christ is with him in heaven, because such sanctification is more worthy of heaven than of earth. The throne of God, the bridal chamber of the Spouse, the house of the Lord, the tabernacle of Christ, is worthy to be where Christ is: heaven is more worthy than earth to guard so precious a treasure. Such integrity deserves to be suc-ceeded only by incorruptibility, certainly not by disintegration or decay. That most holy body left as food for worms? I would be afraid to say so because I cannot even think it. That incomparable gift of grace drives such thoughts from my mind, and reflection upon many texts of Scripture invites me to say so. The Truth once said to his servants: 'Where I am, there shall my servant be also.'[16] If this is the general rule for all who serve Christ through faith and works, how much more specially does it apply to Mary! Surely she served him and minis-tered to him in every way, carrying him in her womb and bringing him forth to the world, feeding and warming him, putting him to rest in the manger, hiding him on the flight to Egypt, following him from childhood to the cross, never being far from where he was. She could not doubt his divinity, knowing that she had conceived him not by man's seed but by the breath of God. She was unhes-

---

[14] John 17:21.   [15] John 17:24.   [16] John 12:26.

itatingly confident of her Son's power as of the power of God when, as the wine ran short at the wedding, she said to him: 'They have no wine.'[17] She knew what he could do—what he did immediately by working a miracle.

"Behold Mary the servant of Christ in faith and works! If she is not where Christ wants his servants to be, where will she be? And if she is there, will it be by an equal grace? And if it is by an equal grace, is this fair of God, who renders to each according to merit? If in her lifetime Mary deserved so much greater grace than all others, will her grace be the less when she is dead? Of course not! If the death of all the saints is precious, Mary's is certainly beyond all price. In my judgment, therefore, it must be confessed that Mary was assumed into the joy of eternity by the loving will of Christ, and received with more honor than the rest since by grace he honored her more than others; and that after death she was not brought down to the common human lot—rot, the worm, the dust—because she had begotten her Savior and the Savior of all. If God's will chose to preserve unscathed the garments of the three young men in the fiery furnace, why would he deny to his own mother what he chose for someone else's clothing? For pity's sake alone he willed that Jonah should be uncorrupted in the belly of the whale; why will he not by grace preserve Mary uncorrupted? Daniel was saved from the ravenously hungry lions; is not Mary to be saved, having been endowed with such great merits and dignities?

"We know that all the benefits we have named could not have been saved by nature, but we do not doubt that for the sake of Mary's integrity grace could do more than nature could. Christ therefore made Mary rejoice soul and body in himself, her own Son, nor did he allow the ill of corruption to touch her whose integrity had suffered no corruption in bearing so great a Son. Thus she upon whom so great graces had been showered should have life in its fullness, since she gave life to her Son, who is the Life of all. If then I have spoken as I should, approve, O Christ, you and yours! If not, forgive me, I beg, you and yours!"

[17] John 2:3.

120. Saint Bernard

Bernard, Bernardus, comes from *ber*, a well or spring, and *nardus*, nard, which, as the *Gloss* on the Canticle of Canticles[1] says, is an herb humble, warm in nature, and sweet-smelling. Saint Bernard was warm in his fervent love, humble in his dealings with others, a spring in the outflow of his doctrine, a well in the depth of his knowledge, and sweet-smelling in the fragrance of his good renown.

His life was written by William, abbot of Saint Thierry, an associate of Saint Bernard, and by Arnold, abbot of Bonneval.

Bernard was born in Burgundy at the castle of Fontaines, the child of noble and very religious parents. His father, Celestin, was a knight valorous in worldly affairs and equally devout in his relations with God. His mother was called Aleth. She bore seven children, six sons and a daughter, all her sons future monks, her daughter promised to the religious life. As soon as she had brought forth a child, she offered him or her to God with her own hands. She did not allow her babies to be nursed by other women: it was as though she wished, with her milk, somehow to infuse them with her own goodness. As her children grew up and as long as they were under her care, she trained them for the desert, and fed them with coarse, common food as if to send them out to the wilderness as soon as possible.

While she was still carrying her third son, Bernard, she had a dream that was a presage of things to come: she saw in her womb a little dog, white except for its red back, and the puppy was barking. She told a certain man of God about this dream, and he responded prophetically: "You will be the mother of a very good dog, who will be the watchman of the house of God and will bark against its foes, for he will be a renowned preacher and will cure many by grace of the medicine of his tongue."

When Bernard was still a small boy, he fell seriously ill with pains in his head. A woman came to assuage his pain with her incantations, but he indignantly shouted at her and drove her away. God's mercy did not fail the child's zeal, and he rose at once and realized that he was completely relieved of his illness.

In the holy night of the Lord's nativity the boy Bernard was in the church, waiting for the morning office, and asked those with him at what hour of the

---

[1] The book called the Song of Solomon in the King James and Revised Versions is called Solomon's Canticle of Canticles in the Douay.

night Christ was born. Then and there the Infant Jesus appeared to him as though being born again from his mother's womb. Remembering that experience, Bernard, as long as he lived, was always convinced that this was the hour at which the Lord was born. From that time on he was graced both with a deeper sense of all that pertained to the Lord's birth and a more abundant eloquence in treating it; and later on, among the earliest of his written works, he produced a remarkable little book in praise of the Blessed Mother and her Child, in which he explained the Gospel lesson that begins: "The angel Gabriel was sent from God. . . ."[2]

The ancient Enemy, seeing the boy's salutary resolution, attacked his determination to live a chaste life and set many tempting traps in his path. Once, for instance, Bernard was gazing rather fixedly at a woman until suddenly, blushing at what he was doing, he rose as a stern avenger against himself and jumped into a pool of ice-cold water. There he lay until he was almost frozen, but by God's grace the heat of fleshly lust was wholly cooled in him. About that same time a girl, egged on by the devil, jumped into the bed where he was sleeping. When he became aware of her presence, he moved over calmly and silently, leaving to her the side of the bed he had been occupying, and, turning to the other side, went back to sleep. The woman put up with this expectantly for some time, then began touching and teasing him, but he remained motionless. Finally, impudent though she was, she blushed with shame, felt a flood of horror mixed with admiration, got out of bed, and hurried away.

On another occasion he was a guest in the house of a certain matron, and she was so impressed by the young man's good looks that she burned with desire for him. She had his bed made up in a separate room, but then, in the night, went to him without a sound or a qualm. The minute he felt her presence, however, he shouted: "Thieves! Robbers!" This made the woman flee and awakened the whole household. Lamps were lighted, the thief was sought but not found, and everybody went back to bed and to rest—all, that is, except the unhappy woman, who could not sleep. She rose again and sought Bernard's bed, but again he called out: "Thieves! Robbers!" Again the thief was hunted, but was not identified by the only one who knew who the real thief was. The woman tried a third time but was repulsed, and, overcome by fear and despair, finally gave up. The next day, as he renewed his journey with his companions, they made fun of him a little, asking what made him dream of thieves so often. He told them: "I really faced a thief's designs on me last night, because my hostess tried to rob me of my chastity, a treasure that, once lost, can never be recovered!"

It was already clear to Bernard that there was no safety in living with the Serpent. He began to think about fleeing the world and decided to enter the Cistercian Order. His brothers learned of this and used every means of dissuad-

[2] Luke 1:26.

ing him, but the Lord conferred such grace upon him that not only did he hold fast to his purpose of conversion, but won all his brothers and many others to serve the Lord in the religious life. Only his brother Gerard, a stalwart knight, considered his words idle and turned a deaf ear to his warnings. Bernard, however, already afire with faith and wondrously spurred by his zealous love for his brother, said to Gerard: "I know, brother, that misfortune alone can make you able to understand what I am saying to you!" He pressed his finger to his brother's side and said: "The day will come soon when a lance will pierce your side and will make a way to your heart for the counsel that you now reject!" A few days later Gerard was caught by enemies, received a lance-thrust at the point in his side where his brother's finger had rested, and was held, shackled, in captivity. Bernard went to him and was not allowed to get close to him, but called out: "Brother Gerard, I know that very soon you and I are going to enter the monastery!" That very night the shackes fell from his feet, the door opened of itself, and Gerard walked out happily and told his brother that he had changed his mind and wanted to become a monk.

In the year of the Lord 1112, the fifteenth from the founding of the Cistercian Order, Bernard, the servant of the Lord, who was then twenty-two years old, entered the Order with more than thirty companions. When Bernard was leaving his father's house with his brothers, Guy, the eldest, saw his youngest brother, Nivard, still a child, playing in the square with other boys. "Hello there, brother Nivard!" he called. "From now on our land and all we own is yours to take care of!" The lad gave an answer that was not at all childish, saying: "So all of you will have heaven and you leave me nothing but earth? That's certainly not a fair division!" Nivard continued to live with his father for a while, then followed his brothers.

Once he had entered the Order, Bernard, the servant of God, was so completely absorbed in the life of the spirit that he hardly used his bodily senses. He lived a whole year in the novices' cell and yet did not know that it had a vaulted ceiling. He passed very often in and out of the monastery church, which had three windows in the apse, yet he thought there was only one.

The abbot of the Cistercians sent some of his monks to build a house at Clairvaux and appointed Bernard to be their abbot. He lived there for a long time in extreme poverty, often making food out of the leaves of beech trees. The servant of God denied himself sleep to an extent beyond human endurance. He used to complain that the time spent sleeping was time lost, and considered sleep to be rightly compared to death: as sleepers looked dead to the eyes of men, so the dead looked like sleepers to God. If Bernard heard a monk snoring more loudly or lying more restlessly than normal, he could hardly bear it with patience, and claimed that such a monk slept in a carnal or worldly manner.

He took no pleasure in eating, and only fear of fainting made him take food, which he did as if it were a form of torture. It was his custom after eating to think about how much he had eaten, and if he felt that he had taken even a little more than usual, he did not allow the fault to go unpunished. He had so mastered the cravings of gluttony that he had largely lost even the ability to distinguish different tastes. If, for example, oil was mistakenly put before him and he drank it, he was not aware of it until he wondered why his lips felt oily. Raw blood was served to him by mistake, and he is known to have used it day after day in place of butter. He used to say that the only thing he tasted was water, and that was because it cooled his cheeks and throat.

He confessed that whatever he knew about the Scriptures he had learned while meditating and praying in the woods and the fields, and he sometimes said that among his friends he had no teachers except the oaks and the beeches. Finally he admitted that at times, as he meditated and prayed, the whole of Scripture appeared to him as though spread open and explained. He himself relates, in his sermons on the Canticle of Canticles, that once while he was in the very act of preaching, he tried to fix in his memory some thought suggested to him by the Holy Spirit, so that he might use it at another time—not that he did not trust the Holy Spirit's inspiration, but that he feared to trust himself too much. But a voice came to him and said: "As long as you cling to that one thought, you will not receive another."

In the matter of dress, poverty always pleased him, slovenliness never. The latter he took to be a sign of a careless mind or inordinate self-esteem or a will to attract other people's attention. He often repeated a proverb that he always had at heart: "Anyone who does what no one else does, all men will wonder at him." He wore a hair shirt for many years, as long as he could keep it a secret, but when he felt that it was known, he put the shirt off and dressed like everybody else. He never laughed but that it seemed he was forcing himself to laugh rather than to suppress laughter, and had to spur his laughter rather than to curb it.

He used to say that three kinds of patience were needed—one to bear insults, one to put up with damage to one's goods, and one to submit to bodily injury; and he proved that he had these three kinds by three examples. For instance, he had written a letter to a certain bishop by way of friendly admonition, and the bishop, extremely resentful, wrote back a very sharp letter that began: "I bid you good health and not the spirit of blasphemy," as if Bernard had written out of a spirit of blasphemy. Bernard replied: "I do not believe that I have the spirit of blasphemy, and I know that I have not wished to speak irreverently, especially to a prince of my people." Then a certain abbot had sent Bernard six hundred silver marks for the construction of a monastery, but on the way the whole sum was stolen by brigands. When Bernard heard of this, all he said was: "Blessed be God, who has spared us this burden! As for those who made off with the money, may they not be blamed too severely, both because human greed drove them to the deed, and because the size of the sum imposed a very strong temptation on them."

For a third example: a canon regular came to Bernard and asked him insistently to receive him as a monk. The saint did not consent and urged him to return to his church. "Well, then," said the canon, "why do you so strongly recommend the pursuit of perfection in your books, if you do not grant it to one who yearns for it? If I had your books in my hands, I would tear them to pieces!" Bernard: "In none of my books have you read that you cannot be perfect in your cloister. What I have commended in my books is reform of morals, not changes of place." The canon, furious, rushed at him and struck him in the face so hard that redness followed the blow and swelling followed the redness. The people who were present quickly set upon the sacrilegious assailant, but the servant of God stopped them, calling out and adjuring them in Christ's name not to touch him or do him any injury.

To those who wanted to enter the novitiate he regularly said: "If what you are eager to lay hold of are the things that are within you, leave outside here the bodies you have brought from the world! Only spirits are allowed inside, the flesh is of no avail."

His father, who had stayed alone in his house, came to the monastery and there, advanced in years and having lived a good life, died a peaceful death. His sister, who was married, worldly, and in spiritual danger amidst riches and pleasures, once came to the monastery to visit her brothers, having with her a proud retinue and splendid trappings. Bernard shrank from her as from a net spread by the devil to catch souls and would not consent to go out to her. When she saw that none of her brothers came to meet her—except one of them who was the porter at the door, who called her a dressed-up dunghill—she broke into tears. "Though I am a sinner," she said, "Christ died for such as I; and because I know that I am a sinner, I seek the counsel and conversation of those who are good. If my brother despises my flesh, let the servant of God not despise my soul! Let him come out, let him command, and whatever he commands I will do!"

With this promise in hand, Bernard and his brothers went out to her, and, because he could not separate her from her spouse, he forbade her all worldly show and reminded her of their mother as a model for her imitation. Then he let her depart. She went home and changed so quickly that in the midst of the world she led the life of an anchoress, alienating herself from everything worldly. Finally, by dint of much prayer, she obtained her husband's consent and, being dispensed by the bishop, entered a monastery.

There was a time when the man of God fell so seriously ill that he seemed about to breathe his last. He was rapt in ecstasy and saw himself being presented before God's judgment seat, while Satan stood opposite him and peppered him with malicious charges. When Satan had exhausted his list and it was the man of God's turn to speak for himself, fearless and unperturbed he said: "I admit I am unworthy, and unable by merits of my own, to gain entrance to the kingdom of heaven. On the other hand, my Lord has won the kingdom by a twofold right, namely, by inheritance from his Father and by the merits of his passion. The first he has reserved for himself but the second he gives to me; and by that gift I assert my right and shall not be confounded!" These words threw the Enemy into confusion, the meeting was closed, and the man of God came to himself.

Bernard mortified his body by so much abstinence, toil, and watching in the night that he continually suffered poor health and even very serious illness, and could follow the conventual routine only with great difficulty. One time when he was laid low with illness, his brother monks prayed for him so persistently that he felt restored to some extent, but he called them all together and said: "Why do you cling so to me, miserable man that I am? You are stronger than I and you have prevailed, but spare me, I beg of you, spare me and let me go!"

Several cities elected the man of God to be their bishop, chief among them Genoa and Milan. Neither acceding to their pleas nor making false excuses, he said that he was not his own man but was destined to the service of others. His brother monks, moreover, acting on the saint's advice, had anticipated such situations and had armed themselves with the sovereign pontiff's authority, so that no one could deprive them of the one who was their joy.

Once when he had gone to visit his brothers the Carthusians and they had been greatly edified by him in every respect, just one thing had raised a small doubt in the mind of the prior of the place: it struck him that the saddle on which Bernard rode was of fine workmanship and showed no evidence of poverty. The said prior mentioned this to one of the visiting monks and he to Bernard himself. He was taken aback and asked what saddle they were talking about: he had ridden from Clairvaux all the way to the Grande Chartreuse and had never noticed the saddle. He rode along the Lake of Lausanne for a whole day without even seeing the lake, or not seeing that he saw it. Then in the evening his companions were talking about the lake, and he asked them where this lake was—a question that made them wonder.

The lowliness of his heart surpassed the sublimity of his renown, and the whole world could not exalt him so much as he lowered himself. He was considered the highest by all, and the lowest by himself; and whereas all ranked him above themselves, he considered himself above no one. He often said that when the highest honors and the favors of the peoples were showered upon him, he felt that some other man had been put in his place and he himself was absent, or that this was a dream. When he was with the simple brothers, on the other hand, he was happy to enjoy and share their friendly humility and to be himself again. Indeed he was always to be found either praying or reading or writing or meditating, or edifying his brothers by talking to them.

Once when he was preaching to the people and they were paying devout attention to his every word, a tempting thought crept into his mind: "Now you're preaching at your best and people are listening to you willingly, and they all esteem you as a wise man." But the man of God, feeling himself beset by this idea, paused for a moment and thought whether he should go on with his sermon or end it. At once, strengthened by God's help, he silently answered the

Tempter: "You had nothing to do with my beginning to preach, and nothing you can do will make me stop," and calmly continued to the end of his sermon.

One of the monks, who in his earlier life had been a rake and a gambler, was goaded by a malignant spirit and wanted to return to the world. When Saint Bernard could not dissuade him, he asked him what he would do for a living. "I know how to play at dice," the monk answered, "and I'll make a living that way!" Bernard: "If I give you some capital, will you come back now and then and divide the profit with me?" The monk agreed gladly and promised to do as requested. Bernard ordered that he be given twenty sols, and off he went. The saint did this to be able to bring him back, and that is what happened. The man lost all he had and came crestfallen to the door of the monastery. His coming was announced to the man of God, who joyfully went out to him and held out his scapular spread wide to receive his share of the winnings. "I didn't win anything, father," he said, "and was stripped even of our capital. But take me back, if you will, in place of the money." Bernard kindly responded: "If that's the way things are, it's better that I get you back than that I lose both you and the capital!"

Once when blessed Bernard was riding along a road, he met a countryman, to whom he spoke sadly about a matter that was on his mind, namely, the instability of the human heart at prayer. The peasant, hearing this, immediately formed a low opinion of him and said that in his own prayer he always kept his heart firm and stable. Bernard wished to change the man's mind and temper his bold overconfidence, so he said to him: "Go aside a little way and, with all the attention you can bring to it, begin to pray the Lord's Prayer; and if you are able to finish it without any distraction or wandering of the heart, the beast I'm riding will be yours without doubt or question. But you must give me your word that if any other thought comes to you, you won't hide it from me." Happy with the offer, and feeling that he already owned the animal, the man withdrew, recollected himself, and began to recite the Our Father. He was not halfway through the prayer when a distracting thought stole into his heart: "The saddle . . . will I get the saddle with the mount, or not?" Becoming aware of the distraction, he hurried back to Bernard, told him the selfish thought that had come to him as he prayed, and from then on was not so rashly sure of himself.

Being young and listening to bad advice, Brother Robert, one of his monks and a close relative, left Clairvaux and took himself off to Cluny. The venerable father hid his feelings about this for some time, then decided to recall the young monk by letter. He was dictating the letter in the open air and another monk was putting it down in writing, when a sudden rainstorm came over and the writer started to fold up the paper. Bernard: "This is the work of God! Go right ahead with your writing!" The monk therefore wrote the letter in the midst of the shower as if there were no shower: it was raining all around, but at that spot the power of charity warded off the annoyance of the rain. Then an unbelievable cloud of flies invaded a monastery built by the man of God, making life unbearable for the monks. Bernard said: "I excommunicate the flies!" The next morning not a single fly was found alive.

The pope sent Bernard to Milan to reconcile the Milanese to the Church. When the saint reached Pavia on the return journey, a man brought his wife, who was possessed of a devil, to him. The devil, speaking through the poor woman's mouth, began to insult the man of God, saying: "This eater of leeks and devourer of cabbages won't get me out of my little old woman!" Bernard sent the woman to the church of Saint Syrus, but Saint Syrus wished to defer to his guest and so wrought no cure, so the woman was brought back to blessed Bernard. Then the devil began to babble through the woman's mouth, saying: "Little old Syrus will not expel me and neither will little old Bernard throw me out!" But as soon as Bernard began to pray, the wicked spirit said: "How glad I would be to get out of this old woman, tormented as I am inside her! How gladly I would leave her, but I cannot, because my great master will not let me!" Bernard: "And who is this great master?" The devil: "Jesus of Nazareth!" The man of God: "Have you ever seen him?" The answer: "Yes!" The saint: "Where did you see him?" The devil: "In glory!" The saint: "And you were in glory?" The devil: "Indeed I was!" The saint: "How is it that you left?" The devil: "Many of us fell with Lucifer!" All this talk came in a lugubrious tone from the old woman's mouth for all to hear. Then the man of God asked the devil: "Would you like to go back to that glory?" But the spirit, with a harsh laugh, said: "It's too late now!"

Bernard prayed, and the demon went out of the woman; but when the man of God left the place, the devil again took possession of her. Her husband ran after Bernard and told him what had happened. He ordered the man to tie a paper around his wife's neck, with these words written on the paper: "In the name of our Lord Jesus Christ I forbid you, demon, to presume to come near this woman from now on!" This was done, and the spirit no longer dared to molest the woman.

In Aquitaine there was a pitiable woman possessed of a wanton demon, an incubus, who for six years abused her and treated her with incredible lust. The man of God was passing through the region, and the demon sternly forbade the woman to go to him, adding the threat that the saint could do her no good, and that after he left, the demon, who had been her lover, would persecute her most cruelly. Nevertheless she went confidently to the man of God and told him, with tears and groans, what she was suffering. Bernard: "Take this staff of mine and put it in your bed, and if he can do anything then, let him try it!" She did as ordered, and when she lay in bed, the demon came in promptly but did not dare to undertake the usual activity, nor even to approach her bed; but he threatened her sharply, saying that when the saint was no longer there, he, the demon, would exact a fearful revenge. When she reported this to Bernard, he called the whole populace together and ordered them to come with lighted candles in their hands. Then, with the assembly joining in, he excommunicated the demon and forbade him thenceforth to come near this or any other woman. So the woman was completely freed of her trouble.

The man of God was in the same province as a delegate with a specific task to perform, namely, to reconcile the duke of Aquitaine to the Church, but the duke absolutely refused to be reconciled. The saint went to the altar to celebrate the mass, while the duke, still under excommunication, stood outside expectantly. When the man of God had said the *Pax Domini*,[3] he placed the Body of the Lord[4] on the paten and, taking it with him, went outside. There, his face ablaze and fire in his eye, he marched up to the duke and spoke fearsome words. "We have pleaded with you," he said, "and you have spurned us! Look here, the Son of the Virgin has come to you, he who is the Lord of the Church you are persecuting! Here is your judge, in whose name every knee must bend! Here is your judge, into whose hands that soul of yours will fall! Will you despise him as you despise his servants? Resist him if you can!" Hearing this, the duke was bathed with sweat. His limbs gave way under him, and he threw himself at the saint's feet. Bernard nudged him with his foot and ordered him to stand up and hear God's sentence. He rose all atremble and thereafter fulfilled all that the holy man prescribed.

The servant of God went into the kingdom of Germany to calm some civil strife, and the archbishop of Mainz sent a venerable cleric to accompany him. When the cleric told him that his master had sent him, the man of God replied: "Another master sent you!" The cleric wondered what that meant and affirmed that his master the archbishop of Mainz had sent him. To the contrary, the servant of Christ said: "You are mistaken, my son, you are mistaken! A greater master, Christ himself, sent you!" The cleric understood and said: "Do you think I want to become a monk? Not at all! No such thing has entered my mind!" But what followed? In the course of that journey the cleric bade farewell to the world and received the habit from the man of God.

Bernard had received a knight of the noble class into the Order, and this new monk followed the man of God for some time but then began to be bothered by a very grave temptation. Seeing how depressed he was, one of his brother monks asked him the reason for his sadness. "I know," he answered, "I know I will never be happy again!" This monk told the servant of God what the other had said, and the saint prayed for him with special fervor, whereupon the one who had been so sorely tempted and so disheartened looked as much happier and jollier than the rest as before he had been sadder. When the concerned brother reminded him in a friendly way of what he had said about being sad, he answered: "Although I said then that I never again would be happy, now I say that I shall never again be sad!"

---

[3] The peace of the Lord (be with you).
[4] The consecrated wafer.

Saint Malachy, the bishop of Ireland, whose virtuous life was written by Saint Bernard, died a happy death in Bernard's monastery, and the man of God celebrated his funeral mass. By divine revelation he knew that Malachy was already in glory. So, inspired by God, he changed the form of the post-communion prayer and, in a joyous voice, said: "O God, thou hast made blessed Malachy the equal of thy saints in merit. Grant, we beseech thee, that we, who celebrate the feast of his precious death, may imitate the examples of his life." When the cantor suggested that Bernard had made a mistake, he said: "No mistake! I know what I'm saying!" Then he went and kissed the sacred remains.

At the approach of Lent a large number of young students came to visit Bernard, and he urged them to give up their vanities and licentiousness at least during the holy season. They would not listen to a word of this, so he ordered them to drink a toast that went: "Here's to souls!" They drank the toast, and a sudden change came over them. They ended their visit and, though they had refused to mend their ways even for a short season, thereafter gave their whole lives to God.

At last blessed Bernard, happily looking forward to his death, said to his brother monks: "I bequeath to you three things to be observed, three things that I, in the course of my life, have kept in mind and have done my best to observe. I have wished to give scandal to no one, and if scandal occurred, I have kept it secret as best I could: I have always trusted the opinion of others more than my own: I have never sought to avenge an injury. Charity, humility, patience—these are the three things I leave you." Finally, after he had wrought many miracles, had built 160 monasteries, and had compiled many books and treatises, in the sixty-third year of his life, with his spiritual sons around him, he went to his eternal rest in the year of the Lord 1153.

After his death he manifested his glory to many. Thus he appeared to the abbot of a certain monastery and admonished him to follow him. The abbot followed him, and the man of God said to him: "See, we have come to Mount Lebanon. You stay here, and I am going to climb the mountain!" The abbot asked him why he intended to climb, and he said: "I want to learn!" Wondering, the abbot asked: "What do you want to learn, father? We believe that you are second to none in knowledge today!" Bernard: "Here below there is no knowledge, no grasp of what the truth is: above there is fullness of knowledge . . . above, a true conception of the truth." With these words he disappeared. The abbot noted the date and found that the man of God had migrated from the body on that day.

God wrought many other, indeed almost innumerable miracles, through his servant.

---

121. Saint Timothy

Timothy (Timotheus) might come from *timorem tenens*, holding fear, or from *timor* and *theos*, God, hence fear of God. That fear is aroused in every holy man, as Gregory says, when he considers where he has been, where he will be, where he is, and where he is not: where he was, because in sin; where he will be, in judgment; where he is, in misery; where he is not, in glory.

Timothy was severely tortured by the prefect of the city of Rome under Nero. His open wounds were sprinkled with quicklime, but amid these tortures he gave thanks to God. Two angels stood by him and said: "Raise your head toward heaven and see!" He looked and saw the heavens opened, and Jesus holding a jeweled crown and saying to him: "You will receive this crown from my hand." A man named Apollinaris witnessed this and had himself baptized, whereupon the prefect, seeing that both of them persevered in confessing Christ, had them beheaded, about A.D. 57.

---

122. Saint Symphorian

The name Symphorian is formed from *symphonia*, symphony. The saint indeed, was like a musical instrument, emitting a harmony of virtues. In this instrument, however, there were three qualities. A musical instrument, as Averrhoës says, should be of hard material in order to resonate, mellow in order to hold the note, and wide to give breadth of sound. Thus Symphorian was hard to himself in his austerity, mellow toward others in his gentleness, and wide in the broad reach of his charity.

Symphorian was a native of Autun. When he was still an adolescent, he was so serious in his conduct that he seemed to anticipate the mien and manners of older men. The pagans had a custom of celebrating the feast of Venus and parading her statue before the prefect Heraclius. Symphorian was present, and, for refusing to worship the goddess, he was given a prolonged flogging and thrown into prison. When he was brought out and ordered to sacrifice, being promised a wealth of gifts if he did so, he said: "Our God knows how to reward merit and also how to punish sins. The life we are to pay to Christ as a debt, let us pay it out of piety! Repentance is late when it consists of trembling with fear under the baleful glare of a judge. Your gifts, laced with the sweetness of honey, turn to poison in the minds of the erroneously credulous. Your greed grasps at everything and possesses nothing, because, by the arts of the devil, it is caught in the snare of a sorry profit. Your joys are like glass: they begin to shine and are shattered."

The irate judge then pronounced sentence and ordered Symphorian to be put to death. As he was being led to the place of execution, his mother called down from the wall, saying: "My child, my child, remember eternal life! Look up and see the Lord reigning in heaven, where this life is not taken away but exchanged for a better." He was beheaded, and Christians took his body away and buried it with honors.

So many miracles occurred at his tomb that he was held in high honor even by the pagans. Gregory of Tours tells us that a Christian carried away three bloodstained pebbles from the place where the martyr had shed his blood. These three pebbles he placed in a silver box and put the box in a wooden casket. This was kept in a castle, and later the castle was totally destroyed by fire, but the aforementioned casket was brought out of the ruins undamaged and unmarked.

The saint suffered about A.D. 270.

---

123. Saint Bartholomew

Bartholomew (Bartholomeus) is interpreted as son of one who suspends the waters, or son of one who suspends himself. The name comes from *bar*, which means son, *tholos*, height, and *moys*, water. So Bartholomew is the son of one who holds the waters on high, i.e., a son of God, who lifts up the minds of the doctors so that they may pour down the waters of their teaching. The name is not Hebrew but Syriac. The first interpretation indicates three kinds of suspension found in Bartholomew. He was suspended in the sense that he was lifted above love of the world, or in that he was sustained by the love of heavenly things, or in that he was totally supported by grace and the help of God. The second interpretation indicates the depth of his wisdom. Regarding the depth of his wisdom, Dionysius, in his *Mystical Theology*, says: "The divine Bartholomew says that there is much in theology, the science of God, and yet there is very little, and that the Gospel is broad and abundant, and yet concise." Dionysius means that Bartholomew wants to show that from one perspective everything can be affirmed of God, while from another, everything is more properly negated.

Bartholomew the apostle went to India, which is at the end of the earth, entered a temple where there was an idol named Astaroth, and began to stay there like a pilgrim. In this idol there dwelt a demon who said that he cured the sick, though he did not really cure them but merely stopped hurting them. Now, however, when the temple was filled with sick people and daily sacrifices were offered for the infirm who were brought even from distant regions, they could obtain no response from the idol. They therefore went to another city where an idol named Berith was worshiped, and asked this idol why Astaroth would give them no response. Berith answered: "Our god is bound with fiery chains and does not dare to breathe or speak since the moment when the apostle Bartholomew came in." They said: "Who is this Bartholomew?" The demon: "He is a friend of almighty God, and he came into this province to rid India of all its gods!" And they: "Give us a sign by which we can pick him out!" The demon told them: "His hair is dark and curly, his complexion fair, his eyes wide, his nose even and straight, his beard thick, with a few gray hairs. He is clad in a white, short-sleeved garment with purple tassels, and a white cloak decorated with purple gems at the corners. He has worn the same clothes and sandals for twenty years, and they show no signs of wear or dirt. He kneels a hundred times a day to pray, and as many times at night. Angels walk with him and never allow him to get tired or hungry. He is always cheerful and joyous in countenance and spirit. He foresees all and knows all, speaks and understands the language of every people. At this moment he knows what we are talking about. When you look for him, he will let you see him if he so wishes, but if he does not so wish, you will not be able to find him. Moreover I beg you, when you do find him, ask him not to come here and have his angels do to me what they have done to my comrade!"

These people spent two days looking for the apostle but never caught sight of him. Then a man who was possessed of the devil cried out: "Bartholomew, apostle of God, your prayers are burning me!" The apostle: "Be still, and get out of that man!" And the man was freed at once. Polemius, the king of that region, heard of this. He had a daughter who was given to violent fits, so he sent to the apostle and asked him to come and cure her. Bartholomew went and found the girl tied down with chains because she tried to bite anyone who came near her. He ordered her released, and when the attendants were afraid to approach her, he said: "I already hold in bonds the demon that was in her! What are you afraid of?" So they took off her chains and set her free. The king then loaded camels with gold and silver and precious stones, and sent people in search of Bartholomew, but he was nowhere to be found. The next morning, however, he appeared to the king, who was alone in his chamber, and said to him: "Why were you looking for me all day with gold and silver and precious stones? Such things are a necessity to those who seek earthly goods, but I desire nothing that is of the earth or of the flesh."

Then Saint Bartholomew began to teach the king much about the way our redemption was accomplished. He showed him, among other things, that Christ conquered the devil in a way that was appropriate and demonstrated his power, his justice, and his wisdom. It was appropriate in that the devil, who had conquered the son of a virgin, namely, Adam, who was formed out of the virgin earth, should be conquered by the Son of the Virgin. The victory demonstrated Christ's superior power, since he ejected the devil from the lordship that belonged to Christ, which the devil had usurped by bringing down the first man. And as the conqueror of a tyrant sends his adjutants to erect monuments in his honor and to do away with those of the tyrant, so Christ the victor sends his messengers everywhere to eliminate worship of the devil and to spread the religion of Christ. There was justice, in that the one who had laid hold of man by inducing him to eat the forbidden fruit should lose his hold on mankind through being conquered by a man who fasted. Wisdom was demonstrated, since the devil's tricks were bested by the arts of Christ. The devil's trick consisted in snatching Christ up the way a falcon snatches a bird, and leaving him in the desert. If he fasted there but did not get hungry, then undoubtedly he would be God: if he did grow hungry the devil would conquer him with food, as he had conquered the first man. But as things turned out, Christ, because he did get hungry, could not be recognized as God, nor could he be conquered, because he did not yield to the devil's temptation and eat bread.

When he had preached the mysteries of faith to the king, Bartholomew told him that if he chose to be baptized, he would show him his god bound in chains. The following day, therefore, when the pagan priests were offering sacrifice to the idol close by the king's palace, the demon began to cry out, saying: "Stop, you poor fools, stop sacrificing to me, or you may suffer worse torments than those I am suffering. I am wrapped about with fiery chains by an angel of Jesus Christ, whom the Jews crucified thinking they could put an end to him by death. But he took death, our queen, captive, and vanquished our prince, the author of death, with fiery chains!" All then took ropes with which to pull down the idol, but they could not. The apostle, however, commanded the demon to come out of the idol and demolish it. Out he came, and by himself destroyed all the idols in the temple. The apostle prayed and cured all the sick, then dedicated the temple to God, and ordered the demon to depart and go to the desert.

Now an angel of the Lord appeared and flew around the temple, inscribing the sign of the cross with his finger at the four corners and saying: "Thus says the Lord: 'As I have cleansed all of you of your infirmities, so this temple will now be rid of all foulness and of its inhabitant, whom my apostle has bidden to go off to a desert place.' First I will show him to you. Do not be afraid when you see him, but make the sign of the cross on your foreheads as I have inscribed it on these stones!" Then he showed them an Ethiopian blacker than soot, with a sharp face, a thick beard, hair reaching down to his feet, blazing eyes that flashed sparks like a fire-reddened iron, shooting sulphurous flames from his mouth and eyes. His hands were clamped in red-hot gyves behind his back. The angel said to him: "Because you heeded the vision of the apostle and shattered all the idols as you left the temple, I shall release you to go to some place where no man dwells, and there you may stay until the Judgment Day!" So the demon, freed of his bonds, disappeared with much clatter and howling, and the angel of the Lord flew up to heaven as all watched.

After that the king was baptized with his wife and children and all his people, resigned his kingship, and became a disciple of the apostle. At this all the priests of the temples gathered together and went to King Astyages, brother of King Polemius, and charged Bartholomew with the loss of their gods, the leveling of the temple, and the deception of the king by tricks of magic. King Astyages, indignant, dispatched a thousand men to take the apostle prisoner. When Bartholomew was brought before him, the king said: "So you are the one who subverted my brother!" The apostle: "I did not subvert him, I converted him!" The king: "As you made my brother abandon his gods and believe in your God, so I shall make you abandon your God and sacrifice to my god!" Bartholomew: "I bound the god your brother worshiped—bound him in chains—showed him thus bound, and forced him to demolish the idol. If you can do the same to my God, you will be able to make me bow before your idol. Otherwise I shall reduce your gods to splinters! And, as for you, believe my God!"

He had not finished saying this when word came to the king that his god Baldach had fallen and was lying in fragments. Hearing this, the king tore the purple robe he was wearing, and ordered the apostle to be beaten with clubs and flayed alive. Christians then took his body and gave it honorable burial. King Astyages and the temple priests were seized by demons and died. King Polemius was ordained bishop, fulfilled the episcopal office laudably for twenty years, and then, full of virtues, died a peaceful death.

There are various opinions about the kind of death Bartholomew suffered. Saint Dorotheus says that he was crucified. These are his words: "Bartholomew preached to the people of India. He also gave them the Gospel according to Matthew written in their own language. He died in Albana, a city of Greater Armenia, being crucified head downward." Saint Theodore says that he was flayed. In many books, however, we read that he was beheaded. This disagreement can be resolved by saying that he was crucified, then, before he died, taken down and, to intensify his suffering, flayed alive, and finally had his head cut off.

In A.D. 831 the Saracens invaded Sicily and devastated the island of Lipari. The body of Saint Bartholomew was enshrined there, and they broke into his tomb and scattered his bones. His remains, by the way, came to the island in the following manner. The pagans in Armenia saw that due to the frequent occurrence of miracles his body was greatly venerated, and this displeased them profoundly. They therefore put the body into a leaden coffin and tossed it into the sea, and by God's will it reached the aforesaid island. The Saracens dispersed the saint's bones, but after they left Lipari, the apostle appeared to a monk and said: "Get up and collect my bones, which have been scattered!" The monk answered him: "For what reason should we collect your bones or pay you any honor, since you allowed us to be overrun and did nothing to help us?" Bartholomew: "For a long time, due to my merits, the Lord spared this people, but their sins grew so grievous that they cried to heaven, and I could no longer obtain pardon for them." The monk asked him how he could find his bones among so many others, and the saint said: "Go and look for them at night, and when you see any that shine like fire, gather them up right away!" Everything happened just as the apostle had said. The monk found the bones, collected them, and put them on a ship bound for Benevento, the principal city of Apulia, whither the ship carried them. Some say the relics are now in Rome, but the Beneventani still insist that they have that body.

A woman brought a jug of oil to have it put in a lamp at Saint Bartholomew's shrine, but, tilt the jug as they might, nothing came out of it. The sacristans put their fingers into the jug and felt that there was oily liquid in it, and someone exclaimed: "I think the apostle does not want this oil used in his lamp!" So they went and poured it into another lamp and it flowed out freely.

The emperor Frederick razed Benevento and gave orders to destroy all the churches in the city, intending to transfer the whole city to another location. Then a certain man came upon a group of men dressed in white robes and shining brightly; they were talking among themselves and seemed to be having a serious discussion. Astonished at what he saw, the man asked who they were, and one of them answered: "That is Bartholomew the apostle, with the other saints whose churches stood in the city. They came together to confer, and to agree upon the punishment to be visited on the one who had driven them from their abodes. They have arrived at an unalterable sentence: that man must go before God's judgment seat without delay, to answer to God the Judge for all those deeds!" A short time later the emperor came to a miserable end.

We read in a book of the miracles of the saints that there was a certain master who was accustomed to celebrate solemnly the feast of Saint Bartholomew. Once, as he was preaching on the feast day, the devil appeared to him in the form of a very alluring young woman. When the master's eyes fell on her, he invited her to dinner, and while they were at table, the girl used all her wiles to make him desire her. Now blessed Bartholomew came to the door of the house in the guise of a pilgrim and begged insistently to be admitted for the love of Saint Bartholomew. The girl objected to this, so a loaf was carried out to the pilgrim by a messenger, but he refused to accept it. Instead he asked the master, via the messenger, to tell him what property or quality, in his opinion, was unique in man. The master said it was the power to laugh, but the young woman said: "No, it is sin! Man is conceived in sin, born in sin, and lives in sin!" The pilgrim approved the master's reply but noted that the woman's was more profound. He sent a second request, this time to tell him where on earth was the place, measuring not more than one foot, where God manifested the greatest miracles. The master replied: "The place where the cross stood. There God worked his wonders." "No," said the girl, "it is the human head, in which the world exists, as it were, in miniature." The apostle approved both answers, but sent in a third question: "What is the distance between the peak of heaven and the bottom of hell?" The master said that he did not know, but the woman broke in: "I'm caught! I know how far it is, because I fell the whole distance, and it is fitting that I show it to you!" Then the devil cast himself into hell with a dreadful shriek. When they looked for the pilgrim, he was not to be found.

A very similar story is told about Saint Andrew.

Blessed Ambrose, in the Preface he wrote for this apostle, sums up his legend as follows.

"O Christ, you have deigned wondrously to show your majesty to your disciples who preach to the world your trinity in the one divinity! Among those preachers your benign foresight directed blessed Bartholomew, whom you honored with a special gift of virtues, to a far distant people, and that people, remote from you as they had been in their human affairs, he merited, by his increased preaching, to bring close to you. Oh, with what praises this wonderful apostle should be celebrated! To him it was not enough to sow the faith in the hearts of nearby peoples. As if with winged feet he penetrated to the farthest borders of the lands of the Indies! He came with an innumerable throng of sick people into a devil's temple and there prevented the demon from curing anyone. Oh, how wonderful the evidence of this man's virtues! By a simple command he silenced an adversary whose long speeches exhausted his hearers! He freed a king's daughter from demonic possession and gave her back to her father loosed from her bonds and cured of her ills. Oh, how sublime the miracle of his sanctity, when he compelled the ancient enemy of the human race to shatter his own image! How worthy to be counted among the heavenly host is he for whom an angel descended from heaven to give full confirmation to his miracles! The angel showed the enchained demon in his ugly deformity to all and inscribed the Lord's saving cross on the stone. King and queen are baptized together with the people of twelve neighboring towns and follow you, our Father God, body and soul! And in the end, when the apostle is denounced by the priests of the temples, the tyrant brother of the neophyte Polemius has him, steadfast as always in the faith, beaten, flayed, and subjected to a bitter death. And the apostle, manfully facing the perils of death, carries the triumph of that glorious contest into the joys of heaven." So Ambrose.

Saint Theodore, abbot and eminent doctor, says, among other things, about this apostle: "Bartholomew, the blessed apostle of God, first preached in Lycaonia, later in India, and lastly in Albana, a city of Greater Armenia, where he was flayed alive and beheaded, then buried there. When he was being sent to preach, he heard this, I think, from the Lord: 'Go, my disciple, go and preach, go out and fight, you are fit to face dangers! I accomplished my Father's works. I was the first witness. Now you fill up what is still needed, imitate your Master, emulate your Lord, put your blood with his blood, give flesh for flesh! What I have suffered and borne for you, suffer! Your weapons are good will in toil, gentleness toward those who wrong you, patience amidst the things that pass.' The apostle did not refuse. As a faithful srvant consenting to his master's command he went forward rejoicing, as the light of the world to dispel the darkness, as the salt of the earth to preserve the insipid pagans, as a tiller of the earth to bring to fruition a spiritual crop. The apostle Peter does great progidies: Bartholomew performs mighty miracles. Peter is crucified head downward: Bartholomew, after being flayed alive, has his head cut off. As clearly as Peter grasps the meaning of mysteries, so deeply is Bartholomew able to penetrate them. They both make the Church fruitful, they weigh equally on the scale of divine graces. Bartholomew, at the center of the sacred number twelve, is in accord by his sermonizing with those preceding him and those following, as the strings of the harp make harmony. All the apostles, dividing the world among themselves, were constituted shepherds of the King of kings. Armenia, from Eiulath to Gabaoth, was Bartholomew's lot and portion. See him using his tongue as a plow to cultivate the spiritual soil, hiding the word of faith in the depths of hearts, planting the gardens and vineyards of the Lord, grafting on healing remedies for the sufferings of men, weeding out harmful thorns. He cuts down the forests of impiety, he builds fences of sound doctrine.

"But what payment do they make to him for all these services? For honor, dishonor; for blessing, malediction; for gifts, pain; for a reposeful life, a most bitter death! After he underwent unbearable tortures, his skin was pulled off as if to make a bag. After he had departed this world, he still cared for his killers, inviting the lost by miracles and beckoning them in with marvels. But nothing would check their bestial mind or draw them back from evil. What do they do next? they vent their rage upon his sacred body! The sick despise their healer, the lame the one who led them by the hand, the blind their guide, the shipwrecked their pilot, the dead their reviver. How? By throwing his holy body into the sea! Then his coffin, along with the coffins of four other martyrs, which had been treated the same way and cast into the sea, was driven from the coasts of Armenia. So, over great distances, with these four leading the way for the apostle and being at his service, so to speak, they came to the island called Lipari, close to Sicily: this was revealed to the bishop of Ostia, who was there at the time. Thus the great treasure came to one very poor, this priceless pearl to one without nobility, this most brilliant light to one lost in gloom.[1] The other four coffins went to other places, leaving the holy apostle on the said island. Of the four martyrs already referred to, the apostle sent one, namely, Papinus, to the city of Mylae in Sicily, another, Lucianus, to Messina, and the remaining two to Calabria—Gregory to the city of Colonna, Achatius to the city called Cales, and these cities enjoy their protection to this day. Saint Bartholomew's body was welcomed with hymns and praises and candles, and a magnificent temple was built to house it. A volcanic mountain contiguous to the island, which did harm to those who lived nearby because it erupted with fire, stretched itself invisibly a distance of a mile or more and hovered around the sea, so that even today it looks to those who see it like a figuration of fleeing fire.

"Hail, O blessed of the blessed, thrice blessed Bartholomew! You are the splendor of Divine light, the fisherman of holy Church, expert catcher of fish endowed with reason, sweet fruit of the blooming palm tree! You wound the devil who wounds the world by his crimes! May you rejoice, O sun illumining the whole earth, mouth of God, tongue of fire that speaks wisdom, fountain ever flowing with health! You have sanctified the sea by your passage over it, you have purpled the earth with your gore, you have mounted to heaven, where you shine in the midst of the heavenly host, resplendent in the splendor of undimmable glory! Rejoice in the enjoyment of inexhaustible happiness!" Thus Theodore.[2]

---

124. Saint Augustine

Augustine received his name either on account of his high dignity or because of the fervor of his love, or again due to the etymology of the name. He was *augustinus* by his high rank, because, as Augustus the emperor had excelled above all kings, so Augustine, as Remy says, surpasses all doctors. Other doctors

---

[1] The meaning here is obscure.
[2] Saint Theodore the Studite, d. A.D. 826.

are compared to the stars: "They that instruct many to justice [shall shine] as stars for all eternity."[1] But Augustine is compared to the sun, as is clear from the epistle that is sung in his honor, since "as the sun when it shines, so did he shine in the temple of God."[2] Secondly, his name befitted the fervor of his love, because, as the month of August is fervent with the heat of the weather, so Augustine is fervent with the fire of the love of God. In his *Confessions* he says of himself: "You have pierced my heart with the arrow of your love"; and in the same book: "Sometimes you put into my innermost being a very unaccustomed affection—I know not what sweetness—which, if it be made perfect in me, I know not what it will be unless it will be eternal life."

Thirdly, there is the etymology of the name. *Augustinus* comes from *augeo*, I increase, *astin*, city, and *ana*, above. Hence Augustine is one who increases the city on high, wherefore we sing of him: "*qui praevaluit amplificare civitatem*"—he who is powerful enough to enlarge the city. About this city he himself says in the eleventh book of the *City of God*: "The city of God has origin, knowledge, happiness. If one asks whence the city comes, God founded it; if whence its wisdom comes, it is enlightened by God; if whence its happiness, it has God to enjoy. From him it has subsistence and measure, contemplating him it has its light, inhering in him, its pleasure. It sees and loves, it flourishes in God's eternity, it shines in God's truth, it has enjoyment in God's goodness." Or, as the *Glossary* says, the name Augustine means magnificent, happy, excellent. The saint was magnificent in his life and excellent in his teaching, and is happy in eternal glory.

His life was compiled by Possidius,[3] bishop of Calama, as Cassiodorus says in his *Book of Illustrious Men*.

The eminent doctor Augustine was born in Carthage,[4] a city in the province of Africa, the son of very honorable parents. His father was Patricius, his mother, Monica. He was so learned in the liberal arts as to be considered a philosopher of the highest order, and a brilliant rhetorician. By himself he studied and understood the books of Aristotle and all the books on the liberal arts that he could read, as he testifies in his *Confessions*, saying: "Wicked slave of evil desires as I then was, on my own and unaided I read all the books they call liberal—all, at any rate, that I could read.[5] In the same book he says: "Whatever concerns the art of speaking and debating, or the dimensions of figures, or music and num-

---

[1] Dan. 12:3.

[2] Ecclus. 50:7 (Douay): probably from the first reading (hence "epistle") in an ancient mass for the feast of Saint Augustine.

[3] Not Possidonius, as in the text.

[4] He was born in Tagaste, in the Roman province of Africa, of which Carthage was the principal city.

[5] *quoscumque legere potui*—meaning, no doubt, all that were available to him.

bers, I understood without great difficulty and with no help from anyone. You know, O Lord my God, that all quickness in understanding and sharpness in learning are your gifts, but that did not lead me to worship you, because knowledge without love does not edify, but puffs up one's pride." He fell into the error of the Manicheans, who hold that Christ was a phantasm and deny the resurrection, and persisted in that error for nine years, while he was still an adolescent. His attachment to trifles was such that he said that a fig tree wept when a leaf or a fig was plucked.

When he reached the age of nineteen, he read a book by a certain philosopher[6] in which it was said that the world's vanity should be shunned and philosophy pursued. He liked the book very much but regretted that the name of Jesus Christ, which he had learned from his mother, did not appear in it. All this time his mother wept for him and tried to bring him around to the truth of faith. Once, as we read in the third book of the *Confessions*, she had a vision in which she saw herself standing on a wooden rule, grief-stricken, and a young man stood beside her and asked the cause of her sadness. "I mourn for the loss of my son," she told him. "Be reassured," he replied, "because where you are, there he is." And she looked and saw her son at her side. When she told Augustine about this vision, he said: "You're mistaken, mother, you're mistaken! He did not say what you quote him as saying; he said that where I am, there you are." "No, my son," she said, "what he said to me was, 'Where he is, you will be,' not, 'Where you are, there he will be.'"[7] His mother continued her efforts and, as Augustine testifies in the same book of the *Confessions*, importuned a certain bishop to deign to intercede for her son. Won over by such insistence, the bishop answered, and his words were prophetic: "Go confidently! It is impossible that the son of so many tears should perish!"

After Augustine had taught rhetoric for a number of years in Carthage, he left secretly for Rome without letting his mother know and in Rome attracted many pupils. Monica had followed him to the Carthage city gate, intending either to dissuade him or to go with him to Rome, but he managed to divert her attention and got away by night. When she discovered this in the morning, she filled the ears of God with her cries. Every day, morning and evening, she went to the church and prayed for her son. At that time the Milanese[8] appealed to Symmachus, the prefect of Rome, to send them a teacher of rhetoric. The man of God Ambrose was bishop of that city. In response to the people's request Augustine was sent to Milan. His mother, however, could not rest and, overcoming all sorts of difficulties, came to join him. She found him neither a convinced Manichean nor truly a Catholic. Augustine had begun to follow Ambrose and frequently heard him preach. He paid the closest attention to the

---

[6] According to Graesse (550n) "Others add 'Cicero.'"

[7] Monica's answer is here translated exactly as Graesse's text has it, including the obvious contradiction: cf. *Confessions* 3.11.

[8] Graesse has *Athenienses*, which cannot be right.

bishop's sermons, waiting to hear what he might say either against the heresy of the Manicheans or in its favor. The time came when Ambrose spoke at length against that error, refuting it with clear reasons and sound authorities, and the error was driven from Augustine's heart once and for all. What happened to him after this, he himself tells us in the *Confessions*: "When I first came to know you, [Christ] you assailed my weak sight, turning your brightness blindingly upon me. I shuddered with love and horror, and found myself to be far from you, in a region of unlikeness, and seeming to hear your voice as from on high, saying: 'I am the food of the full-grown! Grow and you will eat me, and you will not change me into yourself like the food of your body, but you will be changed into me.'"

The way of Christ pleased him then, but he still hung back from entering by those narrow paths, until the Lord put it into his mind to go to Simplicianus, in whom the light, namely, divine grace, shone. To him he could confide his anxieties regarding the proper mode of living in order to walk in God's ways, on which some went one way and some another. What he had to do in the world now gave him no pleasure in comparison with the sweetness of God and the beauty of his house, which he loved. Simplicianus began to exhort him, saying: "How many mere boys and girls serve God within the Lord's church, and you are not able to do what this one and that one do! Or, in truth, do they do this in and of themselves and not in their God? Why do you insist on standing all by yourself when you do not succeed in standing at all? Cast yourself upon him and he will welcome you and save you!"

In the course of their conversations the memory of Victorinus came up. Simplicianus was delighted and told how Victorinus, still a pagan, came to Rome— the fame of his wisdom earned him the very great honor of having a statue of himself in the forum—and how he repeatedly claimed that he was a Christian. When Simplicianus said to him: "I will not believe you unless I see you in church!" he jokingly replied: "So! Is it walls that make a man a Christian?" But at length he came into the Church, and a book was given to him privately so as not to embarrass him. It was the custom to give such a book, which contained the Credo or symbol of faith, so that he could read and proclaim it. He mounted a platform and recited his faith at the top of his voice, while all Rome marveled and the Church rejoiced, and the throng cried out: "Victorinus! Victorinus!" They shouted suddenly and as suddenly fell silent.

At this time Pontitianus, a friend of Augustine's, came over from Africa and told about the life and miracles of the great Anthony, who had died not long before under Emperor Constantine.[9] Augustine was so stirred by these men's examples that, troubled both in his looks and in his mind, he ran to Alypius and loudly exclaimed: "Now we've heard this! What are we waiting for? These are people without education and they rise up and seize heaven, while we, with all

---

[9] Constantius II, 351–363. Anthony died in 356.

our learning, are sinking into hell! Is it that we are ashamed to follow because they have gone ahead of us? Should we not be ashamed if we do not at least follow them?"

He ran out into the garden and, as he recalls in the same book, threw himself down under a fig tree and, weeping inconsolably, lamented aloud: "How long, how long will it be 'Tomorrow, tomorrow! Not right now, hold on a little while?'" His "now" had no end, and the "little while" went on and on. He reproached himself for procrastinating, as he wrote further on in the same book: "Woe is me! You are high in the heights and deep in the depths and you never draw back from us, and we barely succeed in returning to you! Act, Lord, do, and awaken us and call us back! Come for us and seize us and draw us with your perfume and your sweetness! I feared to be relieved of all the impediments that stood in my way, as I should have feared to be impeded by them. Late have I loved, you, O Beauty so ancient and so new! Late have I loved you! You were within me and I was outside, and I looked for you outside, and, unbeautiful as I am, I rushed after those beauties, which you have created! You were with me and I was not with you! You called and clamored and broke into my deafness, you sparkled and shone and chased away my blindness! You have let me breathe in your fragrance and I pant after you! You have touched me and I burn to enjoy your peace!" As he wept so sorrowfully, he heard a voice saying to him: "Take and read, take and read!" Quickly he opened the book of the apostle, and his eye first fell on the chapter where it is said: "Put ye on the Lord Jesus Christ, and make not provision for the flesh, to fulfill the lusts thereof."[10] And immediately every shadow of doubt was blown away.

Meanwhile he suffered a toothache so severe, as he himself says, that he was almost ready to agree with the opinion of the philosopher Cornelius, that the highest good of the soul is in wisdom, and the body's highest good is in feeling no pain. The toothache was so bad that he could not speak, wherefore, as he notes in his *Confessions*, he wrote on wax tablets, asking all to pray for him that the Lord might mitigate his suffering. So everyone knelt in prayer, and the pain subsided at once.

He wrote a letter to Saint Ambrose, conveying his wish to become a Christian and asking him to tell him which books of the Bible he should read in order to better prepare himself. Ambrose recommended the prophet Isaiah as most suitable, since that prophet had predicted the Gospel and the calling of the Gentiles. Augustine read the first chapters of the book, but did not understand it and put it aside to be read later, when he would have learned more about the sacred writings. When the Easter season came, his mother's merits and Ambrose's preaching bore fruit, and Augustine, then thirty years old,[11] with his friend Alypius and his son Adeodatus, a bright boy whom he had fathered in his youth

[10] Rom. 13:14.
[11] Thirty-three, actually.

when he was still a Gentile and a philosopher, received holy baptism. Then Ambrose, we are told, sang *Te Deum laudamus*, and Augustine responded *Te Dominum confitemur*,[12] and so, alternately, they composed the hymn and chanted it to the end, as Honorius also testifies in his book which is called *Speculum Ecclesiae*.[13] In some books, however, *Canticle Composed by Ambrose and Augustine* is given as its ancient title.

Now that he was so wondrously confirmed in the Catholic faith, Augustine relinquished all his worldly hopes and left behind the schools that he had governed. In his *Confessions* he tells how sweet was the love of God that he enjoyed thereafter. He says: "You have pierced my heart with the arrow of your love, and I carried your words transfixed in my loins. The examples of your servants, whom you brought from darkness to light and from death to life, crowded into the heart of my thought, burned there, and took away all heaviness and languor. To me as I came up out of the vale of tears and sang the gradual canticle,[14] you gave sharp arrows and devastating coals. In those days I could not have enough of the wonderful sweetness of considering your high design for the salvation of the human race. How much I cried, hearing your hymns and canticles suavely resounding in the church. I was poignantly moved by the voices, and those voices flowed into my ears and your truth flowed smoothly into my heart, and the tears ran down, and they did me much good. That was the time when those chants were composed in the church of Milan. And I called out from the depth of my heart: 'In peace in the selfsame I will sleep and I will rest.'[15] For you are the selfsame, you do not change, and in you there is rest and the forgetting of all labors. I read that whole Psalm[16] and I burned—I, who had been a bitter, blind opponent, ranting against these words that are honeyed with the honey of heaven and luminous with your light. Now I pined for such words of Scripture. Christ Jesus, my helper, how sweet it suddenly was for me to be without the sweetness of my treasured trifles! I had been afraid of losing them, and now it was a joy to be without them! You threw them out from me, you, the true and highest sweetness! You threw them out and came in in their stead, you, sweeter than all pleasures, but not to flesh and blood, brighter than all lights, yet more inward than any secret, more exalted than all honors, but not to those who exalt themselves!"

After this he set out for Africa, taking with him Nebrodius, Evodius, and his loving mother, but while they were in Ostia on the Tiber, his mother died. After her death Augustine went home to his estates in Africa, where, with those

[12] "We praise thee as God, we acknowledge thee as the Lord"—the opening verses of the *Te Deum*.

[13] Mirror of the Church.

[14] One of the Gradual Psalms or Canticles (Psalms 120–134), also called Songs of Degrees, or of Steps.

[15] Ps. 4:9 (Douay).

[16] Psalm 120, the one referred to above as the Gradual Canticle.

who stayed with him, he devoted himself to fasting and praying to God, wrote books, and taught the unlearned. His fame spread abroad, and he was admired both for his books and for his way of life. He was careful not to visit any city that was without a bishop, for fear he might be forced to assume that office. At this time there was in Hippo a very wealthy man, who sent word to Augustine that if he came and preached the Word to him, he might renounce the world. When Augustine heard this, he hurried to Hippo. Valerius, the bishop of that city, knew Augustine's reputation and, despite his resistance, ordained him a priest in his church. There were those who took his reluctance and his tears as a sign of pride, and told him, by way of consolation, that although the position of a priest was beneath his deserts, it was nonetheless a step toward the episcopate. Augustine immediately established a monastery for clergy and began to live according to a rule drawn up by the holy apostles. About ten bishops were elected from this monastery. Bishop Valerius, being a Greek and not very familiar with the Latin language and letters, commissioned Augustine to preach before him in his church, contrary to the usage of the Eastern Church. Many bishops protested at this, but Valerius paid no attention so long as through Augustine he was getting done what he himself was not able to do.

About this time he spoke against and refuted Fortunatus, a Manichean priest, and other heretics, expecially the Donatists, who insisted on rebaptism of lapsed Catholics, and the Manicheans. Thus he completely nullified their influence. Valerius began to fear that some other city would carry Augustine off and make him bishop, so he persuaded the archbishop of Carthage to let him resign from his office, and to promote Augustine to be the bishop of the church of Hippo. Augustine refused time after time to agree to this, but finally yielded to pressure and pleas and assumed the episcopal office. That this should not have been done to him while his bishop was alive he later both said and wrote, having learned after his ordination that the procedure was forbidden by decree of a council. He deplored what had been done and did not want it to happen to anyone else. He also did his best to persuade the bishops in council to make a law requiring that the statutes of the fathers be fully made known to those about to be ordained. We read that at a later time he said of himself: "I feel that the Lord was never so angry with me as when, though I was unworthy even to be put at an oar, he placed me at the helm to govern the Church."

His clothing, footwear, and vestments were neither too elegant nor too poor, but modest and suitable. We read that he said about himself: "I admit that I am ashamed of a costly garment, and so, if one is given to me, I sell it, so that since the garment can't belong to everybody, its price may be shared by all." His table was frugal and sparse, but along with the herbs and vegetables there was meat for the sick and other guests. At the table he preferred reading or good talk to feasting, and against the plague of malicious gossip he had inscribed the following verse on the table:

Quisquis amat dictis absentum rodere vitam
Hanc mensam indignam noverit esse sibi.[17]

Indeed, one time some of his fellow bishops, close friends of his, set their tongues to making derogatory remarks, and he had harsh words for them, saying that unless they desisted, he would either erase the inscription or leave the table. Another time he had invited some of this friends to a meal, and one of them, more curious than the rest, went into the kitchen and found nothing but cold food. He came back to Augustine and asked what dishes the master of the house had ordered for dinner. Augustine, who had no curiosity about such things as food, answered: "I don't know any more than you do!"

He said that he had learned three things from Saint Ambrose. The first was never to court a woman for someone else; the second, never to encourage someone who wanted to be a soldier; the third, to accept no invitations to dinner parties. The reason for the first is that the two might not be suited to each other and might come to quarreling; for the second, that soldiers might be given to calumny and others might put the blame on him; for the third, that he might perhaps overstep the limits of temperance.

Such was his purity, such his humility, that in his book of *Confessions* he confesses and humbly accuses himself to God of sins so slight that we would think little or nothing of them. Thus, for instance, he accuses himself of playing ball as a boy when he should have been at school; or of being unwilling to read or study unless held to it by his parents or his tutors; or of enjoying, when he was still young, the reading of poets' fables, such as the story of Aeneas, and of weeping for Dido when she died of love; or of having stolen something from his parents' pantry or table to give to his playmates; or of cheating to win in their games. He accuses himself of stealing a pear from a tree near his own vineyard, when he was sixteen years old. In the same book he confesses the slight pleasure he sometimes felt in eating, and says: "You, Lord, taught me that I should go to take food as though it were some kind of medicine. But when I pass over from the annoyance of needing to eat to the restfulness of satiety, in that very passage the trap of concupiscence is set for me, for that passage itself is a pleasure, and there is no other passage than this one, which need forces me to take. I have to eat and drink for my health, and this dangerous enjoyment adds itself as an accompaniment and often tries to go beyond, so that it is for this pleasure that I do what I say I do and want to do only for my health's sake. Excess in drinking is far from me: have pity on me lest it come near me. Intoxication sometimes overtakes your servant: have pity, that it may be far from me. And who is there, Lord, who is never carried a little beyond the bounds of need? Whoever he is,

---

[17] Whoever likes to gnaw at the lives of those absent / Will know that at this table there is no place for him.

he is certainly great, may he glorify your name! But I am not great, because I am a sinful man!"

He suspected that he might be too fond of odors, and says: "I am not too much drawn by the allurement of aromas: when they are absent I do not miss them, when they are present I do not repulse them, being ready to do without them forever. That is how I see myself, and I may be mistaken, for no one should be so sure of himself in this life, which is rightly called a total temptation. Let him who has been able to go from bad to good not go from good to bad." About the sense of hearing he confesses: "The pleasures of the ear involved me and captivated me very tenaciously, but you released and freed me. When it happens that I am moved by the singing more than by the content of the song, I confess my sin and would prefer not to hear the singer." He also accuses himself with regard to the sense of sight, for instance, of taking too much pleasure in watching a dog run, or of enjoying, as he walked through the fields, the sight of hunters hunting, or of spending too much time at home watching spiders trap flies in their webs. He confesses these faults before the Lord, and says in the same place that they distracted him from good meditations and interrupted his prayers.

He accuses himself of an appetite for praise, and of being lured by vainglory. He says: "Anyone who wishes to be praised by men while you, Lord, reproach him, will not be defended by men when you judge him, nor rescued by them when you condemn him. A man is praised because of some gift that you have given him, yet he rejoices that he, rather than the gift, is praised. Daily, without respite, we are attracted by these temptations. The human tongue is a furnace for every day. Nevertheless I would not want approval voiced by someone else to increase my enjoyment of any good that is in me; but, I admit, not only does praise increase the enjoyment, but blame diminishes it. I am sometimes saddened, however, by being praised, when what is praised in me is something that displeases me, or when minor or slight good things are given more praise than they deserve."

The holy man put down the heretics so relentlessly that they publicly declared it would be no sin to kill Augustine, any more than it would be to kill a wolf, and they added that all the killers' sins would be forgiven by God. He put up with many plots against him, for instance, when they set up an ambush on a road he was expected to travel, but by God's providence they were wrong about the road and could not find him.

He always had his fellow poor in mind and liberally shared with them any goods he might have. Sometimes, for the sake of the poor and the captives, he had vessels used in divine service broken and melted down for distribution to those in need. He never wanted to buy a house or a field or a villa for himself. He refused to accept many legacies left to him, and said that they belonged to the children and kinfolk of the deceased rather than to him. He felt no love or concern for property that he held in the name of his church, and kept his thoughts day and night on the Scriptures and the things of God. He was not interested in new buildings, firmly refusing to burden his mind with them, in order to keep it free from material cares and to devote it to continuous meditation and assiduous reading. He did not, however, deter others who wished to do building, unless he thought their plans were too ambitious.

Augustine had high praise for those who longed for death, and in this regard often cited the examples of three bishops. Ambrose, when he was near death and was asked to pray for an extension of his life, answered: "I have not lived in such a way as to be ashamed to live among you, nor do I fear death, because the Lord is good." He spoke of another bishop, who, when he was told that the Church had great need of him and therefore the Lord should let him stay with it, said: "If I am never to die, very well, but if I am to die sometime, why not now?" He also said that Saint Cyprian told this about another bishop, that when he was suffering with a grave malady, he prayed that his health might be restored. A handsome young man appeared to him trembling with indignation, and said: "You are afraid to suffer, you are unwilling to die! What shall I do with you?"

The saint would have no woman, not even his own sister or his brother's daughters, living in his house, though they all served God as he did. His reasoning was that, though there could be no suspicion concerning his sister or his nieces, such persons could not be without other women whom they needed, and men might come to visit them, which could cause the weaker ones among them to be disturbed by human temptations, or certainly to be put to shame by men's wicked suspicions. He never was willing to talk with a woman alone, unless some secret was involved.

He did well by his relatives, not to make them rich but to supply or lighten their needs. Rarely was he willing to intercede for someone in writing or by word of mouth, keeping in mind a certain philosopher who, in consideration of his own reputation, seldom did many favors for his friends and often said: "Heavy weighs the power that's called upon." When he did intervene for someone, he modulated his style so as not to impose a burden but to merit the favor sought by the courtesy of his request. He preferred to settle differences between people he did not know rather than between friends of his, because in passing judgment for strangers he would be free to point to the guilty party and so make a friend of the one for whom, justice being done, he gave a favorable judgment, but between friends he was sure to lose one of them, namely, the one against whom he had to decide.

He was invited by many churches and preached in them, converting many people from error. From time to time he used to digress from the theme of his sermon, and he said that God ordered him to do this to promote the salvation of some particular person. This happened in the case of a businessman among the Manicheans, who was listening to Augustine preaching. The man of God digressed to speak against that heresy, and the merchant was converted.

It was at this time that the Goths sacked Rome, and Christians suffered much at the hands of these idolators and infidels. This prompted Augustine to write the book *The City of God*. In it he showed that the just are bound to be oppressed in this life while the impious flourish. The book treats of the two cities, Jerusalem and Babylon, and their kings, the king of Jerusalem being Christ, the king of Babylon, the devil. Two loves, he says, build the two cities: the city of the devil is built by love of self growing into contempt of God, and the city of God by love of God growing into contempt of self.

In those days, namely, in A.D. 440, the Vandals occupied the province of Africa, ravaging all without respect for sex, rank, or age. They reached Hippo and laid siege to the city with a strong force. Amid these tribulations Augustine, more than others since he was now in old age, lived a most bitter and mournful life. His tears were his bread, flowing day and night, as he saw some killed, others in flight, churches widowed of their priests, cities demolished and their inhabitants scattered. In the midst of these misfortunes he consoled himself with a sentence from a certain wise man: "The man who thinks it a great thing that sticks and stones fall and that mortals die is not a great man." He called his brothers together and said to them: "I have asked the Lord either to rescue us from these perils or to grant patience to bear them, or to receive me out of this life, lest I be compelled to witness so many calamities."

As it happened, he obtained the third petition. In the third month of the siege he fell ill with fever and took to his bed. Realizing that the dissolution of his body was imminent, he had the seven Penitential Psalms written out and hung on the wall opposite his bed, and lying there he read them and wept constantly and copiously. In order that he might devote himself more freely to God, and that no one should distract his attention, ten days before his death he ordered that no one be admitted to his presence, unless the doctor came in or food was brought to him. But one sick man did get in and begged him to cure him of his infirmity. Augustine answered: "What are you talking about, my son? Do you think that if I could do what you ask, I would not do the same for myself?" The sick man insisted nonetheless, declaring that in a vision he had been ordered to come to the saint and receive his health. Seeing the man's faith, Augustine prayed for him and he was made well.

He cured many persons who were possessed of the devil, and performed a great many other miracles. In the twenty-second book of *The City of God* he mentions two of his miracles as if they were someone else's, saying: "I know of a certain young woman in Hippo, who anointed herself with oil into which a priest who was praying for her had let his tears drop, and in an instant she was delivered of the devil." In the same book he says: "I also know a bishop who prayed for a youth without seeing him, and at once the youth was freed of the devil." There seems to be no doubt that he was talking about himself but for humility's sake would not use his name. In the same book of *The City of God* he says that there was a man who was due to undergo surgery and was in great fear that he would die under the knife. The sick man prayed to God with much weeping, and Augustine prayed with him and for him. The man recovered his health completely without an incision.

At last, when his end was near, he taught this memorable rule, namely, that no man, no matter how high his merit might be, should die without confession and the Eucharist. The last hour came, and Augustine, sound in all his members, sight and hearing unimpaired, in the seventy-seventh year of his life and the fortieth of his episcopate, with his brothers around him and praying, migrated to the Lord. He made no last will and testament, since, as the poor man of Christ, he had nothing to bequeath. He flourished in the years around A.D. 400.[18]

Thus Augustine, that shining light of wisdom, that bulwark of the truth and rampart of the faith, incomparably surpassed all the doctors of the Church, both in native gifts and in acquired knowledge, excelling by the example of his virtues and the abundance of his teaching. Hence Saint Remy, commemorating Jerome and several other doctors, concludes as follows: "Augustine outdid them all in genius and knowledge, for, although Jerome admitted that he had read six thousand volumes of Origen, Augustine wrote so many that no one, working day and night, could write his books, nor even succeed in reading them." Volusianus, to whom Augustine wrote a letter, says of him: "Anything that Augustine happened not to know is not in the law of God."

Jerome wrote in a letter to Augustine: "I am not able to respond to your two short works, most learned and brilliant with every splendor of eloquence as they are. All that genius can say or assume or draw from the fountains of the Scriptures has there been said and treated. But I beg Your Reverence to allow me to say something in praise of your genius." In his book *Of the Twelve Doctors*, Jerome writes as follows about Augustine: "Augustine the bishop, flying like an eagle over the mountain peaks and not attending to what is at their foot, discoursed in clear language about the broad spaces of the heavens, the length and breadth of the lands, and the circle of the seas." And Jerome's reverence and affection for Augustine appear from the letters he wrote to him, in one of which he says: "To the holy lord and most blessed father Augustine, Jerome sends greetings. At all times I have venerated Your Beatitude with the honor due you, and have loved the Lord our Savior dwelling in you, but now, if I may, I add to the sum and bring my veneration to its fullness, lest we let one hour pass without a mention of your name." In another letter to the same: "Far be it from me to dare to question anything in Your Beatitude's books. I have enough to do to correct my own without criticizing anyone else's."

Gregory also, in a letter to Innocent, the prefect of Africa, writes as follows about Augustine's works: "I am gratified by your interest and your request that I send you my commentary on holy Job; but if you wish to gorge yourself on delicious fare, read the treatises of blessed Augustine, your compatriot, and by

[18] Augustine was born in 354, was ordained bishop in 395, and died in 430.

comparison with his fine flour you will not ask for my bran." In his *Register* he says: "We read that blessed Augustine would not live in the same house with his sister, saying: 'The women who are with my sister are not my sisters.' The caution of that learned man should teach us an important lesson."

In Ambrose's Preface we read: "In Augustine's dying we adore your magnificence, O Lord! Your power works in all, so that this man, fired by your Spirit, was not led astray by flattering promises, because you had imbued him with every kind of piety, and to you he was altar, sacrifice, priest, and temple." Blessed Prosper, in the third book of *The Contemplative Life*, speaks about him as follows: "Saint Augustine the bishop was keen of mind, suave in his eloquence, thoroughly familiar with secular literature, industrious in his labors for the Church, clear in everyday discussions, well organized in all his activities, acute in solving problems, careful in arguing with heretics, catholic in expounding our faith, cautious in explaining the canonical Scriptures." Bernard writes: "Augustine was the mighty hammer of heretics."

After his death, when the barbarians overran that region and profaned the churches, the faithful took Augustine's body and transported it to Sardinia. About A.D. 718, 280 years after the saint's death, Liutprand, the deeply religious king of the Lombards, heard that the Saracens were depopulating Sardinia, and sent a formal delegation there to take the holy doctor's relics to Pavia. Having paid a high price, they obtained the saint's body and brought it as far as Genoa. When the devout king learned of this, he went with great joy to that city and reverently met and accepted the body. However, when they wanted to carry it farther, they could not move it from the place until the king had made a vow that if Augustine allowed him to go on from there, he would build a church at that place in his honor. Once the vow was made, the body was carried away without difficulty, and Liutprand fulfilled his vow and had a church constructed as promised. The same miracle occurred a day later in a country villa called Cassella in the diocese of Tortona, and the king built a church there in honor of Saint Augustine. In addition he granted the villa itself and all its appendages to be owned in perpetuity by those who would serve that church. By this time the king saw that it pleased the saint to have a church built in his name wherever his body had rested. Liutprand feared that Augustine might choose for his final resting place a location other than the one the king wanted, so he arranged for the erection of a church everyplace where he and the relic were given hospitality overnight. So the sacred body was finally brought into Pavia, welcomed with much jubilation, and enshrined with honors in the church of Saint Peter, which is called Golden Heaven.

A miller who had a special devotion to Saint Augustine was suffering from an abscess in the leg and prayed earnestly to the saint for help. Augustine appeared to him in a vision and rubbed the leg with his hand, completely healing it. The miller awoke to find himself cured, and gave thanks to God and Saint Augustine.

A boy was sick with the stone and the physician recommended that the stone be cut out, but the boy's mother, fearing that her son would die, invoked Augustine's aid. No sooner had she finished her prayer than the boy passed the stone with his urine and was completely cured.

In the monastery called Elemosina, on the vigil of Saint Augustine's feast day, a monk was rapt in spirit and saw a shining cloud coming down from heaven. On the cloud was seated Saint Augustine, arrayed in pontifical vestments. His eyes were like two rays of the sun, lighting up the whole church, and a marvelous aroma filled the building.

Saint Bernard was once assisting at matins and fell asleep for a moment during the reading of a treatise of Saint Augustine. He saw a beautiful young man standing there, out of whose mouth gushed such a torrent of water that it seemed to be filling the whole church. Bernard had no doubt that this was Augustine, who watered the Church with the fountain of his teaching.

A man who loved Augustine deeply paid the monk who was guardian of the saint's body a large sum of money, for which the monk was to give him a finger from the body. The monk took the money but gave the man a finger, wrapped in silk, from another dead body, pretending that it was Augustine's finger. The man accepted the relic piously and worshiped it with devotion, frequently touching it to his mouth and eyes and clasping it to his bosom. Seeing his faith, God mercifully and miraculously gave him one of Saint Augustine's fingers, throwing away the supposititious one. When the man returned to his home country, many miracles occurred there, and the fame of the relic spread to Pavia. When the aforesaid monk declared that the finger belonged to some other dead man, the saint's tomb was opened and it was found that a finger was indeed missing. The abbot learned of this, took the monk's charge away from him, and punished him severely.

In the monastery of Fontaines in Burgundy there was a monk who was particularly devoted to Saint Augustine, read his writings zealously, and derived spiritual nourishment from them. For a long time he had petitioned the saint not to let him leave this life except on the day when his sacred feast was celebrated. Then, two weeks before the saint's feast day, the monk was stricken with a high fever and on the vigil of the feast was laid out on the ground to await death. And behold, a number of men, decorous and splendid in appearance and wearing white garments, entered the church in procession, followed by a venerable man clothed in pontifical vestments. A monk who was in the church was astounded at the sight of the procession, and asked the marchers who they were and where they were going. One of them said that Saint Augustine, with his canons, was on his way to his dying devotee to take his soul to the kingdom of glory. Then the solemn procession entered the infirmary, and after some time the monk's soul was released from his body, and his dear friend, shielding it from the grasp of the enemy, led it into the joys of heaven.

We also read that once, while Augustine was still alive in the flesh and was reading, he saw a demon going past him carrying a book on his shoulders. He immediately adjured the spirit to show him what writings were hidden in the book. The demon asserted that the sins of men were written there, and that he collected them from all over and kept a record of them. Augustine ordered him to let him read anything about his own sins that might be written in the book. The demon pointed to a page, but Augustine saw nothing there except that he had once forgotten to recite compline, the last hour of the divine office. So the saint required the demon to wait for him there, and he went into the church and devoutly said compline and completed the usual prayers, then went back and told the evil one to show him that page again. The devil quickly opened the book, found the page blank, and said angrily: "You have duped me shamefully, and I am sorry I showed you my book, because you wiped out your sin by the power of your prayers." Having said this, he vanished in confusion.

Some malicious persons had wronged a woman, and she went to blessed Augustine to seek his advice about the matter. She found him studying and addressed him reverently, but he neither looked at her or gave her a word of response. Thinking that perhaps due to his holiness he did not want to look a woman in the face, she came close and carefully explained her errand, but he did not turn to her or answer a word. So she left, sorely disappointed. The next day, while Augustine was celebrating mass and the woman was present, she was rapt in ecstasy at the elevation of the Lord's Body and saw herself placed before the tribunal of the most holy Trinity. Augustine also was there, standing with bowed head and discoursing most attentively and sublimely about the glory of the Trinity. Then a voice spoke to her, saying: "When you went to Augustine, he was absorbed in thinking about the glory of the Trinity and thus was completely unaware of your presence. But go back to him confidently! You will find him kindhearted, and he will give you helpful advice." The woman did as directed, and Augustine heard her kindly and gave her wise counsel.

It is also told that a certain holy man was rapt in spirit and looked upon the saints in glory, but did not see Augustine. He asked one of the saints where Augustine was, and the saint answered: "Augustine resides in the highest heaven, and there expatiates on the glory of the most excellent Trinity."

Some men of Pavia were held in confinement by the marquis of Malespina, who would allow them no water, his purpose being to extort a large ransom from them. Some of the men were almost at the point of death, some were drinking urine, but there was one, a youth, who was very devoted to Saint Augustine, and called upon him for help. Augustine appeared to the youth, took him by the right hand, and led him out to the Gravelone River. There, dipping a vine leaf in the water, he cooled the youth's tongue with it, and the young man, who had almost been ready to drink urine, now would have thought little of a draft of nectar.

The provost of a certain church, who was devoted to Saint Augustine, had been suffering from an illness so serious that he had to keep to his bed. When the saint's feast day was at hand and the bell rang for the vespers of the vigil, the priest prayed assiduously to Saint Augustine, whereupon the saint appeared to him in white vestments, addressed him three times by name, and said: "You have called on me so often, and here I am! Get up quickly and celebrate the evening office in my honor!" The provost astonished everyone by rising hale and hearty, going into the church, and devoutly conducting the service.

A shepherd had a malignant ulcer between the shoulders and was so ill with it that all his strength was gone. He prayed to Saint Augustine, who appeared to him in a vision, laid his hand on the afflicted spot, and healed it perfectly. At a later time the same man lost his eyesight. He besought Augustine's help, and one day about noon the saint appeared, rubbed the man's eyes, and restored his sight.

About the year A.D. 912, a band of more than forty men from Germany and France, all suffering from various infirmities, set out for Rome to visit the tombs of the apostles. Some of them were so bent over that they had to push themselves along on small sleds, some supported themselves with crutches. Blind men were guided by others, and there were some with crooked hands and feet. They crossed the mountains and reached a place called Carbonaria, and went on to a place called Cana, three miles from Pavia. There Saint Augustine, vested in pontificals, came out of a church built in honor of Saints Cosmas and Damian, met and greeted the men, and asked where they were going. When they told him, he said: "Go into Pavia and ask your way to the monastery of Saint Peter, called Golden Heaven, and there you will obtain the mercy you desire." The pilgrims asked him his name, and he answered: "I am Augustine, once bishop of the city of Hippo," and vanished from their sight. They went into Pavia and, arriving at the monastery, learned that Augustine's body rested there, and raised their voices in a unanimous appeal: "Saint Augustine, help us!" Aroused by this clamor, townspeople and monks flocked together to see this great spectacle. The sick men's arteries became distended and burst, and their blood flowed in such quantities that from the monastery entrance to the saint's tomb the floor was awash. When the infirm came to the tomb, all were restored to health, as if there had never been any defect in their bodies.

From that time on the fame of Saint Augustine grew, and multitudes of sick people came to his tomb, recovered their health, and left pledges of their gratitude, with the result that in time these pledges filled Saint Augustine's chapel and the portico of the church, making it difficult to get in and out, and the monks perforce stored them elsewhere.

Note that there are three things that worldly people yearn for, namely, riches, pleasures, and honors. Such was the perfection of that holy man that he despised riches, rejected honors, and shrank from pleasures. He himself affirms that he despised riches, in his book of *Soliloquies*, where Reason asks him: "Do you not

131

covet any wealth?" and he answers: "Not now, anyway! I am thirty years old and for the last fourteen years I have ceased to desire it, and am concerned only to have enough to live on. One book of Cicero easily convinced me that riches are not at all to be desired." That he rejected honors he testifies in the same book. Reason asks him: "What about honors?" Augustine answers: "I admit that it is only lately, indeed in these last days, that I have ceased to desire them." Pleasures and riches he despised, notably the pleasures of the bed and the table. Reason asks about the first in the same book: "What about a wife? Would you not be delighted with a beautiful, virtuous, compliant, wealthy wife, especially if you were sure she would be no trouble to you?" Augustine answers: "Much as you depict her and heap her with every good quality, I have decided that there is nothing I should flee from as much as I should from a bedfellow!" Reason: "I was not asking about what you have decided, but whether you are attracted in that direction." Augustine: "I want absolutely nothing of the sort, desire nothing, even recall such things with horror and disgust!" As to the second, Reason asks: "What about food?" Augustine: "Don't bother asking about food and drink or baths or other pleasures of the body! All I want of them is what can give me hope of good health."

125. The Beheading of Saint John the Baptist

The feast of the Beheading of John the Baptist, as we find in the book *De mitrali officio*, was instituted in celebration of four events. The first is the beheading itself, the second, the collection and cremation of the saint's bones,[1] the third the finding of his head, the fourth, the translation of one of his fingers and the dedication of a church in his honor.

First, then, the feast celebrates John's beheading, which came about in the following way. We have from the *Scholastic History* that Herod Antipas, son of Herod the Great, was on his way to Rome and stopped to visit his brother Philip. He made a secret agreement with Herodias, Philip's wife, who, according to Josephus, was the sister of Herod Agrippa, that on his return journey he would repudiate his own wife and wed Herodias. This, however, was no secret

---

[1] The Graesse text has *capitis* (of the head) here, surely an error.

to the wife of this Herod Antipas, the daughter of Aretas, king of Damascus. She did not wait for her husband's return but went as fast as she could to her own homeland. Herod meanwhile came back and took Herodias away from Philip, thus making enemies of King Aretas, Herod Agrippa, and Philip.

John the Baptist took Herod to task for this, on the ground that according to the law he had no right to marry his brother's wife while his brother was alive. Because of the severity of John's rebuke and because John, by his preaching and baptizing, attracted a large following, Herod chained him and put him in prison. He also wished to please his wife but feared to lose the allegiance of John's followers. What he really wanted to do was to kill John, but was afraid of the people. Indeed, both Herodias and Herod longed to find an opportunity to get rid of John, and they seem to have arranged secretly between themselves that Herod would invite the leading men of Galilee to a banquet in honor of his birthday, and would have Herodias's daughter dance for them, after which Herod would swear to give her anything she asked for, and she would ask for the head of John. On account of his oath he would have to grant her request but would pretend to be saddened because he had sworn. That there had been this conspiracy and false pretense seems to be suggested by what the *Scholastic History* says: "It is entirely credible that Herod and his wife had secretly plotted John's death on this occasion. Likewise Jerome in the *Gloss*: "He therefore swore to find an occasion to put John to death, because if the girl had asked for the death of her father or mother, Herod would not have yielded."

So the banquet is held, the girl is present, she dances for the company, everyone is pleased, the king swears that he will give her whatever she asks, she follows her mother's instructions and demands the head of John. Two-faced Herod feigns sadness because of his oath—because, as Rabanus says, he had to do what he had sworn to do. But the sadness was only on his face. In his heart he was delighted. He excused his crime by citing his oath, thus doing an impious deed under cover of a show of piety. So the headsman is dispatched, John loses his head, the head is given to the daughter and presented by the daughter to her adulterous mother.

Augustine, in a sermon he preached on the beheading of John the Baptist, uses Herod's oath as the occasion for a story with a moral. He says: "I heard this story from an innocent and trustworthy man. When someone refused to return something he had lent him or something that was owed to him, he was distressed and provoked the borrower to swear. The borrower swore and the lender lost. That night the lender had a vision in which he was brought before the Judge, who asked him: 'Why did you provoke the man to swear an oath when you knew he would swear falsely?' The lender answered: 'He refused to give me what was mine!' The Judge: 'It would have been better to lose what was yours rather than to make him lose his soul by swearing falsely!' He was then punished by being laid on the ground and beaten so severely that when he awoke the traces of the whipping were visible." Thus Augustine.

It was not, however, on this day that John was beheaded, but during the Days of Unleavened Bread in the year preceding the passion of Christ. It was right, therefore, that on account of the mysteries of the Lord which mark that season, the lesser event should yield to the greater and be celebrated at another time.

In connection with the beheading, John Chrysostom exclaims: "John is the school of virtues, the guide of life, the model of holiness, the norm of justice, the mirror of virginity, the stamp of modesty, the exemplar of chastity, the road of repentance, the pardon of sinners, the discipline of faith—John, greater than man, equal of angels, sum of the Law, sanction of the Gospel, voice of the apostles, silence of the prophets, lantern of the world, forerunner of the Judge, center of the whole Trinity! And so great a one as this is given to an incestuous woman, betrayed to an adulteress, awarded to a dancing girl!"

Herod did not escape punishment: he was condemned to exile. The *Scholastic History* has it that the other Herod, namely, Agrippa, was a man of valor but impoverished—so poor, indeed, that in desperation he went into a tower intending to starve himself to death. When his sister Herodias heard of this, she begged her husband, Herod Antipas, to get his brother out of the tower and to provide for his needs. He did this, but while the two were celebrating together, Herod the tetrarch became overheated with wine and began to scoff at the other over the favors he had done him. Agrippa deeply resented this insult, so he went to Rome and won the favor of Caius Caesar, which led the emperor to grant him two tetrarchies, Lisania and Abilene, and to send him back, wearing the royal diadem, to be king of Judea.

Herodias, seeing that her brother now had the title of king, importuned her husband with demands that he go to Rome and procure a similar title for himself. But he was a very rich man and felt no need of promotion, preferring his life of leisure to honors that involved work. But his wife won in the end, and he went to Rome, taking her with him. Agrippa, getting word of this, wrote to the emperor, telling him that Herod had cultivated a friendship with the king of the Parthians and was determined to rebel against the Roman Empire. In proof of this charge he submitted that Herod had in his cities weapons enough to equip seventy thousand armed men. Having read the letter Caius questioned Herod, as if he had information from a different source, about the state of his affairs, and asked, among other things, whether it was true, as the emperor had heard, that Herod had such a large store of arms in his cities. Herod made no effort to deny this. Thereupon Caius took to be true what Herod Agrippa had written, and sent Antipas into exile, but granted permission to his wife to return to her own country, since Herodias was Herod Agrippa's sister and Agrippa was very dear to Caius. Herodias, however, chose to accompany her husband into exile, saying that she had shared his good fortune and would not abandon him in adversity. They were therefore deported to Lyons and ended their days there in misery. This we learn from the *Scholastic History*.

The second event commemorated by this feast is the burning and gathering, or collection, of Saint John's bones. According to some sources, his bones were burned on the very day of his martyrdom and were partly recovered by the faithful. Hence he suffered, as it were, a second martyrdom, since he was burned in his bones. Therefore the Church celebrates this second martyrdom on this day. In the twelfth book of the *Scholastic* or *Ecclesiastical History*, we read that John's disciples had buried his body at Sebaste, a city in Palestine between Elisaeus and Abdias, and that many miracles had occurred at his tomb. For this reason the pagans, by order of Julian the Apostate, scattered his bones, but the miracles did not cease, and the bones were collected, burned, and pulverized, and the ashes thrown to the winds to be blown over the fields, as both the above-mentioned histories report.

Bede, however, says that the collected bones were scattered still more widely, and so a second martyrdom seemed somehow to be suffered. Some people represent this, not knowing that they are doing so, when on the feast of the Baptist's birth they gather bones from here and there and burn them. In any case, the bones were collected to be burned, as both the *Scholastic History* and Bede have it, and some monks came from Jerusalem secretly, mingled with the pagans, and managed to carry off many of the relics. These they delivered to Philip, bishop of Jerusalem, who afterwards sent them to Anastasius,[2] bishop of Alexandria. Still later, Theophilus, bishop of the same city, enshrined the bones in a temple of Serapis, which he had purged and consecrated as a basilica in honor of Saint John. This from Bede and the *Scholastic History*. Now, however, the relics are devoutly worshiped in Genoa, and Popes Alexander III and Innocent IV, after verifying the facts, have signified their approval by granting privileges.

As Herod, who ordered the beheading of John, suffered the penalty for his crimes, so the divine vengeance was visited upon Julian the Apostate, who ordered the burning of the martyr's bones. How Julian was punished is told in the story of Saint Julian, which follows the chapter on the Conversion of Saint Paul.[3] A full account of the origins, the reign, the cruelty, and the death of this Julian the Apostate is contained in the *Tripartite History*.

Constantius, brother to Constantine the Great by the same father, had two sons, Gallus and Julian. When Constantine died, his son Constantius raised Gallus to the rank of caesar but later put him to death. This made Julian fearful, and he became a monk but also began to consult soothsayers to learn whether he might eventually be emperor. Afterwards Constantius made Julian a caesar and sent him to Gaul, where he scored many victories. One day he was passing between two columns, between which a laurel crown was suspended by a cord. The cord broke and the crown fell on Julian's head, fitting him neatly. The

[2] Graesse notes that the Ed. Pr. has "Athanasius."
[3] It follows the chapter on Saint Paula.

troops cheered, this being a sign that he would be emperor. The soldiers began to call him Augustus, and since there was no crown available with which to crown him, a soldier took off a necklace he was wearing and placed it on Julian's head. Thus the army made him emperor.

From then on, Julian abandoned his pretense of being a Christian, opened the temples of the idols, offered sacrifice to them, and appointed himself high priest of the pagan cult. He also had all crosses thrown down and destroyed; yet once it happened that dew fell on his clothing and on that of the others with him, and each drop of dew took the shape of a cross. After Constantius died, Julian, wanting to please everyone, allowed all to practice whatever religion they chose. He also dismissed all the eunuchs, barbers, and cooks from his household—the eunuchs because his wife had died and he had not taken another, the cooks because he preferred simpler fare, the barbers because, he said, one barber could serve many people. He wrote a number of books in which he defamed the emperors who had ruled before him. When he dismissed cooks and barbers, he acted like a philosopher, not an emperor; when he slandered or praised, he acted as no philosopher or emperor would.

Once, when Julian was sacrificing to the idols, the mark of a cross encircled by a crown was seen in the entrails of a slaughtered sheep. This sight stirred fear in the ministers, who interpreted it as foretelling the future unity, victory, and perpetuity of the cross. Julian reassured them, saying that this was a sign that Christianity should be kept down and not allowed to expand outside the circle. Another time, when he was offering sacrifice in Constantinople to the goddess Fortuna, Maris, the bishop of Chalcedon, who in his old age had lost his sight, approached him and called him a blasphemer and apostate. Julian answered him: "Well, your Galilean hasn't been able to cure you!" Maris: "I thank God for that, because he deprived me of my sight so that I would not have to look upon you, stripped of all religion as you are!" Julian had nothing to say to that and moved away.

In Antioch he had the sacred vessels and cloths brought together, threw them on the ground, sat on them, and soiled them. Very soon he was stricken in those parts of his body, with worms crawling out and gnawing at his flesh, and he suffered that condition for the rest of his life. And a prefect, also named Julian, having robbed the churches of their sacred vessels at the emperor's command, made water on them, saying: "Look there at the vessels in which Mary's Son is served!" Instantly his mouth became an anus and functioned as such thereafter.

Julian the Apostate was entering the temple of Fortuna, and the ministers of the temple were sprinkling water as a ritual cleansing upon those entering. Valentinian saw a drop fall on his mantle and angrily struck the minister, saying that the water did not purge but stained him. Julian saw this happen, and ordered Valentinian to be taken into custody and banished to the desert. Valentinian was a Christian, and as a reward he merited to be elevated to the empire.

136

As a mark of his hatred of Christians, Julian ordered the temple of the Jews to be restored, and allotted large sums of money for the building. But when a large supply of stones had been brought to the site, a wild wind blew and scattered the stones, a violent tremor shook the earth, and fire burst out from the foundations and consumed a great many people. Another day the sign of the cross appeared in the sky, and the Jews' clothing was covered with black crosses.

Julian invaded Persia, came to Ctesiphon, and laid siege to the city. The king offered to relinquish a part of his kingdom to the emperor if the latter would withdraw his troops, but Julian would not hear of it. Following the ideas of Pythagoras and Plato about the transmigration of souls, he thought that he possessed the soul of Alexander, or rather that he was another Alexander in another body. But suddenly a spear flew through the air and buried itself in his side, and of that wound he died. To this day no one knows who hurled the spear. Some say it was thrown by an invisible hand, others by an Ishmaelite shepherd. Still others think the assailant was a soldier who was worn out with the long marches and with hunger; but whether by man or by angel, obviously it was the command of God that was carried out. Calixtus, who was close to Julian, said that the emperor was struck by a demon. So much we learn from the *Tripartite History*.

The third event commemorated by today's feast is the finding of the head of John the Baptist, because, it is said, his head was indeed found on this day. We read in the eleventh book of the *Ecclesiastical History* that John was chained and beheaded in a castle in Arabia called Macheronta. Herodias, however, had John's head taken to Jerusalem and, as a precaution, buried close to Herod's palace, because she feared that the prophet would return to life if his head was buried with his body. In the time of Emperor Marcian, who, according to the *Scholastic History*, began to reign in A.D. 453, Saint John revealed the whereabouts of his head to two monks who had come to Jerusalem. They hurried to the palace that had been Herod's, and found the head rolled up in haircloth sacks—the cloth, I suppose, that he wore in the desert. When they were on their way back to their homeland with the head, a potter from the city of Emissa, who was running away from poverty, joined them on the road. The potter carried the pouch containing the sacred head, which the monks had entrusted to him, but he was admonished by Saint John to get away from them, and he went back to Emissa with the head. As long as he lived, he kept the relic in a cave and venerated it there, and he prospered not a little. When he was dying, he committed the relic to his sister's care, enjoining secrecy upon her, and she passed it on to her successors.

A long time passed, and Saint John revealed the presence of his head to the monk Saint Marcellus, who was living in the aforementioned cave. Here is how the revelation came about. While Marcellus was asleep, he seemed to see great crowds singing Psalms as they filed by, and saying: "Behold, Saint John the

Baptist is coming!" Then he saw blessed John, who was accompanied by an attendant at his right and another at his left, and the saint blessed all who approached him. Marcellus went to him and prostrated himself at his feet, and the saint raised him, held him by the chin, and gave him the kiss of peace. Marcellus asked him where he had come from, and John answered: "I have come from Sebaste!"

When Marcellus awoke, he wondered much about this vision. Then, another night when he was asleep, someone came and awakened him, and, once awake, he saw a star shining in the entrance to his cell. He got up and tried to touch the star, but it quickly moved to another part of the cave, and he followed it until it came to rest over the spot where John the Baptist's head was buried. Marcellus dug down and found the urn containing the holy treasure. Now a bystander refused to believe what he heard and presumed to touch the urn, but his hand immediately shriveled and stuck to the urn. His companions prayed for him and his hand came free but was still misshapen. John then appeared to him and said: "When my head has been deposited in the church, you shall touch the urn and be restored to health." The man did this and was whole again.

When Marcellus told the bishop of that city—the bishop's name was Julian—all that had happened, they took up the relic and brought it into the city. From that time on, the Beheading of Saint John was solemnly celebrated annually there, on the day of the year when the head was found and dug up, or so we gather from what the *Scholastic History* says. Later on, however, it was transferred to Constantinople. We read in the *Tripartite History* that when Valens was emperor, he ordered the sacred head to be put in a wagon and translated to Constantinople. When the vehicle came close to Chalcedon, it could not be moved a foot farther, no matter how hard the oxen were goaded, so the cortege had to halt and deposit the relic at that point. At a later time, Emperor Theodosius wished to move it again. He found a virgin lady who had been appointed its custodian, and asked her to allow him to take the sacred head away. She consented, thinking that as in the time of Valens the relic would not allow itself to be moved, but the pious emperor wrapped it in purple, took it to Constantinople, and built a beautiful church for it. Thus the *Tripartite History*. Still later, in Pepin's reign, the head was transferred to Poitiers in France, where by John's merits many dead were restored to life.

Just as Herod was punished for beheading John, and Julian for burning his bones, so also Herodias was punished for instructing her daughter to ask for the head, and the girl for doing so. There are some, indeed, who say that Herodias was not sentenced to exile and did not die in exile, but that when she had the head in her hands and taunted it gleefully, by God's will the head breathed in her face and she expired. This is the popular tale, but what was said above, namely, that she was exiled with Herod and died in misery, is what the saints hand on in their chronicles, and therefore is to be believed. As for her daughter, she was walking over an icy pond when the ice gave way under her and she was drowned, though one chronicle says that the earth swallowed her alive. This is understandable, since it is said of the Egyptians who were drowned in the Red Sea: "The earth swallowed them."[4]

The fourth event commemorated by today's feast is the translation of one of Saint John's fingers and the dedication of a church. The finger with which he pointed to the Lord[5] could not, we are told, be burned. This finger was recovered by the aforesaid monks, and later, as the *Scholastic History* has it, Saint Thecla took it into the Alps and deposited it in the church of Saint Maximus. John Beleth adds his testimony, saying that the aforementioned Saint Thecla brought the finger overseas to Normandy and there built a church in honor of Saint John. According to this author, the church was dedicated on this day, for which reason the lord pope decreed that this day should be solemnized throughout the world.

In a city of France called Marienna,[6] a lady who was very devoted to John the Baptist prayed earnestly to God that at some time a relic of Saint John might be given to her. Her prayers were not being answered, so she took confidence in God and bound herself by an oath not to eat until she received what she was asking for. After she had fasted for some days, she saw a wonderfully shining thumb lying on the altar, and joyfully accepted it as a gift from God. In no time three bishops were present, each wanting a part of the thumb, whereupon they were astonished to see three drops of blood fall on the cloth on which the relic lay, and each bishop rejoiced at having merited one drop.

Theodelinda, queen of the Lombards, built and endowed a noble church at Monza, near Milan, in honor of Saint John the Baptist. Some time later, as Paul states in his *History of the Lombards*, the emperor Constantine, also called Constans, wanted to take Italy from the Lombards and consulted a holy man, who had the spirit of prophecy, about the outcome of the war. The holy man prayed during the night and gave his answer in the morning: "The queen built the church in honor of John, and John intercedes continually for the Lombards. Therefore they cannot be conquered. There will come a time, however, when that place will no longer be honored, and then they will be conquered." And so it happened in Charlemagne's time.

Gregory, in his *Dialogues*, tells us that a man of great virtue named Sanctulus had assumed the custody of a deacon whom the Lombards had captured, on condition that if the deacon escaped, he, Sanctulus, would accept capital punishment in his stead. Then Sanctulus forced the deacon to flee and be free. For this, Sanctulus was sentenced to death and led to the place of execution, and the strongest headsman, of whom there was no doubt that with one stroke he could sever the head, was chosen to carry out the sentence. Sanctulus extended his

---

[4] Exod. 15:12.

[5] In art, John the Baptist is frequently portrayed pointing one finger at Christ.

[6] Graesse notes that the Ed. Pr. has Mamerena, while "others read Maurienna or Marienna." Such uncertainty about place names and proper names is not infrequent in the text.

neck, and the executioner, mustering all his strength, raised his arm, holding the sword aloft. At that moment Sanctulus said: "Saint John, get hold of him!" Instantly the striker's arm became stiff and inflexible, and held the sword heavenward until he swore an oath never again to strike a Christian. The man of God then prayed for him, and at once he was able to lower his arm.

※

126. Saints Felix and Adauctus

Felix, a priest, and his brother, also named Felix and also a priest, were brought before Diocletian and Maximian. The older of the two was led to the temple of Serapis to offer sacrifice there, but he blew into the face of the statue, which fell to pieces immediately. He was taken to a statue of Mercury and blew on it with the same result. For a third trial he faced a statue of Diana, and down it came. He was tortured on the rack and then, for a fourth time, led to a sacrilegious tree, there to offer sacrifice. Instead he knelt and prayed, then blew on the tree, which promptly was torn up by the roots and demolished the altar and the temple as it fell.

Word of this came to the prefect, and he ordered Felix to be beheaded at that place and his body to be thrown to the wolves and dogs. Then a man sprang forth from the crowd and freely avowed himself to be a Christian. They embraced each other and were executed together then and there.

The Christians did not know the name of the second man and called him *Adauctus*, which means added on or joined to, because he was joined to Saint Felix in winning the crown of martyrdom. The Christians buried the two in the hole left by the falling tree. The pagans tried to dig them up but were seized by the devil. The martyrs suffered about A.D. 287.[1]

---

[1] The second Felix is forgotten. Such duplication of names may result from actual multiplicity of homonyms, or from similar stories coming from different quarters. It may also be that there were two Felixes, about one of whom nothing was known.

127. Saints Savinian and Savina

Savinian and Savina[1] were the children of Savinus, a member of the high nobility but a pagan, who fathered Savinian by his first wife and Savina by his second, and derived their names from his own.

Somewhere Savinian read the verse: "Thou shalt sprinkle me, Lord, and I shall be cleansed; thou shalt wash me and I shall be made whiter than snow,"[2] and wondered what it meant but could not understand it. He went into his bedroom and sat in sackcloth and ashes, saying that he would prefer to die rather than to live and not understand the meaning of those words. An angel appeared to him and said: "Do not fret yourself to death, because you have found favor with God, and when you have been baptized you will be whiter than snow, and then you will understand what now puzzles you."

The angel left him and he was happy, and thereafter spurned the veneration of idols. His father rebuked him severely for this and often said to him: "It would be better for you to be the only one to die for not adoring the gods than to have all of us involved in your death!" Savinian therefore left home secretly and went to the city of Troyes. When he arrived at the Seine and prayed the Lord that he might be baptized in the river, he was baptized there, and the Lord said to him: "Now you have found what you have labored so long to find!" Savinian then drove his staff into the ground, and, after he had prayed, the staff produced a profusion of leaves and flowers, while a crowd of people looked on. Thereupon 1,108 men believed in the Lord.

Emperor Aurelian heard about this and sent a squadron of soldiers to take Savinian prisoner, but when they found him praying, they were afraid to come near him. The emperor dispatched a troop larger than the first, but they, finding him at prayer, knelt and prayed with him, then rose and said: "The emperor desires to see you!" When he was brought in and refused to sacrifice, at Aurelian's command he was bound hand and foot and beaten with iron bars. "Increase the torments if you can," said Savinian. The emperor ordered him to be taken to the center of the city and seated, bound, on a bench, under which wood should be stacked and drenched with oil, then ignited, and that would be the end of Savinian. But then the monarch saw him standing in the middle of the flames and praying. Stupefied, he fell on his face, then stood up and said to the

---

[1] The preferred spelling is Sabinian, Sabina, but Jacobus's spelling is retained here. At the end of this chapter Jacobus recognizes another Saint Sabina, who was revered as a Roman martyr.
[2] Ps. 50(51):9.

saint: "You foul beast, are you not satisfied with the souls you have deceived? Must you strive to deceive even us by your magical tricks?" Savinian: "Many more souls, and you yourself, are to believe in the Lord through me!"

The emperor now blasphemed the name of God, and gave orders that on the next day Savinian was to be bound to a stake and shot through with arrows; but when the orders were carried out, the arrows hung in the air to either side of him, and not one of them touched him. So the emperor came to him and asked: "Where is your God? Let him come now and rescue you from these arrows!" But instantly one of the arrows jumped out and struck the emperor in one eye, blinding it completely. This angered him, and he ordered the saint back to prison, to be beheaded the following day. Savinian, however, prayed to God that he might be transferred to the place where he had been baptized. His chains fell off, the door of the prison opened, and he walked through the soldiers and set out for the bank of the Seine. This was reported to Aurelian, who commanded that he be pursued and beheaded. Seeing the soldiers coming, Savinian walked over the water as if it were stone, and came to the spot where he had been baptized. The soldiers made their way across, but then feared to strike him, and he said to them: "Don't be afraid to strike me, and take some of my blood to the emperor, so that he may receive his sight and acknowledge the power of God." They cut off his head, but he picked it up and carried it for forty-five paces.

When the emperor touched the wounded eye with the blood, he was cured immediately and said: "The God of the Christians is truly good and great!" A woman who had been blind for forty years heard about this, so she had herself carried to that place and prayed there. Her sight was restored at once. Savinian was martyred about A.D. 279, on the first day of February. Savinian's story, however, is given here simply as an adjunct to the story of his sister Savina, since the feast is celebrated principally in her honor.

Savina, then, wept every day for her lost brother and prayed to the idols for him. At length an angel appeared to her in her sleep and said: "Don't cry, Savina! Give away all your possessions, and you will find your brother raised to the highest honors!" When she awoke, she asked her foster sister: "My friend, did you hear or see anything?" "Yes, ma'am," was the response, "I saw a man talking to you, but I don't know what he said." Savina: "You won't tell anyone?" The other: "Of course not! Do anything you like, but don't kill yourself!"

The two women started out the next morning. After the father had made every effort to find Savina and had failed, he raised his hands to heaven and said: "If you are a God powerful in heaven, destroy my idols! They have not been able to save my children!" Then the Lord thundered, and broke and crushed all the idols, and many people, seeing this, believed.

Savina went to Rome and was baptized by Pope Eusebius. She cured two blind men and two paralytics, and lived in Rome for five years. Then an angel appeared to her in her sleep and said: "What are you doing, Savina? You gave up all your riches, yet here you are, living in luxury! Get up and go to the city of Troyes, where you will find your brother!" Savina said to her maidservant: "We must not live here any longer." The servant: "Madam, where do you want to go? Everybody here loves you, and you want to die a wanderer?" Savina: "God will provide for us!"

Taking a barley loaf with her, she set out and reached Ravenna. She went to the house of a certain rich man, whose daughter was being mourned as if she were already dead. Savina asked a servingwoman to allow her to stay in the house. The woman answered: "My lady, how could you be a guest in this house, when my mistress's daughter is dying and everyone is grief-stricken?" "She will not die because of me," said Savina. She entered the house, took the girl's hand, and brought her to her feet completely cured. The family pressed her to stay with them, but she would have none of it.

When she came within a mile of Troyes, she said to her maid: "Let's rest here for a while." Then from the city came a noblemen named Licerius, who asked her: "Where are you from?" She answered: "I'm from here, from this city." Licerius: "Why do you lie to me, since your accent shows that you're a stranger here!" Savina: "Sir, it's true that I am a stranger, and that I'm looking for my long-lost brother Savinian!" "The man you're looking for," he answered, "was beheaded for Christ, and I know where he's buried." Savina prostrated herself in prayer, saying: "O Lord, you have always preserved me in chastity. Do not allow me to weary myself any longer with journeying! Do not let me move my body beyond this place! I commend to you my servant, who has borne so much on my behalf. I could not see my brother here, but grant that I may be found worthy to see him in your heavenly kingdom!" And, having finished her prayer, she migrated to the Lord.

Her maidservant, seeing her dead, began to weep because she had no means of burying her. The aforementioned man sent a herald through the city, calling for men to come and bury a woman from another land. Men came and gave her honorable burial.

On this day the feast of a Saint Sabina is celebrated. She was the wife of a soldier named Valentine, and was executed under Hadrian because she refused to sacrifice.

128. Saint Lupus

Lupus, a native of Orléans, came of royal stock and shone with all the virtues. He was elected archbishop of Sens and distributed almost all he had to the poor. One day he had invited more people than usual to his table, and the wine ran short. Lupus said to the steward: "I believe that God, who feeds the ravens, will fill up our charity." At that moment a messenger came and announced that a hundred casks of wine stood outside the door.

All the members of his official family censured him severely, claiming that he was much too fond of the daughter of his predecessor, a virgin and devout servant of God. Lupus, in the presence of his detractors, held the young woman and kissed her, saying: "What other people say does no harm to one whose conscience is clear," for he knew that she loved God ardently, and he loved her with a perfectly pure affection.

When Clothar, king of the Franks, invaded Burgundy and sent his marshal against the people of Sens to besiege the city, Saint Lupus went into the church of Saint Stephen and began to ring the bell. When the enemy troops heard it, such terror seized them that they thought they would not escape death unless they fled.

In the end the king won the realm of Burgundy and sent another high officer to Sens, but blessed Lupus did not come out to meet him with gifts. The envoy was offended and denounced him to the king, and the king sent Lupus into exile, where the saint enhanced his renown by his teaching and his miracles. Meanwhile the people of Sens put to death another bishop who had usurped Saint Lupus's place, and petitioned the king to have Lupus return from exile. When the king saw this rightful bishop, weakened and worn out by exile, God changed his heart. He threw himself at Lupus's feet and begged his pardon, and sent him back to his city with many gifts. When Lupus went to Paris, the doors of the prisons opened and the prisoners' chains fell off, allowing them to meet the saint in crowds. One Sunday, while he was celebrating mass, a jewel fell from heaven into his sacred chalice. The king kept the jewel among the saint's relics.

King Clothar heard that the bell of Saint Stephen's church had wonderful sweetness of sound, and sent to have it brought to Paris so that he might hear it more often. But this displeased Saint Lupus, and as soon as the bell was out of the city of Sens, it lost the sweetness of its tone. When word of this reached the king, he immediately ordered the bell returned, and at the seventh milestone from the city it rang with its usual dulcet sound. Therefore Saint Lupus went out to meet it, and what he had grieved at losing he welcomed back with honor.

One day he had made the rounds of the city's churches as was his custom, and when he got home, his clerics were haranguing each other because they were bent on committing sin with women. He went to the church and prayed for them, and in no time all sting of temptation left them, and they came before him and begged for his pardon.

At last, renowned for his virtues, Lupus fell asleep in peace. He flourished in the years around A.D. 610, in the time of Heraclius.

---

129. Saint Mamertinus

While still a pagan, Mamertinus once was worshiping the idols when he lost one of his eyes and one of his hands became paralyzed. He thought he had offended his gods, and went to the temple to placate them. On the way he met a monk named Savinus, who asked him the cause of his affliction. He answered: "I have offended my gods and am on my way to pray to them, that what they have taken away in anger they may restore to me in kindness." Savinus: "You are mistaken, brother, if you think the demons are gods. Go to Saint Germain, bishop of Auxerre, follow his counsel, and you will be healed at once."

Mamertinus set out again in haste, and came to the sepulcher of bishop Saint Amator and a number of other saintly bishops. It started to rain, and he took shelter for the night in a small cell built above the tomb of Saint Concordian. There he fell asleep and had a wonderful vision, in which he saw a man come to the opening of his cell and invite Saint Concordian to come to the feast that Saint Peregrinus, Saint Amator, and other bishops were holding. Saint Concordian answered from his tomb: "I can't come now, because I must stay and protect a guest from the serpents that live here." The man went and reported what he had heard, then came back and said: "Rise, Concordian, and come, taking with you Vivian the subdeacon and Julian the acolyte to perform their functions. Alexander will take care of your guest." Mamertinus then saw Saint Concordian take him by the hand and lead him to the company of the other bishops. Saint Amator asked Concordian: "Who is this man who came in with you?" Concordian: "He is my guest." Amator: "Put him out! He's unclean, and cannot be with us!" Mamertinus was about to be expelled, but prostrated himself before Saint Amator and besought his mercy, whereupon Amator ordered him to go quickly to Saint Germain. When he awoke, he hurried off to Saint Germain and knelt before him, asking forgiveness. When he told the bishop all that had happened to him, they went together to blessed Concordian's tomb, removed the stone, and found a tangle of snakes that were over ten feet long. These fled in different directions, Germain commanding them to go to places where they would not dare to harm anyone.

At last Mamertinus received baptism and was cured of his ills. He then became a monk in the monastery of Saint Germain and succeeded Saint Allodius as abbot. In his time there was in the monastery a holy monk named Marinus, whose obedience Mamertinus wished to test. He therefore assigned Marinus to the meanest work in the monastery, which was to care for the cattle. While the holy man watched over his steers and cows in a woodland, he radiated such holiness that the birds of the forest came to him and pecked food out of his hand. A boar pursued by dogs once took refuge in his cell; he snatched the boar away from the pursuers and then set it free. Another time thieves robbed him, taking away with them even his clothes and leaving him only one poor tunic, but he ran after them, calling out: "Come back, my masters, come back! I found a coin in the hem of my tunic, and you may perhaps have need of it." Back they came and took the tunic and the coin, leaving him completely naked. The robbers set out in haste for their hiding place, but after marching all night they found themselves back at Marinus's cell. He greeted them and welcomed them kindly to his dwelling, washed their feet, and provided for their needs as well as he could. They were dumbstruck at the thought of the way they had treated him, and every one of them was converted to the faith.

One time some younger monks who lived with him set a trap for a she-bear that was preying on the sheep, and in the night the animal was caught in the trap. Saint Mamertinus sensed what had happened, so he rose from his bed and went out to the bear. "What are you doing, poor beast!" he said. "Hurry away from here or you will be caught!" He loosed the trap and the bear ran off.

When Mamertinus died, his body was being transported to Auxerre, but the cortege reached a certain villa and could not move a step farther until a man lying in prison found his chains suddenly broken, jumped up free, came to the corpse, and helped the others to carry it into the city. There the body was given honorable burial in the church of Saint Germain.

130. Saint Giles

Aegidius is the Latin form of the name Giles. *Aegidius* is formed from *a*, meaning without, *geos*, earth, and *dyan*, brilliant or godlike. Saint Giles was without the earth by his disdain for earthly things, brilliant by the light of his knowledge, and godlike by the love that causes the lover to be like the beloved.

Giles, or Aegidius, was born in Athens of royal stock and was instructed in the sacred writings from childhood. One day as he was on his way to church, he came upon a sick man lying beside the road and asking for an alms. He gave the sick man his coat, and as soon as the man put it, on he was cured of his illness. Another time, as he was returning home from church, he met a man who had been bitten by a snake, but Giles prayed for him and drove out the poison. Then a man possessed of the devil was in church with the rest of the people, disturbing the faithful with his clamor, but Giles drove the devil out and cured the man. Later, when his parents had fallen asleep in the Lord, he made Christ the heir of his patrimony.

Fearing the perils of being praised by men, Giles left the city and secretly made his way to the seacoast. From the shore he saw sailors who were in danger of shipwreck, and calmed the storm by his prayer. The sailors came ashore and, learning that he wanted to go to Rome and out of gratitude for what he had done for them, promised that they would take him aboard without payment. He got as far as Arles and stayed there for two years with Saint Caesarius, the bishop of that city. There he cured a man who had been stricken with fevers for three years. Then, seeking solitude, he left Arles surreptitiously and stayed for a long time with Veredonius, a hermit known for his holiness. There, by his merits, he put an end to the barrenness of the soil. The fame of his miracles spread widely, and, always aware of the danger of human adulation, he left Veredonius and penetrated farther into the desert, where he found a cave and a small spring. There was also a doe ready to hand, and she came at certain hours and nourished him with her milk.

The king's men came hunting in that area and saw the doe. Caring nothing for other game, they pursued her with their dogs, and the doe, hard pressed, took refuge at her foster son's feet. Giles wondered why the animal was whining and whimpering, which was not at all like her, so he went out, and, hearing the hunt, prayed the Lord to save the nurse he had provided. No dog dared come closer than a stone's throw, and the pack returned to the huntsmen barking and howling vehemently. Night drew on and the hunt turned for home. They came back the next day, but their labors were thwarted again, and they returned home as before.

Word of this reached the king, and, suspecting how matters stood, he came out with the bishop and a throng of huntsmen. When the dogs did not dare to come close to the doe but turned tail howling, the huntsmen surrounded the place, which was so thickly overgrown with thorn bushes as to be impenetrable. One of them incautiously shot an arrow, hoping to drive out the quarry, but instead inflicted a serious wound on the man of God as he prayed for his doe. The soldiers then cut a way through the brambles and came to the hermit's cave. There they found the old man wearing a monk's habit, white-haired, venerable with age, and the doe stretched out at his feet. Only the bishop and the king, having ordered the rest to stay back, came to him on foot. They asked him who he was and where he came from, and why he had chosen so dense a wilderness, and who had dared to wound him. When he had answered all their questions and they had humbly begged his pardon, they promised to send a physician to care for the wound and offered him many presents. But he refused medical care and spurned the gifts, which he did not even look at. Rather, knowing that power is made perfect in weakness, he prayed the Lord not to restore his health as long as he lived.

The king came often to visit the man of God and to receive from him the food of salvation. He offered Giles great wealth, but Giles refused to accept it and proposed instead that he use the treasure to build a monastery where the monastic way of life could be followed to the letter. The king did this, and Giles, finally yielding to the royal tears and entreaties, undertook the rule of the monastery.

Now King Charles heard of Giles's renown, invited the saint to visit him, and welcomed him reverently. In the course of their conversations about the soul and salvation, the king asked his visitor to pray for him, because he had committed an enormous crime, which he dared not confess even to the saint himself. The following Sunday, while Giles was celebrating mass and praying for the king, an angel of the Lord appeared to him and deposited on the altar a scroll on which it was written that the king's sin was forgiven due to Giles's prayer, provided that the king was truly repentant, confessed his sin, and abstained from committing it thereafter. Furthermore, anyone who had committed a sin and prayed to Saint Giles to obtain pardon should have no doubt that by the saint's merits the sin was forgiven. Giles gave the scroll to the king, and Charles acknowledged his sin and humbly prayed for pardon.

The saint, now more honored than ever, set out on his return journey. At Nîmes he restored to life the son of the chief man of that city, who had just died. A short time later he foretold the destruction of his monastery by enemies and went to Rome, where he obtained from the pope not only a privilege for his church, but two cypress-wood doors on which the images of the apostles were carved. These he lowered into the Tiber, commending them to God's guidance.

When he was back at his monastery he cured a paralytic at Tiberone. In the port he found the two doors described above, and, thanking God for having preserved them from the perils of the sea, placed them at the entrance to his church, both as an ornament to the church and as a memorial of its union with the see of Rome.

In due time the Lord revealed to him through the Spirit that the day of his death was imminent. He made this known to his brothers and asked them to pray for him, then happily fell asleep in the Lord. Many testified that at the moment of his death they had heard the angels singing as they bore his soul to heaven. Giles flourished around A.D. 700.

---

131. *The Birth of the Blessed Virgin Mary*

The glorious Virgin Mary took her origin from the tribe of Judah and the royal stock of David. Matthew and Luke do not set forth the lineage of Mary but that of Joseph—who had nothing to do with the conception of Christ—because the usage of the sacred writers is said to have been to weave the series of generations of males, not of females. It is perfectly true, nevertheless, that the Blessed Virgin descended from the lineage of David: this is obvious because, as Scripture often testifies, Christ was born of the seed of David. Since, therefore, Christ was born of the Virgin alone, it is plain that the Virgin herself was born of David, through the line of Nathan.

Among David's sons there were two, Nathan and Solomon. Of the line of Nathan, son of David, as John of Damascus testifies, Levi begot Melchi and Panthar, Panthar begot Barpanthar, Barpanthar begot Joachim, and Joachim was the father of the Virgin Mary. Nathan took a wife from the line of Solomon, and of her begot Jacob. When Nathan died, Melchi of the tribe of Nathan, son of Levi and brother of Panthar, married the deceased Nathan's wife, the mother of Jacob, and of her begot Heli. Thus Jacob and Heli were brothers born of the same mother, Jacob being of the tribe of Solomon and Heli of the tribe of Nathan. Heli of the tribe of Nathan died without issues, and Jacob his brother, who was of the tribe of Solomon, took Heli's wife and raised up seed to his brother,[1] begetting Joseph. Joseph therefore was by birth the son of Jacob of the

---

[1] Cf. Mark 12:19.

line of Solomon, and by law the son of Heli of the line of Nathan: in other words, the son born according to nature was the son of the father who begot him, but, according to the law, the son of the deceased.[2] Thus John Damascenus.

We also find, in the *Ecclesiastical History* and in Bede's *Chronicle*, that all the genealogies of Hebrews and aliens were kept in the Temple's secret archives. Herod ordered the burning of these records, thinking that he might be able to pass himself off for a noble if, in the absence of proof to the contrary, he was thought to be Israelite by race. There were also some who were called *dominici* ("men of the Lord") because they were closely related to Christ and were from Nazareth. These *dominici* worked out, as well as they could, the order of Christ's human ancestry, partly from what they had learned from their forefathers and partly from some books that they had at home.

Joachim took a wife named Anna, who had a sister named Hismeria. This Hismeria was the mother of Elizabeth and Eliud, and Elizabeth was the mother of John the Baptist. Eliud was the father of Eminen, and Eminen the father of Saint Servatius, whose body is in the town of Maastricht on the Meuse, in the diocese of Liège. Anna is said to have had three husbands, Joachim, Cleophas, and Salome. Of Joachim, her first husband, she gave birth to one daughter, Mary, the mother of the Lord, whom she gave in marriage to Joseph, and who bore and brought forth Christ the Lord. Joachim died and Anna married Cleophas, Joseph's brother, and of him had another daughter, whom she likewise called Mary and who was married to Alpheus. This Mary bore her husband four sons, namely, James the Less, Joseph the Just also called Barsabas, Simon, and Jude. After the death of her second husband Anna took a third, namely, Salome, of whom she had another daughter, whom she also called Mary and whom she gave as wife to Zebedee. This Mary had two sons by her husband, namely, James the Greater and John the Evangelist. All this is summed up in the following verses:

> Anna solet dici tres concepisse Marias,
> Quas genuere viri Joachim, Cleophas, Salomeque.
> Has duxere viri Joseph, Alpheus, Zebedaeus.
> Prima parit Christum, Jacobum secunda minorem,
> Et Joseph justum peperit cum Simone Judam,
> Tertia majorem Jacobum volucremque Joannem.[3]

---

[2] I.e., the deceased first husband of the mother. Part of the confusion in this genealogy is due to its failure to include Mathan or Matthan, described in Matt. 1:15 as the father of Jacob. Our author identifies this Mathan with one of the Nathans he cites. This point does not entirely dispel the confusion, though it helps to achieve the purpose of the genealogy, which is to confirm the Davidic ancestry of Mary and Jesus.

[3] Anna is usually said to have conceived three Marys, / Whom [her] husbands, Joachim, Cleophas, and Salome, begot. / The Marys were taken in marriage by Joseph, Alpheus, Zebedee. / The first Mary bore Christ, the second, James the Less, / Joseph the Just with Simon and Jude, / the third, James the Greater and John the Wingèd.

But now a question arises: how could Mary be a cousin of Elizabeth, as has been said elsewhere? It is clear that Elizabeth was the wife of Zachary, who was of the tribe of Levi, and according to the Law a man had to choose a wife from his own tribe and family, but Luke testifies that Elizabeth was of the daughters of Aaron.[4] According to Jerome, Anna was from Bethlehem, which belonged to the tribe of Judah, but keep in mind that both Aaron and Joiada the high priest took wives of the tribe of Judah, which proves that the priestly and kingly tribes were always joined to each other by ties of blood. It may be, as Bede says, that this sort of relationship, by which women were given in marriage from one tribe to another, developed in later times, so that it would be manifest that Mary, who descended from the royal tribe, had a bond of kinship with the priestly tribe. Therefore blessed Mary was of both tribes. God willed that these privileged tribes should be mingled with each other by reason of the mystery, because the Lord Christ was to be born of them, and Christ, king and priest, would offer himself for us, would rule his followers as they struggled amid the evils of this life, and would crown them after they had won the fight. This is also suggested by the name of Christ, which means anointed, because in the Old Law only priests, kings, and prophets were anointed. Hence we are called Christians after Christ, and are also called a chosen generation and a kingly priesthood.[5] And when it was said that women should be wedded only to men of their own tribe, it is clear that this was ordered so as not to upset the distribution of the land by lot. Since the tribe of Levi had no share in this distribution among the other tribes, the women of that tribe could marry whomever they wished.

Blessed Jerome says in the Prologue to his *History of the Birth of the Virgin* that in his early youth he had read the story in some book, and many years later was asked to put it in writing, so he wrote it down as he remembered it from his early reading. Joachim, a Galilean from the town of Nazareth, took Saint Anna, a native of Bethlehem, as his wife. They were both righteous and walked without reproach in all the commandments of the Lord. They divided all their goods into three parts, one part being reserved for the Temple and its ministers, one for transient strangers and the poor, and the third for their own needs and those of their household. They lived for twenty years without offspring and made a vow to the Lord that if he granted them a child, they would dedicate it to the service of God. With this in mind they went up to Jerusalem for the three principal feasts. Once, when Joachim and his kinsmen traveled to Jerusalem for the feast of the Dedication, he went with the others to the altar to make his offering. When the priest saw him, he angrily ordered him away and upbraided him for presuming to approach the altar of God, declaring that it was not proper for one who was subject to the Law's curse to offer sacrifice to the Lord of the Law, nor for a sterile man, who made no increase to the people of God, to stand among men who begot sons.

[4] Luke 1:5.
[5] 1 Peter 2:9.

Joachim, seeing himself thus rejected, was ashamed to go home and face the contempt of his kinsmen, who had heard the priest's denunciation. Instead he went and lived with his shepherds. Then one day an angel appeared with great brilliance to him when he was alone. He was disturbed by the apparition, but the angel told him not to be afraid and said: "I am an angel of the Lord, sent to announce to you that your prayers have been heard and your alms have ascended in the sight of the Lord. I have seen how you were put to shame, and heard the reproach of childlessness wrongly put upon you. God punishes not nature but sin, and therefore, when he closes a woman's womb, he does this in order to open it miraculously later on, and to make it known that what is born is not the fruit of carnal desire but of the divine generosity. Did not the first mother of your race suffer the shame of childlessness until she was ninety years old, and yet bore Isaac, to whom was promised the blessing of all nations? Was not Rachel barren for a long time and yet bore Joseph, who had power over all Egypt? Who was stronger than Samson or holier than Samuel? Yet they both had sterile mothers. Believe these reasons and examples, which show that delayed conceptions and infertile childbearing are usually all the more wonderful! So then, your wife will bear you a daughter and you will call her Mary. As you have vowed, she will be consecrated to the Lord from infancy and filled with the Holy Spirit from her mother's womb. She will not live outside among the common people but will abide in the Temple at all times, lest any sinister suspicion be aroused about her. And, as she will be born of an unfruitful mother, so, miraculously, the Son of the Most High will be born of her. His name will be Jesus, and through him all nations will be saved. And let this be a sign to you: when you arrive at the Golden Gate of Jerusalem, Anna your wife will be there waiting for you. She has been worried because you were so late and will be glad at the sight of you." With these words the angel left him.

Meanwhile Anna was weeping bitterly, not knowing where her husband had gone, when the same angel appeared to her, revealed to her the same things he had told Joachim, and added that, for a sign, she should go to Jerusalem's Golden Gate, where she would meet her husband as he returned. So they met as the angel had predicted, and were happy to see each other and to be sure they were to have a child. They adored God and went to their home, joyfully awaiting the fulfillment of the divine promise. Anna conceived and brought forth a daughter, and they called her name Mary. When she was weaned at the age of three, the parents brought her to the Lord's Temple with offerings. Around the Temple there were fifteen steps, corresponding to the fifteen Gradual Psalms, and because the Temple was built on a hill, there was no way to go to the altar of holocaust, which stood in the open, except by climbing the steps. The virgin child was set down at the lowest step and mounted to the top without help from anyone, as if she were already fully grown up.

Having made their offering, Joachim and Anna left their daughter in the Temple with the other virgins and went home. Mary advanced steadily in all holiness. Angels visited her every day, and she enjoyed the vision of God daily.

In a letter to Chromatius and Heliodorus, Jerome says that the Blessed Virgin had made a rule for herself: the time from dawn to the third hour she devoted to prayer, from the third to the ninth hour she worked at weaving, and from the ninth hour on she prayed without stopping until an angel appeared and brought her food.

When Mary was in her fourteenth year, the high priest publicly announced that the maidens who were reared in the Temple and had come of age should return to their homes and be legally joined with their husbands. The other girls obeyed this edict. Only the Blessed Virgin Mary answered that she could not do so, both because her parents had dedicated her to the service of the Lord and because she herself had vowed her virginity to God. The high priest was perplexed: he did not intend, by impeding the fulfillment of a vow, to go against the Scripture that says: "Make your vows to the Lord your God and perform them,"[6] nor did he dare to introduce a custom not usual in the nation. A feast of the Jews was imminent, and he called the elders together to consult them. They were unanimous in their decision that in so doubtful a matter the counsel of the Lord should be sought. They prayed earnestly, and the high priest went inside to consult the Lord. Presently a voice sounded from the Holies for all to hear. It said: "Each unmarried but marriageable man of the house of David is to bring a branch to the altar. One of these branches will bloom and the Holy Spirit in the form of a dove will perch upon its tip, according to the prophecy of Isaiah. The man to whom this branch belongs is, beyond all doubt, the one who is to be the virgin's spouse."

Joseph, of the house of David, was among the other men, but it seemed incongruous to him that a man of his advanced age should take so tender a young woman to wife, and he alone withheld his branch when the others placed theirs on the altar. So it was that nothing happened as the divine voice had predicted, and the high priest thought to consult the Lord a second time. The voice responded that the only man who had not brought his branch was the one to whom the virgin was to be espoused. Therefore Joseph brought his branch forward, it flowered at once, and a dove came from heaven and perched upon it. So it was clear to all that Joseph was to be Mary's husband.

Once the espousals were accomplished, Joseph went back to his home city of Bethlehem to get his house ready and to make the necessary arrangements for the wedding. Mary, on the other hand, returned to her parents' home in Nazareth, together with seven virgins of her own age and breeding, whom the high priest had assigned to her because of what the miracle had shown. And in those days the angel Gabriel appeared to her as she prayed, and announced to her that she was to be the mother of the Son of God.

The day of the Blessed Virgin's birth was unknown to the faithful for a long time. Then, as John Beleth tells it, there was a holy man, diligent in the practice of contemplation, who, every year on the eighth day of September, heard, as he

[6] Ps. 75:12 (76:11).

prayed, the joyous choirs of angels chanting solemn paeans. He devoutly prayed to know why he heard this annually on this day and on no other. He received a response from God, that on this day the glorious Virgin Mary had been born to the world, and that he should make this known to the children of Holy Church so that they might join the court of heaven in celebrating her birthday. He passed this knowledge on to the supreme pontiff and others, and they, fasting and praying and searching the Scriptures and ancient documents to ascertain the truth, decreed that this day should be celebrated throughout the world in honor of holy Mary's birth.

There was a time when the octave of Mary's birth was not solemnized, but Pope Innocent, a native of Genoa, instituted its celebration, for the following reason. After the death of Pope Gregory, the Romans locked all the cardinals in a conclave so that they would elect a successor more quickly. But when they had not reached an agreement after several weeks, and had to endure many abuses inflicted by the Romans, they made a vow to the Queen of heaven that if by her intercession they agreed on a choice and would be free to go home, they would decree that the long-neglected octave of her birthday should be celebrated from then on. So they elected the lord Celestin and were set free. Celestin, however, died in less than a month, and their vow was translated into law by the lord Innocent.

Note that the Church solemnizes only three birthdays, namely, those of Christ, of holy Mary, and of John the Baptist. These three birthdays mark three spiritual births, for we are reborn in water with John, in penance with Mary, and in glory with Christ. Since the rebirth of baptism in adults must be preceded by contrition, as must the rebirth in glory, these two birthdays rightly have vigils, but penance is itself a vigil, and therefore our rebirth in penance does not call for a vigil. All three, however, have octaves, because they all look forward to the octave of the resurrection.

There was a knight who was dauntless in combat and also fervently devoted to the Blessed Virgin. On his way to a tournament he came to a monastery built in honor of the Virgin and went in to hear mass; but one mass succeeded another, and for the Virgin's honor he did not want to miss any of them. Finally he left the monastery and rode as fast as he could toward the field of the tourney. And behold, he was met by knights coming back from the field, and they congratulated him for jousting so well. All who had been there said the same, and all applauded his mastery in the lists. There were also some who said he had captured them, and they surrendered to him forthwith. The knight, a man of discernment, saw that the courtly Queen had honored him in a courtly way. He explained what had happened, returned to the monastery, and thereafter soldiered for the Son of the Virgin.

A certain bishop, who held Blessed Mary in the highest reverence and piety, was on his way in the middle of the night to a church of the Virgin, to make a visit of devotion. And lo! the Virgin of virgins, accompanied by a great chorus of virgins, came to meet the bishop, received him with high honor, and began to lead him toward the church to which he was going. Two of the maidens from the choir led the chant, and sang:

> Cantemus Domino, sociae, cantemus honorem,
> Dulcis amor Christi resonet ore pio.[7]

The whole chorus of virgins took up the chant, repeating the verses, while the two leaders sang the next two in time:

> Primus ad ima ruit magna de luce superbus,
> Sic homo cum tumuit, primus ad ima ruit.[8]

Thus they led the man of God in procession to the church, the two leaders always intoning the verse and the rest responding.

A woman who had lost her husband had her only son, whom she loved tenderly, for consolation. It happened, however, that the son was captured by enemies and imprisoned in chains. When she heard this, she wept inconsolably, and prayed incessantly to the Blessed Virgin, to whom she was much devoted, to obtain her son's liberation. Then, seeing that her prayers were not answered, she went alone into a church where there was a sculptured image of Blessed Mary, and, standing in front of the image, she addressed it in these terms: "O Virgin blessed, I have often asked you for the liberation of my son, and so far you have not come to the aid of this pitiable mother. I have sought your patronage for my son and see no return for my prayers. Therefore, as my son has been taken away from me, I will take your Son away from you and hold him in custody as a hostage for mine." She then went up and took the image of the Child from the Virgin's lap, went home with it, wrapped it in spotless cloths, and hid it in a cupboard, which she locked carefully. Thus she could rejoice at having a good hostage for her son and guarded it closely.

The following night the Blessed Virgin appeared to the young man and opened the door of the prison. She told him to get up and leave, and said: "Son, you will tell your mother to give my Son back to me as I have given hers back to her." The youth walked out, went to his mother, and told her how the Virgin had set him free. Overjoyed, she took the image of the Child, went to the church, and returned her Son to Mary, saying: "I thank you, my lady, for restoring my only son to me, and now I return your Son to you, because I acknowledge that I have received my own."

There was a thief who committed many robberies, but had deep devotion to Blessed Mary and often greeted her with prayers. Once, however, he was caught in a robbery and sentenced to be hanged. When he was hanged, the Virgin was

---

[7] Let us sing to the Lord, dear companions, let us carol his honor; / Let the sweet love of Christ resound in pious song.

[8] As [Lucifer] the proud one fell first from the great light into the depths, / so the first man, when he was swollen with pride, fell into the abyss.

immediately at his side, and for three days, as it seemed to him, she held him up as he hung, so that he sustained no injury. But then the men who had hanged him, passing by and finding him alive and cheery of mien, thought that they had not adjusted the noose properly and prepared to finish him off with the sword, but the Blessed Virgin held back the swordsman's weapon and they could do the criminal no harm. They learned from him how Blessed Mary had come to his aid. Wondering, they took him down and, for love of the Virgin, let him go free. He went off and entered a monastery, where he spent his remaining years in the service of the mother of God.

There was a cleric who loved the Blessed Virgin devotedly and recited her hours faithfully. When his parents died, having no other offspring they left their whole estate to him. His friends then pressed him to take a wife and manage his heritage. On the appointed day he was on the way to his wedding and was passing a church, when he remembered his service to Mary, went into the church, and began to say her hours. The Blessed Virgin appeared to him and, as if angry, said: "O foolish, unfaithful man! Why are you leaving me, your friend and spouse, for another woman?" The cleric was filled with remorse at this, but he returned to his companions, hiding his distress, and went through with the wedding. At midnight, however, he left everything behind and fled from his house, entered a monastery, and devoted himself to Mary's service.

The priest of a certain parish, a man of virtuous life, knew no other mass than the mass of the Blessed Virgin Mary, which he celebrated day after day in her honor. This was brought to the bishop's attention, and he called the priest in immediately. The priest told him that he did not know any other mass. The bishop scolded him harshly, called him an impostor, suspended him from his parish duties, and forbade him to celebrate Mary's mass. The following night Blessed Mary appeared to the bishop, rebuked him severely, and asked why he had treated her servant so badly. She added that he would die within thirty days unless he reinstated the priest in his parish. The bishop, shaken, summoned the priest, begged his pardon, and ordered him to celebrate no other mass than the one he knew, the mass of the Virgin Mary.

There was a cleric who was vain and dissolute, yet loved the mother of God devotedly and recited her office piously and promptly. One night, in a vision, he saw himself standing before God's judgment seat and heard the Lord saying to those present: "It is yours to decide what judgment the man who is looking at you deserves. I have tolerated his conduct for a long time and to this day have seen no sign of amendment in him." Then the Lord, with unanimous approval, pronounced a sentence of damnation upon the cleric. But now he saw the Blessed Virgin rise and say to her Son: "Loving Son, I ask your clemency for this man. Mitigate his sentence of damnation, and, as a favor to me, let him live, although what he really deserves is death." "I grant your petition," the Lord answered, "on condition that from now on I see him amend his ways." The Virgin turned to the man and said: "Go and sin no more, that nothing worse befall you!" The man awoke, changed his way of living, became a religious, and spent the rest of his life in good works.

In Sicily, in the year A.D. 537, as we have the story from Fulbert of Chartres, there was a man named Theophilus, who served a bishop as his administrator. Theophilus managed the Church's affairs so ably that when the bishop died, the whole populace acclaimed him as worthy of the episcopate. He was content to remain as administrator, however, and preferred to have someone else ordained as bishop. But in time this new bishop deprived Theophilus, all unwilling, of his office, and Theophilus fell into such despair that, in order to regain his honorable post, he sought the advice of a Jewish sorcerer. The sorcerer summoned the devil, who came immediately. Thereupon Theophilus, at the demon's command, renounced Christ and his mother, repudiated the Christian faith, wrote a statement of his renunciation and repudiation in his own blood, signed and sealed the script, and gave it to the demon, thus pledging himself to his service. The next day, by the devil's manipulation, Theophilus was taken back into the bishop's good graces and reinstated in his dignities of office.

In time, however, the good man came to his senses and regretted what he had done, and, with all the devotion of his heart, had recourse to the glorious Virgin. At a certain moment Blessed Mary appeared to him, upbraided him for his impiety, ordered him to renounce the devil, and made him confess his faith in her and in Christ, the Son of God, and in the whole Christian doctrine. So she brought him back into her favor and her Son's, and, in token of the forgiveness granted him, appeared to him again and returned the scroll he had given to the devil, placing it on his breast as a sign that he need not fear he might still be in the demon's service, and that through her intervention he was a free man. Theophilus, having received this gift, was overcome with joy. He went before the bishop and the whole populace, and gave a full account of the above events. All were filled with admiration and gave praise to the glorious Virgin, and Theophilus, three days later, fell asleep in the peace of the Lord.

A man and his wife had an only daughter whom they gave in marriage to a young man, and, for love of their daughter, brought the son-in-law into their house along with his wife. The girl's mother, for love of her daughter, cared for the young man so kindly that the bride's love for her husband was no greater than the mother-in-law's for her son-in-law. That being the situation, evil-minded people began to say that the woman was not doing this for her daughter's sake but was trying to take her daughter's place in the young man's affections. This false rumor unsettled the woman's mind, and, fearing it would turn into a public scandal, she parleyed with two countrymen, promising to pay each of them twenty sols if they would secretly strangle the son-in-law.

One day, therefore, she hid the two in the cellar of her house, sent her husband out on some business or other, and dispatched her daughter on some other errand. Then she asked the young man to go to the cellar and bring up some wine, and he was strangled by the two malefactors. The mother-in-law laid him out in her daughter's bed and covered him up as if he were sleeping. The husband and the daughter came home and were seated at the dinner table, and the mother told her daughter to awaken her husband and call him to dinner. When the young wife found the dead body, she raised an outcry, the whole family fell to lamenting, and the murderess feigned to lament with the others. But in time she grieved over the crime she had committed and confessed the whole story to a priest. Sometime later a dispute arose between the woman and the priest, and he accused her of the murder of her son-in-law. When the young man's parents learned of this, they had her brought to justice, and the judge condemned her to die by fire. The woman, considering the fact that her end was near, had recourse to the mother of Christ, went to the Virgin's church, and prostrated herself in tears and prayer. In a short time she was forced to come out and was thrown into a blazing fire, and all saw her standing in the middle of the flames unhurt and unharmed. The dead man's kinsmen thought the fire was not big enough and fetched wood to throw on it, but, seeing that the woman was still unscathed, attacked her with lances and spears. The judge was stupefied at what was going on and checked their assaults, but, examining her carefully, he found no sign of the fire on the woman, or other mark except the wounds from the lances. Her own people then carried her back to her house and revived her with salves and baths. But it was not God's will that she should suffer suspicion and disgrace any longer, and after she had persevered for three days in praising the Virgin, God called her forth from this life.

---

132. Saints Cornelius and Cyprian

Cornelius is interpreted as one who understands circumcision. Pope Cornelius understood circumcision and, understanding it, lived cut off from all superfluous, though permitted, goods, and even from necessary ones. Or the name comes from cornu, horn, and leos, people, hence the horn, or fortitude, of the people. Cyprian comes from cyprus, which means mixture, and ana, above; or it comes from cyprus, meaning sadness or inheritance. Saint Cyprian had a supernal mixture of grace and virtue, sadness for sins, and an inheritance of heavenly joys.

Pope Cornelius, successor to Saint Fabian, was sent into exile with his clergy by Decius Caesar, and while in exile received letters of support and comfort from

Saint Cyprian, bishop of Carthage. In time he was brought back from exile and set before Decius. When he continued unshaken in the faith, the emperor had him beaten with leaded whips, and ordered him to be brought to the temple of Mars to offer sacrifice there, or to submit to the sentence of death. A soldier asked the pope, on his way to execution, to turn aside to the soldier's house and pray for his wife, who had lain paralyzed for five years. He prayed and the woman was cured, whereupon twenty soldiers, together with the woman and her husband, believed in the Lord. By command of Decius they were taken to the temple of Mars, but they spat upon the idol and were martyred with Saint Cornelius.

Cyprian, bishop of Carthage, was brought before the proconsul Patronus in that city. When nothing could make him abjure his faith, he was sent into exile, then recalled by Angliricus, the proconsul who had succeeded Patronus, and by him sentenced to death. When the sentence was pronounced, Cyprian gave thanks to God. He came to the place of execution and ordered his ministers to pay the headsman fifteen gold pieces. Then he was given a blindfold and with his own hands covered his eyes with the cloth, and so received the crown of martyrdom, about A.D. 256.

133. Saint Lambert

Lambert was noble by birth and more noble by the holiness of his life. From his earliest years he was instructed in letters. He was so beloved for his sanctity that he was considered worthy to succeed Theodard, who had been his teacher, as bishop of Maastricht. King Childeric had great affection for him and always treated him as the dearest of all the bishops. There were those who envied him, and their malice increased, though without reason, until they drove him out of his see and deprived him of the honors due him. In his place they installed Feramund as bishop. Lambert entered a monastery and lived a most meritorious life there for five years.

One night as he rose from prayer, he unwittingly made some noise on the pavement, and the abbot, hearing it, said: "Let whoever made that noise go immediately to the cross." Lambert, clad in a hair shirt, ran barefoot to the cross and stood motionless in the snow and ice. Then in the morning, when the monks were warming themselves after matins, the abbot noticed Lambert's absence. One of the brothers told him that the bishop was the one who had gone to the cross, so the abbot had him brought inside, and with all the monks begged his forgiveness. Not only did the man of God pardon them kindly; he preached sublimely to them on the virtue of patience.

Seven years later Feramund was expelled, and by order of Pepin Saint Lambert was brought back to his see, where he displayed his power by word and example, as before. Then two miscreants began to heap troubles on him, and friends of the pontiff killed them, as they deserved. At the same time Lambert took Pepin to task concerning a lewd woman he was keeping. A man named Dodo, brother of the woman and a blood relative of the two who were killed, was also a domestic in the king's palace. He gathered a corps of armed men and surrounded the bishop's house, meaning to avenge the death of his kinsmen on the saint himself. Lambert was at prayer when a servant came to tell him what was going on, and the bishop, trusting in God, snatched up a sword to drive the attackers away. But on second thought, judging that it was better to conquer by standing firm and dying than to stain his sacred hands with the blood of the impious, he threw the weapon aside, and admonished his attendants to confess their sins and suffer death patiently. The malefactors rushed upon Saint Lambert as he knelt in prayer, and killed him, about A.D. 620. When the murderers left, some of the bishop's people, who had escaped, secretly brought his body to the cathedral church by ship, and gave it burial while the whole city mourned.

---

134. Saint Adrian and His Companions

Adrian suffered martyrdom in the reign of the emperor Maximian. When Maximian was offering sacrifice to the idols in the city of Nicomedia, he issued an order that all the citizens should hunt out the Christians; whereupon, either for love of the promised money or for fear of punishment, neighbors informed on neighbors and relatives delivered their own kinsmen to the torture. Thus thirty-three Christians, captured by the pursuers, were brought before the king,[1] who said to them: "Have you not heard of the punishments we have decreed against Christians?" They answered: "Yes, we've heard, and we've laughed at the stupidity of your decree!" The king was angry at this, and ordered them to be whipped with raw thongs and to have their mouths beaten in with stones, after

---

[1] In this chapter and elsewhere, Jacobus sometimes wrote "king" for "emperor."

which each one's confession of faith was to be recorded, and all were to be imprisoned in chains.

Adrian, the commander of the guard, was impressed by their constancy and said to them: "I adjure you by your God, tell me what reward you expect for enduring these torments." The saints told him: "No eye has seen, nor ear heard, nor the heart of man conceived, what God has prepared for those who love him perfectly."[2] At this, Adrian jumped in among them and said: "Record me with these, because I too am a Christian!" The emperor heard this and, since Adrian refused to offer sacrifice, ordered him to be chained and imprisoned.

When Natalia, Adrian's wife, heard that her husband was in prison, she tore her garments, weeping and sobbing loudly. But when she learned that he was jailed for confessing the faith of Christ, she was filled with joy, ran to the prison, and began to kiss her husband's bonds and those of his companions. She too was a Christian, but on account of the persecution had made no public show of the fact. She said to her spouse: "Blessed are you, my lord Adrian, because you have found riches that were not left to you by your parents, riches which those who have much will not have at that time when there will no longer be borrowing and lending, when no one will liberate another—not a father his son nor a mother her daughter, nor a servant his master nor a friend his friend, nor riches their owner." She exhorted him to spurn all earthly glory, to pay no heed to friends or relatives, and always to fix his heart on the things of heaven. Adrian said to her: "Go home, my sister, and when the time for our passion comes, I will call for you, so that you may witness our end." So she commended her husband to the other saints, bidding them encourage him, and returned home.

A short time later Adrian, learning that the day of his passion was at hand, gave money to the guards and left the saints who were with him as pledges, then started for home to call his wife as he had promised, so that she might witness their martyrdom. Someone, however, saw Adrian outside the prison, and hurried ahead to break the news to Natalia, saying: "Adrian has been set free and is on his way here." Natalia did not believe what she heard, and said: "But who could have freed him of his chains? May it not happen to me that he be freed and separated from those saints!" Even as she spoke, one of her servants came and said: "See, my master has been released."

Natalia thought that Adrian had fled from martyrdom and wept most bitterly; and when she saw him, she rose quickly and shut the door against him, saying: "May he who has run away from God keep away from me! Let it not be my lot to speak to the man who with his own mouth has renounced his Lord!" And through the door she said: "O godless wretch, who forced you to undertake what you could not finish? Who separated you from the saints? Who misled you and made you give up the covenant of peace? Tell me, why did you run away before the fight began, even before you saw the opponent? How have you been wounded, when no arrow has yet been shot? And I . . . I was wondering that

---

[2] Cf. 1 Cor. 2:9.

someone from the godless people, the race of the impious, would be offered to God! Alas, alas! Unhappy, miserable woman that I am! What shall I do, I who am joined to this man from a heathen race? It has not been granted me that for the space of an hour I should be thought of as the wife of a martyr, but rather that I should be called the wife of a renegade. How brief was my exaltation! And now my shame will last forever!"

As Adrian listened to this, his joy was boundless. He was amazed that this young woman, a beauty and a noble, to whom he had been married for fourteen months, could speak as she was speaking. He heard her all the more gladly as her words made him desire martyrdom more ardently. But when he saw that her distress was getting out of control, he said: "My lady Natalia, open the door for me! I have not run away from martyrdom as you think. I came to call you, as I promised I would!" But she did not believe him and said: "See how this deceiver beguiles me, how this other Judas lies! Away from me, wretch! Or shall I kill myself? Will that satisfy you?"

She still did not open the door, and Adrian said: "Open to me quickly, because I must go, and you will see me no more, and you will grieve that you did not see me alive. I gave the holy martyrs as pledges for my return, and if the guards don't find me when they come for me, the saints will bear their own torments and mine too!" Natalia opened the door and they fell into each other's arms, then went together to the prison, where for seven days Natalia cleansed the saints' sores with fine linens.

On the appointed day the emperor ordered the prisoners to be brought before him. Because they were weakened by the punishments they had endured, they were carried in like animals. Adrian followed them with his hands manacled. Then he alone, now carrying his own rack, was presented to the caesar. Natalia stayed close to him and said: "See to it, my lord, that you don't stumble when you see the torments! You will suffer for a moment now, but immediately you will exult with the angels."

Adrian refused to offer sacrifice and was cruelly beaten, and Natalia ran joyfully to the saints who were in prison, saying: "See, my lord and master has begun his martyrdom!" When the emperor warned him not to revile his gods, Adrian answered: "If I am tortured because I revile beings who are not gods, how will you, who revile the true God, be tortured!" The emperor: "Seducers taught you to say these things!" Adrian: "Why do you call them seducers? They are teachers of the truth." Natalia ran to the others and reported her husband's answers to them.

Now the king had Adrian beaten by the four strongest men available, and Natalia speedily carried back all his tortures, questionings, and responses to the other martyrs who were still in confinement. Adrian was so severely scourged that his entrails spilled out, and he was again put in chains and remanded to jail. He was a young man twenty-eight years of age, delicate, handsome. When Natalia saw her husband lying there, wounded from head to foot, she put her hand under his head and said: "You are blessed, my lord, you who have been made worthy to be counted among the saints. You are blessed, light of my life, you who suffer for him who suffered for you. Go forth now, my sweet, to see his glory!"

The emperor learned that many women were ministering to the saints in prison, and gave orders that they could no longer get in to do so. Natalia cut off her hair and dressed as a man, and continued to be helpful to the imprisoned saints. Her example induced other women to do the same. She asked her husband to pray for her when he was in glory, that the Lord would keep her untouched and would soon call her out of this world. The emperor found out what the women were doing, and issued orders that an anvil be brought and that the martyrs have their legs broken on it and so die. Natalia feared that Adrian would be terrified by the others' suffering, and asked the executioners to begin with him. He therefore had his feet cut off and his legs broken, and Natalia asked him to allow a hand to be cut off as well, so that he would be on a par with the other saints, who had suffered more than he had. When this was done, Adrian breathed his last, and the others stretched out their feet, died, and migrated to the Lord.

The emperor ordered that the bodies of the martyrs be burned, but Natalia hid Adrian's hand in her bosom. When the saints' bodies were cast into the fire, Natalia wanted to throw herself in with them, but a very heavy rainstorm broke out and extinguished the flames, leaving the holy bodies unscathed. The Christians, after taking counsel among themselves, had the bodies transferred to Constantinople, until, when peace was restored to the Church, they were brought back with honor. The martyrs suffered about A.D. 280.

Natalia continued to dwell in her house and kept Adrian's hand with her, having it always at the head of her bed for her life's consolation. Some while later the tribune, seeing Natalia so beautiful, so rich, and so noble, obtained the emperor's permission and sent ladies to her to seek her consent to marry him. "Who could possibly outdo me in honor," she said, "when I become the wife of so great a man? But I beg that I may be given a delay of three days to prepare myself." She said this in order to flee from the city, since she had prayed God to keep her untouched. Then suddenly she fell asleep, and one of the martyrs appeared to her, comforted her kindly, and bade her go to the place where the bodies of the martyrs had been kept.

She woke up and, taking with her nothing but Adrian's hand, boarded ship with many Christians. The tribune was informed of this and, with a company of soldiers, pursued her by ship, until a contrary wind rose and forced them to turn about, many of them being washed overboard. Then at midnight the devil, in the guise of a pilot in a phantom vessel, appeared to those who were with Natalia. Imitating a pilot's manner, he asked them: "Where do you come from and where are you headed?" They replied: "We come from Nicomedia and are headed for Constantinople." The answer came: "You are on the wrong bearing.

Bear left and correct your heading!" He was trying to make them run aground and perish; but as they were about to trim sail, Adrian, sitting in a small skiff, suddenly appeared to them and told them to stay on course, adding that it was the evil spirit who had spoken to them. He then set out ahead of them to show them the right course. When Natalia saw Adrian leading the way, her joy knew no bounds.

So they sailed into Constantinople before dawn. Natalia entered the house where the martyrs' bodies were preserved and placed Adrian's hand beside his body. Then, having said a prayer, she went to sleep. Adrian appeared to her and bade her come with him into eternal rest. She wakened and told her attendants about the dream, then bade them farewell and breathed her last. The faithful took her body and placed it with the remains of the martyrs.

---

135. Saints Gorgonius and Dorotheus

Gorgonius and Dorotheus held high office in Diocletian's palace at Nicomedia, but gave up their rank in order to follow their King more freely and made it clear to all that they were Christians. The emperor was very displeased by this news. He found it hard to accept the loss of men of their quality, raised in the palace as they had been, and distinguished for their nobility of blood and of behavior. But neither threats nor blandishments could change their commitment to the faith, so they were stretched on the rack, their flesh was torn with whips and iron hooks, and vinegar and salt were poured on their open wounds. They bore all this without flinching. Next they were roasted on grates but seemed to lie there as if on a bed of flowers, feeling no hurt. Finally, at the emperor's command, they were hanged by the neck, and their bodies exposed to wolves and dogs; but they remained untouched and were buried by the faithful. They suffered about A.D. 280.

Many years later the body of Saint Gorgonius was translated to Rome. In the year A.D. 766, the bishop of Metz, a nephew of King Pepin, transferred the body to France and entombed it in the monastery at Gorze.

136. Saints Protus and Hyacinthus

Protus and Hyacinthus were personal slaves to Eugenia and were her companions in the study of philosophy. She was the daughter of Philip, who belonged to the highest Roman nobility. He was appointed by the Senate to be prefect of Alexandria, and took with him his wife Claudia, his sons Avitus and Sergius, and his daughter Eugenia. In time Eugenia knew all there was to know in the liberal arts and letters, and Protus and Hyancinthus, who had studied with her, were proficient in all branches of knowledge.

When Eugenia was fifteen years old, Aquilinus, the son of the consul Aquilinus, asked for her hand in marriage. Her answer was: "A husband is to be chosen not for his ancestry but for his morals." Then Saint Paul's writings came into her hands, and she gradually became Christian at heart. At that time Christians were allowed to live on the outskirts of Alexandria. One day Eugenia was on her way to the family villa for a spell of recreation, when, in passing, she heard Christians chanting:

> Omnes Dii gentium daemonia,
> Dominus autem caelos fecit.[1]

She said to her servants Protus and Hyacinthus, who had studied with her: "We worked our way with meticulous attention through the philosophers' syllogisms, Aristotle's arguments and Plato's ideas, the precepts of Socrates, and, to be brief, whatever the poets sang, whatever the orators or the philosophers thought; but all that is wiped out by this one sentence. A usurped authority has used words to make me your mistress, but the truth makes me your sister. Let us then be brothers, and follow Christ!"

The proposal was deemed acceptable, and Eugenia put on men's clothing and went to a monastery. Helenus, a man of God, was the head of this monastery, and Helenus would not allow a woman to come near him. Once when he was arguing with a heretic and the argument grew too heated for his liking, he had a huge fire built and lighted, the purpose being to prove that the one of them who passed through the fire without being burned had the true faith. Helenus went first into the fire and emerged unharmed, but the heretic refused to run the risk and was driven out by all. When Eugenia approached Helenus and said she was a man, he replied: "Rightly do you call yourself a man, because you act like a man though you are a woman." Her true sex was revealed to him by God.

---

[1] All the gods of the Gentiles are demons, / but the Lord made the heavens.

Eugenia therefore, together with Protus and Hyacinthus, received the monastic habit from Helenus, and thenceforth was called Brother Eugene.

When Eugenia's father and mother saw that her carriage had come home empty, they were grief-stricken and had a search made for their daughter, but she could not be found. They asked soothsayers what had happened to her, and their answer was that the gods had taken her up among the stars. The father therefore had a statue made of her and ordered everyone to worship it. Meanwhile she and her two companions persevered in the fear of God, and when Helenus died, Brother Eugene was elected to replace him.

At this time there was in Alexandria a rich and noble woman named Melancia. Brother Eugene had cured her of the quartan fever by anointing her with oil in the name of Jesus Christ. In return for this favor Melancia sent many gifts, which were not accepted. The lady took for granted that Brother Eugene was a man and visited him often, and, seeing how elegantly youthful and personally attractive he was, fell heatedly in love with him. Losing no time, she devised a plan whereby she could get him to lie with her. She pretended to be ill and sent word to him, asking that he deign to come and pay her a visit. He went, and she let him know how ardently she loved him and wanted him, begged him to come to her, then grasped him and kissed him, urging him to join her in bed. Brother Eugene was horrified and said: "You are well called Melancia, for the name says that you are filled with black perfidy and are the dark daughter of darkness, friend of the devil, leader of pollution, fuel of lust, sister of perpetual torment, and daughter of eternal death!"

Melancia, thwarted and afraid that word of her crime might get abroad, decided to be the first to accuse and cried out that Eugene was trying to violate her. Then she went to Philip the prefect and issued a complaint, saying: "A certain treacherous young man, a Christian, came in under pretext of remedying my illness, but set upon me shamelessly and was about to ravish me, and would have satisfied his lust upon me had not one maid, who was in the room, come to my rescue." The prefect, incensed at what he heard, sent a troop to bring in Eugene and the other servants of Christ bound in chains, and set a date on which all of them were to be thrown to the wild beasts in the arena. He summoned them before him and said to Eugene: "Tell us, you basest of criminals, is that what your Christ taught you—to do the works of corruption, and madly and shamelessly to assault our women?" Eugenia, lowering her head so as not to be recognized, answered: "Our Lord taught chastity, and to those who guarded their integrity he promised eternal life. We can show that this Melancia is a false witness, but it is better that we suffer than that she, once convicted, be punished and we lose the reward of our patience. In any case, have the maid who, she says, witnessed the crime, come in and testify, so that from her mouth her mistress's lies may be refuted."

The maid was brought in, but, being instructed by Melancia, she stoutly maintained that the man had tried to take his pleasure with her mistress; and all the other servants, likewise corrupted, told the same story. At this, Eugenia said: "The time for silence is past, it is now time to speak. I will not allow this wanton woman to impute crime to the servants of Christ and boast of her deception. To make sure that truth shall prevail over mendacity and wisdom conquer malice, I will show the truth, not out of personal pride but for the glory of God!" So saying, she opened her robe from the top to the waist, and was seen to be a woman. She said to the prefect: "You are my father, Claudia my mother, the two who are sitting with you, Avitus and Sergius, are my brothers, I am your daughter Eugenia, and these two are Protus and Hyacinthus."

When her father heard this and gradually recognized his daughter, he and her mother rushed to embrace her, and many tears were shed. They clothed Eugenia in cloth of gold and raised her on high, and fire came down from heaven and consumed Melancia and her coconspirators. Thus Eugenia converted her father, mother, brothers, and the whole household to the faith of Christ. Her father was dismissed from the prefecture but was ordained bishop by the Christians, and, persevering in faith and prayer, was put to death by the pagans.

Claudia returned to Rome with her sons and Eugenia, and they converted many to Christ. By order of the emperor, Eugenia was bound to a great stone and cast into the Tiber, but the stone broke loose and she walked unharmed over the waves. Then she was thrown into a roaring furnace, but the fire went out and she came forth refreshed. She was shut up in a dark jail, but a splendid light shone around her. After she had been there for ten days without food, the Savior appeared to her, held out a shining white loaf, and said: "Take food from my hand! I am your Savior, whom you have loved with your whole heart. On the day when I came down upon earth, I myself will take you up." On the day of the Lord's birth, therefore, a headsman was sent and cut off her head. Later she appeared to her mother and foretold that Claudia would follow her on the Sunday. Sunday came, and Claudia, rapt in prayer breathed her last. Protus and Hyacinthus, when they were dragged to the temple, shattered the idol with a prayer and, when they refused to sacrifice, achieved their martyrdom by being beheaded. They suffered under Valerian and Gallus, about A.D. 256.

137. The Exaltation of the Holy Cross

This feast is called the Exaltation of the Holy Cross because on this day the faith and the holy cross were raised to the heights.

It should be noted that before Christ's passion the wood of the cross was a cheap wood, because crosses used for crucifixions were made of cheap wood. It was an unfruitful wood, because no matter how many such trees were planted on the mount of Calvary, the wood gave no fruit. It was an ignoble wood, because it was used for the execution of criminals; a wood of darkness, because it was dark and without any beauty; a wood of death, because on it men were put to death; a malodorous wood, because it was planted among cadavers.

After Christ's passion, however, this wood was exalted in many ways. Its cheapness passed into preciousness, so Saint Andrew the apostle exlaimed: "Hail, precious cross!" Its unfruitfulness gave way to fertility, as in the Song of Solomon (7:8): "I will go up into the palm tree, and will take hold of the fruit thereof." What had been ignoble became sublime, as Augustine says: "The cross, which was the gibbet of criminals, has made its way to the foreheads of emperors." Its darkness turned to light, as Chrysostom says: "Christ's cross and his scars will, on the Day of Judgment, shine more brightly than the sun's rays." Its death passed into eternal life, and we sing:

Ut unde mors oriebatur, inde vita resurgeret.[1]

Its stench became an odor of sweetness: "While the king was on his couch, my nard, i.e., the holy cross, gave forth its fragrance."[2]

The feast of the Exaltation of the Holy Cross is solemnly celebrated by the Church because on that day the Christian faith itself was exalted to the heights. In the year A.D. 615, the Lord allowing his people to be scourged by the savagery of the pagans, Chosroës, king of the Persians, subjected all the earth's kingdoms to his rule. When he came to Jerusalem, however, he withdrew in fear from the sepulcher of the Lord but took away a piece of the holy cross that Saint Helena had left there. Chosroës wanted to be worshiped as God. He built a gold-and-silver tower studded with jewels, and placed in it images of the sun, the moon, and the stars. Bringing water to the top of the tower through hidden pipes, he poured down water as God pours rain, and in an underground cave he had horses pulling chariots around in a circle to shake the tower and produce a noise

---

[1] In order that whence death arose, life might rise again (from the preface for the mass of the holy cross).

[2] Song of Sol. 1:12 (RSV).

like thunder. Then he abdicated his kingdom in favor of his son and, profane as he was, settled himself in the tower as in a fane, put the Lord's cross at his side, and decreed that all should call him God. Indeed, we read in the book *On the Mitral Office* that he sat on a throne in the shrine as the Father, put the wood of the cross on his right in place of the Son, and a cock on his left in place of the Holy Spirit. He commanded that he be called the Father.

Emperor Heraclius now marshaled a large army and marched against the son of Chosroës to confront him at the Danube River. Finally the two princes agreed to meet in single combat on the bridge that crossed the river, the victor to take over the empire, both armies being spared any damage. It was also decreed that anyone who came to the assistance of his prince would have his legs and arms cut off and be thrown into the river.

Heraclius offered himself totally to God and commended himself to the holy cross with all the devotion of which he was capable. The two princes fought for a long time, and the Lord granted victory to Heraclius, who thus made the opposing army subject to his command, with the result that all Chosroës's people acknowledged the Christian faith and received holy baptism. Chosroës himself knew nothing of the outcome of the war, because he was hated by all and no one told him about it.

Heraclius journeyed to Chosroës and found him seated on his golden throne. He said to him: "Because you have honored the wood of the holy cross in your own way, you will be spared your life and your reign on condition that you accept the Christian faith and receive baptism, a few hostages being taken as guarantee. If, on the other hand, you consider this beneath you, I will kill you with my sword and cut off your head." Chosroës refused the offer and Heraclius promptly decapitated him; but, since he had been a king, he was given suitable burial. Heraclius found the king's son, a child ten years of age, with him. He had the boy baptized and with his own hands lifted him from the font, then left his father's kingdom to him. But he demolished the tower and allotted the silver to his army as spoils of war, reserving the gold and the jewels for the rebuilding of the churches the tyrant had destroyed.

Now Heraclius carried the sacred cross back to Jerusalem. He rode down the Mount of Olives, mounted on his royal palfrey and arrayed in imperial regalia, intending to enter the city by the gate through which Christ had passed on his way to crucifixion. But suddenly the stones of the gateway fell down and locked together, forming an unbroken wall. To the amazement of everyone, an angel of the Lord, carrying a cross in his hands, appeared above the wall and said: "When the King of heaven passed through this gate to suffer death, there was no royal pomp. He rode a lowly ass, to leave an example of humility to his worshipers." With those words the angel vanished.

The emperor shed tears, took off his boots and stripped down to his shirt, received the cross of the Lord into his hands, and humbly carried it toward the gate. The hardness of the stones felt the force of a command from heaven, and the gateway raised itself from the ground and opened wide to allow passage to those entering. And a most sweet odor, which, from the day and moment when the sacred cross was taken out of Chosroës's tower, had glided across the far reaches of land from Persia to Jerusalem, now made itself felt, and refreshed with the wonder of its perfume all who sensed it. Then the truly devout emperor burst forth in praise of the cross: "O cross, more splendid than all the heavenly bodies, renowned throughout the world, deserving of all men's love, holier than all things else! O cross, you were worthy to carry the ransom of the world! O sweet wood, sweet nails, sweet sword, sweet lance, you were the bearer of sweet burdens! Save the host gathered today in praise of you and signed with your banner!"

Thus it was that the precious cross was brought back to its place, and the miracles of old began again: dead men were raised to life, four paralytics were cured, ten lepers were made clean, fifteen blind people received their sight, demons were driven out, and great numbers were delivered of various infirmities. Heraclius also repaired the churches and endowed them richly. Then he went back to his own land.

Some chronicles, however, give a different version of these events. We read that when Chosroës had occupied all the neighboring kingdoms and had taken Jerusalem together with the patriarch Zachary and the wood of the cross, Heraclius wanted to make a treaty of peace with him, but he swore that he would not make peace with the Romans until they renounced the cross and adored the sun. Then Heraclius, fired with zeal, moved against him with an army, overran the Persians in a series of battles, and forced Chosroës to retreat as far as Ctesiphon. Later Chosroës fell ill with dysentery and wanted to confer the crown on his son Medasas. When his eldest son, Syrois, learned of this, he made a pact with Heraclius, then pursued his father with nobles and put him in chains. He fed the old man with the bread of afflictions and the water of distress, and in the end had him put to death with arrows. Later he dispatched all the prisoners, together with the patriarch and the wood of the cross, to Heraclius, and Heraclius took the precious wood to Jerusalem and eventually to Constantinople. So we read in many chronicles.

The pagan Sybil, as we learn from the *Tripartite History*, had this to say about this same wood of the cross: "O thrice blessed wood, upon which God was stretched!" Perhaps this was said because of the life of nature, grace, and glory that comes from the cross.

In Constantinople a Jew went into the church of Saint Sophia and there looked at an image of Christ. Seeing that there was no one about, the Jew drew his sword and struck the image in the throat. Blood poured out instantly and spattered the Jew's face and head. Terrified, he seized the image, threw it down a well, and fled. A Christian met him and asked: "Where are you coming from, Jew? You've killed a man!" "Not true!" said the Jew. But the man said again: "Of course you've committed a murder and that's why you're spattered with blood!" The Jew: "Truly the God of the Christians is great, and everything confirms faith in him. I have not stabbed a man but an image of Christ, and straightaway the blood gushed out from his throat!" The Jew then led the man to the well and they retrieved the sacred image, and it is said that the wound in Christ's throat can be seen to this day. The Jew became a Christian without delay.

In the city of Berith in Syria, a Christian who occupied a house on an annual rent had hung a picture of the crucified Christ on the wall facing his bed and there regularly said his prayers. At the end of the year, however, he moved to a different house and forgot to take the picture with him. A Jew rented the first house and invited one of his fellow tribesmen to dinner on a certain day. In the course of the festivities the guest looked around the house and came upon the picture hanging on the bedroom wall. Trembling with anger he threatened his host, demanding to know why he dared to keep an image of Jesus Christ the Nazarene. The host, who had not even noticed the picture, declared with all the oaths he could muster that he knew absolutely nothing about the image the guest was talking about. The guest, pretending to be satisfied with the answer, took his leave and went to the head man of his tribe, to make charges against the other Jew regarding what he had seen.

The Jews now gathered and went to the house, saw the picture and belabored the householder with insults, manhandled him and expelled him half dead from the synagogue. Then they trampled the picture and renewed upon it all the indignities of the Lord's passion. When they thrust a lance into the image of his body, a copious flow of blood and water issued from it and filled a vase that they held under it. They were amazed and took the blood to their synagogues, and all the sick who were anointed with it were cured immediately. Then the Jews gave the bishop of the city a full account of all that had happened, and every one of them accepted the faith of Christ and holy baptism.

The bishop kept the blood in phials of crystal and glass. He also sent for the Christian to whom the picture belonged, and asked him who had painted so beautiful an image. He said: "Nicodemus painted it and at his death bequeathed it to Gamaliel; Gamaliel left it to Zacheus, Zacheus to James, and James to Simon. So it remained in Jerusalem till the fall of the city. Then the faithful took it into Agrippa's kingdom. From there it was brought into my country by my ancestors and came to me by right of inheritance." This happened in A.D. 750. Then all the Jews consecrated their synagogues, turning them into churches. This is the origin of the custom of consecrating churches: previously only the altars were consecrated.

On account of the above miracle the Church ordained that a commemoration of the Lord's passion be made on 27 November, or, as we read elsewhere, on 9 November. For the same reason a church was consecrated in Rome in honor of the Savior, and there a phial of that blood is preserved and a solemn feast observed.

There have been many evidences of the great power of the cross, even among those not of the faith. Gregory, in the third book of his *Dialogues*, records the experience of Andrew, bishop of the city of Fondi. He had permitted a nun to live in his house, and the ancient enemy began to impress the nun's image so vividly on the bishop's mind that it was as if he were seeing her in person. So, lying in bed, he thought of doing things that should not even be spoken of. Then one day a Jew came to Rome, and when, toward nightfall, he had not found a place to stay, he took shelter in the temple of Apollo. He feared the sacrilegious nature of the place and, though he had no faith in the cross, took care to protect himself with the sign of the cross. In the middle of the night he woke up and saw a horde of evil spirits going forward to do obeisance to a potentate, who walked in front of the rest and sat down in their midst. This potentate then began to hear the case of each of the spirits and to discuss their actions, in order to find out how much evil each one had done.

For the sake of brevity Gregory does not describe the way the discussion was conducted, but it can be deduced from a moral tale that we read in the *Lives of the Fathers*. A man had gone into a temple of the idols, and saw Satan seated and his troops standing around him. Then one of the wicked spirits came forward and adored him. "Where have you come from?" Satan asked. "I was in a certain province," the spirit replied, "and there stirred up many wars, caused much disturbance and shedding of blood; and I have come to report to you." Satan: "How much time did this take you?" The spirit: "Thirty days." Satan: "Why so long?" And he ordered his assistants to beat him with scourges as hard as they could. A second demon came up, adored Satan, and said: "My lord, I have been at sea, rousing up violent storms, sinking many ships, killing a lot of people." Satan: "How long did this take you?" The answer: "Twenty days." Satan: "So much time to do so little?" And he ordered a like beating. A third came and said: "I was in a city and incited fights at some wedding feasts, and much blood was spilled, and once I killed the bridegroom himself; and I came to report to you." Satan: "How long did it take you to do that?" "Ten days!" Satan: "Couldn't you wreak more havoc than that in ten days?" And whipping was ordered. Now the fourth came forward and said: "I stayed in the desert for forty years, devoted all my efforts to one monk, and at long last I have got him to commit one sin of the flesh!" Satan rose from his throne, kissed the spirit, took his crown off his own head and placed it on the other's, had him sit beside him, and said: "You have shown skill and courage, and have accomplished more than the others!" That, or something like it, is how the aforesaid discussion went, though Gregory passed over the details.

To return to Bishop Andrew . . . When each of the spirits in the temple of Apollo had reported what he had done, one more leapt into the middle and described the sort of carnal temptation he had aroused in Andrew's mind regarding that nun, adding that the day before, at the hour of vespers, he had got the bishop to go so far as to give the woman a friendly pat on the back. The head spirit exhorted him to finish what he had started, and so to win the palm among all the others, for bringing about the ruin of a bishop.

Satan also ordered his minions to find out who the man was who had had the presumption to sleep in Apollo's temple. By this time the Jew was all atremble, but when the spirits who were sent to seek him out saw that he was signed with the mystery of the cross, they cried out in terror: "He is an empty vessel, indeed, but it's sealed!" At this outcry the horde of malign spirits disappeared. The Jew went in haste to the bishop and recounted the incident in full detail. The bishop groaned with remorse, put all the women out of his house, and baptized the Jew.

Gregory also tells us in the *Dialogues* that a certain nun went into the garden, saw a fine lettuce, and was so hungry for it that, forgetting to bless it with the sign of the cross, she bit into it avidly. She was immediately seized by the devil and fell down. However, when blessed Equitius came to her, the devil cried out: "What have I done? I was sitting on the lettuce and she came and bit me!" Equitius ordered him out, and the spirit made his exit forthwith.

In the eleventh book of the *Ecclesiastical History* we read that the pagans had painted the arms of Serapis on house walls in Alexandria. Emperor Theodosius ordered the emblems to be obliterated and signs of the cross to be painted instead. When they saw this, the Gentiles and the priests of the idols asked for baptism, saying: "A tradition handed down by the ancients says that the gods they worshiped would stand until appeared the sign in which is life." And among the characters of their writing, one, which they called sacred and which, they said, stood for eternal life, had the form of a cross.

---

138. Saint John Chrysostom

John, surnamed Chrysostom, the Golden-mouthed, a native of Antioch, was the son of Secundus and Anthusa, both of whom were of noble descent. The *Tripartite History* gives a full account of his life, his ancestry, his character, and the persecutions he suffered.

John early engaged in the study of philosophy but later gave that up to devote himself entirely to the sacred writings. He was ordained a priest and was considered too severe because of his zeal for chastity. He was blunt rather than gentle, and, because of his concern for doing the right thing at the moment, was incapable of looking forward prudently to the consequences of his actions. Those who did not know him well found him arrogant in conversation, but he was an excellent teacher, remarkable in his ability to expound and clarify, and peerless as an upholder of strict morality.

In the reign of Arcadius and Honorius, caesars, and the pontificate of Damasus in the see of Rome, John was ordained bishop of Constantinople. By his determination to reform the life of the clergy all at once, he aroused their hatred: they shunned him as a madman and maligned him for all to hear. He never invited guests to dine with him, nor did he wish to be invited by others, so the word was that he acted this way because his table manners were atrocious. Or, said others, he invited no one to share his meals because he permitted himself only the most exquisite and expensive foods. The truth was that his strict abstinence often caused him severe pains in head and stomach, and so he avoided festive banquets.

The people loved him for the sermons he gave in church, and they paid no attention to the things his rivals said about him. Hostility toward him grew, however, when he began to direct his criticism to persons in high places, and one episode brought matters to a head. Eutropius, the emperor's provost, who held the rank of consul, wanted to avenge himself on some persons who had fled to churches for sanctuary. He therefore had the emperor make a law abolishing such refuge and providing that those who had already availed themselves of it could be taken out of the churches. But not long afterwards Eutropius himself fell into disfavor with the emperor and fled to a church for sanctuary. Bishop John, hearing of this, came and found him hiding under an altar, whereupon he made a speech denouncing Eutropius and addressed his harsh reproaches to Eutropius himself. John's failure to take pity on the unfortunate man, and the fact that he continued to upbraid him, turned many against the bishop, while the emperor seized Eutropius and had him beheaded. For a variety of reasons John criticized and reprehended many men immoderately, and the number of his enemies increased.

Theophilus, bishop of Alexandria, was anxious to depose John and wanted to put a priest named Isidore into his place, so he was looking for grounds to justify the bishop's deposition. The people, however, defended John and eagerly received the nourishment of his teaching. John continued to compel the priests to fashion their lives on Church laws, saying that those who disdained to live by priestly standards should not enjoy the honor of priesthood. He not only governed the city of Constantinople with a strong hand, but strove to put order in several adjacent provinces by imposing appropriate laws backed by imperial authority. When he learned that in Phoenicia sacrifices were still being offered to demons, he sent clerics and monks there and saw to it that all the heathen temples were destroyed.

At that time there was a certain Gaimas, by race a Celt, by character a barbarian. He was carried away by his tyrannical ambition and perverted by the Arian heresy, yet was made the commandant of the army. Gaimas asked the emperor to give him and his followers one church inside the city. The emperor was willing and, in order to put a rein on the man's tyranny, asked John to grant him one church. But John, strong in virtue and aflame with zeal, said: "O Emperor, do not allow this, or give what is holy to dogs, and do not be afraid of this barbarian! Order both of us to be called, and in private hear what we say to each other. I will put a bit on his tongue that will stop him from making such presumptuous demands!"

The emperor was happy to hear this and summoned the two for the next day. When Gaimas requested one church for himself, John said: "The house of God is open to you everywhere, and no one is keeping you from praying!" Gaimas: "I belong to another sect, and I have the right to demand a temple for myself and my people. I have taken on many labors for the Roman state, therefore my petition should not be spurned!" John: "You have received many rewards—rewards that exceeded your deserts. You have been made commandant of the army, and more than that you wear the toga of a consul. You ought to keep in mind what you were before and how you are now regarded, how poor you were in the past and how rich you are now, what clothes you used to wear and how splendidly you are now attired. Therefore, since minimal labors have brought you maximum return, do not be ungrateful to the emperor who honors you!" That was enough to close Gaimas's mouth and force him to keep silent.

John continued to govern the city of Constantinople with a firm hand, but Gaimas, now coveted the empire itself; and since he could accomplish nothing by day, he sent his barbarians by night to burn down the emperor's palace. Then John's way of protecting the city became apparent. A great crowd of armed angels in bodily shapes appeared confronting the barbarians, who promptly took to their heels. When they reported this to Gaimas, he could not understand it, since he knew that his regular troops were garrisoned in other cities. He sent the barbarians out the following night, and they were again put to flight by the vision of angels. Finally Gaimas himself went out, saw the miracle, and fled, thinking that these troops hid by day and guarded the city by night. He went to Thrace, assembled a large army, and pillaged the land; the people were terrified by the ferocity of the barbarians. The emperor therefore imposed upon Saint John the burden of going as his ambassador to Gaimas, and John, putting old grudges out of his mind, set out with alacrity. Gaimas was touched by the saint's trustfulness and, forgetting his resentments, went out a great distance to meet him. He took John's hand and held it over his own eyes in a gesture of humility, and bade his sons embrace the bishop's sacred knees. Such indeed was the power of John's virtue: he could reduce even the most terrible men to humility and fear.

At that time a dispute arose about whether or not God had a body. Many were the disagreements and wordy battles over this question, some holding this view, others, that. Mostly it was the crowds of simple monks who were deceived and said that God was set apart by a bodily form. Theophilus, bishop of

Alexandria, preferred the contrary view. He argued against those in the church who asserted that God had a human form, and preached that God is incorporeal. The Egyptian monks learned of this, left their abodes, and came to Alexandria, where they stirred up sedition against Theophilus, even attempting to put him to death. Their actions frightened Theophilus, and he said to them: "I look at you and see the face of God!" They said: "If you really mean that God's face is like ours, anathematize the books of Origen, which contradict our belief. If you do not do this, you will be in rebellion against the emperors and God himself, and we will see to it that you are disgraced." "Don't do anything violent," said Theophilus, "and I will do what pleases you." Thus he diverted the monks' attack. Note again that the better-trained and perfect monks were not deceived, but the simple monks, excited by the ardor of their faith, rose against their brothers who held the opposite opinion, and killed many of them.

While that was going on in Egypt, John, in Constantinople, flourished in his teaching and was universally admired. Nevertheless the Arians multiplied in numbers and had a church outside the city. On Saturdays and Sundays they came in and sang hymns and antiphons all night in the streets, and at dawn, still singing, they marched through the middle of the city and out through the gates to their own church. They continued to do this in mockery of the orthodox, frequently singing: "Where are those who say that three are one in power?"

John feared that simple folk might be drawn into heresy by these songs, and gave orders that the true believers should gather and sing hymns at night, in order to drown out the singing of the others and to strengthen the faithful in their faith. He also had silvered crosses made and carried with silvered candles. The Arians, fired with zeal and envy, went so far as to commit murder. One night Brison, one of the empress's eunuchs, whom John had assigned to lead the hymn singing, was struck with a stone, but, more than that, a number of people of either party lost their lives. The emperor, disturbed by this disorder, prohibited the Arians from singing hymns in public.

At that time Severian, bishop of Gabala, a man honored by his peers and a favorite of the emperor and the empress, came to Constantinople and was warmly welcomed by John; and when John traveled to Asia, he left his church in Severian's care. But Severian was unfaithful to his trust and curried favor with the people. Serapion, one of John's clergy, took care to notify John about this. Then, once when Severian was passing in front of him, Serapion did not rise, and Severian, indignant, shouted: "If this fellow Serapion does not die, Christ was not born in human nature!" When John heard of this, he came back to Constantinople and ejected Severian from the city as a blasphemer. The empress was gravely displeased. She had John summoned and asked him to make peace with Severian. He refused to do so until she brought her infant son Theodosius and laid him on the bishop's knees, begging him and solemnly appealing to him to pardon Severian.

About that same time Theophilus, bishop of Alexandria, unjustly banished Dioscorus, a saintly man, and Isidore, who previously had been his friend. The two came to Constantinople and recited the facts to the emperor and to John. John held the men in high regard but was unwilling to take their side until he knew more about the case. A false rumor reached Theophilus, however, to the effect that John was in league with Dioscorus and Isidore and was supporting their cause. This aroused Theophilus's anger, and he marshaled all his forces, not only to avenge himself on the two men but to depose John from his see. Concealing his real intention, he sent word to the bishop of each city, saying that he wished to condemn the works of Origen. Making a pretense of friendship, he cozened Epiphanius, the holy and esteemed bishop of Cyprus, and asked him to condemn Origen's books as he himself was doing. Epiphanius, whose sanctity kept him from suspecting the other's craftiness, summoned his bishops to Cyprus and forbade the reading of Origen. Then he wrote to John, urging him to stop reading those books and to confirm what had been ordered. John, however, paid little attention to this. He went on teaching the doctrine of the Church, at which he excelled, and felt no concern about the plots that were being woven around him.

Finally Theophilus let his long-concealed hatred of John be known, and made it clear that he wanted John deposed. The bishop's enemies, and many clergymen and palace officials, thought the time opportune and did their best to have a council convoked at Constantinople against John. Then Epiphanius came to Constantinople, bringing with him the condemnation of Origen's works. Out of regard for Theophilus he declined John's offer of hospitality. Some bishops, owing to their reverence for Epiphanius, subscribed to the condemnation of Origen, but many more refused to do so. Among the latter was Theotinus, bishop of Sichia, a man renowned for the rectitude of his life, who responded to Epiphanius as follows: "Neither will I do injury to him who long since went to his rest, nor do I presume to risk being guilty of blasphemy by condemning works that our predecessors did not see fit to reject, and in which I also find no wrong doctrine. Those who heap insults on these works do not know themselves. Athanasius, defender of the Council of Nicaea against the Arians, appealed to this man as a witness of his own faith. He put Origen's books on a level with his own, and said: 'Origen, that admirable, tireless man, gives us this testimony to the Son of God, asserting that he is coeternal with the Father.'"

John had not taken it amiss when Epiphanius, acting outside the rules, performed an ordination[1] in his church, but asked him nevertheless to stay with him among the bishops. Epiphanius answered that he would neither stay with him nor pray with him unless he, John, dismissed Dioscorus and subscribed to the

---

[1] Or "issued an ordinance"; *facere ordinationem* could mean either one, both here and below. It is also not clear whether *in sua ecclesia* refers to Epiphanius's church or to John's.

condemnation of Origen's books. John refused to comply, and Epiphanius was turned against him by the saint's enemies. Epiphanius condemned Origen's works and pronounced a judgment against Dioscorus, and began to defame John as their defender. John sent the following message to him: "You have done many things contrary to the rules, O Epiphanius! First you performed an ordination in a church that belongs under my jurisdiction; second, on your own authority you have celebrated the sacred mysteries; again, when I invited you, you made excuses; and finally, you trust overmuch in yourself. Therefore take care lest there be an uprising among the people and the danger of it fall upon you!"

Having received this message, Epiphanius left the city, but before he set out for Cyprus, he sent word to John: "I hope you will not die a bishop." To this John responded: "I hope you never reach your homeland." Both hopes were realized: Epiphanius died on his way home, and John in time was deposed from his see and finished his life in exile.

At the tomb of this very holy man Epiphanius, demons were driven out of the possessed. He was a man of wondrous liberality toward the poor. Once he gave away all the church's money and nothing was left for himself. Then a stranger came along, offered the saint a bag full of money and went his way, and no one knew where he came from nor where he went. Another time a couple of poor men decided to trick Epiphanius into giving them some money. One of them lay stretched out on the ground, and the other stood over him and wept, as if he were dead, and complained that he had no money to pay for his friend's burial. Epiphanius came by, prayed that the dead man might rest in peace, and supplied the other with funds for the burial. Then he consoled the mourner and went his way. The man shook his companion and said: "Get up, get up! Today let us feast on the fruit of our labors!" He shook him again and again, and saw that he was dead, so he ran after Epiphanius and told him what had happened, also begging him to revive his friend. Epiphanius spoke words of consolation to the man, but did not raise his friend to life, lest it should seem too easy to delude God's ministers.

After Epiphanius took his leave, John learned that it was Eudoxia, the empress, who had turned Epiphanius against him. Outspoken as usual, the bishop preached a sermon to his flock, in which he inveighed against all women in very rude terms. Everybody took it that the diatribe was aimed at Eudoxia. The empress heard about it and complained to Arcadius, saying that the indignities aimed at his wife were sure to recoil on him. The emperor took umbrage at this and ordered that a synod be called to act against John. Theophilus therefore quickly convoked the bishops, and all John's enemies flocked together, calling him haughty and arrogant. The bishops then meeting in Constantinople were no longer concerned with Origen's writings, but were open in their opposition to John and sent for him to appear before them. John considered them enemies to be avoided and proclaimed that a universal synod must be called. The other bishops cited him four times more, but he still stayed clear of them and demanded a synod. They therefore condemned him, on no other ground than that he had not obeyed their summons.

The people of the city learned what was happening and were on the verge of rioting in protest. Meanwhile they would not allow their bishop to be taken out of the church, and demanded that the case be referred to a larger council. The emperor, however, gave orders that John was to be brought out and deported into exile, and he, fearing an outbreak of sedition, gave himself up to be exiled before the people knew what he was doing. When the news did get out, there was a wave of popular protest so serious that even many of his enemies were moved to be sorry for him, and said that he was a victim of calumny, whereas a short time before they had longed to see him deposed.

Now Severian, of whom mention has been made above, preached a sermon in church, in which he spoke ill of John, saying that even if he had committed no other crime, his pride could be a sufficient reason to depose him. This intensified popular opposition to the emperor and the bishops, and Eudoxia felt bound to ask the emperor to recall John from exile. Then a great earthquake shook the city, and the common opinion was that this happened as a result of John's expulsion. So legates were sent to ask him to come back quickly, in order to help the endangered city by his prayers, and to calm popular unrest. Then others were sent, then still others, to persuade him to return. When despite his reluctance they brought him home, the whole populace went out to meet him with lanterns and torches. John refused, however, to occupy his episcopal throne, saying that this should be by synodal decree and that those who had condemned him should revoke their sentence. But the people were eager to see him once more on his throne and to hear the words of their teacher. The popular will prevailed, and he had to resume his seat and preach to the people.

For Theophilus it was time to get away quickly. Just as he reached Hierapolis, the bishop of that city died, and a saintly monk named Lamon was elected. Lamon hastily went into hiding, but Theophilus pressed him to accept the election. Lamon promised, saying: "Tomorrow, what pleases God will be fulfilled." Therefore they came to his cell the next day, insisting that he receive the episcopate. He said: "Let us first pray to the Lord." He prayed, and finished his prayer and his life at the same moment.

John meanwhile continued his preaching uninterruptedly. At that time a silver statue was set up in the square in front of the church of Saint Sophia in honor of Eudoxia Augusta, and the knights and nobles of the city engaged in public games there. This displeased John exceedingly, since he saw it as dishonoring the church. He therefore raised his voice in denunciation as fearlessly as ever. It might have been appropriate to plead with the princes to put an end to such exercises, but he did nothing of the kind. Rather, turning loose the full force of his eloquence, he lashed out at those who ordered the games. The empress again took this as a personal insult and renewed her efforts to have a synod called into session. John, hearing about this, launched into the most famous of his homilies, the one that begins: "Again Herodias is raging, again she is perturbed, again she yearns to receive the head of John in a dish." This added considerably to Eudoxia's indignation. There was also a man who tried to kill John, was seized by the people, and turned over to be judged; but the prefect, to save him from death, spirited him away. Another man, the servant of a certain priest, rushed upon the bishop in an effort to kill him. A bystander tried to restrain him, but the attacker struck this man down and two others as well, killing them. This drew a large and clamorous crowd, and the man dealt fatal blows to several more. In the midst of this turmoil the people kept John safe, standing guard around his house day and night.

Eudoxia now won her point. Bishops convened in Constantinople, and John's accusers began to malign him with dire intent. Christmas was at hand, and Arcadius sent word to John that unless he had been cleared of all the charges against him, he, the emperor, would not receive communion from him. The bishops, however, could find nothing against him, unless it was that he had presumed to sit in the episcopal chair without the decree of a council. Then Easter was drawing near, and the emperor informed him that he could not stay in the same church with John, since two councils had condemned him. John therefore stayed home and no longer went down to his church. Those who took John's part were called Johannites. Finally the emperor had John expelled from the city and taken into exile in a poor village in the Pontus region, at the edge of the Roman Empire, an area threatened by cruel barbarians.

But the merciful Lord did not allow his faithful champion to linger long in such a place. Pope Innocent got word of the situation and was disturbed by it. He had it in mind to call a council and wrote to the clergy of Constantinople, forbidding them to ordain anyone as a successor to John. John, meanwhile, was worn out with long travel, suffered very painful headaches, and found the heat of the sun unbearable. So it was that at Cumana, on the fourteenth day of September, that holy soul was released from the body. At the hour of his death a tremendous hailstorm descended on Constantinople and its environs, and everyone said that this was an expression of God's anger over John's unjust condemnation. Eudoxia's sudden death bore out this thought: she died four days after the hailstorm.

After the death of this man who was teacher and doctor to both East and West, the bishops of the West would have no communion with those of the East until these latter placed the sacred name of John with those of his predecessors. Moreover, Theodosius, most Christian son of the aforementioned Arcadius, who had both the name and the piety of his grandfather Theodosius, had the sacred relics of this doctor of the Church transferred to the royal city in the month of January, on which occasion the faithful people met the cortege with lanterns and torches. Theodosius worshiped the saint's relics, praying earnestly for his parents Arcadius and Eudoxia, that the wrong they had unwittingly done might be forgiven them. Both parents had died in the meantime.

This Theodosius was a most benign ruler. He never sentenced to death those who did him any wrong, saying: "Would it were possible for me to recall the dead to life!" His court seemed like a monastery. He recited matins and lauds and read the sacred books. His wife, who wrote poems in the heroic meter, was named Eudoxia. He had a daughter also called Eudoxia. He gave his daughter in marriage to Valentinian, whom he made emperor.

All this information is extracted from the *Tripartite History.* John Chrysostom died about A.D. 400.

✳

---

139. Saint Euphemia

The name Euphemia comes from *eu*, which means good, and *femina*, woman. A good woman is helpful, righteous, and pleasing, because goodness implies these three qualities. Thus Saint Euphemia was helpful in her relations with others, righteous by her virtuous way of life, and pleasing to God by her contemplation of heavenly mysteries. Or *euphemia* has the same meaning as *euphonia*, sweet sound, and sweet sound is produced in three ways, namely, by the voice in singing, by the stroke of the hand, as in playing the harp, and by blowing, as in the organ. Saint Euphemia made sweet sound with the voice of her preaching, with the strokes of good works, and with the breath of her inward devotion.

In the reign of Diocletian, Euphemia, the daughter of a senator, saw how Christians were being tortured and mangled in various ways. She went straight to Priscus, the judge, publicly proclaimed her Christianity, and by the example of her constancy gave strength to resist even to men. While the judge was putting Christians to death one after the other, he ordered more of them to be present, so that by witnessing the tortures endured by those who refused, they might at least be terrified into offering sacrifice. He had the saints cruelly mutilated in Euphemia's presence, but their steadfastness only strengthened her own resolve, and she declared aloud that the judge was doing her an injustice. Priscus was delighted, thinking that she was willing to offer sacrifice, and asked her how he was wronging her. She answered: "I am of noble birth, and I want to know why you put these nobodies, these common folks, ahead of me, letting them reach Christ and attain the promised glory before I do!" The judge: "I thought you had come to your senses! I was glad you had remembered your rank and your sex!"

Priscus therefore consigned her to prison, and the next day, when the others were brought out in chains, she came out unfettered. Again she complained vehemently: why was she alone spared the chains, contrary to the emperor's law? So she was beaten and remanded to prison. The judge followed her and wished to take his pleasure of her, but she resisted manfully, and the power of God paralyzed his hand. Priscus thought he was under some kind of spell. He sent his head steward to promise her all sorts of things if she would do his will, but the man was unable to open the jail door with keys or to break into it with an ax, and finally was seized by a demon, screamed, tore his own flesh, and barely escaped with his life.

Then Euphemia was brought out and placed on a wheel, the spokes of which were filled with burning coals. The man who operated the wheel stood under it and had given a signal to those who turned it: when he made a certain sound they should all pull together, causing the fire to erupt and the spokes to tear the woman's body apart. But by God's will the tool by which he controlled the wheel fell from his hand, and the sound it made set the pullers to pulling, and the wheel crushed the man and left Euphemia standing on it unharmed. Grieving, the dead man's kinsmen lit a fire under the wheel, intending to burn Euphemia and the wheel together, but the wheel burned and an angel freed her from it and carried her to a high place, where she again stood unscathed.

Apellianus said to the judge: "The power these Christians have can be overcome only by iron. I advise you therefore to have her beheaded." They put ladders up and one man went up to take hold of her, but at once he was stricken with paralysis and was brought down half dead. Another man, this one named Sosthenes, climbed up but was converted as he reached her. He begged her to pardon him, drew his sword, and called down to the judge that he would kill himself rather than touch this woman, whom angels were defending.

Euphemia was finally taken down, and Priscus told his chancellor to round up all the ruffians he could find, and to let them enjoy her as long as they liked, until she died exhausted. But when the chancellor went in to her, he found her praying and many shining virgins around her, and she spoke to him and he was converted to the Christian faith. So the judge had her hung up by her hair, and when she persisted in her refusal, he ordered her to be put back in prison and deprived of food for seven days, at which time she would be crushed like an olive between great millstones. For seven days she was fed by an angel, and when on the seventh day she was placed between the stones, she prayed and the stones were reduced to the finest powder.

Priscus was shamefaced at being outdone by a mere girl and had her thrown into a pit where there were three wild beasts so ferocious that they would swallow any man. The beasts were gentled at once. They came running to the virgin and, by twining their tails together, made a sort of chair for her to sit on. Thus they threw the judge into utter confusion. Indeed he was almost dying with frustration when a headsman came in to avenge the offense given to his master. This he did by driving his sword into Euphemia's side, thus making her a martyr for Christ.

To reward the headsman for his service, the judge draped him in a silk garment and girded him with a gold belt, but as the man went out, he was snatched by a lion and devoured by the same. When a search was made for him, nothing was found except a few of his bones, the torn garment, and the gold belt. As for Priscus himself, he chewed on his own flesh and was found dead. Saint Euphemia was buried with honor in Chalcedon, and by her merits all the Jews and Gentiles in Chalcedon believed in Christ. She suffered about the year A.D. 280.

Ambrose, in his Preface, speaks of this virgin as follows: "The gentle, triumphant virgin Euphemia, retaining the miter of virginity, merited to be crowned with the crown of martyrdom. By her prayers the hostile enemy was defeated, and Priscus her adversary was outdone. The virgin was plucked unhurt from the fiery furnace, hard stones reverted to dust, wild beasts turned gentle and bent their heads, and every kind of torture was overcome by her prayer. At the very end, pierced by the point of the sword, she left the bondage of the flesh and joyfully joined the celestial choir. This sacred virgin, O Lord, commends your Church to you. She intercedes for us sinners. May this virgin, this little unspoiled servant in your house, also offer our vows to you."

***

140. Saint Matthew, Apostle

Matthew had two names, Matthew and Levi. Matthew (Matthaeus) is interpreted as hasty gift, or as giver of counsel. Or the name comes from *magnus*, great, and *theos*, God, hence great unto God, or from *manus*, hand, and *theos*, hence the hand of God. Saint Matthew was a hasty gift by his speedy conversion, the giver of counsel by his salutary preaching, great unto God by the perfection of his life, and the hand of God by the writing of his gospel. Levi is interpreted as taken up, or attached, or added to, or placed with. The saint was taken up from the work of exacting taxes, attached to the company of the apostles, added to the group of the evangelists, and placed with the catalog of the martyrs.

Matthew the apostle was preaching in Ethiopia in a city called Nadaber, and found two sorcerers named Zaroës and Arphaxat. These two worked their arts upon whomever they wished in such a way that the victim seemed to be deprived of the functioning of his limbs and of his sanity. This made the sorcerers so proud that they got people to worship them as gods. When the apostle arrived in the aforesaid city, he was given hospitality by the eunuch of Queen Candace, whom Philip had baptized. He soon exposed the magicians' artifices, so that whatever they did to harm men the apostle turned into benefits.

The eunuch asked Matthew how he happened to speak and understand so many languages, and he explained that after the descent of the Holy Spirit upon the apostles, he found that he possessed knowledge of all languages. Thereafter, whereas those whose pride had made them want to build a tower reaching to heaven had to stop building because of the confusion of languages, so the apostles, by their knowledge of all languages, were able to build a tower not of stones but of virtues, by which all who believed could ascend to heaven.

Now a man came to say that the sorcerers had come with two dragons, which belched forth sulfurous fire from mouth and nostrils and killed many people. The apostle shielded himself with the sign of the cross and confidently went out to meet these beasts. The minute the dragons saw him, they fell asleep at his feet, and he said to the sorcerers: "Where is your magical power now? Wake them up if you can! If I had not prayed to the Lord, I would have turned back upon you the harm you had thought to inflict upon me." And when all the people had gathered together, Matthew ordered the dragons in Jesus' name to go away, and off they went, harming no one.

Now the apostle began to preach a great sermon to the people about the glory of the earthly paradise, telling them that it had stood above all the mountains and had been close to heaven; that in it there were no thorns or brambles, and lilies and roses did not wither; that old age never came, and people always stayed young; that there the angels played upon their instruments, and that when the birds were called, they obeyed at once. The apostle went on to say that mankind had been expelled from this earthly paradise, but that through the birth of Christ they had been recalled to the paradise of heaven.

While Matthew was saying all this, suddenly a loud cry of mourning arose for the king's son, who had died. When the sorcerers could not revive him, they convinced the king that his son had been taken up into the company of the gods, and that therefore a statue should be made and a temple erected in his honor. But the aforesaid eunuch had the magicians kept in custody and called for the apostle, who by his prayer restored the youth to life. The king, whose name was Egippus, saw this and sent a message throughout his kingdom, saying: "Come and see God hiding in the likeness of a man!" They came, bringing gold crowns and various kinds of votive offerings in order to sacrifice to Matthew, but he checked them, saying: "What are you doing, men? I am not a god but a servant of the Lord Jesus Christ!" He persuaded them to expend the gold and silver they had brought on the building of a great church. They completed the church in thirty days, and the apostle presided in it for thirty-three years and converted all Egypt. King Egippus was baptized with his wife and the whole people. Matthew dedicated Ephigenia, the king's daughter, to God, and put her at the head of more than two hundred virgins.

Hirtacus succeeded Egippus. Hirtacus lusted after the virgin Ephigenia, and promised the apostle the half of his kingdom if he could prevail upon her to become his wife. Matthew told him to follow the custom of his predecessor and come to church on Sunday, where Ephigenia and the other virgins would also be present, and he would hear about the blessings of lawful marriage. The king was happy and hastened to comply, thinking that the apostle would persuade Ephigenia to marry him. With the virgins and the whole populace present, Matthew preached at great length on the good of matrimony. The king praised what he heard, because he believed that it had been said in order to make Ephigenia desire marriage. But then, after calling for silence, Matthew went back over his sermon, and said: "Since marriage is good as long as the union is kept inviolate, all of you here present know that if one of his servants dared to usurp the king's spouse, he would deserve not only the king's anger but death as a penalty, and this not because he had married a wife, but because by taking his master's spouse he was guilty of violating matrimony. So it is with you, O king! You know that Ephigenia has become the spouse of the eternal King and is consecrated with the sacred veil. How can you take the spouse of One who is more powerful than you and make her your wife?"

When the king heard this he was beside himself with rage and stamped out of the church. The apostle, unafraid and unmoved, encouraged his hearers to be patient and steadfast. Ephigenia was prostrated with fear, but he gave her and the other virgins his blessing. After the ceremony of the mass was concluded, the king sent a swordsman, who found Matthew standing before the altar with his hands raised to heaven in prayer. He stabbed the apostle in the back, killing him and making him a martyr. The people found this out and thronged to the royal palace, intent on setting it and everything in it afire, but the priests and the deacons restrained them, and they all celebrated Saint Matthew's martyrdom joyfully.

Hirtacus then sent ladies to Ephigenia to plead his cause, and the sorcerers worked their charms upon her, but none of these efforts succeeded in weakening her resolve. He therefore had a huge fire ignited around her house, hoping to put her and her virgins to death, but the apostle appeared to them and turned the fire away from their house and toward the king's palace. It swept through the building and consumed all in it, the king barely escaping with his only son. The son was immediately seized by the devil but ran to the apostle's tomb, confessing his father's crimes. The father was stricken with a loathsome leprosy that could not be cured, so he took his life with his own sword. The people established Ephigenia's brother, whom the apostle had baptized, as their king, who reigned for seventy years and installed his son as his successor. He aided the spread of the Christian religion and filled the whole province of Ethiopia with churches of Christ. As for Zaroës and Arphaxat, they fled into Persia the very day the apostle raised the king's son to life, but the apostles Simon and Jude overcame them there.

Note that there are four things about Matthew that deserve special consideration. The first is the quickness with which he obeyed. When Christ called him, he quit his customhouse immediately to become a follower of Christ and nothing else, not fearing his superiors though he left his accounts unfinished. This readiness to obey led some to misinterpret it, as Jerome points out in his commentary on this place in Matthew's gospel.[1] Jerome says: "Porphyrius and the emperor Julian discern in this text either the ineptitude of a lying historian or the folly of those who immediately followed the Savior, as if without rhyme or reason they followed anyone who called them. So many manifestations of power and so many miracles had preceded this moment of encounter, and no doubt the apostles had seen these wonders before they believed; and surely the brightness and majesty of Christ's hidden divinity, which shone even in his human face, could draw men to him the first time they saw him. If we say that a magnet has the power to attract rings and iron filings, how much more could the Lord of all creatures draw to himself anyone he wished to draw." Thus Jerome.

The second notable thing about Matthew is his generosity, or liberality, because he quickly arranged to hold a great feast in his house for the Lord. This feast was great not only on account of lavish preparation, but for four other reasons. Firstly, there was the thought that inspired it: Matthew welcomed Christ with great affection and desire. Secondly, there was the mystery: the feast indicated a great mystery, which the *Gloss* on Luke points out: "Whoever welcomes Christ into his interior abode is nourished with the greatest delights of overflowing pleasures." Thirdly, it was a great feast by reason of the great teachings that Christ imparted there, such as "I will have mercy and not sacrifice," and "They that are in health need not a physician, but they that are ill."[2] Fourthly, the feast was great by reason of the persons invited, because truly great persons, namely, Christ and his disciples, were guests.

The third quality worthy of note in Matthew is his humility, which was manifested in two ways. Firstly, he let himself be known as a tax-gatherer, a publican. The other evangelists, as the *Gloss* says, did not put in his common title, in order to spare him shame and to guard the honor of an evangelist, whereas he, following the prescription that the just man is his own first accuser, calls himself Matthew the publican.[3] Thus he showed that no convert ought to be uncertain about his salvation, since a publican suddenly became an apostle and evangelist. Secondly, he proved his humility by his patience in bearing

---

[1] Matt. 9:9. [2] Matt. 9:9–13. [3] Matt. 10:3.

insults. When the Pharisees murmured because Christ turned aside to a sinful man, Matthew might well have retorted: "You are the miserable, sinful ones, because, judging yourselves to be righteous, you want nothing to do with the physician, while I should not now be called a sinner, because I have had recourse to the physician of salvation, and I do not hide my wound from him."

The fourth thing to consider about Matthew is the high honor paid in the Church to the gospel that he wrote. His gospel is read more frequently in church than the others, as the Psalms and Paul's letters are heard more often than the other Scriptures. The reason for this is, as James testifies, that there are three kinds of sins, namely, pride, lust, and avarice. Saul, who was called Saul after the exceedingly proud King Saul, sinned by pride when he persecuted the Church beyond measure. David sinned by the sin of lust, when he not only committed adultery but killed Uriah, his most loyal soldier. Matthew sinned by avarice by seeking ill-gotten gains, since he was a tax-gatherer, a keeper of the customs. The customhouse (called *teloneum* in Latin) is, as Isidore says, a place at a seaport where taxes are paid on ships' cargoes and seamen's wages: *telos*, as Bede says, is the Greek word for tax, as *vectigal* is in Latin.

Granted, therefore, that Saul, David, and Matthew were sinners, their repentance so pleased the Lord that he not only forgave their sins but heaped his gifts upon them in greater abundance. He made the cruelest persecutor the most faithful preacher, the adulterer and homicide a prophet and singer of Psalms, the covetous seeker of profit an apostle and evangelist. Therefore the sayings and writings of these three men are recited to us so frequently so that no one who might wish to be converted would despair of pardon, when he sees that such great sinners were also so great in grace.

According to Saint Ambrose, certain things are to be noted about Saint Matthew's conversion, regarding the physician, the sick man who was healed, and the way the cure was effected. In the physician there were three things, namely, his wisdom, which recognized the root of the disease, his kindness, which furnished remedies, and his power, which could change the sick man so suddenly. Of these three things Ambrose, speaking in the person of Matthew, says: "He who knows hidden things can take away the pain in my heart and the pallor of my soul." So much for his wisdom. "I have found a physician who lives in heaven and dispenses remedies on earth." So much for his kindness. "He alone can heal my wounds who has none of his own to heal." So much for his power.

In the sick man who was healed, namely, in Saint Matthew, three things are to be considered, as the said Ambrose demonstrates: the sick man put off his sickness completely, he was grateful to his physician, and he kept himself clean ever after in the good health he had received. Hence Ambrose says: "Matthew now followed Christ, happy and supple, and exulted, saying: 'I no longer carry in me a publican, I no longer carry Levi, I put off Levi after I put on Christ.' That as to the first. 'I hate my race, I flee from my past life, I follow you alone, Lord Jesus, you who heal my wounds.' That as to the second. 'Who shall

separate us from the love of Christ? Shall tribulation? Or distress? Or famine?'"
That as to the third.

How was the cure of the sick man effected? In three ways, according to Saint
Ambrose. First, Christ bound him in fetters; second, he applied a caustic to the
wound; third, he did away with all the rottenness. Hence Ambrose, speaking in
the person of Matthew, says: "I am bound with the nails of faith and the soft
shackles of love. Jesus, take away the rottenness of my sins while you keep me
bound with the fetters of love. Cut away any rot you find in me!" So much for
the first way. "I shall hold every commandment of yours as an applied caustic,
and if the caustic commandment burns, it will be burning away the corruption
of the flesh lest the contagious poison spread; and if the remedy stings, it still
removes the poison of the wound." So much for the second way. "Come
quickly, Lord, cut into the various secret, hidden passions, open the wound
quickly lest the noxious fluid spread, cleanse all that is fetid with a pilgrim bath."
So much for the third way.

Matthew's gospel, written by his own hand, was discovered about A.D. 500
with the bones of Saint Barnabas. Saint Barnabas carried this gospel with him
and placed it on sick persons, and it instantly cured the illness, as much by
Barnabas's faith as by Matthew's merit.

❋

---

141. Saint Maurice and His Companions

Maurice (Mauritius) comes from *mari*, meaning the sea or bitter, *cis*, which
means vomiting or hard, and *us*, a counselor or one who hastens. Or the name
comes from *mauron*, which, according to Isidore, is the Greek word for black.
Saint Maurice had bitterness from dwelling in misery and being put far from his
native land; he vomited in the sense that he rejected everything superfluous; he
was hard and firm in bearing the torments of his martyrdom; he was a counselor
in the exhortation he addressed to his troops; he was one who hastened by his
fervor and the multiplication of his good works; and he was black in his contempt of self.[1]

[1] Maurice is the first saint to be portrayed as a black man in Western Christian iconography, and
the first such image was a statue dated 1240–1250, erected on the facade of the cathedral of Magde-
burg. Jacobus wrote in the early 1260s, but probably his reason for saying that Maurice was black was
simply the "etymological" one given in the text. The subject of blackness in Christian iconography
is studied by J. Devisse and illustrated in *The Image of the Black in Western Art*, vol. 2, part 1 (New
York: William Morrow, 1979), esp. 164f.

The passion of these saints was written and compiled by Saint Eucherius, bishop of Lyons.

It is said that Maurice was the commander of the holy legion called "Theban." The soldiers were called Thebans after their city, the name of which was Thebes. This was the region toward the East, beyond the border of Arabia, a land powerful and wealthy, fertile and fruitful, and pleasantly wooded. The inhabitants of the region are said to be tall and sturdy, expert in arms, brave in warfare, shrewd and witty, and richly endowed with wisdom. The city had a hundred gates and was situated above the Nile River, which flows out of the earthly paradise and is called Gyon. Of this city it is said: "Behold old Thebes, lying crushed with her hundred gates."

Here James, brother of the Lord, preached the Gospel of salvation and perfectly taught the people the faith of Christ. Diocletian and Maximian, however, who began to reign in A.D. 277, were determined to wipe out the Christian religion and sent letters to this effect to all the provinces where Christians dwelt. They wrote: "If there was something to be decided or known, and the whole world was marshaled on one side and Rome alone on the other, the whole world would flee in defeat, and Rome would stand alone at the peak of knowledge. Why do you, poor little folk, resist her commands and draw yourselves up so stubbornly against her statutes? Therefore either accept belief in the immortal gods, or the immutable sentence of condemnation will be pronounced against you."

The Christians received these letters but sent the messengers back without an answer. Diocletian and Maximian were angry at this, and dispatched orders to all the provinces that all men capable of bearing the weapons of war should muster and should subdue all those who were rebelling against the Roman Empire. The emperors' letters were delivered to the people of Thebes, and these people, in obedience to God's command, rendered to Caesar the things that are Caesar's and to God the things that are God's. They recruited a choice legion of 6,666 soldiers and sent them to the emperors to help them in waging just wars—not therefore to suppress Christians but rather to defend them. The commander of this sacred legion was the illustrious Maurice, and its standard-bearers were Candidus, Innocent, Exuperius, Victor, and Constantine. Diocletian now sent Maximian, his associate emperor, to Gaul with an immense army, to which he attached the Theban legion. Pope Marcellinus had admonished the Thebans that they should rather perish by the sword than violate the Christian faith which they had made their own.

When the whole army had crossed the Alps and come to Octodurus, the emperor commanded that all who were with him should offer sacrifice to the idols and should unanimously take an oath against Rome's rebellious subjects, but particularly against Christians. When the holy soldiers heard this, they withdrew a distance of eight miles from the army and made camp along the Rhone in a pleasant place called Agaune. When Maximian learned of this, he sent soldiers to tell them to come quickly and offer sacrifice to the gods with the others. The Thebans answered that, being Christians, they could not do this. The emperor, fuming with anger, said: "An insult to heaven is added to the contempt directed at me, and as I am despised, so is the Roman religion! Let these willful soldiers know that I can avenge not only myself but my gods!" The emperor then sent his soldiers to deliver the order that either the Thebans were to sacrifice to the gods or every tenth one of them was to be beheaded. The saints then joyfully hastened forward, one after the other bending his neck to receive the headsman's deathblow.

Now Saint Maurice rose in their midst and addressed them: "I rejoice with you because you are all ready to die for the faith of Christ. I have allowed your fellow soldiers to be put to death because I saw you prepared to suffer for Christ, and I have kept the command the Lord gave Peter: 'Put your sword into its sheath!'[2] Now that the bodies of our comrades form a barricade around us and our garments are reddened with their blood, let us follow them to martyrdom! Therefore, if you agree, let us send our answer to Caesar: 'We are your soldiers, Emperor, and we have taken arms to defend the commonwealth. There is no treason in us, no fear; but we will not betray the faith of Christ.'" Receiving this message, the irate emperor ordered a second decimation of the Thebans.

When that had been done, Exuperius the standard-bearer picked up a banner and, standing amidst the troops, said: "Maurice, our glorious leader, has spoken to us about the glory of our comrades. Now let me say that Exuperius, your standard-bearer, has not taken arms to resist dying for Christ! I say, let our right hands throw aside these carnal weapons and be armed with virtues, and, if it please you, let us send this reply to the emperor: 'We are your soldiers, O Emperor, but we freely profess that we are Christ's servants. To you we owe military service, to him our innocence. From you we have received wages for our work, from him the beginning of life itself. So for him we are prepared to suffer every torment, and we will never give up our faith in him!'" The impious emperor now commanded his army to surround the whole legion so that not one man should escape. The soldiers of Christ were therefore surrounded by the soldiers of the devil, struck down by murderous hands, trampled by horses' hooves, and consecrated to Christ as his precious martyrs. They suffered about A.D. 280.

By God's will a large number of the Thebans did escape, and went to other regions to preach the name of Christ and to triumph most gloriously in many places. Among them we learn that Solutor, Adventor, and Octavius went to Turin, Alexander to Bergamo, Secundus to Ventimiglia; and there were also Constantius, Victor, Ursus, and a great many others.

When the bloody killers had divided the booty and were making merry together, an old man named Victor happened to pass by and they invited him to join them in the feasting. He asked how they could be having such a jolly

[2] John 18:11.

celebration with so many thousands of dead soldiers lying around, and someone told him that the dead had died for the faith of Christ. Victor sighed and groaned, declaring that he would be blessed if he had been slain with them. As soon as they became aware that the old man was a Christian, they fell upon him and cut him to pieces.

Some time later, and on the same day, the two emperors, Maximian at Milan and Diocletian at Nicomedia, laid aside the purple and retired to private life, leaving the rule to younger men, namely, Constantius, Maximus, and Galerius, whom they made caesars. But in time Maximian wanted to resume his tyrannical rule, but Constantius, his son-in-law, ran him down and hanged him.

The body of Saint Innocent, who belonged to the Theban legion, had been thrown into the Rhone River but was recovered by Bishop Domitian of Geneva, Bishop Gratus of Aosta, Bishop Protasius, and others, and by them buried in a church that they built for the purpose. While the church was under construction and most of the workmen were at mass on Sunday, one of them, a pagan, went on with his work alone. Suddenly the legion of the saints appeared, seized the pagan, beat him, and reproached him for engaging in profane labor and toiling at mechanical tasks on the Lord's day, while the others were occupied in divine service. Being thus corrected, the man ran to the church and begged to be made a Christian.

Ambrose, in his Preface for these martyrs, says: "This troop of faithful men, lustrous with the light of God, came from the ends of the earth to plead happily with you, O Lord! This legion of warriors, fenced about with bodily weapons but also protected by spiritual arms, hastened with watchful constancy to martyrdom. The pestiferous tyrant, in order to terrorize them, massacred every tenth man with the beheading sword and, when the rest clung steadfastly to their faith, ordered all of them to submit to the same penalty. But so ardent was the fervor of their love that, discarding their arms, they knelt before the headsmen and with joyful hearts received the blow that killed them. Among them blessed Maurice, afire with love for your faith, sustained the combat and won the crown of martyrdom." Thus Ambrose.

A woman entrusted her son to the abbot of a monastery where the bodies of some of the Theban martyrs reposed. The boy was there to be instructed, but before long he died, and the mother mourned him inconsolably. Saint Maurice appeared to her and asked why she wept so much for her son, and she replied that as long as she lived, she would never stop mourning her loss. Maurice said: "Do not think of him as being dead! Know that he is living with us. If you want proof of this, come to the service of matins tomorrow and every day, and you will hear his voice among the voices of the monks as they chant the Psalms." The woman followed the saint's admonition and always discerned her son's voice as he sang with the monks.

After King Gontran had retired from worldly pomp and circumstance and had distributed his wealth to the poor and the churches, he sent a priest to obtain for him some sacred relics of the holy martyrs. On his return voyage across the lake of Lausanne a tempest arose and the ship was sinking, but the priest held up the chest containing the relics in the face of the storm, and a serene calm settled over the waves.

In the year A.D. 963 certain monks, acting on behalf of Charles, obtained from Pope Nicholas the bodies of Pope Saint Urban and Saint Tiburtius. On their way home they visited the church of the Theban martyrs, and besought the abbot and the monks to allow them to transport the body of Saint Maurice and the head of Saint Innocent to the church in Auxerre that Saint Germain had long since dedicated to the martyrs.

Peter Damian tells us that in Burgundy there was a certain proud, ambitious cleric who had taken over for himself a church dedicated to Saint Maurice, despite the determined opposition of a powerful knight. One day when mass was being celebrated and the deacon, at the end of the gospel, sang: "Whoever exalts himself will be humbled and whoever humbles himself will be exalted," the wretched cleric scoffed and said: "That is false! If I had humbled myself before my enemies, I would not now have this rich church for myself!" Instantly a flash of lightning darted into the mouth out of which he had spewed these blasphemous words, and that was the end of the blasphemer.

142. Saint Justina, Virgin

The name Justina is derived from *justitia*, justice; and Saint Justina showed her justice by giving to every person what was due to the person—to God, obedience; to the prelate her superior, reverence; to her equals, harmonious relations; to her inferiors, instruction; to her enemies, patience; to the poor and afflicted, compassion and help; to herself, holiness; and to her neighbor, love.

The virgin Justina was born in Antioch, the daughter of a pagan priest. Sitting at her window every day, she listened to the deacon Proclus reading the Gospel and in time was converted by him. Her mother told her father about this as they lay in bed, and when they had fallen asleep, Christ, accompanied by angels, appeared to them and said: "Come to me, and I will give you the kingdom of heaven!" As soon as they were awake, they had themselves baptized with their daughter.

This virgin Justina had long been pursued by a certain Cyprian, and in the end she converted him to the faith. Cyprian had been a magician from childhood:

when he was seven years old, his parents consecrated him to the devil. He practiced the arts of magic, often being seen to change women into beasts of burden and performing many other marvels. He became enamored of Justina, and put his magic to work in order to have her for himself or for a man named Acladius, who also lusted after her. He therefore invoked the demon to come to him and enable him to win the virgin. The demon came and asked him: "Why did you call me?" Cyprian answered: "I love a maiden who is of the Galilean sect. Can you make it possible for me to have her and work my will with her?" The demon: "I was able to throw man out of paradise; I induced Cain to kill his brother; I caused the Jews to put Christ to death; I have brought every kind of disorder among men! How could I not be able to let you have one mere girl and do what you please with her? Take this lotion and sprinkle it around the outside of her house, and I will come and set her heart afire with love for you, and compel her to consent to you."

The following night the demon came to Justina and tried to awaken an illicit love in her heart. Sensing what was happening, she devoutly commended herself to the Lord and covered her whole body with the sign of the cross. Seeing that sign, the devil fled in terror and went and stood before Cyprian. "Why haven't you brought that maiden to me?" Cyprian asked. "I saw a certain sign on her," the demon answered, "and I weakened and all power left me." Cyprian dismissed that demon and called for a stronger one. This one told Cyprian: "I heard your orders and I saw why that other could do nothing, but I will do better and will carry out your will. I will go to her and wound her heart with lustful love, and you will enjoy her as you wish to." So the devil went to Justina and did his best to win her over and inflame her soul with sinful desire. But Justina again devoutly commended herself to God and dispelled all temptation with the sign of the cross, then blew upon the devil and drove him away. The spirit departed in confusion and fled to Cyprian. Cyprian: "Where is the virgin I sent you after?" The demon: "I admit I'm beaten, and I'm afraid to say how! I saw a certain terrible sign on her and at once lost all my strength!"

Cyprian scoffed at him and sent him away. Then he summoned the prince of demons and, when he came, said to him: "What is this power of yours that's so low that a mere girl can overcome it?" Said the devil: "I will visit her and disturb her with various fevers. I will inflame her spirit with hotter passion and spread hot spasms throughout her body. I'll get her in a frenzy and put fearful phantasms before her eyes. And in the middle of the night I will bring her to you!"

Then the devil gave himself the appearance of a young woman and went to Justina, saying: "I come to you because I want to live in chastity with you; but tell me, I beg of you, what will be the reward of our effort?" The holy virgin answered: "The reward is great, the labor light." "Then," said the devil, "what about God's command to increase and multiply and fill the earth? I fear, my good friend, that if we persist in virginity, we shall nullify God's word. By being disdainful and disobedient we shall bring grievous judgment upon ourselves, and while we expected a reward, we will incur torment!" The virgin began to have serious doubts, induced by the devil, and she felt more strongly stirred by the heat of concupiscence, so much so that she rose and was on the verge of going out. But then she came to herself and recognized who it was that was speaking to her, so she shielded herself with the sign of the cross, then blew on the devil, causing him to melt like a candle. Thereupon she felt herself freed of all temptation.

Next the devil transfigured himself into a handsome young man and came into the room where Justina was lying in bed. Shamelessly he leapt into her bed and tried to envelop her in his embrace. This made Justina recognize the presence of a malignant spirit, so she quickly made the sign of the cross, and again the devil melted away. Then, God permitting, the demon sapped her strength with fevers, and killed many people along with their herds and flocks. He also made possessed persons predict that a great wave of death would sweep through Antioch unless Justina consented to marry. For that reason the entire citizenry, beset as they were with disease, gathered at her parents' door and demanded that Justina be given in marriage so that the city could be delivered of this great peril. But Justina absolutely refused, and all were under the threat of death, but in the seventh year of the plague she prayed for them and drove out the pestilence.

Now the devil, seeing that he was making no headway, changed himself to look like Justina in order to besmirch her good name, and deceived Cyprian, boasting that he would bring Justina to him. Then, but this time looking like the virgin, he came running to Cyprian as if languishing with love for him and wanting to kiss him. Cyprian, thinking of course that it was Justina, was overwhelmed with joy and said: "Welcome, Justina, loveliest of women!" But the minute he pronounced the name of Justina, the devil could not bear it and vanished in a puff of smoke.

Cyprian, aggrieved at having been fooled, yearned the more ardently for Justina and took to watching at her door. Sometimes he changed himself by magic into a woman, sometimes into a bird, but when he came close to that door, he no longer looked like a woman or a bird: he was Cyprian. Acladius, too, was changed by diabolic art into a sparrow and flew to the virgin's windowsill, but as soon as she looked at him, he was no longer a sparrow but Acladius, and he felt trapped and frightened because he could neither fly nor jump from such a height. Justina feared that he might fall and break to pieces, so she had him brought down by a ladder, and warned him to give up his mad adventure or be punished for breaking the law against trespass.

All these apparitions, of course, were nothing but devilish artifices, and none of them served the devil's purpose; so, defeated and confused, he went back and stood before Cyprian. Cyprian said to him: "So you too are beaten! What kind of power do you have, you wretch, that you can't overcome a simple girl or have any control over her? To the contrary, she defeats all of you and lays you low! But tell me one thing, I beg of you: where does her greatest strength come from?" The demon answered: "If you will swear never to desert me, I will reveal to you the power behind her victory." Cyprian: "What shall I swear by?" The demon: "Swear to me by my great powers that you will never desert me!" Cyprian: "By your great powers I swear to you that I will never desert you."

Now the devil, being reassured, told Cyprian: "That young woman made the sign of the cross, and at once all my strength ebbed away. I could do nothing, and like wax melting at a fire I melted away." Cyprian: "Therefore the Crucified is greater than you?" The demon: "Greater than all! And all of us and all those we deceive he turns over to be tormented in the fire that never dies out!" Cyprian: "Therefore I too should become a friend of the Crucified, so as not to incur so awful a punishment!" The devil: "You swore to me by the power of my army, by which no one can swear falsely, that you would never desert me!" Cyprian answered: "I despise you and all your devils, and I arm myself with the saving sign of the Crucified!" Instantly the devil fled in confusion.

Then Cyprian went to the bishop. When the bishop saw him, he supposed that he had come to lead Christians into error, and said to him: "Be satisfied, Cyprian, with misleading those who are not of the faith! You can do nothing against the Church of God, for the power of Christ is unconquerable." Cyprian: "I am sure that Christ's power cannot be conquered." And he told the bishop all that had happened to him, and had the bishop baptize him. Thereafter Cyprian made great progress both in knowledge and in holiness of life, and when the bishop died, Cyprian was ordained to take his place. He established the holy virgin Justina in a monastery and made her the abbess over many holy virgins. Saint Cyprian often sent letters to the martyrs and strengthened them in their struggles.

The prefect of that region heard of the renown of Cyprian and Justina and had them brought before him. He asked them if they were willing to sacrifice to the idols. When they persisted firmly in the faith of Christ, he ordered them to be put in a heated caldron filled with wax, pitch, and fat, but this only refreshed them and inflicted no pain. Then a priest of the idols said to the prefect: "Command me to stand in front of the caldron, and I will outdo all their power!" He went close to the caldron and said: "Great are you, O god Hercules, and you, Jupiter, father of the gods!" And behold, fire poured out and consumed the priest. Cyprian and Justina were taken out of the caldron, sentenced, and beheaded together. Their bodies were thrown to the dogs and lay for seven days, then were transported to Rome, and now, we are told, repose in Piacenza. They suffered under Diocletian, on the twenty-sixth day of September, A.D. 280.

143. Saints Cosmas and Damian

The name Cosmas comes from *cosmos*, which means form or adorned. Or, according to Isidore, *cosmos* is the Greek word for clean, as is the Latin word *mundus*. Saint Cosmas was a form, an example to others; he was adorned with good virtues and clean of all vices. Damianus, or Damian, is derived from *dama*, a humble, gentle beast, or the name comes from *dogma*, doctrine, and *ana*, above, or from *damum*, which is sacrifice. Or Damianus is equivalent to *Domini manus*, the hand of the Lord. Saint Damian was mild of manner, had supernal doctrine in his preaching, was a sacrifice in the mortification of his flesh, and was the hand of the Lord in the healing cures he brought about.

Cosmas and Damian were brothers, born of a pious mother, Theodoche by name, in the city of Egea. They learned the art of medicine, and received such grace from the Holy Spirit that they cured the illnesses not only of men and women but of animals, not taking any payment for their services. A lady named Palladia, however, who had spent all she had on doctors, came to the saints and by them was fully restored to health. She therefore offered a modest gift to Saint Damian and, when he declined to accept it, appealed to him with solemn oaths. He then accepted the gift, not that he was greedy for the money but to satisfy the donor's kind intention, as well as to avoid seeming to dishonor the name of the Lord, since the woman had adjured him in that name. When Saint Cosmas learned of this, he gave orders that his body was not to be buried with his brother's, but the following night the Lord appeared to Cosmas and explained Damian's reason for his action.

Word of the brothers' fame reached Lisias, the proconsul, and he had them summoned and asked them their names, their native land, and their possessions. The holy martyrs replied: "Our names are Cosmas and Damian; we have three brothers named Antimas, Leontius, and Euprepius; Arabia is our homeland; and as for earthly fortunes, Christians do not acquire them." The proconsul ordered them to fetch their brothers, and then to sacrifice to the idols together.

When the five brothers unanimously refused to sacrifice, Lisias commanded that they be tortured in their hands and feet. They made light of these torments, and he ordered them to be bound with chains and thrown into the sea, but at once they were drawn out by an angel and set before the judge. This official gave thought to the matter and said: "By the great gods, it is by sorcery that you conquer, because you mock at torments and calm the sea! Therefore teach me your magic arts, and in the name of the god Adrian I will follow you." No sooner had he said this than two demons appeared and struck him in the face with great force, and he cried out: "I beg you, good men, to pray for me to your God!" They prayed, and the demons disappeared.

The judge said: "You see how angry the gods are with me because I thought of leaving them. Now therefore I will not suffer you to blaspheme my gods!" He ordered them to be thrown into a huge fire, but the flame not only left the martyrs unharmed, but leapt out and slew many bystanders. The brothers were then stretched on the rack, but their guardian angel kept them uninjured, and the torturers, tired of beating them, returned them to the judge. He in turn had three of the brothers put back in prison, but ordered Cosmas and Damian to be crucified and stoned by the crowd. The stones turned back upon the throwers and wounded a great number. The judge, now beside himself with rage, had the three brothers brought out and ranged around the cross, while four soldiers shot arrows at Cosmas and Damian, still crucified; but the arrows turned and struck many, while the holy martyrs remained untouched. The judge, defeated at every turn, was at death's door from frustration and had the five brothers beheaded in the morning. The Christians, remembering what Saint Cosmas had said about not burying him with Damian, wondered how the martyrs wanted to be buried, when suddenly a camel appeared on the scene, spoke in a human voice, and ordered the saints to be entombed in one place. They suffered under Diocletian, who began to reign about A.D. 287.

A peasant, after hours of working at the harvest, fell asleep in the field with his mouth open, and a snake slipped into his mouth and down to his belly. The man woke up and felt nothing, and went on home, but by evening suffered severe pains in the stomach. He uttered pitiful cries and invoked the aid of Cosmas and Damian, saints of God, but the pain grew worse and he ran to the church of the holy martyrs. There he suddenly fell asleep, and the snake slipped out of his mouth as it had slipped in.

A man who was about to set out on a long journey commended his wife to the care of the holy martyrs Cosmas and Damian, and gave her a sign that she could rely on if at any time he called her. Afterwards the devil, knowing the sign the husband had given, got himself up as a man, showed the woman the sign, and said: "Your husband sent me to you from that city to conduct you to him." She was afraid to go, and said: "I recognize the sign, but I am commended to the holy martyrs Cosmas and Damian, so you must swear to me on their altar that you will take me safely to him." The devil immediately swore as requested. The woman went with him, and when they came to a secluded spot, the devil wanted to throw her off her horse and kill her. When she felt danger coming, she exclaimed: "O God of saints Cosmas and Damian, help me! I trusted them and followed this man!" Instantly the saints appeared with a host of men clad in white and set the woman free. The devil vanished. They said to her: "We are Cosmas and Damian, in whom you trusted, and we hurried to come to your assistance."

Pope Felix, a predecessor of Saint Gregory, built a noble church in Rome in honor of Saints Cosmas and Damian. In this church there was a man, a devoted servant of the holy martyrs. One of the man's legs was totally consumed by a cancer. While he was asleep, the two saints appeared to their devoted servant, bringing salves and surgical instruments. One of them said to the other: "Where can we get flesh to fill in where we cut away the rotted leg?" The other said: "Just today an Ethiopian was buried in the cemetery of Saint Peter in Chains. Go and take his leg, and we'll put it in place of the bad one." So he sped to the cemetery and brought back the Moor's leg, and the two saints cut off the sick man's leg and inserted the Moor's in its place, carefully anointing the wound. Finally they took the amputated leg and attached it to the body of the dead Moor.

The man woke up, felt no pain, put his hand to his leg, and detected no lesion. He held a candle to the leg and could see nothing wrong with it, and began to wonder whether he was himself or somebody else. Then he came to his senses, bounded joyfully from his bed, and told everyone about what he had seen in his dreams and how he had been healed. They sent at once to the Moor's tomb, and found that his leg had indeed been cut off and the aforesaid man's limb put in its place in the tomb.

✳

---

144. Saint Fursey, Bishop

Fursey, a bishop, whose story Bede is believed to have written, reached his final hour after a life that shone with every virtue and goodness. As he was about to breathe his last, he saw in a vision two angels coming to him to carry his soul to heaven, and a third, armed with a shining shield and a gleaming sword, going ahead of him. Then he heard demons shouting: "We must go first and stir up wars in his path!" As these went ahead, they turned around and hurled fiery darts at him, but the leading angel caught them on his shield and extinguished them. Then the demons blocked the angels' way and said: "This man often spoke idle words and therefore should not go unpunished to enjoy eternal life." The angel retorted: "If you cannot accuse him of more serious vices than that, he will not perish for trifles."

Then the devil said to them: "If God is just, this man will not be saved, for it is written: 'Unless you be converted and become as little children, you shall not enter into the kingdom of heaven.'"[1] The angel made an excuse for him, saying: "His heart was right, but human custom kept him quiet." The demon: "Since he accepted evil due to custom, let him accept punishment from the supreme Judge!" The holy angel said: "Let us seek judgment from God!" With the angel fighting for him, the adversaries were put down.

Then the demon said: "A servant who knows the will of his master and does not do it will receive many a hard blow." The angel: "In what did this man fail to fulfill the will of his Lord?" The demon: "He accepted gifts from the wicked." The angel: "He thought that every one of them had done penance." The demon said: "He should first have verified their perseverance in penance and then received the fruit." The angel answered: "Let us submit the case to God!" The demon gave up but returned to the fray, saying: "Until now I've been intimidated by God's truthfulness, as when he promised that any wrong that is not atoned for on earth will be punished hereafter. But this man once accepted a coat from a usurer and was not punished, so where is the justice of God?" The angel: "Silence! You do not know God's secret judgments. As long as there is hope of repentance, the mercy of God accompanies a man." The devil: "But there is no place for repentance here!" The angel: "You do not know the depth of God's judgments."

Then the devil struck Fursey so hard that after he came back to life, he always bore the mark of the blow. What the demons did was to pick up one of the people they were torturing in the fire and throw him at Fursey, whose cheek and shoulder were burned by the contact. Fursey recognized the man who was thrown at him as the one from whom he had accepted the coat. The angel said: "What you once set afire has burned you. If you had not received a gift from this man who died in his sins, his punishment would not have burned in you." So it was by God's permission and order that Fursey received this blow for having accepted the man's coat.

Now another demon said: "There is still a narrow gate for him to pass through, and there we will be able to overpower him—namely, the Law 'You shall love your neighbor as yourself.'"[2] The angel responded: "This man did much good for his neighbors." "That is not enough, unless he also loved himself," the adversary retorted. The angel: "The fruit of love is to do good works, because God renders to each according to his works."[3] The demon said: "Because he did not fulfill the Law by loving, he will be damned." The battle went on, and the holy angels were victors over the horde of the evil.

The devil spoke again: "If God is not wicked and any transgression of his word displeases him, this man will not escape punishment, for he promised to renounce the world, and, to the contrary, he loved the world, going against what is said: 'Love not the world, nor the things which are in the world.'"[4] The

---

[1] Matt. 18:13.   [2] Matt. 22:39.   [3] Rom. 2:6.
[4] 1 John 2:15.

holy angel responded: "He loved the things that are in the world not for himself, but because he could give them to people in need." The devil replied: "No matter how or for what reason he loved them, it was against the divine command!"

The adversaries were defeated again, and the devil resorted to more subtle accusations, saying: "It is written: 'If you do not speak to warn the wicked from his wicked way, his blood I will require at your hand';[5] but this man did not warn sinners as he should have done." The holy angel responded: "When the hearers pay no heed to the word, the teacher's tongue is tied, and when he sees that his preaching is despised, he does well to know that when it is not the time to speak, it is better to say nothing." So the demons lost in each phase of the confrontation, until by the Lord's judgment the angels were triumphant and the adversaries were vanquished, and the holy man was enveloped in bright light.

Bede tells us that one of the angels said to Fursey: "Look down on the earth!" He saw a gloomy valley far beneath him, and four fires in the air at some distance from each other. The angel told him: "These are the four fires that are burning up the world. One is the fire of falsehood, because men promise in baptism to renounce the devil and all his pomps, but they do not fulfill the promise. The second is the fire of greed, because men put the world's riches ahead of the love of heavenly goods. The third is the fire of discord, which makes people not hesitate to hurt their neighbors over the slightest thing. The fourth is the fire of impiety, of ruthlessness, which makes people think nothing of robbing and defrauding the weak and defenseless." Then the fires drew together and formed one blaze, which came closer to Fursey and made him afraid. He said to the angel: "This fire is coming very close to me!" The angel: "What you did not ignite will not burn in you, because that fire tests each man according to the merits of his works, for as the body is burned by illicit pleasures, so it will be burned by the punishment it deserves."

At last Fursey was brought back to his body, while all were mourning because they thought he was dead. He lived for some while longer and finished his life laudably in doing good works.

[5] Ezek. 3:18.

145. Saint Michael, Archangel

Michael is interpreted as meaning "Who is like to God?" and it is said that when something requiring wondrous powers is to be done, Michael is sent, so that from his name and by his action it is given to be understood that no one can do what God alone can do: for that reason many works of wondrous power are attributed to Michael. Thus, as Daniel testifies, in the time of the Antichrist Michael will rise up and stand forth as defender and protector of the elect. He it was who fought with the dragon and his angels and expelled them from heaven, winning a great victory. He fought with the devil over the body of Moses, because the devil wanted to keep the body hidden so that the Jewish people might adore Moses in place of the true God. Michael receives the souls of the saints and leads them into the paradise of joy. In the past he was prince of the synagogue but has now been established by the Lord as prince of the Church. It is said that it was he who inflicted the plagues on the Egyptians, divided the Red Sea, led the people through the desert, and ushered them into the Promised Land. He is held to be Christ's standard-bearer among the battalions of the holy angels. At the Lord's command he will kill the Antichrist with great power on Mount Olivet. At the sound of the voice of the archangel Michael the dead will rise, and it is he who will present the cross, the nails, the spear, and the crown of thorns at the Day of Judgment.

The sacred feast of Michael the archangel celebrates his apparition, his victory, his dedication, and his memorial. There have been several apparitions of this angel. He first appeared on Mount Gargano. In Apulia there is a mountain named Gargano near the city called Sipontus. In the year of the Lord 390 there was, in the aforesaid city of Sipontus, a man named Garganus, who, according to some books, took his name from the mountain, or from whom the mountain got its name. This man was rich, and had sheep and cattle beyond counting. Once when the herd was grazing on the flanks of Mount Gargano, it happened that one bull separated himself from the rest and climbed to the top of the mountain. When the herd came in and this bull's absence was discovered, the landowner mustered a band of his people to track it up the mountain trails, and they finally found the animal standing in the mouth of a cave at the top. The owner, annoyed at the bull for having wandered off alone, aimed a poisoned arrow at it, but the arrow came back, as if turned about by the wind, and struck the one who had launched it. This dismayed the townsmen, and they went to the bishop and asked him what he thought of the strange occurrence. The bishop bound them to a three-day fast and admonished them to direct their questions to God. They did, and Saint Michael appeared to the bishop and said: "Know that it was by my will that the man was struck by his arrow. I am the archangel Michael, and I have chosen to dwell in that place on earth and to keep it safe. I wished by that sign to indicate that I watch over the place and guard it." The bishop and the townspeople formed a procession and went to the cave, but, not presuming to enter, stood around the entrance, praying.

The second apparition is described as having occurred about A.D. 710. At a place close to the sea, called Tumba, about six miles from the city of Avranches, Michael appeared to the bishop of that city and ordered him to build a church at the aforesaid place, at which church, as at Mount Gargano, the memory of Saint Michael the archangel was to be celebrated. When the bishop was uncertain about the exact place where the church should be built, the archangel instructed him to build at a spot where he would find that thieves had hidden a bull. The bishop also had doubts about how large the church should be, and was ordered to use as a measure the circuit marked by the bull's hoofprints. On the site there were two boulders so massive that no human strength could move them. Then Michael appeared to a man and ordered him to go to the place and remove the rocks. The man went there and moved the stones so easily that they seemed to have no weight at all. When the church was built, they brought from Mount Gargano a cutting from the mantle Saint Michael had spread over the altar there and a slab of the marble on which he had stood, and placed them in his new church. And since there appeared to be a scarcity of water there, upon the angel's advice they broke a cleft into a very hard rock at the site, and such a stream of water poured out that even now it more than meets every need. This apparition is solemnly celebrated in that place on the sixteenth day of October.

We are told that in this same place there occurred a miracle which is worthy of being remembered. The mountain on which Saint Michael's church was built is surrounded on all sides by the ocean, but twice on the saint's feast day a path is opened to allow the people to walk over. One such day, when a large throng was crossing to the church, it happened that a woman who was pregnant and close to her time went with them. Then the tide came in with a rush, and the crowd, terrified, made for the shore, but the pregnant woman could not move fast enough and was caught by the waves. The archangel Michael, however, kept her unharmed, in such a way that she brought forth her son in the welter of the sea and nursed him there in her arms. Then the waters again opened a path for her, and she walked joyfully ashore with her child.

We read that the third apparition took place in Rome during the reign of Pope Gregory. The pope had instituted the Greater Litanies because the inguinal plague was raging in the city, and he was praying devoutly for the people when he saw, above the castle that in the past was called the Tomb of Hadrian, an angel of the Lord who was wiping a bloody sword and returning it to its sheath. Saint Gregory understood from this that his prayers were heard by the

Lord, and he built a church there in honor of the angels: the castle is still called the Castle of the Holy Angel. This apparition is celebrated on 8 May, together with the apparition on Mount Gargano, when Michael gave victory to the people of Sipontus.

The fourth apparition consists in the hierarchies of the angels. The first hierarchy is called Epiphany, or higher apparition, the middle one is called Hyperphany, or middle apparition, and the lowest is called Hypophany, or lower apparition. The word hierarchy comes from *hierar*, sacred, and *archos*, prince, hence sacred prince. Each hierarchy includes three orders. The highest includes Seraphim, Cherubim, and Thrones; the middle one, as Dionysius assigns them, contains Dominations, Virtues, and Powers; and the lowest, according to the same Dionysius, comprises Principalities, Angels, and Archangels. This ordering and ranking of the angels can be understood by its similarity with the organization of a royal court. Among the king's ministers, some, such as chamberlains, counselors and assessors, work in immediate contact with him: the orders in the first hierarchy are similar to these. Other officials have duties pertaining to the overall government of the kingdom, not to one particular province: of this class are the commanders of the militia and the judges in the courts of law, and they are similar to the orders in the second hierarchy. There are also minor officials, for instance, prefects, bailiffs, and the like, who are put in charge of a particular part of the kingdom: these are similar to the orders of the lowest hierarchy.

Among the angels, the three orders in the first hierarchy are those that are close to God, with no intermediary, and are wholly turned to him. For this relationship three things are necessary: first, the highest love, and this is attributed to the Seraphim, whose name means afire with love; second, perfect knowledge, which characterizes the Cherubim, whose name means fullness of knowledge; third, perpetual comprehension or enjoyment, which belongs to the Thrones, whose name means seats, because God sits in them and rests, as he grants them to rest in him.

The three orders in the middle hierarchy are leaders and rulers over the universe of men as a whole. This rule has three elements. It consists first in presiding or commanding, and this belongs to the order of Dominations, whose role it is to be at the head of those inferior to them, to direct them in all divine ministries, and to give them all necessary commands, as we read in Zechariah: "One angel said to the other: 'Run, say to that young man, Jerusalem shall be inhabited as villages without walls.'"[1] The second element consists in the works to be done, and this applies to the order of Virtues, for whom nothing that is commanded is impossible, because it is given to them to be able to rise above all difficulties encountered in the service of God. Therefore the power to work miracles is attributed to them. The third element consists in getting rid of obstacles and resisting attacks, and this pertains to the order of the Powers, who are charged

---

[1] Zech. 2:4.

with driving off opposing powers, as we read in Tobit: "The angel Raphael took the devil and bound him in the desert of Upper Egypt."[2]

The three orders of the lowest hierarchy are those whose sphere of influence is fixed and limited. Some of them have authority in only one province, and these are of the order of Principalities, or Princes, like the prince of the Persians, who ruled over Persia, about whom we read in the tenth chapter of Daniel. Some were commissioned to rule over a multitude of people, as, for example, over one city, and these are called Archangels. Some had a single person placed in their charge, and these are called Angels. Hence Angels are said to make minor announcements, for the reason that their ministry is limited to one man, but Archangels are said to announce great events, because the good of a multitude is of greater importance than that of one individual.

Gregory and Bernard agree with Dionysius regarding the assigned functions of the orders of the first hierarchy, because the assignment of function corresponds to the fruit it produces, namely, ardent love for the Seraphim, profound knowledge for the Cherubim, and perpetual possession of God for the Thrones. They appear to differ, however, regarding the assigned functions of two orders in the middle and lowest hierarchies, namely, of the Principalities and Powers. Gregory and Bernard start from the assumption that the status of master is awarded to the middle hierarchy and that of ministry to the lowest. In this perspective, angels have mastery over three groups: some are masters over angelic spirits, and these are called Dominations, some over good men, and these are called Principalities, and some over demons, and these are called Powers. Here the order and levels of dignity are obvious. Ministry also is of three kinds, namely, the performance of works, the teaching of great matters, and the teaching of less important ones. The first ministry belongs to the Virtues, the second to Archangels, the third to Angels.

There was a fifth apparition of the archangel Michael, and we read about it in the *Tripartite History*. Not far from Constantinople there is a place where the goddess Vesta was worshiped in the past, but where now there stands a church built in honor of Saint Michael, for which reason the place itself is called Michaelium. A man named Aquilinus was overtaken by a raging fever known for the redness that accompanies it. The doctors gave him a potion to break the fever, but he vomited it and continued to vomit whatever he ate or drank. Knowing that he was near death, he had himself carried to the place mentioned above, thinking that there he would either die or be relieved of his malady. Saint Michael appeared to him and told him to prepare a mixture of honey, wine, and pepper and to dip everything he ate in this mixture, and he would be wholly cured. He did as directed and was indeed made well, although it seems contrary to medical science to administer hot drinks to the feverish. This we read in the *Tripartite History*.

---

[2] Tob. 8:3.

Secondly, this feast is called Victory. Michael and his angels have won many victories. The first is the one that the archangel Michael bestowed on the people of Sipontus in the following way. Some time after the finding of the cave at the top of Mount Gargano, the Neapolitans, who were still pagans, organized an army and began to make war on the people of Sipontus and Beneventum, a town some fifty miles from Sipontus. The bishop advised these people to seek a three-day truce, which would give them time to fast and to pray to their patron Michael for help. On the third night Michael appeared to the bishop, told him that the prayers had been heard, promised him victory, and ordered that the enemy be met at the fourth hour of daylight. As the battle was joined, Mount Gargano was shaken by a violent earthquake, lightning flashed uninterruptedly, and a dark cloud blanketed the whole peak of the mountain. Six hundred of the enemy troops fell before the swords of the defenders and the fiery lightning flashes. The rest, recognizing the power of the archangel, abandoned the error of idolatry and bent their necks to the yoke of the Christian faith.

The second victory was won by the archangel Michael when he drove the dragon, i.e., Lucifer, and all his followers out of heaven, a battle about which the Book of Revelation tells us: "There was a great battle in heaven. Michael and his angels fought with the dragon, and the dragon fought with his angels, and they prevailed not."[3] For when Lucifer wanted to be equal to God, the archangel Michael, standard-bearer of the celestial host, marched up and expelled Lucifer and his followers out of heaven, and shut them up in this dark air until the Day of Judgment. They are not allowed to live in heaven, or in the upper part of the air, because that is a bright and pleasant place, nor on the earth with us, lest they do us too much harm. They are in the air between heaven and earth, so that when they look up and see the glory they have lost, they grieve for it, and when they look down and see men ascending to the place from which they fell, they are often tormented with envy. However, by God's design they come down upon us to test us, and, as has been shown to some holy men, they fly around us like flies. They are innumerable, and, like flies, they fill the whole air. Hence Haymon says: "As philosophers have said and as our doctors agree, the air is as full of demons and wicked spirits as a ray of sunlight with specks of dust." Still, innumerable as they are, Origen is of the opinion that their numbers lessen when we conquer them, with the result that when one of them is defeated by a holy man, the tempter can no longer tempt that man to fall into the vice into which he had failed to draw him.

The third victory is the one that the angels win over the demons every day, when they fight for us and save us from the demons' effort to tempt us. The angels do this in three ways: first, by curbing the power that belongs to the demons. The Book of Revelation tells us about the angel who bound the demon and cast him into the bottomless pit;[4] and in Tobit we read about

---

[3] Rev. 12:7–9.   [4] Rev. 20:1–3.

the angel who bound a demon in the desert of Upper Egypt.[5] This binding is nothing less than the curbing of the demon's power. The second way is by cooling concupiscence. This is what is meant by the passage in Genesis which says that an angel touched the sinew of Jacob's thigh and it shrank.[6] The third way is by impressing on our minds the memory of the Lord's passion. This is what Revelation means where we read: "Do not harm the earth or the sea or the trees, till we have sealed the servants of our God upon their foreheads";[7] and in Ezekiel we find: "Mark *Tau* upon the foreheads of the men that sigh."[8] *Tau* is the Greek letter that is written in the shape of a cross, and those who are marked with this sign have no fear of the avenging angel. Hence we read in the same place: "Upon whomsoever you shall see the sign *Tau*, kill him not."[9]

The fourth victory is the one that Michael the archangel is to win over the Antichrist when he kills him. Then Michael the great prince, as Daniel[10] calls him, will rise and stand forth, a valorous aid and protector against the Antichrist. The Antichrist, as the *Gloss* says on the text in Revelation, "I saw one of his heads as it were slain to death,"[11] will pretend to be dead and will hide for three days, then will appear and say that he is resurrected, and, with demons carrying him by their magical arts, will rise in the air, and all will be amazed and will adore him. Finally he will go to the top of Mount Olivet, according to the *Gloss* on the words in 2 Thessalonians, "And then that wicked one shall be revealed, whom the Lord Jesus shall kill."[12] He will sit in his tent and on his throne, at that place from which the Lord ascended, and Michael will come and slay him. This fight and this victory are understood, according to Gregory, as referring to the text in Revelation mentioned above: "There was a great battle in heaven, etc." And what is said about Michael's threefold battle is understood as referring inclusively to the fight he had with Lucifer when he expelled him from heaven, the one with the demons to keep them from doing us too much harm on earth, and the one we are talking about here—the battle with the Antichrist at the end of the world.

Thirdly, this feast is called Dedication, due to the fact that on this day the archangel Michael revealed that he himself had dedicated the place on Mount Gargano, already described. When the people of Sipontus came back after defeating their enemies and achieving such a magnificent victory, they began to have doubts about whether they should dedicate the cave or even enter it. The bishop therefore consulted Pope Pelagius about this, and the pope answered: "If indeed it behooves man to dedicate that church, it should be done on this date, the day on which victory was granted us. If, on the other hand, it would please Michael to have something else done, he is the one to tell us what his will is in the matter." The pope, the bishop, and the people joined in a three-day fast, and on this very day Michael appeared to the bishop and said: "There is no need for

[5] Tob. 8:3.   [6] Gen. 32:24–25.   [7] Rev. 7:3.
[8] Ezek. 9:4.   [9] Ezek. 9:6.   [10] Dan. 12:1.
[11] Rev. 13:3.   [12] 2 Thess. 2:8.

you to dedicate this church, because I myself founded it, built it, and dedicated it." He ordered the bishop to enter the church with the people on the following day. There they were to pray to Michael and acknowledge him as their special patron.

Michael told the bishop that for all to have a sign of the consecration he had spoken of, they should come up from the eastern side and through a rear entrance, and there they would find the marks of a man's footsteps imprinted in the marble. So, the next day, the bishop and the entire populace climbed to the place and went inside. They found themselves in a vast cavern, in which two altars stood on the south side and one to the east. This last altar was of imposing dimensions and was covered all around with a red mantle. Mass was then celebrated, and after receiving holy communion the people went their several ways rejoicing. The bishop appointed priests and clerics to celebrate the divine office there continually. In this same cave a clear, sweet water flowed. The people drank it after communion and were cured of whatever diseases they had. When the pope was informed of these events, he decreed that this day should be celebrated throughout the world in honor of Saint Michael and all the blessed spirits.

Fourthly, this feast is called a Commemoration of Saint Michael: by it, however, we commemorate all the angels and honor all of them together. There are many reasons for our honoring and praising the angels. They are our guardians, our servants, our brothers, and our fellow citizens; they carry our souls into heaven; they present our prayers before God; they are the noble soldiers of the eternal King and the consolers of the afflicted.

First, then, we owe them honor because they are our guardians. To every man two angels are given, one good and the other bad, the bad one to test him and the good one to protect him. The good angel is deputed to an infant in the womb and immediately after birth, is with him or her in adult life. Man needs an angel as guardian in these three stages of life. He could die while still in the womb and therefore be damned. After being born but before adulthood it may not be possible for him to be baptized; and as an adult he can be drawn to a variety of sins. The devil deceives the mind by false reasoning, entices the will by seduction, and overpowers virtue by violence. Therefore it was necessary that a good angel be deputed to each man as guardian, to instruct and direct him against falsehood, to exhort and incite him to good and defend him against cajolery, and to protect him against violent oppression.

The guardianship of the angel can be said to have a fourfold effect upon a man. The first is that his soul makes progress in gaining grace, and the angel does this in the soul in three ways. One is by removing every obstacle to doing good, as in Exodus, where we see that the angel slew every firstborn in the land of Egypt.[13] The second is that the angel shakes us out of our slothfulness, as we see in Zechariah, where we read: "The angel of the Lord waked me, like a man that

---

[13] Exod. 12:29.

is wakened out of his sleep."[14] The third is that the angel leads man to, or leads him back to, the path of penance, which is shown in figure when the angel leads Tobias away safely and brings him back safely.[15]

The second effect of the angel's protection is that it keeps man from falling into the evil of sin, and this the angel does in three ways. The first way is by preventing him from committing a sin that he is thinking of committing, as in the case of Balaam, who was on his way to curse Israel but was halted by an angel.[16] The second way is by reproaching wrongdoers for a wrong already done, as is shown in the Book of Judges, when the angel reproached the sons of Israel for their disobedience, and they lifted up their voices and wept.[17] The third way is by doing violence, as it were, to put a stop to the commission of sin, as when angels violently forced Lot and his wife to leave Sodom[18]—"Sodom" here standing for habitual sin.

The third effect is that if someone falls he is made to get up again, and this the angel brings about in three ways. The first way is by moving the sinner to repentance, and we see this in Tobias,[19] when Tobias, instructed by the angel, anoints his father's eyes, i.e., his heart, with the gall of the fish, which represents repentance. The second way is the purging of the lips in preparation for confession, as is indicated when the angel cleanses Isaiah's lips with a live coal.[20] The third way is by rejoicing when penance is done for sin, as we read in Luke[21] that there will be more joy in heaven over one sinner who repents than over ninety-nine righteous who need no repentance.

The fourth effect is to preserve us from falling into sin as deeply or as often as the devil would have us do, and the angel accomplishes this in three ways: by curbing the demon's power, by mitigating our concupiscence, and by impressing on our minds the memory of the Lord's passion.

Secondly, we must honor the angels because they are our servants. They minister to us, as we read in Hebrews: "Are they not all ministering spirits, sent to minister for them who are to receive the inheritance of salvation?"[22] All are sent for our sake—the highest orders to the middle orders, these to the lowest ones, and the lowest to us. This sending of the angels is in accord, firstly, with the kindness of God, because it shows how much he loves our salvation, since he directs and dispatches the noblest spirits, those who are joined to him in intimate love, to procure salvation for us. Secondly, their mission also befits the angels' love for us, for it is of the nature of ardent love to desire intensely the welfare of others. For this reason Isaiah said: "Behold, Lord, here am I! Send me!"[23] The angels can help us because they see us in need of their aid, with bad angels warring against us. Thus the law of angelic love requires that they be sent to us. Thirdly, their sending also meets the neediness of mankind. The good

---

[14] Zech. 4:1. [15] Tob. 5:20. [16] Num. 22–24, esp. 22:12, 22–31
[17] Judg. 2:1–4. [18] Gen. 19, esp. vv. 15–17. [19] Tob. 11:8.
[20] Isa. 6:6–7. [21] Luke 15:7. [22] Heb. 1:14.
[23] Isa. 6:8.

angels are sent to inflame our hearts with love. As a figure of this we read that they were sent in a fiery chariot. They are sent also to enlighten our understanding and bring us to knowledge, as is shown in a figure in the angel who held an open book in his hand.[24] And they come to strengthen any weakness in us to the limit of our need, as we see in 1 Kings, where we read that the angel brought to Elijah a cake baked on hot stones and a jar of water, and Elijah ate and drank, and walked in the strength of that food forty days and forty nights, to Horeb the mountain of God.[25]

Thirdly, we should honor the angels because they are our brothers and fellow citizens. All the elect are assumed to the angelic orders, some to the highest, some to the lowest, and some to the middle orders, according to the diversity of their merits. The Blessed Virgin is, of course, above all of them. Saint Gregory, in one of his homilies, confirms this truth. He says: "There are some of the chosen who grasp but little knowledge yet ceaselessly share what they know with their brothers, and these run in the order of the Angels. There are some elect who succeed in grasping the highest of the secrets of heaven and in making them known, and these are with the Archangels. There are those who perform wondrous signs and works of power, and these are assumed among the Virtues. There are some who, by virtue of their prayer and the force of the power they have received, put the evil spirits to flight, and these are with the Powers. Some surpass the merits of most of the elect and rule over them, and these are allotted a place among the Principalities. There are those who so completely dominate all vices in themselves that by right of their purity they are called gods among men, as the Lord said to Moses: 'Behold I have appointed thee the God of Pharaoh.'[26] These are with the Dominations. There are some elect on whom the Lord sits as upon his throne and examines the deeds of others, and since these rule the holy Church, the weak actions of the rest of the elect are judged by them: they are with the Thrones. There are some of the chosen who are more filled with the love of God and neighbor than the rest, and it falls to their lot to merit a place among the Cherubim, because *cherubim* means plenitude of knowledge, and, according to Paul, love is the fulfilling of the law. And there are those who are fired with the love of contemplating the things of heaven and pant with the sole desire of their Creator, who want nothing of this world, feed only on the love of eternity, throw away all earthly things, rise in their minds above all things temporal, who love and burn and in that very ardor find rest, who burn by loving and glow by speaking and make any whom their word touches burn with the love of God. These receive their inheritance not elsewhere than among the Seraphim." So Gregory.

Fourthly, we are to honor the angels because it is they who bear our souls up to heaven, and this they do in three ways. The first is by preparing the way, so we read in Malachi: "Behold I send my angel, who will prepare the way before

---

[24] Rev. 10:2, 8.   [25] 1(3) Kings 19:6–8.   [26] Exod. 7:1.

your face."[27] The second is by conveying the souls to heaven along the prepared way; so Exodus: "Behold I will send an angel, who shall go before thee and keep thee in thy journey, and bring thee into the land which I promised to thy fathers."[28] The third is by putting the souls in their place in heaven; so Luke: "It came to pass that the beggar died and was carried by the angels into Abraham's bosom."[29]

Fifthly, the angels are to be honored because it is they who present our prayers before God. First, they do indeed present our prayers to God; Tobias: "When thou didst pray with tears and didst bury the dead, I offered thy prayer to the Lord."[30] Second, they plead our cause for us; Job: "If there shall be an angel speaking for him, one among thousands, to declare man's uprightness, he shall have mercy on him";[31] and Zechariah: "The angel of the Lord answered and said: 'How long wilt thou not have mercy on Jerusalem and on the cities of Judah, with which thou hast been angry? This is now the seventieth year.'"[32] Third, they report God's sentence to us, as we read in the Book of Daniel that Gabriel flew to Daniel and said: "From the beginning of thy prayers the word came forth" (to which the *Gloss* adds "the word, i.e., God's sentence"), "and I am come to show it to thee, because thou art a man of desires."[33] Bernard, in his book on the Song of Solomon, says of these three services rendered by the angels: "The angel runs as a mediator between God the beloved and the beloved supplicant, offering the supplicant's prayers, and bringing back God's gifts, stirring up the petitioner, appeasing God."

Sixthly, we should honor the angels because they are the noble soldiers of the eternal King, as Job says: "Is there any numbering of his soldiers?"[34] Among the soldiers of a king we see some who are always in the king's presence, to attend him and to sing songs that honor him and lighten his cares. Others guard the cities and strongholds of the realm; others rout the king's enemies. Thus some of the soldiers of Christ always attend upon the King in his court, namely, in the empyrean heaven, and continually sing chants of joy and glory to him, saying: "Holy, holy, holy Lord, God of hosts!"[35] and "Benediction and glory and wisdom to our God for ever and ever!"[36] Others stand guard over the cities, country places, and fortified towns—in other words, the angels who are deputed to guard us and to watch over the chastity of virgins, the continency of married people, and the communities of religious. So we read in Isaiah: "Upon your walls, O Jerusalem, I have set watchmen."[37] Others rout the King's enemies, namely, the demons, and Revelation says: "There was a great battle in heaven, etc."[38] According to one interpretation, this refers to the battle in the Church militant, in which Michael and his angels fight against the dragon.

[27] Cf. Mal. 3:1. [28] Cf. Exod. 23:20. [29] Luke 16:22.
[30] Cf. Tob. 12:12. [31] Cf. Job 33:23–24. [32] Cf. Zech. 1:12.
[33] Cf. Dan. 9:23. [34] Job 25:3. [35] Isa. 6:3.
[36] Rev. 7:12. [37] Isa. 62:6. [38] Rev. 12:7.

Seventhly and lastly, the angels are to be honored because they console those in tribulation. In Zechariah we find mention of "the angel that spoke in me good words, comfortable words";[39] and in Tobias: "Be of good courage: thy cure from God is at hand."[40] This the angels do in three ways. First, they comfort and strengthen, as we find in Daniel. When Daniel had given up and had no strength left, the angel touched him and said: "Fear not, O man of desires, peace be to thee. Take courage and be strong!"[41] Second, they preserve us from impatience: "He will give his angels charge of you, to guard you in all your ways. On their hands they will bear you up, lest you dash your foot against a stone."[42] Third, they cool and allay affliction, and this is typified in Daniel, when the angels of the Lord descended to the three young men in the fiery furnace, and in the middle of the furnace it was as if a dewy breeze were blowing.

146. Saint Jerome

Jerome (Hieronymus in Latin) comes from *gerar*, holy, and *nemus*, a grove—hence a holy grove—or *noma*, a law. Therefore in his legend the saint's name is interpreted as sacred law. He was holy, i.e., firm, or clean, or wet with blood, or set apart for sacred use, as the temple vessels were said to be holy because they were kept apart for sacred uses. Jerome was holy, which is to say firm in doing good, by his long-suffering perseverance. He was clean in his mind through his purity, and wet with blood through his meditation on the Lord's passion. He was set apart for sacred usage in his exposition and interpretation of Holy Scripture. Or he is called a grove after the grove where he lived at times, and a law because of the religious rule that he taught his monks, and also because he expounded and interpreted the sacred law.

The name is also construed as meaning vision of beauty, or one who judges speech. Beauty is manifold. First of all, there is spiritual beauty, which is in the soul, secondly, moral beauty, which consists in propriety of conduct, thirdly, intellectual beauty, which is the beauty of the angels, fourthly, supersubstantial

[39] Zech. 1:12 (Douay).
[40] Tob. 5:13.
[41] Dan. 10:17–18.
[42] Ps. 90(91):11–12.

beauty, which is divine, fifthly, celestial beauty, which is the beauty of the saints in heaven. Jerome had this fivefold beauty and saw it in himself—the spiritual in the variety of his virtues, the moral in the propriety of his way of life, the intellectual in the excellence of his purity, the supersubstantial in the ardor of his love, the celestial in his eternal and excellent charity. He judged speech, whether his own or that of others, his own by carefully weighing his words, that of others by confirming what was true, refuting what was false, and exposing what was dubious.

Jerome was the son of a nobleman named Eusebius and was a native of the town of Stridon, which lay on the boundary between Dalmatia and Pannonia. While still a youth he went to Rome and became thoroughly proficient in the Latin, Greek, and Hebrew languages and letters. In the art of grammar his teacher was Donatus, in rhetoric the orator Victorinus. He labored day and night in the study of the divine Scriptures, drawing deep draughts from them and later pouring out his knowledge in abundance. There was a time, as he wrote in a letter to Eustochium, when he read Cicero by day and Plato by night, because the coarse language of the prophetic books displeased him.

Then, about halfway through Lent, he came down with a fever so sudden and so violent that his whole body was cold and the vital heat throbbed only in his chest. Preparations for his funeral were therefore under way when abruptly he was haled before the judge's tribunal. The judge asked him what his profession was, and he professed without hesitation that he was a Christian. "You lie!" the judge said. "You are no Christian, you are a Ciceronian, for where your treasure is, there is your heart also." Jerome did not answer, and the judge ordered him to be flogged severely. Then Jerome burst out: "Have mercy on me, O Lord, have mercy on me!" The people present pleaded with the judge to pardon the adolescent, who swore an oath and said: "O Lord, if ever I possess or read worldly books again, I will be denying you!" Hearing this, the judge dismissed him, and Jerome of a sudden regained his strength and found himself bathed in tears, and his shoulders terribly bruised from the flogging he had received at the tribunal. From then on he devoted as much study to godly books as previously he had given to pagan works.

At the age of twenty-nine Jerome was ordained a cardinal priest in the church of Rome, and when Pope Liberius died, Jerome was acclaimed by all to be worthy of the pontifical chair. But he had denounced some monks and clerics for their lascivious lives, and they were so resentful that they began to lay snares for him. John Beleth tells us, for instance, that they used a woman's clothing to create a false impression of him. He got up one morning to go to matins, as was his custom, and found at his bedside a woman's gown, which, thinking it was his own, he put on and so proceeded into the church. His adversaries, of course, had done this in order to make it look as if he had a woman in his room.

Jerome now saw how far these people would go in their insane folly, so he gave way to them and went to join Gregory of Nazianz, bishop of the city of Constantinople. After studying the Scriptures with Gregory, he retired to live in the desert. Later he wrote to Eustochium to tell her about his trials there: "How many times, living in the wilderness, in the vast solitude that provides a horrid, sun-scorched abode to monks, have I thought that I was basking amid the delights of Rome! My misshapen limbs shuddered in their sackcloth, my squalid skin had taken on the blackness of an Ethiopian's flesh. Tears all day, groans all day—and if, resist it as I might, sleep overwhelmed me, my fleshless bones, hardly holding together, scraped against the bare ground. I say nothing about food or drink: even the sick have cold water to drink, and to have some cooked food was like a sinful indulgence. All the company I had was scorpions and wild beasts, yet at times I felt myself surrounded by clusters of pretty girls, and the fires of lust were lighted in my frozen body and moribund flesh. So it was that I wept continually and starved the rebellious flesh for weeks at a time. Often I joined day to night and did not stop beating my breast until the Lord restored my peace of mind. I even dreaded my cell, haunted as it was with my thoughts. Angry and stern with myself I plunged alone, deeper and deeper, into the wasteland; and, as the Lord is my witness, from time to time and after many tears I seemed to be in the midst of throngs of angels."

After leading this penitential life in the desert for four years, Jerome went to the town of Bethlehem and offered himself to live, like a domestic animal, at the Lord's crib. He reread his own books, which he had kept safely stowed away, and other books as well. He fasted every day until sundown and gathered many disciples around him to follow the same holy way of life. For fifty-five years and six months he toiled at the translation of the Scriptures. He was a virgin to the end of his life—or so this legend says—but he once wrote about himself to Pammachius: "I hold virginity as high as heaven—not that I have it."

In time the saint was so worn out and weakened that he lay on his cot and had a rope hanging from an overhead beam, by which he pulled himself upright to follow the offices of the monastery as well as he could. One day toward evening, when he was seated with the brethren to hear the sacred lessons read, a lion suddenly limped into the monastery. The other monks fled at the sight of the beast, but Jerome greeted him as a guest. The lion showed him his wounded foot, and Jerome called the brothers and ordered them to wash the animal's feet and to dress the wound carefully. When they set about doing this, they found that the paw had been scratched and torn by thorns. They did what was necessary, and the lion recovered, lost all his wildness, and lived among the monks like a house pet.

By this time, however, Jerome sensed that the Lord had not sent them the lion for the health of the wounded paw, but so that the animal could render them some service. The saint therefore followed the advice of his monks and assigned a duty to the lion. The monks had an ass that carried firewood in from the forest, and it became the lion's chore to lead the ass out to pasture and to watch over her safety. And so it went. Once the care of the ass was enjoined upon the lion, they were constant companions. He guarded her like a faithful shepherd, going with her to pasture and being a most vigilant defender. He looked after his own food and the ass went about her accustomed work, but at fixed hours he led his charge home.

Then one day, when the ass was feeding and the lion fell into a deep sleep, some merchants passed that way with their camels and, seeing the ass unguarded, made off with her at once. When the lion woke up and did not see his companion, he ran hither and yon, roaring, but did not find the ass. He went sadly back to the monastery but was ashamed to go in as he usually did. The monks, seeing him come home late and without his ward, concluded that hunger had made him eat the ass. Therefore they would not give him his usual provisions and said to him: "Get out, and go eat what's left of the poor little ass, and satisfy your gluttony!"

The monks, however, found it hard to believe that the lion had done this bad thing, and they went out to the pastures to see if they could discover any sign of what had happened; but there was none, and they reported the whole matter to Jerome. At his suggestion they turned the ass's work over to the lion and loaded the cut wood on his back. The lion submitted to this patiently. Then one day, when his work was finished, he went out to the fields, running to and fro and hoping to learn what had become of his companion. Then at a distance he saw a train of merchants with their loaded camels, and an ass leading the way: in that region it is usual, in order to keep the camels on the right track when they have a long way to go, to have them follow an ass that leads them with a rope around its neck. The lion recognized his friend and with a terrifying roar rushed upon the caravan and put all the men to flight. Then, still roaring terribly and flailing the ground with his tail, he drove the frightened camels, laden as they were, toward the monastery. The monks saw them coming and notified Jerome, who said: "Wash the feet of our guests, dearest brothers! Offer them food, and above all, await the will of the Lord!"

Now the happy lion began to run around the monastery, prostrating himself before each brother and swishing his tail as if to beg pardon for the perpetrated fault although he had not committed it. Jerome, foreseeing what was about to happen, said to the monks: "Go, brothers, and get ready to provide our arriving guests with whatever they need!" He was still speaking when a messenger came to tell him that some visitors were outside and wanted to see the abbot. When Jerome went out to meet the merchants, they threw themselves at his feet, asking his pardon for the wrong they had done. He brought them kindly to their feet, and admonished them to take what was theirs and not to usurp what belonged to others. They prevailed upon Jerome to accept half their oil in return for his blessing. Reluctantly consenting, he accepted their offer. Furthermore they promised that every year the same measure of oil would be given to the monks, and that their heirs would be ordered to continue this practice.

In earlier times there had been no uniformity in the Church's offices or in the chant. Now Emperor Theodosius, as John Beleth tells us, asked Pope Damasus to charge some learned man with the work of bringing order to the liturgy. The pope, knowing that Jerome was expert in Greek and Hebrew and supreme in all kinds of knowledge, committed this task to him. Jerome distributed the Psalms for the days of the week, assigned a proper nocturne for each day, and specified that the *Gloria Patri* should be sung at the end of each Psalm, as Sigebert says. He also assigned the readings from the gospels and epistles to be sung throughout the cycle of the year, and put rational order into whatever else pertained to the office following the chant. He then sent the whole work from Bethlehem to the sovereign pontiff, and he, with his cardinals, gave it solemn approval and established it as standard for the whole Church in perpetuity. After that, Jerome arranged a tomb for himself at the mouth of the cave where the Lord had lain, and after living for ninety-eight years and six months, he died and was buried there.

The reverence in which Augustine held Jerome is patent in the letters he addressed to him. In one of them he wrote: "To Jerome, most dear lord worthy to be respected and embraced with the sincerest veneration and love, Augustine sends greetings." Elsewhere Augustine wrote of him: "The holy priest Jerome, learned in the Greek, Latin, and Hebrew speech, lived in holy places, and with the sacred writings, to an extreme old age, and, by the nobility of his discourse, shone from the East to the West like the light of the sun." Saint Prosper, in his *Chronicle*, says of him: "The priest Jerome lived in Bethlehem but was famed throughout the world, and served the Church universal with his rare intelligence and learning." To Albigensis Jerome said about himself: "From childhood on I have tried to avoid nothing so much as the prideful spirit and the haughty head that provoke the wrath of God"; also: "I fear all that is too safe"; also: "In the monastery we extend hospitality from the heart, welcome with gladsome countenance all who come to us except heretics, and wash our guests' feet." Isidore in his *Etymologies*, says: "Jerome was expert in three languages, and his interpretation is preferred to those of others because he is both closer to the letter and clearer in his perception of the meaning, and, since it comes from a Christian interpreter, truer." In his *Dialogue*, Severus, a disciple of Saint Martin and a contemporary of Saint Jerome, is held to have written about him: "Besides the merit of his faith and his endowment of virtues, he was so learned, not only in Latin and Greek but also in Hebrew letters, that no one dares to compare himself with him in any branch of knowledge. Against the wicked his fight was unceasing, his struggle relentless. Heretics hate him because he never stops attacking them. Clergy hate him because he berates their sinful lives and their crimes. But all good people admire and love him wholeheartedly. Those who consider him a heretic are insane. He is totally absorbed in study, totally in books. He rests

215

neither by day nor by night: he is always either reading or writing." Thus Severus.

As is clear from these quotations, and as he himself has testified, he had to suffer the hostility of many persecutors and many detractors. How willingly he submitted to this persecution is obvious from what he says in a letter to Asella: "I thank God that I am thought worthy to have the world hate me and prattlers call me an evildoer, but I know how to get to heaven, whether others think well or ill of me"; also: "Would that for the honor of my Lord's name the whole mob of unbelievers might persecute me! Would that this world would rise up more stoutly to shame me! Only let me be worthy to be praised by Christ and to hope for his promised reward! Welcome indeed and desirable is that trial for which Christ's reward is hoped for in heaven, nor is that curse harmful which is transmuted by God's praise."

Jerome died about A.D. 398.[1]

---

147. Saint Remy

Remy (or Remi) is the English form of the Latin name Remigius, and this name is derived from *remigo*, a pilot, or from *remi*, oars, the implements by which a boat is moved, and *gyon*. a grappling or struggle. Saint Remy piloted the Church away from the danger of shipwreck, moved it to the gates of heaven, and struggled for it against the wiles of the devil.

We are told that Remy, who was the bishop of Rheims, converted King Clovis and the Frankish nation to Christ. The king's wife was named Clothilda. She was a devout Christian and strove to convert her husband to the faith, but could not. When she bore a son, she wanted him baptized, but the king firmly forbade it. The queen, however, could not keep quiet about it, and Clovis finally gave in. The child was baptized but died shortly afterward. Then the king said to Clothilda: "It is now clear that Christ is a poor sort of god, since he could not keep alive someone by whom his faith could have been exalted." Clothilda answered: "It's the other way around. I sense that what has happened shows

[1] The saint's dates are ca. 342–420.

how dearly God loves me! I know that he has accepted the first fruit of my womb and has granted my son an infinite kingdom, one better than your own!"

Clothilda conceived again and bore a son, who, like the first, was baptized only after the king's resistance had been overcome; and as soon as the child was baptized he fell ill and his life was despaired of. Clovis said to his wife: "This God of yours is a weak one, since he cannot keep alive anyone baptized in his name. If you bore a thousand children and all were baptized, they would all perish!" But this new son recovered and grew to manhood, and, long after, succeeded his father as king. For the present, however, Clothilda, that woman of faith, persisted in her effort to bring her husband to the faith of Christ, and he was equally persistent in refusing. How in the end he was converted and became a Christian is narrated in the legend for the other feast of Saint Remy, the one celebrated after Epiphany.[1]

After his conversion, King Clovis wanted to endow the church of Rheims. He told Saint Remy that he would give the church as much land as the bishop could walk around while he, the king, had his midday siesta, and Remy started to walk. However, there was a man who operated a mill that was within the bishop's boundaries, and when Remy approached it, the miller angrily ordered him away. Remy said: "Friend, why should it bother you if we share this mill?" But the miller repulsed him, and as soon as the bishop started to walk away, the mill began to turn in the reverse direction. The miller called after him: "Servant of God, come back and we shall share the mill equally!" Remy: "Not for me, not for you!" And the earth opened and swallowed the mill.

Now Remy foresaw that a famine was imminent, and filled a barn with a large supply of grain. Soon some drunken rustics, jeering at the old man's thrift-iness, set fire to the barn. The bishop heard of this and came to the place, and, due to the chill of age and the late hour, warmed himself at the fire and said calmly: "Fire is always good; but those who set this fire, and their posterity, will suffer for it, the men from rupture and the women from goiter!" And so it befell, until Charlemagne dispersed the descendants.

It should be noted that the feast of Saint Remy which is celebrated in January is said to mark the day of his happy death and of the translation of his sacred body. What happened was that after his death his body was being transported on a litter to the church of Saints Timothy and Apollinaris, but as the litter was being carried past the church of Saint Christopher, it suddenly became so heavy that it could not be moved. The bearers, perplexed, prayed the Lord to let them know if perchance he wished that the body be buried in the church of Saint Christopher, where a thousand relics of saints reposed. At once the litter became very light and the body was honorably laid to rest. Many miracles occurred there, and the church was enlarged and a crypt built behind the altar for Saint

---

[1] See chapter 16 above.

Remy's remains, but when the body was unearthed and they tried to place it there, again it could not be moved. The ministers spent the night in prayer until they all fell asleep, and in the morning, on the first day of October, they found that angels had carried the coffin containing the saint's body to the new crypt. Much later, however, the sacred remains, in a silver casket, were enshrined in a more beautiful crypt.

Saint Remy flourished about the year A.D. 490.

---

148. Saint Leger

Leger (or Leodegar) was known for his virtuous life and was considered worthy to be made bishop of Autun. When King Clothar died and the care of the kingdom weighed heavily on Leger, by the will of God and with the consent of the princes he promoted Childeric, Clothar's adolescent brother, as the one fully suited to be king. Ebroin[1] wanted to secure the throne for Theoderic, Childeric's brother, not for the good of the realm but because Ebroin himself had been deposed from power, was hated by all, and feared the hostility of the king and the princes. Because of his fear he petitioned the king for permission and was allowed to retire to a monastery. The king also put his brother Theoderic in confinement to keep him from plotting against the throne. Thus, due to the bishop's holiness and foresight, the realm enjoyed a marvelous peace.

Some time later the king, deceived by disloyal counselors, was aroused to such hatred of the man of God that he sedulously sought both the opportunity to put him to death and the best way to do it. The bishop bore all this calmly and, embracing all his enemies as if they were friends, arranged that the king should celebrate the feast of Easter with him in his episcopal city. That very day, however, it was made known to him that the ruler had ordered him to be done to death on Easter night. Fearing nothing, Leger dined with the king as arranged, but then escaped from his persecutor and fled to the monastery of Luxeuil. There he served the Lord and with unfailing charity waited on Ebroin, who was hiding there under a monk's habit.

[1] Ebroin had been "mayor of the palace," in Merovingian times a position second only to the king's.

A short time later King Childeric died, and Theoderic was raised to the throne. Then Leger, moved by the tears and pleading of his people and constrained by the abbot's command, returned to his episcopal see. At the same time Ebroin abandoned religion and was appointed seneschal to the king. If he had been evil before, he then became more evil and spent all his energy in his effort to bring about Leger's death. He sent soldiers to take him captive, and when the bishop learned this, he went outside his city, wearing his pontifical robes, to face their fury. They laid hold of him and put out his eyes.

Two years later Leger was brought to the royal palace with his brother Garin, whom Ebroin had exiled. He responded wisely and peacefully to Ebroin's derisive taunts, but the wicked man ordered Garin to be stoned to death, and the holy bishop to be marched barefoot for a whole day through a stream that flowed over sharp stones. When he heard that Leger praised God while enduring these torments, he had his tongue cut out and then handed him over to another guard to be held for new tortures. Leger, however, did not lose the power of speech, but applied himself to preaching and exhortation as well as he could. He also foretold when and how he and Ebroin would meet their several ends. A wide and brilliant light circled his head like a crown, and many who saw this asked the bishop what it was; but he prostrated himself in prayer, giving thanks to God, and admonished all the onlookers to mend their lives for the better.

These events came to Ebroin's ears, and his wrath knew no bounds. He sent four swordsmen with orders to behead Leger. As they led him toward a suitable place, he said to them: "There's no need, brothers, to tire yourselves any longer. Do here what the one who sent you wants you to do!" Thereupon three of them were so stricken with remorse that they fell at his feet and begged for pardon, and the fourth, after beheading him, was immediately seized by a demon and cast into a fire, thus coming to a miserable end.

Two more years passed, and Ebroin heard that the holy man's body had become famous for the many miracles that occurred around it. He sent a soldier to find out whether there was any truth to this rumor, and if so to let him know. The soldier, a haughty, arrogant fellow, came to the saint's tomb, kicked it, and exclaimed: "Death to anyone who believes that a dead man can perform wonders!" At once he was snatched up by a demon and died then and there, by his death further confirming the bishop's holiness. News of this threw Ebroin into paroxysms of rage, and he determined afresh to stamp out the saint's renown, but as Leger had predicted, the wicked man was killed wickedly by the sword.

Leger suffered about A.D. 680, in the reign of Constantine IV.

149. Saint Francis

Francis was born in Assisi, he was first named John but later was called Francis. It appears that there were several reasons for this change of names. The first was to call attention to a miracle, because he is known to have received miraculously from God the power to speak in the French language. Hence we read in his legend that whenever he was filled with the ardor of the Holy Spirit, he burst out with ardent words in French. The second reason was to make his mission manifest: his legend says that divine providence conferred this name upon him, in order that by the unusual name awareness of his mystery might be spread more quickly throughout the whole world. Third reason, to indicate the effect that was to follow from his ministry—in other words, to make it known that he, through his own work and that of his sons, was to free and enfranchise many slaves of sin and the devil. Fourth reason, his greatness of soul: the name French, or Frankish, *français* is derived from ferocitas, fierceness, the quality of high-spiritedness and impetuosity, because in the French there is a natural truthfulness and magnanimity. Fifth reason, the saint's virtuosity in speech: his speech was like an ax that chopped out vices. Sixth, the terror he aroused in driving out demons. Seventh, his security in virtue, the perfection of his works, and his honorable dealings with others. It is said that the term *franciscae* is used for the ax-shaped insignia which were carried before consuls in Rome, and which stood for terror, security, and honor.

Francis, servant and friend of the Almighty, was born in the city of Assisi. He became a merchant and, until he was twenty years old, lived a vain and frivolous life. The Lord chastened him with the whip of ill health and quickly made a different man of him, and he began to exhibit the spirit of prophecy. Once he and a number of companions were captured by the Perugians and confined in a horrid prison, where the others bemoaned their fate while Francis alone rejoiced. When his fellow prisoners rebuked him, he answered: "Know that I rejoice now because in time the whole world will worship me as a saint!" Another time he went to Rome for reasons of devotion. When he got there, he put off his fine clothes and dressed in a beggar's rags, then sat with the other beggars at the door of Saint Peter's church and grabbed hungrily for food like any of them. He would have done this more often but was dissuaded because it embarrassed those who knew him.

The ancient enemy tried to turn Francis aside from his virtuous intention and forced the image of a hunchback woman upon his mind, warning him that if he did not give up the way of life he had undertaken, the devil would make him as ugly as she was. Then, however, he heard the Lord comforting him and saying: "Francis, take the bitter instead of the sweet, and despise yourself if you long to know me!" Then he found himself face to face with a leper, the sort of man he utterly abhorred; but, remembering the Lord's word to him, he ran and kissed the afflicted man. The leper instantly vanished. Francis then hastened to the place where people with leprosy lived, devoutly kissed their hands, and left them money.

He went into the church of Saint Damian to pray, and an image of Christ spoke to him miraculously: "Francis, go and repair my house, because, as you see, it has fallen into ruins!" From that moment on his soul melted within him, his compassion for Christ was marvelously fixed in his heart, and he devoted himself zealously to the rebuilding of the Church. He sold all he had and wanted to give the money to a certain priest, but the priest refused to accept it for fear of offending Francis's parents. Francis thereupon threw the money on the ground, treating it as worth no more than dust. His father therefore had him bound and held in custody, whereupon he gave all his money to his father, and with it the clothes off his back. Then he flew naked to the Lord and put on a hair shirt. The servant of God next called in a plain, simple man whom he took as a father, and asked him to bless him whenever his true father heaped curses on him.

His blood brother, seeing Francis at prayer clothed in rags and shivering with the wintry cold, said to a companion: "Tell Francis to give you a penny's worth of his sweat!" Francis heard this and quickly retorted: "In fact I sell it to my Lord!" Another day, hearing what Jesus said to his disciples as he sent them off to preach, Francis rose immediately to carry out to the letter what he had heard, took the shoes off his feet, put on a single cheap garment, and exchanged his leather belt for a length of rope. Then he was walking through the woods in winter when thieves laid hold of him and asked him who he was. He declared that he was the herald of God, so they threw him into the snow, saying: "Lie there, you peasant, herald of God!"

Many people, of noble and of humble birth, both clerical and lay, put away the world's vanities and followed his path. Like a father, this holy man taught them to strive for evangelical perfection, to embrace poverty, and to walk the way of holy simplicity. He also wrote a Rule, based on the Gospel, for himself and his present and future friars: this Rule was approved by the lord Pope Innocent. From then on Francis began with even greater fervor to sow the seeds of the word of God, going about from city to city and town to town.

There was a friar who seemed from the outside to be a man of remarkable sanctity but was not at all like the others in his conduct. He observed the rule of silence so extravagantly that he made his confession with nods of the head, not speaking. All the friars were praising him as a saint when the man of God came along and said: "Leave off, brothers! Do not praise his diabolical illusions to me!

Let him be admonished to confess his sins once or twice a week! If he does not do this, it's all diabolical temptation, fraud, deception!" The friars admonished this brother, but he silenced them with his finger to his lips and shook his head to indicate that he had nothing to confess. After a few days he returned to his peculiar ways, and ended his life in criminal actions.

Once when the servant of God, too tired to walk farther, was riding on an ass, his companion, Friar Leonardo of Assisi, who also was tired, thought to himself: "This man's parents were not so wellborn as mine." At that moment Francis dismounted and said to Leonardo: "It is not right for me to ride and you to walk, because you are of nobler stock than I." Astonished, the friar knelt at Francis's feet and asked forgiveness.

He was walking along the road one day when a certain noble lady, almost running in her haste, came to meet him. Seeing how tired and out of breath she was, he felt sorry for her and asked her what she wanted. The lady said: "Pray for me, father, because I had made a resolution to lead a virtuous life, but my husband prevents me from living up to it and makes every effort to keep me from serving Christ." Francis: "Go home, my daughter, because you will soon receive consolation from him; and in the name of almighty God and in my name, tell him that now is the time of salvation, and later will come the time of just reward." She conveyed the saint's message, and the husband, suddenly changing his attitude, promised to live continently.

For a peasant who was fainting with thirst in the desert, Francis, by his prayer, obtained a spring of water.

Prompted by the Holy Spirit, he disclosed a secret to a friar who was close to him, saying: "Today there is on earth a certain servant of God, for whose sake, as long as he lives, the Lord will not allow famine to scourge the people"; and there is no doubt that that was the situation during the saint's lifetime. But once he was taken away, things changed. Not long after his happy death he appeared to the aforementioned friar and said: " Now you will see the coming of the famine, which, while I was alive, the Lord would not allow on earth."

On Easter Sunday the friars laid the table more carefully than usual, with white linens and glass vessels. When the man of God saw this, he turned away, picked up a poor man's cap that was lying there, put it on his head, and, staff in hand, went out and waited at the door. When the friars sat down to eat, he called out at the door, asking them for the love of God to give an alms to a poor, enfeebled pilgrim. The poor man was called in and entered, sat down on the ground alone, and set his dish in the ashes. The friars were shocked at seeing this, but Francis said to them: "I saw the table all set and decorated, but of the poor men begging from door to door I did not see a single one here."

He loved poverty in himself and in others so much that he always spoke of his Lady Poverty, and, when he saw someone poorer than himself, he envied him and was afraid he might be outdone by him. One day he saw a poor little man passing by and said to his companion: "That man's neediness puts us to shame;

it makes a false show of our poverty. For my riches I chose my Lady Poverty, but you see that she is more glorified in him than in me."

A poor man was walking by, and at the sight of him Francis was moved with compassion, but his companion said to him: "Poor he may be at the moment, but perhaps in the whole province there is no one as rich as he would like to be." The man of God said: "Quick, take off your cloak and give it to that man, and kneel down at his feet and confess your guilt!" And the friar obeyed forthwith.

One day three women, alike in figure and finery, confronted him and greeted him with the words: "Welcome to Lady Poverty!" They disappeared at once and were seen no more.

Once when he went to the city of Arezzo, where civil strife had broken out, he looked down from a high point above the town and saw demons exulting over the disorder below them. Francis called his companion, whose name was Silvester, and said to him: "Go to the city gate, and in the name of almighty God order the demons to leave the city!" Silvester hurried to the gate and called out loudly: "In the name of almighty God and by order of our father Francis, go away, all you demons!" And in a short time the townspeople made peace.

While Silvester was still a secular priest, he had a dream in which he saw a gold cross issuing from the mouth of Francis. Its high point touched the heavens, and its extended arms embraced and held the world from east to west. The priest was smitten with self-reproach, abandoned the world, and became a perfect imitator of the man of God.

While Francis was at prayer, the devil called him three times by name. The saint responded, and the devil added: "In the whole world there is not a single sinner to whom the Lord will not grant pardon if he repents; but if someone kills himself with excessive penances, he will not obtain mercy forever." By a revelation, the saint instantly recognized the lie and the liar, and saw how the demon was trying to cool his ardor to lukewarmness. The ancient enemy, seeing that his effort was of no avail, aroused in Francis a violent temptation of the flesh, but the man of God, feeling this, took off his habit and scourged himself with a coarse rope, saying to his body: "See here, brother ass! Either behave yourself or take a beating!" But the temptation persisted, so the saint went out and threw himself naked into the deep snow. Then he made seven snowballs, which he set in front of him, and spoke again to his body: "Look here," he said, "the biggest ball is your wife, the next four are two sons and two daughters, and the last two are a manservant and a maidservant. Hurry up and clothe them, they're dying of cold! Or, if it bothers you to give them so much attention, then serve the Lord with care!" Thereupon the devil went away in confusion, and the man of God returned to his cell glorifying his Lord.

The lord cardinal Leo of the Holy Cross once invited Francis to be his guest, and he stayed in his house for some time. One night demons came and gave the saint a severe beating. He called his companion and explained the thing to him: "The demons are the Lord's bailiffs, whom he sends to punish excesses. I do not recall an offense that I have not washed away by the Lord's mercy and my penance, but it may be that he has allowed his bailiffs to attack me because the fact that I am lingering in the courts of the powerful could awaken a justified suspicion in my poor little brothers, who may think I am lolling in luxury." So he rose at dawn and left the cardinal's palace.

Sometimes when he was at prayer, he heard troops of demons running around noisily on the roof of the house. When that happened, he ran outside, armed himself with the sign of the cross, and said: "In the name of almighty God I tell you, demons, whatever you are allowed to do to my body, do it! I will gladly submit to whatever it may be, because I have no greater enemy than my body, and you avenge me upon my adversary when, acting for me, you wreak punishment on it." The demons were dumbfounded and scurried away.

A friar who was a close associate of Francis was rapt in ecstasy, and saw, among the other seats in heaven, one that was particularly distinguished and glorious. He wondered who might be the saint for whom so noble a throne was reserved, and heard a voice saying: "That chair belonged to one of the fallen princes and now has been made ready for humble Francis." Emerging from prayer, the friar questioned the man of God, saying: "What do you think of this, father?" Francis: "To myself I seem to be the greatest of sinners." At once the Spirit said in the friar's heart: "Know by this how true your vision was, because humility will raise the humblest of men to the seat that was lost through pride."

The servant of God had a vision in which he saw above him a crucified Seraph, who imprinted the signs of crucifixion upon him, so that he himself seemed to have been crucified. His hands, feet, and side were marked with the signature of the cross, but he with great care hid the stigmata from the eyes of all. There were some, however, who saw them while the saint was alive, and after his death many observed them. That these marks were truly the stigmata of the crucifixion was confirmed by many miracles, of which it will suffice to insert two that occurred after the saint's death.

In Apulia a man named Roger was standing in front of a painting of Saint Francis and began to ask himself whether what he saw was true: had the saint really been honored by such a miracle, or was this a pious illusion or a fraud contrived by his friars? As he turned these thoughts over in his mind, he heard a sound like that of an arrow being shot from a crossbow, and felt that he was painfully wounded in the left hand, though his glove seemed to be undamaged. He took the glove off, found a deep wound such as an arrow would make, and so much heat came from it that he felt he would faint with the pain and the burning. He repented his doubt and testified that he firmly believed in Saint Francis's stigmata. Two days later, as he pleaded with the saint by his stigmata, the man's wound was healed.

This happened in the kingdom of Castille. A man who was devoted to Saint Francis was on his way to assist at the office of compline when he was ambushed by mistake in a trap set for another man and was left half dead of a lethal wound. Then the cruel murderer drove his sword into the man's throat, but could not pull the sword out and went away. From all sides people came running and loudly bewailed the man for dead. Then, when at midnight the bell of the friars' convent rang for matins, the man's wife called out: "Master, get up and go to matins, the bell is calling you!" The man raised his hand as if to summon someone to extract the sword; but, as all looked on, the sword, as if hurled by the hand of a brawny fighter, leapt out and fell at a distance. The man, fully restored to health, stood up and said: "Blessed Francis came to me and touched his stigmata to my wounds, and their sweetness spread over all my hurts and the contact healed them wondrously; and when he was about to go away, I signaled to him to remove the sword, because otherwise I could not talk. So he grasped the sword and hurled it away, and at once, by stroking the wounded throat with his holy stigmata, he cured it perfectly."

In the city of Rome two shining lights of the world, Saint Francis and Saint Dominic, met with the bishop of Ostia, who later became the supreme pontiff. The bishop asked them: "Why do we not make some of your friars bishops and popes, since they stand out from the rest by their teaching and example?" The two saints argued for some time about which of them should respond and how. Humility conquered Francis, keeping him from being the first to answer: it also conquered Dominic, since he humbly obeyed by answering first. Blessed Dominic therefore said: "My lord, my friars have already attained a high status, if they only knew it. For my part, I cannot allow them to be raised higher, lest they pursue marks of dignity other than what they already possess." After him Saint Francis spoke: "My lord, my friars are called Minor, lest they presume to be made greater."

Blessed Francis was filled with the simplicity of the dove. He exhorted all creatures to love their Creator. He preached to the birds and they listened to him; he taught them and they did not fly away without his permission. When swallows were chattering when he was preaching, he bade them be silent and they obeyed. At the Portiuncula a locust that nested in a fig tree next to his cell used to sing at all hours, until the man of God extended his hand and said: "My sister locust, come here to me!" Obediently the locust came up and rested on his hand. "My sister locust, sing! Sing, and praise your Lord!" The locust began to sing and did not hop away until the saint gave permission.

The saint would not handle lanterns and lamps and candles because he did not want to dim their brightness with his hands. He walked reverently on stones out of respect for him who was called Peter, which means stone. He lifted worms from the road for fear they might be trampled underfoot by passersby. Bees might perish in the cold of winter, so he had honey and fine wines set out for them. He called all animals brothers and sisters. When he looked at the sun, the moon, and the stars, he was filled with inexpressible joy by his love of the

Creator and invited them all to love their Creator. He would not have a large crown[1] shaved on his head, and said: "I want my simple brothers to have a share in my head."

A certain man of the world heard the servant of God preaching in the church of Saint Severinus and, by God's revelation, saw Saint Francis pierced through and through by two gleaming swords in the form of a cross, one of them passing from his head to his feet, the other passing through his chest from one out-stretched hand to the other. The man had never seen Francis before but recognized him by this sign. Moved by compunction he retired from the world, entered the Order, and finished his life in holy living.

His eyesight was impaired by his constant weeping, but, to those who urged him not to weep so much, he replied: "The visitation of eternal light is not to be repelled for love of the light we have in common with the flies." His friars pressed him to allow a remedy to be applied to his failing eyes, and he held in his hand an iron surgical instrument heated in the fire. He said: "My brother fire, at this hour be kind to me and cure me! I pray the Lord who created you to mitigate your heat for me." Having said these words, he made the sign of the cross over the instrument, and when it was thrust through the tender flesh from ear to eyebrow, he himself said that he felt no pain.

He was in the desert of Saint Urban when he was stricken with a serious illness, and when he realized that his strength was waning, he asked for a cup of wine, but wine there was none to be had. He was given a cup of water and blessed it with the sign of the cross, and straightaway it was changed into an excellent wine. What the poverty of that desolate place could not supply the holy man's purity obtained, and at the first sip of wine he was healthy again.

He preferred to hear himself reviled rather than praised, and when people extolled the merits of his sanctity, he ordered one of the friars to assail his ears with abusive epithets. The friar, all unwilling, called him a bumpkin, a money-lover, an ignoramus, and a worthless fellow, and Francis cheered and said: "Lord bless you, brother! You have told the truth, and I need to hear such things!" The servant of God wished not so much to be in command as to be subject to authority, not so much to give orders as to carry them out. Therefore he gave up the office of general of his Order, and asked for a guardian, to whose will he would be subject in everything. To the friar with whom he was accustomed to go about he always promised obedience and always kept his promise.

A friar had done something forbidden by the rule of obedience, but then repented. To strike terror in others, however, the man of God ordered the delinquent friar's cowl to be thrown into the fire, and then, when it had been in the fire for some time, taken out and returned to the one it belonged to.

---

[1] The reference is to the tonsure, an area of the scalp shaved as a mark of the clerical or religious state. The tonsure was also called a crown, because there were, and are, various shapes of tonsure, one or more of which might suggest a crown.

The cowl, therefore, was snatched from the flames and showed not a trace of scorching.

Once when Francis was walking through the Venetian marshes, he came upon a large flock of birds singing, and said to his companion: "Our sisters the birds are praising their Creator. Let's go in among them and chant the canonical hours to the Lord!" They walked in among the birds and the birds did not move away, but their chirping was so noisy that the two friars could not hear each other. Francis said: "Sister birds, stop your singing until we pay our debt of praise to the Lord!" The birds were quiet until the friars had sung lauds, after which they received permission and resumed their singing as usual.

He was courteously invited to dinner by a knight, to whom he said: "Brother host, take my advice and confess your sins, because you will soon dine elsewhere." The knight quickly followed this advice, put his house in order, and accepted a salutary penance; and as they went in to dinner, the host suddenly expired.

He came upon a large flock of birds and spoke to them as though they were rational beings, saying: "My brother birds, you owe a great debt of praise to your Creator, who clothes you with feathers, gives you wings to fly with, grants you the purity of the air, and without effort on your part he sustains you." The birds began to stretch their necks toward him, spread their wings, opened their beaks, and fixed their eyes upon him. He walked through the middle of the flock and his cloak touched them, but not one of them moved an inch until, permission given, they all flew away at once.

Francis was preaching at the castle of Almarium but could not be heard because of the loud chirping of swallows that nested nearby. He said to them: "My sister swallows, you've said enough! Now it's my turn to talk, and you keep quiet till the word of the Lord has been spoken!" Obediently they hushed their chatter at once.

The man of God was passing through Apulia and came upon a pouch bursting with coins, lying on the road. His companion wanted to take the pouch and distribute the money to the poor, but Francis would have none of it and said: "My son, it is not right to make off with someone else's property." But the friar insisted vehemently, and Francis, after praying for a moment, ordered him to pick up the pouch, which now contained a viper in place of the coins. Seeing this the friar was afraid but, wishing to obey and to do as ordered, took the pouch in his hands, and a large serpent sprang out. "To the servants of God," said the saint, "money is nothing but the devil and a poisonous snake."

There was a friar who was plagued with temptation. He thought that if he had a script in the father's handwriting, the temptation would be driven away, but he did not dare to broach the matter to the saint. Then came a moment when the man of God called this friar and said to him: "Bring me paper and ink, my son, I want to write words of praise to God." When he had written them, he said: "Take this paper and keep it carefully until the day of your death," and all temptation left the friar at once. When the saint was lying ill, this same friar began to think: "Here our father is approaching death, and what a consolation it would be for me if I could have my father's cloak after he died!" Shortly afterwards Saint Francis called him and said: "I hand this cloak over to you now, and after my death it will be yours by right."

He was the guest of a man of good repute in Alessandria in Lombardy, and his host asked him to eat everything that was set before him, in accordance with the Gospel. In deference to the host's devotion the saint agreed, and the good man hurried off to prepare a fine seven-year-old capon for dinner. While they were eating, an unbeliever came and begged an alms for the love of God. Hearing God's blessed name, Francis sent a leg of the capon out to the beggar. The wretched man kept the gift, and the next day, while the saint was preaching, the fellow showed it to everyone, saying: "Look at the kind of fine food this friar eats, for he gave me this last evening!" But the capon's leg now looked like a fish to all who saw it, and they rebuffed the man as insane. The man was ashamed and asked pardon, and, once he had come to his senses, the meat looked like a capon's leg again.

Once when the man of God was seated at table and heard a reading on the poverty of the Blessed Virgin and her Son, he rose abruptly from the table, sobbing and weeping, and ate the rest of his bread sitting on the bare ground.

He always manifested deep reverence for the hands of priests,[2] hands empowered to produce the sacrament of Christ's Body. He often said: "If I happened to meet at the same time a saint coming down from heaven and some poor little priest, I would hurry first to kiss the priest's hands and would say to the saint: 'Wait for me, Saint Laurence, because this man's hands have handled the Word of life and possess something beyond the human.'"

In his lifetime he was known for his many miracles. Bread that was brought to him to be blessed by him restored health to many sick people. He changed water into wine, which a sick man tasted and recovered his health immediately. And he performed many other miracles.

Finally he was suffering from a long illness and knew that his last days were at hand. He had himself laid on the bare ground and had all the friars who were with him summoned to his presence. He laid his hands on each of them, blessed all present, and distributed to each a morsel of bread in the manner of the Lord's Supper. As was his custom, he invited all creatures to praise God, even exhorting death itself, terrible and hated by all, to join in praise. He met death joyfully and invited her to be his guest, saying: "Welcome, my sister Death!" His last hour came, and he fell asleep in the Lord.

One of his friars saw his soul like a star, as large as the moon and as bright as the sun. The minister of the friars who worked on the farms, whose name was

---

[2] Francis, by reason of humility, chose not to be ordained to the priesthood. He was an ordained deacon.

Augustine, was also in his last hour. He had long since lost the power of speech, but suddenly he cried out: "Wait for me, father, wait! See, I am coming with you!" The brothers asked him what he meant, and he said: "Don't you see our father Francis, who is on his way to heaven?" And he slept in peace and followed the father.

A lady who had been devoted to Saint Francis had gone the way of all flesh, and clerics and priests were present at her bier to celebrate her funeral rites. Suddenly she sat up on the bier and called to one of the priests, saying: "I want to confess, father! I had died and was about to be committed to a horrid dungeon, because I had not yet confessed the sin I shall now reveal to you. But Saint Francis prayed for me and obtained permission for me to return to my body, in order that by confessing this sin I may merit forgiveness, and once I have made the sin known, I shall sleep in peace in the sight of all of you." So she confessed, received absolution, and fell asleep in the Lord.

When the friars at Vicera asked a certain man to lend them a cart, he answered indignantly: "I would sooner skin two of you alive, and Saint Francis with you, than let you use my cart!" But then he came to his senses and chided himself for the blasphemy, fearing God's wrath. Soon his son fell ill and died. When the man saw his son dead, he rolled on the ground in grief, shed tears, and invoked Saint Francis, saying: "I am the one who sinned! You should have laid the scourge to me! O Saint, give back to the one now devoutly beseeching you what you have taken from the one who impiously blasphemed you!" His son arose and put a stop to the breast-beating. "When I died," he said, "Saint Francis led me by a long, dark road, set me down in a beautiful garden, and then said to me: 'Go back now to your father, I won't detain you any longer!'"

A poor man who owed a rich man a sum of money asked the rich man, for the love of Saint Francis, to give him more time to pay. The rich man answered haughtily: "I will shut you up in a place where neither Francis nor anyone else will be able to help you!" And he confined the poor man, chained, in a dark prison. Not long afterwards Saint Francis was there, broke into the prison, undid the man's chains, and brought him home unharmed.

There was a knight who belittled the works and miracles of Saint Francis. Once when he was playing at dice, filled as he was with folly and having no faith, he said to those around him: "If Francis is a saint, let the dice come up eighteen!" On his first throw, three sixes turned up, and in nine subsequent throws he had the same result every time. Then, adding lunacy to folly, he said: "If your Francis be a saint, may my body fall beneath the sword this day; but if he is not a saint, I shall escape unscathed!" In order that his prayer should become a sin, when the game was over, he did his nephew a wrong, and the nephew took a sword and plunged it into his uncle's belly, thus killing him.

A certain man had a leg so far consumed with disease that he could not move, and he called upon Saint Francis with these words: "Help me, Saint Francis! Be mindful of the devotion and the service I have rendered you! I let you ride my ass, I kissed your holy feet and hands, and look! I am dying with the pain of this awful affliction!" The saint soon appeared to him carrying a small stick shaped like a T, and touched the diseased leg with the stick. The abscess broke and the leg healed immediately, but the mark of the T remained imprinted on it. Saint Francis used to sign his letters with this same mark.

In Pomereto, a town in the hills of Apulia, a young girl, the only child of her father and mother, had died, and the mother, who was devoted to Saint Francis, was beside herself with grief. The saint appeared to her and said: "Don't cry, because the light of your lantern, which you mourn because it is extinguished, is to be returned to you through my intercession." The mother, therefore, felt renewed confidence and would not allow the corpse to be taken away. Rather she invoked the name of Saint Francis, took her dead daughter's hand, and raised her up in good health.

In the city of Rome a little boy fell out of a window of his house and was killed, but Saint Francis was invoked and the child was restored to life. And in the city of Susa a house collapsed and crushed a young man to death. His mother besought Saint Francis with her whole heart, and about midnight the youth yawned, got up unhurt, and burst out in words of praise.

Friar James of Rieti had crossed a river with some brothers in a small boat and had put his companions on the other bank. He was preparing to step ashore himself, when the skiff overturned and sank to the bottom. The friars called upon Saint Francis to save the drowning man, and he himself did his best to invoke the saint's aid. Well! The aforesaid friar began to walk on the river bottom as on dry land, took hold of the sunken craft, and brought it to land. His clothing was not dampened, nor had as much as a drop of water clung to his cloak.

※

---

150. Saint Pelagia

Pelagia was first among the women in the city of Antioch—first in possessions and wealth, and in beauty of form. She was also ostentatious and vain in her bearing, and licentious in mind and body.

One day she was promenading through the city with a maximum of display: one could see nothing on her but gold and silver and precious stones, and, as she passed, the air was filled with the aroma of a variety of perfumes. Ahead of her and following her went a retinue of youths and maidens, likewise richly adorned. She was seen by a holy father, Veronus, bishop of Heliopolis (now called Damietta), who began to weep bitterly because the woman put more care into pleasing the world than he did into pleasing God. He threw himself face down on the pavement, beating his brow on the ground, and bedewed the earth with his tears, saying: "Almighty God, pardon me, a sinner, because the attention a courtesan has given to her adornment for one day exceeds the effort of my whole life. Do not let the outward show of a harlot put me to shame in the sight of your awesome majesty! She adorns herself for earthly eyes with the utmost care, whereas I, having resolved to please you, my immortal Lord, fail to do so because of my negligence." To those who were with him he said: "I say to you in truth, God will bring this woman forward against us at the Judgment, because to please her earthly lovers she had painted herself so meticulously, and we give so little care to pleasing our heavenly Spouse!"

Having said these and similar things, Veronus suddenly fell asleep and dreamed that while he was celebrating mass, a black, malodorous dove flew around him, but when he dismissed the catechumens, the dove disappeared. After mass it came back, and the bishop plunged it into a tub of water. The dove came out clean and shining white, and flew away so high that it could no longer be seen, and the bishop woke up.

Then one day he went to the church and preached. Pelagia was present and was so stricken with remorse that she sent a letter to him, in which she said: "To the holy bishop, disciple of Christ, Pelagia, disciple of the devil. If you prove truly to be a disciple of Christ, who, I have heard, came down from heaven for sinners, you will receive me, a sinner but a repentant one." Veronus sent back an answer: "I beg you not to tempt my humility, because I am a sinful man; but if you truly wish to be saved, you may not see me alone, but you will see me along with others."

Pelagia came to him with other people present. She clasped his feet, wept profusely, and said: "I am Pelagia, a sea of iniquity cresting with waves of sin; I am an abyss of perdition; I am a whirlpool, a sink to catch souls. I have misled many and deceived them, and now I shudder at the thought of all this!" The bishop questioned her: "What is your name?" She answered: "At birth I was named Pelagia, but now they call me Margaret, the Pearl,[1] because of the preciousness of my attire." The bishop then raised her kindly, imposed a salutary penance upon her, diligently instructed her in the fear of God, and gave her rebirth in holy baptism.

The devil was present and began to cry out: "Oh, the violence that I suffer at the hands of this decrepit old man! Oh, injustice! Oh, evil old age! Cursed be the day you were born to oppose me and to rob me of my greatest hope!" Then one night, when Pelagia was asleep, the devil came to her and awakened her, and

---

[1] *Margarita* is the Latin word for pearl.

said: "Lady Margaret, what wrong have I ever done you? Have I not made you rich and famous? I ask you, tell me in what way I have disappointed you, and I will quickly make amends. Only, I beg of you, do not abandon me, or I will become an object of shame in the eyes of Christians!" But Pelagia made the sign of the cross and blew at the devil, and he vanished. On the third day thereafter, she prepared and assembled everything she owned and gave it all to the poor. A few days later, without letting anyone know, she left by night and went to Mount Olivet, where she donned the robe of a hermit, moved into a small cell, and served God in strict abstinence. She was held in high esteem and was called Brother Pelagius.

Some time later one of the aforesaid bishop's deacons went to Jerusalem to visit the holy places. The bishop told him that after he had made his visitations, he should look for a monk named Pelagius and go to meet with him, since he was a true servant of God. The deacon did this and was recognized by Pelagia, but she was so emaciated that he did not know her. Pelagia asked him: "Do you have a bishop?" "Indeed I do!" he answered. Pelagia: "May he pray the Lord for me, because he is truly an apostle of Christ!"

Three days later the deacon returned to her cell, but when he knocked at the door and no one answered, he opened the window and found her, and saw that she was dead. He hurried to make this known to the bishop, and he, with the clergy and all the monks, gathered to give solemn burial to the holy man. When they removed the body from the cell and saw that it was the body of a woman, they marveled and gave thanks to God, and gave her honorable burial. She died about A.D. 290.

151. Saint Margaret

Margaret, also called Pelagius, was a very beautiful woman, a virgin, rich and of noble birth. She was raised by her parents and taught to live virtuously with such solicitous care, and such were her integrity and modesty that she took every means to avoid being seen by men. The time came when a young man of the nobility sought her hand in marriage, and both her parents consented. Everything was prepared for the wedding with lavish expenditure for elegance and pleasure. The wedding day arrived, and the young gallants and winsome maidens, and the whole nobility of the city, gathered for the celebration around the elaborately garlanded wedding chamber. God, however, put it in the virgin Margaret's mind to ponder how the loss of virginity was preluded by such abandoned revels. She threw herself weeping on the ground, weighing in her heart the glory of the virgin state as compared with the cares of wedlock, until she repudiated the joys of that kind of life as so much dung. That night she abstained from consorting with her husband, and in the middle of the night, recommending herself to God, she cut off her hair, put on man's clothes, and secretly got away.

After a long journey she came to a monastery and, calling herself Brother Pelagius, was welcomed by the abbot and instructed in the ways of the community. There she lived a holy and deeply religious life. When the director of a convent of nuns died, Pelagius, by the consent of the elders and the abbot's order, and despite her own reluctance, was placed as director of this monastery of consecrated virgins, for whom she continuously and blamelessly provided both bodily and spiritual nourishment.

Meanwhile the devil, envious of her prosperous course, sought to impede it by placing the appearance of wrongdoing in her way. He lured one of the nuns, who worked outside the convent, into a sin of adultery, and in time the roundness of her belly could no longer be hidden. Great were the shame and grief felt by all the nuns and monks of both monasteries; and, since Pelagius was in charge of the convent and the only man on familiar terms with its people, all the monks and nuns condemned him without trial or judgment, forced him out ignominiously, and confined him in a rocky cave. They also appointed the strictest of the monks to supply the prisoner with a minimum amount of barley bread and water. Pelagius bore all this patiently and allowed nothing to disturb her, but thanked God at all times and found comfort in the examples of the saints.

Time passed, and she knew that her end was near. She therefore wrote the following letter to the abbot and the monks: "I am of noble birth. In the world I was called Margaret but took the name Pelagius to help me across the sea[1] of temptation. It was not for purposes of deception that I allowed myself to be taken for a man, as I have shown by my deeds. From the crime of which I was accused I have gained virtue; though innocent I have done penance. Now I ask that the holy sisters bury the one who men did not know was a woman. These women will recognize that I am a virgin, and what they learn from my dead body will be the vindication of my life, though slanderers judged me to be an adulterer."

When the monks and the nuns heard of all this, they ran to the cave, and Pelagius was acknowledged by women to be a woman and a virgin undefiled. Then all did penance, and Pelagius was buried with honor in the nuns' monastery.

---

[1] A pun on the Greek word for sea or ocean, *pelagos*, latinized as *pelagus*.

152. Saint Thais, Courtesan

Thais the courtesan, as we read in *Lives of the Fathers*, was a woman of such beauty that for her many men sold all they possessed and were reduced to penury. Her lovers, driven by jealousy, frequently fought each other at the woman's door and covered the threshold with the blood of young men.

When news of this came to the ears of Abba Paphnutius, he put on layman's clothes, provided himself with some money, and went in search of Thais in a certain Egyptian city. Finding her, he offered her the money as the price of sinning. She took the money and said: "Come with me into this room." He went in and was invited to climb up into a bed spread with costly coverlets, but said to her: "If there is a room farther in, let us go there." She led him through a series of rooms, but he kept saying that he was afraid of being seen. Finally she said to him: "There is a little room that nobody goes to; but if you are afraid of God, there is no place that is hidden to his divinity." When the old man heard this, he asked her: "If you know that, why have you brought so many souls to perdition? You will have to account not only for your own soul but for those others, and you will be damned."

Thais heard what he said. She prostrated herself at the holy man's feet and appealed to him tearfully: "I know there is repentance too, father, and I am sure I shall obtain forgiveness if you pray for me. Please give me three hours' delay, and after that I will go wherever you say and will do whatever you command me." He indicated where she should go, and she brought together everything she had earned by sin, carried it to the center of the city, and, while the people looked on, set the whole afire and burned it to ashes, calling out: "Come, all of you who have sinned with me, and see what I am doing with what you gave me!" What she destroyed was worth four hundred pounds gold.

When the fire had died out, the woman went to the place that Paphnutius had designated. He shut her up in a narrow cell in a monastery of virgins and sealed the cell door with lead, leaving a small window through which meager fare could be passed to her. He further ordered that a bit of bread and a little water be brought her daily by the ministry of others. As the old man was about to leave, Thais asked him: "Father, where do you want me to deposit my water when nature calls?" "In your cell," he answered, "that's all you deserve!" She asked again: "How should I worship God?" He replied: "You are not worthy to say the name of God nor to have the name of the Trinity on your lips. Just kneel and face the East, and repeat over and over: 'O you who made me, have mercy on me!'"

When Thais had been thus confined for three years, Abba Paphnutius took pity on her and went to Abbot Anthony to ask him whether God had forgiven her her sins. Having heard the whole story, Anthony called his disciples together and ordered them to pray all night, each one by himself, so that God might declare to one of them the answer Paphnutius had come to seek. As they all prayed incessantly, Abba Paul, Anthony's chief disciple, suddenly saw in heaven a bed adorned with precious coverlets, watched over by three virgins with shining faces, who stood guard. These three virgins were the fear of future punishment, which had pulled Thais back from evil, shame for sin committed, which had won her pardon, and love of righteousness, which had carried her over to heavenly things. When Paul said to the virgins that so great a favor belonged only to Abbot Anthony, the voice of God responded: "It belongs not to your father Anthony, but to Thais the courtesan!"

When Paul reported this the next morning, Paphnutius, now sure of the will of God, departed rejoicing and went back to the monastery. He broke down the door of Thais's cell, but she asked to be allowed to remain enclosed. He said to her: "Come out, because God has forgiven your sins!" Thais: "God is my witness that as soon as I came into this cell I made a bundle of all my sins and set it before my eyes, and, just as the breath has not left my nostrils, so my sins have not left my eyes, and I have wept all the time, considering them." Abba Paphnutius said: "It is not on account of your penances that God has remitted your sins, but on account of the fear of God that you always had in your heart!" The monk led her out of her cell, and she lived on for a fortnight, then died a peaceful death.

Abba Ephrem wanted to convert another courtesan this same way. When this woman tried shamelessly to entice Saint Ephrem to sin, Ephrem said to her: "Follow me!" She followed him to a place where there was a crowd of people, and he said to her: "Lie down here so that I can copulate with you!" "How can I do that," she said, "with all these people standing around?" "If you are ashamed before men," he said, "should you not be much more ashamed before God, who reveals the secrets of the dark?" The woman walked away in confusion.

153. Saints Dionysius, Rusticus,
and Eleutherius

Dionysius[1] is interpreted as one who flies forcefully; or the name may come from *dyo*, two, and *nisus*, elevation, hence a raising up in two forms, namely, in the body and in the soul. Or the name is derived from *Diana*, Venus, the goddess of beauty, and *syos*, god, hence beautiful to God. Or, as some think, the name comes from *dionysia*, which (as Isidore says) is a kind of black gem that is effective against drunkenness. Saint Dionysius, or Denis, was indeed one who fled forcefully from the world by perfect renunciation, who was raised up by his contemplation of the things of the spirit, beautiful to God by the beauty of his virtues, helpful to sinners against the intoxication of the vices.

Before his conversion, Dionysius had several surnames, He was called the Areopagite after the quarter in Athens where he lived, and Theosophus, one wise in the knowledge of God, Even today wise men among the Greeks call him *Pterigion tou ouranou*, which in Greek means wing of heaven, because he wonderfully flew to heaven on the wing of spiritual understanding. He is also called *Macarius*, which means blessed. After his homeland he is called *Ionicus*. Ionic, as Papias says, is one of the Greek languages; or Ionic, as the same author says, is a metrical foot with two short and two long syllables. All this shows that Dionysius was wise in the knowledge of God through his investigation of secret things, the wing of heaven through contemplation of the things of heaven, and blessed by possession of eternal goods. Moreover, it is known that he was a marvelous orator by his eloquence, a sustainer of the Church by his teaching, short by humility, long in his charity to others. Augustine, in the eighth book of *The City of God*, says that the term *Ionic* designated a school of philosophers. He distinguishes two schools, namely, the Italic, belonging to Italy, and the Ionic, belonging to Greece. Since, therefore, Dionysius was a preeminent philosopher, automatically he was called Ionic.

Methodius of Constantinople wrote his passion and life in Greek, and a Latin version was made by Anastasius, librarian of the apostolic see, as we learn from Hincmar, bishop of Rheims.

Dionysius the Areopagite was converted to the faith of Christ by the apostle Paul. It is said that he was called the Areopagite because he lived in the quarter of Athens called the Areopagus. This was the quarter of Mars, since the temple

---

[1] The name becomes Denis in French and Dennis in English.

of Mars was here. The Athenians designated the different quarters of the city by the names of the gods worshiped in each one. Hence they called the quarter where Mars was worshiped the Areopagus, because *Ares* was the Greek name for Mars. In the same way the section where Pan was worshiped was called Panopagus, and so on; each quarter went by the name of its own god.

The Areopagus was the upper-class section of Athens, where the nobility lived and the schools of liberal arts were established. Dionysius made his home there. He was an eminent philosopher, also called Theosophus, i.e., wise unto God, because of the fullness of his knowledge concerning the divine names. With him lived Apollophanes, who was his fellow philosopher. There dwelt also the Epicureans, who placed the happiness of man solely in bodily pleasure, and the Stoics, who placed it only in the virtue of the spirit.

On the day of the Lord's passion there was darkness over the whole earth, and the philosophers who were in Athens could find no natural cause for this phenomenon. It was not a natural eclipse of the sun, because the moon was not in the region of the sun, and an eclipse occurs only when the moon and the sun come together. At that time, however, the moon was in its fifteenth day, and therefore at its greatest distance from the sun. Moreover, it could not have been a natural eclipse, because an eclipse does not take away the light from every part of the earth, and because an eclipse cannot last for three hours. It is known that this particular eclipse shut off the light over the whole earth, first because Luke the evangelist says so; then because the Lord of the universe was suffering; and finally because the darkness was seen in Heliopolis of Egypt, in Rome, in Greece, and in Asia Minor. Orosius testifies that it was seen in Rome. He says: "When the Lord was nailed to the cross, a tremendous earthquake shook the whole earth, rocks were split asunder in the mountains, and many sections of great cities were flattened by this extraordinary tremor. On that same day, from the sixth hour on, the sun was totally obscured and black night was suddenly drawn over the earth, so that the stars were seen across the whole sky in those daytime hours, or rather in that awful night, or so we are told." Thus Orosius.

The eclipse was seen in Egypt, as Dionysius records in a letter to Apollophanes, in which he says: "A fog of darkness spread uniformly over the earth, and the disk of the sun came back shining clearly. We applied the rule of Philip Arrhideus and found, as was well known, that the sun was not due to suffer an eclipse. I then said to you: 'O sanctuary of vast learning, you do not yet know the mystery of this great thing! I ask you, O Apollophanes, mirror of doctrine, what do you think is the cause of these mysterious events?' To this you answered, with the mouth of a god and a word of more than human meaning: 'O good Dionysius, divine things are being disturbed.' And when Paul thundered to our anxiously attentive ears the day and year of the event that we had noted, I, having learned to read the signs that acclaimed it, surrendered to the truth and was freed of the bonds of falsity." Thus Dionysius. He also recalls this in a letter to Polycarp in which he speaks of himself and Apollophanes, saying: "We were both in Heliopolis at the time, standing together, and unexpectedly saw the moon coming in front of the sun, although it was not the time for an eclipse, and again, from the ninth hour until evening, saw the eclipse beginning in the east and coming to the limit of the sun's course, and again saw the waning and waxing of the light, not from the same but from the diametrically opposite direction." At that time Dionysius had gone to Heliopolis with Apollophanes to study astrology, and later returned from there.

We know from Eusebius that the eclipse was also seen in Asia. In his *Chronicle* he states that he had read in the pagan writings that in Bithynia, a province of Asia Minor, there had been a great earthquake, and a darkening of the sun such as had never happened before, and that at the sixth hour daylight had turned to pitch-dark night, so that the stars were seen in the skies. At Nicaea, a city in Bithynia, the earthquake had leveled all the buildings. Finally, as we read in the *Scholastic History*, the above events led the philosophers to say that the God of nature was suffering. Elsewhere we read that they said: "Either the order of nature is overturned, or the elements are lying, or the God of nature is suffering and the elements are suffering with him." And in other writings we read that Dionysius said: "This dark night,which we regard as something new, signals the coming of the whole world's true light."

The Athenians then built an altar to that god and put above it the title: "TO THE UNKNOWN GOD." Every altar had a title placed above it, indicating to which god it was dedicated. When the people wanted to offer holocausts and victims to the god, the philosophers said: "The god needs none of our goods; but kneel before his altar and offer him your supplications, because he does not want sacrifices of animals but piety of spirit."

When Paul came to Athens, the Epicurean and Stoic philosophers engaged him in debate. Some said: "What does this sower of words mean to say?" Others said: "He seems to be announcing new divinities." So they conducted Paul to the philosophers' quarter, the Areopolis, in order to subject this new teaching to scrutiny. They said: "You are bringing new things to our ears, and we want to know what these novelties mean." The Athenians, indeed, enjoy nothing so much as either to say or to hear something new. As Paul walked around among the shrines of the gods and saw an altar dedicated to the Unknown God, he said to the philosophers: "The god whom you worship unknown, I announce to you as the true God, who made the heavens and the earth." Then he said to Dionysius, who struck him as being more learned in divine matters than the rest: "Who, Dionysius, is this unknown God?" Dionysius answered: "He is the true God, who has not shown himself as the other gods have. He is unknown to us and hidden from us, yet in the age to come he will be,[2] and he will reign forever." Paul: "Is he a man, or only a spirit?" Dionysius: "He is God and man,

---

[2] Possibly an echo of Exod. 3:14 ("God answered: I am who am") and/or John 8:58 ("Before Abraham was, I am").

but is unknown because his life is in heaven only." Paul: "He is the God I preach to you! He came down from heaven, took flesh, endured death, and on the third day rose from the dead."

As Paul and Dionysius were debating, by chance a blind man passed by, and Dionysius said to Paul: "If you say to this blind man: 'In the name of my God, see!' and he sees, I will believe immediately. But do not use magic words, because it may be that you know words that would have this effect. Therefore I will dictate the form of words you are to use. You will say to him: 'In the name of Jesus Christ, born of a virgin, crucified, dead, who rose from the dead and ascended into heaven, see!'" But, in order to eliminate any possibility of suspicion, Paul told Dionysius to address these very words to the blind man. Dionysius did so, and the blind man instantly received his sight.

Dionysius and his wife Damaris and their whole household were baptized forthwith. Having received the faith, Dionysius was instructed by Paul for three years and then ordained bishop of Athens. He preached constantly, and converted the whole city and most of its surrounding territory to the faith of Christ.

It is said that Paul revealed to Dionysius what he, in ecstasy, had seen in the third heaven, as Dionysius himself seems to insinuate in more than one place. Hence he discoursed upon the hierarchies of the angels, their orders, ranks, and functions, so brilliantly and clearly that you would not think he had learned all this from someone else, but that he himself had been rapt to the third heaven and there had looked upon all he described. He shone with the spirit of prophecy, as appears from the letter he sent to John the Evangelist, who was in exile on the island of Patmos, in which he foretold that John would return from exile, and said: "Rejoice, O truly beloved, truly amiable and desirable and lovable, O greatly beloved!" And further on: "You will be released from your prison in Patmos, you will return to the land of Asia, and, by imitating the goodness of God in your life, will hand down an example to those who will live after you." He was present at the dormition[3] of Blessed Mary, as he suggests in his book *The Divine Names*.

When Dionysius learned that the emperor Nero had imprisoned Peter and Paul in Rome, he put another bishop in his place and went to Rome to visit the apostles. When they had happily migrated to the Lord, Clement became supreme pontiff. After a time Clement sent Dionysius to France, giving him Rusticus and Eleutherius as associates. He arrived in Paris and there converted many to the faith, built a number of churches, and installed clerics of various ranks. The priests of the idols more than once aroused the people against him and they came after him with weapons to assault him, but the grace of God shone so brightly in him that as soon as they saw him, they either put away their fury and groveled at his feet, or were overcome with fear and fled from his presence.

---

[3] Dormition, a "falling asleep," term used to describe the death of the Blessed Virgin Mary.

The devil was alarmed to see that while the number of his own worshipers was decreasing day by day, converts to the faith were multiplying and the Church was winning the fight. He therefore provoked Emperor Domitian to such a state of anger that the emperor issued a decree that anyone who found out that a given person was a Christian must either force that person to sacrifice to the idols or be put to all sorts of torture. The prefect Fescenninus was dispatched from Rome to Paris to deal with the Christians there and found blessed Dionysius preaching to the people. At once he had the saint taken captive, beaten, mocked, and spat upon, then bound with the toughest thongs and brought before him with Saint Rusticus and Saint Eleutherius. When they were steadfast in confessing the true God, a noblewoman came forward and charged that these three men had grossly and shamefully deceived her fickle husband into accepting the faith. The husband was sent for with all speed, and when he too persevered in confessing God, he was unjustly put to death, while the saints were scourged by twelve soldiers, loaded with a great weight of chains, and cast into prison.

On the following day Dionysius was stretched naked on an iron grill over a blazing fire, and he sang to the Lord, saying: "Thy word is refined by fire, and thy servant has loved it."[4] Then he was removed from the fire and thrown to wild beasts that were hungry, not having been fed. They rushed at him, but he made the sign of the cross over them and they became tame and gentle. He was thrown into an oven, but the fire went out and he was unhurt. They nailed him to a cross and left him there in torment for a long time, then took him down and returned him to prison with his two companions and many of the faithful. Dionysius celebrated mass in the prison and was giving holy communion to the prisoners, when the Lord Jesus, surrounded by a brilliant light, appeared to him, took the bread, and said to him: "Receive this, my beloved, because your reward is very great with me."

After this the saints were again presented to the judge and tortured anew. Finally, before the idol of Mercury, the heads of the three were cut off with swords in confession of the Holy Trinity. Instantly the body of Saint Dionysius stood up, took his head in its arms, and, with an angel and a heavenly light leading the way, marched two miles, from the place called Montmartre, the hill of martyrs, to the place where, by his own choice and by God's providence, he rests in peace. Great was the melodious chanting of angels that resounded there, and many who heard it believed. Among them was Laertia, wife of the prefect Lubrius, who cried out that she was a Christian. She was beheaded then and there by the pagans, and died baptized in her own blood. Her son Virbius, who served in the army at Rome under three emperors, finally returned to Paris, was baptized, and was numbered among religious men.

[4] Cf. Ps. 118:140 (Douay).

The infidels were afraid the Christians would bury the bodies of Saints Rusticus and Eleutherius, so they ordered them thrown into the Seine. A certain noblewoman invited those who were carrying the bodies to stop for lunch, and while they were feasting, she furtively whisked the bodies away and had them buried secretly on her property. Later on, when the persecution had ceased, she retrieved them and gave them honorable burial beside the body of Saint Dionysius. They suffered under Diocletian in A.D. 96, Dionysius then being ninety years old.

About the year A.D. 815, in the reign of Louis, son of Charlemagne, ambassadors of Emperor Michael of Constantinople brought to King Louis, among other gifts, Dionysius's books *On the Hierarchy*, translated from the Greek into Latin. They were received with joy, and nineteen ill persons were cured the same night in the church of Saint Denis.

Once when Bishop Regulus of Arles was celebrating mass, he added, to the names of the apostles in the canon of the mass, the words *et beatis martyribus tuis Dionysio, Rustico et Eleutherio*.[5] He said these words though, as far as he knew, these servants of God were still alive, and then began to wonder why he had pronounced their names in the canon. And behold, while he was still wondering, three doves, with the martyrs' names written in blood on their breasts, appeared and perched on the cross above the altar. The bishop studied the doves thoughtfully, and intuition told him that the saints had migrated from their bodies.

About A.D. 644, as a certain chronicle has it, Dagobert, king of the Franks, who reigned long before Pepin, had from childhood held Saint Dionysius in fervent veneration. When as a child he feared the anger of his father Chlothar, he ran and hid in the church of Saint Denis. Dagobert succeeded his father and eventually died, and a certain holy man had a vision in which he saw the deceased king's soul being borne to judgment, and many saints charging him with having stripped their churches. The wicked angels therefore wanted to carry the soul off to punishment, but Saint Denis stood by, and through his intervention Dagobert's soul was freed and escaped punishment. It may be that his soul returned to his body and there did penance.

King Clovis once irreverently uncovered the body of Saint Denis, broke off an arm bone, and took it away. In no time he lost his mind.

Note also that Hincmar, bishop of Rheims, says, in the letter he wrote to Charles, that the Dionysius who was sent to Gaul was Dionysius the Areopagite, as was said above. John Scotus makes the same assertion in a letter to Charles. This cannot be questioned, therefore, on the ground that the dates are contradictory, as some have tried to argue.

---

[5] . . . and with thy blessed martyrs . . .

154. Saint Callistus

Pope Callistus suffered martyrdom in A.D. 222, under Emperor Alexander. At that time a fire was sent by God and reduced the higher part of the city of Rome to ashes, and the left hand of a gold statue of Jove was melted away. Then all the priests went to Alexander and demanded that the angry gods be placated by sacrifices. They were offering sacrifice on a calm morning—it was Jove's day[1]—when lightning struck from heaven. Four priests of the idols died, Jove's altar was reduced to rubble, and the sun turned so dark that the populace of Rome fled outside the walls.

The consul Palmadius learned that Callistus and his clergy were in hiding across the Tiber, and asked permission to do away with the Christians in order to purge the city, since it was due to them that this calamity had befallen it. Permission granted, he marched his soldiers across the river in pursuit of the Christians, but the soldiers were stricken blind. Palmatius, terrified, reported this to Alexander. The emperor then commanded that the whole populace come together on Mercury's day to offer sacrifice to this god, in order to obtain an answer from him regarding these happenings. As this order was being carried out, a temple virgin named Juliana was seized by a demon and cried: "The God of Callistus is the true and living God, and he is enraged by our filthy practices!" When Palmatius heard this, he crossed the Tiber and went to the city of Ravenna, found Saint Callistus, and was baptized by the pope, together with his wife and family.

When this news reached the emperor, he had Palmatius arrested and turned him over to Simplicius, a senator. The senator's task was to win him over by flattering him with the argument that the republic could not do without him. Palmatius was persevering in prayer and fasting when a soldier came to him and promised that if Palmatius cured his paralytic wife, he would accept the faith at once. Palmatius prayed and the woman was cured. She ran to Palmatius and said: "Baptize me in the name of Christ, who took me by the right hand and lifted me up!" Callistus came and baptized the woman and her husband, along with Simplicius and a great many others.

The emperor's response to all this was to have all the baptized beheaded, and to keep Callistus for five days without food or drink. He saw, however, that the saint looked stronger than ever, so he ordered him to be flogged every day, then

---

[1] The days of the week were named after the Roman gods—Luna, Mars, Mercurius, Jupiter (Jove), Venus—and still are, in the Romance languages.

thrown from a window, then chained to a large stone and dropped down a well. Asterius, a priest, raised his body from the well and buried it in the cemetery of Calipodius.

✳

---

155. Saint Leonard

Leonardus means the perfume of the people, from *leos*, people, and *nardus*, which is a sweet-smelling herb; and Leonard drew people to himself by the sweet odor of his good renown. Or the name comes from *legens ardua*, one who chooses the hard tasks; or again, it comes from *leo*, the lion. The lion has four characteristics. He has fortitude, and this fortitude is (as Isidore says) in his breast and in his head. So Saint Leonard had fortitude in his heart by the curbing of evil thoughts, and in his head by his tireless contemplation of the things of heaven. Secondly, the lion has sagacity, and this in two ways: he sleeps with his eyes open, and he erases his tracks when he runs away. So Leonard was watchful in labor and action, and, while awake, slept by the quiet of contemplation. In himself he also erased every trace of worldly attachment. Thirdly, the lion has a special power in his voice. The lion cub is born dead, but on the third day the lion roars at it and it comes alive. Moreover, his roar stops every other animal stock-still. So Leonard restored to life many who were dead in sin, and many who were dead in their bestial way of life he fixed firmly in the way of good works. Fourthly, the lion has fear in his heart, because (according to Isidore) he fears two things, namely, the noise of wheels and the crackling of fire. So Leonard feared and, because he feared it, avoided the noise of mundane busyness, wherefore he took refuge in the desert, shrank from the fire of earthly greed, and disdained all treasures that were offered him.

Leonard is said to have lived about the year A.D. 500. Saint Remy, archbishop of Rheims, lifted him from the baptismal font and instructed him in salutary disciplines. His parents held first rank in the palace of the king of France. The king held Leonard in such high favor that any prisoners whom he visited were straightway released from bondage. As the fame of his holiness spread abroad, the king compelled him to stay with him for a long time, until he might bestow a bishopric on him. But Leonard refused to accept this, and, longing for solitude, left everything and went to Orleans, where he preached with his brother Lifard.

After they had lived for some time in a monastery, Lifard decided to lead a solitary life on the banks of the Loire, and Leonard, guided by the Holy Spirit, proposed to preach in Aquitaine. So they kissed and parted.

Leonard preached here and there, wrought many miracles, and lived in a forest close by the city of Limoges, where the king had a hunting lodge. It happened one day that the king was hunting there, and the queen had come out to enjoy the sport. Then suddenly she was seized with the pangs of childbirth and her life was in danger, while the royal retinue wept and groaned over the queen's condition. Leonard, who was walking through the forest, heard the sounds of mourning and, moved with pity, hastened toward the source of the sound. The king called him into the lodge and asked him who he was, and he said he had been a disciple of Saint Remy. This raised the monarch's hopes: he thought that anyone instructed by so good a teacher could be relied on. He brought Leonard in to the queen, asking him to pray both for her well-being and for the safe delivery of the child. Leonard prayed, and his petitions were granted.

The king now offered Leonard much money, but Leonard refused the offer and urged the monarch to distribute the money to the poor, saying: "I do not need any of this. What I desire is only to live in the forest and serve Christ alone, shunning all the riches of this world." The king then wanted to grant him the whole forest, but he answered: "I do not accept the whole forest, but I ask you to convey to me only as much as I can ride around on my ass in one night." To this the king willingly agreed.

A monastery was therefore built, and for a long time Leonard lived there with two monks who had joined him, living an austere life. Water was available no nearer than a mile away, but Leonard ordered a dry well dug at the monastery, and in answer to his prayers the well filled with water. He called the place Nobiliacum, because it had been given to him by a noble king. There his many miracles won him fame. Any prisoner who invoked his name saw his bonds loosened and went free with no one interfering. Such persons brought their chains and fetters to Leonard, and many stayed with him and served the Lord there. Seven families of his own noble line sold all their possessions and stayed with him, each family settling in its own section of the forest, and their example attracted a great many others.

At last the holy man Leonard, renowned for his many virtues, migrated to the Lord on the sixth day of November. After many miracles had occurred at his tomb in the monastery, it was revealed to the clergy there that since the church was too small to accommodate the throngs that frequented it, they were to build a church at another location and to transfer the saint's body there with due honors. The clerics and the people gave themselves to fasting and prayer for three days, then looked around and saw that the whole province was covered with snow except the one place where Saint Leonard wished to rest. That place, they discovered, was bare. The saint's relics were transferred to the new site, and the number of miracles the Lord wrought there through him is evidenced by the variety of chains and fetters hanging before his tomb.

In order to strike terror into miscreants, the viscount of Limoges had had a very heavy chain made, and ordered it hung from a beam that jutted from the wall of his tower: anyone who, with that chain around his neck, was left exposed to the vicissitudes of the weather for very long, died not one but a thousand deaths. It happened, however, that a man who had been in service to Saint Leonard was shackled with this chain though he had done no wrong. When he was about to breathe his last, he put his whole heart into a plea to Saint Leonard, begging him, who had freed many others, to come to the aid of one who had been his servant. At once the saint, clad in a white robe, appeared to him and said: "Don't be afraid, you are not going to die! Get up, and carry that chain with you to my church! Follow me, because I will lead the way!" The man got to his feet, gathered up the chain, and followed Saint Leonard, who went on ahead to his church. As soon as they came to the door, blessed Leonard left him. He went into the church that the saint had caused to be built, told everyone what had happened to him, and hung the huge chain in front of Leonard's tomb.

There was a man who lived in Saint Leonard's monastery at Nobiliacum and was devoted to the saint, and this man was made captive by a tyrant. The tyrant said to himself: "That Leonard frees everybody, and the strength of iron melts before him like wax in front of a fire. If I put my man in chains, Leonard will be on hand at once and will set him free. If, on the other hand, I manage to keep the fellow, I will get a thousand pounds' ransom for him. I know what I'll do! I'll have a deep pit dug under my tower, and I'll put my man, gyved and fettered, at the bottom of the pit. Then I'll have a wooden hut built over the mouth of the pit and station armed soldiers in it. Even though Leonard breaks iron, he has never yet gone underground."

The tyrant carried out his scheme, and the poor captive called loudly and often upon Saint Leonard. Night came and with it Leonard, who overturned the hut in which the soldiers lay asleep, and shut them up under it like dead men in a sepulcher. Then, with much light shining around him, he went into the pit, clasped his devotee's hand, and asked: "Are you asleep or awake? Here I am, Leonard, for whom you were calling!" The man, startled, said: "My lord, help me!" Leonard quickly broke the chains, took the man in his arms, and carried him out of the tower. Once outside, they chatted as one friend to another, and the saint led the man to Nobiliacum and his house.

There was a man who, upon his return from a pilgrimage to Saint Leonard, was taken captive in Auvergne and locked in a cage. He pleaded with his captors, telling them that since he had done them no wrong, they ought to let him go for the love of Saint Leonard. They answered that unless he paid them a copious ransom he would not get out. He replied: "That's between you and Saint Leonard, to whom I am committed, as you know!" The following night Saint Leonard appeared to the commander of the stronghold and commanded him to release the pilgrim. This man woke up in the morning, dismissed the vision as a dream, and had no thought of setting the prisoner free. The next night the saint presented him with the same command, and again he refused to obey. On the third night Saint Leonard took the pilgrim and led him outside the fortress, and immediately the tower and half the castle collapsed and crushed many, leaving only the recalcitrant chief, whose legs were broken, to welter in his own confusion.

A knight had been imprisoned in Brittany and invoked the aid of Saint Leonard. The saint appeared at once in the middle of the house, where all there saw and recognized him and marveled at the sight. The saint entered the jail cell, broke the bonds, placed the chains in the knight's hands, and led him out through those present, while they looked on, dumbfounded.

There was another Leonard, likewise a monk and equally virtuous, whose body rests at Corbigny. He was the abbot of his monastery but so humbled himself that he seemed the lowest of all. Since almost the whole populace flocked to him, a few envious people convinced King Chlothar that unless he took precautions, the kingdom of France would suffer considerable damage through Leonard, who, they said, was gathering a large following under the pretext of religion. The king, all too ready to believe them, ordered the expulsion of Leonard. Soldiers came after him, but his words impressed them so poignantly that they promised to become his disciples at a future time. The king repented and asked for pardon, and had the detractors stripped of their goods and honors. He also conceived a great affection for Leonard and at the saint's prayer restored the detractors to their former dignity. Like the other Leonard, this one also obtained of God that any who were held in prison and invoked his name would quickly be released.

One day, as he lay prone in prayer, a large serpent crawled up beside him, so long that it stretched from his feet to his chest. This did not make the saint interrupt his prayer, but once he had finished it, he said to the reptile: "I know that from the time you were created, you have done all you could to trouble men; but now, if power over me has been given to you, do to me whatever I have deserved." At these words the serpent leapt out through the saint's cowl and fell dead at his feet. Later, after having made peace between two bishops, he predicted that he would die the next day. This was about A.D. 570.

156. Saint Luke, Evangelist

Luke, Lucas in Latin, is interpreted as rising up, or elevating; or the name comes from *lux*, light. Saint Luke was one rising above love of the world and elevating himself to the love of God. He was the light of the world in that he shed light on the whole universe: "You are the light of the world."[1] The light of the world is the sun itself, and this light has sublimity in its place: "The sun when it riseth to the world in the high places of God."[2] The light is sweet to look upon: "Light is sweet, and it is delightful for the eyes to see the sun."[3] Light moves swiftly: "The earth is vast and heaven is high and the sun is swift in its course."[4] Light is useful in its effect, because, according to the philosopher, man engenders man, and so does the sun. Luke has sublimity through contemplation of heavenly things, he was delightful in the sweetness of his conversation and swift in the fervor of his preaching; and he gave useful service through the writing down of his doctrine.

Luke was a Syrian, a native of Antioch and a practitioner of medicine. Some would have it that he was one of the Lord's seventy-two disciples. Jerome, however, says that Luke was a disciple of the apostles, not of the Lord; and since the *Gloss* on Exodus 25 notes that he did not receive the faith from the preaching of the Lord but came to it after the resurrection, it is more likely that Luke was not one of the seventy-two, despite the fact that some think he was.

So great was the perfection of his life that he was very well ordered in his relation to God, to his neighbor, to himself, and to his appointed task. As a sign of this fourfold ordering he is described as having four faces, namely, those of a man, a lion, an ox, and an eagle. Ezechiel says[5] that each of the four living creatures in his vision had four faces and four wings. In order to have a clearer idea of this, imagine an animal with a square head like a cube of wood, and on each of the four sides of the cube a face—on the front, the face of a man, on the right side that of a lion, on the left side that of a calf, and on the back, that of an eagle. Because the eagle's face stood higher than the others due to the stretched neck, the eagle's neck being long, it is said that the eagle was uppermost. Each of these animals had four wings, because, since we are imagining the animal as squared and the square has four edges, there was a wing on each edge.

[1] Matt. 5:14.   [2] Ecclus. 26:21.   [3] Eccles. 11:7.
[4] 3 Esd. 4:34. The Latin Vulgate includes this book as "added to the series of the canonical books," printed after the New Testament and numbered 3 Esdras (1 and 2 Esdras are canonical). The RSV has it among the Apocrypha as 1 Esdras.
[5] Ezek. 1:5, 10.

According to the holy fathers, these animals represent the four evangelists, and each animal had four faces because each evangelist wrote about the humanity, the passion, the resurrection, and the divinity of Christ. Yet the four faces are distributed among the four evangelists by a sort of attribution. According to Jerome, Matthew is represented by the face of a man because he dwells mostly on the humanity of Christ. Luke is represented by a sacrificial calf because he treats of Christ's priesthood. Mark is figured as a lion because he wrote more clearly about the resurrection, and lion cubs, we are told, lie as though dead until the third day after birth, when the lion wakes them up with his roaring; also Mark is the lion because he began his gospel with the roar of the Baptist's preaching. John is represented in the eagle, flying higher than the others by writing about Christ's divinity. Christ, about whom he wrote, was also signified in these four figures—his humanity because he was born of a virgin, his passion in the sacrificial calf, his resurrection in the lion, and his ascension in the eagle.

These four faces, which represent Luke as they do the other evangelists, show the four ways in which, as we saw above, his life was well ordered. The face of a man shows that he was rightly ordered in relation to his neighbor, whom one should instruct by right reasoning, attract by gentleness, and support generously, since man is a rational, gentle, and liberal animal. The face of the eagle shows that he was rightly ordered in relation to God, because in him the eye of the intellect was fixed on God through contemplation, the beak of his desire was sharpened toward God by meditation, and old age was thrown aside like the eagle's, by rejuvenation.[6] The eagle, indeed, is a sharp-eyed bird that can look into the sun without blinking an eye and from a marvelous height can see tiny fishes in the sea. If its beak becomes too hooked, making it difficult to catch fish, the eagle rubs it against a stone and makes it more suitable for use in feeding. When he is burned by the heat of the sun, the eagle plunges at great speed into a body of water, thus casting off old age, while the sun's heat cleans away the film from his eyes and lightens his feathers. The lion's face shows that Luke was rightly ordered in relation to himself, because he had nobility in his honorable conduct, sagacity in foiling the plots of his enemies, and readiness to suffer in his compassion for the afflicted. The lion, indeed, is a noble animal, since he is the king of beasts; he is cunning, because he wipes out his tracks with his tail so that no one can follow him when he flees; he is familiar with suffering, because he is susceptible to the quartan fever.

The face of the calf or the ox shows that Luke was rightly ordered in relation to his appointed task, which was to write his gospel. On that work he proceeded slowly, unhurriedly, beginning as he did with the birth of the forerunner and the birth and infancy of Christ, and so, step by step, moving toward the final consummation. He proceeded judiciously. Writing after two other evangelists, he supplied what they had omitted and omitted what they had treated sufficiently.

---

[6] Cf. Ps. 103:5.

He gave special attention to the Temple and to sacrifice, as is clear in the beginning, the middle, and the end of his gospel. Moreover, the ox is a slow-moving animal and has cleft hooves, and this signifies the discernment of those who offer sacrifice.

That blessed Luke was well ordered in the four ways already mentioned becomes still more obvious as one looks more deeply into the various aspects of his life. Firstly, he was well ordered in his relation to God. Man, according to Saint Bernard, is rightly related to God in three aspects, namely, in his desire, his thought, and his intention. His desire must be holy, his thought clean, and his intention right. Luke's desire was holy because he was filled with the Holy Spirit. Jerome, in his Prologue to Luke's gospel, says: "He died in Bithynia, full of the Holy Spirit." His thought was clean: he was a virgin in body and mind, and this shows the purity of his thought. He had rectitude of intention, because he sought the Lord's glory in everything he did. Regarding the last two qualities, Jerome's Prologue to the Acts of the Apostles says: "[Luke was] without wrongdoing, abiding in virginity" (this refers to cleanness of thought). "He chose above all to serve the Lord," i.e., the Lord's honor, and this refers to rightness of intentions.

Secondly, his relations with his neighbor were in good order. Such good order exists when we pay our neighbor what we owe him. According to Richard of Saint Victor we owe our neighbor three debts, namely, we owe him what we can do for him, what we know, and what we wish for him; and these three lead to a fourth, namely, what we do for him. Saint Luke was well ordered in these four respects. He gave to his neighbor what he could give in the way of help, as we see in his always being at Paul's side in every kind of trouble, never leaving him, and thus helping him in his preaching. So Paul wrote in his letter to Timothy: "Luke alone is with me."[7] When Paul says "with me," he indicates the kind of help Luke gives him, namely, as his assistant and defender. When he says "Luke alone," he indicates that Luke is constant in his attachment. Again Paul says of Luke: "Not only that, but he has been appointed by the churches to travel with us in this gracious work which we are carrying on."[8]

The second debt—what he knew—he paid in giving good counsel; i.e., he made his knowledge available to his neighbor when he put in writing what he knew of apostolic and evangelical doctrine for the use and service of his fellows. Luke says this about himself in the prologue of his gospel: "It seemed good to me, having followed all things from the beginning, to write an orderly account for you, most exellent Theophilus, that you may know the truth concerning the things of which you have been informed."[9] How he shared his knowledge in giving good counsel is shown by what Jerome says in his Prologue, namely, that Luke's words are medicine to the languid soul.

---

[7] 2 Tim. 4:11.   [8] 2 Cor. 8:19.   [9] Luke 1:3–4

Third debt—what he wished and desired for his neighbors—he paid by desiring eternal salvation for them. "Luke, the most dear physician, salutes you," says Paul, meaning "desires eternal salvation for you."[10] And fourth debt—what we do for our neighbor—this, too, Luke paid. He gave the Lord hospitality, thinking that he was caring for a pilgrim, and exhibited toward him every kindness that charity called for. This was when Luke was Cleopas's companion on the road to Emmaus, as some say he was, including Gregory in his *Moralia*, though Ambrose says it was someone else, and even gives his name.

Thirdly, Luke was well ordered in relation to himself. There are, according to Bernard, three qualities that best put order in a man's management of his own life, namely, a sober life-style, just action, and a pious sense, i.e., a sense of God's presence in our lives. Each of these three, as Bernard says, is divided three ways. One's life-style will be sober if one lives continently, sociably, and humbly. One's action will be just if it is straightforward, discreet, and fruitful—straightforward by good intention, discreet by moderation, and fruitful by edification. A pious sense there will be if our faith senses God as all-powerful, all-wise, and all-good, so that we believe that by his power our weakness is aided, by his wisdom our ignorance is corrected, and by his goodness our wickedness is washed away. Thus Bernard.

In all those ways Luke was in perfect order. His way of living was sober, and this in three respects. He lived continently, for, as Jerome says in his Prologue to Luke's gospel, the evangelist had neither wife nor child. He lived sociably, as we see from what the last chapter of his gospel says about Luke and Cleopas (if we accept the opinion stated above): "That very day two of them were going to a village named Emmaus and talking with each other."[11] His sociability is indicated by the word "two" and the word "disciples," because they were "disciplined," in other words, morally correct. His humility is suggested by the fact that his companion's name, Cleopas, is given, but his own is suppressed—because it is the opinion of some that Luke omitted his name for humility's sake.

Secondly, his action was just. It was just by intention, as indicated by the prayer in the mass of his feast: "[He] bore continually in his body the mortification of the cross for the glory of your name." It was just by discretion, indicated by moderation and signified by the image of the ox, whose hoof is cleft, thus expressing the virtue of discretion or discernment. And his action was fruitful because it was edifying; it bore such fruit for his neighbors that he was held "most dear" by all. Hence Paul calls him "Luke, the most dear physician."[12]

Thirdly, Luke possessed a pious sense, because he believed, and professed in his gospel, that God is all-powerful, all-wise, and all-good. Of the first two he

[10] Col. 4:14.
[11] Luke 24:13–14.
[12] Col. 4:14.

wrote in chapter 4: "They were astonished at his doctrine, for his speech was with power."[13] Of God's goodness he says: "Jesus said, 'None is good but God alone.'"[14]

Fourthly and last, Luke was well ordered in relation to his appointed task, that of writing his gospel. This is shown by the fact that his gospel is permeated by much truth, filled with much usefulness, adorned with much charm, and confirmed by many authorities. There are three kinds of truth, namely, truth of life, truth of justice, and truth of doctrine. Truth of life consists in making the hand do what the tongue says, truth of justice in making the sentence fit the case, truth of doctrine in making the idea agree with reality. Luke's gospel is permeated by this threefold truth, because in his gospel this truth is fully expounded.

Luke shows that Christ had this multiple truth in himself, and that he taught it to others. He uses the testimony of adversaries to prove that Christ had the truth in himself, as we see in chapter 20, when the Sadducees say to the Lord: "Teacher, we know that you speak and teach rightly" (the truth of doctrine), "and show no partiality" (the truth of justice), "but truly teach the way of God"[15] (the truth of life: the good life is called the way of God). But his gospel also shows that Christ taught this threefold truth. He taught the truth of life, which consists in observing the commandments of God. Hence we read in chapter 10: "You shall love the Lord your God with all your heart . . . and your neighbor as yourself. . . . Do this and you will live."[16] And in chapter 18 we read: "A ruler asked him: 'Good Teacher, what shall I do to inherit eternal life?' And Jesus said: 'You know the commandments—do not commit adultery, do not kill,' etc."[17] Christ also taught the truth of doctrine. To some, who were perverting the truth of doctrine, he said: "Woe to you, Pharisees, for you tithe (meaning, you teach others to tithe) mint and rue and every herb, and you neglect justice and the love of God"; and, in the same place: "Woe to you, lawyers! You have taken away the key of knowledge; you did not enter yourselves, and you hindered those who were entering."[18] And thirdly, the truth of justice is taught: "Render to Caesar the things that are Caesar's, and to God the things that are God's";[19] and "As for these enemies of mine, who did not want me to rule over them, bring them here and slay them before me!"[20] And in chapter 13, where it is question of the Judgment, we read that the Judge will say to the accursed: "Depart from me, all you workers of iniquity."[21]

Second, just as Luke's gospel is permeated with truth, it is also filled with much usefulness. Its author was a physician, to signify that he prescribed a very healthful medicine for us. There are three kinds of medicine: some cures, some preserves, some improves. In his gospel Luke shows us that the heavenly physi-

[13] Luke 4:32.   [14] Luke 18:19.   [15] Luke 20:21.
[16] Luke 10:27–28.   [17] Luke 18:18.   [18] Luke 11:42, 52.
[19] Luke 20:25.   [20] Luke 19:27.   [21] Luke 13:27.

cian has prescribed these three medicines for us. The medicine that cures diseases is penance, which cures every spiritual sickness. Luke shows that the celestial doctor has provided this medicine, for he says: "The Spirit of the Lord has sent me to heal the contrite of heart, to preach deliverance to the captives," etc.[22] Also: "I have not come to call the righteous, but sinners, to repentance."[23] The medicine that improves, i.e., that increases good health, consists in the observance of the counsels, for the counsels make people better and more perfect. Luke shows that the physician has prescribed this medicine for us when he says: "Sell all that you have and distribute to the poor";[24] also: "From him who takes away your cloak, do not withhold your coat as well."[25] The preservative medicine is that which saves us from falling, and this consists in avoiding the occasion of sinning and the company of sinners. The physician prescribes this medicine when he says: "Beware of the leaven of the Pharisees,"[26] teaching us to shun bad company.

It can also be said that Luke's gospel itself is filled with usefulness, since in it the power of every kind of wisdom is contained. Here is what Ambrose says about this: "Luke enfolded all the powers of wisdom into his gospel story. What he taught has to do with nature, when he discloses that the Lord's incarnation was the work of the Holy Spirit. David also teaches this natural wisdom when he says: 'Send forth thy Spirit and they shall be created.'[27] In the same vein, Luke taught that darkness came over the whole land, the sunlight failed, and the earth trembled, during the passion of Christ. He taught moral wisdom when, in the Beatitudes, he set forth the ways of moral living.[28] He taught rational wisdom when he said: 'He who is faithful in a very little is also faithful in much.'[29] Without this threefold wisdom—the natural, the moral, and the rational—there can be no faith, there can be no mystery of the Trinity." Thus Ambrose.

Third, Luke's gospel is also adorned with much charm, for his style and manner of speaking are indeed charming and decorous. If someone wants what he says or writes to have grace and charm, then, as Augustine says, it must be pleasing, clear, and touching. If his words are to please, they should be eloquent; to be clear, they should be easy to follow; to touch hearts, they should be fervent. Luke had these three qualities in his writing and in his preaching. On the first two, Paul said: "With him [Titus] we have sent the brother (the *Gloss* adds 'Barnabas or Luke') whose praise is in the gospel through all the churches."[30] That he was praised points to his eloquence; "through all the churches" indicates that he could be understood wherever he preached; that he spoke fervently follows from the fact that he had an ardent heart, since he said: "Did not our hearts burn within us while he talked to us on the road?"[31]

[22] Luke 4:18–19.	[23] Luke 5:32.	[24] Luke 18:22.
[25] Luke 6:29.	[26] Luke 12:1.	[27] Ps. 103(104):30.
[28] Luke 6:20ff.	[29] Luke 6:10.	[30] 2 Cor. 8:18 (Douay).
[31] Luke 24:32.		

Fourth, Luke's gospel is confirmed by many authorities. The authority of many guarantees it. This gospel was ordered by the Father, who says, as in Jeremiah 31: "Behold, the days are coming, when I will make a new covenant with the house of Israel and the house of Judah, not like the covenant which I made with their fathers; but this is the covenant which I will make with the house of Israel after these days, says the Lord, I will put my law within them and I will write it upon their hearts."[32] This literally refers to the doctrine contained in the gospel. The doctrine was also corroborated by the Son, as we read in chapter 21: "Heaven and earth will pass away, but my words will not pass away."[33] Thirdly, this gospel was inspired by the Holy Spirit, as Jerome, in his Prologue on Luke, says: "Spurred by the Holy Spirit. he wrote this gospel in Achaia."

Fourthly, it was prefigured by angels, notably by the angel about whom it is said in the Book of Revelation: "I saw an angel of God flying through the midst of heaven, having the eternal gospel."[34] This gospel is called eternal because it is made from eternity by Christ, who is eternal; it has eternal things as its material, eternal life as its end, and eternity as its duration. Fifthly, it was foretold by the prophets. The prophet Ezechiel foretold it when he said that one of the living creatures had the face of a calf, by which Luke's gospel was represented, as we said before. Ezechiel also says that he saw a book that was written within and without, and there were written in it lamentations and canticles and woe.[35] We are to understand that this book is Luke's gospel, which is written within through the depth of the mystery it encloses, and outwardly by the history of events that it lays open. It contains the lament of Christ's passion, the song of his resurrection, and the woe of damnation, as we see in chapter 11, where woe is predicted for many.

Sixthly, this gospel was disclosed by the Virgin Mary. The Blessed Virgin kept all these things in her heart, pondering them diligently, as we read in chapter 2 of Luke,[36] in order to be able to communicate them to writers, as the *Gloss* on this passage says: "She kept in her memory everything she knew about the Lord and what the Lord did and said, so that when the time came to preach or write about the incarnation, she could adequately make known all that had been said and done, to those who sought information." So Bernard also, assigning a reason for the angel's announcing to Mary that Elizabeth had conceived, says: "This announcement was made to Mary so that when it was necessary to teach about the Savior's coming at one time and the forerunner at another, she, remembering the times and sequence of events, could better disclose the truth to the writers and preachers of the Gospel, since she was fully instructed by heaven about all the mysteries from the beginning."

[32] Jer. 31:31–33.　　[33] Luke 21:33.　　[34] Rev. 14:6.
[35] Ezek. 2:9–10 (Douay).
[36] Luke 2:19, 51.

It is believed, therefore, that the evangelists questioned Mary about many things, and that she gave them sure answers. This would be particularly true in Saint Luke's case. It is believed that he turned to her as to the ark of the testimony and from her received sure knowledge about many things, above all about matters that concerned her alone, such as the angel's annunciation of the birth of Christ and similar things, which Luke alone relates in his gospel.

Seventhly, Luke got information from the apostles. He had not been with Christ to witness all the Lord's actions and miracles, so he wrote his gospel relying on what the apostles, who had been present, told him. Luke himself suggests this in his prologue, when he says that he had compiled "a narrative of the things which have been accomplished among us, just as they were delivered to us by those who from the beginning were eyewitnesses and ministers of the word."[37] It was customary to have two kinds of testimony, namely, what was seen and what was heard; so the Lord (as Augustine says) wanted to have two witnesses to what they had seen, namely, Matthew and John, and two to what they had heard from others, namely, Mark and Luke. Furthermore, since the testimony of eyewitnesses is firmer and more certain than that based on hearsay, therefore, as Augustine says, the two gospels written by eyewitnesses are put first and last, and the other two, based on hearsay, are put in between, being weaker than those on the ends, which, being surer than the other two, undergird and support them.

Eighthly, Luke's gospel was marvelously approved by Paul, when he quoted it in confirmation of what he himself was saying. Hence Jerome, in his book *On Illustrious Men*, says: "There are some who surmise that every time Paul, in his epistles, says 'according to my gospel,' he is referring to Luke's book." Paul also expressed wondrous approval of this gospel when he mentioned Luke in 2 Corinthians, saying: ". . . whose praise is in the gospel through all the churches."

We read in the *History of Antioch* that at a time when the Christians who lived in Antioch had abandoned themselves to all sorts of shameful conduct, they were besieged by a horde of Turks and were sorely tried by hunger and misery. But then they were fully converted to the Lord by contrition and penance, and a man radiant of aspect and clothed in white garments appeared to someone praying in the church of Saint Mary of Tripoli. The visitor was asked who he was, and he said he was Luke and had come from Antioch, where the Lord had mustered the hosts of heaven and the apostles and the martyrs to fight for his pilgrims. The Christians therefore took heart and cut the Turkish horde to pieces.

[37] Luke 1:2.

157. Saints Chrysanthus and Daria

Chrysanthus, the son of Polimius, a man of high rank and distinction, had been instructed in the Christian faith and had become a Christian. His father could not persuade him to return to the worship of idols, so he had him locked up in a room, and put five damsels in with him to seduce him with their amorous wiles. Chrysanthus, however, prayed God not to let him be overwhelmed by that wild beast, namely, carnal concupiscence. What then happened was that the aforesaid damsels fell into a deep sleep and could take neither food nor drink; but when they were led out of the room, they took both eagerly.

Then Daria, a most decorous virgin who was dedicated to the goddess Vesta, was asked to go in to Chrysanthus and restore him to the gods and his father. She went in, and Chrysanthus reprehended her for the pompousness of her garb. Her response was that she was arrayed that way not for vain show, but to win him back to the gods and his father. Chrysanthus again rebuked her, this time for worshiping as gods beings whom their own authors often described as vicious men and wanton women. Daria replied that the philosophers had given the elements human names in order to confer some standing upon them. Chrysanthus: "If one man worships the earth as a goddess, and another, a peasant, plows it, obviously the earth gives more return to the peasant than to the worshiper; and the same can be said of the sea and the other elements."

Chrysanthus and Daria, whom he had now converted, were united by the bond of the Holy Spirit but pretended to be wedded in the flesh. They proceeded to convert a great many people to Christ, including the tribune Claudius, who had been Chrysanthus's tutor, with his wife and children, as well as a number of other soldiers. Chrysanthus was therefore locked up in a fetid dungeon, but the stench was changed into a sweet odor. Daria was consigned to a brothel, but a lion that had escaped from the amphitheater stood guard at the brothel door. A man was sent to corrupt the virgin, but the lion caught him and seemed to be looking to Daria to be told what to do with his captive. She ordered the lion to do the man no harm and to allow him to come to her.

The man was quickly converted and ran through the city shouting that Daria was a goddess. Huntsmen were dispatched to recapture the lion, but they were all taken captive by the beast, laid at the virgin's feet, and by her converted. The prefect then ordered a roaring fire to be built at the entrance to the cell, in order to consume both the lion and Daria. The lion gave thought to this, was dismayed, and by roaring obtained the saint's permission to go wherever he wanted to go, provided he did not hurt anyone.

The prefect inflicted a variety of tortures on Chrysanthus and Daria, but none of them did the slightest harm to the two saints. Finally these inviolate spouses were dumped into a pit and crushed with earth and stones, and so were consecrated as martyrs to Christ. This took place in the time of Carus, bishop of Narbonne, who became bishop in A.D. 211. In Narbonne their feast is celebrated with special solemnity.

---

158. The Eleven Thousand Virgins

The martyrdom of the eleven thousand virgins came about in the following way. In Britain there was a most Christian king named Notus or Maurus, who had a daughter called Ursula. Ursula was distinguished for her virtuous life, her wisdom, and her beauty, and her fame took wing and spread far and wide. The king of Anglia, who had great power and had subjected many nations to his rule, heard of this virgin's renown and declared that he would be very happy to have her married to his one and only son. The young man agreed warmly to this proposal. They therefore sent ambassadors of state to the virgin's father. These made large promises and lavished flattering words, to which they added dire threats about what would happen if they were to return empty-handed to their lord.

King Notus was sorely troubled for several reasons: he thought it improper to hand over a woman who was signed with the Christian faith to a worshiper of idols; he knew that she herself would never give her consent; and he was mortally afraid of the other king's savagery. His daughter, however, acting under God's inspiration, persuaded him to yield to the aforesaid king's request, but on the following conditions: the king and her father were to assign to her ten carefully chosen virgins as companions, and to her and each of the ten the company and service of a thousand virgins; triremes should be rigged and provisioned for their transportation; an interval of three years should be given her to fulfill her dedication to virginity; the young man himself should be baptized and during the three years receive instruction in the faith.

There was wisdom behind her proposal: given the difficult conditions, the king might change his mind about having her for his son, or, given this opportunity, she might dedicate all those virgins to God with herself. The suitor, however, readily accepted the conditions and insisted that his father do likewise. He was baptized forthwith and ordered that everything else should be carried out as quickly as possible. Her father gave orders that his daughter, whom he loved dearly, should have men in her entourage, to give her and her battalions any help they might need.

From all sides, then, the virgins flocked together, and men, too, hurried to see this great spectacle. Many bishops also came to be with the virgins and to travel with them. One of the bishops was Pantulus, bishop of Basel, who led them to Rome, came back with them, and with them accepted martyrdom. Saint Gerasina, queen of Sicily, also came. She had married a very cruel man, a veritable wolf, whom she transformed into a lamb. She was the sister of Bishop Macirisus and of Daria, Saint Ursula's mother. Ursula's father wrote her a letter in which he gave her an idea of Ursula's secret purpose, and Gerasina, inspired by God, immediately put the affairs of the kingdom in the hands of one of her sons, and took ship and sailed to Britain, having with her her four daughters, Babilla, Juliana, Victoria, and Aurea, and her little son Adrian, who for love of his sisters attached himself to the pilgrimage. At her invitation, virgins gathered from various countries, and Gerasina, continuing as their leader, eventually suffered martyrdom with them.

In accordance with the compact, the virgins were assembled and the well-stocked triremes made ready. Now the queen disclosed the secret to those who had become, as it were, her fellow soldiers, and all took the oath of this new knighthood. They engaged in the customary preludes of war. They ran hither and they ran yon. At times, simulating the conditions of war, they pretended to flee the field of battle. They took part in all sorts of contests, trying whatever came to their minds and leaving nothing neglected. Sometimes they came in at midday, sometimes barely before dark. Princes and primates came to witness this unusual spectacle, and all were filled with admiration and joy. Ursula in time converted all the virgins to the faith.

Then, in the space of one day, with a fair wind blowing, they arrived at a port of Gaul named Tyella, and from there went on to Cologne. In Cologne an angel of the Lord appeared to Ursula and predicted that the full count of virgins would return to that city and there would win the crown of martyrdom. Following the angel's orders they set out for Rome and landed at Basel, left the ships there, and continued to Rome on foot. Pope Cyriacus[1] rejoiced at their coming. He himself was from Britain and had many blood relations among the virgins, so he and the entire clergy of Rome welcomed them with high honor. That very night it was divinely revealed to the pope that he would gain the palm of martyrdom with them. He kept this knowledge to himself and baptized many of the virgins who had not yet received the sacrament.

When Cyriacus, the nineteenth pope after Peter, had ruled the Church for one year and eleven weeks, he saw that the time was opportune. He called his

---

[1] Not listed in the *Acta apostolica*.

court together and informed them of his resolution, and there, in the presence of all, resigned his dignities and his office. Everyone protested, especially the cardinals, who thought he must be out of his wits to abandon the glory of the pontificate and go off with a lot of silly women. He, however, stood firm and ordained a holy man called Ametos[2] to succeed him as pope. Because he had left the apostolic see against the wishes of the clergy, the said clergy expunged his name from the catalog of popes, and thenceforth the sacred chorus of virgins lost all the favor they had enjoyed with the Roman curia.

Meanwhile two wicked commanders in the Roman army, namely, Maximus and Africanus, seeing this great multitude of virgins and noting that many men and women were hurrying to join them, were afraid that their influence would make the Christian religion flourish overmuch. The two therefore studied the women's itinerary closely and sent messages to Julius, their kinsman, the chief of the Hunnish tribe, telling him to lead his army against the virgins, since they were Christians, and slaughter them when they reached Cologne. Blessed Cyriacus left Rome with this noble company of virgins. Vincent, a cardinal priest, followed him, as did James, who had gone from Britain, his homeland, to Antioch, and there had held the dignity of the archepiscopal office for seven years. James had come to make a visitation to the pope then reigning, and had already left the city when he heard of the virgins' arrival and hastened back to join them, and to share their journey and their martyrdom. Maurisius, bishop of the city of Levicana, who was the uncle of Babilla and Juliana, as well as Follarius, bishop of Lucca, and Sulpicius, bishop of Ravenna, who were then in Rome, also joined the aforesaid virgins.

Ethereus, who was pledged to be blessed Ursula's husband, had stayed in Britain and now, by an angelic message, received the Lord's order to urge his mother to become a Christian. His father Ethereus had been baptized and had died within a year, and his son had succeeded to the kingdom. When the holy virgins and the aforesaid bishops were on their way back from Rome, Ethereus was admonished by the Lord to go out and meet his plighted spouse, and to receive the crown of martyrdom with her in Cologne. In obedience to the divine command he had his mother baptized, and then, with his mother and his little sister Florentina and Bishop Clement as well, went out to meet the virgins and to proceed with them to martyrdom. Marculus, the bishop of Greece, and his niece Constantia were now directed by a vision to go to Rome, where they too joined the virgins, to be with them and to share their martyrdom. Constantia had been betrothed to the son of a king, but he had died before the wedding and she had vowed her virginity to the Lord.

All the virgins, therefore, with the above-named bishops, traveled back to Cologne but found the city under siege by the Huns. The barbarians saw them, rushed upon them with wild yells, and, like wolves ravaging a flock of sheep, slew them all. Having butchered the rest, they came at last to blessed Ursula.

Likewise unlisted.

258

Their chief was dazzled by her wondrous beauty. He tried to console her over the death of her companions and promised that he would make her his wife. But she scorned his offer, and he, seeing that she despised him, transfixed her with an arrow and so consummated her martyrdom. One of the virgins, whose name was Cordula, was so frightened that she hid all night in the ship, but in the morning surrendered of her own volition and so received the crown; but her feast was not celebrated because she had not suffered with the others. She therefore appeared long afterwards to a recluse, ordering her to see to it that her solemnity was observed the day after the feast of the virgins.

Their passion took place in the year A.D. 238. There are some, however, who maintain that the events above related could not have occurred at that date. Sicily, they reason, was not a kingdom, nor was Constantinople, at the time when the queens of these kingdoms are alleged to have been with the virgins. It is therefore thought to be more likely that this wholesale martyrdom took place when Huns and Goths were warring upon each other, long after the reign of the emperor Constantine—namely, in the time of the emperor Marcian (as we read in one chronicle). Marcian reigned in the year A.D. 452.[3]

A certain abbot asked the abbess of Cologne to give him the body of one of the virgins, which he promised to enshrine in a silver casket in his monastery church, but for a whole year he kept the body on the altar in a wooden box. Then one night, while the abbot was singing matins with his community, that virgin descended bodily into the sanctuary and, after bowing reverently before the altar, walked out through the middle of the choir while the monks looked on in astonishment. The abbot ran to the wooden box and found it empty, so he went to the place from which they had taken the body, and there it was. The abbot begged forgiveness and the present of that body or another, promising most seriously that he would have a precious casket made for it right away. He got nothing.

A certain religious who had great devotion for these virgins was gravely ill, and one day saw a most beautiful virgin appearing to him and asking if he recognized her. He marveled at the vision and admitted that he did not recognize her at all, and she said: "I am one of the virgins for whom you have such devotion. We want you to be rewarded for this, and so, if for love of us and in our honor you will recite the Lord's Prayer eleven thousand times, you will have us to protect and console you at the hour of your death." She disappeared, and the monk fulfilled the condition as fast as he could. Then he called the abbot and had himself anointed,[4] and, as soon as he was anointed, said loudly that they should all go away and make room for the sacred virgins. The abbot asked what

---

[3] The confusions, historical and geographical, in this legend are not unusual in the *Golden Legend*, nor in similar literature of the period, and they do not in the least diminish the main point of the story, which is the virtue, sanctity, and Christian courage of these virgins, so marvelously multiplied. A succinct and informative examination of this legend is given in *Butler's Lives of the Saints* (New York: P. J. Kenedy & Sons, 1963), 4:165–168.

[4] I.e., given the last rites.

this was about, and the monk gave him a full account of the virgin's promise. All left him, and when they came back a little later, found that he had migrated to the Lord.

---

159. Saints Simon and Jude, Apostles

Simon means obedient, or one who bears sadness. This Simon had two surnames; he was called Simon Zelotes, the Zealot, and Simon the Cananean, after Cana of Galilee, where the Lord changed water into wine. Zelotes is the equivalent of Cana, because *cana* means zeal. Simon was obedient with regard to the commandments by acting in accordance with them; he bore the sadness of the afflicted by his compassion; he had zeal for souls by his constant fervor.

Jude (Judas) is interpreted as confessing, or glorious, or it comes from *jubilum dans*, one who gives jubilation. Jude was a confessor of the faith; he had the joy of the kingdom and the jubilation of inward joy. He had several surnames. He was called *Judas (frater) Jacobi*, Judas the brother of James, because he was the brother of James the Less. Secondly, he was called Thaddeus, which means one who lays hold of the prince; or it comes from *thadea*, a royal garment, and *deus*, God. Thaddeus was a royal garment of God by the ornament of his virtues, and by this garment he laid hold of Christ. Or Thaddeus comes from *tam Deus*, i.e., great God, which he was by adoption. Thirdly, the *Ecclesiastical History* calls him *Lebbaeus*, which sounds like *cor*, heart, or *corculus*, little heart. therefore one who cultivates, takes care of, his heart; or *Lebbaeus* is like *lebes*, a basin. Jude is called heart for his greatheartedness, little heart for his purity, a basin for the fullness of his graces, because he merited to be a basin or vase of virtues and grace.

The passion and legend of Simon and Jude Thaddeus was written in Hebrew by Abdias, bishop of Babylonia, who was ordained a bishop by the apostles themselves, Tropeus, a disciple of Abdias, translated it into Greek, and Africanus put it into Latin.

Simon the Cananean and Jude, also called Thaddeus, were brothers of James the Less and sons of Mary of Cleopas, who was married to Alpheus. Thomas sent Jude to Abgar, king of Edessa, after the Lord's ascension. The *Ecclesiastical History* tells us that the said King Abgar had dispatched a letter to our Lord Jesus Christ. The letter read as follows: "King Abgar, son of Euchanias, to Jesus the good

Savior, who has appeared in the region of Jerusalem, greetings. I have heard about you and the cures you effect, that you do this without medicaments or herbs, and that with a word you cause the blind to see, the lame to walk, lepers to be cleansed, and the dead to live again. Having heard all this, I have decided in my mind that you are either a god and have come down from heaven to do what you do, or you are the Son of God and so do these things. For this reason I write to ask you to be kind enough to come to me and cure me of the illness from which I have long suffered. I have also learned that the Jews are murmuring against you and plotting to do away with you. Come therefore to me, because I have this city, a modest but honorable one and large enough for both of us."

The Lord Jesus answered Abgar in these words: "Blessed are you, who have believed in me though you had not seen me, for it is written of me that those who do not see me will believe, and those who do see me will not believe. As for what you have written to me asking me to come to you, I tell you that I must finish all the work I was sent to do, and later be welcomed back by him who sent me. Therefore when I have been assumed, I shall send one of my disciples to you to cure you and give you new life." That is what we read in the *Ecclesiastical History*.

Abgar thus realized that he was not to see Christ face to face. Therefore, according to an ancient history as attested to by John of Damascus in Book IV, he sent a painter to Jesus to make a portrait of the Lord, so that even though he, Abgar, could not see him in the flesh, he could at least imagine him by looking at his portrait. But when the artist came to Jesus, the radiance of the Lord's countenance was so intense that he could not see his face clearly nor fix his eyes upon it, and so could not make the portrait as ordered. Seeing this, Jesus took a linen cloth that belonged to the artist and pressed it to his face, leaving his image imprinted on it, and sent this to the king. The same ancient history describes this image, as John of Damascus testifies. It showed the Lord as having fine eyes and a fine brow, and a long face slightly tilted forward, which is a sign of maturity.

It is said that the letter written by our Lord Jesus Christ had such power that no heretic or pagan could live in Edessa, nor did any tyrant dare to harm the city. Indeed, if at any time a hostile tribe raised an armed hand against Edessa, a child stood atop the city gate and read the letter, and the enemy horde either fled in terror or sued for peace. This actually happened in the past, or so we are told. At a later time Edessa was captured and profaned by the Saracens, all miraculous help being withheld because of the wave of sinfulness that had spread throughout the East.

After Christ's assumption into heaven (as we read in the *Ecclesiastical History*), Thomas the apostle sent Thaddeus (also called Jude) to King Abgar, as the Lord had promised. When Thaddeus came to the king and said that he was the promised disciple of Jesus, Abgar saw in his face a marvelous, godlike splendor. Amazed and frightened at the sight, he adored the Lord, and said: "Truly you are a disciple of Jesus the Son of God, who made me this promise: 'I will send you one of my disciples to cure you and give you life.'" Thaddeus: "If you believe in the Son of God, you will obtain all that your heart desires." Abgar: "I do verily believe and would willingly put to death the Jews who crucified him, if I had that possibility and the Roman authority did not interfere." Now Abgar, as we read in some books, was a leper. Thaddeus therefore took the Savior's letter and rubbed the king's face with it, and at once the leprosy was completely cured.

Jude Thaddeus subsequently preached in Mesopotamia and Pontus, and Simon in Egypt. Then they both went to Persia and there found the two sorcerers, Zaroës and Arphaxat, whom Matthew had driven out of Egypt. Baradach, commander of the king of Babylonia's army, was about to go and make war upon the Indians but could get no response from his gods. He went to the temple of a neighboring city and there received a response, to wit, that because of the apostles who had come there, the gods could not answer him. The commander had a search made for the apostles, found them, and asked them who they were and for what purpose they had come. They answered: "If you want to know our race, we are Hebrews; if our state of life, we confess our Christianity; if our reason for being here, it is for the sake of your people's salvation." The general replied: "When I come back victorious, I shall hear you!" The apostles: "It would be more fitting that you should know the One by whose help you may be able to conquer the rebels, or at least to find them eager to make peace." The commander: "I see that you are more powerful than our gods! Well, then, tell us how the war will end!" The apostles: "So that you may know that your gods are liars, we command them to give their answers to your questions. When their answers show that they know nothing, we shall have proof that they lie about everything!" The answer came through the sorcerers—to wit, that it would be a widespread war with large numbers of people killed on both sides.

The apostles began to laugh. The commander said to them: "You laugh, but I am gripped with fear!" The apostles: "There's nothing to be afraid of, because peace came here with us. Tomorrow at the third hour of the day, legates from the Indies will come to you and bow peaceably to your power!" At this the priests of the idols laughed derisively, and said to the commander: "These men say this to make you feel secure, and you will relax your guard and the enemy will overrun you!" The apostles: "We did not tell you to wait a month, but one day. Tomorrow you will be the victor, and there will be peace."

The commander placed all parties under guard, so that if the outcome showed that what the apostles had said was true, they would be honored for it and the others would be punished for their crime. The following day what the apostles had predicted actually happened. The commander then wanted to put the priests to death by fire, but the apostles forbade this, because they had been sent not to kill the living but to bring the dead to life. The commander was overwhelmed with surprise because they would not let the priests be killed and would not accept a share of their possessions, and he brought the pair to the king, saying: "These two are gods hiding under the appearance of men!" Then, with the two magicians present, he told the king all that had happened. The magicians, beside themselves with envy, said that the apostles were workers of evil and were subtly plotting against the kingdom. The commander said to them: "Try them, if you dare!" The magicians: "If you want to see that in our presence men cannot speak, let some of your most eloquent men come in, and if they manage to speak in our presence, you will know that we have no skills at all!"

A large group of lawyers were brought before the sorcerers, and they became so mute that they could not even nod to indicate that they could not speak. Next the sorcerers said to the king: "We will show you that we are gods when we let these people speak but make them unable to walk, then allow them to walk but make them unable to see, even with their eyes open!" They proceeded to do all that they had said, and the commander brought the lawyers, all ashamed and bewildered, to the apostles. When the lawyers saw them clothed in rags, they had nothing but contempt for them. Simon said to them: "It often happens that worthless stuff is kept in gold, jeweled cases, and precious, gem-studded neck-laces are stored in cheap wooden boxes. Anyone who wishes to become the possessor of a thing will not pay much attention to the container but to the thing it contains. Therefore promise that you will quit the worship of idols and adore the one and invisible God, and we will mark your foreheads with the sign of the cross. Then you will be able to show that the sorcerers are frauds."

The apostles marked the lawyers' foreheads, and they again appeared before the king with the sorcerers present. Not only were these unable to outwit the lawyers, but the lawyers made fools of the sorcerers, who, enraged, caused a wriggling mass of serpents to appear. At once, at the king's order, the apostles came in. They filled their mantles with the reptiles, then threw them upon the magicians, and said: "In the name of the Lord you shall not die, but the snakes will gnaw at your flesh and you will grunt and moan with pain." The serpents began to eat their flesh and the magicians howled like wolves, whereupon the king and the others asked the apostles to let the animals kill the magicians. The apostles' answer was: "We were sent to bring the dead back to life, not to bring death upon the living."

Simon and Jude then prayed, and commanded the serpents to draw out all the venom they had injected, then to go back where they belonged. The magicians felt greater pain when the serpents sucked out the venom than they had when they were being bitten. The apostles told them: "You will feel pain for three days. On the third day you will be healed, so that then at last you may abandon your malice." When the magicians had gone three days without food or drink, and—so acute were their sufferings—without sleep, the apostles came and said to them: "The Lord does not stoop to accept forced service. Therefore get up cured, and be on your way, free to do whatever you wish." They persisted in their malice, however, and went away to stir up all Babylonia against Simon and Jude.

Some time after this, the daughter of a duke conceived out of fornication and gave birth to a son. She defamed a certain holy deacon, saying that he had violated her and was the father of her child. When her parents wanted the deacon dead, the apostles entered the case and asked when the child had been born. They answered: "Today, at the first hour of the day!" The apostles said: "Bring the infant here, and see that the deacon whom you accuse is here also." They did so, and the apostles said to the newborn: "Tell us, child, in the name of the Lord, if this is the deacon's doing!" The infant: "That deacon is chaste and saintly, and has never defiled his flesh." The parents then insisted that the apostles find out who was the author of the crime, but they replied: "It is ours to absolve the innocent, not to bring ruin on the guilty."

At that time two savage tigresses that had been kept in separate cages escaped and devoured everyone they encountered. Then the apostles came to them and in the name of the Lord made them as meek as lambs.

Simon and Jude wanted to leave that region but the people asked them to stay, and they stayed for a year and three months, within which period more than sixty thousand people, not counting children, were baptized. The magicians already described went to a city called Samir, where there were seventy high priests of the idols. They set the priests' minds against the apostles, urging them either to compel the holy men to sacrifice to the idols, or to put them to death. When the apostles had traversed the whole province and arrived at the city, the pontiffs, with the entire populace, took them captive and carried them to the temple of the Sun. The demons began to shout: "What is there between us and you, apostles of the living God? When you come in, we are burned by the flames!" Then an angel of the Lord appeared to the apostles and said: "Choose one or the other, sudden death for these, or your own martyrdom!" The apostles: "Adored be the mercy of God! May he convert these men, and lead us to the palm of martyrdom!"

Silence fell, and the apostles said: "So that you may know that these idols are full of demons, watch! We command the demons to come out and each one of them to shatter his own image!" And immediately, to the utter amazement of all, two black and naked figures[1] came out of the idols, smashed them, and with wild cries departed. The pagan priests rushed upon the apostles and killed them. At that very hour, the skies being brilliant and serene, such lightnings flashed down that the temple was split from top to bottom into three segments, and the two sorcerers were turned to ashes by the heat of the lightning. The king had the apostles' bodies transferred to his city, and in their honor built a church of admirable grandeur.

---

[1] "Figures" is substituted here for the "Ethiopians" of the text.

Numerous sources tell us that Simon was nailed to a gibbet in the shape of a cross. Isidore says this in his book *On the Death of the Apostles*. The same testimony is given by Eusebius in his *Ecclesiastical History*, by Bede in his treatise *On the Acts of the Apostles*, and by Master John Beleth in his *Summa*. These authors say that when Simon had preached in Egypt, he returned to Jerusalem. After the death of James the Less, Simon was unanimously elected by the other apostles to succeed him as bishop of Jerusalem. He is said to have raised thirty dead persons to life, wherefore it is sung of him:

> Ter denos mortuos
> Fluctibus mersos
> Humanae vitae reddidit.[2]

When he had ruled the church at Jerusalem for many years and had reached the age of 120, Trajan being emperor and Atticus consul at Jerusalem, the consul arrested Simon and had him tortured. In the end he ordered him nailed to a cross, and all the bystanders, including the judge, marveled that an old man of six score years could bear the torment of the cross.

Some authors, however, say—and this is the truth of the matter—that it was not this Simon who bore the martyrdom of the cross and was the bishop of Jerusalem, but another Simon, the son of Cleopas the brother of Joseph. Eusebius, bishop of Caesarea, testifies to this in his chronicle. Isidore and Bede say the same in their chronicles. Isidore and Eusebius corrected what they had previously written in their chronicles, as is clear from Bede, who, in his *Retractations*, reproaches himself for having held the other opinion. Usuard also gives this same testimony in his *Martyrology*.

✳

160. Saint Quentin

Quentin, noble by birth and a Roman citizen, went to the city of Amiens and performed many miracles there. By order of Maximian, prefect of the city, he was taken prisoner and beaten until the executioners fainted from their exertions. Then he was jailed, but an angel set him free, and he went to the center

---

[2] Three tens of dead / drowned by the waves / he restored to human life.

of the city and preached to the people. Arrested again, he was stretched on the rack until his veins burst, then was whipped with raw thongs, then had boiling oil, pitch, and grease poured over his wounds. All this he bore patiently, meanwhile mocking the judge, who resented this and gave orders to force lime, vinegar, and mustard into his mouth. Even this did not move him, and he was taken to Veromandum. There the judge had two nails pounded into his body from head to legs, and ten pegs driven under his fingernails. Finally he was beheaded.

Quentin's body was cast into the river and lay hidden for fifty-five years, then was found by a noble Roman lady. Here is how that happened. The lady was absorbed in prayer one night, when an angel alerted her and directed her to hasten to the stronghold of Veromandum, there to search for the body of Saint Quentin and bury it with honors. With a large company she went to the said place and they all prayed devoutly, whereupon the saint's body, incorrupt and sweet-smelling, rose to the surface of the river. The lady saw to the burial and in return for that service recovered her eyesight. She had a church built there and then returned home.

---

161. Saint Eustace

Eustace was first called Placidus. He was the commanding general of Emperor Trajan's armies. Though a worshiper of idols, he was assiduous in doing works of mercy, and his wife was his partner both in worship and in good works. They had two sons, and their father saw to it that the boys were trained in a manner befitting their high station.

Placidus's constant care for those in need merited him the light of grace that led him to the way of truth. One day when he was hunting, he came upon a herd of deer, among which one stag stood out by his size and beauty, and this deer broke away from the others and bounded into a deeper part of the forest. Leaving his soldiers to follow the rest of the herd, Placidus gave his full effort to pursuing the stag and did his best to catch it. The deer kept well ahead of him, however, and finally stopped at the top of a high peak, Placidus, coming near, pondered how he might capture the animal. As he studied it, he saw between its antlers what looked like the holy cross, shining more brightly than the sun. Upon the cross was the image of Jesus Christ.

Christ then spoke to Placidus through the stag's mouth, as once he had spoken through the mouth of Balaam's ass. The Lord said: "O Placidus, why are you pursuing me? For your sake I have appeared to you in this animal. I am the Christ, whom you worship without knowing it. Your alms have risen before me, and for this purpose I have come, that through this deer which you hunted, I myself might hunt you!" There are others, however, who say that these words were pronounced by the image which appeared between the stag's antlers.

Having heard what was said, Placidus was stricken with fear and fell from his horse. After an hour, however, he came to himself, rose from the ground, and said: "Let me understand what you were saying, and I will believe you." The Lord said: "I am the Christ. I created heaven and earth. I made light to rise and be separate from darkness. I set seasons and days and years. I formed man from the slime of the earth. For the salvation of the human race I took flesh and appeared on earth. I was crucified and buried, and on the third day I rose from the dead."

Placidus, having heard these words, again fell to the ground and said: "Lord, I believe that you ARE, that you have made all things, that you convert the erring." The Lord said to him: "If you believe, go to the bishop of the city and have him baptize you." "Lord," said Placidus, "do you want me to make all this known to my wife and my sons, so that they also may believe in you?" "Yes," said the Lord. "Tell them, and let them be cleansed with you. Then you yourself come here tomorrow morning, and I will appear to you again and tell you more fully what the future holds for you."

Placidus went home, found his wife in bed, and began to tell her what he had to tell, but she burst out, saying: "My master, I too saw him this past night, and he said to me: 'Tomorrow you and your husband and your sons will come to me!' So now I too know that he is Jesus the Christ!" And right then, in the middle of the night, they went to the bishop of Rome. He baptized them with great joy, giving Placidus the name Eustace and his wife the name Theospis, and called his sons Agapetus and Theospitus.

Morning came, and Eustace, as he had done before, set out for the hunt. Coming near to the place he knew, he dismissed his soldiers on the pretext that their task was to pick up the tracks of some game. Then, standing in the same place, he saw the same vision as before and, prostrating himself on the ground, said: "I implore you, Lord, show your servant what you promised to show him!" The Lord: "Blessed are you, Eustace, for accepting the bath of my grace, because now you have overcome the devil! Now you have trampled on the one who had deceived you! Now your faith will be seen! The devil, because you have left him, will fight furiously against you. You will have to bear many hardships in order to receive the crown of victory. You will have to suffer much, in order to be brought low from the lofty vanity of the world and be exalted again in the riches of the spirit. Do not lose courage, nor look back upon your former eminence, because, through your trials, you are to become another Job.

But when you have been humbled, I will come to you and restore you to your erstwhile glory. Tell me, therefore! Do you wish to endure trials now or at your life's end?"

Eustace gave his answer: "Lord, if so it is to be, order the trials to befall us now, but grant us the patience to bear them!" The Lord: "Be of good heart! My grace will guard your souls." Then the Lord ascended to heaven, and Eustace went home and told all to his wife.

Within a few days a lethal plague gripped the men and women who served in his house and killed them all, and not long afterwards his horses and herds perished. Then some lawless men, seeing him despoiled and desolate, broke into his house at night, laid hands on everything they found, and robbed him of his gold and silver and all his goods. Eustace gave thanks to God and, having nothing left, fled by night with his wife and sons: dreading the shame of destitution, they decided to go to Egypt. The king and all the senators were shocked at the loss of their commander-in-chief, especially since they could find no equal to replace him.

The fugitives made their way to the sea, boarded a ship, and sailed away. Eustace's wife was a beautiful woman, and the ship's captain lusted after her. When it was time to pay their passage and they had nothing to pay it with, the captain commanded that the woman be held on board. He intended to make her his own, but Eustace absolutely refused to agree. When he persisted in his refusal, the master gave his crew the idea of throwing Eustace overboard so that they could have his wife; and Eustace, unable to resist further, sadly left her to them and went ashore with his sons. Weeping, he said to the boys: "Woe to me, woe to you, that your mother is given over to a man who is not of our race!"

They came to a river in flood, and the father did not dare attempt to cross with the two boys at the same time, so he left one and carried the other across. But the river was over its banks, so Eustace put ashore the boy he was carrying and started back to rescue the other. As he reached the middle of the stream, a wolf ran out, snatched the boy his father had just put ashore, and disappeared into the forest. Eustace, despairing of this child, turned again to go to the other one, but a lion came and carried the boy away. Unable to go after either son, since he was out in the middle of the river, the father began to mourn and tear his hair, and might have abandoned himself to the waters had not divine providence restrained him.

Meanwhile some shepherds saw the lion carrying the boy off alive and went after him with their dogs. By God's will the beast dropped the child unhurt and got away. On the other side of the river huntsmen raised the hue and cry in pursuit of the wolf, and freed the boy, unharmed, from the animal's jaws. As it happened, the huntsmen and the shepherds were of the same village, and they kept the boys with them and took care of them.

Eustace, however, did not know that this had happened, and went his way weeping and saying: "Alas, alas! Once I flourished like a tree, but now I am almost leafless! Woe is me! Once I was surrounded by a multitude of soldiers, but now I am left alone, and even the company of my sons is denied me! I remember, Lord, that you told me it was my lot to be tried as Job was tried, but it seems to me that even more ills have come to me than to him. Even if he was stripped of his possessions, he could at least have dung to sit on, but I have not even that! He had his friends to share his misery, but I have only the fierce beasts that stole my sons. Job's wife was left to him, I am bereft of mine. Give pause, O Lord, to my tribulations, and set a guard over my mouth, lest my heart incline to evil words, and I be cast out of thy sight!" He went on and came to a certain village, where he stayed and, for a pittance, watched over the fields of those men for fifteen years, while in the next village his sons were growing up and did not even know that they were brothers. The Lord also kept Eustace's wife in his care. The ship's captain, that foreigner, never took her to wife but died leaving her untouched.

In those years the emperor and the Roman people were constantly harassed by enemies. The emperor remembered Placidus, who had fought so valiantly against those same foes, and was saddened to think of the sudden change that had overtaken his general. So he sent many soldiers to different parts of the world, promising wealth and honors to those who would find Placidus. Two men who had served under the former commander came to the village where he was living. Eustace saw them coming across the field, recognized them by their gait, and was disturbed by the memory of his own former high status. He said to the Lord: "Lord, I see these men who were with me, whom I had not hoped ever to see again! Please grant that I may again see my wife! I cannot ask for my sons, because they were eaten by wild beasts." And a voice came to him, saying: "Have confidence, Eustace, because you will soon have back your high honors, and your sons and your wife will be returned to you!"

He went to meet the two soldiers, who did not recognize him at all. They greeted him and asked if he knew a stranger whose name was Placidus and who had a wife and two sons. He professed not to know them. He invited the soldiers, however, to be his guests and waited on them. Then, recalling his former rank, he could not contain his tears, but went outside and washed his face before returning to serve them. Meanwhile the two men looked at each other questioningly, and one said: "Doesn't that man look a lot like the one we're looking for?" "He certainly does," the other said. "We'll watch closely, and if he has a scar on his head like the one our general had, he's the one!" They looked and saw the scar, and knew that Eustace was the man they were looking for, so they jumped up and embraced him and asked about his wife and children. He told them that his sons were dead and his wife in captivity. Then the neighbors hurried in as though to enjoy a bit of theater, and the soldiers boasted about their general's prowess and the glory that had been his. They also informed him of the emperor's order and clothed him in fine garments.

A fifteen-days' journey brought them back to Rome, and the emperor, learning that Eustace was approaching, hurried to meet him and embraced him warmly. He told them all that had happened to him, and they took him immediately to military headquarters and ordered him to take charge. He surveyed his forces and found that they were far fewer in number than he needed in order to face so many foes, so he ordered recruits to be called up from every city and village. Thus it happened that the place where the two sons had grown up was called upon to furnish two recruits. The local people considered the two young men to be the most fitted for military service, and sent them up. Eustace was very pleased to see these two physically robust and morally upright candidates, and assigned them to places in his immediate circle. Off they went to war and won a great victory, and Eustace granted the troops three days of rest in a place where, though he did not know this, his wife kept a modest inn. By God's will the two youths were quartered in this inn, but they were not aware that their hostess was also their mother.

Around midday the two were lounging outside and chatting about their early years, while the mother, seated at a little distance, listened intently. The older son said to the younger: "I can't remember anything about my childhood, except that my father was the commander of the armies, and my mother was a very beautiful woman. They had two sons, me and a younger one—he was very handsome too—and our parents took us one night and we boarded a ship going I don't know where. When we got off the ship, our mother stayed on board, I don't know why. Our father was crying as he carried the two of us and came to a river, which he crossed carrying my younger brother, leaving me behind on the riverbank. When he was on his way back to get me, a wolf came and ran off with my brother, and, before my father could reach me, a lion came out of the forest, seized me, and dragged me into the woods. Sheepherders snatched me from the lion's mouth and brought me up on their own land, as you know. I never could find out what became of my father and the boy." Hearing all this, the younger brother began to weep, and said: "By God, from what I hear, I am your brother, because the men who brought me up said the same thing—that they had snatched me from a wolf!" So they fell into each other's arms, and kissed, and wept.

The mother, having heard the story as the older son told it, spent hours wondering whether these could be her sons. The next day she went to the commander and questioned him, saying: "I beg of you, my lord, to order me returned to my native land, because I am a Roman and therefore a foreigner here." As she spoke to the commander, she noticed certain distinguishing marks and recognized her husband. Unable to control herself, she threw herself at his feet and said: "I pray you, my lord, tell me about your early life, because I think you are Placidus, commander of the armies, and are also called Eustace, whom the Savior converted when you were still Placidus. You underwent one trial after another. Your wife—and I am she—was taken from you at sea but was preserved from degradation. I had two sons, whose names were Agapetus and Theospitus." While she spoke, Eustace studied her carefully and saw that she was indeed his wife. Tears of joy and mutual embraces followed, and he glorified God who comforts the afflicted.

Then his wife said to him: "My master, where are our sons?" He said: "They were carried off by wild beasts." And he told her how he had lost them. "Thank God!" she exclaimed. "I think that as God has given us the gift of finding each other, he will also give us the joy of recognizing our sons!" Eustace: "I told you they were carried off by wild beasts!" She: "Yesterday I was sitting in the garden and listening to two young soldiers telling each other about their childhood, and I think they are our own sons! Ask them! They'll tell you!" Eustace sent for them and, upon hearing an account of their young years, knew that they were indeed his sons. He and their mother embraced them, floods of tears were shed, and kisses exchanged time after time. The whole army cheered and rejoiced, both because these people had been reunited and because the barbarians had been conquered.

When Eustace returned to Rome, Emperor Trajan had died and Hadrian, a still more guilty tyrant, had succeeded him. Hadrian staged a magnificent welcome for the commander and laid on a sumptuous banquet, celebrating his victory and the finding of his wife and sons. The next day the emperor led a procession to the temple of the idols, to offer sacrifice in thanksgiving for the victory. The emperor noticed that Eustace did not offer sacrifice either for the victory or for the recovery of his family, and exhorted him to do so. Eustace answered: "I worship Christ as God and I sacrifice to God alone!" This made Hadrian angry. He had Eustace, together with his wife and their sons, placed in the arena, and had a ferocious lion loosed upon them. The lion came running to them, lowered his head as though adoring them as saints, and meekly withdrew. Then the emperor had a brazen bull heated and ordered the four saints enclosed in it alive. Praying and commending themselves to the Lord, they entered the bull and so rendered their souls to the Lord.

Three days later their bodies were taken out of the bull in the emperor's presence. The bodies were intact, nor had the heat of the fire touched the hair or any other part of them. Christians took the sacred remains, buried them in a most honorable place, and built an oratory there. The martyrs suffered on 1 November, or, according to others, on 20 September, in the reign of Hadrian, which began about A.D. 120.

162. All Saints

The Feast of All Saints was instituted for four purposes. The first was connected with the dedication of a certain temple; the second was to supply for the omission of many saints from the calendar; the third was to atone for neglect in honoring the saints; the fourth was to make it easier to obtain the favors for which we pray.

The feast was indeed instituted in connection with the dedication of a certain temple. When the Romans were masters of the whole world, they built a very large temple, in the middle of which they set up their idol. Then around the perimeter they arranged the statues of the gods of the provinces, the faces turned to the idol of Rome and the eyes fixed upon it. If from time to time a province rebelled, at once, they say, by some trick of the devil, the statue of that province turned its back on the Roman idol, as if to give notice that the province no longer accepted Roman rule. What happened next was that the Romans quickly dispatched a large army and subjugated the rebellious state. The Romans, however, were not satisfied with having only the images of all the provincial gods in the capital, and temples were built to most of them in Rome itself to show that the gods had made the people of Rome conquerors and masters of all the provinces. But because there were too many idols for each to have its own temple, the Romans pushed their insane display to the point of erecting a temple higher and more marvelous than the rest in honor of all the gods, and called it the Pantheon, which means "all gods" and comes from *pan*, meaning all, and *theos*, meaning god. To complete the people's delusion, the priests of the idols pretended that they had been advised by Cybele, whom they called the mother of all the gods, that if they wished to obtain victory over all nations, they should build this magnificent temple to all her children.

The foundation of this temple was laid in a circle to signify the eternity of the gods. But because the vault would be too wide to support, the builders, each time the walls had reached a certain height, filled the interior with earth into which, it is said, coins were thrown, and so they proceeded until the wonderful temple was completed. Then it was announced that anyone who wished to carry away the earth could keep the money he found in it; whereupon crowds of people came hurrying, and the building was cleaned out in no time. Finally the Romans erected a gilded bronze pinnacle at the top of the dome, around the inside of which, so the story goes, emblems of all the provinces were sculpted, so that anyone who came to Rome could see in which direction his province lay. In time, however, this pinnacle fell down and left a large opening in the roof.

In the reign of the emperor Phocas, about the year 605, long after Rome had accepted the faith of Christ, the emperor ceded the temple described above to Pope Boniface IV, the third pope after Saint Gregory the Great. Boniface had the statues and everything connected with the cult of idols removed, and, on the twelfth day of May 609, consecrated the building in honor of Blessed Mary and all the martyrs. He gave it the title of Sancta Maria ad Martyres, but now it is popularly known as Santa Maria Rotonda. At that time no feast days were solemnized in honor of sainted confessors, but the crowds that came for this particular feast were so great that food ran out and the people could not stay for the celebration. A later Pope Gregory therefore moved the May feast to the first day of November, when supplies were ample after the harvest and the vintage was finished. He also decreed that the new feast was to be celebrated throughout the world, and that this day should be solemnly observed in honor of all the saints. Thus the temple that had been built for all the idols was now dedicated to all the saints, and where a horde of false gods had been worshiped, a multitude of saints was now praised.

The second purpose of the feast is to supply for omissions. We have in fact omitted many saints, not celebrating feast days or making memorials of them. Indeed we could not have feasts for all the saints. For one thing the number of them has multiplied until it is almost infinite. Besides that, we are weak and because of our weakness could not put up with so many celebrations. And then there is not enough time in the year: as Jerome says in the letter that prefaces his *Calendar*, there is not one day except the first of January that could not have five thousand martyrs assigned to it. Therefore the Church with good reason has ordered that since we cannot solemnize the saints one by one, we shall at least honor them generally and all together.

But why is it an established rule that we must mark the saints' feasts on earth? Master William of Auxerre gives six reasons for this in his *Summa de officiis*. The first is the honor due the divine majesty, because when we pay honor to the saints, we honor God in the saints and proclaim that he is admirable in them. Whoever pays honor to the saints pays special honor to him who made them saints. The second reason is that we need help in our weakness. Because we cannot obtain salvation by ourselves, we need the intercession of the saints, and it is right that we should honor them in order to gain their assistance. So we read in 1 (3) Kings, chapter 1:30, that Bathsheba (whose name means "wall of plenty" and stands for the Church triumphant) by her prayers obtained the kingdom (i.e., the Church militant) for her son. The third reason was to increase our own sense of security—in other words, to have the glory of the saints recalled to us on their feast day, and thus to build up our own hope and confidence. If mortals like ourselves could by their merits be so lifted up, it follows that we can do likewise, because "the hand of the Lord is not shortened that it cannot save" (Isa. 59:1). The fourth reason was to offer an example for our imitation. When the saints are celebrated on their feast days, we are inspired to imitate them, i.e., to follow their example by making little of earthly goods and setting our hearts on the things of heaven. The fifth reason was to allow a fair exchange. The saints make festival in heaven over us, for there is joy before the angels of God and holy souls over one sinner doing penance, and so we should make a fair return by celebrating their feasts on earth. And Master William's sixth reason is to assure our own honor, because when we honor the saints, we are taking care of our own interests and procuring our own honor. Their feast day honors us. When we pay tribute to our brothers, we honor ourselves, since love makes all things to be in common, and all things are ours, in heaven, on earth, and in eternity.

In addition to these reasons John of Damascus, Book IV, chapter 7, gives others as to why the saints and their bodies and relics ought to be honored. Some of his reasons are based on the dignity of the saints, some on the preciousness of their bodies. Their dignity, he says, is fourfold: they are God's friends, his children, his heirs, and our leaders and guides. And here are his authorities: for the first, John 15:15: "No longer do I call you servants, but I have called you friends"; for the second, John 1:12: "he gave power to become children of God"; for the third, Rom. 8:17: "if children, then heirs of God." Regarding the fourth he says: "How much trouble you would go to in order to find a guide to present you to a mortal king and speak to him on your behalf! But the leaders of the whole human race, who appeal to God for all of us, are they not to be honored? Of course they are, as also are those who build temples to honor God and to venerate the saints' memory."

Other reasons are based on the preciousness of the saints' bodies. John of Damascus gives four such and Augustine adds a fifth, all demonstrating how precious the bodies of the saints are. Their bodies were God's repository, Christ's temple, the alabaster vase of spiritual ointment, divine fountains, and the organ of the Holy Spirit. They were God's repository; Damascenus: "These became the repositories of God, pure cenacles." Their bodies were Christ's temples, whence it follows that God dwelt in their bodies by way of the intellect, as the apostle says (1 Cor. 3:16): "Do you not know that you are God's temple and that God's Spirit dwells in you?" God is spirit! How then could God's living temples, his living tabernacles, not be honored? Chrysostom also says about this: "Man delights in building houses, God's delight is in the company of the saints." So Ps. 25:8: "I have loved, O Lord, the beauty of thy house." What beauty? Not the beauty of a variety of splendid marbles, but that which a variety of living graces bestows. The former beauty pleases the eye of the body, the latter gives life to the soul; the former lasts only for a time and beguiles the eyes, the latter builds up the spirit unto eternity. Third, the saint's body is the alabaster vase of spiritual ointment, and Damascenus says: "The relics of the saints give out a sweet-smelling ointment, and let no one disbelieve it. If water gushed out of the hard stone of the cliff in the desert, and water came out of the jawbone of an ass to quench Samson's thirst, it is all the more believable that a fragrant ointment should flow from the martyrs' relics for those who thirst for

God's power, to the honor of the saint, which is from God." Fourth, the fountains of God. The same John of Damascus says: "The saints, living in the truth, stand freely present in assistance before God. Christ, the master of his saints, has provided us with their relics as salutary springs from which flow manifold benefits." Fifth, the organ of the Holy Spirit. Augustine gives this reason, saying, in his *City of God*: "The bodies of the saints are to be treated not with disdain but with the greatest reverence, because, while they were alive, the Holy Spirit used them as so many organs for the doing of every good work." So the apostle says (2 Cor. 13:3): "Since you desire proof that Christ is speaking in me . . . "; and of Stephen it is written (Acts 5:10): "They could not withstand the wisdom and the Spirit that spoke." In the same vein Ambrose, in the *Hexaemeron*: "Here is something priceless—that a man could be the organ of the divine voice, and with the body's lips utter divine pronouncements."

The third reason for the institution of the feast of All Saints is to make amends for our negligences. Granted that we do observe the feasts of a relatively small number of saints, even then we often do so carelessly, and through ignorance or negligence omit many things. If therefore we have been neglectful in the celebrations we have performed, in this general solemnization we can make up for our omissions and purge ourselves of negligence. This reason seems to be touched upon in a sermon recited in the Church's office for this day, in which we hear: "It is decreed that on this day the memory of all the saints shall be brought to mind, in order that anything which human frailty, due to ignorance or negligence or preoccupation with some detail, may have less than fully carried out in the solemn celebrations of the saints, shall be compensated in this general solemnization."

Note that there are four categories—apostles, martyrs, confessors, and virgins—among the saints of the New Testament whom we celebrate in the cycle of the year, and whom today we honor all together. Rabanus points out that the four quarters of the world stand for the four categories, the East for apostles, the South for martyrs, the North for confessors, and the West for virgins.

The first category is that of the apostles, whose dignity and excellence appear in that they surpass all the other saints in four ways. Firstly, they are preeminent in dignity, being wise commanders in the Church militant, powerful members of the eternal Judge's court, and gentle shepherds of the flock of Christ. Bernard: "It was proper that such pastors and teachers, men gentle and powerful and wise, be given authority over the human race: gentle so as to take hold of me kindly and mercifully, powerful so as to protect me strongly, wise so as to lead me to life by the way that goes straight to the city on high." The apostles excel, secondly, by preeminence of power, about which Augustine says: "God gave the apostles power over nature to cure it, over demons to drive them out, over the elements to change them, over souls to release them from their sins, over death that they might make little of it, and above the angels' power, because the apostles could consecrate the Lord's body." Thirdly, they excel in the prerogative of sanctity. On account of their sublime holiness and the fullness of grace in them, the life and conduct of Christ shone in them as in a mirror, and he was known in them as the sun is known in its rays, a rose in its fragrance, or fire in its heat. In his commentaries on Matthew, Chrysostom says: "Christ sent the apostles as the sun sends its rays, as a rose spreads the odor of its fragrance, and as a fire sprays its sparks, so that as the sun appears in its rays and a rose is known to be present by its perfume, as fire is sighted by its sparks, so the power of Christ is known in the apostles' virtues." Thus Chrysostom. Fourthly, the apostles excel in the efficacy of their work. Speaking of the apostles, Augustine says of this efficacy: "The most abject, the most unlearned, the fewest in number are ennobled, enlightened, and multiplied. They bring the most fluent orators, the most renowned geniuses, the most numerous legions, and the wonderful skills of the most eloquent authors and teachers under the yoke of Christ."

The second category of saints comprises the martyrs, whose dignity and excellence are demonstrated by the fact that they suffered in many ways, and fruitfully, and with constancy. They suffered in many ways, because besides the martyrdom of blood they endured a threefold bloodless martyrdom. Of this triple martyrdom Bernard says: "There is a threefold unbloody martyrdom, namely, abstinence in the midst of abundance, which David practiced, generosity in poverty, exhibited by Tobit and the poor widow, and chastity in youth, which was Joseph's way in Egypt." Gregory also speaks of a triple bloodless martyrdom. There is patience in adversity, of which he says: "We can be martyrs without the sword, if we practice patience of spirit." There is compassion for the afflicted, about which he says: "Anyone who suffers over another's needs bears a cross in his mind." There is love of enemies, and he says: "To endure shameful treatment and to love one who hates you is a martyrdom in the hidden depth of thought."

Martyrdom is fruitful. For the martyrs themselves its fruits are the remission of sins, the accumulation of merits, and the gaining of eternal glory. They bought these blessings at the price of their blood, and therefore their blood is precious, i.e., full of price or value. Of the first and second Augustine says in the *City of God*: "What is more precious than the death on account of which sins are forgiven and merits accumulated?" In his commentary on John he says: "Christ's blood is precious without sin, yet he also makes precious the blood of the martyrs, for whom he gave his blood in payment. If he did not make the blood of his servants precious, it could not be said that the death of his servants is precious in the sight of the Lord." (Cf. Ps. 115:14 [116:15].) Similarly Cyprian: "Martyrdom is the end of sin, the stopping point of peril, the guide of salvation, the master of patience, the house of life." And, regarding the third fruit of martyrdom to those who endure it, Bernard says: "Three things make the death of the saint precious—rest from labor, joy in newness, certainty about eternal life."

The death of the martyrs is useful and fruitful for us, too, and in two ways. They are given to us as models for the struggle that is life; Chrysostom: "O Christian, you are a dainty soldier if you think you can win without a fight or conquer without combat. Put forth your best effort, fight strenuously, strive mightily in this battle. Consider the pact, weigh the agreement, know what it means to be a soldier—the pact to which you gave your name. By this pact all have fought, by this agreement all have conquered, in this militia all have triumphed!" Thus Chrysostom.

The martyrs are also patrons to help us, which they do both by their merits and by their prayers. Regarding their merits Augustine says: "Oh, boundless kindness of God, which allows the martyrs' merits to be our support! He tests them in order to instruct us, he spends them to buy us, he wills that their torments aid our progress." And about their prayers Jerome writes against Vigilantius: "If the apostles and the martyrs, while they were still in their bodies and had to be concerned for themselves, could pray for others, how much more can they do after winning their crowns, their victories, their triumphs! One man, Moses, obtained pardon from God for 600,000 warriors, and Stephen obtained forgiveness for Paul and many others; but after they begin to be with Christ, they can do much more. The apostle Paul said that 276 lives in the ship were saved by his prayers. Is he likely to have less power now that he is freed from the body with Christ?"

Lastly, the martyrs suffered with constancy. Augustine: "The soul of the martyr is a sword shining with charity, sharpened with truth, brandished with the power of a fighting God—a sword that has fought wars, has bested troops of gainsayers in argument, has struck down its foes and laid adversaries low." Likewise Chrysostom: "The tortured have shown more strength than the torturers, the torn limbs have conquered the claws that tore them."

The third category of saints is that of the confessors. Their dignity and excellence are manifest in that they have confessed God in three ways, namely, in the heart, in the mouth, and in works. The heart's confession is insufficient unless it is expressed in speech, as Chrysostom, commenting on Matthew, proves with four reasons. About interior confession he says: "The root of confession is faith in the heart, and confession is the fruit of faith. As long as the root is alive in the ground, it must produce branches and leaves; otherwise you may be sure that the root has dried in the ground. So also as long as faith is whole in the heart, it always sprouts in oral profession; if confession has withered in the mouth, you may be sure that faith has already dried up in the heart." His second reason runs as follows: "If it is to your profit to believe in your heart without confessing your faith before men, then it profits an unbelieving hypocrite to confess Christ even though he does not believe in his heart. If it does him no good to confess without faith, then neither do you gain anything by believing without declaring your belief." Here is his third reason: "If it is enough for Christ that you know him although you have not confessed him before men, then let it be enough for you that Christ knows you even though he does not confess you before God. If being known by him is not enough for you, then neither is your belief enough for him." And for a fourth argument he says: "If faith in the heart were sufficient, God would have created only a heart for you. Now, however, he has also created a mouth for you, in order that you may believe in your heart and confess with your mouth."

Thirdly, the confessor saints have confessed God by their works. How anyone can confess or deny God by works is shown by Jerome: "They profess that they know God, saying, 'Christ is wisdom, justice, truth, holiness, fortitude.' Wisdom is denied by foolishness, justice by wickedness, truth by mendacity, holiness by shamelessness, fortitude by cowardice. As many times as we are conquered by vices and sins, so many times we deny God; and conversely, as often as we do some good, we confess God."

The fourth category is that of the virgin saints. Their dignity and excellence are evidenced first by the fact that they are the brides of the eternal King. Ambrose: "Who could imagine beauty greater than that of her who is loved by the King, approved by the Judge, dedicated by God, always a spouse, always unwed?" Second, because they are compared to the angels; Ambrose: "Virginity surpasses the condition of human nature, because through it human beings are associated with the angels, yet the virgins' victory is greater than the angels', because angels live without flesh but virgins triumph in the flesh." Third, because they are more illustrious than all the faithful, as Cyprian says: "Virginity is the flower of the seed of the Church, the beauty and ornament of spiritual grace, a happy disposition for praise and honor, a work integral and incorrupt, the image of God, and again with reference to God's holiness the more illustrious portion of the flock of Christ." Fourth, because they are preferred before married women. This excellence, which virginity has over marital union, is evident from many comparisons between the two states. Marriage fertilizes the womb, virginity makes the spirit fruitful; Augustine: "It is a noble thing to choose, while still in this life, to imitate the life of the angels rather than to increase in this life the number of mortals. More fruitful and happier is the fecundity that fosters the spirit than that which swells the belly." The latter brings forth sons of sorrow, the former, sons of joy and exultation; Augustine: "Continence itself is never sterile, it is the fruitful mother of sons of joy begotten of you, O Lord!" Marriage fills the earth with children, virginity fills heaven; Jerome: "Nuptials fill the earth; virginity, paradise." From the former comes a multitude of cares, from the latter a plenitude of calm; Gilbert: "Virginity is the silencer of worries, the peace of the flesh, the ransom from vices, the reign of the virtues." The one is good, the other better; Jerome to Pammachius: "There is as much difference between marriage and virginity as there is between not sinning and doing good; or, to put it more briefly, between good and better." The one is compared to thorns, the other to roses; Jerome to Eustochium: "I praise marriage, but because it begets virgins to me; I gather a rose from thorns, gold from the earth, from the shell a pearl!" Fifth, because virgins enjoy many privileges. They will have golden crowns, they alone will sing the canticle, they will wear the same garments that Christ wears, they will always march after the Lamb himself.

The fourth and last reason for the institution of the feast of All Saints is to make it easier for us to have our prayers heard. On this day we honor all the saints universally in order to have them interceding for us all together, and thus to obtain the mercy of God more readily, because if it is impossible for the prayers of many not to be heard, it is surely impossible that with all the saints praying for us their prayers would not be granted. This reason is brought out in the collect of the day's mass, which says: "With the great host of those interceding for us, grant us the desired abundance of your mercy." The saints intercede for us by their merits and by their good will. Their merits help us and they desire the fulfillment of our wishes, but this only when they know that what we wish for is in accordance with God's will.

That on this day all the saints come together to intercede universally for us was shown in a vision which, we are told, occurred a year after the institution of the feast. On this day the warden of the church of Saint Peter devoutly went around to all the altars and implored the help of all the saints. When he got back to Saint Peter's altar he rested for a short while and was rapt in ecstasy. In a vision he saw the King of kings seated on a high throne, surrounded by all the angels. Then the Virgin of virgins came forward, wearing a gleaming diadem and followed by an innumerable multitude of virgins and the continent. The King rose immediately to meet her and placed a throne beside his own for her to be seated. Then came a man clad in camel skins, whom a large number of ancients followed, and after them another man wearing pontifical vestments and accompanied by a chorus of men similarly attired. Next a great army of soldiers advanced, and then a vast throng of men and women of every race. All gathered before the King's throne and knelt to adore him. The man in pontifical robes then intoned matins, and the rest joined in the chant.

The angel who was guiding the aforementioned warden now explained the vision to him. The Virgin at the head of the procession, he said, was the mother of God with her train of virgins, the man in camel skins was John the Baptist with the patriarchs and prophets, the one in the robes of a pontiff was Saint Peter with the other apostles, the soldiers were the martyrs, the rest of the crowd, the confessors. All these people had come before the King to thank him for the honor done them by mortals on this day, and to pray for the whole world. Then the angel led the warden to another place and showed him people of both sexes, some reclining on golden beds, others at tables enjoying delicious viands, still others naked and needy, begging for help. This place, the angel said, was purgatory. Those enjoying abundance were the souls for whom their friends provided plentiful aid, whereas those in need had no one who cared for them. The angel therefore commanded the warden to make all this known to the supreme pontiff, and to inform him that he was to establish after the feast of all the saints a day of commemoration for the souls of all the departed, on which day those who had no one to pray for them would at least share in the general commemoration.

✳

163. The Commemoration of All Souls

The commemoration of all the faithful departed was instituted in order that those who have no special suffrages offered for them may be helped by this general memorial, as was demonstrated in the revelation already described.[1] Peter Damian says that Saint Odilo, abbot of Cluny, learned that voices and howls of demons were heard near a volcano in Sicily, and that the souls of the dead were being snatched from the demons' grasp by the power of alms and prayers. The abbot ordered that after the feast of All Saints a commemoration of the dead be made in his monasteries. Later this practice was approved throughout the Church.

Regarding this custom two points should be considered specifically. The first concerns the persons in need of purgation—who they are, by whom they are purged, and where they are purged. The second concerns the sacrifices and suffrages made in their behalf: these will be discussed further on.

Those who are to be purged fall into three classes. The first consists of those who die before they have completed the penance imposed on them. However, if while on earth they had contrition of heart great enough to erase their sins, they would pass freely to heavenly life although they had not completed satisfaction, because contrition is the greatest satisfaction for sin and the best way to be cleansed of sin. Jerome: "What counts with God is not length of time but depth of sorrow, not abstinence from food but mortification of the vices."

Those who have not been contrite enough and who die before completing their penance are punished most grievously in the fire of purgatory, unless some of their dear ones take the satisfaction upon themselves. For this commutation to be of avail, four conditions must be met. The first is required of the one who

---

[1] At the end of the chapter (162) on All Saints.

commutes the penance, namely, his authority, because the commutation must be done by the authority of a priest. The second is required of those for whom the commutation is made, namely, need, because they must be in a situation such that they cannot make satisfaction for themselves and so need help. The third is charity, required of the one who takes the commutation upon himself, because without charity the satisfaction he offers would not be meritorious or satisfactory. The fourth must be met by the penance or punishment imposed, namely, proportionality: a lesser penalty must be commuted to a greater, because a penalty borne by the sinner in person is more satisfactory to God than one borne by someone else.

There are, in fact, three kinds of penalty or penance: personal, i.e., borne by the sinner himself and voluntarily, and this is the most satisfactory; penance borne by the person himself but not voluntarily, because it is done in purgatory; and penance borne voluntarily by someone else, and this is less satisfactory than the first kind because it is not done by the sinner himself, but more satisfactory than the second kind because it is voluntary. If, however, the person for whom satisfaction is assumed dies, he still is punished in purgatory, but, due to the punishment he endures personally and the penalty satisfied by others for him, he is freed more quickly, because God counts both payments as one sum total. Thus if the person owed a penance of two months in purgatory he could, due to suffrages offered by others, be freed in one month; but he is never released from purgatory until the debt is paid in full. Once it is fully paid, the payment belongs to the one who made it and is credited to him. If he does not need it, it goes into the Church's treasury or benefits the souls in purgatory.

The second class of those who go down to purgatory comprises those who indeed have completed the satisfaction imposed upon them, but that satisfaction was not sufficient, due to the ignorance or carelessness of the priest who imposed it. Unless the depth of their contrition supplies the difference, these souls will make up in purgatory what was lacking in the satisfaction they offered in this life. God, who knows how to match punishments to sins in right proportion, adds a sufficient penalty lest some sin go unpunished. The penance enjoined by the priest is either too much or just enough or too little. If it is too much, the excess is credited to the doer for an increase of glory; if it is just right, the whole debt is discharged; if it is not enough, what is left is made up according to the demands of divine justice.

About those who repent only at the very end of their lives, hear what Augustine thinks: "One who is baptized in his last hour leaves this life sure of salvation; a man of faith who has led a good life leaves this life secure; one who has done penance and is reconciled while in good health leaves this life secure: about those who repent only at the last moment I myself am not sure. Therefore take what is certain and leave what is uncertain." Augustine speaks this way because there are those who repent out of necessity rather than out of free will, for fear of punishment rather than for love of glory.

The third class of those descending into purgatory includes those who take wood, hay, and stubble with them, in other words, who are bound by a fleshly attachment to their earthly goods although they love God more than wealth. The carnal affections that bind them to houses, wives, and possessions, although they put nothing above God, are signified by the wood, hay, and stubble, and those who carry them will suffer the fire a longer time, like wood, or a shorter, like hay, or a minimum, like stubble. That fire, as Augustine says, though it is not eternal, nevertheless is so fierce, so hot, that it is more painful than anything anyone ever suffers in this life. Never was such pain felt in the flesh, dreadful as were the torments endured by the martyrs.

As to our second question about the suffering souls, namely, by whom they are purged, be it known that purgation and punishment are the work of wicked angels, not of good ones, for good angels do not harass good people but bad people, whereas bad angels harass both good and bad people. It is, however, believable that the good angels frequently visit and console their brothers and fellow citizens in purgatory and exhort them to suffer patiently. The souls also have another consoling remedy in that they await with certainty the glory to come. Their certainty about glory is less than that of the souls who are already in heaven, but they are more certain than those still living on earth. The certainty of those who are in heaven waits for nothing and fears nothing. They already possess all they might expect of the future, and there is nothing they can be afraid of losing. The certainty of those still alive on earth, on the contrary, is mixed with expectancy and fear, but that of the souls in purgatory is midway between: they are expectant because they await the future glory, but have no fear because, while they are confirmed in freedom of choice, they also know that they cannot commit sin. They too have another consolation, knowing that prayers and sacrifices are being offered for them. Yet it might be closer to the truth to believe that the punishment of purgatory is not inflicted by bad angels, but by command of God's justice and his breath making it happen.

In answer to the the third question, namely, where purgation takes place, be it said that the souls are purged in some place located near hell and called purgatory. This is the opinion held by most learned men, although others think the place is in the air and in the torrid zone. However, by divine dispensation different places are sometimes appointed for different souls, and this for a number of reasons—either because their punishment is lighter or their liberation faster, or for our instruction, or because their sin was committed in this particular place, or on account of the prayer of some saint.

First, the place can be for a lighter punishment. Thus, according to Gregory, it was revealed to certain people that some souls are punished simply by being kept in darkness. Or their earlier liberation can be the reason for the place, so that they are able to make their needs known to others and to seek their help, and thus be delivered sooner from their punishment. We read, for instance, that in the autumn season some of Saint Theobald's fishermen pulled in a large block of ice instead of a fish. They were happier about this catch than they would have been with a fish, because the bishop suffered great pain in his feet; so they put the ice under his feet and this gave him much relief. One time, however, he heard a human voice coming from the ice. He adjured the voice to identify itself, and it said: "I am a soul punished in this refrigerant for my sins, and I could be freed if you would say thirty masses for me on thirty consecutive days without interruption." The bishop said half the number of masses and was vesting for the next one when it happened that due to diabolical incitement all the townspeople started fighting with each other. The bishop was called to the scene to calm the discord and, putting off the sacred vestments, omitted the mass that day. He began again and had completed two-thirds of the masses when a huge army, or what looked like one, laid siege to the city, which forced the bishop to omit that day's mass. Beginning a third time, he had said all but one of the thirty masses and was about to celebrate the thirtieth when his house and grounds seemed to burst into flame. His servants called on him to get out quickly, but he said: "Let the whole place burn down! I will not put off this mass!" The minute the mass was finished the ice melted, and the fire that they had thought they saw vanished like a phantasm and did no damage.

A particular place may also be appointed for our instruction, for instance, so that we may know that a great punishment can be visited on sinners after death. Thus we read about something that happened in Paris, as Peter Cantor of Paris tells it. Master Silo had a colleague, a scholar who was very ill, and Silo asked him urgently to come back after he died and tell him, Silo, how things were with him. Some days after his death the scholar appeared to Silo, wearing a cape made of parchment written all over with sophisms, and woven of flames inside. The master asked who he was and he answered: "I am indeed the one who promised to come back to you." Asked how things were with him he said: "This cape weighs upon me and presses me down more than if I were carrying a tower on my shoulders. It is given to me to wear on account of the pride I had in my sophisms. The flames that flare inside it are the delicate, mottled furs I used to wear, and they torture and burn me." The master, however, thought that this penalty was fairly light, so the dead man told him to put out his hand and feel how light the punishment really was. He held out his hand and the scholar let a drop of his sweat fall on it. The drop went through the master's hand like an arrow, causing him excruciating pain. "That's how I feel all over," the scholar said. Master Silo, alarmed by the severity of the other man's punishment, decided to abandon the world and enter the religious life; and the next day he recited the following couplet to his class:

Linquo choax ranis, cra corvis, vanaque vanis.
Ad logicam pergo, quae mortis non timet ergo.[2]

And so he left the world behind him and took refuge in religion.

---

[2] I leave croaking to the frogs, cawing to the crows, vanities to the vain. / Therefore I stay with logic, which fears not the *ergo* of death.

Fourthly, a place of punishment might be chosen because crime had been committed there. According to Augustine, souls were sometimes punished in the places where they had sinned, as appears from an incident that Gregory relates in the fourth book of his *Dialogues*. A certain priest went to the baths and found a man he did not know waiting to serve him. The man continued to be attentive to him, and one day the priest brought him a blessed loaf as a benediction and as payment for his services; but the man said: "Why do you give this to me, father? This bread is holy and I cannot eat it. I used to own this place, and was sent here after I died to suffer for my sins. But I ask you to offer this bread to almighty God for my sins, and you will know that your prayers have been heard when you come to bathe and you do not find me here." The priest offered the Host of salvation for him during a whole week, and when he returned to the bath, the man was not to be found there.

Fifthly, the place may be chosen in answer to a saint's prayer. Thus we read that Saint Patrick once prayed that a purgatory be opened underground for certain souls. You will find an account of this after the chapter on Saint Benedict.

Our second major question is about the sacrifices offered for the holy souls. Three points are to be considered: first, about the sacrifices themselves, i.e., what is offered; second, for whom they are offered; and third, who offers them.

Regarding the sacrifices offered in aid of the souls in purgatory, know that there are four kinds which are of maximum benefit, namely, the prayer of the faithful and of friends, almsgiving, the sacrifice of the mass, and the observance of fasts. That the prayer of the faithful and of friends is helpful to the souls is borne out by the story of Paschasius, a man known for his sanctity and virtue, as Gregory tells it in the fourth book of his *Dialogues*. It happened that two men were elected to the papacy at the same time. The Church finally came to an agreement on which one was the true pope, but Paschasius mistakenly preferred the other and clung to this opinion as long as he lived. When he died, a man possessed by an evil spirit touched a sacred vestment that was spread over the bier and was cured instantly. A long time later Germanus, bishop of Capua, went to take the baths for his health and found the aforesaid deacon Paschasius standing there waiting to serve him. Germanus was frightened at the sight of so holy a man and asked him what he was doing there. He answered that he was being punished there because in the case of the two popes he had held on too stubbornly to his opinion. "I ask you to pray the Lord for me," he added, "and you will know that your prayer has been granted if you come back here and do not find me." The bishop prayed for him, and when he returned to the place a few days later, Paschasius was no longer there.

Peter of Cluny tells us that there was a priest who celebrated mass every day for the dead. He was denounced for this to the bishop, who suspended him from his ministry. When the bishop was marching in procession with pomp and ceremony through the cemetery on his way to matins, the dead rose against him, saying: "This bishop gives us no masses and, more than that, has taken our priest away from us! But if he does not mend his ways, he will certainly die!" The bishop not only absolved the priest but thereafter willingly offered masses for the dead.

Another example, this one from the Cantor of Paris, shows how grateful the dead are for the prayers of the living. There was a man who, as he walked through the cemetery, always recited the *De profundis* for the dead. Once, when he was running away through the cemetery with his enemies after him, the buried, each one armed with the tool proper to his craft, quickly rose and defended the fleeing man with might and main. His pursuers, terrified, retreated in haste.

That the second kind of suffrage, namely, almsgiving, is of benefit to the souls can be seen clearly from the twelfth chapter of 2 Maccabees. There we read that the mighty man Judas Maccabeus sent twelve thousand silver drachmas to Jerusalem for sacrifice to be offered for the sins of the dead, thinking well and religiously concerning the resurrection. And another episode related by Gregory in the fourth book of the *Dialogues* shows how well almsgiving serves the dead. There was a knight who had died and lay lifeless, but his soul soon returned to his body and he narrated what had happened to him. He said that he came to a bridge below which a black, murky, fetid river flowed. On the other side there were fair meadows beautified by sweet-smelling herbs and flowers, and in the meadows groups of men could be seen, clothed in white and luxuriating in the perfume of the many fragrant flowers. This bridge was there for a test: if any unrighteous persons tried to cross it, they slipped and fell into the river, while the just went across surefooted to the pleasant fields beyond. The knight declared that he had seen on the bridge a man named Peter who was lying on his back lashed to a great bundle of iron. Asked why he was there in that condition, Peter replied that he was being punished because when he had been ordered to torture a condemned man, he had done so more because his cruel nature enjoyed it than because he was obeying orders. The knight also said he had seen a pilgrim who came to the bridge and crossed it with the same degree of confidence as had been the measure of his purity of life. Not so with another pilgrim whose name was Stephen. When he tried to cross, his foot slipped and half his body hung over the side of the bridge. Then some hideous beings rose out of the river and tried to pull him down by the legs, while some truly beautiful men clothed in white tried to haul him up by the arms. The scuffle was still going on when the knight came back to life, so he could not say who had won this test of strength. The combat, however, makes it clear that sins of the flesh were competing with generosity in almsgiving. Stephen was being pulled down by his lower parts and upward by his arms, which shows that he had loved giving alms but had not perfectly resisted the vices of the flesh.

As to the third kind of suffrage, namely, the sacrifice of the mass, many examples show the very great benefit it brings to the dead. In the fourth book of his

Dialogues Gregory tells us that when one of his monks, Justus by name, was dying, he admitted to Gregory that he had secretly kept three gold coins, and he died bemoaning this fault. Gregory ordered the monks to bury the deceased with his three gold pieces in a dunghill, and to say: "May your money go to perdition with you!" Later Gregory had a monk offer mass for the departed brother for thirty days, not missing a day. When this order had been carried out, the monk who had died appeared to another monk on the thirtieth day. The other monk asked: "How is it with you?" "Very bad till today," he answered, "but now all goes well because I received communion this morning."

The offering of the host is shown to benefit not only the dead but the living. Some men were digging silver out of a cliff when the rock fell in and killed all but one, who found himself in a sort of cave in the cliff and so escaped death, but he could not get out. His wife, thinking him dead, had a mass celebrated for him every day and daily offered a loaf of bread and a jug of wine with a lighted candle. The devil appeared to her for three successive days in the form of a man and asked her where she was going. When she explained what she was about, he said: "Don't bother going to all this trouble, the mass has already been said." So for three days she did not go to mass or have one offered. Then, some time later, someone else was digging for silver in the same cliff and heard a voice from below, saying: "Don't dig too hard! There's a big rock right over my head and it might fall on me!" Frightened, the one digging called a lot of people to hear the voice, and when he started to dig again, the voice was heard speaking. The bystanders came closer and said: "Who are you?" The entombed man answered: "Go easy with the pick and shovel! A big rock might fall on me!" They dug from the side and found him safe and unharmed, pulled him out, and asked how he had survived so long. He said that a loaf, a jug of wine, and a lighted candle had been given to him every day but three. Hearing this, his wife rejoiced, realizing that her offering had kept him alive, and that it was the devil who had deceived her and prevented her from having the mass said on those three days. This took place, as Peter of Cluny attests, near the village of Ferrières in the diocese of Grenoble.

Gregory also tells the story of a seaman who suffered shipwreck and was lost at sea. A priest said mass for him, and in the end he came back from the sea unharmed. When asked how he had escaped, he said that while he was being tossed about by the waves and was nearly at the end of his strength, someone came to him and gave him a loaf. When he had eaten the bread, his strength was renewed, and he was picked up by a passing ship. Then it was learned that he had received the bread at the very hour when the priest had offered the host for him.

The fourth kind of suffrage, namely, the observance of fasts, benefits the dead, as Gregory asserts. Treating of fasts along with the other three kinds of suffrage, he says: "The souls of the dead are released by four means—offerings by priests, prayers of the saints, alms given by friends, and fasting by kinsmen. Penances performed by their friends also are helpful." A certain august doctor has related that a woman whose husband had died was left desperately poor, and the devil appeared to her and said that he would make her rich if she did his will. She promised to do so. He demanded four things: she was to lead men of the Church, who were housed with her, to commit fornication; to take in poor people by day and put them out empty-handed at night; to interfere with people's praying in church by talking loudly; and not to make confession about any of this to anyone. At length, when she was near death and her son begged her to confess her sins, she told him what the facts were and said that she could not confess, and that confession would do her no good. The son tearfully insisted and promised to do penance for her, and she, conscience-stricken, sent him for the priest; but before the priest arrived, a swarm of demons rushed in upon her, and, overwhelmed with fear and horror, she died. Her son confessed his mother's sin and accepted and fulfilled a seven-year penance, and at the end of the seven years his mother appeared and thanked him for her deliverance.

The Church's indulgences also help the dead. A delegate of the apostolic see persuaded a valorous knight to fight in the service of the Church in Albigensian territory and granted him a forty days' indulgence for his deceased father. The knight served out his forty days, at the end of which time his father appeared to him brighter than light and thanked him for obtaining his release from purgatory.

The second point about the suffrages offered for the departed concerns those for whom the sacrifices are made, and here again four questions arise. To whom are these suffrages beneficial? Why are they beneficial? Are they equally beneficial to all? How can those benefited know that sacrifices have been made for them?

In answer to the first question, Augustine says that those who depart this life are either very good or very bad or mediocre. Therefore the suffrages done for the very good are acts of thanksgiving, those done for the very bad are in some way consolations for the living, those for the middling have the value of expiation. The very good are those who fly heavenward immediately and are free of both fires, hell and purgatory. The very good fall into three classes—the newly baptized, the martyrs, and the perfect. This third class consists of those who have built perfectly with gold, silver, and precious stones—i.e., with love of God, love of neighbor, and good works—to such a point that they had no thought of pleasing the world but only of pleasing God. They may have committed venial sins, but the fervor of their charity burned away the sin in them like a drop of water on a hot stove. Thus they never take anything with them that needs to be burned away. Anyone therefore who prays for or offers some other suffrage for a deceased person in any of these three classes insults that person, because, as Augustine says, whoever prays for a martyr wrongs the martyr. But if one were to pray for a very good person without being sure whether that person had gone straight to heaven, those prayers would be equivalent to acts of thanksgiving and would add to the merit of the one praying, according to the text of Ps. 34:13: "My prayer shall be turned into my bosom."

To these same three kinds of very good persons heaven is opened immediately upon their death, nor do they have to suffer any purgatorial fire. This is signified by three to whom heaven was opened. First, to Christ at his baptism; Luke 3:21: "When Jesus had been baptized and was praying, the heaven was opened." This means that heaven is opened to all those baptized either as infants or in adulthood, so that if they leave this life, they fly at once to heaven. By virtue of Christ's passion baptism cleanses away all sins, original, mortal, and venial. Second, to Stephen at his stoning; Acts 7:56: "Behold, I see the heavens opened." This means that heaven is opened to all martyrs, so that when they die, they go straight to heaven, and if they had anything to be burned away, it would be cut down by the scythe of martyrdom. Third, to John the most perfect; Apoc. 4:1: "I looked, and lo, in heaven an open door!" This means that for the perfect, who have totally completed all penance and have committed no venial sins, or if they have committed any, these have been consumed by the fervor of their charity, heaven is opened promptly and they go in to reign forever.

The very bad are those who sink at once into the depths of hell. For them, if their damnation is certain, no suffrages of any kind are to be offered, according to what Augustine says: "If I knew my father was in hell, I would no more pray for him than I would for the devil." If, however, suffrages were offered for any of the damned whose damnation was in doubt, the suffrages would not benefit them in the least. They cannot be freed from their pains; their punishment cannot be mitigated or lessened. Their damnation cannot be suspended for a time or even for a moment. They cannot be strengthened to bear their suffering more lightly. In hell there is no redemption.

The mediocre are those who take with them some inflammable materials—wood, hay, stubble—or who, caught unawares by death, cannot complete the sufficient penance imposed upon them. They are neither so good that they do not need our help nor so bad that suffrages would not benefit them. The sacrifices made for them are their expiation. Hence these are the only ones for whom such sacrifices can be useful. In instituting such suffrages the Church has usually observed three orders of numbers of days, namely, the seventh, the thirtieth, and the anniversary. The reason for this is stated in the book *De mitrali officio*. The seventh day is observed so that the souls of the departed may arrive at the eternal Sabbath of rest, or so that all the sins may be remitted which they committed in life, life being lived seven days at a time, or that they may be forgiven for the sins they committed with the body, which is composed of four elements, and with the soul, which has three powers. The thirtieth day—the number thirty being composed of three decades—is singled out so that their offenses against faith in the three Persons of the Blessed Trinity and the ten commandments of the Decalogue may be purged in them. The anniversary is observed so that from the years of calamity they may come to the years of eternity. Thus, as we celebrate the anniversary of the saints to their honor and our own profit, we mark the anniversary of the departed to their benefit and our devotion.

Next we asked why suffrages offered for the dead actually help them. There are three reasons for this. The first is unity. The dead are one body with the Church militant, and the goods of the latter must be common to all. The second is their dignity. While they were living on earth, they merited to have suffrages benefit them, and it is right that since they helped others, they should be helped by others. The third reason is their need, because in their present state they are unable to help themselves.

As to whether the suffrages are of equal advantage to all the dead, let it be known that if they are offered for particular persons, they are more beneficial to those persons than to others. If they are offered for all souls in general, those whose lives made them more worthy of help will receive more if they are in equal or greater need.

Can the dead know that sacrifices have been made to help them? According to Augustine there are three ways by which they may know this. The first is by divine revelation: God himself may reveal it to them. The second is that the good angels may make it known. These angels, who are always with us and observe all our actions, can descend to the souls in an instant and notify them of our aid. The third is through notice brought by souls leaving this world, because they can make this and other things known to the souls in purgatory. There is also a fourth way, namely, by what their own experience reveals to them, because when they feel relief from their suffering, they know that suffrages have been offered for them.

The last question concerns those who make the sacrifices and provide the suffrages by which the souls in purgatory are aided. If these suffrages are to benefit the souls, they must be done by persons who are in charity, because if they are offered by evil people, they cannot be helpful. We read that a certain knight, lying in bed with his wife one night while bright moonlight streamed through the window, began to wonder why rational man does not obey his Creator whereas nonrational creatures do. Then he began to think disparagingly about a fellow knight, a boon companion now dead, when suddenly the dead man entered the room and said to him: "Friend, don't have evil suspicions about anyone, and forgive me if I have wronged you in any way." Asked about his present state, he said: "I have a lot to atone for, mainly because I desecrated a cemetery by wounding a man there and stealing his cloak. I have to wear the cloak all the time, and it weighs me down more than a mountain would." Then he begged his former friend to have prayers offered for him. The friend asked him whether he wanted the prayers to be offered by one particular priest, and he said nothing but shook his head negatively. Would he prefer that a certain hermit pray for him? "Yes, indeed," he answered, "I do want him to pray for me."

This was promised him, and he went on: "And I tell you that two years from this very day you too will die!" With that he disappeared, and the knight changed his way of life for the better and fell asleep in the Lord.

Note that suffrages done by bad people cannot be profitable to the dead unless they are sacramental works such as the celebration of mass, which cannot be invalidated though the minister be wicked, or unless the deceased person while alive, or a friend, had entrusted a sum to be spent for him to someone else, even though this trustee be a bad person. In this case the trustee would do well to make proper use of the sum right away, lest what happened to another man in like circumstances should happen to him. We read that one of Charlemagne's knights, who was about to go to war against the Moors, asked a cousin of his to sell his horse and give the money to the poor in case he should die in battle. The knight was killed, but the cousin liked the horse so much that he kept it for himself. Not long after the knight's death he appeared like a radiant sun to his cousin and said: "Good cousin, you made me suffer in purgatory for a week by not selling my horse and giving the money to the poor as I told you to, but you won't get away with it! This very day, while I, purged of sin, go into the kingdom of God, the devils will carry your soul to hell!" and lo, of a sudden an uproar as of lions, bears, and wolves was heard in the air, and the demons laid hold of the cousin and carried him off.

---

164. The Four Crowned Martyrs

The four crowned martyrs were Severus, Severianus, Carpophorus, and Victorinus, who, by order of Emperor Diocletian, were beaten to death with leaded scourges. The names of these four were not known at the time but were learned through the Lord's revelation after many years had passed. Then it was decreed that they should be commemorated following the names of five other martyrs, namely, Claudius, Castorius, Symphorian, Nicostratus, and Simplicius, who had suffered two years after the martyrdom of the above-named four.

These five saints were all skilled in the art of sculpture and refused to fashion an idol for Diocletian or to offer sacrifice in any way. The emperor therefore ordered them to be placed alive in lead coffins and thrown into the sea, about A.D. 287. Before the names of the earlier four were known, Pope Melchiades decreed that these should be honored following the names of the later five and should be called the Four Crowned. Even after their names had become known, custom prevailed and they are still remembered as the Four Crowned.

---

165. Saint Theodore

Theodore suffered martyrdom in the city of the Marmanites, under Diocletian and Maximian. When the judge ordered him to offer sacrifice and to return to the army, Theodore replied: "I am a soldier in the service of my God and of his Son Jesus Christ!" The judge: "So your god has a son?" Theodore: "Yes!" The judge: "Might we know him?" Theodore: "Indeed you can know him and come to him!"

Theodore was granted a delay to prepare to offer sacrifice. Instead he entered the temple of the Mother of the Gods by night, set fire to the temple, and burned it to the ground. He was accused of this by someone who had seen him, and was shut up in a jail to die there of hunger. The Lord appeared to him and said: "Be confident, Theodore my servant, because I am with you!" Then a throng of men in white robes came to him though the doors were closed, and chanted the Psalms with him. When the jailers saw this, they fled in terror. Theodore was brought out and invited to offer sacrifice, but said: "Even if you burn my flesh with fire and inflict other tortures on me, I will not renounce my God as long as there is breath in my body."

The judge then commanded that Theodore be hung from a limb and have his flanks torn so cruelly with iron hooks as to expose the ribs. As he hung there, the judge said to him: "Theodore, do you want to be with us or with your Christ?" Theodore: "With my Christ I was and I am and I will be!" So a fire was lighted around him and in the fire he breathed his last, yet his body was not harmed by the flames. This happened about A.D. 287. A sweet odor spread everywhere and a voice was heard saying: "Come, my beloved, enter into the joy of your Lord!" Many also saw the heavens opened.

166. Saint Martin, Bishop

Martinus is like *Martem tenens*, one who makes war, namely, against vice and sin; or the name is like *martyrum unus*, one of the martyrs, because Martin was a martyr at least by desire and by his practice of mortification. Or the name is interpreted as one who angers or provokes or dominates; and Martin, by the merit of his holiness, angered the devil and made him envious, provoked God to be merciful, and dominated his body by continuous penances. Reason, or the spirit, ought to dominate the flesh, as Dionysius says in his letter to Demophilus, just as a master dominates his slave, a father his son, and a mature person a frivolous adolescent.

The saint's life was written by Severus, surnamed Sulpicius, whom Gennadius numbers among illustrious men.

Martin was born in the town of Sabaria in Pannonia but grew up in Pavia, Italy, with his father, who was a military officer. Martin served in the army under the caesars Constantine and Julian, but a military career was not his own choice. Even in childhood he was inspired by God, and at the age of twelve, against his parents' wishes, he fled to a church and asked to be accepted as a catechumen. He would have become a hermit, but his youth and lack of bodily strength forbade it. Then the caesars decreed that the sons of veterans should take their fathers' places in the legions. Martin was pressed into service at the age of fifteen, with only one man to serve him, although more often it was Martin who took off his man's boots and cleaned them.

Once, in the wintertime, he was passing through the city gate of Amiens when a poor man, almost naked, confronted him. No one had given him an alms, and Martin understood that this man had been kept for him, so he drew his sword and cut the cloak he was wearing into two halves, giving one half to the beggar and wrapping himself in the other. The following night he had a vision of Christ wearing the part of his cloak with which he had covered the beggar, and heard Christ say to the angels who surrounded him: "Martin, while still a catechumen, gave me this to cover me." The holy man saw this not as a reason for pride, but as evidence of God's kindness, and had himself baptized at the age of eighteen. Moreover, he stayed in the army for two years more at the urging of his superior officer, who promised that when his term of office expired, he too would renounce the world.

At that time the barbarians were breaking through the empire's frontiers, and Emperor Julian offered money to the soldiers who would stay and fight them.

Martin had had enough of soldiering and refused the profferred bonus, saying to the emperor: "I am a soldier of Christ, and I am forbidden to fight." Julian was indignant and said that Martin was refusing not for motives of religion but because he was afraid of getting into a war. Martin, who knew no fear, retorted: "If my refusal is attributed not to faith but to cowardice, I will stand forth tomorrow morning at the line of battle, unarmed, and, in the name of Christ, protected not by shield or helmet but by the sign of the cross, shall walk safely through the enemy's lines." He was put under guard immediately to ensure that he would face the barbarians unarmed, as he had said. But the next day the enemy sent legates to convey their surrender of all men and materials, so there can be no doubt that this bloodless victory was due to the holy man's merits.

After resigning from the army Martin went to Hilary, bishop of Poitiers, and by him was ordained acolyte. Then the Lord ordered him in a dream to visit his parents, who were still pagans. Setting out, he predicted that he would suffer many ordeals on the way. As he crossed the Alps he fell among robbers, but when one of them aimed a blow at Martin's head, another robber held back the hand that wielded the sword. The saint's hands were tied behind his back, and he was given into the custody of one of the brigands, who asked him if he was afraid. He answered that he had never felt so safe, because he knew that God's mercy was at hand especially in times of trial, and then went on to preach to the robber and converted him to the faith of Christ. The converted robber put him back on the road and afterward finished his days in praiseworthy living.

When Martin was passing through Milan, the devil met him in the form of a man and asked him where he was going. He replied that he was going wherever the Lord called him to go, and the devil said: "Wherever you go, the devil will be there to oppose you!" Martin answered him: "The Lord is my helper, I will not fear what man can do to me!"[1] The devil vanished instantly.

Martin converted his mother, but his father clung to his error. The Arian heresy, however, was advancing everywhere, with Martin almost alone to resist it, and he was beaten in public and cast out of the city. He went back to Milan and founded a monastery there, but was driven out by the Arians and went to the island of Gallimaria with a single priest as companion. There he happened to eat hellebore, a poisonous herb that was mixed in with other herbs. This made him so ill that he felt close to death, but he dispelled all pain and danger by the power of his prayer.

Learning that blessed Hilary had returned from exile, Martin went to Poitiers and established a monastery near the city. In the monastery there was an unbaptized catechumen. Martin came back to the monastery after a short absence and found that the catechumen had died without baptism. He had the body brought to his cell and prostrated himself upon it, and by his prayer recalled the man to life. This same man used to say that when he had died, he was sentenced to

[1] Ps. 117(118):6.

remain in a place of darkness, whereupon two angels reminded the Judge that this was the man for whom Martin was praying at that moment, and the Judge ordered the angels to take him back and return him alive to Martin. The saint also restored to life another man who had fallen into a pit and died.

The people of Tours were without a bishop, and they begged Martin, reluctant though he was, to be ordained as their bishop. Some among the assisting bishops disapproved of his choice on the ground that he was small of stature and unattractive in appearance: the most outspoken among the objectors was a bishop named Defensor, a name that meant defender. Since there was no lector present, one of the bishops took the Psalter and read from the first Psalm he opened to: "Out of the mouth of infants and of sucklings thou hast perfected praise, to destroy the enemy and the defender."[2] No one rose to support Bishop Defensor's objection. Martin was ordained bishop but could not abide the tumult of the city, so he built a monastery about two miles outside the walls and lived there in strict austerity with eighty disciples. No one drank wine there unless illness compelled him, and soft garments were considered a crime. Many cities chose their bishops from among these men.

A cult began to develop around an unknown who was alleged to be a martyr. Bishop Martin could learn nothing about his life or his merits; so one day he stood at the tomb and prayed the Lord to make known who was buried there and what had been his merits. Turning to his left he saw a pitch-black shade standing there. The shade, challenged by Martin, said that he had been a robber and had been put to death for his crimes. Martin therefore ordered the immediate destruction of the altar that had been raised beside the tomb.

We also read in the *Dialogue* of Severus and Gallus (where many details are supplied which Severus omitted in his *Life* of Saint Martin) that at one time Martin went to Emperor Valentinian about something he needed; but the emperor knew that the bishop was going to ask for something that he did not want to grant him, so he had the palace doors closed and barred. Martin, having been repulsed once and again, wrapped himself in sackcloth, sprinkled ashes on his head, and denied himself food and drink for a week. Then, bidden by an angel, he went to the palace and made his way to the emperor, no one interfering. Valentinian saw him coming and, angry because he had been admitted, did not rise to acknowledge his presence until flames burst out from the royal throne and set the imperial posterior afire. At that the emperor, though still irritated, rose to greet Martin and admitted that he had felt the power of God. He granted all the bishop wanted before the latter had time to ask, and offered him many gifts that Martin did not accept.

In the same *Dialogue* we read how he brought a third dead man back to life. A young man had died, and his mother, weeping, pleaded with Saint Martin to revive her son. Martin was standing in the middle of a field surrounded by a

---

[2] Cf. Ps. 8:3 (Douay).

multitude of pagans, but he knelt down and prayed, and the boy arose in the sight of all. Thereupon all those pagans were converted to the faith.

Inanimate, vegetable, and nonrational beings also obeyed this holy man. Inanimate beings like fire and water did his bidding. Once, when he had set fire to a temple, the wind was blowing the flames toward an adjacent house. Martin went up on the roof of the house and faced the approaching flames. Immediately the fire turned against the wind, so that there seemed to be a conflict between the two elements. We also read in the same *Dialogue* that a ship was sinking, and a merchant who was not yet a Christian exclaimed: "May the God of Martin save us!" A great calm settled over the sea at once.

Vegetable creatures likewise. . . . In a certain place Martin had seen to the demolition of a very ancient temple, and he wanted to cut down a pine tree that was dedicated to the devils. The country people and the pagans objected, and one of them said to him: "If you have so much confidence in your God, we will cut down the tree, and you let it fall on you. If your God is with you as you say, you will escape injury." He agreed. They cut through the tree and it began to fall toward the spot where he waited, but he made the sign of the cross against it and the tree fell in the opposite direction, almost crushing the people who had taken a place they thought was safe. At the sight of the miracle they all were converted to the faith.

As for nonrational animals, they very often obeyed the saint, as again we read in the *Dialogue*. Once he saw a pack of dogs chasing a little rabbit. He called to the dogs and they stopped their pursuit, halting in their tracks as if they were tied there. Another time he had gone to bathe in a river where there was a water snake, and he said to the snake: "In the Lord's name I command you to go back where you came from!" At the saint's word the reptile turned around and crossed to the opposite bank. Martin groaned: "Serpents listen to me and men do not!" A dog was barking at one of the saint's disciples, and the disciple said to the dog: "In Martin's name I order you to be quiet!" The dog stopped as if his tongue had been cut out.

Martin was a man of deep humility. In Paris he once came face to face with a leper from whom all shrank in horror, but Martin kissed him and blessed him, and he was cured. His dignity was great: he was said to be equal in dignity with the apostles, and this due to the grace of the Holy Spirit, who descended upon him in the appearance of fire to strengthen him, as had happened to the apostles. The aforesaid *Dialogue* tells us that once, when he was sitting alone in his cell and Severus and Gallus, his disciples, were waiting outside, they were struck with wonder at hearing several voices speaking in the cell. Later they asked Martin about this, and he said: "I will tell you, but I ask you not to tell anybody else. Agnes, Thecla, and Mary came to talk with me." And it was not only on that day, but frequently, that, as he admitted, these saints came to visit him, and the apostles Peter and Paul often came as well.

He was very just, giving to each his due. Once when he was invited to dine by Emperor Maximus, the cup was offered first to Martin, and everyone expected that he in turn would pass it to the king. But he passed the cup to the priest who was with him, considering no one more worthy to drink after the bishop, and deeming it unjust to put the king or the king's close associates ahead of a priest.

His patience was inexhaustible and was maintained in all circumstances. Even though he was the priest highest in rank, his clerics often treated him rudely without being reprimanded, nor did he for that reason exclude them from his charity. No one ever saw him angry, nor grieving, nor laughing. Nothing was heard from his lips but Christ, never was aught in his heart but piety, peace, and mercy.

We read in the same *Dialogue* that once, clad in a rough garment and a long black cloak, he was riding along a road on his donkey. A troop of cavalry rode toward him and the horses took fright and bolted, throwing their riders to the ground. The soldiers made for Martin, whom they pulled from his mount and beat soundly. The saint said nothing and turned away from them, and they were all the more incensed because he did not seem to feel their blows or to have any high regard for themselves. Then their own mounts stood as if rooted in the ground, immovable as boulders despite spur and whip, until the men went back to the bishop and confessed the wrong they had unwittingly done him. Then he gave them leave, and their horses started off at a lively trot.

He was assiduous in prayer. Indeed, we read in his legend that no hour or minute passed which he did not devote either to prayer or to sacred reading. Whether at work or at reading he never took his mind from prayer. As the smith, while working the iron, strikes the anvil from time to time to ease his labor, so Martin, whatever he might be doing, made all of it a prayer.

He lived a very austere life. Severus, in a letter to Eusebius, tells how Martin once stopped overnight at a villa in his diocese, and the clergy there prepared for him a bed with a mattress filled with straw. When he lay down on it, he shuddered at the unaccustomed softness, since he usually slept on the floor with only a single hair cloth over him. Unhappy at this unintended misunderstanding, he rose, threw aside all the straw, and stretched out on the bare ground. In the middle of the night all that straw burst into flame. Martin, awakened, tried to get out of the room but could not, and the flames caught him and set his garment afire. He returned to his wonted refuge of prayer, made the sign of the cross, and stood untouched amidst the flames; and whereas moments before he had felt the pain of their burning, now they seemed as refreshing as dew. The monks were awakened by the fire and came running, expecting to find Martin burned to death, but instead led him out unharmed.

His compassion for sinners was unbounded. He took to the bosom of his merciful understanding all who wished to repent. The devil himself took issue with Martin for admitting to penance those who fell once, and Martin answered: "If you yourself, poor wretched being, would stop trying to bring men down, and would repent of your deeds, I, trusting in the Lord, would promise you Christ's mercy!"

There was no limit to his compassion for the poor. The *Dialogue* tells us that Martin was on his way to the church for the celebration of some feast and was followed by a poor man who was just about naked. The bishop asked the archdeacon to find some clothes for the man, but the archdeacon deferred doing this, and Martin went into the sacristy, took off his tunic, gave it to the beggar, and told him to be off. The archdeacon then advised the bishop to proceed with the ceremony, but Martin said that he could not go ahead until the poor man—meaning himself—got some clothes to wear. The archdeacon did not understand, since the bishop was wrapped in his cope and the other could not see that he had nothing under it, and anyway, he observed, there was no poor man there. "Fetch me a tunic," Martin said firmly, "and then there will be no poor man here looking for clothes!"

The archdeacon, resentful, went to the marketplace and for five coins bought a cheap, short tunic—the kind called *paenula, paene nulla*, almost nothing. Angrily he threw the garment at Martin's feet. The bishop went behind a screen, put the tunic on—the sleeves coming only to his elbows and the lower edge only to his knees—and, so vested, went on to celebrate the mass. While he was celebrating, a globe of fire appeared over his head and was seen by many people. (For this reason Martin is said to be on a par with the apostles.) To his account of this miracle Master John Beleth adds that when the bishop raised his hands to God, as is done in the mass, the sleeves of the tunic slipped back, since his arms were not thick or fleshy and the tunic reached only to his elbows, and so his arms were left bare. Then, miraculously, angels brought him gold armlets set with jewels, and the bare arms were decently covered.

The saint once noticed a sheep that had been shorn, and said: "That sheep has obeyed the Gospel mandate. She had two tunics and gave one of them to someone who had none. You should do likewise!"

Martin displayed much power in driving out demons and often did expel them from the possessed. In the aforesaid *Dialogue* we read that there was a cow that was possessed by the devil, and she roared and raged and gored many people. Once this cow rushed in a fury at Martin and his company as they passed on the road. Martin raised his hand and ordered the cow to halt. Halt she did, and he saw a demon sitting astride her. Martin rebuked the demon, saying: "Get off her back, O evil one, and stop tormenting this harmless animal." The spirit departed immediately. The cow then fell to her knees at the bishop's feet and then, at his behest, ambled peaceably back to the herd.

Martin had a subtle sense for discerning demons. No matter what form, image, or disguise they assumed, he saw them openly and uncovered. Sometimes they presented themselves in the person of Jove, frequently as Mercury, occasionally as Venus or Minerva, but he berated them all by their proper names. Mercury gave him the most trouble. He said that Jove was brutish and dull. Once the devil appeared to him in the semblance of a king, clothed in purple, wearing a diadem and golden shoes, serene and smiling of mien. For a long time neither one spoke. Then the devil said: "Martin, acknowledge him whom you adore! I am Christ and am about to come down upon the earth, but I chose to manifest myself to you in advance." Martin marveled at this but maintained his silence, and the spirit spoke again: "Martin, why do you hesitate to believe, since you see me? I am CHRIST!" Then the saint, instructed by the Holy Spirit, said: "The Lord Jesus Christ did not predict that he would come empurpled and wearing a glittering crown. I will not believe that Christ has come unless he is as he was when he suffered, unless he bears the stigmata of the cross!" At these words the devil disappeared, leaving the cell filled with a horrid stench.

Martin knew the time of his death well in advance and revealed it to his brothers. Meanwhile he visited the diocese of Candes, to reconcile some differences there. On the way he saw diving birds watching for fish and catching some, and he said: "This is the way demons work. They trap the unwary, they catch some before they know it, they devour their catch and can never get enough." So he ordered the birds to go away from the water and seek some desert place, and off they flew in a great flock toward the hills and the forests.

When he had spent some time in the above-named diocese, his strength began to fail, and he told his disciples that his days were numbered. They wept and asked him: "Why are you deserting us, father? To whom are you leaving us, orphans? Fierce wolves will ravage your flock!" Moved by their entreaties and tears, Martin wept with them and prayed: "Lord, if I am still needed by your people, I do not refuse the labor! Thy will be done!" He really was not sure which he preferred, because he wanted neither to leave these people nor to remain separated from Christ any longer. Therefore when fevers racked him for some time and his disciples asked him to let them put some straw in the bed where he lay in sackcloth and ashes, he said: "My sons, the only proper way for a Christian to die is in sackcloth and ashes. If I leave you any other example, I shall have sinned." His eyes and his hands he kept always pointed to heaven, and never let his unconquered spirit slacken in prayer. He lay always on his back, and when his priests begged him to let them ease his poor body by turning him on his side, he said: "Leave me as I am, brothers! Let me keep my eyes on heaven rather than on earth, so that my spirit may always be directed toward the Lord!" Even as he said this, he saw the devil standing by and said: "What are you here for, bloody beast? You will find nothing deadly in me, and Abraham's bosom will welcome me!" And with these words, in the reign of Arcadius and Honorius, which began about A.D. 395, and in the eighty-first year of his life, he yielded his spirit to God. His face shone as though he was already glorified, and many heard choirs of angels singing around him.

At his death the people of Poitiers and the people of Tours came together, and a bitter altercation broke out between them. The people of Poitiers said: "He is our monk, we want him back!" Those of Tours responded: "From you he was taken by God, to us he was given!" In the middle of the night, the Poitiers people being sound asleep, the men of Tours passed the saint's body through a window and ferried it by the Loire to the city of Tours, where there was great rejoicing at its reception.

Blessed Severinus, bishop of Cologne, was making the rounds of the holy places after matins on Sunday, as was his custom, when, at the hour of Saint Martin's passing, he heard angels singing in heaven. He called his archdeacon and asked him if he heard anything. The archdeacon said he heard nothing, but the archbishop told him to listen intently. He stretched his neck upwards and strained his ears, raising himself on his toes and steadying himself with his staff while the archbishop prayed for him, and he said he heard some voices in the heavens. Said the archbishop: "It is my lord Martin who has migrated from the world, and now the angels are carrying him to heaven!"

There were demons there, too, and they tried to hold Martin back, but they found nothing with which to charge him and withdrew nonplussed. The archdeacon took note of the day and the hour, and learned that this was indeed the time when Martin had breathed his last. The monk Severus, who wrote his life, had fallen into a light sleep after matins, and, as he states in a letter, Martin appeared to him clothed in white robes, his face alight, his eyes shining like stars, his hair purpled, holding in his right hand the book that Severus had written about his life. Martin blessed him and he saw the saint rising to heaven, and Severus, wishing he could have gone with him, woke up. After that, messengers came with the news that Martin had died that same night.

On that day Saint Ambrose, bishop of Milan, was celebrating mass, and fell asleep at the altar between the reading of the prophecy and the epistle. No one presumed to awaken him, and the subdeacon would not dare read the epistle without his order. Two or three hours passed before they aroused Ambrose, saying: "Time is passing and the people are getting tired of waiting. May it please your lordship to have the clerk read the epistle?" "Don't be upset," Ambrose said, "my brother Martin has gone to heaven, and I have been at his funeral and was leading the final prayers, but you disturbed me and I could not sing the last response." They noted the day and the hour, and found that that was when Saint Martin had departed to heaven.

Master John Beleth says that the kings of France used to carry Martin's *cappa*, or cloak, into battle; wherefore the guardians of the cloak were called *cappellani*, or chaplains.

In the sixty-fourth year after Martin's death, blessed Perpetuus enlarged his church magnificently and wished to rebury the saint's body there, but, despite fasts and vigils and several futile efforts, they could not move the sarcophagus.

They were about to leave it where it was when a beautiful old man appeared to them and said: "What are you waiting for? Don't you see Saint Martin ready to help you as soon as you put your hand to the task?" Then, with them, he put his hand under the stone, and they lifted the sarcophagus with ease and speed and set it where it is now venerated. The old man did not appear again.

Odo, abbot of Cluny, relates that when the transferral took place, the bells in all the churches rang though no one pulled the ropes, and all the lamps and candles came alight though no one touched them. It is also said that there were two partners, one of whom was blind and the other paralyzed, and the blind man hauled the cripple around in a cart and the cripple told him where to go. By begging this way they made a good living. Then they heard that many infirm people were cured when they came close to Saint Martin's body, and especially when the body was carried around the church, and they began to fear that the said body might be carried close to the house where they lived, and they by chance might be made whole—which they did not want to happen, because it would deprive them of their income. So they moved their domicile to another street, thinking that the sacred body was never carried that way. But just as they were moving, they met the body being carried in procession, and since God bestows blessings even on those who do not ask for them, the two partners found themselves completely cured against their will and were sorely aggrieved at this turn of fortune.

Ambrose has this to say about Saint Martin: "Blessed Martin destroyed the temples of pagan error, raised the banners of piety, restored the dead to life, drove wild demons from the bodies of the possessed, and raised up those who suffered from various maladies with the remedy of good health. He was found to be so perfect that he clothed Christ in the poor beggar and dressed the Lord of the world in a garment that he himself had received as an alms. O happy largesse, by which divinity was clothed! O glorious dividing of the cloak that clothed a soldier and a King! O priceless gift, that was worthy to be worn by divinity! Rightly, Lord, did you confer on this man this reward for confessing your name! Rightly did the savagery of the Arians bow before him! Rightly did the love of martyrdom arm him against fear of the persecutor's torments! What shall he, who deserved to clothe God and see him in return for the half of a cloak, receive for the offering of his whole body? So he brought medicine to the hopeful, to some by his prayers and to others by the mere sight of him!"

167. Saint Brice

Brice, one of Saint Martin's deacons, had no respect for the saint and heaped abuse upon him. Once when a beggar was looking for Martin, Brice told him: "If you're looking for that madman, look upwards! He's the one who like a fool is always looking toward heaven!" When the poor man had obtained what he needed from Martin, the holy man called Brice and said to him: "Do I look like a raving fool to you, Brice?" Brice was ashamed and denied that he had said anything like that, but Martin answered: "Was not my ear at your mouth when you said it at a distance? But now I tell you the truth! I have it from the Lord that you are to succeed me as bishop, but be it known to you that you will suffer much adversity in this office!" Brice laughed at this and said to others: "Wasn't I telling the truth when I called him a raving fool?"

After Martin's death Brice was elected bishop, and, though still haughty and outspoken, was devoted to prayer and kept his body chaste. When he had been bishop for thirty years, a woman who dressed like a religious and did his laundry for him conceived and bore a son. At that the whole town gathered at the bishop's door carrying stones and shouted: "All these years, out of respect for Saint Martin, we have pretended not to notice your lascivious life, but now we can no longer kiss those polluted hands!" He denied their accusations vehemently and said: "Bring the infant here to me!" The child, now thirty days old, was brought, and Brice said to him: "I adjure you by the Son of God to say, in the presence of all here, whether I begot you!" The infant replied: "Not you! You are not my father!" The people then pressed Brice to ask the child who his father was, but Brice declared: "That's not my affair! I did what I was called upon to do!"

The people then attributed all this to magic and said: "You are falsely called our shepherd, and we will no longer have you ruling over us!" But Brice wanted to prove his innocence and carried burning coals in the fold of his mantle to Saint Martin's tomb while all the people watched. He threw the coals aside and his mantle was undamaged, and he said: "As my garment was not scorched by the coals, so is my body clean of contact with a woman." The people, however, did not believe him, so they showered him with insults and expelled him from his see. Thus Saint Martin's prediction was fulfilled.

Brice then went sorrowing to the pope in Rome and stayed with him for seven years, doing penance for the wrongs he had done to Saint Martin. The people of Tours selected Justinian for their bishop and sent him to Rome to defend his right to the see against Brice's. But Justinian died on the way to

Rome in the city of Vercelli, and the Tours people put Armenius in his place. At the end of the seven years, however, Brice, supported by the pope's authority, returned to his diocese. He halted overnight six miles away from Tours, and Armenius expired that same night. Brice learned of his death by a revelation. He awakened his retinue, telling them to come with him in haste to the burial of the bishop of Tours. As Brice entered the city by one gate, the dead bishop was carried out by another. When Armenius had been buried, Brice resumed his place as bishop and presided for seven years. He led a praiseworthy life and in the forty-eighth year of his episcopate fell asleep peacefully in the Lord.

168. Saint Elizabeth

The name Elizabeth is interpreted as meaning My God has known, or the seventh of my God, or the satiety of my God. Elizabeth was called by a name meaning My God has known because God knew her, in other words, God observed her with pleasure and approved her, i.e., infused her with the knowledge of himself. Secondly, Elizabeth means the seventh of my God. Saint Elizabeth had the seventh of God, either because she practiced the seven works of mercy; or because she now is in the seventh age, the age of those who are at rest, and is about to come at last to the eighth age, namely, the age of rising from the dead; or because of the seven states of life in which she lived. She was first in the state of virginity, secondly, in the state of marriage, thirdly, in widowhood, fourthly, in the active state, fifthly, in the contemplative state, sixthly, in the state of consecrated religious life, and seventhly, in the state of glory. These seven states are brought out in her legend, so that it can be said of her as it is said of Nabachudonosor in the Book of Daniel: "Seven times shall pass over you."[1] Thirdly, Elizabeth is called the satiety of my God, for God filled and sated her with the splendor of truth, the sweetness of benignity, and the strength of eternity. Hence Augustine, speaking about the heavenly city in his book *On the City of God*, says: "In God's eternity is its strength, in God's truth its light, and in God's goodness its joy."

[1] Dan. 4:29.

Elizabeth, illustrious daughter of the king of Hungary, was noble by birth and still more noble by her faith and her devotion to religion. She ennobled her already noble lineage by her example, shed light on it by her miracles, and embellished it with the grace of her holiness. The Author of nature somehow raised her above nature. As a child growing up surrounded by regal privileges and pleasures, she either spurned the things children love, or directed them to God's service, showing how much her tender childhood was strengthened by her simplicity, and how sweet was the devotion of her earliest years. As a child she applied herself to serious concerns, shunning idle games, avoiding worldly success and prosperity, and advancing always in reverence toward God. When she was only five years old, she spent so much time praying in church that her companions and her maids could hardly get her out to play. Her servants and playmates noticed that when one of them in the course of a game went into the chapel, Elizabeth followed her, profiting by the opportunity to get into the church; and when she entered, she would kneel down or lie full length on the floor. She had not yet learned to read but often spread the Psalter open before her, pretending to read so that no one would disturb her. Sometimes she stretched herself on the ground beside other girls, playing at measuring herself against them, but also to display reverence for God. When playing the game of rings or any other game, she put her whole trust in God. When as a little girl she won something in a game or acquired a new possession in some other way, she divided it among poor children, urging them to say frequently the Our Father and the Hail Mary.

Elizabeth grew in age and even more in the intensity of her devotion. She chose the Blessed Virgin, mother of God, as her patroness and advocate, and Saint John the Evangelist as the guardian of her chastity. When papers with the names of the several apostles written on them were placed on the altar and then distributed at random among the girls, Elizabeth prayed three times and always received the paper with Saint Peter's name on it as she wanted to, because her devotion to that saint was so fervent that she would never deny anything to anyone who asked in his name. For fear that worldly successes might attract flattery to her, she daily gave away some token of her prosperity. When she won in some game, she called a halt and said: "I don't want to play any more! I leave the rest for the sake of God!" When invited to dance with other girls she would dance one round, then would say: "Let's let one round be enough and give up the rest for God," thus tempering the girls' taste for such vain pastimes. She abhorred too much show in dress and loved modesty in all such matters.

Elizabeth imposed upon herself the daily recitation of a certain number of prayers, and if she was too busy to complete the number during the day and was put to bed by her maids, she stayed awake until she had fulfilled her promise to her heavenly spouse. She observed solemn feast days with so much devotion that she would not allow her long sleeves to be stitched on her dress under any pretext until after the celebration of mass. She forbade herself the wearing of gloves before noon on Sunday, wishing thereby both to defer to the sacred solemnity and to satisfy her own devotion. For this same purpose it was her custom to impose such practices upon herself by vow, so that no one would be able to dissuade her from carrying out her intention. She assisted at liturgical services with such reverence that when the gospel was read, or the host consecrated, she removed her sleeves if they had been stitched on, and put aside her necklaces and any ornaments she was wearing on her head.

She lived out her state of virginity prudently and innocently, but was compelled to enter the state of marriage in obedience to her father's order. Thus she gained the thirtyfold fruit,[2] keeping the faith of the Trinity and obeying the Ten Commandments. She consented to conjugal intercourse, not out of libidinous desire but out of respect for her father's command, and in order to procreate and raise children for the service of God. Thus, while bound by the law of the conjugal bed, she was not bound to enjoyment. This is obvious from the fact that she made a vow in Master Conrad's[3] hands, that if she survived her husband she would practice continence for the rest of her life.

Elizabeth therefore was married to the landgrave[4] of Thuringia, as befitted her royal dignity but also as God's providence ordained, namely, that she might thus lead many to the love of God and might give instruction to the ignorant. Although her state of life was changed, there was no change in the way she intended to live. How great her devotion and humility toward God was, how strict her austerity and self-denial, how abundant her generosity and compassion for the poor, it will be the purpose of what follows to demonstrate.

She was so fervently devoted to prayer that she sometimes hurried to arrive in church ahead of her maids, as if wishing by some secret prayer to win a particular favor from God. She often rose during the night to pray, though her husband begged her to spare herself and give her body some rest. She had an arrangement with one of her maids who was closer to her than the others, that if by chance she overslept, the maid would wake her up by touching her foot. Once by mistake she touched the landgrave's foot. He woke up with a start but understood what had happened, and patiently put up with it and pretended not to have noticed anything. In order to make her prayers a rich sacrifice to God, Elizabeth often sprinkled them with a profusion of tears, but she shed her tears happily and without any unseemly change of countenance, weeping with sorrow and rejoicing at the sorrow; and this beautified her visage with gladness.

So profound was her humility that for the love of God she never shunned menial or lowly work, but did it with unbounded devotion. She once took an ugly sick man and clasped his filthy head to her bosom, then cut his hair and

[2] Cf. Mark 4:8, 20.
[3] For Master Conrad, see below.
[4] A title equivalent to "count."

washed his head, while her maids stood by laughing. On Rogation Days[5] she always walked in the procession barefoot and wearing a plain woolen garment. At the station churches she sat among the poorest women to hear the sermon, as if she too were poor and of low estate. When she went to be churched[6] after childbirth, she never made a show of jewelry or gold-embroidered gowns, as other women did. Following the example of Mary the immaculate mother, she carried her child in her arms and humbly offered him at the altar with a lamb and a candle, thus showing her distaste for worldly pomp and modeling her behavior after that of the Blessed Mother. Then, when she returned to her house, she gave the clothing she had worn in church to some poor woman.

As a further manifestation of her humility, Elizabeth, unsurpassed though she was in freedom and high station, submitted herself in obedience to a priest called Master Conrad. Conrad was a very poor man but was known for his knowledge and piety. With her husband's consent and the marriage right safeguarded, she pledged herself to obey Master Conrad so unreservedly that she would fulfill any order of his with reverence and joy. Her purpose was to gain merit and to imitate the example of her Savior, who became obedient even unto death. For instance, on one occasion Master Conrad had ordered her to attend a service at which he was to preach, but the marchioness of Meissen came to visit and Elizabeth missed the service. Conrad took her disobedience so amiss that he would not forgive it until, stripped to her shift, she was soundly flogged, along with some of her servants who had committed some fault.

Elizabeth took on herself so much abstinence and privation that her body was wasted with vigils and disciplines and fasting. Frequently she avoided her husband's bed and went without sleep in order to spend the night in contemplation and to pray to her heavenly Father in secret. When sleep overcame her, she slept on mats strewn on the floor. When her husband was away she passed the whole night in prayer with her heavenly spouse. Often, too, she had her servingwomen flog her in her bedroom, in return for the scourging her Savior had borne for her and to quell all carnal desire.

Such was Elizabeth's temperance in matters of food and drink that at her husband's table, laden as it was with a variety of tasty dishes, she sometimes ate nothing but a bit of bread. Master Conrad forbade her to eat any food about which she had the slightest qualm of conscience, and she obeyed this behest so meticulously that however abundant the delicious foods might be, she and her servingmaids partook of coarser fare. At other times she sat at table and divided and moved the food around on her plate, so as to seem to be eating and to ward off any notion that she was superstitious: thus, by her urbanity, she put all the guests at their ease. When they were traveling and she was worn out with the

---

[5] See chapter 70, "The Greater and Lesser Litanies."

[6] After giving birth, a woman came to the church to offer thanksgiving and to receive a special blessing.

length and labors of the journey, and she and her husband were offered foods that might not have been honestly acquired, she accepted none of them and patiently ate stale black bread soaked in hot water, as her maids did. For this reason, indeed, her husband had assigned funds to her, sufficient to provide for her living and that of some few of her women, who chose to follow her example in everything. Frequently, too, she refused what was served at the royal table and asked for the provisions of ordinary people. The landgrave was tolerant of all of this and said that he would gladly do the same himself if he were not afraid of upsetting the whole household.

Elizabeth's position was one of the highest dignity, but her whole desire was to share poverty with the poor, so that she might make return to Christ for his poverty and the world might have no claim on her. Sometimes, when she was alone with her servingwomen, she put on cheap, dingy clothing, covered her head with a shabby kerchief, and said to them: "This is how I will go about when I have attained the state of poverty." She checked her own appetite with a tight rein of abstinence but was openhanded in her generosity to the poor, never letting anyone go hungry and supplying the needs of all so liberally that she was acclaimed as the mother of the poor.

Blessed Elizabeth put her utmost effort into the performance of the seven works of mercy, hoping to inherit the everlasting kingdom and to reign there perpetually, and to possess the Father's blessing with the saints gathered at his right hand. She clothed the naked and provided raiment for the burial of poor people and strangers, as well as for infants at their christening. Often she lifted children of the poor from the baptismal font and sewed clothing for them with her own hands: having become their godmother, she then did more for them. On one occasion she gave a rather elegant dress to a poor woman, who was so overwhelmed with joy at the sight of such a magnificent gift that she fell to the ground and was thought to be dead. Blessed Elizabeth, seeing her lying there, was sorry she had given her so fine a present, fearing that she had thus been the cause of her death, but she prayed for her and the woman stood up fully recovered. Often, too, she spun wool in company with her servants, in order to receive the glorious fruit of these good labors, giving an example of true humility, and an alms to God out of the toil of her own body.

She fed the hungry. Once, when the landgrave had gone to the court of Emperor Frederick, then being held at Cremona, Elizabeth collected the whole year's crop from his barns, called in the poor from all sides, and provided for their daily needs, because the cost of living had risen and they were threatened with famine. When poor people ran out of money, she often sold her jewelry in order to help them. Indeed she regularly drew from her own resources and those of her faithful servingwomen to have something put aside for the poor.

She gave drink to the thirsty. Once she was serving beer to poor people, and after everyone had been served, the jug was still as full as it had been before she started.

She provided shelter for pilgrims and poor people. She had a very large house built at the foot of the high hill on which her castle stood, and there took care of numbers of the ill and infirm despite the difficulty of getting up and down the hill. While with them she saw to all their needs and exhorted them to patience. Bad air always distressed her, but for God's love, even in the heat of summer, she did not shrink from the smells and sores of the sick, but applied remedies to their wounds, dried them with the veil from her head, and treated them with her own hands, although her maids could hardly bear to watch her.

In this same house Elizabeth saw to it that children of poor women were well fed and cared for. She was so gentle and kind to them that they all called her Mother and, when she came into the house, followed her around as if she were in fact their mother, and crowded about her to be as close to her as possible. She also bought some small dishes and cups and rings and other glass toys for the children to play with. She was riding up the hill, carrying these things in the fold of her cloak, when they came loose and fell to the rocks below, but not one of the toys was broken.

Elizabeth visited the sick. Her compassion for their sufferings ruled her heart so much that she often went looking for their lodgings and visited them solicitously, entering their poor abodes as if she were at home, not deterred by the strangeness of the locale or bothered by the distance she had to go. She provided for their needs and spoke words of consolation to them, thus earning reward in five ways, namely, by honoring them with her visit, by the fatigues of the journey, by the warmth of her compassion, by her words of consolation, and by the generosity of her donations.

She concerned herself with the burial of the poor, devotedly going to their funerals, covering their bodies with clothes that she herself had made, and on one occasion cutting up the large linen veil she was wearing and wrapping the corpse of a poor person with part of it. She prepared them for interment with her own hands and piously stayed for the rites at the grave.

The piety of her husband deserves praise for his part in all these doings. He had many interests to attend to but was devout in honoring God, and, since he could not personally get involved in such activities, gave his wife the freedom and the means to do whatever served the honor of God and made for the salvation of his soul. Blessed Elizabeth wanted very much to see her husband turn the use of his arms to the defense of the faith, and by her salutary exhortations persuaded him to go to the Holy Land. There the landgrave, a faithful prince, devout and renowned for the integrity and sincerity of his faith, lost his life and received the reward of his good works.

Elizabeth now piously embraced the state of widowhood, taking care not to be defrauded of the reward of a widow's continence and to gain the sixty-fold fruit by observing the Decalogue together with the seven works of mercy. But as soon as the news of her husband's death spread throughout Thuringia, she was denounced by some of the landgrave's vassals as a prodigal, wasteful woman and was shamefully banned from her country. Thus her patience was brought fully to light, and her long-standing desire for poverty was fulfilled.

She went by night to the house of an innkeeper and was given shelter where the pigs usually rested, and for this she gave thanks to God. In the morning she went to the house of the Friars Minor and asked them to sing a *Te Deum*, in thanksgiving for the troubles that had befallen her. The following day she was ordered to go with her children into the house of one of her enemies, where she was given a very small room to live in. The man and woman whose house it was treated her so meanly that she bade farewell only to the walls, saying: "I would gladly give my good wishes to these people, if they had been kind to me." Having no place else to go she went back to the innkeeper's house, sending her children to various places to be cared for. She had to go along a path filled with mud, with only stepping-stones to walk on, and came face to face with an old woman whom she had befriended many times; but the old woman would not let her pass and she fell into the mud. Nothing daunted, she came up rejoicing and laughing, and shook the mud out of her clothes.

Now her aunt, who was an abbess, took pity on Elizabeth's poverty and brought her to the bishop of Bamberg, who was her uncle. He received her with due honor and shrewdly gave her hospitality in his house, planning to get her married again. The servingwomen who had vowed continence with her learned of the bishop's intention and wept as they reported it to blessed Elizabeth; but she reassured them, saying: "I trust in the Lord, for love of whom I have vowed perpetual continence. He will keep my resolution firm, will ward off all violence, and will defeat the schemes of men. If perchance my uncle wishes to wed me to another, I will set my mind against him and contradict him verbally; and if no other way of escape is left to me, I will cut off my nose, because no one would have me, thus disfigured."

By the bishop's order she was taken against her will to a castle, to stay there until she consented to marry, and she wept and commended her chastity to the Lord. But now, by God's will, her husband's bones were returned from overseas, and the bishop had Elizabeth brought back to give loving welcome to her spouse's remains. The bishop met the landgrave's bones in a procession of honor, and blessed Elizabeth gave them welcome with devotion and much shedding of tears. She then turned to the Lord and said: "I give you thanks, O God, for deigning to console miserable me by the reception of the bones of my spouse whom you loved. You know, O Lord, that I loved him dearly, as he loved you, yet for love of you I deprived myself of his presence and sent him to relieve your Holy Land. Delightful as it would be for me to live with him still, even were we reduced to go begging through the whole world, yet I would not give one hair of my head to have him back against your will, nor to recall him to this mortal life. I commend him and me to your grace."

Now, lest she lose the hundredfold fruit which is given to those who strive for evangelical perfection and are transferred from the left hand of misery to the right hand of glory, Elizabeth put on religious dress, namely, robes of plain gray, low-grade material. She observed perpetual continence after her husband's death, embraced voluntary poverty, and would have begged from door to door had not Master Conrad forbidden her. Her habit was so shabby that her gray cloak had to be lengthened and the holes in the sleeves of her tunic patched with cloth of a different color. When her father, the king of Hungary, heard of the destitution in which she was living, he sent a knight to persuade her to return to her paternal home. When the knight saw her dressed in such poor attire, sitting humbly and spinning thread, he was overcome with confusion and wonder, and exclaimed: "Never has a king's daughter been seen in such tawdry clothes, nor any royal personage spinning wool!"

Blessed Elizabeth absolutely refused to return with the knight, preferring to live in poverty with the poor rather than to be surrounded with riches with the rich. Then in order that her spirit might move totally to God and her devotion be unhampered by distraction or impediment, she prayed the Lord to fill her with contempt for all temporal goods, to take from her heart her love for her children, and to grant her indifference and constancy in the face of every insult. When she had finished her prayer, she heard the Lord saying to her: "Your prayer has been favorably heard." Elizabeth told her women: "The Lord has heard my voice graciously, because I regard all temporal things as dung, I care for my children no more than for others around me, I make light of all contempt and disrespect, and it seems to me that I no longer love any but God alone."

Master Conrad often imposed disagreeable and contrary things upon her, and separated from her company any persons to whom she seemed to feel a particular attachment. Thus he sent away from her two servingmaids who had grown up with her and were her loyal and dear friends: many tears were shed on both sides over this separation. The holy man took these measures in order to break her will and allow her to direct her whole desire to God, and to guard her from being reminded of her past glory by any of her servants. In all these matters she was quick in obedience and steadfast in patience, in order to possess her own soul by patience, and by obedience to be crowned with victory.

Blessed Elizabeth also said: "For God's sake I fear mortal man as much as I ought to fear the heavenly judge. Therefore I choose to give my obedience to Master Conrad, a poor, undistinguished man, rather than to some bishop, so that every occasion of worldly consolation may be taken away from me." Once when she had yielded to the earnest request of some nuns and had visited their convent without obtaining permission from her spiritual master, he had her flogged so severely that the marks of the lashes were still visible three weeks later. To her women she said, for their consolation as well as for her own: "The sedge grass lies flat when the river is in flood, and when the water recedes, the sedge straightens up. So, when some affliction befalls us, we should bow to it humbly and, when it passes, be lifted up by spiritual joy to God." Her humility was such that she would not allow her servants to address her as "lady" but insisted that they use the singular forms,[7] as is usual when speaking to inferiors. She washed the dishes and other kitchen utensils, and, lest her maids prevent her from doing so, had them carried to different places. She also said: "Could I have found a more menial way of life, I would have chosen it."

For the rest, in order to possess the best part with Mary, Elizabeth gave herself diligently to contemplative prayer. In this prayer she had special graces to shed tears, to have frequent visions of heaven, and to light the fire of love in others. At times when she was happiest she shed tears of joyous devotion, so that happy tears seemed to flow from her eyes as from a serene fountain. She seemed to be weeping and rejoicing at the same time, never letting tears change or mar her face. She said of those who looked gloomy when they wept: "Do they want to frighten the Lord away? Let them give to God what they have to give him with joy and good cheer!"

She often had visions of heaven in the course of her prayer and contemplation. One day in the holy season of Lent she was in church and had her eyes fixed intently on the altar, as if she were gazing at the very presence of God. This went on for a time, and the divine revelation refreshed and comforted her. When she got home, she was so weak that she rested on the lap of one of her maidservants and gazed through the window at the heavens, and such joyousness swept over her face that she burst out laughing. Then, after she had for some time been filled with joy by this vision, suddenly she was weeping. Opening her eyes again, the earlier joy was renewed in her, and when she closed them again, back came the flood of tears. This went on till compline, as she lingered in these divine consolations. She did not speak a word for a long time, then suddenly exclaimed: "So, Lord, you wish to be with me and I with you, and I want nothing ever to separate me from you!"

Later on her servants asked her to tell them, for the honor of God and their own edification, what was the vision she had seen. Conquered by their insistence, blessed Elizabeth said: "I saw the heavens opened, and Jesus leaning toward me in a most kindly way and showing me his loving face. The sight of him filled me with ineffable joy, and when it was withdrawn, I could only mourn my loss. Then he, taking pity on me, gave me again the joy of seeing his face and said to me: 'If you wish to be with me, I will be with you.' And you heard my answer." And when she was asked to tell about the vision she had seen at the altar, she answered: "It is not for me to tell the things I saw there, but I was in great joy and looked upon the wonderful works of God!"

It often happened that when she was at prayer, her face was radiant and from her eyes beamed light like the rays of the sun. Often, too, the fervor of her prayer was such that it lighted the fire of love in others. She saw a young man fastidiously dressed, and called him to her, saying: "You look to me as if you were leading a dissolute life, when you ought to be serving your creator! Do you

---

[7] I.e., thou, thee, thy, etc.

want me to pray to God for you?" "Oh yes," he answered, "I beg you to do so!" She thereupon gave herself to prayer and urged him to pray for himself, but the young man cried: "My lady, stop praying! Please stop!" But she prayed the more intently, and the youth cried more loudly: "Stop! I'll collapse! I'm on fire!" He was indeed so heated that he was dripping and steaming with sweat, and contorting his body and flailing with his arms like a madman. Several bystanders tried to hold him and found his clothing soaked with sweat, and his body too hot to touch, while he continued to cry out: "I'm on fire all over! I'm consumed!" Saint Elizabeth finished her prayer, and the young man no longer felt the heat. He came to himself and, enlightened by divine grace, entered the Order of Friars Minor. This incident showed that the fiery fervor of her prayer could inflame someone who was cold at heart; this young man, accustomed to the pleasures of the flesh and not yet ready for the joys of the spirit, could not understand what had happened.

Elizabeth, having reached the summit of perfection through Mary's contemplative prayer, did not give up Martha's laborious activity, as we have shown by her devotion to the seven works of mercy. Indeed, after taking the veil of religion, she practiced those works as assiduously as before. She had received two thousand marks for her dowry. Now she gave some of that to the poor and with the rest built a large hospital at Marburg. This made people regard her as a prodigal spendthrift, and many called her insane. When she gladly accepted these insults, they accused her of being so happy because she had put the memory of her husband out of her heart too quickly.

After the hospital was built, she committed herself to serving the poor like a simple servingwoman. She ministered solicitously to their needs, bathing them, putting them to bed, covering them, and cheerfully saying to her own maids: "How fortunate we are, to be able to bathe our Lord and cover him!" In waiting on the sick she humbled herself so completely that when a poor child who had only one eye and was covered with scabs came into the hospital, she took him in her arms to the privy seven times in one night and willingly washed his bedclothes. Again there was a woman with a horrible leprosy whom she bathed and put to bed, cleansing and bandaging her sores, applying remedies, trimming her fingernails, and kneeling at her feet to loosen her shoes. She prevailed upon the sick to confess their sins and to receive holy communion, and when one old woman flatly refused, she had her whipped to change her mind.

When Elizabeth was not busy with caring for the sick, she spun wool that was sent to her from a monastery, and divided the money she earned among the needy. At a time when everyone was poor, Elizabeth received five hundred marks from her dowry and set about distributing the money to those in need. She lined them all up, tied an apron on, and began the distribution, having made a rule that if anyone changed place in the line in order to receive a second time, that person's hair would be cut off. It happened that a girl named Radegund, who was admired for the beauty of her tresses, came to the hospital, not to receive an alms but to visit her sister who was ill. Since she did not get on line, she was brought to blessed Elizabeth for breaking the rule, and Elizabeth ordered her hair cut off, despite her sobs and her struggles. Then some of those present said that the girl was not at fault, but Elizabeth said: "At least from now on she won't be able to flaunt her curls at dances or indulge in similar vanities." She asked Radegund if she had ever thought of entering the religious life, and the girl answered that she would have done so long since if she were not so proud of her hair. Elizabeth: "It is dearer to me that you have lost your hair than if my son had been raised to the Empire!" Radegund took the religious habit and stayed on with Elizabeth, leading a praiseworthy life.

A poor woman gave birth to a daughter, and blessed Elizabeth lifted the baby from the sacred font and gave her her own name. Then she saw to the mother's needs and gave her the sleeves taken from her maid's coat to keep the infant warm. She also gave her shoes to the mother. Three weeks later the woman deserted her child and secretly went off with her husband. When Elizabeth got word of this, she had recourse to prayer, and the man and wife were unable to go a step farther, but had to come back to her and beg her forgiveness. She reproached them for their ingratitude, as they deserved, then turned the baby over to them to be cared for, and provided them with the necessary means.

The time was drawing near when the Lord intended to call his beloved out of the prison of this world, and to receive her, who had despised the kingdom of mortals, into the kingdom of the angels. Christ appeared to her and said: "Come, my beloved, to the eternal dwelling prepared for you!" She was brought low with fever and lay with her face turned toward the wall, and those who stood around her heard her humming a sweet melody. When one of her maids asked her what this meant, she answered: "A little bird perched between me and the wall, and sang so sweetly that I too had to sing." Throughout her illness she was always cheerful and prayed all the time. The day before she died she said to her attendants: "What would you do if the devil came near you?" After an interval she cried out three times : "Go away!" as if chasing the devil. Then she said: "It is almost midnight, the hour when Christ chose to be born and when he lay in his crib." And as the moment of her departure drew near, she said: "Now is the time when almighty God calls those who are his friends to the celestial nuptials!" Another interval, and she breathed her last and slept in peace, in the year of our Lord 1231.

Although her venerable body lay unburied for four days, no unpleasant odor came from it, but rather a pleasant aroma that refreshed everyone. Then flocks of small birds that had never been seen there before clustered on the roof of the church. Their melodies were so sweet and their harmonies so varied that their music, which, as it were, accompanied the saint's obsequies, won the admiration of all who heard it. Loud was the mourning of the poor, deep the devotion of all the people. Some cut off wisps of her hair; others clipped shreds from her graveclothes, to be kept as precious relics. Her body was placed in a monument from which oil is said to have flowed afterwards.

A number of events surrounding the saint's death manifest the height of sanctity that she had attained. Consider first the singing of the little bird and the driving away of the devil. The bird that perched between Elizabeth and the wall, and sang so sweetly that she sang with it, we take to have been her angel, who was delegated to be her guardian and also to assure her of eternal joy. Sometimes, to increase the consternation of the damned, their eternal punishment is revealed to them before they die; and to the elect their eternal salvation is at times revealed to enhance their consolation. Elizabeth's singing at that moment was evidence of the immense joy which that revelation stirred in her, a joy so great that it could not be contained in her heart but manifested itself in the dulcet sound of her voice. The devil, too, comes to dying saints to find out whether he has any right over them, but since he had no hold over Elizabeth, he fled ignominiously.

Second, her cleanness and purity were made manifest by the sweet odor that came from her body; since in her lifetime her body shone with cleanness and chastity, in death it gave out a fragrant aroma.

Third, her excellence and high dignity were manifested by the joyful singing of the birds. We believe that the birds that sang jubilantly on the ridge of the church roof were angels sent by God to carry her soul to heaven and to honor her body with celestial caroling. Just as a swarm of demons convenes around dying unrepentant sinners to torment them with terror and to whisk their souls off to hell, so a multitude of angels gathers around the good at the hour of death to comfort them and conduct their souls to the heavenly realm.

Fourth, the depth of blessed Elizabeth's mercy and pity was manifested by the flow of oil. Oil flowed from her dead body because in her lifetime she abounded in works of mercy. Oh, how largely the spirit of pity must now flow in the vitals of one from whose body lying in the dust oil was found flowing!

Fifth, the occurrence of numerous miracles manifests Elizabeth's power and merit before God. After she had passed from her body, God glorified her with a multiplicity of miracles, some of which will be related here, many being omitted for the sake of brevity.[8]

In a monastery in the diocese of Hildesheim, Saxony, there was a Cistercian monk named Henry. He was so ill and suffered so much pain that all the monks felt compassion for him and were disturbed by his cries of distress. One night there appeared to him a venerable lady dressed in white garments, who told him that if he wished to recover his health, he should dedicate himself by vow to Saint Elizabeth. The following night the same lady appeared and gave the same advice. Since the abbot and the prior were both away from the monastery, the

---

[8] The reason given for the omission is Jacobus's.

monk made the vow after consulting his immediate superior. The third night the lady appeared and made the sign of the cross over him, and he was cured. When the abbot and the prior heard of this, they began to wonder about Henry's health but were in serious doubt about whether he should keep his vow, since no monk is allowed to make vows or assume such obligations without permission. The prior added that demons often appeared to monks, who were deluded by them into making such forbidden vows *sub specie boni*—under the semblance of good—and that therefore the said monk should be advised to strengthen his unstable mind by confession. The following night, however, the same lady as before appeared to Henry and said: "You will always be ill until you fulfill your vow!" Immediately his illness returned and he was tortured with pain. The abbot, upon hearing of this turn of events, gave the monk the necessary permission and ordered that enough wax be given to him to make the required image. Again Henry's health was restored, and he zealously fulfilled his vow and suffered no recurrence of his malady.

In the diocese of Mainz a young woman named Benigna asked a servant to give her a drink, and the servant, annoyed, gave it to her, saying: "Take it and drink the devil!" It seemed to Benigna that a burning brand was going down her throat, and she cried out that she had pains in her neck. Then her belly swelled up like a balloon, and she felt as if some animal was running around inside her. She moaned miserably and uttered demented cries, and was thought to be possessed of the devil. In that condition she lived for two years. Then she was brought to Saint Elizabeth's tomb and a vow was made for her there. She was placed atop the tomb and looked to be lifeless, but when they gave her a morsel of bread to eat and some blessed water to drink as she lay there, to the astonishment and delight of all she rose up cured.

A man in the diocese of Utrecht, whose name was Gederic, had lost the use of one hand, which was paralyzed. He visited Saint Elizabeth's tomb twice without obtaining a cure but went with much devotion a third time with his wife. On the way he met an old man of venerable aspect, saluted him, and asked where he came from. The old man said that he came from Marburg, where the body of Saint Elizabeth rested, and where many miracles occurred. Gederic told him about his paralyzed hand, and the aged man raised his hand and blessed him, saying: "Go with confidence, you will be healed, provided you put your infirm hand into an opening hollowed out in the stone at the head of the tomb; and the farther you thrust your hand in, the speedier your cure will be; and at that moment have Saint Nicholas in mind, because he works as companion and associate of Saint Elizabeth in her miracles." He added that those who, having put down their offerings, left the saints' shrines immediately, made a foolish mistake, because it pleased the saints when their aid was sought with perseverance. With that the old man disappeared and they saw him no more. They went on their way to Marburg, wondering about his appearance and disappearance, but fully confident that they would obtain the cure they sought. Gederic therefore followed the old man's advice, putting his hand in under the stone at the head of the tomb, and, when he withdrew it, it was perfectly sound.

A man of the diocese of Cologne, Herman by name, was being held in prison by the judge. He commended himself totally to God, and called upon Saint Elizabeth and Master Conrad to come to his aid, with all the devotion of which he was capable. The following night they both appeared to him, surrounded by brilliant light, and consoled him in many ways. Finally his sentence was carried out and he was hanged on a scaffold a Teutonic mile from town. The judge, however, gave the parents permission to take the body down and bury it. The grave was prepared and the convict's father and uncle laid the body in it, meanwhile invoking Saint Elizabeth's patronage in favor of the dead man. To the stupefaction and admiration of all present, the man who had been dead arose alive.

A schoolboy called Burchard, from the diocese of Mainz, was fishing, but carelessly fell into the river and drowned. He was pulled out after quite a while, but the body was rigid, without feeling or motion, and showed no signs of life, so he was judged to be dead by the men who had found him. Then the merits of Saint Elizabeth were invoked, and, wonderful to behold, the boy was restored to life and health.

A boy three and a half years old, whose name was Hugolin, of the diocese of Mainz, died on the road, and his body lay rigid and lifeless. His mother carried him a distance of four Teutonic miles, imploring Saint Elizabeth with all devotion, and the boy returned to life and health.

A four-year-old boy fell into a well, and a man who came to draw water noticed the body submerged and lying at the bottom. He got the boy out with some difficulty and determined that he was dead. The indications of death were the length of time the boy had been in the water, the rigidity of the body, the horrible staring eyes and gaping mouth, the blackened skin, the swollen body, and the utter absence of movement and feeling. The man therefore pronounced a vow to Saint Elizabeth, invoking her help for the deceased, and the boy recovered the life he had had. There was also a girl who fell into a river, and when she was pulled out, she was quickly restored to life by Saint Elizabeth's merits.

A man named Frederick, of the diocese of Mainz, was an expert swimmer. While swimming in a certain body of water he saw a poor man who had been cured of blindness through Saint Elizabeth's intercession, and began to make fun of him, contemptuously splashing water in his face. The man resented this and said: "That holy lady who obtained this grace for me will take my revenge on you, and you will not come out of the water until you are dead and drowned." The swimmer thought little of this threat and swam away insolently into deep water, but suddenly lost all his strength, could not help himself, and sank to the bottom like a stone. After a long time he was found and lifted from the water, and loud was the lamentation for him. Some of his kinsmen, however, made a vow to Saint Elizabeth on his behalf and devoutly sought her assistance; and quickly he began to breathe and rose alive and well.

A certain John, also of the Mainz diocese, was apprehended with a thief, though he himself had not committed any crime, and was sentenced to be hanged. He begged those around him to pray to Saint Elizabeth, asking her to help him as he deserved. He was hanged nonetheless but heard a voice speaking over him: "Take heart, have confidence in Saint Elizabeth, and you will be freed." At once, while the other man remained suspended, John's noose broke and he fell heavily from a height, but suffered no injury, though a new shirt he was wearing was torn. Rapturously he prayed: "O Saint Elizabeth, you freed me and made me fall on a patch of soft ground!" There were those, however, who said that he should be hanged again, but the judge said: "Whom God has set free I will not allow to be hanged a second time!"

A lay brother named Volmar, in a monastery in the diocese of Mainz, was extremely religious and afflicted his body so severely that for twenty years he wore a leather-and-iron corset next to his skin, and lay on sticks and stones to rest. He was working in the mill when his hand got caught and the millstone mangled it so badly that the flesh was torn away on both sides, the bones and tendons were shredded, and the hand looked as if it had been mashed in a mortar. The pain of the injury was so intense that Volmar asked to have the hand cut off. He frequently invoked Saint Elizabeth's aid, having throughout his life been devoted to her, and one night she appeared to him and asked: "Do you want to be healed?" "Oh, please, I do!" he answered. She took his hand, mended the sinews, brought the bones together in place, restored the flesh on either side, and rejoined the hand to the wrist. In the morning the brother found his hand perfectly repaired and showed it, so mended, to the whole community, to the amazement of all.

A five-year-old boy named Dietrich, in the diocese of Mainz, was born blind but by Saint Elizabeth's merits received the light; but he had no eyelids and the skin grew over his eyes, covering them completely and leaving no sign that there were any eyes beneath. His mother brought him to Saint Elizabeth's sepulcher, rubbed his face over the eyes with earth from the tomb, and invoked the saint's merits on her son's behalf. And behold, the unbroken skin split open, and two small eyes, clouded and bloodshot, looked out. Thus the boy obtained the blessing of eyesight through the merits of Saint Elizabeth.

A girl of the same diocese, whose name was Beatrice, for a long time was afflicted with a number of woeful infirmities. In time a hump grew on her back and a tumor in her chest. She was so bent over that she could not stand erect and had to support her body by resting her hands on her knees. Her mother managed to carry her in a sort of basket to Saint Elizabeth's tomb and they stayed there for ten days, unable to find any remedy for the child's ills. The mother lost her temper and complained to Saint Elizabeth, saying: "You hand out all these favors to everybody else and you don't even listen to wretched me! I'll go home and turn as many people as I can away from coming to visit you!" Still angry, she started out and walked a mile and a half, while the daughter groaned with pain. Then the child fell asleep and saw a beautiful lady with a radiant face, who lightly touched her back and chest, and said: "Get up, child, and walk!" The girl woke up and found herself cured of all curvature and deformity. She told her mother about the vision, and they both rejoiced and were glad. Then back they went to Saint Elizabeth's tomb, where they gave thanks to God and left the basket in which the child had been carried.

A woman of the same diocese, whose name was Gertrude, for many years was paralyzed in both legs and suffered curvature of the spine. In a dream she was advised to go to Saint Nicholas and implore the help of his merits. She had herself carried to the church of Saint Nicholas and found one of her legs cured. Later, almost beside herself with pain, she was brought to Saint Elizabeth's monument and placed upon her tomb, and was quickly and completely made well. Still in the same diocese, a woman named Scintrude lost her sight for a year and had to be led about by the hand; but she commended herself to Saint Elizabeth with all devotion and recovered her sight.

A man named Henry, of the diocese of Mainz, being deprived of his eyesight, visited Saint Elizabeth's tomb and received the benefit of a complete cure. Later the same man suffered hemorrhage so grave that his family thought he would die. But someone brought him some earth from Saint Elizabeth's tomb, he mixed it with water and drank it, and his health was restored completely.

Mechtilde, a girl of the diocese of Trier, was blind and deaf and could neither talk nor walk. Her father and mother dedicated her to Saint Elizabeth, and the saint gave her back to them perfectly cured. They all then praised the great works of God and Saint Elizabeth. A woman named Hedwig, of the diocese of Trier, was completely blind for a year and for her cure invoked Saint Elizabeth's merits. She was led to the saint's tomb and there recovered the sight of one eye, but, when she was home again, felt excruciating pain in the other. She invoked the saint's merits again, and Elizabeth appeared to her and said: "Go to the altar, wipe your eyes with the corporal,[9] and you will be healed." She did as ordered and was cured.

A man named Theoderic, of the diocese of Mainz, was so gravely stricken in the knees and legs that he could not get about unless supported by others. He made a vow to visit the sepulcher of Saint Elizabeth with offerings. Although he lived only ten miles from her shrine, it took him all of eight days to get there. When he had stayed at the tomb for four weeks without obtaining a cure, he started home, but stopped on the way and sought rest lying beside another sick man. Then in a dream he saw someone come and pour water over him. He woke up and said angrily to the man next to him: "Why did you pour water all

---

[9] A linen cloth on which the consecrated elements are placed in the mass.

over me?" The man replied: "I did not pour water over you, but I think the shower will be the cause of your well-being." Theoderic stood up and found himself made a whole man, whereupon he threw his crutches over his shoulder and marched back to give thanks at Saint Elizabeth's tomb. Then he went home to his family, rejoicing.

※

169. Saint Cecilia

The name Cecilia may come from *coeli lilia*, lily of heaven, or from *caecitate carens*, lacking blindness, or from *caecis via*, road for the blind, or from *coelum* and *lya*, a woman who works for heaven. Or the name may be derived from *coelum* and *laos*, people. For Saint Cecilia was a heavenly lily by the modesty of her virginity. She is called a lily because of her shining cleanness, her clear conscience, and the aroma of her good renown. She was a road for the blind by giving good example, a heaven through her continual contemplation, and a worker for heaven by her application to good works. Or she is called heaven because, as Isidore says, the philosophers have said that heaven is revolving, round, and fiery, and Cecilia was revolving in a constant circle of good works, round in her perseverance, and fiery with the warmth of her charity. She was free of blindness through the splendor of her wisdom. She was a heaven of the people because in her, as in a spiritual heaven—the sun, the moon, the stars—people saw how to imitate heaven, namely, by the perspicacity of her wisdom, the magnanimity of her faith, and the variety of her virtues.

Cecilia, that illustrious virgin, was born into a noble Roman family and raised in the faith of Christ from infancy. She always carried Christ's gospel in her bosom, prayed continually by day and by night, and besought the Lord to preserve her virginity. She was betrothed to a young man named Valerian and the wedding day was set, but Cecilia wore a hair shirt next to her flesh beneath her cloth-of-gold outer garments. While the musical instruments sounded, she sang in her heart to the Lord alone, saying: "Let my heart and my body be undefiled, O Lord, that I may not be confounded"; and she fasted for two or three days at a time, commending her fears to God. Finally came her wedding night, and she and her spouse retired to the silence of the bridal chamber. She addressed him: "O sweetest and most loving young man, I have a secret to confess to you, on condition that you swear to keep this secret entirely to yourself." Valerian swore that no necessity would make him reveal it, nor any reason force him to betray it. Then she said: "I have a lover, an angel of God, who watches over my body with exceeding zeal. If my angel senses that you are touching me with lust in your heart, he will strike you and you will lose the flower of your gracious youth. If, on the other hand, he knows that you love me with sincere love, he will love you as he loves me, and will show you his glory."

Valerian, guided by God's will, said: "If you want me to believe you, show me this angel of yours, and if I see for myself that he is really an angel, I will do as you are exhorting me to do; but if I see that you love another man, I will finish off both of you with my sword!" Cecilia told him: "If you will believe in the true God and promise to be baptized, you will be able to see him. Go therefore to the third milestone from the city on the Appian Way, and say to the poor people you will find there: 'Cecilia has sent me to you to have you show me an aged holy man named Urban, because I carry secret orders for him which I will pass on to him.' When you see this Urban, tell him everything I have said, and after you have been purified by him, come back to me and you will see the angel!"

Valerian set out and, following the directions given to him, found his way to Saint Urban the bishop, who was hiding among the tombs of the martyrs. When he had told him all that Cecilia had said, Urban raised his hands to heaven, wept, and said: "Lord Jesus Christ, sower of chaste counsel, accept the fruit of the seeds that you sowed in Cecilia! Lord Jesus Christ, good shepherd, Cecilia your hand-maid has served you like a busy bee: the spouse whom she received as a fierce lion, she has sent to you as a gentle lamb!" And now there appeared to them an aged man clothed in garments as white as snow, holding a book written in gold letters. When Valerian saw this, he was so afraid that he fell as if dead, but was raised to his feet by the old man and read in the book: "One Lord, one faith, one baptism, one God and father of all, who is above all and through all and in all of us."[1]

When Valerian had read those words, the old man asked him: "Do you believe that this is so, or do you still doubt?" Valerian exclaimed: "There is nothing else under heaven that could be more truly believed!" The old man vanished forthwith. Valerian was baptized by Urban and went back to find Cecilia talking to an angel in her room. The angel held two crowns of roses and lilies in his hand, one of which he gave to Cecilia and the other to Valerian, saying: "Guard these crowns with spotless hearts and clean bodies, because I have brought them to you from God's heaven. They will never wither nor lose their sweet odor, nor can they be seen by anyone except those whom chastity pleases. And you, Valerian, since you have trusted good counsel, ask whatever you wish and you will have it!" Valerian: "There is nothing dearer to me in this life than the love

---

[1] Eph. 4:5. Graesse has "One God, one faith," etc.

of my only brother. I ask therefore that he may join me in acknowledging the truth!" The angel: "Your petition pleases the Lord, and you will both come to him with the palm of martyrdom."

At this moment Tiburtius, Valerian's brother, came in, smelled the strong odor of roses, and said: "I wonder where this odor of roses and lilies is coming from at this season! Their aroma could not penetrate me more sweetly if I were holding the flowers in my hands! I confess to you that I am so refreshed that of a sudden I feel totally changed!" Valerian said: "We have crowns that your eyes cannot see. They bloom with florid color and snowy whiteness. At my prayer you perceived their odor. So also, if you believe, you will be able to see them." Tiburtius: "Am I hearing this in dream, Valerian, or are the things you are saying true?" Valerian: "We've been living in dream, but now we dwell in the truth!" Tiburtius: "How do you know this?" And Valerian: "An angel of the Lord has taught me, and you will be able to see him if you choose to be purified and to renounce the worship of idols!" Ambrose testifies to this miracle of the crowns of roses in his Preface, where he says: "Saint Cecilia was so filled with the heavenly gift that she accepted the palm of martyrdom, cursing the world along with the pleasures of marriage. Her witness is the confession she evoked from her spouse, Valerian, and from Tiburtius, both of whom, O Lord, you crowned by an angel's hand with sweet-smelling flowers. A virgin led these men to glory, and the world recognized how powerful commitment to chastity can be." Thus Ambrose.

Cecilia then showed him plainly that all idols were without feeling or speech, and Tiburtius responded, saying: "Anyone who does not believe this is a brute beast!" Cecilia kissed his breast and said: "Today I declare that you are my kinsman, for just as the love of God has made your brother my husband, so has contempt for the idols made you my kinsman. Go therefore with your brother to be purified and made able to see the faces of angels!"

Tiburtius said to his brother: "I beg of you, brother, tell me who it is that you are leading me to." Valerian: "To Urban the bishop!" Tiburtius: "Are you talking about the Urban who has been condemned to death so many times and is in hiding somewhere? If that man is found, he will be burned alive and we will be caught in his flames, and, while we are looking for God in heaven, we will bring burning fury upon us on earth!" To this, Cecilia responded: "If this life were the only life, we would be right in fearing to lose it, but there is another and a better life, which is never lost and which the Son of God has told us about. All things that were made, the Son begotten of the Father has established in being, and all the things that are established, the Spirit who proceeds from the Father has enlivened. This Son of God came into the world and showed us, by his words and his miracles, that there is another world." Tiburtius: "Surely you assert that there is only one God! How then can you testify that there are three?" Cecilia's answer: "Just as in human knowledge there are three powers, namely, thought, memory, and understanding, so in the one divine being there can be three persons."

Then she began to instruct him about the coming of the Son of God and his passion, and to show the many ways in which his passion was fitting. "The Son of God was held in bonds," she said, "in order to free humankind from the bonds of sin. He was accursed, that accursed mankind might be blessed. He allowed himself to be mocked in order to free man from being made a mockery by the demons. He submitted to receiving a crown of thorns on his head so as to lift the capital sentence from us. He tasted the bitter gall to cure our taste for the sweet things of life. He was stripped of his garments to cover our first parents' nakedness. He was hung upon a tree to undo the evil done at the tree!" Tiburtius said to his brother: "Have pity on me and lead me to the man of God so that I may receive purification!" So he was purified, and thereafter often saw the angels of God and obtained whatever he prayed for.

Valerian and Tiburtius now devoted themselves to works of mercy and gave burial to the bodies of saints whom the prefect Almachius had put to death. Almachius summoned them and asked them why they buried those who were condemned for their crimes. Tiburtius: "Would that we might be the slaves of those whom you call condemned! They despised what seems to be and is not, and have found what is not seen to be, and is!" The prefect: "And what is that?" Tiburtius: "That which seems to be and is not is everything in the world that leads man to nonbeing. What is not seen to be and is, is the life of the righteous and the punishment of the wicked." Almachius: "From what you say, I think you are out of your mind!"

Then he had Valerian brought before him and said to him: "Since your brother is not right in his head, you at least may be able to answer us reasonably. It is clear that you are wrong in many ways, since you spurn all joys and are attracted to everything hostile to enjoyment." To this, Valerian said that in wintertime he had seen idle men mocking and making fun of those who work in the fields, but in the summer, when the glorious fruits of their labor are ready for harvesting, he had seen those who were thought to be foolish rejoicing, and those who seemed to be clever beginning to weep. "We too," he went on, "who bear shame and hard work, will in the future receive glory and an eternal reward, while you, who enjoy what is transitory, in the future will face eternal grief." The prefect: "So we, unconquered and unconquerable princes, will have eternal sorrow, and you, the rabble, will possess perpetual joy?" Valerian: "You are not princes, but little men, insignificant, born in our time, soon to die, and due to give a stricter account to God than any of us!"

At that Almachius retorted: "Why do we go on arguing in circles? Offer libations to the gods and go scot-free!" The saints answered: "We offer sacrifice to the true God every day." "What is his name?" the prefect demanded. Valerian: "You will not be able to find his name, even if you take wings and fly!"

"Then Jupiter is not a name of God?" the prefect asked. Valerian: "It is the name of a murderer and debaucher!" Almachius: "Therefore the whole world is in error, and you and your brother alone know the true God!" Valerian: "We are not alone! An innumerable multitude has accepted this holy truth!"

The brothers were handed over to the custody of Maximus, who said to them: "O purple flower of youth, O loving brothers, how is it that you hasten to your deaths as to a banquet?" Valerian answered that if Maximus promised to believe in Christ, he would see the glory of their souls after they died. Maximus: "If what you have said really happens, may I be consumed by fiery lightning if I do not profess my faith in that one true God whom you adore!" And in the event, Maximus, his whole household, and all the executioners accepted the faith and were baptized by Urban, who came to them secretly.

Dawn ended the night, and Cecilia exclaimed: "Hail, soldiers of Christ, cast aside the works of darkness and put on the arms of light!" Then, at the fourth milestone from the city, at the statue of Jupiter, the brothers refused to offer sacrifice and were beheaded. Maximus swore that in the hour of the saints' passion he had seen shining angels, and the martyrs' souls going forth like virgins from the bridal chamber, and the angels carrying them heavenwards. When Almachius learned that Maximus had become a Christian, he had him beaten to death with leaded thongs. Saint Cecilia buried his body with those of Valerian and Tiburtius.

Almachius now made a move to get possession of the brothers' properties and had Cecilia, as Valerian's wife, brought before him, commanding her either to sacrifice to the idols or to incur the sentence of death. Her servants wailed at the thought and urged her to yield, on the ground that a maiden so fair and so noble should not commit herself to death. She said to them: "Good folks, I am not losing youth but exchanging it, giving up clay and receiving gold, abandoning a hut for a palace, leaving a narrow corner of the street for a wide-open, light-filled plaza. If someone offered you a gold piece for a copper, would you not accept it readily? God, indeed, gives back to us a hundred for one. Do you believe what I'm saying?" "We believe," they answered, "that Christ, who has such a handmaid as you are, is truly God!" Bishop Urban was thereupon sent for, and more than four hundred people were baptized.

Almachius again summoned Saint Cecilia and asked her: "What is your status in life?" "I am freeborn and of noble descent," she said. Almachius: "I'm asking about your religion!" Cecilia: "Then your interrogation began badly, because the one question called for two answers." Almachius: "Where do your presumptuous answers come from?" "From a clear conscience and unfeigned faith!" she retorted. Almachius: "Don't you know where my power comes from?" Cecilia: "Your power is a balloon filled with wind! Prick it with a pin and it collapses, and what seemed rigid in it goes limp." Almachius: "You began with insults, and with insults you continue!" Cecilia: "You cannot speak of insults unless what is said is false! Show me the insult, if what I said was false!

Otherwise blame yourself for uttering a calumny! We, who know the holy name of God, cannot deny it, and it is better to die happy than to live unhappy." Almachius: "What makes you speak so proudly?" Cecilia: "It is not pride but constancy!" Almachius: "Unhappy girl, don't you know that the power to give life or to take life away is given to me?" Cecilia: "Now I can prove that you have lied against what is known to everyone! You can indeed take life away from the living, but you cannot give life to the dead. Therefore you are a minister of death, not of life!" Almachius: "Stop this wild talk and offer sacrifice to the gods!" Cecilia: "I don't know where you lost your eyes! What you call gods are nothing but lumps of stone, as we all see. Put your hand out and touch them, and you will know with your fingers what you can't see with your eyes!"

Almachius, now angry, ordered her to be brought to her house, and there to be burned in a boiling bath for a night and a day. She lay in the bath as in a cool place, without feeling as much as a drop of perspiration. When the prefect heard this, he commanded that she be beheaded in the bath. The headsman struck her three times in the neck but could not cut her head off; and because the decree forbade striking a fourth blow, he left her bleeding and half dead. She lived for three days, during which time she gave all her possessions to the poor. All those whom she had converted she commended to Bishop Urban, saying: "I asked for a delay of three days so that I might commend all of us to your beatitude and have you consecrate my house as a church."

Saint Urban buried her body where bishops were buried, and consecrated her house as she had requested. She suffered about A.D. 223, in the reign of Emperor Alexander. Elsewhere we read that she suffered in the reign of Marcus Aurelius, who ruled about A.D. 220.

---

170. Saint Clement

The name Clemens comes from *cleos*, which means glory, and *mens*, mind. Saint Clement had a glorious mind, in other words a mind cleansed of all stain, adorned with every virtue, and now graced with the fullness of happiness. This happiness, as Augustine says in his book *On the Trinity*, consists in this, that in heaven our being will not be subject to death, nor our knowing to error, nor our love to resistance. Or the name comes from *clementia*, clemency, and the saint was a very clement man. Or, as the *Gloss* tells us, *clemens* means mild, just, mature, and pious; and Clement was just in action, mild in speech, mature in his relations with others, and pious in his intentions.

Clement himself inserted the story of his life, especially up to the point where the account shows how he came to succeed Saint Peter as supreme pontiff, in his *Itinerarium*. The rest of his life story is drawn from the records of his acts, which are commonly available.

Clement, the bishop of Rome, was born of noble Roman stock. His father's name was Faustinianus, his mother's, Macidiana. He had twin brothers, one of whom was called Faustinus, the other, Faustus. Macidiana, his mother, was a woman of striking beauty, and her husband's brother burned with desire for her and annoyed her with his daily attentions, to which she gave not the slightest hint of consent; yet she shrank from making the situation known to her spouse, for fear of stirring up enmity between the two men. She therefore conceived the idea of absenting herself from her homeland until this illicit affection, which was fanned by the sight of her presence, had had time to cool. In order to obtain her husband's assent to this plan she cannily invented a dream, which she related to Faustinianus as follows: "In my dream I saw a man standing beside me and ordering me to leave the city as soon as possible, taking with me the twins, Faustinus and Faustus, and to stay away until he commanded me to return home. If I did not do this, I would perish with the two children."

The husband was alarmed by this and sent his wife and sons, with a large retinue, to Athens, to live there and have their sons educated there. The father kept his youngest son, Clement, to be a comfort to him. The mother and the two boys sailed away, but one night their ship was wrecked and Macidiana, without the children, was cast up on a rocky island, She supposed that the boys had been drowned, and would have cast herself into the sea for grief had she not hoped she might recover their bodies. When she realized that she would not find her children either dead or alive, she cried and screamed, tore her hands with her teeth, and would accept consolation from no one. Many women came to her and told her of their own misfortunes, but this did nothing to mitigate her grief. One of the women, however, told her that her own husband, still a young man and a seaman, had perished at sea, and that for love of him she had refused to remarry. This proved to be of some comfort to Macidiana, and she went to live with this woman, earning her day-to-day living by the work of her hands. But in a short time her hands, which she had injured so seriously by biting them, were without feeling or movement, and she could work no longer. Moreover, the kind woman who had taken her in became paralyzed and could not get out of bed. Macidiana was forced to beg, and she and her hostess lived on whatever she was able to bring home.

A year had passed since the mother and the twins had left Rome, and the father sent messengers to Athens to look for them and bring back news of their doings, but the messengers never returned. Finally, after he had sent still others and they had come back with the word that they had found no trace of the woman and the children, Faustinianus left his son Clement in the care of tutors, and he himself boarded ship to hunt for his wife and offspring, but he also never returned.

Thus orphaned, Clement for twenty years could learn nothing about what had become of his father, his mother, and his brothers. He was an assiduous student of letters and scaled the highest peak of philosophy. He ardently wished for and studiously sought a way of convincing himself that the soul is immortal. With this in mind he frequented the schools of the philosophers, rejoicing when it seemed to him that his immortality was proved, and saddened when the conclusion was that he was mortal.

Then Saint Barnabas came to Rome and preached the Christian faith. The philosophers derided him as a fool and a know-nothing. One of them, however—according to some it was Clement the philosopher—at first mocked Barnabas and scorned his preaching, and by way of making a fool of him proposed a question to him, saying: "The mosquito is a tiny animal. Why therefore does it have six feet and wings as well, whereas the elephant, a huge beast, has no wings and only four feet?" Barnabas: "Foolish fellow, I could very easily answer your question if you seemed to be asking it in order to learn the truth; but it would be absurd to talk to all of you here about creatures, since you know nothing about the one who gives being to creatures. You do not know the Creator, so it is right and just that you should be in error about his creatures!" These words so touched the heart of Clement the philosopher that he received instruction in the Christian faith from Barnabas and then hurried to Judea to visit Saint Peter. The apostle completed his instruction in the faith of Christ and gave him clear proofs of the soul's immortality.

At that time Simon Magus, the magician, had two disciples, Aquila and Nicetas by name, but they saw through his frauds, left him to take refuge with Saint Peter, and became his disciples. Peter questioned Clement about his origins, and Clement told him about his mother, his brothers, and his father, adding that as far as he knew, his mother and brothers had been lost at sea, and his father had died, either of grief, or, like the others, in a shipwreck. Hearing this account, Peter could not restrain his tears.

Peter went to Antander with his disciples, and from there to an island six miles offshore, where Macidiana, Clement's mother, lived. On the island stood some marvelously high glassy columns, and Peter and the others were admiring these columns when a beggar woman approached them. Peter asked her reproachfully why she did not work with her hands, and she answered: "These hands that I have just look like hands! They are so weakened by my biting them that they have lost all feeling, and I wish I had thrown myself into the sea, so as not to go on living!" Peter: "Why do you say that? Don't you know that the souls of those who do away with themselves are punished grievously?" Macidiana: "If only I could be sure that souls do live after death, I would gladly kill myself, just to see my sweet children at least for one hour!" Peter asked her why she was so sad and she told him the whole story, whereupon Peter said: "There is a young man named Clement with us, and he has told us that what you say happened to you happened also to his mother and brothers!"

The woman was so benumbed with surprise at this information that she fell in a faint, and, when she came to herself, wept and said: "I am that youth's mother!" She threw herself at Saint Peter's feet and begged him to let her see her son as soon as possible. Peter said to her: "When you see him, restrain yourself for a short time, until our ship carries us away from this island!" She promised to do so, and Peter took her hand and led her to the ship where Clement was. When Clement saw Peter approaching hand in hand with a woman, he began to laugh; but as soon as Macidiana came close to her son, she could contain herself no longer, but clasped him in her arms and kissed him repeatedly. Clement thought the woman was out of her mind and pushed her away indignantly, then turned to Peter with a show of displeasure. Peter: "What are you doing, son? Don't push your mother away!" When Clement heard this, he burst into tears, dropped down beside the prostrate woman, and recognized his mother. Then, at Peter's order, they brought the woman who had befriended Macidiana and who lay paralyzed, and he cured her immediately. Now Clement's mother asked him about his father, and he answered: "He left Rome to look for you and never came back!" At hearing this she only sighed, the great joy she felt over finding her son outweighing her other woes.

Nicetas and Aquila had been absent while all this was going on, but now appeared and saw a woman in Peter's company. "Who is this?" they asked. Clement answered them: "This is my mother, whom God has given back to me with the help of Peter, my master." Peter then told them all that had happened. Hearing this, Nicetas and Aquila stood up abruptly, shaken to the core, and said: "O God, lord and ruler, is what we have heard true or is it a dream?" Peter: "My sons, we are not raving! What you heard is true!" The two young men rubbed their faces and said: "We are Faustinus and Faustus, and our mother thought we were lost at sea!" And they rushed to embrace their mother and covered her face with kisses.

Macidiana said: "What's the meaning of this?" Peter: "They are your sons, Faustinus and Faustus, who you thought perished in the sea!" What she had heard filled the mother with such joy that she was beside herself and fell in a faint, then came to herself and said: "My darling sons, tell me how you escaped!" They said: "When the ship broke up, we clung to a plank, and some pirates picked us up and took us into their boat. Then they changed our names and sold us to an honest widow whose name was Justina, and she treated us as if we were her own sons, and had us educated in the liberal studies. Finally we took up philosophy and joined Simon Magus, who had been a student with us. In time we saw through his frauds, deserted him completely, and, through Zacheus's good offices, became Peter's disciples!"

The following day Peter took the three brothers, namely, Clement, Aquila, and Nicetas, and went off to a secluded place to pray. There a venerable but poor old man spoke to them as follows: "I pity you, brothers! Though your motives are good and pious, I consider you seriously wrong, because there is no God, there is nothing to worship, there is no providence in the world. Everything is controlled by chance and the aspect of the planets at the moment of your birth. I am sure of this out of my own knowledge of astrology, in which I am more learned than most. Therefore make no mistake! Whether you pray or not, what the stars determine for you will be your fate!"

As the old man talked, Clement studied his face, and it suddenly struck him that he had seen this man somewhere before. Peter told the three brothers to continue the discussion, and they went on at length to demonstrate the reality of providence by sound reasoning. Out of reverence they several times addressed him as father, until Aquila said to his brothers: "Why are we calling him father, since we have a commandment to call no man father on earth?"[1] Then, turning to the aged man, he said: "Don't be offended, father, that I have corrected my brothers for calling you father, for we do have a commandment not to give that name to any man on earth." When Aquila had said this, everybody present, including the old man and Peter, laughed; and when Aquila asked them what they were laughing about, Clement told him: "You yourself addressed him as father—the very thing you blamed us for!" But Aquila questioned this, saying: "Truly I don't know whether I called him father or not!"

When the question of providence had been discussed at some length, the old man said: "I would indeed believe that there is a providence, but my conscience forbids me to give consent to this belief. I know my horoscope and that of my wife, and I know that what they determined for each of us has happened to us. Let me tell you the position of the planets at my wife's birth, and you will see the aspect that determined what actually happened to her. At her birth she had Mars with Venus above the center, the moon in descent in the house of Mars and in the borders of Saturn. That alignment makes women commit adultery, makes them fall in love with their own slaves, travel to distant parts, and perish in the water. All this happened. My wife fell in love with a slave, and, fearing danger and disgrace, went off with him and perished at sea. Indeed, as my brother told me, she first fell in love with him and, when he would have nothing to do with her, turned to the slave to satisfy her lust. Nor should she be blamed for this, since her stars compelled her to do as she did." He went on to tell about her dream, and how she and her children had perished in a shipwreck.

His sons were poised to throw themselves upon him and tell him what had really happened, but Peter stopped them, saying: "Quiet, till I give you the word!" Then he said to the old man: "If today I deliver to you your wife, chaste as ever, and your three sons, will you believe that there is nothing to astrology?"

[1] Matt. 23:9.

The reply: "Just as you cannot posssibly do what you have promised, so it is impossible that anything can happen outside the influence of the stars." Peter said to him: "Look! Here is your son Clement, and here are your twin sons Faustinus and Faustus!" At this the old man's limbs gave way, and he fell to the floor giving no sign of life. His sons bent over him and kissed him, fearing that he might not breathe again. He recovered, however, and heard in detail all that had happened. Then suddenly his wife came in weeping and called out: "Where is my husband and lord?" As she continued to cry out like a woman demented, her husband ran to her, shedding copious tears, and began to embrace and kiss her.

Now the family was reunited, and a messenger came to inform them that Apio and Ambio, two close friends of Faustinianus, were the guests of Simon Magus. Faustinianus was overjoyed to hear of their arrival and went to visit them. Shortly another messenger came to tell them that one of Caesar's ministers had arrived in Antioch to hunt down all magicians and put them to death. Then Simon Magus, out of hatred for the two brothers who had been his disciples and had left him, impressed his own likeness on their father's face, so that he would be taken for Simon, not for Faustinianus, and the emperor's ministers would arrest and execute Faustinianus in place of Simon himself. Simon then took off for far places. When Faustinianus went back to his sons and to Peter, the sons were terrified to see Simon's face while they heard their father's voice. Peter was the only one who saw the other man's natural face, and when the sons and the wife, thinking it was Simon, were fleeing from him and cursing him, Peter asked them: "Why are you cursing your father and fleeing from him?" They answered that it was because he looked like Simon the Magician: Simon had made some unguent and applied it to Faustinianus's face, and by magical arts imposed his own features on him. Faustinianus complained and said: "What has happened to wretched me, that in one day I am recognized by my wife and sons, and yet cannot rejoice with them?" His wife tore her hair and his sons shed floods of tears.

While Simon was in Antioch, he had slandered Saint Peter as much as he could, calling him a malign artificer and a murderer, and had worked the people up to such a pitch of hostility toward Peter that they were ready to tear at his flesh with their teeth. Peter therefore said to Faustinianus: "Since you look like Simon, go to Antioch, speak about me favorably before the whole populace, and, speaking as Simon, retract everything he has said against me. Then I will come to Antioch, rid you of that alien face, and, in the sight of all, restore your own visage to you!"

It is not to be believed, however, that Peter ordered Faustinianus to lie, since God certainly does not need our lying. Clement's *Itinerarium*, which contains these details, must therefore be an apocryphal book and, despite what some may be pleased to think, is not to be credited with regard to such details as the above. Yet, when Peter's words are weighed carefully, it can be said that he did not tell

328

Faustinianus to say that he was Simon Magus, but to let the people see the face that had been imposed on him, and thus, speaking as if he were Simon, to say good things about Peter and revoke the bad things Simon had said about him. In other words, he said he was Simon not according to the reality but according to appearances. So what Faustinianus said, as quoted below—"I, Simon, etc."— should be understood as "that is, as far as appearances go, I seem to be Simon." He was Simon, but putatively.

So Faustinianus, father of Clement, went to Antioch, convoked the populace, and said: "I, Simon, declare to you and confess that I was wrong in what I said about Peter. He is neither a seducer nor a sorcerer but has been sent for the salvation of the world. Therefore, if from now on I say anything against him, chase me out as a seducer and sorcerer. Now I do penance, because I acknowledge that I spoke falsely. I warn you therefore to believe Peter, lest you and your city perish!" When Faustinianus had carried out all Peter's orders and had given the people reason to love Peter, the apostle arrived and prayed over him, completely effacing the likeness of Simon from him. The populace of Antioch, thereupon, welcomed Peter warmly and with much honor, and raised him to the episcopal chair.

Now it was Simon himself who arrived in the city and called the people together. "I marvel," he said to them, "that after I had instructed you in salutary rules of action and had warned you against that deceiver Peter, you have not only listened to him but have made him your bishop." The whole crowd, now roused to fury, challenged him, saying: "In our eyes you are a monster! Day before yesterday you were saying how penitent you were, and now you are trying to bring us to ruin with yourself!" They rushed at him and promptly chased him, shamefaced, out of the city. Clement tells this story, inserting it in his book about himself.

After these events Saint Peter went to Rome and, knowing that his passion was imminent, ordained Clement as bishop to succeed him. When the prince of the apostles died, Clement, a farsighted man, took precautions for the future. He foresaw the possibility that some future pope would take what Peter had done as an example and would select and install his successor in the Church, thus making the Lord's sanctuary a sort of hereditary possession. Clement therefore yielded his place as bishop of Rome first to Linus, then to Cletus. There are some who assert that Linus and Cletus were not supreme pontiffs but merely coadjutors to Peter, and as such merited inclusion in the catalog of popes. After them Clement was elected and compelled to preside. He was so obviously a good and holy man that he pleased Jews and Gentiles as well as all Christian peoples. He had a written list of the names of poor Christians in the several provinces and would not allow those whom he had cleansed by the sanctification of baptism to be subjected to the humiliation of public beggary.

Clement had consecrated the virgin Domitilla, niece of Emperor Domitian, with the sacred veil, and had converted Theodora, wife of Sisinnius, a friend of the emperor, Theodora having promised to lead a chaste life thereafter. Sisinnius, driven by jealousy, secretly entered the church where his wife worshiped, wanting to know what it was that made her visit the church so often. As he entered, Saint Clement intoned a prayer and the people responded, and Sisinnius was stricken blind and deaf. At once he told his servants: "Take hold of me and lead me outside!" The servants led him all around the inside of the church but could not reach any door. Theodora saw them wandering about, but at first kept out of their way, thinking that her husband might recognize her. Finally she asked the servants what they were doing, and they said: "Our master wanted to see and hear forbidden things, and was stricken blind and deaf." Theodora resorted to prayer, asking God to allow her husband to go outside; and after praying, she said to the servants: "Go now and take your master home!"

When they had left, Theodora told Saint Clement what had happened. At her request the saint went to Sisinnius, and found him with his eyes open but seeing nothing and hearing nothing. Clement prayed for him and his sight and hearing were restored; and when he saw Clement standing beside his wife, he flew into a rage and suspected that he was being fooled by magical tricks. He therefore ordered his men to sieze Clement, saying: "He blinded me so that he might go in to my wife!" His men were to bind the saint hand and foot and drag him away; but they wound their bonds around columns and stones that were lying there, thinking, as Sisinnius also thought, that they were binding Clement and his clerics and dragging them around. Then Clement said to Sisinnius: "To things that are stones you give the name of gods, so you deserve to drag stones!" Sisinnius thought Clement was in bonds and said to him: "I'll have you killed!" But Clement walked away after asking Theodora to continue praying for her husband until the Lord visited him. Saint Peter appeared to Theodora as she prayed, and said: "Through you your husband will be saved, in order that what my brother Paul said, namely, that 'the unbelieving husband is sanctified by the believing wife,'[2] may be fulfilled." Having said this, he disappeared.

Now Sisinnius called his wife and begged her to pray for him and to summon Saint Clement. The saint came, instructed Sisinnius in the faith, and baptized him and 313 persons of his household. Many nobles and friends of Emperor Nerva were also converted to the Lord by this Sisinnius.

The official in charge of the sacred funds now gave out a lot of money, bribing a mob to start a riot against Saint Clement. Mamertinus, the urban prefect, could not tolerate such disturbances, so he had Clement brought before him. He rebuked the saint and tried to bend him to his own point of view, but Clement said: "I wish you would listen to reason! If a pack of dogs comes barking at us and they try to bite us, they still cannot take away from us our being men of reason while they are irrational dogs. A riot stirred up by ignorant men shows that it has nothing certain or true behind it!"

[2] I Cor. 7:14.

Mamertinus wrote to Emperor Trajan about Clement and received a reply to the effect that either Clement should offer sacrifice or Mamertinus should send him into exile across the Sea of Pontus,[3] adjacent to the city of Chersonesus. Then the prefect, weeping, said to Clement: "May your God, to whom you offer pure worship, come to help you!" The prefect assigned a ship to him and provided for all his needs, and many clerics and lay people followed him into exile. He landed on an island and found two thousand Christians who had been sentenced to quarry marble there. The moment they saw Clement, they burst into tears. He consoled them and said: "For no merit of mine has the Lord sent me to you to be the chief jewel in your crown of martyrdom!"

The prisoners told him that they had to carry water on their shoulders a distance of six miles, and he said to them: "Let us all pray to our Lord Jesus Christ to open for his confessors a spring and veins of water here in this place, that he, who struck the rock in the desert and water came forth abundantly,[4] may grant us a fountain of water, and we may rejoice in his goodness to us!" When he had finished his prayer, he looked around and saw a lamb standing, with his foot raised as if to indicate a certain spot to the bishop. Clement understood that this was the Lord Jesus Christ and that he alone could see him, so he went to the spot and said to those following him: "Strike the ground in this place, in the name of the Father and of the Son and of the Holy Spirit!" But since none of them knew where the lamb stood and nothing happened, Clement took a short stick and struck a light blow at the spot where the lamb's foot rested. Instantly a flood of water erupted and swelled into a stream. Then, as all rejoiced, Saint Clement said: "The stream of the river makes the city of God joyful."[5] The fame of this spread abroad and many people came to the site, and in one day over five hundred received baptism from him. They then tore down the temples of the idols and built seventy-five churches within one year.

Three years later, Emperor Trajan, whose reign began in A.D. 106, heard about all this and sent a general to take action. Finding that all the people were ready and glad to accept martyrdom, the general yielded to numbers and settled for one man. He had Clement thrown into the sea with an anchor fastened around his neck, saying that the Christians would not be able to worship him as God. A great crowd stood at the water's edge, and Cornelius and Probus, Clement's disciples, bade all the people pray that the Lord would show them the martyr's body. At once the sea drew back three miles, and all walked out dry-shod and found a small building prepared by God in the shape of a temple, and within, in an ark, the body of Saint Clement and the anchor beside him.

It was revealed to Clement's disciples that they were not to remove his body. Every year thereafter, at the date of his passion, the sea receded three miles and

---

[3] Pontus Euxinus, the Black Sea.

[4] Cf. Exod. 17:6; Num. 20:11.

[5] Ps. 45:5(46:4).

stayed back for a week, affording dry passage to those who came. In one of these annual solemnities a woman went out to the shrine with her little son, and the child fell asleep. When the ceremony was finished and the sound of the inrushing tide was heard, the woman was terrified and forgot her son in her hurry to get ashore with the rest of the crowd. Then she remembered, and loud were the cries and lamentations she addressed to heaven, wailing and running up and down the beach, hoping she might see the child's body cast up by the waves. When all hope was gone, she went home and mourned and wept for a whole year. Then, when the sea drew back, she was the first to reach the shrine, running ahead of the crowd to see whether she might find some trace of her son. She prayed devoutly at Saint Clement's tomb, and when she rose from prayer she saw the child asleep where she had left him. Thinking that he must be dead she moved closer, ready to gather up the lifeless body; but when she saw that he was sleeping, she quickly awakened him and, in full sight of the crowd, lifted him in her arms. She asked him where he had been throughout the year, and he said he did not know if a year had passed and thought that he had slept soundly for one night.

Ambrose, in his Preface, says: "When the wicked persecutor was forced by the devil to inflict torment on blessed Clement, he did not inflict torment but bestowed triumph. The martyr was thrown into the waves to drown, but this was his path to reward, as by the waters Peter, his master, reached heaven. In the waves Christ showed his approval of both of them, calling Clement up from the depths to the palm of victory, and lifting Peter up to the heavenly kingdom lest he be drowned in the same element."

Leo, bishop of Ostia, tells us that during the reign of Michael, emperor of the New Rome, there was a priest who was called Philosophus because he was so learned, even as a child. This priest arrived in Chersonesus and questioned the people in the town about the things narrated in Clement's story, but most of the people were not natives of the city and admitted that they knew nothing about Clement. The miraculous recession of the sea had long since ceased to happen, due to the sinfulness of the inhabitants. Even before that, the barbarians invaded the area and on the occasion of the sea's withdrawal had destroyed the small temple, leaving the ark containing the body to be covered over by the waves, as was also called for by the townspeople's wrongdoing. Wondering at this, Philosophus went to a small city called Georgia and accompanied the bishop, the clergy, and the people to an island on which the martyr's body was thought to be. There they started to dig in search of the relics, singing hymns and praying as they worked, and by a divine revelation they found the body and the anchor with which the martyr had been cast into the sea. They took all this to Chersonesus. Then the aforesaid Philosophus went to Rome with Saint Clement's body, and it was placed with due honor in the church that is now named after Saint Clement. Many miracles occurred there. Another chronicle has it, however, that the sea left that particular place dry, and blessed Cyril, bishop of the Moravians, transferred the body to Rome.

171. Saint Chrysogonus

Chrysogonus was in prison by order of Emperor Diocletian, and Saint Anastasia provided for his needs. Then Anastasia's husband put her in very strict confinement, and she wrote the following letter to Chrysogonus, who had instructed her in the faith: "Anastasia to Chrysogonus, holy confessor of Christ. I have taken upon myself the yoke of a godless husband, whose bed, God pitying me, I have avoided by feigning illness, and day and night I walk in the footsteps of our Lord Jesus Christ. My husband has used my patrimony to gain prominence, but he is squandering it in unworthy ways and with shameful idolaters. He treats me as a sorceress and blasphemer, and keeps me under such close guard that I suspect I shall soon lose this temporal life, for there is nothing left for me but to breathe my last and succumb to death. I know that that death will glorify me, but I am sorely tried at the thought that my wealth, which I had consecrated to God, is used by scoundrels to no good purpose. Farewell, man of God, and remember me."

Chrysogonus wrote her in reply: "Take care not to be disturbed that you, a God-fearing woman, are beset by adversity, for you are not being deceived, but tried. Soon a time more to your liking will come. Christ will turn to you, and after the darkness of night you will see God's resplendent light, and after winter's cold, a golden, tranquil season will follow for you. Farewell in the Lord, and pray for me."

In time Anastasia's treatment became so harsh that she was scarcely given a morsel of bread, and she felt that she was about to die. She wrote to Chrysogonus: "Anastasia to Chrysogonus, Christ's confessor. My bodily life is soon to end. May he receive my soul for whose love I bear these trials, about which you will learn from this old woman, my messenger." He wrote back: "What is always true is that darkness precedes the light, and so health returns after sickness and life is promised us after death. One end finishes off the adversities and the prosperities of this world, lest despair overrule the sad, or elation the glad. The little ships of our bodies sail one and the same sea, and our souls do the work of the sailors under the one pilot of the body. The ships of some are held together by strong chains and survive the pounding waves of life undamaged, whereas other ships, constructed of fragile wood, are close to foundering even in calm weather yet finish their voyage. You then, O handmaid of Christ, cling with your whole heart to the trophy of the cross, and prepare yourself for the work of God."

Diocletian meanwhile was in the area of Aquileia and was putting many Christians to death. He had Chrysogonus brought before him and said: "Sacrifice to the gods, and assume the powers of your prefecture and the consulship that is yours by birth!" Chrysogonus answered: "I adore one God in heaven and spurn your honors as dirt!" So sentence was pronounced and he was led away and beheaded, about A.D. 287. Saint Zelus, a priest, buried his body with the head.

172. Saint Catherine

Catherine comes from *catha*, which means total, and *ruina*, ruin; hence "total ruin." The devil's building was totally demolished in Saint Catherine: the edifice of pride by her humility, that of carnal concupiscence by the virginity which she preserved, and that of worldly greed, because she despised all worldly goods. Or Catherine's name may be taken for *catenula*, a small chain, for by her good works she fashioned a chain for herself by which she climbed to heaven. This chain or ladder has four steps, which are innocence of action, cleanness of heart, contempt for vanity, and speaking of the truth. The prophet proposes these one by one: "Who shall ascend into the mountain of the Lord? . . . The innocent in hands, and clean of heart, who hath not taken his soul in vain, nor sworn deceitfully to his neighbor."[1] How these four steps were present in blessed Catherine's life will be clear as we read her story.[2]

Catherine, the daughter of King Costus, was fully instructed in all the liberal studies. Emperor Maxentius had summoned all the people, rich and poor alike, to Alexandria to offer sacrifice to the idols, and was persecuting the Christians who refused to do so. When Catherine, then eighteen years old and living alone in a palace filled with treasure and servants, heard the bellowing of animals and the hurrahs of the singers, she quickly sent a messnger to find out what was going on. Learning the facts, she took some people from the palace with her and, arming herself with the sign of the cross, went out and saw many Christians about to offer sacrifice because they were afraid to die. Deeply grieved by what she saw, she boldly made her way into the emperor's presence and spoke as

[1] Ps. 23(24):3, 4.

[2] According to *Butler's Lives of the Saints* (New York: P. J. Kenedy & Sons, 1963), 4:420, Catherine's dates are unknown and there is no documentation regarding her life or her death. The popularity of her cult in the Middle Ages may be judged from the length and detail of this chapter.

follows: "Both the dignity of your rank and the dictates of reason counseled me, Emperor, to present my greeting to you if you were to acknowledge the Creator of the heavens and renounce the worship of false gods." Standing at the temple entrance, she argued at length with the emperor by syllogistic reasoning as well as by allegory and metaphor, logical and mystical inference. Then she reverted to the common speech and said: "I have taken care to propose these thoughts to you as to a wise person, but now let me ask you why you have vainly gathered this crowd to worship the stupidity of idols. You wonder at this temple built by the hands of artisans. You admire the precious ornaments that in time will be like dust blown before the face of the wind. Marvel rather at the heavens and the earth, the land and the sea and all that is in them. Marvel at their ornaments, the sun and the moon and the stars, and at their service—how from the beginning of the world until its end, by night and by day, they run to the west and go back to the east and never grow weary. Take note of all these things, and then ask, and learn, who it is who is more powerful than they; and when by his gift you have come to know him and have been unable to find his equal, adore him, give him the glory, because he is the God of gods and the Lord of lords!" And she went on to discourse at length and with wisdom about the incarnation of the Lord.

The emperor was so amazed that he could make no reply to her, but recovered himself and said: "Please, O woman, please let us finish our sacrifice, and afterwards we will come back to this discussion." He then had her accompanied to the palace and guarded carefully. He was overwhelmed with admiration of her knowledge and the beauty of her person. She was indeed lovely to behold, of truly incredible beauty, and was seen by all as admirable and gracious.

The emperor came to the palace and said to Catherine: "We have heard your eloquence and admire your knowledge, but were so intent upon worshiping the gods that we were unable to follow all you said. Now let us start by hearing about your ancestry." "It is written," Saint Catherine replied, "that one should neither speak too highly of oneself nor belittle oneself: foolish people do that, being teased by a taste for hollow glory. But I avow my parentage, not boastfully but for love of humility. I am Catherine, only daughter of King Costus. Though born to the purple and quite well instructed in the liberal disciplines, I have turned my back on all that and taken refuge in the Lord Jesus Christ. On the other hand, the gods you worship can help neither you nor anybody else. O unhappy devotees of idols that when called upon in need are not there, who offer no succor in tribulation, no defense in danger!"

"If things are as you say they are," the emperor answered, "then the whole world is in error and you alone speak the truth! However, since every word is confirmed in the mouth of two or three witnesses, no one would have to believe you even if you were an angel or a heavenly power, and all the less since obviously you are but a frail woman!" Catherine's reply was: "I implore you, Caesar, do not let yourself be carried away by anger, lest dire disturbance overturn a wise man's mind, for the poet says, 'If you are ruled by the mind you are king, if by the body you are slave.'" "I see now," said the emperor, "that you are bent on ensnaring us with your perfidious cunning, as you try to prolong this discussion by quoting the philosophers."

Maxentius was now aware that he could not compete with Catherine's learning, so he secretly sent letters to all the masters of logic and rhetoric, ordering them to come quickly to the court at Alexandria, and promising them huge rewards if they could best this female demagogue with their arguments. Fifty orators, who surpassed all mortal men in every branch of human knowledge, came together from various provinces. They asked the emperor why they had been summoned from so far away, and he told them: "We have a girl here who has no equal in understanding and prudence. She refutes all our wise men and declares that all our gods are demons. If you can get the better of her, you will go home rich and famous!"

At this, one of the orators broke out in a voice trembling with indignation: "O deep, deep thinking of the emperor, who on account of a trifling dispute with one girl has gathered men of learning from the ends of the earth, when any one of our pupils could have silenced her with the greatest of ease!" But the caesar retorted: "I could indeed have forced her to sacrifice or got rid of her with a round of torture, but I thought it better to have her refuted once and for all by your arguments." So the masters said: "Have this maiden brought before us! Let her be put to shame for her rashness, let her realize that she had never even seen wise men before!"

When Catherine was informed about the contest that awaited her, she commended herself totally to God, and at once an angel of the Lord stood by her side and admonished her to stand firm, assuring her that she could not be defeated by these people; and more than that, she would convert them and set them on the road to martyrdom. She was then brought into the presence of the orators. To the emperor she said: "Is it fair for you to array fifty orators against one girl, promising the orators rich returns for winning, and forcing me to fight without any hope of reward? Yet my reward will be the Lord Jesus Christ, who is the hope and crown of those who fight for him."

The debate began, and when the orators said that it was impossible for God to become man or to suffer, Catherine showed that this had been predicted even by pagans. Plato affirms a God beset and mutilated. The Sibyl, too, speaks as follows: "Happy that God who hangs from a high tree!" The virgin went on to contradict the orators with the utmost skill and refuted them with clear and cogent reasoning, to the point that they, dumbstruck, found nothing to respond and were reduced to silence. This drove the emperor to fresh outbursts of fury, and he began to rail at them for letting a young girl make fools of them. Then one, the dean of the others, spoke out: "You must know, Caesar, that no one has ever been able to stand up to us and not be put down forthwith; but this young woman, in whom the spirit of God speaks, has answered us so admirably that either we do not know what to say against Christ, or else we fear to say anything at all! Therefore, Emperor, we firmly declare that unless you can propose a more tenable opinion regarding the gods whom hitherto we have worshiped, we are all converted to Christ!"

Hearing this the emperor, beside himself with rage, gave orders to burn them all in the middle of the city. With words of encouragement the virgin strengthened their resolution in the face of martyrdom and diligently instructed them in the faith; and when they were troubled because they would die without being baptized, she told them: "Have no fear, the shedding of your blood will be counted for you as baptism and crown!" They armed themselves with the sign of the cross and were thrown into the flames, thus rendering their souls to the Lord; and it happened that not a hair of their heads nor a shred of their garments was as much as singed by the fire. Then the Christians buried them.

The tyrant now addressed the virgin: "O damsel nobly born, take thought to your youth! In my palace you will be called second only to the queen. Your image will be erected in the center of the city, and you will be adored by all as a goddess!" "Stop saying such things," Catherine answered, "it is a crime even to think them! I have given myself as his bride to Christ, and he is my glory, he my love, he my sweetness and my delight. Neither blandishments nor torture will draw me away from his love!" The emperor's anger surged back in full, and he ordered her to be shut up for twelve days in a dark cell and left to suffer the pangs of hunger. He then left the city to attend to affairs of state.

Then the queen, afire with love, hastened at nightfall to the virgin's cell accompanied by the captain of the guard, whose name was Porphyrius. When the queen entered, she saw the cell filled with indescribable brilliance, and angels ministering to the virgin's wounds. Catherine began at once to preach to her about the joys of heaven, converted her to the faith, and predicted a martyr's crown for her. Thus they went on talking until past midnight. Porphyrius, having heard all this, threw himself at the saint's feet and along with two hundred soldiers, acknowledged the faith of Christ. Moreover, since the tyrant had ordered that Catherine be left for twelve days without food, Christ sent a shining dove from heaven and refreshed her with celestial viands during those days. Then the Lord appeared to her with a multitude of angels and virgins, and said: "O daughter, recognize your Creator, for whose name you have undergone a toilsome conflict. Be constant, because I am with you!"

Upon his return the emperor had Catherine brought before him. He expected to find her worn out by the long fast but instead saw her more radiant than ever. He thought someone had fed her in the prison, and this made him so angry that he ordered the guards to be tortured. The virgin, however, said to him: "I received food from no man, but Christ fed me by an angel." The emperor: "Take to heart, I beg of you, the warning I am giving you, and give me no more of your dubious answers. We have no wish to own you as a mere servant. You will be a powerful queen in my realm, chosen, honored, triumphant!" Catherine: "Now you yourself pay attention, I pray you, and, after judicious consideration of my question, give an honest decision: whom should I choose—one who is powerful, eternal, glorious, and honored, or one who is weak, mortal, ignoble, and ugly?" Indignantly Maxentius retorted: "Now you choose one or the other for yourself: offer sacrifice and live, or submit to exquisite torture and die!" Catherine: "Whatever torments you have in mind, don't waste time! My one desire is to offer my flesh and blood to Christ as he offered himself for me. He is my God, my lover, my shepherd, and my one and only spouse."

Now a certain prefect urged the furious ruler to have prepared, within three days, four wheels studded with iron saws and sharp-pointed nails, and to have the virgin torn to pieces with these horrible instruments, thus terrorizing the rest of the Christians with the example of so awful a death. It was further ordered that two of the wheels should revolve in one direction and the other two turn in the opposite direction, so that the maiden would be mangled and torn by the two wheels coming down on her, and chewed up by the other two coming against her from below. But the holy virgin prayed the Lord to destroy the machine for the glory of his name and the conversion of the people standing around; and instantly an angel of the Lord struck that engine such a blow that it was shattered and four thousand pagans were killed.

The queen, who until then had not shown herself and had watched what was going on from above, now came down and berated the emperor severely for his cruelty. The monarch was enraged and, when the queen refused to offer sacrifice, commanded that she first have her breasts torn off and then be beheaded. As she was led away to her martyrdom, she begged Catherine to pray God for her. "Fear not, O queen beloved of God," the saint answered, "for today you will gain an eternal kingdom in place of a transitory one, and an immortal spouse for a mortal." The queen, thus strengthened in her resolve, exhorted the executioners not to tarry but to carry out their orders. They therefore led her out of the city, tore off her breasts with iron pikes, and then cut off her head. Porphyrius snatched up her body and buried it.

The following day, when an unsuccessful search was made for the queen's body and the tyrant for that reason ordered many to be questioned under torture, Porphyrius burst in and declared: "I am the one who buried the servant of Christ, and I have accepted the Christian faith!" At this Maxentius, out of his wits, uttered a terrible roar and exclaimed: "O me, wretched as I am and to be pitied by all, now even Porphyrius, sole guardian of my soul and my solace in all my toil, even he has been duped!" And when he turned to his soldiers, they promptly responded: "We too are Christians and are ready to die!" The emperor, drunk with rage, ordered them all to be beheaded with Porphyrius and their bodies to be thrown to the dogs. Next he summoned Catherine and told her: "Even though you used your magical arts to bring the queen to death, if you have now come to your senses, you shall be first lady in my palace. Today therefore you shall either offer sacrifice to the gods or lose your head." Her answer was: "Do anything you have a mind to do! You will find me prepared to bear whatever it is!"

She was thereupon sentenced to death by beheading. When she was led to the place of execution, she raised her eyes to heaven and prayed: "O hope and glory of virgins, Jesus, good King, I beg of you that anyone who honors the memory of my passion, or who invokes me at the moment of death or in any need, may receive the benefit of your kindness." A voice was heard saying to her: "Come, my beloved, my spouse, see! Heaven's gates are opened to you and to those who will celebrate your passion with devout minds. I promise the help from heaven for which you have prayed."

When the saint had been beheaded, milk flowed from her body instead of blood, and angels took up the body and carried it from that place a twenty-days' journey to Mount Sinai, where they gave it honorable burial. (An oil still issues continuously from her bones and mends the limbs of all who are weak.) She suffered under the tyrant Maxentius or Maximinus, whose reign began about A.D. 310. How Maxentius was punished for this and other crimes is told in the legend of the Finding of the Holy Cross.[3]

It is said that a certain monk from Rouen journeyed to Mount Sinai and stayed there for seven years, devoting himself to the service of Saint Catherine. He prayed insistently that he might be worthy to have a relic from her body, and suddenly one of the fingers broke off from her hand. The monk joyfully accepted God's gift and carried it back to his monastery.

It is also told that a man who had been devoted to Saint Catherine and often called upon her for help became careless in the course of time, lost his devotion, and no longer prayed to her. Then one time when he was at prayer, he saw in a vision a procession of virgins going by, and among them one who seemed more resplendent than the rest. As this virgin came closer to him, she covered her face and so passed in front of him with her face veiled. Being deeply impressed by her beauty he asked who she was, and one of the virgins answered: "That is Catherine, whom you used to know, but now, when you do not seem to know her, she has passed you by with her face veiled as one unknown to you."

It is worthy of note that blessed Catherine is admirable in five respects: first in wisdom, second in eloquence, third in constancy, fourth in the cleanness of chastity, fifth in her privileged dignity.

Firstly, she is seen to be admirable in her wisdom, for she possessed every kind of philosophy. Philosophy, or wisdom, is divided into theoretical, practical, and logical. The theoretical is divided, according to some thinkers, into three parts—the intellectual, the natural, and the mathematical. Saint Catherine had

---

[3] Above, chapter 68.

the theoretical in her knowledge of the divine mysteries, which knowledge she put to use especially in her argument against the rhetoricians, to whom she proved that there is only one true God and whom she convinced that all other gods are false. She possessed natural philosophy in her knowledge of all beings below God, and this she used in her differences with the emperor, as we have seen. The mathematical she displayed in her contempt for worldly things, because, according to Boethius, this science is concerned with abstract, immaterial forms. Saint Catherine had this knowledge when she turned her mind away from every material love. She showed that she had it when in answer to the emperor's question she said: "I am Catherine, daughter of King Costus. Though born to the purple . . . ," and so on; and she used it principally with the queen, when she encouraged her to despise the world, to think little of herself, and to desire the kingdom of heaven.

The practical philosophy is divided into three parts, namely, the ethical, the economic, and the public or political. The first teaches how to strengthen moral behavior and adorn oneself with virtues, and it applies to people as individuals; the second teaches how to put good order into the life of the family, and applies to the father as head of the family; the third teaches how to rule well over the city, the people, and the commonwealth, and applies to governors of cities. Saint Catherine possessed this threefold knowledge; the first since she organized her life in accordance with all right moral standards, the second when she ruled in a praiseworthy manner the large household that was left to her, the third when she instructed the emperor wisely.

The logical philosophy also is divided into three parts, the demonstrative, the probable, and the sophistic. The first pertains to philosophers, the second to rhetoricians and dialecticians, the third to sophists. Clearly Catherine possessed this threefold knowledge, since it is written of her that she argued many matters with the emperor through a variety of syllogistic conclusions, allegorical, metaphorical, dialectical, and mystical.

Secondly, Catherine's eloquence was admirable: it was abundant when she preached, as we have seen in her preaching, and extremely convincing in her reasoning, as appeared when she said to the emperor: "You wonder at this temple built by the hands of artisans." Her speech had the power to attract the hearer, as is clear in the instances of Porphyrius and the queen, whom the sweetness of her eloquence drew to the faith. She was skillful in convincing, as we see in her winning over the orators.

Thirdly, consider her constancy. She was constant in the face of threats, meeting them with disdain, as, when the emperor threatened her, she replied: "Whatever torments you have in mind, don't waste time . . ."; or again, "Do anything you have a mind to do, you will find me prepared. . . ." She was firm in dealing with offers of gifts, which she scorned, as when the emperor promised to make her second only to the queen in his palace and she retorted: "Stop saying such things! It is a crime even to think them!" And she was constant under tortures, overcoming them, as we saw when she was put in a dungeon or on the wheel.

Fourthly, Catherine was admirable in her chastity, which she preserved even amidst conditions that ordinarily put chastity at risk. There are five such conditions: abundant wealth, which softens resistance, opportunity, which invites indulgence, youth, which leans toward licentiousness, freedom, which shakes off restraint, and beauty, which allures. Catherine lived with all these conditions yet preserved her chastity. She had a huge abundance of wealth, which she inherited from her very rich parents. She had opportunity, being the mistress surrounded all day long by servingpeople. She had youth and freedom, living in her palace alone and free. Of these four conditions it was said above that Catherine, when she was eighteen years old, lived alone in a palace filled with treasure and servants. She had beauty, as was noted: "She was lovely to behold, indeed of incredible beauty."

Lastly, she was admirable by reason of her privileged dignity. Some saints have received special privileges at the time of death—for instance, a visitation by Christ (Saint John the Evangelist), an outflow of oil (Saint Nicholas), an effusion of milk (Saint Paul), the preparation of a sepulcher (Saint Clement), and the hearing of petitions (Saint Margaret of Antioch, when she prayed for those who would honor her memory). Saint Catherine's legend shows that all these privileges were hers.

Doubts have been raised by some as to whether it was under Maxentius or under Maximinus that Catherine's martyrdom took place. At that time there were three emperors, namely, Constantine, who succeeded his father as emperor, Maxentius the son of Maximianus, named emperor by the pretorian guard at Rome, and Maximinus, who was made caesar in parts of the East. According to the chronicles Maxentius tyrannized the Christians in Rome, Maximinus in the East. It seems therefore, as some authors hold, that a scribe's error may have put Maxentius in place of Maximinus.

173. Saints Saturninus, Perpetua, Felicity, and Their Companions

Saturninus was ordained bishop by disciples of the apostles and sent to the city of Toulouse. When he arrived and the demons ceased to give responses, one of the pagans said that unless Saturninus was killed, they would obtain nothing from their gods. They therefore apprehended Saturninus, and, when he refused to sacrifice, tied him to a bull's legs and drove the animal from the highest point of the capitol, precipitating him down the steps to the bottom. Thus Saturninus, with his skull shattered and his brains spilled out, happily consummated his martyrdom. Two women gathered his body and hid it in a deep cavern for fear of the pagans, but his successors later transferred it to a more honorable place.

There was another Saturninus, whom the prefect of Rome held in prison for a long time, starving him. Then he had him lifted upon a rack and beaten with thongs, clubs, and scorpions, and his flanks burned with torches. Finally he was taken down from the rack and beheaded, about A.D. 286, under Maximian.

There was still another Saturninus, in Africa, the brother of Saint Satyrus, who suffered martyrdom with his brother, Revocatus, the latter's sister Felicity, and Perpetua, a woman of noble birth: their passion is commemorated at another time. Here we can say that when the proconsul told them to sacrifice to the idols and they refused, they were put in jail. Perpetua's father came running in tears to the prison and said: "Daughter, what have you done? You have brought dishonor on your family! No one of your lineage has ever been in jail!" When she told him that she was a Christian, he rushed at her and tried to gouge her eyes out, then went away shouting wrathfully.

Blessed Perpetua had a vision that night and told her companions about it in the morning: "I saw a marvelously high golden ladder raised up to heaven, but the ladder was so narrow that only one person, and that one small, could mount it. On the right and left sides of the ladder knives and swords were attached, so that the one ascending could not look down or to either side, but had to hold himself straight and look up toward heaven. Below the ladder lay a huge, hideous dragon, for fear of which no one dared to ascend. I also saw Satyrus, who, having reached the top of the ladder, looked back at us and said: 'Don't be afraid of that dragon, but climb confidently and be with me!'" Hearing this, all gave thanks, knowing that they were called to martyrdom.

They were therefore brought before the judge but refused to sacrifice. The judge had Saturninus and the other men separated from the women, and asked

Felicity: "Do you have a husband?" "Yes," she answered, "but I have nothing to do with him!" The judge: "Have pity on yourself, young woman, and live, especially since you have a child in your womb!" Felicity: "Do to me whatever you wish, but you will never get me to do your will!" Then the parents of blessed Perpetua and her husband came, bringing Perpetua's infant child, whom she was still nursing. When her father saw her standing before the prefect, he fell on his face and cried: "My sweetest daughter, have pity on me and on your sad, sad mother and on your pitiable husband, who will not be able to live without you!" Perpetua, however, was unmoved. Then her father laid her son upon her shoulder, and he and her mother and husband held her hands and wept, kissing her and saying: "Have mercy on us, daughter, and stay alive with us!" But she threw the infant from her and repulsed her parents, saying: "Get away from me, you enemies of God, because I do not know you!"

Seeing the martyrs' constancy, the prefect subjected them to a long scourging and put them in jail. The saints, however, were mainly concerned for Felicity, who was eight months pregnant. They prayed for her, and suddenly the birth pains came upon her and she brought forth a son, alive. One of the jailers said to her: "If giving birth makes you suffer so much, what will you do when you come before the prefect?" Felicity answered: "I suffer this for myself, but then God will suffer for me!"

The martyrs were brought out of the prison with their hands tied behind their backs and their buttocks bared, dragged through the streets, and finally thrown to the wild beasts. Satyrus and Perpetua were devoured by lions, Revocatus and Felicity by leopards, and blessed Saturninus had his head cut off, about A.D. 256, under Emperors Valerian and Gallienus.

※

---

174. Saint James the Dismembered

Saint James, called the Dismembered because of the way he was martyred, was noble by birth and yet more noble by his faith. He was a native of the city of Elape in the land of the Persians, born of most Christian parents and wedded to a most Christian wife. To the king of the Persians he was well known, and stood first among his peers. It happened, however, that he was misled by the prince and his close friendship with him, and was induced to worship the idols. When his mother and his wife found this out, they wrote him a letter, saying: "By doing the will of a mortal man, you have deserted him with whom there is life; to please one who will be a mass of rottenness, you have deserted the eternal fragrance; you have traded truth for a lie; by acceding to a mortal's wish you have abandoned the judge of the living and the dead. Know therefore that from now on we are strangers to you and will no longer live in the same house with you."

When James read this letter, he wept bitterly and said: "If my mother and my wife have become strangers to me, how much more must I have estranged God?" He therefore inflicted harsh penances on himself in expiation of his fault. Then a messenger went to the prince and told him that James was a Christian, and the prince sent for him. "Tell me," he said to James, "are you a Nazarene?" "Yes," James answered, "I am a Nazarene." The prince: "Then you are a sorcerer!" James: "Far be it from me to be a sorcerer!" The prince threatened him with many kinds of torture, but James said: "Your threats do not bother me, because just as the wind blows over a stone, your anger goes quickly in one ear and out the other!" The prince: "Don't be a fool, or you may die a dreadful death!" James: "That is not death but should rather be called sleep, since in a short time resurrection is granted." The prince: "Don't let the Nazarenes deceive you by telling you that death is a sleep, because even great emperors fear it!" James: "We do not fear death, because we hope to pass from death to life!"

Upon the advice of his friends, the prince now sentenced James to death member by member, in order to strike fear into others. When some people wept out of compassion for him, he said: "Don't weep for me, but mourn for yourselves, because I go on to life, while eternal torment is your due!"

Now the torturers cut off the thumb of his right hand, and James cried out and said: "O Nazarene, my liberator, accept this branch of the tree of your mercy, for the husbandman trims the dry branches from the vine in order to let it grow stronger and be crowned with more fruit!" The headsman said: "If you wish to give in, I shall spare you and bring ointments for your wound." James: " Haven't you ever examined the trunk of a tree? The dry tendrils are cut away, and in due season, when the earth warms, each nub left by the pruning puts forth a new shoot. If therefore the vine is thought to need pruning in order to grow and bear fruit as the seasons revolve, how much greater the need of a man of faith who is grafted into Christ the true vine!"

The torturer cut off the forefinger, and James said: "Accept, O Lord, the two branches that your right hand planted." The third finger was cut off, and James said: "I am now set free from the threefold temptation, and I will bless the Father, the Son, and the Holy Spirit. With the three youths rescued from the fiery furnace I will confess you, O Lord, and amidst the choir of the martyrs I will sing Psalms to your name, O Christ!" The fourth finger was severed, and James said: "Protector of the sons of Israel, you were foretold in the fourth blessing.[1] Accept from your servant the confession of the fourth finger as blessed in Judah." The fifth was cut off, and he said: "My joy is complete."

Then the executioners said to him: "Now is the time to spare your soul, lest you perish. And don't be sad because you've lost one hand. Many men have only one hand, yet abound in wealth and honors!" Blessed James responded: "When shepherds shear their sheep, do they take off the fleece from the right side and leave the left side unsheared? And if the sheep, a dumb animal, wants to lose all its fleece, how much the more should I, a rational man, not think it beneath me to die for God?" Therefore those impious men proceeded to amputate the little finger of his left hand, and James said: "You, Lord, were great, but you chose to become little and least for us, and therefore I give back to you the body and the soul that you created and redeemed by your blood." The seventh finger was taken, and James said: "Seven times a day I have given praise to the Lord."[2] The eighth was removed and he said: "On the eighth day Jesus was circumcised, and the Hebrew male child is circumcised on the eighth day in order to pass over to the ceremonies of the Law: so let the mind of your servant pass over from these uncircumcised men with their unclean foreskins, and let me come and look upon your face!" The ninth finger was cut off and he said: "At the ninth hour Christ yielded up his spirit on the cross, and so I, Lord, confess you in the pain of the ninth finger and give you thanks!" The tenth was taken, and he said: "Ten is the number of the commandments, and J[3] is the initial letter of the name Jesus Christ."

Then some of the bystanders said: "O you who were so dear to us in the past, just profess their god before the consul so that you can go on living; and even though your hands are cut off, there are expert physicians who will be able to ease your pain!" To them James said: "Far be it from me to be guilty of so unspeakable a deception! No one who puts his hand to the plow and looks back is fit for the kingdom of God!"[4] The angry torturers came and cut off the great toe of his right foot, and James said: "Christ's foot was pierced and blood poured out!" They took the second toe and he said: "Great above all days is this day to me, for today I shall be turned and go to almighty God." They cut off the third toe and threw it in front of him, and James smiled and said: "Go, third toe, to your fellow toes, and as the grain of wheat bears much fruit, so you at the last day will rest with your companions." The fourth went, and he said: "Why are you sad, my soul, and why do you disquiet me? I hope in God for I will still give praise to him, the salvation of my countenance and my God."[5] The fifth was

---

[1] Cf. Gen. 49:8–12, Jacob's blessing on Judah.

[2] Cf. Ps. 118(119):164.

[3] The Latin text has *Iota*, which is the *ninth* letter of the Greek alphabet, but *Yod*, the corresponding Hebrew letter, is *tenth* in the Hebrew alphabet, as *J* is in the Roman.

[4] Luke 9:62.

[5] Cf. Ps. 42(43):5.

taken, and he said: "Now I shall begin to say to the Lord that he has made me a worthy companion to his servants."

Then they went to the left foot and took off the little toe, and James said: "Little toe, be comforted, because the big and the little will all rise again, and not a hair of the head will perish. How much less will you, the littlest, be separated from your fellows!" The second was taken, and James said: "Destroy the old house, a more splendid one is being prepared." After the third, he said: "The anvil is made more solid by the blows of the hammer." The fourth toe was amputated, and he said: "Comfort me, God of truth, for I trust in you and in the shade of your wings I will hope until iniquity passes away."[6] The fifth went, and he said: "Look upon me, O Lord, I offer sacrifice twenty times!"

Next, the executioners cut off James's right foot, and he said: "Now I shall offer a gift to the King of heaven, for love of whom I endure these pains." They cut off the left foot and he said: "It is you who work wonders, Lord! Hear me and save me!" They cut off his right hand, and he said: "May your mercies help me, O Lord!" After the left hand, he said: "You are the God who work wonders." Off with his right arm, and he said: "Praise the Lord, my soul, in my life I will praise the Lord, I will sing to my God as long as I shall be!"[7] Now his left arm, and he said: "The sorrows of death surrounded me, and in the name of the Lord I will be avenged." Next it was the right leg, which they cut off at the thigh. Blessed James, stricken with unspeakable pain, cried out, saying: "Lord Jesus Christ, help me, because the groans of death have surrounded me!" And he said to the torturers: "The Lord will clothe me with new flesh, upon which the wounds you inflict will not be able to leave a stain." They were exhausted, having toiled from the first to the ninth hour of the day at dismembering blessed James, but now they returned to their task, taking off the calf of the left leg up to the thigh. Blessed James cried out: "O Lord and Ruler, hear me half alive, Lord of the living and the dead! Fingers, Lord, I have none to hold out to you, nor hands to extend to you; my feet are cut off and my knees demolished, so that I cannot kneel to you, and I am like a house that is about to fall because the columns that support it have been taken away. Heed me, Lord Jesus Christ, and lead my soul out of prison!"

When James had said this, one of the executioners cut off his head. Then Christians came secretly, seized his body, and buried it with honors. He suffered on the twenty-seventh day of November.

[6] Cf. Ps. 56(57):2.
[7] Ps. 145:2.

175. Saint Pastor

Saint Pastor lived in the desert for many years, mortifying himself by rigorous abstinence. When his mother wished to see him and his brothers and they would not allow it, she watched for the day and suddenly stood in front of them as they went toward the church, but they turned from her and went back into the monastery, closing the door in her face. She stood at the door, wept aloud, and called to them. Pastor came and said to her through the door: "What are you shouting about, old woman?" She heard his voice and called out still more loudly, weeping and saying: "I want to see you, my sons! What harm can it do if I see you? Am I not your mother, who suckled you, and now I am old and white-haired?" Her son answered: "Do you want to see us here or in the other world?" She replied: "If I am not to see you here, I shall see you there, my sons!" Pastor: "If you can with peace of mind bear not seeing us here, there is no doubt that you will see us there!" So the mother went away rejoicing and saying: "If I am sure to see you there, I don't want to see you here!"

The judge of that province was anxious to see Abbot[1] Pastor, but Pastor would not see him, so he held the young son of the monk's sister as a criminal and put him in jail, saying: "If Pastor comes and intercedes for him, I'll let him go." The boy's mother came weeping to the old monk's door, and when Pastor did not answer her, she said: "Even if you have a heart of iron and can feel no compassion, at least let sympathy for your own flesh and blood bend you, because the boy is my only child!" He sent word to her: "Pastor begot no sons, therefore feels no sorrow!" The mother went away grieving, and the judge said to her: "Let Abbot Pastor at least say the word, and I will release your son!" Pastor's message to him was: "Examine the case according to law! If he is found guilty of a crime worthy of death, let him die forthwith; if not, do whatever pleases you!"

He taught his brothers as follows: "To be on one's guard, to examine oneself, and to have discernment, these are operations of the soul; poverty, tribulation, and discernment are the works of the solitary life. For it is written: 'If these three men, Noe, Job, and Daniel, shall be [in a land that shall sin against me], they shall

---

[1] The Latin title *abbas*, here (and elsewhere in this work) translated abbot, corresponds to the Aramaic word *abba*, father, and in Eastern usage could apply to religious men in general, whether monks or hermits, and was sometimes used by bishops. The title was not restricted, as in Western usage, to the heads of religious-order communities like the Benedictine abbeys, also called monasteries.

deliver their own souls by their justice, says the Lord of hosts.'[2] Noe personifies those who have nothing, Job those who bear tribulation, Daniel those with discernment. If a monk hates two things, he can be free of this world." To a brother who asked what the two things were, he said: "Bodily comfort and empty glory. If you wish to find rest in this world and in the next, in every instance say: 'Who am I?' And judge no one!"

One of the brothers in the community had committed an offense, and his superior, upon the advice of a solitary, expelled him. When the brother wept despairingly, Pastor called him in, consoled him kindly, and sent word to that solitary, saying: "I have heard about you and want to see you. Please take the trouble to visit me." When the hermit came, Pastor said: "There were two men, each of whom had a kinsman die, but one of the men left his own dead and went to share the other man's grief." The hermit heard and understood the message, and was sorry for the advice he had given.

When one of the monks told Pastor that he was disturbed and wished to leave the monastery, because he had heard something about another monk which had not edified him, Pastor told him not to believe what he had heard, because it was not true. The monk insisted that it must be true because Brother Faithful had told him. Pastor: "The one who told you was not faithful, because if he were faithful, he would never have said such things." But the monk retorted: "I saw it with my own eyes!" Pastor then asked him what the difference was between a mote and a beam, and the monk said that a mote was a speck and the beam was a heavy length of wood. Pastor: "Take it to heart that your sins are that beam, and the other monk's fault is like this little speck!"[3]

Then there was a monk who had committed a grave sin. He wished to do a three-year penance for it and asked Abbot Pastor if that was much. Pastor: "It is much." Asked if he would order a penance of one year, he answered: "It is much." Those standing by suggested as little as forty days, and Pastor said: "It is much!" Then he added: "If a man repents his sin with his whole heart and does not repeat it, the Lord will accept three days of penance."

He was asked about the Gospel text: "Whosoever is angry with his brother without cause shall be in danger of the judgment,"[4] and he said: "Whatever the wrong that your brother has chosen to do you, don't be angry with him until he tears out your right eye. If you do otherwise you are angry with him without cause. If, however, someone tries to take you away from God, for that you shall be angry with him."

Pastor also said: "Anyone who is given to complaining is no monk; one who holds a grudge in his heart is no monk; one who has a bad temper is no monk; one who returns evil for evil is no monk; one who is conceited and loquacious is no monk. The true monk is always humble, kindly, and full of charity, and

[2] Cf. Ezek. 14:14, 13.
[3] Cf. Matt. 7:3–5.
[4] Matt. 5:22.

always and everywhere has before his eyes the fear of God, lest he sin." Another time he said: "If there are three men together, and one of them leads a quiet life, another is ailing and gives thanks, and the third serves the ailing one with sincerity of heart, these three are as alike as if they were the work of the same hand."

One of the brothers complained to him that he was bothered with thoughts that put his soul in danger. Abbot Pastor pushed him out into the cold air and said: "Spread your cloak and catch the wind!" The brother: "I can't!" Pastor: "Neither can you keep those thoughts from entering your mind. What you have to do is to resist them!" Still another monk asked him what he should do with his inheritance, and he told the brother to come back to him in three days. When he came back, Pastor said: "If I tell you to give it to the clergy, they will squander it on high living. If I suggest giving it to your kinsfolk, you will get no thanks for it. If I say to give it to the poor, you will be sure it's safe. But do whatever you like with it! It's none of my business."

We find all this in the *Lives of the Fathers*.

---

176. Saint John, Abbot

Episius had been living in the desert for forty years, and Abbot John asked him how much progress he had made during those years. He replied: "From the day I began to live as a solitary, the sun has never seen me eating." John responded: "Nor me angry!"

In the same book[1] and on a similar note we read that when Bishop Epiphanius set meat before Abbot Hilarion, Hilarion said: "Pardon me, but from the day I took this habit I have never eaten anything slain." To this the bishop replied: "From the day I received this habit, I have never allowed anyone to go to sleep having a grievance against me, nor have I slept having a grievance against anyone." "Forgive me," Hilarion said: "you are better than I!"

John wanted to be like the angels, doing no work and devoting himself without interruption to God, so he put off his clothes and spent one week in the desert. By then he was perishing with hunger and wounded from head to foot with the stings of mosquitoes and wasps, so he went to a brother monk's door and knocked. The brother called out: "Who's there?" John: "It's John!" The

---

[1] *Lives of the Fathers.*

brother responded: "It can't be! John became an angel and is no longer seen among men!" John: "But I really am John!" His brother did not open the door and left him outside to endure another night. Then he opened the door and said: "If you are a man, you have to go to work again in order to eat and live, but if you are an angel, why do you want to get back into your cell?" John said: "Forgive me, brother, I have sinned."

When Abbot John was dying, the brethren asked him to leave them some salutary and memorable saying in lieu of a heritage. He groaned and said: "I have never done what I did because I myself wanted to do it. I have never ordered others to do anything that I have not first done myself."

All this we read in the *Lives of the Fathers*.

---

177. Saint Moses, Abbot

A monk asked Abbot Moses for a saying he might live by, and Moses said: "Sit in your cell and it will teach you all there is to know!" When an aged, infirm monk wanted to go to Egypt so as not to be a burden to his brothers, Moses said to him: "Don't go, because you'll fall into fornication." The old man was disappointed and said: "My body is dead, and you say such things to me!" So he went to Egypt and there a young woman, a virgin, piously took care of him. When he recovered his strength, he ravished her, and the woman bore a son. The old monk took the boy in his arms, and on a great feast day, which was celebrated in the church at Syrte, he walked into the midst of his brother monks. They all wept, and he said: "Do you see this child? He is the son of disobedience! So be on your guard, brothers, because I did this in my old age. And pray for me!" Then he went to his cell and resumed his former way of life.

When another aged monk said to his brothers: "I am dead," one of the others said: "I won't be sure of that till you leave your body. You may say you are dead, but Satan is not dead!"

A brother had sinned, and they sent for Abbot Moses. He went to them carrying a sack of sand on his back. They asked what this was for, and he said: "It's my sins, and they follow behind me so that I don't see them, and I've come today to judge another man's sins!" The monks saw the point and forgave their brother.

We read a similar story about Abbot Prior. When the monks were talking about one of their number who had sinned, Prior said nothing, but went and slung a sack of sand over his shoulder, carrying a small packet of the same sand in front of him. Asked what this meant, he said: "The large lot of sand stands for my sins, which I carry behind me so that I don't think about them. This small packet stands for my brother's sins, which are out in front of me so that I can think about them all the time and judge my brother. Yet I ought always to carry my own sins before my eyes, to repent of them and ask God's pardon for them!"

When Abbot Moses was ordained priest and they put a white vestment over him, the bishop said: "The abbot is now whitened!" Moses added: "Outwardly, my lord! Would it were inwardly!" The bishop had a mind to test Moses further and said to his clerics that when Moses came up to the altar, they should drive him away with insults, and then follow him out and listen to what he would say. So they pushed him outside and heard him say to himself: "They were right to do this to you, you dusty, sooty old woman, because, since you are not a man, why did you presume to present yourself among men?"

All this is taken from the *Lives of the Fathers*.

---

178. Saint Arsenius, Abbot

Arsenius was still living in his ancestral palace, and prayed to be directed toward salvation. As he prayed, he heard a voice saying: "Flee away from men and you will be saved." He therefore embraced the monastic life. Then, as he prayed, he heard: "Arsenius, get away, keep silence!"

Regarding this need for quiet, we read in this same book[1] that there were three brothers who had become monks, and one of them chose to make peace among the quarrelsome, the second to visit the sick, and the third to lead a quiet life in solitude. The first did what he could, but, faced with human contentiousness, he could not please everybody. Overcome with the futility of his efforts, he went to visit the second brother, whom he found weary in spirit and unable to carry out the commandment.[2] They agreed to visit the third brother, who

---

[1] *Lives of the Fathers.*
[2] Cf. Matt. 25:43.

lived in solitude. When they told him their troubles, he poured water into a basin and said: "Look into the water while it's stirred up!" A minute later he said: "Now look into it, and see how quiet and limpid it is!" They looked and saw their faces reflected in the water, and he said: "So it is that those who live their lives among other people do not see their own sins, but when they live in quiet, they are able to see them."

Another man came upon a man in the desert who was naked and was eating grass like an animal. The naked man ran away, but the other pursued him, calling out: "Wait for me! I'm following you for God's sake!" The answer: "And I am running away from you for God's sake!" The pursuer threw away his cloak, and the pursued waited for him and said: "Because you threw away that worldly, material thing, I waited for you!" The pursuer: "Tell me what I must do to be saved!" The other answered: "Flee from men and keep silence!"

An aged noble lady was moved by devotion to go and see Abbot Arsenius. Archbishop Theophilus also asked Arsenius to allow the woman to see him, but he flatly refused. Finally she hurried to the monk's cell, found him outside the door, and prostrated herself at his feet. Highly indignant, he lifted her up and said: "If you want to see my face, look at it!" She was overcome with confusion and shame, and would not look at his face. The old man said: "How could you, a woman, have dared to take such a sea voyage? Now you will go back to Rome and tell other women how you saw Abbot Arsenius, and they will come here as you did, wanting to see me!" She replied: "If, God willing, I get back to Rome, I will not allow any other woman to come here. All I ask of you is to pray for me and always to have me in memory." Arsenius: "I pray God to wipe the memory of you out of my heart!"

Hearing this, the lady was deeply distressed, and, when she returned to the city, her distress made her ill with fever. The archbishop heard about this and went to console her, but she said: "See, I am dying of grief!" The archbishop: "Don't you know that you are a woman, and the enemy attacks the saints through women? That is why the old man spoke as he did! He prays for you all the time!" She was consoled by this knowledge and joyfully went home to her own.

Of another father we read that a disciple said to him: "You're old now, father! Let us together go a little closer to the world!" He answered: "Let us go where there are no women!" The disciple said: "And where is there a place that has no women in it, unless it's the wilderness?" The answer: "Then take me to the wilderness!" Another monk had to carry his aged mother across a river and before doing so wrapped a cloth around his hands. His mother asked him: "Why have you covered your hands, my son?" The son: "A woman's body is fire, and when I touched you, it brought to mind the memory of other women!"

Throughout his life, Arsenius, when he sat down to the work at hand, kept a cloth in his bosom with which to dry the tears that flowed frequently from his eyes. He stayed awake all night, and in the morning, when natural weariness made him want to sleep, he would say to sleep itself: "Come on, you wicked slave!" Then he sat down for a brief nap, getting up almost immediately. He also said: "One hour's sleep is enough for a monk, provided he's a fighter!"

When Saint Arsenius's father, a noble senator, was about to die, he made a will leaving a large bequest to his son. A messenger named Magisterianus brought the will to Arsenius, who was disposed to tear it up. The messenger fell at his feet and begged him not to do that, because it would cost him his head. Arsenius: "I was dead before he died! How could he, now that he is dead, make me his heir?" And he returned the will, refusing to accept any part of the inheritance.

Once Arsenius heard a voice saying to him: "Come, and I will show you the works of men!" He was led to a place where he saw an Ethiopian[3] cutting wood, and making a bundle of it so large that he could not carry it; so he cut more wood and added it to the bundle, and did the same thing time after time. Arsenius also saw a man drawing water from a lake and pouring it into a cistern that had a hole in it, so that the water ran back into the lake; but the man kept trying to fill the cistern. Then Arsenius was shown a temple, and two men on horseback riding side by side with a wooden beam laid across their saddles. They were trying to ride into the temple but could not, because the beam, carried crosswise, would not fit through the door. His guide then explained, saying: "The two men are those who bear the yoke of righteousness pridefully and are not humbled, and therefore remain outside the kingdom of God. The woodcutter is the man guilty of many sins, who, instead of doing penance and atoning for his sins, adds wickedness to wickedness. The man drawing water is the man who performs good works but, because he mixes bad ones in with them, loses his good works."

It was Arsenius's custom that on the Sabbath evening, with the Lord's day coming on, he turned his back to the setting sun and stood, with his hands raised to heaven, until the rising sun threw light on his face. Then he sat down.

All this from the *Lives of the Fathers*.

---

[3] In the *Golden Legend* the term Ethiopian refers to any black man and is usually pejorative in implication.

179. Saint Agathon, Abbot

Abbot Agathon put a pebble in his mouth and kept it there for three years, until he learned to keep silence.

Another monk, upon joining the community, said to himself: "Be like the ass! The ass is flogged but says nothing, suffers maltreatment and does not respond. Do likewise!"

Another monk, when ordered away from the table, made no response and went. Later he was asked about this and said: "I have fixed it in my heart that I am no better than a dog. When the dog is chased, he goes outside!"

Agathon was asked what virtue involved the most labor, and answered: "For me there is no labor equal to that of praying to God, because the enemy labors always to destroy the prayer of the one praying. In other forms of labor a man gets some rest, but the man who prays faces a continuous combat."

A monk asked Agathon how he should live with the brothers. Agathon said: "Live as you lived the first day you were here, and share your confidences with no one, for there is no passion worse than that sort of intimacy; it is the mother of all the passions."

He also said: "The wrathful man, were he to awaken the dead, pleases neither man nor God, because of his bad temper. There was a monk who had a bad temper, and he said to himself: 'If I lived alone I would not be moved to anger so easily.' Then it happened that he was filling a pitcher with water and spilled the water, started again and spilled again, started a third time and spilled a third time. By then he was so angry that he smashed the pitcher. Then he came to his senses and realized that it was the same demon of bad temper that had tricked him, and he said to himself: 'Here I am alone, and anger still got the best of me. I'll go back to the community, because I will need hard work and patience and God's help, wherever I am!'"

On the other hand, there were two monks who lived together for many years and could never be provoked to anger. Once one of them said to the other: "Let's have a quarrel, the way men of the world do!" The other monk replied: "I don't know how to start a quarrel!" Said the first: "I put a tile on the table between you and me, and I say: 'This tile is mine!' Then you say: 'No, it's mine!' And that's the way to start a quarrel." So the brother set a tile between them. One of them said: "This tile is mine!" The other said: "No, it's mine!" The first said: "Oh, all right, it's yours. Take it with you!" And off they went, unable to generate a quarrel between them.

Abbot Agathon was a wise and understanding man, tireless at work, sparing of food and frugal in dress. He said: "I have never gone to sleep holding in my heart a grievance against anyone, nor have I allowed anyone to go to sleep having anything against me."

When he was dying, Agathon lay motionless, keeping his eyes open, for three days. When the brothers nudged him, he responded: "I stand in the presence of divine judgment!" They said to him: "Are you afraid?" Agathon: "I have done all I could, with God's help, to keep his commandments, but I am a man, and I do not know whether what I have done has pleased the Lord." They said: "Don't you have confidence in your works, which were in accordance with God's will?" Agathon: "I presume nothing until I come before him. God's judgments are not the same as men's judgments." They wanted to question him further, but he said: "Show some charity and don't talk to me any longer, because I am busy!"

Having said this, he joyfully breathed his last, for they saw him collecting his spirit, as one does when one is about to greet one's dearest friends.

This from the *Lives of the Fathers*.

✳

180. Saints Barlaam and Josaphat

Barlaam's history was studiously compiled by John of Damascus. Barlaam, by God's grace working in him, converted King Josaphat to the Christian faith. At a time when all India was teeming with Christians and monks, a certain very powerful king named Avennir came to power and persecuted the Christians, and especially the monks. Then it happened that a noble, who was a friend of the king and ranked highest in the royal entourage, was moved by divine grace to leave the palace and enter a monastic order. When the king heard of this, his anger was aroused. He had the desert searched to find his man and, when he was found, had him brought before him. The former courtier, who in the past had always worn splendid robes and had enjoyed great wealth, came in covered with a cheap tunic and emaciated from fasting. The king addressed him: "O foolish man, you have lost your mind! Why have you exchanged honor for degradation? Look, you have made yourself the butt of children's jokes!" The man replied: "If you wish to hear my reasons for doing this, send your enemies far away from you!" The king asked him who these enemies were, and he said: "They are anger and greed, which keep you from seeing the truth! Have prudence and equity sit in to hear what will be said!" "Very well," said the king. "Now speak!"

He began: "Fools despise the things that are real as if they did not exist, and strive to apprehend things that don't exist as if they were real. People who have not tasted the sweetness of what is real cannot learn the truth about what is not!" He went on to speak much about the mystery of the incarnation and about the faith, until the king said: "If I had not promised, before you started, to exclude anger from having any part in this discussion, believe me, I would now turn you over to the executioners to be burned alive! Get up, then, and get out of my sight! I may condemn you to a painful end if I still find you around!" The man of God went away sad, regretting that he had not been granted martyrdom.

Meanwhile a beautiful boy was born to King Avennir, who had been childless. The infant was given the name Josaphat. The king called together a huge throng to offer sacrifice to the gods in thanksgiving for the birth of his son and summoned sixty astrologers to question them about the child's future. They all predicted that he would be powerful and rich—all except one, wiser than the rest, who said: "This child who is born to you, O King, will not reign in your kingdom but in an incomparably better one, because, as I see it, he will worship as a believer in Christ's religion, which you are persecuting!" This he said not out of his wisdom but because God inspired him.

The prediction alarmed the king, who had a magnificent palace built in a remote city, in which Josaphat was to dwell. With him the king lodged a number of handsome youths, ordering them never to mention death or old age or sickness or poverty to his son, or anything else that might sadden him. They were always to speak of pleasant things, so that the boy's mind might be fully occupied with joyful thoughts, all concern about the future being crowded out. If any of those ministering to the son fell ill, the king ordered him removed at once, and a hale and hearty substitute put in his place. Not a word about Christ was ever to be spoken to the royal child.

At this time there was with the king another man who secretly was a devout Christian, and who held high rank among the king's associates. One day when he and the king were hunting together, he came upon a poor man lying on the ground, one of his feet having been gnawed by a wild beast. The wounded man asked this knight to take him into his household, saying that he might benefit by so doing. The knight said: "I'm willing to take you in, but I don't see how you can be helpful to me." The other answered: "I am a word-doctor. If someone is injured by something said against him, I know how to apply the appropriate remedy!" The knight thought that this did not make much sense, but for God's sake took the man into his house and cared for his wound.

Now there were others, jealous and malicious men, who saw that this particular knight was in high favor with the king, and they accused him to the king not only of having gone over to the Christian faith, but also of scheming to seize the throne for himself and of soliciting the crowd and buying their support. "But if you, O King, want to find out whether this is true," they said, "call him in privately, and talk to him about the beauty of this present life, so soon to be ended. Tell him that you are of a mind to relinquish the glory of reigning, and to put on the habit of the monks whom you have been persecuting. Then see what his response will be!"

The king did exactly as these advisers had directed, and the other man, unaware of the ruse, burst into tears, praised the king's proposal, dwelt on the vanity of the world, and counseled him to carry out his plan as soon as possible. This convinced the king that what the others had told him was true, but, angry as he was, he made no answer to the knight. This man, however, pondering how seriously the king had taken his words, went away fearful. Then, remembering that he had a word-doctor available, he told him all that had happened. The answer was: "Be it known to you that the king suspects, on the basis of what you said to him, that you want to usurp his throne. Go therefore, cut off your hair, take off those clothes and put on a hair shirt, and go to the king at daybreak. When he asks what this means, you will answer: 'Behold, O King, I am ready to follow you, for though the road you wish to take is a difficult one, being with you I will find it easy. So, as you have had me as a companion in prosperity, so you will have me in adversity. Now, therefore, I am ready! What are you waiting for?'" The knight followed these instructions. The king was stunned, punished the slanderers, and heaped new honors on his friend.

Josaphat, the king's son, who was brought up in the palace built for him, was now a young adult and was well instructed in all branches of knowledge. He wondered why his father had shut him off as he had, and confidentially asked one of his servingmen, whom he trusted, about this. He told the man that not being allowed to go outside the palace made him so sad that neither food nor drink had any taste for him. Word of the son's unhappiness came to the father and worried him, so he had suitable horses prepared and sent cheering choruses ahead of the young prince as he rode forth. He also gave strict instructions that no unpleasant sight was to confront Josaphat. One day, however, in the course of his ride, he was met by a leper and a blind man. Astonished as he was at this encounter, he asked who these people were and what was their trouble, and his attendants answered that those were ills that could befall anyone. "Do they happen to everybody?" he asked. They said no, and he responded: "Are those who are to suffer such things known in advance, or are the incidents unpredictable?" They said: "Who can know what is in store for him?" This unusual event left Josaphat distraught.

Another time Josaphat came upon a very old man whose face was deeply wrinkled, who could not stand up straight, and who drooled and babbled through his toothless gums. Stunned at the sight, he wanted to know how such a thing could happen, and when he learned that old age brought on such conditions, he said: "And what will be the end of this man?" They said: "Death!" "Is death for everybody," he asked, "or only for some?" He learned that all men must die, and asked: "In how many years do these things happen to us?" They told him: "Old age comes on at eighty or a hundred, and death follows." The prince turned all this over and over in his mind and was much depressed; and though he pretended to be cheerful in his father's presence, he yearned to be directed and instructed in these matters.

Now there was a monk, perfect in life and reputation, living in the desert in the land of Sennaar. The monk's name was Barlaam. Barlaam knew by the Spirit what was going on around the king's son, so he put on a tradesman's garb and went into that city. He sought out the man who was Josaphat's tutor and said to him: "I am a merchant, and I have a precious stone to sell. This stone restores sight to the blind and hearing to the deaf, makes the mute able to speak, and infuses wisdom into the foolish. Take me therefore to the king's son, and I will sell him the stone." The tutor: "You seem to be a man of mature good sense, but what you say does not make sense. I know stones, however, so show me the stone, and if it turns out to be what you say it is, you will gain high honors from the prince!" Barlaam: "The stone has still another power, namely, that if someone who does not enjoy good eyesight and does not live a chaste life inspects the stone, the stone loses all its powers. Though I'm no expert in medical matters, I can see that you have eye trouble, but on the other hand I hear that the king's son leads a pure life and has beautiful, healthy eyes." The tutor: "If that's the way things are, don't show me the stone, because my eyes are not good and I wallow in sin!" The tutor then sent word to the king's son and quickly brought Barlaam into his presence. The prince received him reverently, and Barlaam said to him: "Prince, you did well when you paid no attention to my poor appearance." He then told him the following story.

"There was once a great king who was riding in his gilded chariot. On the road he met some men clothed in tattered garments and weak from hunger. He jumped down from his chariot, threw himself at their feet and worshiped them, and then stood up and showered them with kisses. The noblemen in the king's suite were offended by these actions but, not daring to express their disapproval to the king himself, told his brother how the king had done things unworthy of his majesty. The king's brother reproved him for this.

"Now it was this king's custom, when someone had been sentenced to die, to send a herald to stand at the condemned man's door and sound the trumpet that was reserved for such occasions. Evening fell this day, and the king had his herald sound the trumpet at his brother's door. Hearing the sound, the brother despaired of his life, could not sleep that night, and made his last will and testament. In the morning he donned black attire, and went with his wife and children to stand weeping at the palace door. The king had his brother brought in and said to him: 'Foolish fellow, if you are so frightened by your brother's herald when you know you have done him no wrong, how should I not fear the heralds of my God, against whom I have sinned for so long, when they remind me of death more loudly than any trumpet and announce to me the coming of the awesome Judge?'

"This king then ordered the making of four caskets, two of them to be covered with gold on the outside but filled with putrid bones of the dead, the other two to be coated outside with pitch, but filled with precious stones and pearls. Then he summoned the nobles who, he knew, had complained about him to his brother, had the four caskets set up before them, and asked them which caskets were the more valuable. They judged that the golden ones were more valuable, and the other two of little worth. The king ordered the golden caskets opened, and an intolerable stench issued from them. The king said to the nobles: 'Those caskets are like the men who are clad in glorious garments but inwardly are full of the uncleanness of vice.' He had the other caskets opened, and a very pleasant odor came from them. Said the king: 'These are like the very poor men to whom I paid honor. Although they are covered with poor clothes, from within they emanate the perfume of all the virtues, but you pay attention only to what you see on the outside, and give no thought to what is within.' Therefore, prince, according to that king you did well in giving me kind welcome."

Barlaam then launched into a long sermon about the creation of the world, man's fall, the incarnation of the Son of God, his passion and resurrection, treating at length also about the Day of Judgment, the reward of the good, and the punishment of the wicked. He sternly denounced those who served the idols, and illustrated their foolishness by another example, as follows.

"A hunter had caught a small bird called a nightingale and was about to kill it, when a voice was given to the bird, who said: 'What will you gain, O man, by killing me? You will not be able to fill your belly by eating me! But if you release me, I will give you three bits of advice that, if you adhere to them carefully, will be very helpful to you!' Astonished at hearing what the bird had to say, the hunter promised that he would set her free if she gave him this advice. The nightingale responded: 'One, never bother trying to get possession of a thing that is completely beyond your grasp; two, never grieve over losing a thing that cannot be recovered; three, never believe the unbelievable. Observe these three rules and it will be well with you.'

"The hunter set the nightingale free as he had promised, and as she fluttered about in the air, she said to him: 'Worse luck to you, man! You took bad advice and you've lost a great treasure today, because I have in my belly a pearl larger than an ostrich egg!' The man regretted exceedingly that he had released the bird and tried to recapture her, saying: 'Come into my house! I will show you every kindness and then release you honorably!' The nightingale: 'Now I know for certain that you are a fool, because you have followed not one of the three things I told you. You are grieving about losing me irretrievably; you are trying to catch me though you cannot follow my path; and on top of that you believed that I had so large a pearl inside me, when the whole of me would not match the size of an ostrich egg!' So those who trust in idols are fools, because they adore things that their own hands have shaped, and give the name of guardian to things they themselves must guard!"

Barlaam went on to inveigh against the deceptive pleasures and vanities of the world, adducing many examples to prove his point. He said: "Those who yearn for pleasures of the body and allow their souls to die of hunger are like the man who fled from a unicorn that he feared would devour him, and fell into a deep abyss; but as he fell he caught hold of a small bush and set his feet on a slippery, shaky ledge. Looking around, he saw two mice, one white and one black, gnawing at the root of the bush he had hold of, which would very soon be chewed through. At the bottom of the abyss he saw an awful dragon breathing fire, the monster's jaws gaping with the desire to devour him. On the ledge on which his feet had a perch, he saw the heads of four vipers protruding. Then he looked up and caught sight of drops of honey oozing from the branches of his bush; and, oblivious of the dangers that besieged him on all sides, he gave himself entirely to enjoying the sweetness of that little bit of honey.

"Now the unicorn is a figure of the death that constantly pursues men and seeks to lay hold of them. The abyss is the world, full of all evils. The bush is the life of each man or woman, the life that throughout the hours of the day and the night is being eaten away by a white and a black mouse, and comes closer and closer to being cut off. The ledge with the four vipers is the body made up of four elements; when the elements get out of order, the compound of the body is dissolved. The awful dragon is the mouth of hell, yawning to devour all men. The sweetness of the drops of honey is the deceptive pleasures of the world, by which man is seduced, so that he has little awareness of the danger in which he lives."

Barlaam added another example, saying: "Those who love the world are like the man who had three friends, of whom he loved one more than himself, the second as much as himself, and the third very little if at all. This man found himself in great danger and, being summoned by the king, ran to the first friend to seek his help, reminding him of how much he had always loved him. The friend said: 'Man, I don't even know who you are! I have other friends with whom I am to dally today, and I will continue to possess them as friends. I can let you have two small hair shirts, though, and you can cover yourself with them.' Embarrassed, the man went to the second friend and begged him for help. The friend answered: 'Your troubles are of no concern to me, and I have enough worries of my own. However, I will accompany you as far as the gates of the palace and then come straight back to attend to my own business.'

"The man, now saddened and desperate, went to the third friend. Crestfallen, he said: 'I don't know what to say to you. I have not loved you as I should have, but I'm surrounded by troubles and have lost my friends, and I beg of you to lend me your help and to grant me your pardon.' With a cheerful smile the man answered: 'Believe me, I hold you as a cherished friend and am not unmindful of your kindnesses to me, slight as they may have been. I shall go in ahead of you and intercede for you with the king, lest he hand you over to your enemies.'

"Now the first friend is the possession of riches, for which a man will incur many perils, yet when death, the end, comes, all he gets from his riches is a few poor cloths for his burial. The second friend is composed of wife, children, and parents, who come only as far as the grave and then return home to take care of their own affairs. The third friend is made up of faith, hope, charity, almsgiving, and all the good works that can go in ahead of us when we go out of our bodies, can intercede with God for us, and can free us from hostile demons."

Barlaam added still another example, which went as follows. "In a certain great city there was a custom by which a foreigner, an unknown man, was elected as prince. He was given all power to do whatever he wished, everything was allowed him, he ruled the land without any law to go by. So this man enjoyed every delight and thought that this would go on forever. But it always happened that within a year the citizens rebelled against him, dragged him naked all around the city, and then shipped him off to exile on a remote island, where he found neither food nor clothing and was beset by hunger and cold. One year, as usual, a foreigner was elected, but this man knew all about the citizens' custom. So he sent a great store of treasure ahead to the island, and when, at the end of the year, he was exiled there, he enjoyed limitless pleasures of all kinds, while the other exiles perished from hunger. Now that city is the world, and the citizens are the princes of darkness who entice us with the world's false pleasures. Then, while we seem to be in complete command, death supervenes, and we are plunged into the place of darkness. On the other hand, we can send riches ahead of us to the place of eternal life, by putting them now into the hands of the poor."

The king's son, now fully instructed by Barlaam, wished to leave his father immediately and follow his instructor. "If you do that," Barlaam told him, "you will be like a young man who refused to marry a noblewoman. He ran away and came to a place where he saw a young woman, the daughter of a very poor old man, working hard and singing praise to God. 'What are you doing, woman?' he asked her. 'Poor as you are, you thank God as if you had received great gifts from him.' She replied: 'As a little medicine often cures a grave illness, so thanksgiving for small gifts can become the source of large ones. Moreover, the gifts which are outside of us are not ours, but those that are inside us are ours, and I have received many such gifts from God. He made me to his own image and likeness, he gave me understanding, he called me to his glory and has already opened the gate of his kingdom to me. It is right that I should praise him for so many and such great gifts!'

"The young man saw how wise the maiden was, and asked her father for her hand in marriage. The father: 'You cannot take my daughter in marriage, because you come of rich and noble parentage and I am a poor man.' But the young man insisted, and the old man said: 'I can't give you my daughter and have you carry her off to your father's house. She is all I have!' The answer: 'I will stay with you and live as you live!' He took off his fine clothes and put on some of the old man's rags, stayed with him, and made the girl his wife. After her father had tested him for a long time, he took him into the bridal chamber, showed him a huge mass of treasure, and gave him the lot."

Josaphat said: "I see myself in that story, and I think you were really talking about me. But tell me, father, how old you are and where you live, because I wish never to be separated from you!" Barlaam: "I am forty-five years old and I live in the desert in the land of Sennaar." Josaphat: "Father, you look more like seventy to me!" Barlaam: "If you want to know my age counting from birth, you have figured it correctly, but the years I spent in worldly vanity I do not count as years of my life, because then my inner man was dead, and I count them as years of death, not of life." Josaphat wanted to follow Barlaam back to the desert, but Barlaam said: "If you do this, I will have to give up your company and will bring persecution on my brother monks. Wait for the opportune time, and then you will come to me." Barlaam therefore baptized the king's son, completed his instruction, and kissed him, then went back to his own land.

When the king learned that his son had become a Christian, he was overcome with grief. Then one of his friends, whose name was Arachis, comforted him and said: "O King, I know an aged hermit named Nachor, who shares our religion, and who resembles Barlaam in every detail. We will have this hermit pretend to be Barlaam, and he will begin by defending the Christian faith, but then will allow himself to be bested in argument and will revoke all he has taught, and so the king's son will come back to us." This aforesaid noble, the king's friend, mustered a large army and set out in search, he said, of Barlaam; but he found his hermit and noised it about that he had taken Barlaam. Josaphat, the king's son, heard that his master had been captured and wept bitterly, but afterwards learned by divine revelation that the man captured was not Barlaam.

King Avennir went to Josaphat and said: "My son, you have brought great sadness upon me, you have dishonored my white hairs and taken away the light of my eyes. Why have you done this, my son, and why have you abandoned the worship of my gods?" Josaphat answered: "Father, I fled the darkness and ran to the light, abandoned error and acknowledged the truth. Do not labor in vain, therefore! You will not be able to call me back from Christ. Know that that is impossible, as it is impossible for you to touch the height of heaven with your hand, or to dry up the waters of the deepest sea!" The king said: "Who is it that has brought these ills upon me but I myself, by always treating you more generously than any father ever treated his son? And in return for this, the perversity of your will and your unbridled contentiousness have made you rage against my head. The astrologers were right when they said at your birth that you would be arrogant and disobedient to your parents! But now, unless you do as I bid you, you will give up your claim to be my son. I will no longer be your father but your enemy, and I will do to you what I have never done before, even to my enemies!" Josaphat: "Why, O king, are you saddened because I have become a sharer of good things? What father has ever appeared to regret his son's well-being? Therefore I shall no longer call you father, but, if you turn against me, I shall flee from you as I would from a viper!"

The king, livid with anger, left his son and told his friend Arachis how hard-headed Josaphat was. Arachis advised him not to use harsh words to his son, because bland and friendly speech would have more attraction for him. The next day, therefore, the king went to Josaphat, embraced him, and kissed him, saying: "My dearest son, honor your father's white hairs! Respect your father! Don't you know that it is good to obey your father and make him happy, and bad, on the contrary, to provoke him? Those who provoke their fathers come to a bad end!" Josaphat: "There is a time for loving and a time for obeying, a time for peace and a time for war. We certainly should not obey those who are trying to turn us away from God, even if they are mother or father."

Seeing how determined Josaphat was, the king said: "I see that you persist in disobeying me! Come at least, and let us both believe the same truth! This Barlaam who has misled you is by me held captive. Let our people and your people come and meet Barlaam, and I will send out a herald to persuade the Galileans not to be afraid to come. Then let the argument begin, and if your Barlaam prevails, we will accept your beliefs, but if our people win, you will agree with us!" Josaphat agreed to this proposal, and the king and his men arranged with Nachor, the pseudo-Barlaam, the way the encounter should proceed: Nachor would first pretend to defend the faith of the Christians and then would allow himself to be outdone in debate.

Now the parties convened, and Josaphat said to Nachor: "You know, Barlaam, how you taught me. If you now successfully defend the faith you taught me, I shall hold to it as long as I live, but if you are defeated, I shall avenge my humiliation on you. I'll cut out your heart and your tongue and feed them to the dogs, to dissuade others from presuming to lead the sons of kings into error!" These words made Nachor not only sad but fearful. He saw that he had fallen into the pit he had dug . . . that he was caught in his own trap. After some thought, he decided that in order to escape the threat of death it would be better to be on the side of the king's son, for the king had told him in public to defend his faith fearlessly. Then one of the king's masters rose and said: "Are you Barlaam, who led the king's son astray?" "I am Barlaam," he answered, "but I did not lead the king's son into error, I set him free from error!" The master: "Men of renown, admirable men, have adored our gods. How can you dare to rebel against them?" Nachor: "Chaldeans, Greeks, and Egyptians have been wrong in calling creatures gods. The Chaldeans thought the elements were gods, whereas the elements were created to be useful to men, so the Chaldeans were subject to their domination and were corrupted by many passions. The Greeks think that wicked men are gods—Saturn, for instance, who, they say, ate his sons, and cut off his male parts and threw them into the sea, and from them Venus was born, and Saturn was bound by his son Jupiter and cast into the infernal regions. Jupiter also is described as king of the gods, yet it is said that he was often transformed into various animals in order to commit adultery. They say that Venus too was an adulteress, for at times she had Mars as her lover, at other times, Adonis. The Egyptians worshiped animals, namely, the sheep, the calf, the pig, and suchlike. Christians, on the other hand, worship the Son of the Most High, the Son who came down from heaven and assumed the flesh of man." Nachor went on to defend the beliefs of Christians and to back them up with sound reasoning, so that the pagan masters were dumbfounded and knew no way to answer him.

Josaphat was delighted that the Lord had defended the truth through an enemy of the truth, but the king was furious. He ordered the meeting adjourned, as though these matters would be taken up again the following day. Josaphat said to his father: "Either let my master stay with me tonight so that we can work out the answers we will use tomorrow, and you take your people with you and confer with them, or else you leave your men with me and take my man. Otherwise you would not be doing justice but violence." Thereupon the king left Nachor with his son, still hoping that Nachor would be able to win him over. However, when Josaphat got home, he said to Nachor: "Don't think I don't know who you are. I know you are not Barlaam but Nachor the astrologer!" He began then and preached the way of salvation to Nachor, converted him to the faith, and in the morning sent him off to the desert, where he received baptism and led the life of a hermit.

A sorcerer named Theodas heard what had been going on, and went to the king and promised him that he would make his son return to the laws of his father. Avennir: "If you succeed in this, I will have a gold statue raised to you, and I will offer sacrifice as to the gods!" Theodas: "Remove all his men from around him, and order charming, lavishly dressed women to be with him all the time, waiting on him and pampering him and never leaving him alone; and I will send one of my spirits to him to set the fire of lust aflame in him, because nothing can so surely seduce young men as the faces of women. There was a king," Theodas went on, "who had a newborn son, and learned physicians told him that if within ten years the child saw either the sun or the moon, he would lose his eyesight. The king therefore had a cave cut out of solid rock and had his son kept there for ten years. When that time had passed, the king ordered all kinds of things to be set before the boy, so that he might know their names and all about them. Therefore gold and silver, precious stones, gorgeous garments, royal steeds, and all sorts of things were shown to him, and when he asked the name of each object, the servants indicated the proper word. When the boy asked what was the word for women, the king's swordbearer, as a jest, said they were demons who seduced men. When the king asked his son what he liked best of all that he had seen, he answered: 'What else, father, but those demons

364

who seduce men? Nothing else set my soul on fire the way they did!' So don't think there is any other way than this to outwit your son!"

The king therefore had all Josaphat's attendants ejected, and put lovely ladies into his company to stir up his sexual desires at all times. He had no one else to look at, no one to talk to or eat with. The evil spirit sent by the sorcerer entered into the young man and lighted a furnace of fire inside him. Thus the evil spirit inflamed him internally and the women fanned his ardor externally. The youth, feeling himself beset, was sorely troubled and commended himself wholly to God, whereupon he received consolation from above and all temptation left him.

Now a damsel of great beauty, the daughter of a king but bereft of her royal father, was sent in to Josaphat. The man of God preached to her, and she replied: "If you wish to save me from serving the idols, be joined to me in the bonds of marriage, for Christians do not abhor wedlock, they praise it, because their patriarchs and prophets and their apostle Peter all had wives!" His response was: "Woman, it's useless for you to recite these things to me! Christians are allowed to marry, but not those who have promised Christ to preserve their virginity." She: "If that's the way you want things to be, so be it, but if you wish to save my soul, grant me one tiny petition: lie with me tonight, that's all, and I promise you I will become a Christian! For if, as you say, there is joy before the angels of God over one sinner who repents,[1] is not a great reward due the one who brings about the conversion? Just do what I want this one time, and so you will save me!" Thus she battered heavily upon the tower of his soul.

The demon saw this and said to his fellows: "You see how strongly that lass has shaken this man's resolution, while we haven't been able to shake him at all! Come, then! Let us find the right time and attack him with all our might!" The holy young man sensed how closely he was hemmed in, with concupiscence tugging at him and concern for the salvation of one girl—suggested, of course, by the devil—disturbing him. He burst into tears, and gave himself to prayer. While he was praying, he fell asleep and saw himself being led into a meadow blooming with beautiful flowers, where the leaves of the trees, stirred by mild breezes, gave out a soft whisper and a wondrous odor, where there was fruit lovely to look at and delicious to taste, where seats studded with gold and jewels and couches adorned with priceless coverings were placed here and there, and the clearest of waters flowed by. Then he was brought into a city whose walls were of gleaming gold, and where ethereal hosts sang canticles that the ears of mortals have not heard. Then a voice said to him: "This is the abode of the blessed!" The men who were leading him started to take him away, but he asked them to allow him to stay where he was. They said: "You will come here at the cost of great labors, if indeed your strength holds out!" Then they led him to a

[1] Cf. Luke 15:7, 10.

pitch-black place filled with a foul smell, and a voice said: "This is the abode of the wicked!" When he awoke, the beauty of that maiden and the others seemed to him more fetid than dung.

The evil spirits returned to Theodas, who upbraided them for their failure, and they said: "Before he made the sign of the cross, we assailed him and gave him much trouble, but once he had shielded himself with that sign, he came after us fully armed!" Then Theodas went in with the king to Josaphat, hoping that he might at last persuade him. But the aforesaid sorcerer was captured by the one he wanted to capture, was converted by him, received baptism, and thereafter led a praiseworthy life.

The king, in despair, took the advice of his friends and conferred the half of his kingdom on his son. Josaphat's one desire was to retire to the desert, but he agreed to reign for a time in order to spread the Christian faith, and in his cities he erected churches and crosses and converted all the people to Christ. Even his father finally was convinced by his son's reasoning and adopted the faith of Christ, was baptized, and yielded his whole kingdom to Josaphat. Thereafter he devoted himself to good works and finished his life virtuously.

Josaphat proclaimed that Barachias was to be king, and tried many times to flee, but he was always caught by the people. Finally, however, he did get away. As he went across the desert, he gave his royal trappings to a poor man and kept only the poorest raiment for himself. The devil set many traps for him. Sometimes he rushed at him with drawn sword, threatening to strike him dead unless he desisted; at other times he appeared to him in the form of some wild beast, with gnashing of teeth and hideous howls; but Josaphat said: "The Lord is my helper, I will not fear what man can do to me."[2] Josaphat lived in the desert for two years, wandering about, but unable to find Barlaam. At last, however, he found a cave and, standing at the entrance, said: "Bless me, father, bless me!" Hearing his voice, Barlaam hurried out, and they embraced each other fervently. Josaphat recounted all his experiences to Barlaam, who offered heartfelt thanks to God. Josaphat lived there for many years in marvelous austerity and virtue. Barlaam ended his days in peace about A.D. 380. Josaphat, having abdicated his throne at the age of twenty-five, lived the life of a hermit for thirty-five years, until, adorned with many virtues, he died in peace and was laid to rest beside Barlaam's body. When this news reached King Barachias, he went with a large army and, reverently taking up the two bodies, transferred them to his city. There many miracles have occurred at their tomb.

[2] Ps. 117(118):6.

============ ✳ ============

181. Saint Pelagius, Pope
The History of the Lombards

Pope Pelagius was a very holy man who fulfilled his office in a praiseworthy manner, finally going to his eternal reward full of good works. This Pelagius was the first pope of that name, not the immediate predecessor of Pope Saint Gregory. John III succeeded Pelagius I, Benedict I followed John, then came Pelagius II, then Gregory I.

It was during the reign of Pelagius I that the Longobards, or Lombards, came into Italy; and because many do not know the history of this people, I have decided to insert their story here as Paul, the historian of the Lombards, compiled it and as its details are recorded in various chronicles.

The Lombards were a very prolific German tribe that came from the shores of the northern ocean. From the island of Scandinavia they fought their way circuitously through various lands until they came to Pannonia, where, not daring to go farther, they established what they intended to be their permanent homeland. They were first called Winuli, later Longobardi, the Lombards.

While they were still settled in Germany, their king, Agilmund, found seven baby boys, whom their mother, a prostitute, after bringing them forth in one birth, had thrown into a fish pond to die. The king came upon them by chance and was turning them over with his spear when one of the babies grasped the blade with his hand. Seeing this, Agilmund was astonished and had the infant cared for. He named him Lamissio and predicted a great future for him. Lamissio in fact grew up to be a man of such prowess that the Lombards made him their king when Agilmund died.

About this time, i.e., the year 480 after the Lord's incarnation, an Arian bishop (as Eutropius tells us) was baptizing a man named Barba, and used the formula: "I baptize thee, Barba, in the name of the Father, through the Son, in the Holy Spirit," meaning to show that the Son and the Holy Spirit were inferior to the Father, as the Arians maintained. What happened? The baptismal water instantly vanished, and the candidate for baptism took refuge in the true church.

Saints Medardus and Gildardus flourished at this time. They were uterine brothers born the same day, were consecrated bishops on the same day, and died and were taken up by Christ on the same day.

We read in a certain chronicle that at an earlier date, about 450, when the Arian heresy was spreading through Gaul, the unity of substance of the three persons of the Blessed Trinity was demonstrated by a miracle, as Sigibert records it. The bishop of the city of Bazas was celebrating mass when he saw three limpid drops of water, all of the same size, fall on the altar, flow together, and join to form a most beautiful precious stone. The bishop put the stone into the center of a gold cross, and immediately the other gems fell out. Sigibert adds that this particular jewel looked dull to the wicked but brilliant to the good, and that it gave health to the sick and increased the devotion of all who venerated the cross.

At a later time a strong, willful king of the Lombards, whose name was Alboin, made war on the king of the Gepidae, crushed his army, and killed the king. The son who succeeded to the kingship set out with a strong force to attack Alboin and avenge his father's death, but Alboin led his army against him, won the battle, and killed the son, out of whose skull he made a bowl that he bound with silver and used as a drinking cup. He also captured Rosamond, the king's daughter, and made her his wife.

In those days Justin the Younger ruled the empire. As commander of his armies he appointed Narses, a eunuch and a powerful, valiant man. Narses marched against the Goths, who had overrun all of Italy, conquered them, killed their king, and restored peace throughout the land. These great services won him the bitter enmity of the Romans, who lodged false charges against him, and the emperor dismissed him. Sophia, the emperor's wife, humiliated Narses by making him spin yarn and pluck wool with her maidservants. He responded to this treatment by saying to Sophia: "I will weave such a web around you that you will not be able to break through it as long as you live."

Narses got away to Naples and from there summoned the Lombards, inviting them to abandon the poor soil of Pannonia, and to come and take possession of the fertile land of Italy. When he received this message, Alboin left Pannonia and entered Italy with the Lombards, in the year of our Lord 568.

It was the custom of the men of this tribe to wear very long beards, and we are told that once, when scouts were on their way to spy on them, Alboin ordered the women to let down their hair and gather it around their chins, so that the scouts would think that they too were bearded men. Hence this people were called Longobards (Longbeards), *barda* being the word for beard in their language. Others say that when the Winuli were about to fight the Vandals, they called upon a man who had the spirit of prophecy, asking him to pray for their victory and to bless them. The seer's wife advised them to meet under the window where he was accustomed to pray in the morning facing the East, and to have their women tie their hair under their chins. When the seer opened his window and saw all these people, he exclaimed: "Who are all these Longobards?" His wife had also said that those whom he called by that name would be victorious.

The Lombards ravaged Italy, taking most of its cities and slaughtering the inhabitants. After a three-year siege they captured Pavia, where King Alboin had sworn he would kill all the Christians. But when he was about to enter the city, his horse fell to its knees and could not get to its feet no matter how much the spurs were put to it, until, at a Christian's admonition, the king forswore his oath. Then the Lombards took Milan and in a short time subjugated almost all of Italy except Rome and Romanilia (Romagna), so called as if to say "the other Rome" because it had always been united to Rome.

Once, when he was in Verona, Alboin made a great feast and called for the cup he had fashioned out of the king's skull. Then he had his wife, Rosamond, drink from it, saying: "Drink with your father!" When Rosamond learned what he meant, she conceived a violent hatred for him. One of Alboin's generals had had carnal intercourse with a maidservant of the queen; and one night when the king was absent, Rosamond went into this maid's room and, pretending to be the maid, called the general to come to her. When he came, the queen lay with him and afterwards said: "Do you know who I am?" He said she was his little friend, and the queen answered: "Not at all! I am Rosamond, and this night you have done a deed such that either you will have to kill Alboin or you will die by Alboin's sword. What I want you to do, therefore, is to avenge me on my husband, who killed my father, made a drinking-bowl out of his skull, and made me drink from it."

This the general was unwilling to do but promised to find someone else to handle the business. So the queen took away the king's weapons and fastened his broadsword in its scabbard, which hung at the head of his bed, in such a way that it could not be drawn out. Then, at a time when Alboin was asleep, the murderer tried to get into his bedchamber. Hearing the noise, the king jumped from his bed and reached for his sword, but, being unable to draw it, defended himself manfully with the scabbard. The assailant, however, being well armed, overcame the king and slew him. Then he made off with all the palace treasure and fled to Ravenna (so it is said), taking Rosamond with him. Now the lady set eyes on the very handsome prefect of Ravenna and wanted him for her husband, so she put poison in her lover's wine. He drank, tasted the bitterness, and ordered the woman to drink the remainder. She refused. He drew his saber, forced her to drink, and so the two of them perished.

In time another king of the Lombards, Adalaoth (Authari) by name, adopted the Christian faith and was baptized. Theodelinda, the Lombard queen and a most devout Christian, erected a magnificent church at Monza. It was to this Theodelinda that Pope Gregory addressed his *Dialogues*. She converted her husband, Agilulf, to the faith: he had been duke of Turin and became king of the Lombards. The queen persuaded him to make peace with the Roman Empire and the Church, and on the feast of Saints Gervasius and Protasius peace was established between the Romans and the Lombards. Pope Gregory decreed that the verse *Loquetur Dominus pacem in plebem suam* (The Lord will speak peace unto his people) be sung in the mass of that feast. The peace and the conversion of the Lombards were further confirmed on the feast of the Birth of John the Baptist.

Theodelinda had a special devotion to Saint John, to whose merits she attributed the conversion of her people; and it was revealed to a holy man that this saint was the patron and defender of the Lombard nation.

Pope Gregory died and was succeeded by Sabinian, after whom came Boniface III and Boniface IV. At the latter's request the emperor Phocas donated the Pantheon[1] to the church of Christ about A.D. 610. Phocas had already decreed, at Boniface III's request, that the Roman see was the head of all the churches, because the church at Constantinople was claiming that it was the first among the churches.

It was in the time of Boniface IV, about the year of the Lord 610, when Phocas was dead and Heraclius reigned in his place, that Magumeth (Mahomet, Muhammad), a false prophet and sorcerer, began to lead into error the Agarenes or Ishmaelites, whom we call Saracens. This, as we read in a history of Magumeth and in a certain chronicle, came about in the following way. A very famous cleric, who was angry because he had been unable to obtain the honors he desired in the Roman Curia, took flight to the regions beyond the sea and drew great numbers of followers after him by his deceptions. He met Magumeth and told him that he wished to put him at the head of his people. He then put seeds and the like into Magumeth's ear, and trained a dove to pick them out. The dove became so accustomed to this that whenever it saw Magumeth, it lighted on his shoulder and thrust its beak into his ear. Then the cleric called the people together and told them that he would put over them the man whom the Holy Spirit, in the form of a dove, would point out. He secretly released the dove, which flew straight to Magumeth, perched on his shoulder, and put its beak to his ear. Seeing this, the people thought it was the Holy Spirit descending upon him and bringing him the words of God. In this way Magumeth deluded the Saracens, and under his leadership they invaded the kingdom of the Persians and swept through the eastern empire as far as Alexandria. This at least is the popular story, but the following account is closer to the truth.

Magumeth drew up his own laws, into which he inserted certain things from both the Old and the New Testaments. He lied to the people, telling them that he had received these laws, with their elements from the sacred Scriptures, from the Holy Spirit, in the form of a dove they often saw flying about over his head. The fact was that in earlier years he had plied the trade of a merchant and had traveled through Egypt and Palestine with his camels, dealing with Christians and Jews from whom he learned the Old and New Testaments. That is why the Saracens use the Jewish rite of circumcision and abstain from eating the flesh of pigs. To give a reason for the latter observance, Magumeth said that the pig was spawned from camel dung after the Deluge, and therefore was unclean and not to be eaten by a clean people.

---

[1] As stated in the chapter on All Saints, the Pantheon, originally built by the Romans to honor all their gods, became a Christian church to honor all the martyrs, and eventually all the saints.

The Saracens believe, as do Christians, in one and only one all-powerful God, creator of all things. The false prophet also taught, blending truth with error, that Moses was a great prophet but Christ a greater, the highest of all prophets, born of the virgin Mary by the power of God without the seed of man. He also said in his *Alcoran* (Koran) that when Christ was a child, he created live birds out of the slime of the earth. But then Magumeth mixed in some poison, teaching that Christ had not truly suffered or risen from the dead: it was some other man who looked like Christ who had done this or at least had died.

Then there was a matron named Cadigan (Khadija) who ruled the province of Corocanica. Seeing this man who was accepted and protected by Jews and Saracens alike, she took it that the divine majesty was hidden in him, and, being a widow, she married him. Thus Magumeth became the ruler of that whole province. By his feats of magic he fooled not only the lady in question, but also the Jews and Saracens, so completely that he could publicly proclaim himself to be the Messiah promised in the Law. Thenceforth, however, Magumeth began to suffer frequent epileptic seizures. Seeing this happen, Cadigan was exceedingly sorry that she had married a most unclean man and an epileptic. Wanting to make her feel better, he soothed her with such speeches as this: "I often contemplate the archangel Gabriel as he talks with me, and I cannot bear the brightness of his face, so I grow faint and fall down." And she and the others believed it.

Elsewhere, however, we read that it was a monk named Sergius who instructed Magumeth. Sergius had fallen into the Nestorian heresy and been expelled by the monks, whereupon he went to Arabia and joined company with Magumeth. Still another source tells us that he was an archdeacon in the area of Antioch and was (so they say) a Jacobite: this sect practices circumcision and preaches that Christ was not God but only a righteous and holy man, conceived by the Holy Spirit and born of a virgin. All this the Saracens affirm and believe. In any case it was Sergius who (they say) taught Magumeth much about the Old and New Testaments.

Magumeth's father and mother had died and he spent his childhood years in his uncle's care. For a long time he, like all Arabs, practiced the cult of idols. In his *Alcoran* he testifies that God said to him: "You were an orphan and I adopted you, you long remained in the error of idolatry and I led you out of it, you were poor and I made you rich." The whole Arab people, along with Magumeth, worshiped Venus as their goddess, which explains why the sixth day of the week (*dies Veneris*, the day of Venus) is sacred to them, as the Sabbath is to Jews and the Lord's day to Christians.

Magumeth, enriched by Cadigan's wealth, was so emboldened that he thought of usurping the kingship of the Arabs; but he saw that he could not achieve this by violence, particularly because he was looked down upon by his fellow tribesmen who were taller than he. So he decided to present himself as a prophet, in order to attract by his feigned holiness those whom he could not subjugate by brute strength. In this he was following the advice of the aforementioned Sergius, a very astute man. He kept Sergius out of sight and consulted him on all questions, then passed his answers on to the people as coming from the archangel Gabriel. Thus Magumeth, by pretending to be a prophet, gained control over the entire Arab nation, and they all believed him either willingly or for fear of the sword. This account is more true than what was said about the dove, and is therefore to be accepted.

Sergius then, being a monk, wanted the Saracens to wear the monastic habit, namely, the long outer garment without cowl, and to make many genuflections and pray at regular times, as monks do; and since Jews prayed facing west and Christians facing east, he wanted his people to face south. The Saracens observe all these rules today. Magumeth promulgated many laws dictated to him by Sergius, who took a great part of them from the Mosaic law. Thus the Saracens often bathe themselves, especially as a preparation for prayer: they wash the secret parts, the hands, arms, face, mouth, and all the body's members so as to be clean when they pray. In their prayer they confess one God, who has neither equal nor like, and Magumeth his prophet. They fast for one whole month in the year. For that month they take food at night but not during the day, so that from the hour when they can distinguish black from white until sunset no one dares to eat or drink or soil himself by contact with his wife. Once the sun has set and until dawn the next day, they are allowed food and drink and intimacy with their own wives. The sick and infirm are not bound by the law of fast.

They are commanded to go once a year, as a profession of faith, to the house of God, which is in Mecca, and there to adore God. They must also walk around this house in seamless garments and throw stones through the windows by way of stoning the devil. They hold that Adam built this house and that it was a place of prayer for all his children and for Abraham and Ishmael, until finally Magumeth took it over for himself and all his peoples.

They may eat all meats except pork, blood, and carrion. They may have four legitimate wives at one time, and may repudiate any one of them and take her back again as many as three times, but must never exceed the number of four wives. It is licit for them, however, to have as many concubines or female slaves as they wish, and to sell them when they wish, unless one or the other is pregnant. Their law allows them to take wives from among their own kin so as to increase the offspring of the bloodline and to tighten the bond of friendship among them. When there is a contest over property, the person bringing the action must prove his case by the testimony of witnesses; the defendant must establish his innocence by oath.

A man who is caught with an adulteress is stoned together with her; one who sins with any other woman receives eighty lashes. Magumeth, however, made it known that God had sent him a message with the angel Gabriel, giving him permission to approach other men's wives in order to beget virtuous men and prophets. It happened that one of his servingmen had a beautiful wife, whom he had forbidden to talk with his master. Then one day he found her in conversation with Magumeth and promptly sent her away. The prophet welcomed her and counted her among his other wives; but, fearing that people might murmur about this, he pretended that a paper had been brought to him from heaven, in which it was written that if someone repudiated his wife, she would become the wife of anyone who accepted her. The Saracens observe that as law to this day. A thief is punished the first and second times by being whipped, the third time a hand is cut off, the fourth he loses a foot. Abstinence from wine at all times is prescribed.

To all who observe these and other commandments, God, they declare, has promised paradise, a garden of delights watered with full-flowing streams, in which they will have everlasting dwellings. They will not suffer from cold or heat, will dine on every kind of food, will find instantly before them whatever they may ask for, will be clothed in multicolored silken robes. They will enjoy the company of the most beauteous virgins and will lie down amidst all delights. Angels will stroll about among them acting as cupbearers, carrying gold and silver vessels and serving milk in the gold and wine in the silver, saying: "Eat and drink in gladness!" Magumeth says that in paradise they will have three rivers, of milk, honey, and the best spiced wine, respectively. They will also see most beautiful angels, so large that it is a day's journey from one of their eyes to the other.

For those who believe neither in God nor in Magumeth there will be, they assert, the pain of hell for ever. No matter what sins one may have committed, if on the day of his death he believes in God and Magumeth, the prophet will intervene at the judgment and the sinner, they say, will be saved.

The benighted Saracens affirm that this false prophet had the spirit of prophecy above other men, and that he had ten angels helping and protecting him. They add that before God created heaven and earth, he had the name of Magumeth before his eyes, and that if Magumeth had not been destined to exist, neither heaven nor earth, nor paradise would ever have existed. They also falsely assert regarding him that the moon once came to him, and he took it in his lap and divided it into two parts, then put it together again. Moreover, they say that the poisoned flesh of a lamb was once set before him. The lamb spoke to him, saying: "Beware and do not eat me, because I have poison in me." Yet after many years poison was given to him and he perished.

But now let my pen turn again to the history of the Lombards. This people, though they had accepted the Christian faith, were still a serious threat to the Roman Empire. In time Pepin, the Frankish mayor of the palace, died and was succeeded by his son Charles, who was called Tutides. Charles won many victories and left the mayoralty of the palace to his two sons, Charles and Pepin. Charles, the elder son, left worldly pomp and became a monk at Monte Cassino, and Pepin governed the royal palace with a firm hand. Childeric, the king, was no man for his role as ruler, and Pepin consulted Pope Zachary, asking whether the one who was content to be king in name only should be king at all. The pope responded that the one who was in fact governing the realm and doing it well should indeed be called king. Encouraged by this response, the Franks shut Childeric up in a monastery and made Pepin their king, about A.D. 740.

Meanwhile Aistulf, king of the Lombards, had stripped the Roman church of its rule over many of its territories, and Pope Stephen, who had succeeded Zachary, traveled to France to seek King Pepin's aid against the Lombards. Pepin marshaled a large army and marched into Italy, where he besieged Aistulf, from whom he received forty hostages as warranty that he would restore to the Roman church all the lands he had usurped, and would trouble the church no more. When Pepin withdrew, however, Aistulf annulled all his promises; but a short time later he died suddenly while hunting and was succeeded by Desiderius.

Earlier than all this, Theodoric, king of the Goths, who was tainted with the Arian heresy, ruled over Italy by command of the emperor. The philosopher Boethius, a patrician of consular rank, and his son-in-law Symmachus, also a patrician, brought glory to the republic and defended the authority of the Roman senate against Theodoric. Theodoric exiled Boethius and imprisoned him in Pavia, where he wrote his book *The Consolation of Philosophy* and was finally executed. His wife, Elpes by name, is said to have written the hymn in honor of the apostles Peter and Paul that begins *Felix per omnes festum mundi cardines*. She also composed her own epitaph, which reads:

> Elpes dicta fui, Siciliae regionis alumna,
> Quam procul a patria conjugis egit amor;
> Porticibus sacris jam nunc peregrina quiesco,
> Judicis aeterni testificata thronum,

which means: I was called Elpes, native of the region of Sicily, / whom love of my husband carried far from my homeland; / Now a pilgrim I rest before the sacred portals, / having borne witness at the throne of the eternal judge.

Theodoric came to a sudden end, and a holy hermit had a vision in which he saw Pope John and Symmachus, both of whom Theodoric had put to death, plunging him into Vulcan's furnace naked and unshod. Gregory tells about this in his *Dialogues*.

A certain chronicle has it that about A.D. 677 Dagobert, king of the Franks, who reigned long before Pepin, from childhood on held Saint Denis in great veneration and, whenever he feared the wrath of his father Lothar, took refuge in the saint's church. The king died, and a holy man, in a vision, saw his soul brought up for judgment, and many saints accusing him of having robbed their churches. The wicked angels were ready to snatch him away and cast him into hell, but the blessed Denis came forward, and by his intervention the king was freed and escaped punishment. It may be that his soul returned to his body and there did penance. King Clovis irreverently uncovered the body of Saint Denis, broke a bone from his arm, and greedily made off with it: he lost his mind shortly thereafter.

About A.D. 687 the Venerable Bede, priest and monk, shone in England. Although Bede is included in the catalog of the saints, he is called Venerable by the church, and this for two reasons. The first is that when his eyesight was failing due to his extreme age, he is said to have had a guide who led him to towns and villages where he preached the word of God. And once, when they were passing through a valley that was filled with large stones, his disciple, to have fun with him, told him that a great throng was gathered there, silently and eagerly waiting to hear him preach. He therefore preached fervently, and when he came to the conclusion *through all the ages of ages*, the stones, they say, broke out in a loud "*Amen, venerable father!*" So, because the stones miraculously hailed him as venerable, he was known thereafter by that title. Or, as others say, it was the angels who responded: "Venerable father, you have spoken well!" The second reason is that after Bede's death, a clerk who was much devoted to him was working on a verse that he wanted to have inscribed on the saint's tomb. The couplet began: *Hac sunt in fossa*, and for the second line he wrote: *Bedae sancti ossa*, but that did not fit the rhythm of the verse, and the clerk gave a great deal of thought to the problem without finding a suitable solution. Then, after a whole night spent in searching for the right ending, he hastened to the grave and found that angelic hands had carved the inscription, which ran:

Hac sunt in fossa
Bedae venerabilis ossa,

which means, In this grave lie the bones of the venerable Bede.

When the hour of Bede's death approached, on the feast of the Ascension of the Lord, he had himself carried before the altar and there devoutly recited the antiphon *Amen, O Rex gloriae virtutum*. When he had finished it, he breathed his last in peace, and so sweet a perfume pervaded the place that all thought they were in paradise. His body is venerated with fitting devotion in Genoa.

In this same period, around A.D. 700, Racord, king of the Frisians, was about to be baptized. He dipped one foot into the basin but held back the other, asking whether the greater number of his ancestors were in heaven or in hell. Hearing that most of them were in hell he stepped away from the font, saying: "It is more holy to follow the many than the few!" Being thus deluded by the devil, who promised that on the third day thereafter he would give him gifts beyond compare, suddenly on the fourth day he died the eternal death.

It is related that in the Italian Campagna wheat, barley, and beans fell from heaven like rain.

About the year of the Lord 740 the body of Saint Benedict had been translated to the monastery at Fleury and the body of his sister Saint Scholastica to Le Mans. Charles, a monk of Monte Cassino, wanted to bring Saint Benedict's remains back to Cassino, but this move was prevented by miraculous signs from God and by the objections of the Franks.

About this same year 740 there was a tremendous earthquake, which destroyed some cities and moved some others over six miles to outlying lowlands, so we are told.

The body of Saint Petronilla, the daughter of the apostle Peter, was transferred at this time. On her marble tomb there was an inscription written by Saint Peter's own hand, which read: *Aureae Petronillae dilectissimae filiae* (to golden Petronilla, my most beloved daughter). Sigibert records this.

In these years the Syrians invaded Armenia. In earlier times this country had been swept by a plague, and the people, at the urging of Christians, had shaved off their hair in the shape of a cross. Through this sign their health had been restored, and they continued from then on to shave their heads in this fashion.

Pepin the Short, after many conquests, died in 768, and Charles the Great (Charlemagne) succeeded to the throne of the Franks. In his time Pope Hadrian ruled over the see of Rome, and he sent envoys to Charles to seek his help against Desiderius, king of the Lombards, who, like his father Aistulf, was harassing the church. Obediently Charles mustered a large army and came into Italy over the Mont Cenis pass. He laid siege to the royal city of Pavia, took Desiderius prisoner with his wife, his sons, and the princes, sent them into exile in Gaul, and restored to the church all the rights that the Lombards had taken away. In Charlemagne's army there were two stalwart soldiers of Christ named Amicus and Amelius, whose marvelous deeds have been recorded. They fell at Mortaria, where Charlemagne conquered the Lombards and the Lombard kingdom came to an end. Thenceforward that people had to accept the king whom the emperors sent to them.

Charlemagne went to Rome, and the pope convened a synod of 154 bishops. At this synod the pope conferred upon Charlemagne the right of choosing the Roman pontiff and of maintaining order around the apostolic see, and defined that before their consecration the archbishops and bishops throughout the various provinces should receive their investiture from Charlmagne. His sons, moreover, were anointed at Rome, Pepin as king of Italy, Louis as king of Aquitania. Alcuin, Charlemagne's mentor, flourished at this time.

Pepin, Charlemagne's son, convicted of conspiracy against his father, was tonsured as a monk.

About the year of the Lord 780, in the time of the empress Irene and her son named Constantine, a man was digging around the long walls of Thrace (as we read in a certain chronicle) and unearthed a stone coffin. When he had cleaned the coffin and removed the lid, he found a man inside and a scroll that read: "Christ will be born of a virgin and I believe in him, and thou, O Sun, wilt see me again in the reign of the emperors Constantine and Irene."

After the death of Pope Hadrian, Leo, a man universally revered, was raised to the Roman see. Hadrian's kinsmen resented Leo's election. While the pope was celebrating the Major Litanies, they stirred up the populace against him, gouged out his eyes, and cut out his tongue; but God miraculously restored his speech and his sight. Leo took refuge with Charlemagne, who returned him to his see and punished the culprits. Thereupon the Romans, backed by the pope, repudiated the rule of the emperor in Constantinople and by unanimous consent awarded imperial honors to Charlemagne, crowned him emperor by the hand of Pope Leo, and hailed him as Caesar and Augustus. After Constantine the Great the emperors had made Constantinople the seat of the empire, because the aforesaid Constantine had relinquished Rome to the vicars of Saint Peter and decreed that Constantinople was his capital. Due to the dignity of the title, the emperors were still called "Roman emperors" until the time when the Roman Empire was transferred to the kings of the Franks. After that the Eastern rulers were called emperors of the Greeks or of Constantinople; the Westerns bore the title of Roman Emperor.

One very strange thing about the great emperor Charlemagne was that as long as he lived, he would not allow any of his daughters to marry: he said that he could not bear being deprived of their companionship. As his mentor Alcuin wrote about him, he had a happy life in everything else, but in this he felt the malignity of adverse fortune—the writer thus making clear what he meant to say about this matter. Yet the emperor pretended not to be aware that any suspicion was aroused by the situation (though there was a great deal of talk about it), and always had his daughters with him wherever he went.

In Charlemagne's time the Ambrosian office was almost entirely set aside and the Gregorian office was solemnly promulgated, the emperor's authority greatly aiding this change. Augustine tells us in his *Confessions* that Ambrose, at a time when he was harassed by the plots of the Arian empress Justina and was shut up inside his church with his Catholic people, instituted the singing of hymns and Psalms in the Eastern manner, to protect the faithful from weakening with weariness and distress. Later this chant was adopted by all the churches; but Gregory made many changes, additions, and deletions. Obviously the holy fathers could not see immediately to all that pertained to the beauty of the offices, and different fathers gave their attention to different parts. For instance, there have been three ways of beginning the mass. In early times it was opened with a reading from Scripture, as is still done on Holy Saturday. Then Pope Celestine instituted the singing of Psalms to start the mass, and Gregory ordered the chanting of the introit, retaining only one verse of the Psalm that previously had been sung in its entirety. Moreover, in former times the whole congregation stood around the altar forming a crown, as it were, and sang the Psalms together, whence the part of the church near the altar is called the choir. Then Flavian and Theodore determined that the Psalms should be sung antiphonally; they had this manner of singing from Ignatius, who had learned it by a revelation from God. Jerome arranged the Psalms, epistles, gospels, and the greater part of the day and night offices excepting the chant, and Ambrose, Gelasius, and Gregory added the orations and the chant, fitting them in with the lessons and gospels. Ambrose, Gelasius, and Gregory determined that the graduals, tracts, and alleluias should be sung at the mass. The words *laudamus te* and what follows them were added to the *Gloria in excelsis Deo* by Hilary, or, according to other authors, by Pope Symmachus or Pope Telesphorus. Notker, abbot of Saint Gall, was the first to compose sequences in place of the neumes of the *Alleluia*, and Pope Nicholas permitted the singing of these sequences in the mass. Hermannus Contractus of Reichenau composed the *Rex omnipotens*, the *Sancti Spiritus adsit nobis gratia*, the *Ave Maria*, and the antiphons *Alma Redemptoris Mater* and *Simon Barjona*. Bishop Peter of Compostella composed the *Salve Regina*. However, Sigibert says that the sequence *Sancti Spiritus adsit nobis gratia* was composed by Robert, king of the Franks.

According to Archbishop Turpin's description, Charlemagne had a fine figure and a fierce look in his eye. He was eight feet tall, his face was a palm and a half long and his beard a palm, his forehead a foot high. He could split an armored, mounted knight and his horse in half with one blow of his sword, and could take four horseshoes in his hands and easily bend them straight. With one hand he could quickly lift a soldier standing erect from the ground to the height of his head. He ate a whole hare, or two hens, or a goose for his dinner, but took only a little wine mixed with water; in fact he always drank so sparingly that two or three draughts usually sufficed him at a meal. He built many monasteries in the course of his praiseworthy life; and when he died, he made Christ the heir of all he had.

His son Louis (I), a most clement man, succeeded to the empire about the year A.D. 815. During his reign bishops and clergy put off their cinctures woven with gold, their fastidious dress, and other worldly trappings. False charges against Theodulf, bishop of Orleans, were made to the emperor, who put him under arrest at Angers. On Palm Sunday (as we read in a chronicle), a procession was passing the house where Theodulf was confined. He opened a window and, as the throng outside fell silent, sang the beautiful verses he had written, which began: *Gloria laus et honor tibi sit, rex Christe redemptor.* Louis was in the procession and was so pleased with what he heard that he set the bishop free and put him back in his see. Legates from Emperor Michael of Constantinople delivered, among other gifts, Dionysius's book *On the Hierarchy*, translated from the Greek into Latin, to Louis, who accepted it with joy; and that very night nineteen sick people were cured in the saint's church.

Upon Louis's death Lothar (I) succeeded as emperor, but his brothers, Charles and Louis, made war upon him, and the carnage on both sides was such as had not been seen in the kingdom of the Franks within the memory of man. In the end a treaty was drawn up by which Charles became king of France, Louis of Germany, and Lothar, retaining the imperial title, of Italy and that part of France which was called Lotharingia (Lorraine) after him. Lothar later left the empire to his son Louis (II) and took the monastic habit.

In Lothar's time Sergius, a native of Rome, was pope. His name had been Swinemouth, but he changed it to Sergius. From then on it was ordered that every pope should take a new name, not only because the Lord had changed the names of those whom he chose as apostles, but also because as the popes change their names, so they should change in perfection of life; and moreover, no one who is raised to so high a dignity should have to be ashamed of an undignified name.

We read in a chronicle that in the days of this Louis (II), namely, about A.D. 856, a wicked spirit infested a parish in Mainz, beat upon the walls of houses as with a hammer, filled the air with shouting, sowed discord, and beleaguered the people to the point that any house it entered promptly burned to the ground. The priests chanted litanies and sprinkled holy water around, but the Enemy threw stones at them and bloodied more than one. Finally the demon quieted down and admitted that when holy water was sprinkled, he hid under the cape of a certain priest who was like a servant to him, and whom he accused of having sinned with the daughter of the local governor.

At this time the king of the Bulgars was converted to the true faith with his entire nation, and he attained such perfection of life that he appointed his eldest son to the kingship and took the habit of a monk. But his son, behaving like a juvenile, decided to return to pagan worship, whereupon the king took arms again, pursued and captured his son, gouged out his eyes, locked him up in a prison, and established his younger son as king. Then he resumed the sacred habit.

It is said that in Brescia, Italy, blood rained from heaven for three days and three nights. At the same time hordes of locusts appeared in Gaul: they had six wings, six feet, and two teeth harder than stone, and they flew in swarms like an army's front line, advancing four or five miles a day and stripping trees and plants of all leafage. At length they reached the sea of Britain and the wind blew them into the water and drowned them, but the ocean's tides tossed them back on the shore and their rotting polluted the air. This caused a great plague and a famine, and about a third of the population perished.

In the year of the Lord 938, Otto I became emperor. On the solemn day of Easter Otto set up a festive banquet for the princes. Before they were seated, the son of one prince took a dish from the table, as a child might do, and a waiter felled him with a club. The boy's tutor, seeing what had happened, killed the waiter on the spot. The emperor was about to condemn him without a trial, but the tutor threw the emperor to the ground and began to throttle him. When Otto had been snatched from his grasp, he ordered the man to be spared, loudly declaring that he himself was to blame because he had failed to pay due respect to the holy day. So he allowed the tutor to go free.

Otto II succeeded Otto I. Since the Italians often disturbed the peace, he went to Rome and made a great feast on the terrace of the church for all the nobles, magnates, and prelates. While they were enjoying the meal, he had

379

armed men quietly surround them, and then expressed his displeasure concerning breaches of the peace. He had the list of the persons responsible read off, and had them beheaded then and there. Then he compelled the others to go on with the feaSaint

In the year of the Lord 984 Otto III, surnamed the Wonder of the World, succeeded Otto II. According to one chronicle his wife wanted to prostitute herself to a certain count. When the count refused to perpetrate so gross a crime, the woman spitefully denounced him to the emperor, who had him beheaded without a hearing. Before he was executed, the count prayed his wife to undergo the ordeal of the red–hot iron after his death, and thus to prove his innocence. Came the day when the emperor declared that he was about to render justice to widows and orphans, and the count's widow was present, carrying her husband's head in her arms. She asked the ruler what death anyone who killed a man unjustly was worthy of. He answered that such a one deserved to lose his head. She responded: "You are that man! You believed your wife's accusation and ordered my husband to be put to death. Now, so that you may be sure that I am speaking the truth, I shall prove it by enduring the ordeal of the burning iron." Seeing this done the emperor was overwhelmed and surrendered himself to the woman to be punished. The prelates and princes intervened, however, and the widow agreed to delays of ten, eight, seven, and six days successively. Then the emperor, having examined the case and discovered the truth, condemned his wife to death by fire, and as a ransom for himself gave the widow four burgs, naming them Ten, Eight, Seven, and Six after the above-mentioned delays.

After Otto III came the blessed Henry (II), duke of Bavaria, who succeeded to the empire in A.D. 1002. Henry gave his sister, whose name was Gala, as wife to King Stephen of Hungary, who was still a pagan, thus bringing about the conversion of the king and his entire people to the Christian faith. This Stephen was so deeply religious that God glorified him with many miracles. Henry and his wife Cunegund remained virgins, living a celibate life until they fell asleep in the Lord.

The next emperor was Conrad (II), duke of Franconia, who married the niece of Saint Henry. In his time a fiery meteor of wondrous size was seen in the heavens, crossing the sun at sunset and falling to earth. Conrad imprisoned several Italian bishops and, because the archbishop of Milan made his escape, set fire to the outlying section of that city. On Pentecost Sunday, while the emperor was being crowned in a small church outside the city, such a violent storm of thunder and lightning broke out during the mass that some of those present went mad and others died of fright. Bishop Bruno, who celebrated the mass, and others including the bishop's secretary, said that as the mass was proceeding, they saw Saint Ambrose threatening the emperor.

In Conrad's time, about A.D. 1025, Count Leopold, fearing the king's wrath, fled with his wife to an island and hid in a hut in the forest. One day Conrad was hunting in the forest and at nightfall took shelter in this same hut. The countess, who was pregnant and close to childbirth, made him as comfortable as she could and ministered to his needs. That very night the lady gave birth to a son, and the king heard a voice three times, saying: "Conrad, this newborn child will be your son-in-law." In the morning Conrad summoned two squires who were his confidants and told them: "Go and take this infant by force from his mother's arms, split him down the middle, and bring me his heart!" They sped on their errand and snatched the child from his mother's breast; but, moved to compassion by his beauty, they spared his life and placed him at the top of a tree to save him from being devoured by wild beasts. Then they cut open a hare and delivered the heart to the emperor.

That same day a certain duke passed that way and, hearing the child's wailing, had him brought down to him; and since he had no son, he took the infant to his wife and they raised him as their own son and named him Henry. When he was grown up, he was physically handsome, spoke eloquently, and won everyone's favor. The emperor, seeing how fair and prudent the youth was, asked the father to grant him his son, and the young man came to dwell at court; but then Conrad, aware that Henry was favored and commended by all, began to suspect that he might be the child that he had ordered killed and was destined to succeed him. He wanted to be sure that this would not happen, so with his own hand he wrote a letter to his wife and sent it to her with young Henry. The letter read: "As your life is dear to you, as soon as you receive this letter, have the bearer killed."

On his way to carry out his errand the youth stopped to rest in a church and fell asleep on a bench on which he hung the pouch containing the letter. A priest, being curious, opened the pouch and read the letter without breaking the seal. Shocked at the proposed crime, he carefully erased the words "have the bearer killed," and wrote in, "wed our daughter to this man." The queen saw the seal on the letter and recognized the emperor's handwriting, so she convoked the princes, celebrated the nuptials, and gave the daughter to be Henry's wife. The wedding took place at Aix-la-Chapelle. Conrad was stunned when he heard that his daughter was duly married, and by questioning the squires, the duke, and the priest, learned the whole truth of the matter. There was no longer any sense in resisting God's will, so he sent for the young man, approved him as his son-in-law, and decreed that he should reign after him. At the place where the child Henry was born, a noble monastery was built and to this day is called Ursania (Hirschau).

This Henry dismissed all the jesters from his court, and the money previously given to them was allotted to the poor. In Henry's reign there was a schism in the church and three popes were elected. Then a priest named Gratian gave large sums of money to them, they yielded their claims, and Gratian obtained the papacy. Henry proceeded to Rome to put an end to the schism, and Gratian met him and offered him a gold crown to win his favor; but the emperor, concealing his plan, called a synod, convicted Gratian of simony, and put another pope in his place. However, in a book which Bonizo sent to Countess Matilda, it is said that after Gratian, misled by his own simplicity, had bought the pontificate to put an end to the schism, he acknowledged his error and, at the emperor's urging, abdicated his office.

Henry III was the next emperor. In his time Bruno was elected pope and took the name Leo (IX). On his way to Rome to take possession of the apostolic see, he heard the voices of angels singing: *Dicit dominus, ego cogito cogitationes pacis et non afflictionis* (The Lord says, I think the thoughts of peace and not of affliction). He composed chants in honor of many saints. At this time the peace of the Church was disturbed by Berengarius, who held that the body and blood of Christ were not really, but only figuratively, present on the altar. Lanfranc, a native of Pavia and prior of Le Bec, who was the teacher of Anselm of Canterbury, wrote effectively against Berengarius.

Henry IV became emperor in A.D. 1057. In his time Lanfranc reached the height of his fame. Anselm came from Burgundy to benefit by his distinguished teaching. In subsequent years Anselm was known for his virtue and wisdom and succeeded Lanfranc as prior of the monastery at Le Bec. At this time Jerusalem, which had been taken by the Saracens, was recovered by the faithful. The bones of Saint Nicholas were translated to the city of Bari. Concerning this saint we read, among other things, that in a certain church named for the Holy Cross and subject to the priory of Saint Mary of Charity, the new office of Saint Nicholas was not yet being sung, and the brothers earnestly implored the prior to allow them to sing it. The prior absolutely refused and said that it was improper to exchange novelties for the old customs; and when the monks insisted, he angrily retorted: "Begone, brothers! You will never get permission from me to sing these new canticles, which sound like minstrels' songs, in my church!" When the saint's feast day came round, the monks somewhat sadly sang the vigil of matins and went to bed. And behold! Nicholas, terrifying to look upon, appeared to the prior, dragged him from his bed by the hair and threw him to the floor. Then he intoned the antiphon *O pastor aeterne*, beating time to each word with repeated hard blows to the prior's back, laid on with the whip he held in his hand; and in this manner he slowly and in good order sang the antiphon through to the end. The prior, whose cries had awakened the whole community, was carried half dead to his bed. He finally recovered sufficiently to say: "Go, and from now on sing the new legend of Saint Nicholas."

About this time twenty-one monks from the monastery of Molesmes, led by their abbot Robert, sought solitude at Citeaux and, in order to follow a stricter observance of their rule, founded there a new order (Cistercian).

Hildebrand, the prior of Cluny, became pope and took the name of Gregory (VII). While he was still in minor orders, Hildebrand was sent as a legate to Lyons, where he by a miracle convicted the archbishop of Embrun of simony. The archbishop had bribed all his accusers and so could not be convicted, but the legate commanded him to say *Gloria patri et filio et spiritui sancto*. He quickly said *Gloria patri et filio*, but could not say *spiritui sancto* because he had sinned against the Holy Spirit. He confessed his sin and was deposed, and immediately pronounced the name of the Holy Spirit in a loud voice. Bonizo relates this miracle in the book he addressed to the countess Matilda.

When Henry IV died and was buried at Speyer with the other kings, this verse was inscribed on his tomb: *Filius hic, pater hic, avus hic, proavus jacet istic* (the son [lies] here, the father here, the grandfather here, the great-grandfather lies elsewhere). He was succeeded by Henry V in A.D. 1107. This Henry seized the pope and the cardinals, and released them only upon receiving the right of investiture with ring and crosier. During his reign Bernard and his brothers entered the monastery of Clairvaux. In a parish in Liège a sow farrowed a piglet with the face of a man. A hen hatched a four-footed chick.

Lothar (III) succeeded Henry. In his time a woman in Spain brought forth a monster with two bodies joined together, the faces being turned in opposite directions; frontally it was the figure of a man complete with his body and limbs; but its back had the face, body, and limbs of a dog.

The next emperor was Conrad (III), who succeeded in A.D. 1138. In his time Hugh of Saint Victor died, a doctor preeminent in all knowledge and devout in religion. Of him it is told that when he was mortally ill and could not retain any food, he nonetheless pleaded to be given the Body of the Lord. Then the brothers, wishing to calm his uneasiness, brought him an unconsecrated host instead of the Lord's body. Recognizing this by the Spirit, he said: "May the Lord have mercy on you, brothers! Why are you trying to deceive me? What you have brought me is not my Lord!" Astonished, they ran and came back with the sacrament, but he, seeing that he was unable to receive it, raised his hands to heaven and prayed as follows: "May the son ascend to the Father, and my spirit to the God who created it." With these words he breathed forth his soul, and the Body of the Lord disappeared at the same moment. Eugenius the abbot of Saint Anastasius was installed as pope but was driven from the city because the senate had appointed someone else. He went to Gaul, sending Saint Bernard ahead of him, and Bernard preached the way of the Lord and wrought many miracles. Gilbert de la Porrée flourished at this time.

Frederick (I), Conrad's nephew, succeeded him in A.D. 1154. Master Peter Lombard, bishop of Paris, was active in these years. He compiled the *Book of Sentences* and a *Gloss* on the Psalms and Paul's Epistles. Three moons were seen in the sky with a cross in the middle, and shortly afterward three suns were seen.

Alexander (III) was then canonically elected as pope but was opposed by Octavian John of Crema, whose titular church was Saint Callistus, and John of Struma, who were successively elected antipopes and were supported by the emperor. The schism lasted eighteen years, during which time the Germans, who were based at Tusculum to stand by the emperor, attacked the Romans at Monte Porto and slew so many of them between the hours of nones and vespers that never before had so many Romans been killed, though in Hannibal's time so many met death that he shipped to Carthage three coffers filled with rings taken, at his orders, from the fingers of fallen nobles. Many of those killed at Monte Porto were buried in the churches of Saint Stephen and Saint Laurence, and their epitaph read: *mille decem decies sex decies quoque seni*. Emperor Frederick, on a tour of the Holy Land, was bathing in a river and drowned; or, as others tell it, he spurred his horse into the river, the horse fell, and the emperor perished.

Frederick was succeeded by his son Henry (VI) in 1190. In those days there were downpours of rain with thunder and lightning and high winds, storms so boisterous that the oldest men alive could not remember the like. Along with the rain fell squared stones the size of eggs, destroying trees, vines, and crops and killing many people. Crows and great flocks of birds were seen flying through these storms, carrying live coals in their beaks and setting houses afire.

Emperor Henry always dealt tyrannically with the Church of Rome. When he died, therefore, Pope Innocent III opposed the succession of Henry's son Philip, supported Otto, son of the duke of Saxony, and had him crowned king of Germany at Aix-la-Chapelle. Many French barons went overseas to free the Holy Land. They conquered Constantinople. At this time the Orders of Friars Preachers and Friars Minor arose. Innocent sent legates to King Philip of France to get him to invade the Albigensian area in the South and destroy the heretics. Philip took them captive and had them burned at the stake. Finally Innocent crowned Otto (IV) emperor, exacting an oath that he would safeguard the rights of the church. Otto violated his oath the very day he took it, and ordered the pillaging of pilgrims on their way to Rome: the pope excommunicated him and deposed him from the empire. Saint Elizabeth, daughter of the king of Hungary and wife of the landgrave of Thuringia, lived at this time. It is recorded that among a great number of miracles she raised many, namely, sixteen, dead to life and gave sight to a person born blind. It is said that an oil still flows from her body.

After Otto was deposed, Henry's son Frederick (II) was elected emperor and crowned by Pope Honorius (III). He issued very good laws in favor of the church's freedoms and against heretics. He enjoyed an abundance both of riches and of glory, but pride led him to make bad use of his gifts. He turned tyrant against the church, imprisoning two cardinals and making captives of the prelates whom Gregory IX had summoned to a council. The pope therefore excommunicated him. Finally Gregory, crushed by a multitude of tribulations, died, and Innocent IV, a Genoese by birth, convoked a council at Lyons and deposed the emperor. Frederick has since died, and the imperial throne is vacant to this day.

182. The Dedication of a Church

The dedication of a church is celebrated by the Church among the other feast days of the year; and since a church or temple is not only a material thing but a spiritual one, we must here briefly treat of the dedication of this twofold temple. With regard to the dedication of the material temple, three things are to be seen, namely, why it is dedicated or consecrated, how it is consecrated, and by whom it is profaned. And since in the church two things are consecrated, namely, the altar and the temple itself, we must first see why the altar is consecrated, and, secondly, consider the temple.

The altar is consecrated for three purposes. The first is the offering of the sacrament of the Lord, as we read in Genesis (8): "Noe built an altar to the Lord, and taking of all cattle and fowls that were clean, offered holocausts upon the altar." This sacrament is the Body and Blood of Christ, which we offer in memory of his passion, as he himself commanded, saying: "Do this for a commemoration of me." Indeed, we have a threefold memorial of the Lord's passion. The first is in writing, i.e., depicted in the images of the passion of Christ, and this is directed to the eye. Thus the crucifix and the other images in the church are intended to awaken our memories and our devotion, and as a means of instruction; they are the laypeople's book. The second memorial is the spoken word, namely, the preaching of the passion of Christ, and this is addressed to the ear. The third is in the sacrament, which so signally expresses the passion, since it really contains and offers to us the Body and Blood of Christ; and this memorial is directed to the sense of taste. Hence if the depiction of Christ's passion inflames our love strongly and its preaching more strongly, we should be moved more strongly still by this sacrament, which expresses it so clearly.

The second purpose for which the altar is consecrated is the invocation of the Lord's name, as we read in Genesis (12): "Abraham built there an altar to the Lord, who had appeared to him, and called upon his name." The Lord's name is to be invoked, according to the apostle in 1 Timothy 2, either by supplications, which are entreaties for the removal of evils, or by intercessions, which are offered for blessings to be obtained, or by thanksgivings, which are made for the keeping of goods already possessed.

The invocation that is performed on the altar is properly called the mass, *missa* in Latin, which means a sending, because Christ is sent by the Father from heaven and consecrates the host, and is sent by us to the Father to intercede for us. So Hugh says: "The sacred host itself may be called the mass, *missa*, because it is transmitted, first by the Father through the incarnation, and then by us to the

Father, through the passion." Likewise, in this sacrament Christ first is sent to us by the Father by sanctification, through which he begins to be with us, and then by us to the Father in the oblation, by which he intercedes for us.

We may note here that the mass is sung in three languages, Greek, Hebrew, and Latin, to represent the title of the Lord's passion, which was written in these three languages, and also to signify that every tongue should give praise to God, the three languages standing for every tongue. Hence the gospels, epistles, prayers, and chants are in Latin; the *Kyrie eleison* and *Christe eleison* in Greek, and these are repeated nine times to signify that we are to enter the company of the nine orders of angels; and *amen, alleluia, sabaoth,* and *hosanna* are Hebrew words.

Thirdly, the altar is consecrated for the singing of the chant, as is indicated in Ecclesiasticus (47:10–11): "He gave him power against his enemies; and he set singers before the altar, and by their voices he made sweet melody." According to Hugh of Saint Victor, this melody is of three kinds, for there are three kinds of musical sounds, namely, those that are produced by striking, by blowing, and by singing. The first pertains to stringed instruments, the second to the organ, and the third to the voice. This harmony of sound may be applied not only to the offices of the church, but to the harmony of morals; the work of the hands is compared to the striking or plucking of the strings, the devotion of the mind to the blowing of the organ, and vocal prayer to the singing voice. Hugh goes on to say: "What good is the sweetness of the mouth without the sweetness of the heart? You train your voice, train your will as well; you maintain the concord of voices, maintain also the harmony of virtue, so as to be in accord with your neighbor by example, with the Lord by your will, with your teacher by obedience." Therefore these three kinds of music are related to the threefold differences in the offices of the church, as the *Mitrale* says about the church's office, which consists of Psalms, chant, and readings. The first kind of music, then, is made by the touch of the fingers, as with the psaltery and similar instruments, and to this kind psalmody belongs, as the Psalm (150:3) says: "Praise him with psaltery and harp." The second kind is made by the voice, as in singing or reading; thus the Psalm (32): "Sing to him, with a loud noise." The third kind is made by blowing, and this too is related to song, as the Psalm (150:3) says: "Praise him with the sound of trumpet."

There are five reasons or purposes for the consecration of the church building itself. The first is to drive out the devil and his power. In one of his *Dialogues* Gregory relates that when a certain church, which had belonged to the Arians and had been taken back by the faithful, was consecrated and the relics of Saint Sebastian and Saint Agatha were brought into it, the people gathered there felt a pig running around their feet and heading toward the door; but no one could see the pig, and all were filled with wonder. By this the Lord showed, as was clear to all, that an unclean occupant was leaving the place. The following night a loud noise was heard in the church, as if someone were running around on the roof. The second night this noise was still louder, and on the third it was as terrifying as if the whole building was about to fall in. Then the hubbub ceased, and there was no more evidence of the devil's restlessness; but the terrific uproar he had raised showed how reluctantly he vacated a place he had held for so long. Thus Gregory.

Secondly, the church is consecrated in order that those who take refuge in it may be saved. The lords of the land grant this privilege to some churches after they are consecrated, to protect those fleeing to them from pursuit. So the canon prescribes: "The church shall defend those guilty of murder, lest they lose life or limb." That is why Joab fled into the tabernacle of the Lord and laid hold of the horn of the altar.

The third purpose is that prayers offered in the church be surely heard. Thus we read in 3 Kings 8:30 that Solomon, at the dedication of the Temple, said: "Whoever shall pray in this place hear thou in the place of thy dwelling in heaven, and when thou hast heard, thou shalt be propitious." In our churches, however, we worship facing the East, and this for three reasons, according to John of Damascus, Book IV, chapter 5. First, it is our way of showing that we seek our true country; second, we look toward Christ crucified; third, we demonstrate our waiting for the coming of the Judge. So Damascenus says: "God planted the garden of Eden in the East, and when he sent man into exile God made him live to the west away from paradise. So, seeking and looking toward our ancient homeland and toward God, we worship facing the East. Moreover, the crucified Lord faced toward the west, so we worship looking back to him; and when he ascended, he was borne toward the East, and thus the apostles adored him, and he will come again as they saw him going into heaven. Therefore we too pray to him facing the East, awaiting his coming."

The fourth reason for the consecration of the church is to provide a place where praises may be rendered to God. This is done at the seven canonical hours—matins, prime, terce, sext, nones, vespers, and compline. Of course God should be praised at every hour of the day, but we do not have the strength for that, and so it is prescribed that we praise him especially at these hours, which are privileged above the others in several respects. At midnight, when matins are celebrated, Christ was born, taken captive, and mocked by the Jews. At that hour also he harrowed hell, for the *Mitral Office* says that in the middle of the night, using the term broadly, he harrowed hell; and further, he rose before morning light and appeared at the first hour. Hence Jerome says: "I think that the apostolic tradition has persisted, so that at the Easter vigil the people awaiting the coming of Christ should not be dismissed before midnight. Once that time has passed, it may be presumed safe for them to proceed with the celebration of the feast day." Hence we praise God at midnight in the office of matins in order to thank him for his birth, for allowing his capture, and for setting the fathers free, and to await his coming watchfully. And lauds, the Psalms of praise, are added to matins, because it was in the morning that God drowned the Egyptians in the sea, created the world, and rose from the dead. Hence we sing lauds at that hour, in order not to be submerged with the Egyptians in the sea of this world, and to thank God for our creation and his resurrection.

At prime, the first hour of the day, Christ came most often to the Temple, and the people came early in the morning, hastening to hear him, as we read in Luke 21. He was taken before Pilate as soon as it was light; and at that same hour he appeared first to the women after his resurrection. So at this hour we praise God in the office of prime, in order to imitate Christ, to thank him as he rises and appears, and to give the first fruits of the day to God, the maker and source of all things.

At the third hour Christ was crucified by the tongues of the Jews and was scourged at the pillar by Pilate (and it is said that the pillar to which he was bound still shows traces of his blood). At this hour also the Holy Spirit was sent. At the sixth hour Christ was nailed to the cross and darkness came over the whole earth, so that the sun, mourning the death of its Lord, might be covered with somber weeds and might not give light to those who were crucifying the Lord. Likewise at this hour, on the day of his ascension, he sat down with his apostles. It was at the ninth hour that Christ gave up his spirit and the soldier opened his side, that the apostles usually came together for prayer, and that Christ ascended into heaven. On account of these prerogatives we praise God at these hours.

In the evening the Lord instituted the sacrament of his body and blood at the Last Supper; washed his apostles' feet; was taken down from the cross and laid in the sepulcher; manifested himself to the two disciples in the garb of a pilgrim; and for all this the church gives thanks in the office of vespers. At dark he sweated drops of blood, a guard was posted at his tomb, and there he rested, and after his resurrection he brought the message of peace to his apostles; and for these things we give thanks in the office of compline.

Describing how we should pay this debt of thanksgiving to God, Bernard says: "My brothers, in offering the sacrifice of praise let us join sense to words, affection to sense, joy to affection, gravity to joy, humility to gravity, freedom to humility."

Fifthly, the church is consecrated so that the sacraments may be administered there. Thus the church becomes, as it were, the very hostel of God, where the sacraments are contained and administered. One sacrament is administered and given to those who are just coming in, and this is baptism; one, to those who are going out, and this is extreme unction; and some to those who are staying. Of these latter some are ministers, and to them the sacrament of order is given. Some are fighters, and of the fighters some fall, and to them penance is given, while others hold firm, and confirmation gives them strength and boldness of spirit. To all, food is given to sustain them, and this by the receiving of the eucharist. Lastly, lest some stumble, obstacles are removed by the union of matrimony.

Next we must see how the consecration is done, and firstly, the consecration of the altar. This ceremony comprises several actions. First, four crosses are traced with holy water on the corners or horns of the altar; second, the consecrator walks around it seven times; third, holy water is sprinkled on it seven times with hyssop; fourth, incense is burned upon it; fifth, it is anointed with chrism, and sixth, it is covered with clean cloths. These actions signify the virtues that those who approach the altar ought to have. The first of these is the fourfold charity that comes from the cross, namely, love for God, for themselves, for friends, and for enemies, and these four loves are symbolized by the four crosses traced at the four corners of the altar. Of these four horns of charity it is written in Genesis: "Thou shalt spread abroad to the west, and to the east, and to the north, and to the south." Again, the four crosses signify that Christ, by the cross, brought salvation to the four quarters of the world; or again, that we should bear our Lord's cross in four ways, namely, in the heart by meditation, in the mouth by open profession, in the body by mortification, and on the face by frequently making the sign of the cross.

Second, those who mount the altar should watch over their flocks with care and vigilance, as is signified by walking around the altar seven times; so at this point *Invenerunt me vigiles qui circumeunt civitatem* (The watchmen who go about in the city have found me) is sung, because they should watch with care over their flock. Gilbert counts the negligence of a prelate among things worthy of ridicule, for he says: "A ridiculous thing it is . . . a blind watchman, a lame leader, a negligent prelate, an ignorant teacher, a dumb herald." Or these seven turns around the altar signify seven meditations or considerations concerning Christ's sevenfold humility, which we should often turn over in our minds. This sevenfold virtue consisted first, in that being rich, he was made poor; second, he was laid in a manger; third, he was subject to his parents; fourth, he bowed his head beneath the hand of a slave; fifth, he put up with a thieving, traitorous disciple; sixth, he meekly remained silent before a wicked judge; seventh, he mercifully prayed for those who crucified him. Or the seven circuits signify Christ's seven roads—from heaven to his mother's womb, from the womb to the manger, from the manger to the world, from the world to the cross, from the cross to the tomb, from the tomb to limbo, from limbo rising again to heaven.

Third, those who go to the altar should be mindful of the Lord's passion, which is signified by the sprinkling of water; for the seven aspersions stand for the seven times Christ shed his blood. The first was in the circumcision, the second in the prayer in the garden, the third in the scourging, the fourth in the crowning with thorns, the fifth in the piercing of his hands, the sixth in the nailing of his feet, and the seventh in the opening of his side. These aspersions were done with the hyssop of humility and of inestimable charity, for hyssop is an herb lowly and hot. Or again, the seven aspersions signify that in baptism the seven gifts of the Holy Spirit are given.

Fourth, those who approach the altar should be fervent and devout in prayer, as is symbolized in the burning of incense. Incense has the virtue of mounting upward by the lightness of its smoke, of healing by its properties, of binding by its viscosity, and of giving strength by its aromatic odor. Thus prayer rises to the memory of God, heals the soul of past sins by obtaining pardon, imparts caution to the soul as it faces the future, and strengthens it in the present by obtaining God's protection. Or it can be said that incense signifies devout prayer because it ascends to God, Ecclus. 35:21: "The prayer of him that humbleth himself shall pierce the clouds." It offers a sweet odor to God, Apoc. 5:8 ". . . every one of them having harps and phials full of odors, which are the prayers of saints." Devout prayer proceeds from hearts aflame, Apoc. 8:3: "There was given to him much incense, that he should offer the prayers of all saints," and further on, Apoc. 8:5: "The angel took the censer and filled it with the fire of the altar."

Fifth, ministers of the altar should have the brightness of a clear conscience and the odor of good renown, as is signified by the chrism, which is composed of oil and balsam. They should have a pure conscience, to be able to say with the apostle: "For our glory is this, the testimony of our conscience," and a good name, 1 Tim. 3:7: "He must have a good testimony of them who are without." And Chrysostom says: "The clergy should be without stain in word, in thought, in deed, and in reputation, because they are the beauty and the virtue of the church, and if they are evil, they bring shame upon the whole church."

Sixth, they should have the cleanness of good conduct. This is signified by the clean white cloths with which the altar is covered. Clothing is used to cover, to warm, and to adorn. So good works cover the soul's nakedness, Apoc. 3:18: "May you be clothed in white garments, that the shame of your nakedness may not appear." They adorn the soul with honesty, Rom. 13:12–13: "Let us put on the armor of light, let us walk honestly, as in the day." They warm by lighting the flame of charity, Job 37:17: "Are not thy garments hot?" Little would it avail one who went up to the altar, if he had the supreme dignity but the lowest life. Bernard: "A monstrous thing, highest place and lowest life, topmost step and basest status, grave face and frivolous action, much talk and no results, vast authority and inconstancy of spirit."

Having seen how the altar is consecrated, we must now treat of the manner of consecrating the church building; and in this, too, several actions are included. The bishop first goes round the church three times, and each time, when he comes to the door, he strikes it with his crosier and says: "*Attollite portas principes vestras . . .*" (Lift up your gates, O ye princes, and be ye lifted up, O eternal gates; and the king of glory shall enter in!). The church is sprinkled inside and out with holy water. A cross of ashes and sand is made on the floor from one corner on the eastern side obliquely to the corner on the western side, and within this cross the letters of the Greek and Latin alphabets are inscribed. Crosses are painted on the walls of the church and anointed with chrism, and lights are placed before them.

The triple circuit around the building symbolizes the triple circuit that Christ made for the sanctification of the church; for first he came from heaven to earth, second he descended from earth to limbo, and third he returned from limbo, rose, and ascended to heaven. Or it shows that the church is consecrated in honor of the Blessed Trinity. Or again, it denotes the three states of those who are to be saved from within the church, namely, the virgins, the continent, and the married. These three states are also signified in the arrangement of the church building, as Richard of Saint Victor demonstrates; for the sanctuary denotes the order of the virgins, the choir the order of the continent, and the body of the church the order of the married. The sanctuary is narrower than the choir and the choir narrower than the body of the church, because the virgins are fewer in number than the continent, and these than the married. In like manner the sanctuary is holier than the choir, and the choir than the body of the church. Thus Richard.

The thrice-repeated knocking at the door of the church signifies the threefold right that Christ has in the church, by reason of which the door must be opened to him. The church belongs to him by right of creation, of redemption, and of the promise of glorification. Regarding this, Anselm says: "Certainly, Lord, because you made me, I owe myself wholly to your love; because you redeemed me, I owe myself wholly to your love; because you promise me such great things, I owe myself wholly to your love. Indeed, I owe more than myself to your love, inasmuch as you are greater than I, for whom you gave yourself and to whom you promise yourself."

The triple proclamation, "Lift up your gates, O ye princes," denotes Christ's threefold power, namely, in heaven, on earth, and in hell.

The church is sprinkled inside and out with blessed water for three purposes. The first is to drive out the devil, for the blessed water has the particular power to do this. Hence in the rite of exorcism of water are the words: "Water, be exorcised in order to dispel all the power of the Enemy and to exterminate the devil with his apostate angels." This holy water is made from four ingredients, water, wine, salt, and ash, because there are four principal ways of driving the devil away—the shedding of tears, signified by the water, spiritual joy, by the wine, sage discretion, by the salt, and profound humility, by the ashes.

The second purpose is to purify the church itself. All these earthly substances have been corrupted and defiled by sin, and therefore the place itself is sprinkled with the blessed water so that it may be freed, purged, and cleansed of all foulness and uncleanness. This also explains why under the Old Law almost everything was made clean by water.

The blessed water is used, thirdly, to remove every malediction. From the beginning the earth was accursed with its fruit because its fruit was the means by which man was deceived, but water was not subjected to any malediction. Hence it is that Jesus ate fish, but there is no written, explicit record of his eating meat, except perhaps the paschal lamb because of the Law's command, as an example of sometimes abstaining from food that is permitted and at other times eating it. Therefore, in order to remove all malediction and to bring down God's blessing, the church is asperged with blessed water.

Fourthly, the alphabet is written on the floor, and this represents the joining of the two peoples, the Gentiles and the Jews, or it stands for a page of each Testament, or for the articles of our faith. That alphabet, inscribed within the cross in both Greek and Latin letters, represents the union in faith of the pagan and the Jewish peoples that was wrought by Christ by means of the cross. Therefore the cross is drawn from the eastern corner obliquely to the western corner (in the shape of an X) to signify that he who at first was on the right has gone over to the left, and that he who was at the head has been put at the tail, and vice versa. The alphabet also represents a page of each Testament, since both were fulfilled through the cross of Christ, wherefore he said as he died: "It is consummated."

The cross is drawn obliquely because one Testament is contained in the other, and a wheel was in a wheel: Ezek. 1:16. Thirdly, the alphabet represents the articles of faith, for the pavement of the church is like the foundation of our faith, and the characters written on it are the articles of the faith that are taught in the church to the unlettered and the neophytes of both peoples, who should consider themselves to be dust and ashes, as Abraham said in Gen. 18:27: "I will speak to my Lord, although I am dust and ashes."

Fifthly, crosses are painted on the church walls for three purposes. The first is to frighten the demons, who, having been driven out of the building, see the sign of the cross and are terrified by it, so that they do not dare enter there again. Chrysostom says of this: "Wherever the demons have seen the Lord's sign they take flight, fearing the stick that gave them such a beating." The second purpose is to show forth Christ's triumph, for crosses are his banners and the signs of his victory; so, to make it known that the place is subjugated to Christ's lordship, crosses are painted there. Imperial magnificence is manifested in this way: when a city surrenders, the imperial banner is raised in it. We find a figure of this practice in Gen. 28:18, where we read that Jacob raised the stone that he had laid under his head and set it up for a title, i.e., as a monument of proclamation, of memorial, and of triumph. Thirdly, these crosses represent the apostles: the twelve lights placed in front of the crosses signify the twelve apostles, who brought light to the whole world through faith in Christ crucified. Therefore these crosses are illumined and anointed with chrism, because the apostles, spreading faith in Christ's passion, enlightened the whole world with knowledge, inflamed it with love, and anointed it with cleanness of conscience, which the oil denotes, and with the odor of right living, denoted by the balsam.

We come to the third question: by whom is the church profaned? We learn that the house of God was profaned by three men—Jeroboam, Nabuzardan, and Antiochus. In 3 Kings 12:28–29 we read that Jeroboam fashioned two [golden] calves, setting up one of them in Dan and the other in Bethel, which means the house of God. He did this for motives of greed, fearing that the kingdom might return to Roboam. By this is signified that the avarice of the clergy does much to contaminate the church of God, and avarice reigns among the clergy; Jer. 6:13: "From the least even to the greatest, all are given to covetousness"; and Bernard: "From among the prelates show me one who does not pay more attention to emptying the purses of his subjects than to extirpating their vices." The calves are the little nephews whom they place in Bethel, i.e., in God's house.

The church is also profaned by Jeroboam if a church is built out of avarice, meaning out of the ill-gotten gains of usurers and thieves. We read that when a certain usurer had built a church with the profits of his usury and thefts, he put pressure on the bishop to dedicate it. The bishop and his clergy were performing the rite of consecration when the prelate saw the devil standing behind the altar at the throne, wearing episcopal vestments. The devil said to the bishop: "Why are you consecrating my church? Stop immediately! The jurisdiction of this church belongs to me, because it is built out of usury and rapine." The bishop and the clergy fled in terror, and the devil promptly threw down the church with a loud crash.

Similarly Nabuzardan, as we read in 4 Kings 25:9, burned down the house of the Lord. Nabuzardan was the head cook, and stands for those who are addicted to gluttony and the pleasures of the flesh and make gods of their bellies, according to the saying of the apostle, ". . . whose god is their belly" (Phil. 3:19). Hugh of Saint Victor, in his *Claustrale*, shows how the belly can be called a god, saying: "There are those who build temples to the gods, erect altars, ordain ministers to serve them, sacrifice animals, burn incense. For the god of the belly the temple is the kitchen, the altar the table, the ministers the cooks, the sacrificed animals the roasts of meat, the smoke of incense the smell of flavors."

King Antiochus, an exceedingly proud and ambitious man, polluted and profaned God's house, as we read in 1 Maccabees 1. He is a figure of the pride and ambition that are rife among the clergy, who are not eager to serve but to command, and do much to contaminate the church of God. Of their proud ambition Bernard says: "They advance honored with the goods of the Lord, but they bring no honor to the Lord. You see them every day . . . the glamor of harlots, the frippery of stage players, the trappings of royalty, gold in their reins and their saddles, gold in their spurs, their halters more resplendent than their altars."

But just as the church has been profaned by three, so by three it has been dedicated and consecrated. Moses did the first dedication, Solomon the second, Judas Maccabeus the third; and by this it is suggested that in dedicating a church we should have the humility that was in Moses, the wisdom and discernment that were in Solomon, and the commitment to the defense of the true faith that is typified in Judas.

Now let us consider the consecration or dedication of the spiritual temple; and we are that temple, i.e., the congregation of all the faithful, built up of living stones, 1 Pet. 2:5: "Like living stones be yourselves built into a spiritual house." The stones are polished, as the hymn says: "stones made smooth with many hammer blows." They are squared, and the four sides of the spiritual stone are faith, hope, charity, and good works, the sides being equal, because, as Gregory says: "As much as you believe, that much you hope; as much as you believe and hope, that much you love; as much as you believe, hope, and love, so much good will you do."

In this temple the altar is our heart, and on this altar three offerings are to be made to God. The first is the fire of perpetual love, Lev. 6:13: "This is the perpetual fire which shall never go out on the altar," i.e., the altar of the heart. The second offering is the incense of sweet-smelling prayer, 1 Chron. 6:49: "Aaron and his sons will make offerings upon the altar of burnt offering and upon the altar of incense." Thirdly, the sacrifice of justice, which consists in the offering of penance and in the burnt offering of perfect love and in the calf of mortified flesh, of which Ps. 51:21 says: "Then shalt thou accept the sacrifice of justice, oblations and whole burnt offerings; then shall they lay calves upon thy altar."

The spiritual temple that we are is consecrated just as the material temple is. First the high priest, Christ himself, finding the door of the heart closed, goes around it three times, bringing to its memory sins of the mouth, of the heart, and of deeds. Of this triple circuit Isa. 23:16 says: "Take a harp . . . ," the first circuit, ". . . go about the city of the heart . . . ,"[1] the second, ". . . O forgotten harlot," the third. Then he knocks on the closed door three times, to have it opened to him: he knocks on the heart itself with the blows of his benefactions, his counsel, and his lash. Of this triple knocking it is said in Prov. 1:24–25, divine wisdom speaking to the wicked: "I have stretched out my hand . . . ," referring to the benefactions conferred, ". . . and you have ignored all my counsel . . . ," to the counsels inspired in the heart, ". . . and would have none of my reproof," to the lashes inflicted. Or he knocks three times when he stirs the reason to acknowledge sin, the affections to grieve for it, and the will to detest and punish it.

Thirdly, this spiritual temple must be sprinkled three times within and without with water. This threefold wetting is the shedding of tears either inwardly in the heart or sometimes outwardly. For the spirit of a holy man, as Gregory says, is smitten with sorrow at the thought of where he was, where he will be, where he is, and where he is not. Where he was, says Gregory, meaning in sin; where he will be, at the judgment; where he is, in misery; where he is not, in glory. When, therefore, he sheds internal and external tears as he considers that he was in sin and will give account for this at the judgment, then the spiritual temple is sprinkled once with water. When, for the misery in which he is, he is

---

[1] The text of Isaiah does not contain the words "of the heart," here added, probably by Jacobus, for the purpose of the text.

stung to weeping, then he is washed a second time. When he weeps for the glory in which he is not, then a third time he is asperged with water. Or by the watered wine the humility of Christ is symbolized, and by the salt the holiness of his life, which for all is the seasoning of religion. The ashes signify Christ's passion. In these three ways, then, we ought to sprinkle our hearts, namely, by the benefice of his incarnation, which calls us to humility, by the example of his life, which should form us in holiness, and by the memory of his passion, which should spur us to charity.

Fourthly, a spiritual alphabet, i.e., a spiritual scripture, is written in this temple of the heart. What is written there is threefold—the rules governing our actions, the testimony of the divine benefactions, and the accusation of our own sins. Of these three Rom. 2:14 says: "When Gentiles who have not the law do by nature what the law requires, they are a law to themselves," and show that the work of the law is written in their hearts. This is the first evidence. That their conscience makes them aware of this is the second; and the third is their exchange of thought among themselves, accusing or defending themselves.

Fifthly, crosses must be painted, i.e., the austerities of penance must be taken on; and the crosses should be anointed and lighted, because our penances should be borne patiently but also willingly, which the unction signifies, and ardently, signified by the fire. So Bernard: "One who lives in fear bears the cross of Christ patiently; one who advances in hope bears it willingly; one who is perfected in charity embraces it ardently." Bernard also says: "Many see our crosses but they do not see our anointings."

Whoever has these dispositions in himself will truly be a temple dedicated to God's honor. He will be fully worthy to have Christ dwelling in him by grace, so that in the end he will be worthy to dwell in Christ by glory. Which may he deign to grant us who lives and reigns, God for all the ages of ages. Amen.

Here endeth the Golden Legend or Lombardic History of Jacobus de Voragine of the Order of Preachers, bishop of Genoa

INDEX

THE GOLDEN LEGEND

NIHIL OBSTAT: Otto L. Garcia, S.T.D.
                       Censor Librorum

IMPRIMATUR: +Thomas V. Daily, D.D.
                       Bishop of Brooklyn

Brooklyn, New York: August 25, 1992